Ranganathan Series in Library Science, 3

LIBRARY ADMINISTRATION

Some other books by the author

Anuvarga-suchi-kalpa

Classification and communication

Classified catalogue code

Colon classification

Depth classification

Education for leisure

Elements of library classification

Five laws of library science

Grantha-adhyayanartha-hai

Granthalaya-prakriya

Heading and canons

Library development plan

Library legislation

Literature for neoliterates

Organisation of libraries

Philosophy of library classification

Prolegomena to library classification

Public library provision and documentation problems

Rural adult education

Social bibliography

Social education literature

Union catalogue of learned periodical publications in South Asia

Ranganathan Series in Library Science

1 *Library movement in India, a symposium*, ed by P N Kaula

2 *Classified catalogue code with additional rules for dictionary catalogue code*, by S R Ranganathan

3 *Library administration*, by S R Ranganathan

LIBRARY ADMINISTRATION

by

S. R. RANGANATHAN

Published by
Ess Ess Publications
4837/24, Ansari Road
Darya Ganj
New Delhi-110 002

for

Sarada Ranganathan Endowment
For Library Science
Bangalore

Shiyali Ramanriṭa Ranganathan (1892)

First Edition 1935
Second Edition 1959
Second Edition Reprint 1989
Reprinted **2006**

2:8
N58

81-7000-495-0

Rs : 1400 /-

Published by:

Ess Ess Publications

4837/24, Ansari Road, Darya Ganj, New Delhi-110 002
Tel: 011-23260807, 41563444 Fax: 011-41563334
E-mail: info@essessreference.com
url: www.essessreference.com

for

Sarada Ranganathan Endowment for Library Science

702, 'Upstairs', 42nd Cross, III Block, Rajajinagar,
Bangalore-560 010
Ph.no.23305109 E-mail: srels@vsnl.com

Printed in India at:
Printline, New Delhi

To

the memory of

C Sundaram

and

M S Sundaresan

CONTENTS

Extract from *Mahasaraswati* 9

0 Genesis and Conspectus 11

PART 1

Theory of Administration

11 Planning 25

12 Job Analysis 32

13 Routine 37

14 Elimination of Waste 42

15 Correlation 54

16 Time Scheme 57

17 Forms and Registers 62

18 Correspondence, Files and Records 71

PART 2

Distinctive Library Functions

21 Book Selection Section 91

22 Book Order Section 116

23 Periodical Publication Section 151

24 Accession Section 205

25 Technical Section 231

26 Circulation Section 273

27 Reference Section 353

28 Maintenance Section 364

PART 3

General Office Functions

31	Committee Section	419
32	Staff Section	430
33	Staff Council	446
34	Elimination of Waste	448
35	Publicity Section	470
36	Finance Section	473
37	Accounts Section	493
38	Records Section	545
391	Librarian	548
392	Library Profession	551
393	Correspondence Section	553
394	Printing Section	576
395	Binding Section	579
396	Building and Equipment Section	599
397	Stores Section	606
398	Statistical Section	628
	Epilogue	631
	Bibliography	633
	Index	637

Extract from pages 66 to 72 of the

MOTHER

Sri Aurobindo

1928

Mahasaraswati is the Mother's Power of Work and her spirit of perfection and order. The youngest of the Four, she is the most skilful in executive faculty and the nearest to physical Nature. Maheswari lays down the large lines of the world-forces, Mahakali drives their energy and impetus, Mahalakshmi discovers their rhythms and measures, but Mahasaraswati presides over their details of organisation and execution, relation of parts and effective combination of forces and unfailing exactitude of result and fulfilment. The science and craft and technique of things are Mahasaraswati's province. Always she holds in her nature and can give to those whom she has chosen, the intimate and precise knowledge, the subtlety and patience, the accuracy of intuitive mind and conscious hand and discerning eye of the perfect worker. This Power is the strong, the tireless, the careful and efficient builder, organizer, administrator, technician, artisan and classifier of the worlds. When she takes up the transformation and new building of the nature, her action is laborious and minute and often seems to our impatience slow and interminable, but it is persistent, integral and flawless. For the will in her works is scrupulous, unsleeping, indefatigable; leaning over us she notes and touches every little detail, finds out every minute defect, gap, twist or incompleteness, considers and weighs accurately all that has been done and all that remains still to be done hereafter. Nothing is too small or apparently trivial for her attention; nothing however impalpable or disguised or latent can escape her. Moulding and remoulding, she labours each part till it has attained its true form, is put in its exact place in the whole and fulfils its precise purpose. In her constant and diligent arrangement and rearrangement of things her eye is on all needs at once and the way to meet them and her intuition knows what is to be chosen and what rejected and successfully determines the right instrument, the right time, the right conditions and the right process. Carelessness and negligence and indolence she abhors; all scamped and hasty and shuffling work, all clumsiness and a *pue pres* and misfire, all false adaptation and misuse of instruments and faculties and leaving of things undone or half done is offensive and foreign to her temper. When her work is finished, nothing has been forgotten, no part has been misplaced or omitted or left in a faulty condition; all is solid, accurate, complete, admirable. Nothing short of a perfect perfection satisfies her and she is ready to face an eternity of toil if that is needed for the fullness of her creation. Therefore of all the Mother's Powers she is the most long-suffering with man and his thousand imperfections. Kind, smiling, close and helpful, not easily turned away or discouraged, insistent even after repeated failure, her hand sustains our every step on condition that we are single in our will and straightforward and sincere; for, a double mind she will not tolerate and her revealing irony is merciless to drama and histrionics and self-deceipt and pretence. A mother to our wants, a friend in our difficulties, a persistent and tranquil counsellor and mentor, chasing away with her radiant smile the clouds of gloom and fretfulness and depression, reminding always of the ever-present help, pointing to the eternal sunshine, she is firm, quiet and persevering in the deep and continuous urge that drives us towards the integrality of the higher nature. All the work of the other Powers leans on her for its completeness; for she assures the material foundation, elaborates the stuff of detail and erects and rivets the armour of the structure.

CHAPTER 0

GENESIS AND CONSPECTUS

01 First Experience

It was October 1924. The place was the School of Librarianship in the University College, London. There were classes on the various branches of library science. There was a course entitled "Library Routine". C R Sanderson was the lecturer. He was young and brilliant. His manner of exposition was arresting. His mastery of details was impressive. He lighted up the prosaic field of library routine with his powerful personality, analytical mind, and penetrating insight. He made me visualise every piece of work involved in library administration. His lectures equipped me with the power to observe critically and comparatively the way in which the different sections of different libraries were being administered in those days. I observed the day-to-day working of more than a hundred libraries in the United Kingdom. The librarians and the staff of most of these libraries were kind enough to answer my many questions about the why, the what, and the how of the way in which they did their respective pieces of work. This was my first experience in library administration.

011 APPLICATION

I came back to the Madras University Library in July 1925. I found a virgin soii to cultivate. There was no hampering tradition to be fought against. The staff was meagre. They had been looking after the books with considerable care for about ten years. They were willing to move with me in the design of the administrative work, which I took on hand. At the beginning, I did practically every kind of work in the library. This gave me an opportunity to apply the various principles of administration, mentally distilled out of what was absorbed in the United Kingdom.

012 FIFTH LAW IN FULL STEAM

An unexpected event brought me into relation with the then Chief Minister of the Madras State. This resulted in the library getting sumptuous recurring and non-recurring grants for the library. The annual accession shot up from 1,000 to 6,000. The number of periodical publications taken by the library shot up from 200 to 1,200. The annual issue of books shot up from 10,000 to 200,000. The daily attendance shot up from 30 to 600. The staff was gradually increased from 4 to 30. All the staff had to be recruited from among young men fresh from college or school. They had to be fitted into the administration of the library. The Fifth Law of Library Science[1] was thus in full steam.

013 Good in Disguise

This steady and rapid growth of the library in all directions demanded the continued adjustment and development of the organisation of the work, the continued analysis of each piece of work into its ultimate jobs, and the prescription of the routine for each job. The amount of work was, for many years, in excess of the normal capacity of the staff. For, by the time the additional staff needed to cope with a particular amount of work could be got by fighting the way across all the barriers set up by red-tape and the obstructive elements in the top-management, a new higher amount would have been reached. This factor proved to be a good in disguise. Rationalisation of the work became a necessity. Simplification of routine emerged inevitably. Streamlining of the administration became obligatory. Higher productivity had to be pursued in every sphere of work. Standardisation of materials and processes was made consciously or unconsciously. The flow of work had perforce to be taken along the most economical lines.

014 Happy Anticipation

The technique of all these factors in efficient management was not then known. But necessity proved to be as usual a productive mother of invention. The Staff Council and the Sectional Councils were formed out of sheer necessity without any theoretical knowledge or external guidance. They provided the forum for collective thinking in designing a system of administration with the greatest potentiality for productivity. Looking back from our present position in 1959 into those far off years of the 1920's, we find that the design of administration, set up thirty years ago, had anticipated admirably the Canons of Management and Administration being formulated today in the Science of Management. This happy anticipation can be traced only to Providence.

015 Exposition

The Madras Library Association started its School of Library Science in 1929. It was taken over by the University of Madras in 1931 and is still being continued without a break. This School provided a further help in self-education. The task of teaching Library Administration to the students lighted up many a path which had been passed through unconsciously in the day-to-day routine, without any conscious thinking. By 1928 however, the normative principles of Library Science had been formulated. These had also been already expounded in a course of Vacation Lectures of the University of Madras, delivered in December 1928. These principles were called the Five Laws of Library Science. These fundamental laws unified the innumerable details involved in Library Administration. The pulsation of this unity helped in making the exposition of Library Administration pleasurable equally to the teacher and the taught. Teaching the subject in the light of the Five Laws from year to year clarified the thought both in the General Theory of Administration and in its Application to the field of library service.

016 Publication

The Madras Library Association started its Publication Series in 1929, with the object of spreading the essential ideas of Library Science and of directing thought towards the creation of efficient Library Service answering the needs of our country and of the world at large. This activity of the Madras Library Association prompted the gradual writing out of the experience gained during my travel in the United Kingdom, in the administration of the Madras University Library and in teaching the subject. Each chapter was tested by actual application in the day-to-day work and amended wherever necessary. What was thus written out and tested through seven years was published in 1935 as the fifth volume of the Publication Series of the Madras Library Association. This is the Genesis of the first edition of this book.

017 Reception

Though the book contained a forest of details, it enjoyed an unusually good reception in the hands of the library profession in the world. This was evidenced in the book going out of print within two years of its publication. I came across more evidence of it in my frequent travels abroad since 1948. For, I found a well-thumbed copy of it on the work table in many a library in the several countries visited.

02 Edition 2

021 Postponement

Many colleagues in the profession, both at home and abroad, have been all along urging the re-publication of the book. But this has not been possible during the last twenty years. In the first place, writing of new books claimed priority of attention continuously. Secondly, new editions of the basic books *Colon classification*, *Classified catalogue code*, *Organisation of libraries*, *Five laws of library science*, *Prolegomena to library classification*, and *Elements of library classification* had to be brought out more urgently. Thirdly, there was a wish to conduct certain objective studies and experiments in the routine of the work to be done in libraries. Time-study, therbligs, motion-study, areas for further simplification and standardisation, man-power analysis, and mechanisation with the aid of photography, machines, and electronics, were some of the topics which it was the wish to investigate for incorporation in the second edition.

022 Man-Power Analysis

In 1948, I had constructed a Staff-Formula to determine the strength of the staff required in a library in terms of various factors such as accession, circulation, hours of functioning, and so on. The numerical coefficients in this Staff-Formula were all fixed on the basis of guess-work based on unmeasured experience. There was a wish to check up these coefficients by actual measurement. A small beginning was made in this direction in a series of articles entitled *Library man-power analysis* appearing in the *Abgila* and continued in the *Annals of library science*. The first article[2] in the series was by me ; and it expounded the objectives and the plan of the later articles. We did not however have facilities to do time and motion-study with the stop-watch and other instrumental aids. Moreover, neither the size of libraries, nor the magnitude of their daily turn-over, nor the cost of man-power in India, would justify or demand the introduction of photography and other mechanical and electronic aids in library routine. All that could be done was a retrospective estimate of the units of man-hours needed for the routine of the different jobs disclosed by the job-analysis in the first edition of this very book. S Ramabhadran[3] started on this retrospective tabulation of the thousand and odd library jobs. But he found himself unable to complete even this crude attempt at quantitative measurement. Nor could I find the time for it. All these factors had been discouraging a venture into the second edition.

023 Increase in Library Fund

But a new factor appeared a few months ago, which led to the decision to bring out a second edition without waiting for such experimental work and objective investigation to be carried out. I returned home in February 1957, after a long stay in Europe. On my return, I was pleasantly surprised at the enormous provision made by the Government of India for the development of the existing university and research libraries of various kinds, and of libraries in Government Departments. Even more money was said to have been provided for the development of the public library system in the Second Five Year Plan. The formation of new libraries and the increased book-fund were found to be quite in excess of the trained man-power available. The library fund provided could not be utilised in a truly efficient and helpful way.

024 A Bad State of Affairs

It is wrong to neglect the proper training of librarians. It is equally wrong to fail to increase the staff to absorb usefully the vast sum of money provided for the first time in most libraries. There is now utter absence of co-ordination and fore-thought in this matter. Therefore, the public do not get a reasonable return on the public fund turned on to libraries. The attention of the authorities has not been drawn to this bad state of affairs by the library-advisers in the government.

025 Transitory Remedy

In the circumstances, a transitory remedy occurs to me. The small number of the trained librarians we now have should be released as much as possible to the actual service to readers and to the technical processing of books for fitting them for service. This implies that much of the routine in library work should be transferred for the time being to persons with slight or no library training.

026 Urgent Need for Edition 2

This factor made me feel that it might be helpful if a second edition of this book could be brought out quickly to help those entrusted with the routine administrative work in our libraries, old as well as new. I felt that this decision, forced on me largely by Indian requirements, might also incidentally meet the demand of colleagues in other countries for a re-publication of the book.

027 Final Decision on Edition 2

While these factors were engaging my mind, the Asia Publishing House, Bombay agreed to take up the responsibility for publishing the second edition. This was welcome, as we in the Madras Library Association were fully occupied with the printing of new editions of half a dozen other books. The issue of the second edition was thus clinched finally about the end of October 1957. Perhaps, the investigations mentioned in sections 021 and 022 can be completed before the time comes for the third edition. However, this second edition incorporates the changes suggested during the application of the prescribed routine during the last twenty years. The chief among the changes are :

1. The Staff-Formula to determine the strength of staff for a library on the basis of turn-over ;
2. The prescription of routine for Vigilance Work on book orders ;
3. The simplification of the Three Card System in the administration of periodical publications ;
4. The changing of Book Card to a Pocketed Form and of the Reader's Ticket into a Non-Pocketed Plain Card ; and
5. The introduction of the Conscience Box for the collection of overdue charges.

03 A Book for the Work Table

This is not a book to be read through like the *Five laws of library science*. It is, on the contrary, a most prosaic manual full of details. But it has its place on the work table of one who has to carry on the administration of a library from day to day and from hour to hour. To those who do not have to do real work in a library; some of the details elaborated in this manual may appear to be either trivial or pretentious. Library administration has to be so planned and adjusted that the highest accuracy and the greatest promptness and economy are achieved. And these factors cannot be achieved, if the library staff drifts along with its unaided common sense, using the method of trial and error. Actual training of apprentices will convince one of the need for detailed work-sheets. These are provided in every factory. These are equally necessary in administrative work.

031 Demand for the Book

I have been continuously receiving many enquiries about one aspect or another of the day-to-day administration of libraries. While I delight in looking upon such letters as a welcome index of a genuine desire for the scientific management of libraries, I cannot help feeling that a satisfactory answer to such questions could not be given through individual letters. Hence this attempt to lay bare the details of the daily administration of libraries.

04 Local Variation

Libraries vary in size, type and outlook. It would be impossible to write a manual that would exactly fit every kind of library. At any rate, this manual does not claim to be one such. All that is attempted here is to provide certain patterns which can be varied according to local conditions. Here and there examples of local variations are indicated in the form of " subsidiary rules of the Madras University Library". A manual like this should be bound interleaved by the library using it and the blank leaves should be filled up with the subsidiary rules framed to suit the special conditions of the library. In sections 1333 to 1342 are indicated the lines along which the subsidiary rules should be thought out in libraries of different sizes.

05 Scope of the Book

051 Not a Book on Theory

It may also be stated that this manual does not attempt either to discuss or even to state what the outlook of libraries should be, although the details of the day-to-day work depend largely upon the outlook. On the other hand, it assumes the outlook set forth in the *Five laws of library science*.

052 Not a Book on Technique

Nor does this manual attempt to expound the theory or give practical directions regarding the different facets of library work such as book-selection, or classification or cataloguing or reference service. A separate book has been published by me dealing in each one of these techniques.

06 Conspectus

A few words may be devoted to describe the plan of the manual.

061 Theory of Administration

Part 1, dealing with the groundwork is somewhat biased towards the theory of administration. However, this theory is expounded with library administration steadily in view.

062 Facets of Library Administration

Part 2 forms the bulk of this manual. It is devoted to the distinctive facets of library administration.

063 Facets of General Administration

Part 3 deals with those routines which are common to all administrations. Properly speaking, those later chapters would not occupy as much space as they do here, if there were a general book on office administration in our country. In such a case, these later chapters could have been shortened considerably by merely giving references to such a general manual of office administration and by noting down only those variations that are necessary in library administration.

064 Plan of Each Chapter

One chapter is devoted to each *Function*, i e to each of the Sections into which the library staff has to be divided on a functional basis. A chapter is divided into eight parts, corresponding to the eight chapters into which Part 1 is divided. The first part deals with the planning of the work of the Section forming the subject-matter of the chapter and enumerates the different *Factors in Planning*. The second part is devoted to *Job Analysis*. The third part gives the *Routine* for each job. The fourth part indicates the special points that the Head of the Section should bear in mind in order to *Eliminate Waste* and secure efficiency. The fifth part gives in a tabular form the various rules which deal with the points at which the Section comes in contact with the other Sections. In other words, it deals with the *Correlation* of the work of the Section with the work of the other Sections. The sixth part gives in a tabular form a model *Time Scheme* for the performance of the different jobs of the Section. The seventh part enumerates and describes the various *Forms and Registers* required by the Section. The eighth and the last part gives in a tabular form the different *Files* to be maintained by the Section and the way in which they should be classified, numbered and arranged for ready reference.

065 Jobs

It may be stated that the analysis in the second part of the different chapters has isolated nearly 1,000 different jobs (see section 12 for definition) involved in the administration of libraries.

066 Routine

The routine pertaining to all these jobs is described in the third part of the several chapters. It is these parts that will be in constant use by the workers in a library. They occupy, naturally, more than half of the volume.

07 Numbering of Sections

A word about the numbering of the chapters and the sections in this volume. In the *Colon classification*[4] and the *Classified catalogue code*, the decimal notation was used for the purpose. While even that was considered revolutionary by some, I have to confess that the complexity of administrative routine is of a still higher order and has transcended the decimal notation. To use the technical terms developed in the *Colon classification*, the trains of characteristics of analysis to be used in a manual of administration are usually more than two. That is why the decimal notation is not sufficient either to string together or to disclose automatically the points to be covered by this manual. On the other hand, the faceted notation, brought into vogue by the *Colon Classification*, admits of any number of trains of characteristics, and is hence much more powerful. It is found to be both necessary and sufficient.

071 Hospitable and Creative Notation

The function of the notation is not mere enumeration. It will amount to missing one of the most powerful aids to systematic thinking, if the use of notation is restricted to this trivial function. On the other hand, a well-devised notation can whip up thought, secure thoroughness, provide for endless interpolation and extrapolation of paragraphs without altering the number of any of the existing ones and render reference easy. In a word, the notation must be not only hospitable but also creative and expressive.

072 Mnemonic Faceted Notation

The Colon Notation is capable of rendering all this service. Further, on account of its great mnemonic quality, it has led to a considerable economy of thought and secured thoroughness of details in an automatic and effortless way. This is my excuse for having fitted the chapters and the sections of this manual with the faceted mnemonic notation. Those who are familiar with the *Colon classification* will find it to be meaningful. To the others, I would recommend a preliminary study of chapters 01, 02 and the first section of chapter 06 of that book—making altogether not more than seven pages—for understanding the numbering of the chapters and the sections of this manual. It may be stated that a result of the mnemonic numbering is that the numbers used to enumerate the divisions of a topic are not always consecutive.

08 Inspiration from Sri Aurobindo

As the routine parts of the several chapters were getting filled up and faircopied, I had frequent doubts whether a book with such details was worth printing. Once when I was most despondent,

Shri P A Subramania Ayyar, my old headmaster, happened to introduce me to the *Mother* by Sri Aurobindo. And Sri Aurobindo's vivid description of *Mahasaraswati*[5] inspired me and lifted me from the despondence into which I was falling. As far better than any apologia of my own for writing this book of details, I reprint on pages 9 and 10, with his permission, these words of Sri Aurobindo from the *Mother*.

PART 1

THEORY OF ADMINISTRATION

As the Library Grows

How Functions Divide and Subdivide

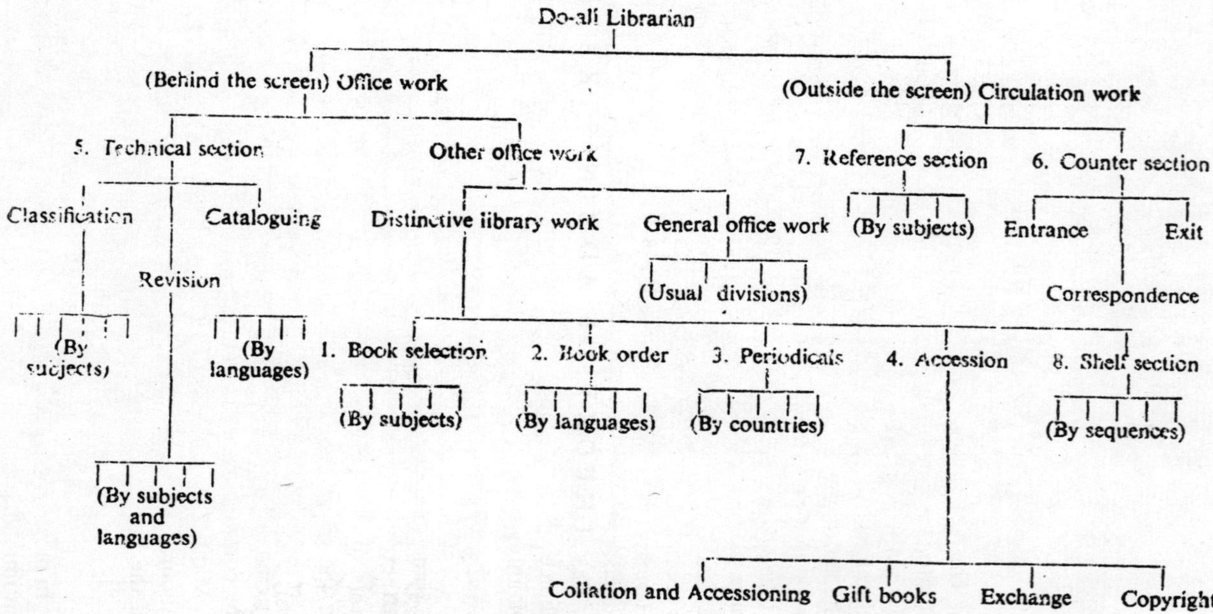

CHAPTER 11

PLANNING

111 Basis of Planning

The first step in organising any administrative force is to organise it into convenient sections according to a carefully thought-out plan. To get a suitable plan is equivalent to finding out an appropriate characteristic as the basis for classifying the entire work cast upon the administrative force. The characteristic chosen will vary with the nature of the business entrusted to the administration. It may be regional or functional or personal or of any other nature—pure or mixed. The science of administration—yes, administration is fast becoming a science in our lifetime—has already developed a special jargon to label the plans, based on different characteristics. Here are some terms, which are current : series plan, parallel plan, functional plan, divisional plan, line and staff plan, and so on.

The Canons of Classification[6] must be borne in mind in the choice of the characteristic which is to be made the basis of the planning of an administration.

112 Functional Planning

Functional planning is found almost universally in nature. All except the very simplest forms of cell life, viz the protista, seem to have learned the advantage of a division of labour. And in the more complex cell colonies, such as animals, we find the degree of specialisation carried so far that the individual cell is fitted only to perform one function, and would quickly perish without the complementary activities of its fellow cells.

Many animals have also learned the advantage of division of labour. From the insect societies to the complex civilisations of the human race we find the principle extensively applied.

1121 MECHANICS OF PLANNING

In most types of administration--and especially in library administration--the basis of planning likely to yield the best results is a functional basis, adapted to the needs of the particular administration and translated into practical shape in the light of other organisational principles. Hence, the first step in planning is to analyse and isolate the different functions to be performed by the staff of the library. Much of the mechanics of planning is thus concerned with the clear presentation of the factors of a situation, so that the situation may be quickly and accurately grasped. Once that is done, the staff can be divided into the necessary number of sections to perform the different functions. The best way of naming each section is to name it by its function.

113 Functional Analysis

The result of such an analysis of the work is set forth in the contents page of this manual. The functions denoted by the numbers 21 to 28 are the distinctive functions of a library administration, while the functions 31 to 398 are functions which are likely to appear in all administrations. The generic names *Distinctive Library Functions* and *General Office Functions* may be applied respectively to these two groups of functions.

The connotation of the terms used to denote the different functions is indicated roughly by the terms themselves. A fuller and more detailed picture of the functions is presented in the respective chapters. The plan of each chapter has already been indicated in section 064. It may be repeated here that each chapter is devoted to a single *Function* and is divided into eight parts. A perusal of the first three parts of each chapter will give a full and detailed view of the function which gives the name to the chapter.

114 Difficulties in the Way

At present many of the functions are being performed under the weight of a non-progressive and crude tradition, involving many wasteful processes. Library administration is particularly hard hit by this state of affairs owing to two causes.

1141 Spending Body

In the first place, a library is a spending department. However much it may remotely contribute to the increase of wealth in the nation, it is not one that directly raises a revenue or earns an income. It is a matter of experience that a department that either raises a revenue or earns a direct income by its operations is indifferent to wastefulness of processes. Comparatively speaking, money is easily forthcoming in its case. On the other hand, a purely spending department like the library department tends to be usually treated in a step-motherly fashion. It is difficult to get the necessary finance. Hence every possible care is to be taken to devise more economical methods of administration.

1142 Dependent Body

In the second place, by its very nature, it is seldom that a library administration is independent. On the contrary, whatever be the nature of a library, other than being a National Central Library, it is likely to be a department of a larger organisation whose central executive usually tends to take advantage of his privileged position and develop a grasping tendency on the one hand and obstructive tactics on the other. As a result of this, a library is at a perpetual disadvantage in developing either its own distinctive functions or the functions common to all administrations along newer, more scientific, and more efficient lines. The library administration thus rests between two opposing forces.

1143 Condition in India

According to Headicar, in the West the library department still continues to be " the Cinderella " of the bigger organisation of which it is a part. It has not yet become what it should be, " the Mecca " of the bigger organisation, nay, " of government itself ".[7] In India, the situation is still worse and will probably continue to be so for a long time. Hence, the library profession here has a much greater handicap than elsewhere in planning its work satisfactorily. It is at once the duty and the privilege of the members of the present generation of the library profession to face and overcome every discouragement and difficulty, and to evolve a healthy tradition of scientifically managing libraries.

1144 Growth in Staff

As a result of a pioneer's dedication, the library profession has often to face frustration in another field as a result of the library being a dependent body. It has been particularly so in India, due to the older generation in positions of power not having had the experience of library service. Further, practically all the libraries are young. They are still at the stage of child-growth. If the staff has sufficient enthusiasm to make the library grow from year to year, it leads to a vexatious situation. The authorities seldom realise how quickly the sanctioned staff is out-numbered. They complain of frequent applications for increase of staff and turn them down. Even with the best of effort, the inadequate staff is unable to render even half the service which they announce and aspire to render. Publicity brings in more readers than can be served and more books than can be organised. The result is complaint and disappointment from all quarters, and ridicule and under-writing by a handful of cynics whose voice drowns the voice of others. Cowardly and selfish librarians feel frustrated and begin to drift at the risk of the library repelling readers. I have seen this phenomenon recur in library after library in the East and in the West alike. Till recently, I had taken this to be as providential and inexorable as an earthquake. Of late, I am able to see some light and think of some means of averting this form of frustration in the growth of a young library and in the spirit of a hard-working, enthusiastic, pioneering staff who put service above self-interests. The means I recommend is that library authorities should once for all agree to a mathematical formula for the staff of library interests in terms of the out-turn of work. Once this formula is accepted, the alteration in the strength of the staff would become mechanical and impersonal. There need not be a recurring opportunity for the play of cynicism and vexation.

This formula is based on my own personal experience in the Madras University Library. I was led to its formulation by my having been invited from 1945 onwards by several libraries for advice on this very question of staff. It was first published in 1948. Since then it has been tested in several places both in India and abroad. It is said to have given satisfaction.

1145 Staff Formula

Let A = Number of volumes Accessioned in a year.
B = Annual Budget allotment in Rupees.
D = Number of periodicals Documented—that is, abstracted and indexed in a year.
G = Number of Gate-Hours for a year.
(One Gate-Hour = One counter gate kept open for one hour.)

H = Number of Hours the library is kept open in a day.
P = Number of Periodicals currently taken.
R = Number of Readers per day.
S = Number of Seats for readers.
V = Number of Volumes in the library.
W = Number of Working days in a year.
[X] = X, if X is one integer.
= The Integer just greater than X, if its fractional part is greater than .25.
= The Integer just smaller than X, if its fractional part is not greater than .25.
SB = Number of persons in Book Section.
SC = Number of persons in Circulation Section.
SL = Number of persons as Librarian and his Deputies.
SM = Number of persons in Maintenance Section.
SP = Number of persons in Periodicals Section.
SR = Number of persons in Reference Section.
ST = Number of persons in Technical—that is Classification and Cataloguing—Section.

Formulae for Staff of Different Sections

SB = A/6000.
SC = G/1500.
SL = HW/1500.
SM = A/3000.
SP = P/500.
SR = [R/50] W/250.
ST = (A+40D)/2000.

Formula for Total Professional Staff

$$SB+SC+SL+SM+SP+SR+ST = \{3(A+20D)+2(G+3P)+2W(H+6[R/50])\}/3000.$$

Formula for Non-Professional Skilled Staff

B/30,000+[S/100].

Formula for Unskilled Staff

$$SB/4+SC/2+SL+SM/4+SP/2+SR/8+A/20{,}000+D/500+B/60{,}000+[S/100]/4+V/30{,}000$$
$$=\{27A+2(B+120D)+40(G+3P)+30{,}000[S/100]+4V+2W(40H+3[R/50]\}/120{,}000.$$

115 As The Library Grows

The question may be asked of what use is an elaborate functional analysis in planning the administrative work of a small library, run by one man—a type that is numerically the greatest in the world. My answer is that even a do-all librarian can discharge his duties with greater ease, thoroughness, and efficiency, if he knows the different functions to be performed, the different jobs to be attended to, and the sequence in which they should be taken up. A well thought-out time-table for the jobs is quite necessary. Again, there is the Fifth Law of Library Science, " A library is a growing organism".[8] The small library of today will soon grow in size and in staff. As it grows, the need for functional planning will become increasingly felt.

1151 Progressive Delegation

As the library outgrows being a one-man concern, a librarian finds that he must delegate to assistants those parts of the work which exceed his own capacity. At first he usually shares with his assistants much of the administrative routine. As the library grows still further, he delegates the entire function of performance. He has professional assistants, non-professional staff and unskilled staff to work under his orders. This stage is reached, we may say, when the strength of the staff grows beyond twenty. Still later, even the work of supervision becomes too great in volume and he is obliged to content himself more and more with indicating plans and objectives, leaving it to the experience of his assistants to find ways of carrying out his plans. This stage is reached as the strength of the staff approaches one hundred. The diagram at the beginning of this part shows the way in which the functions involved in the administration of a library get divided and subdivided as the staff increases. The diagram presents also an articulated view of the different functions.

116 Inequality in Functions

1161 Time Required

Just as all the functions devolve on the do-all librarian at the earliest stage, it is obvious that one and the same person will have to perform more than one function until the staff grows to a sufficient size. Further, all the functions are not of equal magnitude. Hence, two or more of the lighter functions may be assigned to one member of the staff while some of the heavier functions will have, at the same time, to be entrusted to a section of staff consisting of two or more members. This inequality is the result of the unequal demand on time made by the different functions.

1162 Ability Required

There is yet another inequality among the functions. Some functions are of a routine and mechanical nature. Other functions may exact physical exertion. Some are of a high academic order ; while, still others are, in addition to being of an academic nature, dependent for their satisfactory performance on the entire personality of the staff responsible for it.

1163 Number Required

Thus the sections into which the staff of a library will have to be divided will vary considerably in numerical strength. The equipment, the aptitude, and the higher qualities of the members constituting them will also have to vary.

117 Factors in Planning

Before leaving this chapter, it may be stated that the first part of most of the chapters of Parts 2 and 3 will be entitled " Planning". It will enumerate the *Factors* with reference to which the work of the section should be planned. The characteristic forming the basis of the analysis of the factors involved in the function will vary with the function i e will be different in different chapters. Again all the factors may not give rise to the same amount of work or to an equal number of jobs.

CHAPTER 12

JOB ANALYSIS

121 Terminology

1211 JOB

The second part of most of the chapters of Parts 1 and 2 is entitled " Job Analysis". By a *Job* is meant an ultimate piece of work which is best done at a single stretch and whose duration is ordinarily short.

1212 WORK

A number of related jobs constitute an item of *Work*. To each factor enumerated in the " Planning " part of each chapter may correspond a number of related items of work.

1213 SEQUENCE OF CATEGORIES

Thus, as we start from " library administration " and go down step by step along " function", " factor", " work " and arrive at " job", we go through a well-articulated sequence of categories which gradually increase in intension and decrease in extension. In some cases, the step " work " may be absent. In other words, the category " job " may immediately follow the category " factor".

122 Notation for Period

The jobs of each item of work are grouped according to their periodicity. The periods and the notation representing them are as follows :

1	Immediate	5	Weekly
2	Hourly	6	Monthly
3	Casual	7	Quarterly
4	Daily	8	Annual

123 Full Job Number

A word about the structure of the notation representing a job. It is best to begin with a particular example. Let us take the job entitled *Overdue Sheet Filing*. It is a weekly job relating to *Admission Work*, which, in its turn, relates to the factor, *Members*. It is a job that is part of the function of the *Circulation Section*. Its number is 2611:12:54. Here "2" shows that it belongs to a *Distinctive Library Function* and 6 stands for *Circulation Section*, 11 stands for *Members*, 12 stands for *Admission Work*, 5 stands for *Weekly Job* and 4 stands for the specific job, viz. *Overdue Sheet Filing*.

1231 Job vs. Routine

When we speak of the job analysis relating to this job, it will be represented by the number 26211:12:54. Here 2, which is interpolated between 6 and 11, shows that the reference to the job occurs in the "Job Analysis" part of the chapter, 2 being the number of the part dealing with "Job Analysis" in every chapter. Similarly, the routine connected with the job will be numbered 26311:12:54. Here 3, which is interpolated between 6 and 11, shows that the reference to the job occurs in the "Routine" part of the chapter, 3 being the number of the part dealing with "Routine" in every chapter.

1232 Number of Groups of Digits

Now we can describe the structure of the notation representing a job in general terms. It will consist of six groups of digits.

1233 Preliminary Number

The first digit shows whether the job belongs to a Distinctive Library Function or to a General Office Function. This is the *Preliminary Number*.

1234 Function Number

The second group will represent the function. It may be referred to as *Function Number*. It will be of one digit or two digits according as it has no 9 or one 9 at its beginning. Thus, the number of digits in the Function Number is definitely ascertainable from its very appearance. Hence, according to the rules of Colon Classification the function number need not be separated by a ":" from the succeeding group of digits.[2]

1235 FACTOR NUMBER

The third group of digits will represent the *Factor* to which the job relates. It may be referred to as the *Factor Number.* It may be of one or more digits. As it is thus of a varying number of digits, it must be separated by a " : " from the succeeding group of digits.

1236 WORK NUMBER

The fourth group of digits represents the *Work* to which the job belongs. It may be referred to as the *Work Number.* This may be of one or more digits, ie of a varying number of digits. Hence, it has to be followed by a " : ". If there is no Work Number, the colon which is to accompany it may be omitted.

1237 PERIOD NUMBER

Next comes the *Period Number.* From the period table given at the beginning of this part of this chapter, it can be seen that the Period Number is always of one digit. Hence, according to the rules of Colon Classification, it can be followed immediately by the Job Number without an intervening colon.

1238 JOB NUMBER

The sixth group of digits represents the specific job. It may be referred to as the *Job Number.*

1239 FULL NUMBER FOR JOB

Thus a full blown number for a Job will consist of a Preliminary Number, a Function Number, a Factor Number, a colon, a Work Number, a colon, a Period Number, and a Job Number.

It may be stated, further, that in the part of a chapter dealing with " Job Analysis", the digit "2" will be interpolated between the Function Number and the Factor Number. Similarly, in the part of a chapter dealing with " Routine", the digit "3" will be so interpolated.

124 Creative Thinking

The job analysis given in the different chapters does not, however, include a vital piece of work, viz *Creative Thinking.* The qualifications and conditions required for creative thinking often do not harmonise well with those required for effective routine performance. Routine performance usually requires the rapid shifting of attention from one immediate problem to another, leaving little opportunity either for reverie or for continuous concentrated attention to a single idea. If the staff is large enough to release the librarian for this creative work and if his background of past experience could give him the necessary grasp of details, the service of the library will have a chance to improve steadily in quality. But this work of *Creative Thinking* cannot be analysed into definite jobs with definite periodicity. Nor is it desirable that it should be so reduced to routine.

125 Best Day's Work

1251 Job-Sheet

But the situation is quite different in the case of the other ordinary performances. A careful analysis of the work into jobs and a full presentation of the results of analysis are possible. In fact, that is the business of the librarian. The first step in securing effective performance by an individual is to see that he understands and is properly prepared to perform the work. The second step is to create conditions which stimulate him to put forth his best efforts in performance. The two stages are related ; for, the very first essential is interest. Interest, in turn, is closely connected with the understanding of the work and confidence in one's ability to do it well. The setting in of these factors will be facilitated by a ready made job analysis in writing. A job-sheet describing in detail the routine for completing the job should be furnished to the person doing the job. The third sections of the different chapters together form a collection of all the job-sheets.

1252 Friendly Help From Above

The greatest obstacle to harmonious co-operation between the librarian and the staff lies in the ignorance of the librarian as to what really constitutes a proper day's work for a member of the staff, the best day's work that a man could properly do, year in and year out, with efficiency and without undue exhaustion. A close, intimate, personal co-operation between the librarian and his staff is the essence of *scientific administration.* Almost every performance of the staff should be preceded by one or more preparatory acts of the librarian which will enable them to do their work better and quicker than they otherwise could. And each person should be duly taught by and receive the most friendly help from those who are above him, instead of being driven or coerced by his bosses, or left to his own unaided devices.

126 Revision of Analysis

1261 Co-operative Revision

The model analysis shown in the second parts of the different chapters should be examined and revised from time to time. Sectional Meetings of the staff, under the chairmanship of the head of the section, must be convened and the librarian should be present at such meetings and guide the discussion along proper lines. All the jobs, whose routine or time scheme affects two or more sections, should be discussed, in addition, at meetings of the Staff Council. The subordinate finds in such meetings opportunities for self-expression under the direction and co-ordination of the librarian. Good morale results when each member of the staff finds in his work and in such Sectional Meetings an adequate outlet for his creative impulse. In such conditions, there exists—not the suspicious watchfulness and the more or less open warfare which characterises the ordinary types of management—but friendly co-operation between the librarian and the staff.

1262 Changes in the Work-Manual

All the changes in job analysis agreed upon at a Sectional Meeting or by the Staff Council should be carefully drafted or at least scrutinised and approved by the librarian. They must be experimentally put into practice while in the drafting stage and the result should be observed. If any change is found to be desirable, it must be incorporated in the librarian's copy and the section's copy of the manual.

CHAPTER 13

ROUTINE

131 Terminology

By " Routine " is meant those duties of a regular and repetitive nature that are requisite for administrative purposes. The third part of most of the chapters gives the Routine for each of the Jobs relating to the Function of which the chapter treats. In considering the Routine suggested in this manual, it is necessary to bear in mind that the whole of it cannot be exactly suitable to any one set of conditions ; but all the suggestions have been found most necessary and valuable under some one or other ordinary condition.

132 Empirical Approach

The Routine is described in the light of the experience gained during the ten years of training the staff of the Madras University Library. Eighty per cent of the staff were raw recruits, quite unaccustomed to any Routine. This factor provided endless opportunities to observe the idiosyncrasies that men are capable of in performing even the simplest and the obvious Routine, if left to themselves—this is quite apart from the lack of application and the reluctance to do hard work continuously, so characteristic of the youth fresh from the examination-ridden school or college. This situation provided ample opportunities to experiment in many ways and finally fix the Routine with the co-operation and consent of the staff concerned.

133 Need for Revision

Routine, that serves a valuable purpose when initiated, may cease to be useful by some later change in conditions.

1331 EXAMPLE FROM ISSUE WORK

For example, in the earlier years, the Circulation Section had to be inducted in the Routine suited to a " closed " library. As the library began to attract an increasing crowd and as the issue began to mount up by leaps and bounds, the established Routine began to break down from time to time and it had to be varied, against the inertia of established habits. But quite a sharp break had to come in and the existing Routine had to be thrown overboard and replaced by an altogether new one ; because, the authorities of the library were obliged to introduce the open access system and prepare themselves, in conformity with what obtains in open access libraries all the world over, for the small annual loss incidental to such a system, as being less wasteful than increasing the circulation staff indefinitely as the issue increased.

1332 Example from Book-Purchase-Chain

Again, in the earlier years, book selection and book ordering were done once in a year. Consequently cataloguing also came to be done only for a few weeks in the year and there was no classification. This implied also that the bulk of the work of the Accounts Section was concentrated in a few weeks of the year. In those circumstances, the entire staff was moved on from one function to another in the course of the year. This slow method of administering the library was possible in the earlier years as the users were very few and very patient, not knowing what kind of service they could expect from a library. As the library changed its outlook and placed in the forefront prompt and adequate service to the public, the planning of the Routine on an annual basis had to be given up and the weekly basis had to be established for the book-purchase-chain. Books came to be selected and ordered every week. Books arrived every week. They had to be classified, catalogued and released for public use week by week. This change in conditions meant the establishment of an altogether new Routine.

1333 Local Variation

Sometimes a Routine is established to correct some abuse or to gain some experience and with the education of the parties concerned, the value of that Routine becomes too little to be worth maintaining. Hence, it has to be clearly understood that it is not meant that the Routine described in this manual is to be rigidly and mechanically enforced. It has to be looked upon merely as a model. Each library will have to vary it suitably and, whenever necessary, add subsidiary Routine in the light of the strength, the experience, and the ability of the staff.

134 How To Revise

1341 Habit and Prejudice

In setting out to reorganise any Routine, a good deal of preparation is necessary if the transition is to be effected smoothly. Regard must be paid not only to the changing of the methods of Routine involved, but also to the changing of personal habits and to the influence of personal prejudice. If the reorganisation is in good hands, preparatory moves will be made to make ready for the change. This preparatory action is always important, even when the prejudice to be overcome is negligible.

1342 Hasten Slowly

Reorganisation that touches the habits of man should " hasten slowly". The taking on of new habits and the shedding of old habits should be made natural by stimulating the interest of those concerned in the new methods. Any one who has had experience in reorganisation will realise the necessity of keeping an open mind as to the best moves to make and the best sequence in which to make them. Many circumstances may arise to suggest a modification of original plans, and if some desired result can be achieved without disturbing some habits, then this should be done. In any case full notes should be set down of existing methods for future reference, before altering anything. It is quite an important point to consult those who have to carry out the Routine, as to the actual conditions of work. Even if the organiser feels that they cannot be expected to understand the principles of the new lines on which he is working, he will always be the stronger for demonstrating to an interested party—it may be an opposite party—the merits of his proposals. If the organiser can convince the Routine Worker that a modification of Routine is desirable, the results of reorganisation are likely to be better. And on purely selfish grounds, the organiser should aim to have the staff with him by such a step.

1343 Stimulation of the Loyalty of the Staff

To take the staff with him means, or may seem to mean, painfully slow progress, but once this inertia has been overcome, progress will be both rapid and irresistible. But above all, perhaps, the loyalty of the staff will have been stimulated and quite possibly much latent merit in the staff will have been discovered. The staff should willingly realise that it is their duty at this stage to raise points not seemingly provided for by the organiser. Once new methods have become accepted as desirable, it is difficult to be patient with those whose prejudice is longer lived. But even so it is a better policy to circumvent this prejudice than attempt to bear it down by the exercise of authority.

135 Librarian's Duty

Scientific management thus requires considerable thinking, planning, analysis and the previous writing out of the details of procedure on the part of the librarian.

The notion, that the head of a library has only to sign fair copies, and at other moments either drive the staff with the power vested in him or if he is of a soft nature give himself up to private pursuits, should go.

136 Duty of the Staff

While all this is necessary, it is by no means sufficient. No System of Routine, however carefully prescribed, will produce the desired effect, unless its details are faithfully performed by the staff. The unusual opportunity which the library gives to the public to come in constant contact with its working will sharply show forth every little inaccuracy and slovenliness in carrying out the Routine. This danger is very great in libraries. Nothing can be hidden in a library from the public eye. The meticulous performance of the allotted routine with goodwill, interest, and zeal is the only means of ensuring the quality of the service and maintaining the reputation of the library.

1361 Adherence to Time-Table

To mention one or two details, it is of the greatest importance that the time-table for the performance of the different jobs should be strictly observed. Any slackness at any point is likely to appear ultimately as delay in serving the public.

1362 Style of Writing

In spite of the many mechanical contrivances now available,

much writing by hand still remains to be done. A slovenly or irregular hand will, in addition to its being an eye-sore if it catches the public eye, lead to much confusion in charging, discharging and other items of work. Hence, it is necessary that all writing should be neat and clear. All the assistants in a library should remodel their style in conformity with the round detached library hand.[10] The lines should be properly directed. They should be invariably parallel to the edges. It is irritating to find accession numbers, call numbers, headings, and titles written on the catalogue cards or on the books themselves along lines making all imaginable angles with the edges.

137 Accuracy of Work

Another fundamental quality demanded by Library Routine is accuracy. Even a small inaccuracy, for example, in writing the call numbers or accession numbers will create a situation demanding protracted work to discover and set right the inaccuracy at a later stage. Take another example. A most trivial mistake in spelling may effectively hide away a catalogue card from the readers. Those that have had a week's experience in the Circulation Routine can realise what a heartbreak can be caused even by the slightest negligence or inaccuracy in the charging and discharging work.

138 Orderliness

It is well known that a library has to handle thousands of volumes, each being different from the other. Hence, it will be perhaps easily granted that unless orderliness of the highest degree is practised, chaos will soon be the result. But, perhaps, it is not so well known that most of the records in a library are now kept in cards to satisfy the Fourth Law of Library Science, viz " Save the time of the reader " and its corollary, " Save the time of the staff".[11] The card system of records has been shown to reduce the work by about seventy-five per cent. Any apparatus which is so highly evolved and efficient is bound to be extremely delicate. It must be handled with the greatest care and orderliness possible, or endless confusion and chaos will result.

Chapter 14

ELIMINATION OF WASTE

141 Scientific Management

Scientific management requires that, in prescribing the routine as well as in getting it carried out, every possible care must be taken to eliminate waste. Wastage may occur in human personality, in mental energy and in physical energy. Wastage may also occur in materials, in space and in time.

142 Management of Personnel

Of these, the wastage in human personality is the most subtle and elusive and is usually least provided against, although it is the most devastating. When the lower qualities and emotions—a false sense of prestige or the fascination of tyrannical methods—blind the man at the head of affairs, they cause much damage to the personality of the staff.

1421 Philosophy of Force

The trouble may also be due to some false philosophy of management. One such philosophy of moving the staff to action is the philosophy of force. The individual may be presented with hard alternatives, either do a particular thing, or be hurt or made to suffer a loss.

1422 Philosophy of Trickery

Another false philosophy is that of trickery. It ignores the organic nature of human conduct and attempts to deal with every situation *ad hoc*. Both the philosophy of force and the philosophy of trickery sometimes secure results. Both tend to secure these results without bringing into play, or even in opposition to, the personality of the staff. Trickery soon exhausts itself ; force can at best secure only the minimum response, at the cost of an accumulating mountain of grievances, which at last overwhelm the aggressor, as history has repeatedly proved. Force or trickery blesseth neither the chief nor the staff. They both result ultimately in a huge waste in the personality of both.

1423 Philosophy of Leadership

How much more intelligent and how much more human is the philosophy of leadership which enlists the whole personality of the followers. Such a philosophy is hardly compatible with a solitary or predatory attitude which regards others merely as material for exploitation. A social philosophy, on the contrary, holds that individual happiness is best advanced by collective action.

1424 Assent of the Staff

As a first step in the elimination of waste in personality, sane leadership secures the assent of the staff. Thereby, it releases the whole energy instead of a small part. There is no question as to which type of leadership will unfold the personality most fully and eliminate waste therein. But men at the head of affairs have often lacked the patience, the wisdom and the spiritual insight to use the slower but in the end the more productive method of working *with* the staff.

1425 Situation for Use of Force

Force is sometimes justified in one type of situation. When a man is yielding to impulses which in his innermost heart he knows to be anti-social or contrary to obligations whose justice he acknowledges, he will respect force and may even feel gratitude to the chief who wields it. But most of the incentives to effort are social in their nature.

1426 Mutual Adjustment

Now let us examine the interaction among the staff themselves. At first the members do not know and are often suspicious of one another. There are unarticulated and often discordant purposes pulling in various directions. But as good leadership provides the conditions and the stimuli which release the natural social tendencies and habits of the group, these jangling purposes gradually adjust themselves and a common purpose—a " personality " quite definitely recognisable—emerges in the administrative force. It has become a live organism. A small scale repetition of this process takes place every time a new member is grafted on to the living tissues of the group. He is alien and difficult until he has imbibed the customs and the points of view of the group. It is one of the duties of the librarian to minimise the wastage in personality due to these factors.

1427 Maladjustment of Work

Another cause that may lead to wastage in personality is maladjustment of work. If a man cannot do his work well, yet cannot escape doing it, he is likely to come to hate it, and various emotional disturbances mar the performance. The man may attempt to compensate for his own uneasy feeling of inefficiency by activity in other directions in which he imagines he can do better, with the result of meddlesomeness or flightiness. Inferiority reactions may occur in other forms or the individual may simply resign himself to the performance of drudgery, with no interest. Another maladjustment comes when the individual performs work which is too simple for him. Then, he will be bored and inefficiency will set in.

The wastage in personality due to such maladjustments and the importance of the correct adjustment of the individual to the intellectual level of his task are matters of more importance than is commonly realised. It is also a matter of considerable difficulty, because the work of the world must be done and it is not always practicable to give full weight to individual preferences in getting it done. At moments of political and communal recrimination and readjustment, this problem comes to be deliberately ignored. Complete adjustment is also difficult because of the lack of a fully developed technique for measuring individual capacity or assessing individual aptitude. Hence, the success of a management in elimination of waste in this direction, has to depend largely on the judgment and tact of the librarian.

1428 Adjustment of Routine

In conclusion, it may be said that the librarian should deal with every situation and distribute work in such a way that an opportunity is afforded for the personality of each member of the staff to get itself expressed as fully and as artistically as possible in his work. Even routine becomes an enjoyable work of art if the personality of the performer can express itself in it. In such a case, the routine gets adjusted in the most well-proportioned and the most economical way.

143 Factors other than Personnel

While the wastage in human personality is most elusive and requires the full play of the personality of the librarian for its elimination, certain mechanical aids are available to eliminate wastage in other respects, viz mental energy, physical energy, materials, space and time. These aids centre round three ideas, viz standardisation, simplification and recording.

144 Standardisation

Standardisation is the setting up, by authority or common consent, of a quantity, quality, pattern, or method, as a unit of measurement or as an example for imitation. An individual lives his life within severe limits of time, energy and creative power. Hence, every act that can be taken out of the domain of new and therefore uncertain and difficult things, and put in the category of routine and simple acts—approximating to involuntary acts—releases his time and energy to the fulfilment of the creative impulse and thus enlarges his horizon. Hence, standardisation is one of the essential forces which make civilisation possible. Such institutions as the United States Bureau of Standards and the Indian Standards Institution are a tribute for the necessity of standards.

1441 Field for Standardisation

Standardisation can be applied with advantage to nearly all the affairs of business. Wherever a method or an object is used repeatedly, there is likely to be an advantage in standardising the practice and limiting it to a small range of models. Standardisation may be applied to qualities and sizes of materials, to processes and to working procedures of performance. Library administration has to gain not a little by observing the principle of standardisation.

14411 Dewey and Standardisation

Melvil Dewey, the father of librarianship, was one of the first librarians who not only preached standardisation but practised it. Here is an estimate of Dewey's contribution to standardisation :

Out of the determination of Dewey to standardise and simplify " grew the Committee on Co-operation of the American Library Association, which he operated at no profit to himself in Boston. Out of that grew the Readers and Writers Economy Co as a means of manufacturing and distributing time-saving devices for librarians. Out of that finally grew the Library Bureau whose catalogues of equipment quickly overleapt mere convenience for libraries and have resulted in changing the business methods and equipment of every modern office".[12]

1443 Library Materials

The library profession has now standards, on the side of materials, for the book selection card—which is also to serve successively as the book order card, the accession card, and the withdrawal card— the catalogue card, the shelf register card, the book card, the readers' ticket, the book racks, the book shelves, the book trolley, and every kind of records, forms and receptacles.

1444 Library Practices

It has also standardised the procedure to be followed in book selection, in book ordering, in accessioning, in classifying, in cataloguing, in circulation work and in every other piece of work to be done in a library. The routine that is described in the several chapters of this book aims to set up a standard of procedure. The sections dealing with routine are overweighted with details in order to make the standard procedure as definite as possible.

145 Simplified Practice

Next to the principle of standardisation comes the principle of simplification. The smaller the variety of models and sizes which will answer a given need, the lower the wastage. A realisation of this advantage, sharpened by the urgent demands of the world war, led the American business men to seek the guidance of the Department of Commerce and to embark on an extensive programme of simplification. To give an example of their achievement in this matter, where thirty-four varieties and sizes of common brick were made, it was found possible to serve all purposes with one ; where milk bottles were made in forty-nine sizes and types, it was found that nine sizes, all supplied with a single size of cap, would do.[13]

1451 Margin of Tolerance

Reduction of all cases to a single standard or a limited range of standards, presents certain difficulties. We have to reconcile the principle of standardisation to a practical difficulty. Uniformity is foreign to Nature. Among thousands of people all of the same racial type, no two will be found precisely alike. So also in the case of processes. The best that can be aimed at is approximate similarity. In practice some degree of departure from the standard, called " margin of tolerance", must be allowed for. Thus when the standard length of the catalogue card is 5″ it is better to specify it as 5″±.05″ ; by thus fixing the upper limit to the tolerance, we hope to prevent the departure from the standard from becoming violent.

1452 Example of Margin of Tolerance

The general procedure in fixing the margin of tolerance is to ascertain or decide the degree of variation consistent with a desired performance and make the margin as great as can be consistent with this performance. The necessity of tolerance extends to many fields besides the mechanical and the material. Many pieces of work in a library require comparatively exact time standards. For two years, we had a trying time in the Madras University Library when the time standards were rigidly fixed without allowing a margin of tolerance. Not a week passed without each section complaining about the other section as lagging behind time. This produced much irritation and, what is worse, breakdown of performance. About a year ago, the rendering of the time scheme elastic by allowing a reasonable margin of tolerance has produced the necessary change in the atmosphere.

1453 Threshold Value

Tolerance cannot exceed a threshold value, beyond which the desired result will be impossible. The range of the tolerance tends to have a fixed ratio to size, or in other words to follow a geometric rather than an arithmetic rate of increase. In psychology this has been formulated as a law by Weber, who states that the least perceptible difference between one quantity and another bears a constant ratio to the quantity.

1454 India's Special Opportunity

Subject to the provision of such margins of tolerance, the fewer the standards, both of materials and of procedures, the better it will be. India can gain much in her library practice, if her librarians would bear this principle of simplification in mind. It is particularly easy for India, as she has not yet developed any particular standard in the library sphere and practised it for a sufficiently long time, for sentimental interests to develop. The selection of a single method or type as standard and the elimination of unnecessary types would present difficulties in countries where library practice has reached a high level of maturity ; because, it is apt to mean on the part of many individuals and libraries giving up local customs, habits and standards. But in India we are comparatively speaking, free from any such narrow loyalty to local customs, and practices at the present moment. Hence, it is much easier for the library profession in India to arrive at the fewest possible agreed standards of procedure as well as of library apparatus and equipment. The only desiderata are the development of an academic outlook and goodwill, a certain amount of research and above all the suppression of personal pique by individuals in the interest of the establishment of a healthy tradition in the profession.

146 Limitations

This call for standardisation and simplification is not, however, to be interpreted to mean that all individuality in all spheres is to be absolutely suppressed and that everything in a library is to be reduced to a dead level of mechanical routine. This is far from my idea. On the contrary, I hold emphatically that an orderly and satisfactory administrative system should strive to release men and not to enslave them.

Standardisation and simplification are therefore to be carried out only in certain limited spheres. If they are carried beyond these spheres, they are likely to be more harmful than helpful. For, it has to be constantly borne in mind that standardisation is always a compromise. Instinctively one feels, no matter how serviceable the standard article may be, that one puts a certain constraint on one's freedom of action, and some slight shackle on one's individuality in accepting a product built to fit mass needs rather than individual desire. The human mind is not built for repetition. " Life", says Prof Whitehead, " is an offensive against the repetitive mechanism of the universe".[14] The stream of thought must move constantly to new ideas, if it is to continue to flow.

1461 Mechanical Aids and Repetitive Work

Thus the demand both for individuality and for variety sets limits to the extent of standardisation. In those things, which serve the individual as mechanical aids —the type-writer or the tool by which he earns his living, the telephone by which he calls the grocer, or any similar utility—there is no great demand for individuality. All one wants are effectiveness and economy. So it is with repetitive work.

1462 Materials for Enjoyment

But in those things which are somewhat enjoyments in themselves, the average person desires as much exclusiveness, individuality and variety as he can afford. A recognition of this desire indicates roughly certain general limits beyond which the advantages of standardisation do not justify the sacrifice of personal values involved.

1463 Releasing Creative Forces

Thus, standardisation is at best a compromise between the desire for individuality and variety, and the need for economy. Where it merely represents the making habitual and automatic of a necessary activity, standardisation is a net gain to humanity, releasing creative forces to new conquests. The advantages of standardisation, simplification and mechanisation of procedure in all administrations, and particularly in library administration, are similar to what Professor Jacks calls the "Favourable omens" of the present mechanical age. "Whatever the evils of a mechanical age may be", says Prof Jacks in his Hibbert Lectures, "it, nevertheless, provides us with an opportunity for undoing its own mischiefs. Machinery is taking over the burden of human toil, and so liberating our energies and lengthening the time when we are free to use them in ways that are not mechanical. Thus, if mechanism enslaves us while we are immersed in it, at the same time it shortens the hours of our slavery and lengthens the hours when we are free men. Here surely is an opportunity which a wise generation will be quick to seize, and which only a generation sunk in folly could overlook—an opportunity to recover at the *leisure end of life* the freedom, the spontaneity, the creativeness and the joy, which the other end, the mechanical end, tends to thwart and smother."[15]

147 Pick-Up-Work

Elimination of waste of time requires the device of "Pick-Up-Work" in library administration. It is due to the necessity for posting persons at certain points in the library whether there is actual flow of work or not.

1471 Example from Reference Section

For example, the reference librarians have to be posted in the stack room at all hours. But there would be frequently intervals when there may not be any reader at all in the stack room seeking their help. At the same time, as readers may turn up at any moment, they cannot be withdrawn from the stack room. Hence, some pick-up-work must be given to the reference librarians to fill such vacant moments. The pick-up-work must be such that it can be conveniently done in their own places. In the Madras University Library, book selection work is marked out for such Pick-Up-Work for the reference section.

1472 Example from Circulation Section

Again, the circulation assistant cannot leave the counter at any moment even though he may not find sufficient counter work to engage him in certain intervals. The Pick-Up-Work that the Madras University Library is setting apart for him is the correction of the call numbers in the catalogue cards and slips of the volumes whose call numbers have undergone revision.

1473 Scheme of Pick-Up-Work

Each library will have to go carefully into this problem and work out a scheme of Pick-Up-Work, taking into consideration the qualification of the staff who have to be given such work, the adaptability of the work to be done piece-meal at intervals and the points where those members of the staff are stationed.

1474 Responsibility of Head of Section

The fourth part of most of the succeeding chapters deals with the special steps that the head of the section, dealt with in the chapter, should take—the points that he must particularly examine at stated intervals, the kind of statistics that he should collect and build from day to day as a measure of the output of his section, and the diary that he must maintain to enable him to form a clear picture of the regular movement of work in his section and to aid him in making improvements in the standard of procedure in his section and in the formulation of the necessary detailed instructions to the workers.

148 Records of Standards

A step in standardisation is the making of a definite record of the standard. Records are necessary as a substitute and supplement for human memory. Human memories are unreliable. Recollections fuse and diffuse.

Change occurs by imperceptible and unconscious departures from a remembered standard. Only where there is a definite record, is it possible to measure the degree, or note the point of departure from standards.

1481 Manual of Standards

Standard practice instructions, manuals of procedure, job analysis and time schedules furnish illustrations of records of standards. This manual itself is an instance in point. As has already been indicated elsewhere, however much it is overweighted with details, there will still be many points on which each library will have to write out its own supplementary rules. Hence, the copy of a manual like this should be bound interleaved for interpolation of subsidiary rules framed by individual libraries.

1482 Weekly Progress Report

One of the vital duties of the head of a section is to ensure the progress of the work of his section in strict accordance with the approved time scheme. For this purpose he must prepare a weekly time-table for each one of his assistants and himself, showing against each day the different jobs to be performed, arranged in proper time sequence, and indicating wherever possible or necessary the exact hour when a job should be performed or completed. He should scrutinise with the aid of the time-table whether each one of the jobs allotted for the day has been satisfactorily completed. In addition, he should examine and satisfy himself that the week's work is fully and satisfactorily rounded off before the close of the week and he should send a progress report to the librarian through the assistant librarian on the first day of every week. The progress report should state the jobs and the correspondence that are unavoidably left in arrears. Against each such item the reason for the delay and the time when it would be cleared off should be briefly stated.

1483 Diaries

For the preparation of weekly reports, without wastage or dislocation of work, each section, should maintain its own diary of all work done. Diaries are best kept in loose sheets of double foolscap size, fixed to card boards of equal size by gem clips or by any other suitable device. If they are kept in the form of bound books, the verso and the recto of an open page taken together will present the same size.

1484 Daily Diary

If the diary is for daily out-turn, one sheet can be used for one month. The number of horizontal lines should be 38. 31 lines are at the rate of one for each date in the month. The 8th line, the 16th line, the 24th line, the 32nd line and the 36th line are for cumulative totals. The 37th line is for the cumulative total for the year at the end of the preceding month to be brought forward from the diary of the preceding month. The 38th line is for the cumulative total for the year at the end of the current month.

1485 Weekly Diary

If the diary is for weekly out-turn, one sheet can be used for 6 months. The number of horizontal lines should be 32. 26 lines are at the rate of one per week for six months. The 5th line, the 10th line, the 16th line, the 21st line, the 26th line and the 32nd line are for cumulative totals. The diary sheet for the second half of the year is to have, two additional lines, one for bringing forward the cumulative total from the earlier sheet and the other for the final total for the year.

1486 SPECIFICATION FOR HEADINGS OF DIARIES

The fourth part of the different chapters will specify the column headings that should be had in the respective diaries.

1487 DIARY FORMS

The quantity of diary sheets consumed in a year will not justify printing or mechanical duplication. Further the headings may have to be altered from time to time as the distribution of jobs and routine are varied. Hence, the diary forms are to be in manuscript.

CHAPTER 15

CORRELATION

151 Harmony in Work

Elimination of waste requires another factor, namely, the correct correlation of the performances of the different sections which may be referred to as *External Correlation* and also the correct correlation of the performances of the different members of the same section, which may be referred to as *Internal Correlation*. The time is fast going by for the individual achievement of any one man standing alone and without the help of those around him. And the time is coming when all great things will be done by that type of co-operation in which each man performs the function for which he is best suited, each man preserves his own individuality and is supreme in his particular function, and each man loses none of his originality and proper personal initiative and yet is controlled by and must work harmoniously with many other men. Platitudes of this sort are easily expressed and as easily ignored as being a counsel of perfection.

152 Co-ordination and Economy

But the principle of effective correlation assumes special importance in library administration, as the library has to work on all days and for long hours, as the service rendered by the library has to be characterised by an extraordinary degree of promptness and exactness, and as the nature of books is such that accuracy of the highest order is necessary in handling them and in dealing with the various records connected with them at different stages and in different sections. The main essentials to be considered in organising the everyday details in library administration are co-ordination and economy. To an extent economy results from co-ordination. But proper co-ordination may mean an increase of staff and paper work, which may easily appear and still more easily be condemned as extravagance or red-tape ; but the test of economy lies further along the line, as to whether improved administrative correlation is finding expression in over-all increased efficiency in point of quantity or quality or both.

153 Method of Correlating

1531 Staff Council

The librarian should meet the heads of sections at least once in a month to discuss the various matters of inter-sectional adjustment. The formation of Staff Council and regular monthly meetings of the same will be helpful in this matter. I have suggested in the *Five laws of library science*[16] that the Staff Council may consist of the heads of all the sections and in addition one representative of each section. But later experience has shown that the long hours of the library and the shift system, that has to obtain, make it difficult to convene monthly meetings of such a large Staff Council. Hence we changed over in the Madras University Library to the experiment of having only the heads of sections on the Staff Council.

1532 Sectional Meeting

It is desirable to have monthly meetings of the members of a section to discuss and solve all intra-sectional problems. If all such Sectional Meetings are held a few days before the monthly meeting of the Staff Council, it will be possible for the inter-sectional problems also to be well discussed at the respective Sectional Meetings, so that the heads of the sections are well equipped to come to satisfactory and stable decisions on all correlational points brought before the Staff Council. Another method of improving the correlation will be to appoint small *ad hoc* committees to consider specific points and to draft for the consideration of the Staff Council definite rules to help correlation of work between the different sections. Whatever be the machinery set up for the purpose, it is one of the primary duties of the librarian to put his full personality into this work of correlation, so that the best results may be achieved with the least hitch.

154 Articulated Whole

The fifth part of most of the succeeding chapters contains a Correlation Table. It mentions the different rules which represent points of contact between the section dealt with in the chapter and the other sections. The routine described in the several rules figuring in the Correlation Table will be the chief items of routine that will have to be constantly watched and frequently re-examined by the librarian and the Staff Council so that the work of the different sections may be well dovetailed into one another, the correlation between the different sections may always be maintained at as high a level as possible, and the entire work of the library may present a picture of a well articulated whole.

155 Spirit of the Hive

Such a high degree of correlation in the work and the most cordial terms in the relationship of the staff are necessary if the library is to function up to its best. Perhaps, a reference may be made here to the description of the spirit of co-operation that should prevail among the library staff in consequence of the Fifth Law of Library Science—"The Spirit of the Hive" as I have called it in the *Five laws of library science.*[17] "She....departs....Her place is taken at once by an impatient worker, who continues the task that a third will finish, while others close by are attacking the rest of the surface.... ; each one obeying the law of interrupted and successive labour, as though it were an inherent principle of the hive that the pride of toil should be distributed and every achievement be anonymous and common to all."[18]

CHAPTER 16

TIME SCHEME

161 Time Famine

Time is the canvas on which every administrative picture has to be drawn. The canvas, however, is limited and does not offer full amplitude to any administration, and certainly not to library administration. On the contrary, if a library attempts to fulfil the First Three Laws of Library Science, it is obliged to face a perpetual time famine. This has become such a chronic feature of library administration that library science is obliged to devote one of its fundamental laws to time—Save the time of the reader and hence of the staff.

The jobs of the day and of the week are usually such that they can just fill a day or a week without overflowing, if, and only if, they are brought into clearly-understood time-relation with one another. In other words, there must be a properly thought-out time scheme for the jobs. Administration cannot depend upon a fortuitous adjustment of time.

162 How of the Scheme

The first step in proper time-adjustment is to classify the jobs on the basis of their periodicity. Accordingly, jobs have been classified in section 122, as immediate, hourly, casual, daily, weekly, monthly, quarterly, and annual.

1621 MODEL TIME SCHEME

The sixth part of most of the succeeding chapters gives tabular statements showing by way of illustration the distribution of the jobs in time, as it obtained at the time of edition 1 in the Madras University Library. It goes without saying that all the immediate jobs have to be done immediately, that hourly jobs have to be done each hour, and that casual jobs would have to be done as pick-up-work at slack moments. Hence such jobs will not figure in the tabular statements.

1624 DAILY JOBS

There may be a table devoted to daily jobs. This table enumerates the daily jobs in the sequence in which they are best performed. It may happen that some jobs have to be done simultaneously. Such jobs are all shown in a single line or in two or more run-on lines.

The table devoted to weekly jobs gives the jobs to be done in the different days of the week. The jobs assigned to a day are shown in the sequence in which they are best done. They will have to be interpolated between the daily jobs of the day in a convenient manner. A job which has to be done at a particular hour on the allotted day has the hour of the day shown next to it in circular brackets.

1626 Monthly Jobs

In the case of the monthly jobs, the quarterly jobs, and the annual jobs, some indication is made as to the week in which they may be done. They will have to be interpolated between the weekly jobs of the week in a convenient manner.

1628 Periodical Review

Subject to the provision of a comfortable margin of tolerance, as indicated in section 1452, each library should work out a time scheme and the staff should faithfully keep to the time-table. It is the business of the librarian and the Staff Council to review the time scheme periodically and readjust it in the light of the flow of work, change of hands, and the earlier experience in the matter.

163 Junction Mcment

Particular attention should be paid to the fixing of what may be called *Junction Moments*. Junction Moment is a point of time when two or more different jobs have to be done together and in mutual consultation by two or more members of the staff. The problem becomes much more acute, when the different jobs belong to different sections altogether or when the same job has to be done in co-operation by different sections. Each section must work out its time scheme and carry out its duties as close to the scheme as possible so that all the concerned sections may reach the Junction Moment in absolute readiness. Any hitch in this matter is bound to disturb the whole work of the library and may require protracted effort to recover from such a disturbance. The problem of the

Junction Moment is as acute and delicate as the problem of the arrival of all the trains at a junction station according to the scheduled time. As has been already indicated in section 1452, the organisation should give a reasonable margin of tolerance for the work of the different sections, so that all unavoidable deviations from the time schedule, occurring in the different sections, may be made up before the work of the sections reaches the Junction Moment. Here are some examples of the Junction Moment in the Madras University Library :

1631 Example 1

At 5 PM on Wednesdays, the technical section is to hand over the new books of the week to the maintenance section. The technical section keeps the books sorted into different sequences. The maintenance section tallies them and after a rapid scrutiny sends the volumes to their respective places. The " recent additions sequence " is a very popular sequence. Readers know this Junction Moment and they anxiously wait for the new arrivals. Any delay in the work at this Junction Moment is bound to react prejudiciously on the readers. Again the departments of research expect their new supply just after this moment.

1632 Example 2

4 PM Thursdays, is another important Junction Moment. By this time the technical section should have classified the arrivals of the week and detected finally all unintended duplications. The accession section comes to accession the volumes. It has to finish the accession before 5 PM and hand over the related bills to the accounts section. The periodical publication section also is affected by this Junction Moment, as the volumes of periodicals completed during the week have to get accessioned at this time. Thus, four sections meet at this Junction Moment.

1633 Statement of Junction Moments

The Junction Moments are shown in the tables of correlation of the fifth parts of the chapters by the insertion of the time in circular brackets after the Junction Moment jobs. The Junction Moments are also similarly indicated in the time scheme given in the sixth parts of the chapters.

164 Alternative Schemes in Reserve

There is another way in which the organisation will have to imitate the railway to secure the Junction Moment jobs being finished off without a hitch. It is known that the railway has alternative time-tables for the running of a given train in case the normal time-table breaks down completely. Similarly, the library organisation must have alternative distribution of jobs for each section in reserve, so that, if a particular member of the staff is casually prevented from doing his part, the work of the section may be carried through without allowing any repercussion on the Junction Moment. For six months, the Madras University Library worked a scheme of alternative distribution of jobs. We had worked out alternative schemes for distribution of jobs for most of the contingencies that can be reasonably anticipated. Our experience is that it is a source of great relief under trying conditions, whether the trouble is due to unavoidable sudden absence of a member of the staff, or to unusual rush of readers. It saves the head of the section from rushing about in panic and becoming irritable. It enables him to move round, absorbing the situation and *quietly* rearranging the staff, absolutely unperturbed by the conditions which he has to face, so that a spirit of confidence exists throughout.

165 Main Rhythm

It may be stated here that most of the routine in a library is best done on a weekly basis. A day is too short a period and a month is too long. Hence, the majority of the jobs of the library are weekly jobs. Therefore, the greatest possible vigilance should be exercised by the library staff to see that the work is properly rounded off every week. In the Madras University Library, we took Saturday as the first day of the week. Saturday happened to be the busiest day, partly due to the incoming of foreign mail and partly due to the number of visitors to the library being greatest on that day. Sunday came next in heaviness of work. Hence, it would have been inconvenient to clear off arrears and round off the week's work, if we ended the week with a Saturday or a Sunday. On the contrary, it was much more convenient to begin the week with such rush days.

166 Plethora of Holidays

However, there is one factor in India today which disturbs the smooth running of administration on a weekly basis. It is due to the tradition of extravagance that had crept into India in the matter of holidays. The tradition may have been due to political causes. Nevertheless, it leads to much leisureliness, disorderliness, and waste in administration. There is a plethora of holidays, scattered aperiodically throughout the year—Hindu holidays, Muhammadan holidays, Christian holidays, Vaishnava holidays, Roman Catholic holidays, sentimental holidays, and surprise holidays because "A" visits the locality, or "B" was dead, or "C" was once born, or "D" did or did not do something else or "E" lost or won a cricket match. The number of Christian holidays, for example, that India had, was many times greater than what the Christian countries themselves have. To add to this, there is a long list of "late attendance" days and "early closing" days. The result of this is the merciless thwarting of the *Rhythm of Work*.

167 Mute Sun and Cloak of Religion

I am not unaware of the specious arguments, based on pseudo-theories about the influence of the mute tropical sun, that are being advanced to perpetuate this annoying system that has somehow crept in. There are again the arguments masquerading under a religious cloak. Somebody should prick these bubbles and wipe out this baneful tradition. My appeal to the young library profession is that it should take the lead and rescue the enormous time that is being wasted.

CHAPTER 17

FORMS AND REGISTERS

171 Design

Forms are considered by some as unnecessary and are usually condemned as so much red-tape. But if properly designed, forms can be made effective tools to simplify and control work and to save time and cost. To be effective tools, however, forms must be properly designed from the point of view of accomplishing the purpose sought, with a minimum of effort and with the most economic use of materials.

1711 PURPOSE

The first question to be considered in designing the form is the purpose of the form. It must be remembered that forms provide the means of carrying out decisions and policies ; and, they also provide the basis for administrative action.

1712 DESIGN SHEET

Next to purpose, the information to be provided for in the form is to be carefully thought out and recorded systematically in the *Design Sheet*. The Design Sheet is to contain the following information :

1 All the purposes that the form has to fulfil ;
2 The information which must be recorded in the form in order to fulfil each purpose ;
3 The sections and the number of persons by whom the information is to be entered in the form ;
4 The source of the information to be entered in the form ;
5 The time, the frequency and the circumstances attendant on the entry in the form ;
6 Whether pen, pencil, or typewriter, is to be used in filling the form or whether photography is to be used ;
7 The sections and the number of persons by whom each piece of information is to be used and how it is to be used—is it transcribed to another form periodically or is it merely read by some one for information ?

8 When and how frequently and for how long a period is the information to be used ; and
9 The method of sorting the forms and the method of filing them—the information by which they are to be filed and the filing appliances to be used.

The Design Sheet should contain also remarks against each one of the above items, in brief terms, so that it can serve as a check list for consulting all those who come in contact with the form in any way.

1713 Design Work

Having collected all the necessary information and tabulated it in the Design Sheet, we are ready to design the form. The general principle underlying form design is that the recording and the using of information in the form and the handling of the form are to be performed with the greatest economy and with the least number of errors. Accuracy, speed and usefulness are the deciding factors. The following principles may be borne in mind :

1 The headings must be so chosen that the amount of writing to be done in filling the form should be reduced to the minimum possible ;
2 The headings should be in such a form that the information that it shows is definite and whenever possible quantitative ;
3 The headings should be so grouped that they fall in the sequence in which the sections using it normally think of them ; as far as possible one side of the form alone is to be used. If both sides have to be used, an effort should be made to have complete pieces of information on each side of the form to eliminate the necessity for turning ;
4 It is a moot point whether each form should contain printed instructions for its use. In libraries, the headings themselves will constitute the necessary instructions in most cases. If however some extra instruction is necessary in any particular form and if it is printed on one side only, the instructions may be printed on the blank side. This will be necessary only in the case of the forms to be filled by the public. But if the form is to be filled up only by the staff, it may be sufficient

to leave the instructions to the manual of administration ; and

5 The design of the form will depend largely on the type of file used.

51 If vertical files, the filing symbol should be conspicuously put on the leading line and the paper itself should be of proper weight ;

52 If visible files, it has to be decided what information should be visible and whether the form should be visible at the top or at the bottom ;

53 If loose leaf binding is used, sufficient binding margin must be allowed—about an inch or so ;

54 If the forms are to be bound as a book, the amount of margin to be left and the number of pages that should go into a book are to be carefully considered ; whether a verso and the succeeding recto are to be differently paginated or whether the same page number should be borne by them is also to be considered ; and

6 If photography is to be used, multi-purpose Master Copy and a set of associated Masks may be designed. The quantum of work in the libraries of India today and the current cost of clerical labour may not make this economical.

172 Specification

In regard to Specification, attention should be paid to the following :

1 The paper to be used ;

2 The size of the form ;

3 Printing ;

4 The ruling ; and

5 Punching and perforation, wherever necessary.

173 Paper

1731 GRADE

The grade of paper to be used is to be determined in the light of two factors, viz the life of the form and the character of handling.

1732 LIFE

The life of the form may be :

1 Temporary, as in the case of

11 Source selection slips (see rule 217) ;

12 Requisition form for books ;
13 Bespeaking card ;
14 Overdue card (see rule 267) ; and
15 Stores indent forms (see rule 3977).

2 Semi-permanent, as in the case of
21 Book order forms (see rule 227) ;
22 Check cards (see rule 237) ;
23 Admission cards ; and
24 Overdue register sheets (see rule 267).

3 Permanent, as in the case of
31 Accession cards (see rule 217) ;
32 Catalogue cards (see rule 257) ; and
33 The various account books (see rule 377).

1733 Handling

The character of handling may be mild as in the case of accession cards, normal as in the case of the cards of the Periodical Publication Section, or rough as in the case of the catalogue cards in the public catalogue cabinet.

In general, all forms of a permanent nature and all forms that require rough handling for a long period should be on paper of the best quality, while inferior paper may be used for forms of temporary and mild use ; for example, ledger paper is recommended for account books and for the office copy of the catalogue, whereas ordinary writing paper may be used for correspondence, stores indent forms and book selection source slips.

1734 Weight

Again, the weight of the paper to be used is to depend upon the treatment the paper is to receive, the number of carbon copies necessary, the stiffness necessary in order to aid filing, whether the form is to be sent by post and so on. For example, the cards of the Periodical Publication Section and the accession cards are to be made of bristol boards, but the catalogue cards of the public catalogue cabinet are to be of special make with a large percentage of rag, and well pressed and calendered.

1735 Colour

With regard to the colour of the paper, it is better to prefer white or nearly white colour in almost all cases. Colour schemes may have to be adopted for facilitating expeditious routine work. But it is not necessary that the entire card should be coloured. In the Madras University Library, we had experimented with coloured cards for five years. Our feeling is that coloured cards produce exhaustion of the eye much more quickly. At the same time we were convinced also of the great help that the colour scheme gives. We have reconciled these two factors in the following way. Instead of using coloured cards, we use white cards only. But where coloured cards are necessary, the white card has its top edge coloured with the appropriate tint. The application of the colour extends only to about 1/10 of an inch, from the edge. This arrangement secures all the facilities that the colour scheme can give and at the same time relieves the eye from unnecessary strain.

1736 SIZE

The size of the form is a very important factor in effecting savings. Since the time of Melvil Dewey, the opinion of the library profession has been slowly but definitely drawing its weight in favour of 3×5 inches in most of the cases. Such a standardisation of the size of the form is very important, particularly for the ultimate filing of cards or sheets. This standardisation of size is one of the preliminary steps to clear the way for development. To cut cards of 3×5 inches size, it is desirable that libraries purchase boards which are produced to the size 25½×30½ inches. Fifty cards of standard size will cut from one board of this size without any wastage.

While most of the forms in library use are now of the size 3×5 inches, there are still some forms of other odd sizes. There are, for example, letter heads. They cannot obviously be reduced to 3×5 inches size. Further, the practice in India has not yet recognised the value of reducing all letter head sizes to one uniform size. At least two different sizes are in use in most libraries, while three sizes are not uncommon. Again the account books form another problem. The present practice seems to be to keep the account books in folio size. Similarly, certain other forms relating to the staff and account sections continue to be maintained in folio size.

At the other extreme, we have the readers' ticket and the book card which have necessarily to be of a very small size—about 2×1 inches size.

1737 Grade

The following are the only grades recommended : 1 Bristol board, 4 sheets thick ; 2 Ledger paper, double foolscap, 30 lb ; 3 Printing paper, double foolscap, 24 lb ; 4 Printing paper, double foolscap, 21 lb ; 5 Printing paper, double foolscap, 16 lb.

174 Printing

1741 Type-Size

When a form has to be printed, the size of type must be carefully chosen. In all forms intended only for internal use in the library, the smallest possible size may be used, say 6 point type. On the other hand, for forms to be used by the public, slightly larger type may be desirable. Whenever the form is of the standard card size, and much matter has to be printed, 6 point type will have to be used.

1742 Printing of Cards

If a form has to be printed on both sides, care must be taken about the direction in which the successive lines run. If the form is of the card size, in most cases it will be filed vertically so as to stand on one of its longer edges. Hence, the lines should run parallel to the longer edges. Further, as the card will turn on its bottom edge as the axis, the first line at the back of the card will have to be near the bottom edge.

1743 Printing of Other Forms

In the same way, in the case of each form the way in which it will be filed and the axis about which it will turn must be taken into consideration to decide the point where the printing on the back side is to commence.

175 Ruling

Much of staff-time can be saved if proper attention is paid to the ruling of forms. The unit of measure or the distance between two consecutive rules is 1 point or $\frac{1}{72}$ inch. The number of points by which horizontal lines should be spaced must be so decided that the number of rules in a page is five or a multiple of five, in all forms in which the entries are of a-line-an-entry type. The total number of entries are counted very easily if the ruling is standardised in this way. The labour of collecting and building up statistics is thus considerably minimised. From the point of view of the space necessary for writing, 18 point i e ¼ inch spacing is quite common. Hence, the spacing selected for any particular form should be that one in the neighbourhood of ¼ inch, which satisfies the condition that has already been laid down regarding the number of rules that should be had on a page.

1751 Warning

A word of warning may be uttered. The expense of securing proofs for ruling is tremendous and therefore usually prohibitive. It is therefore necessary to have specifications for ruling perfect, since corrections are not possible. It is even more necessary to have accurate specifications for a ruled form than for a form for which a plate is to be made ; for, the loss in case a plate is wrong is merely the cost of the plate, while if the rulings are not specified correctly, the cost is the labour of setting up the machine, the time the machine has been operated and the entire value of the paper.

176 Enumeration

The seventh part of most of the succeeding chapters is devoted to the enumeration and specification of the forms necessary for the work of the section. If one and the same form is likely to be of use in two or more sections, it is described in the chapter devoted to the earliest of the sections. Letter heads and other forms required for general correspondence are described in Chapter 393 "Correspondence Section".

177 Form Number

For convenience of reference, each form is given a *Form Number*. A form number will consist of three groups of digits. Each digit is to be given place value as in decimal fraction.

1771 Size Number

As we proceed from left to right, the first group will represent size. It may be called the *Size Number* and will consist of a single digit as shown in the following schedule :

A Abnormally small size, i e size less than 7.5×13 cms.
C Card size, i e 7.5×13 cms.
O Octavo size, i e 10.5×17 cms.
Q Quarto size, i e 21.5×17 cms.
S Super-size or folio size, i e 21.5×34 cms.

1772 FUNCTION NUMBER

The second group will consist of one digit, two digits or three digits, according as it has no 9, one 9, or two 9's at its beginning. This may be referred to as the *Function Number* and will consist of the number representing the section to which the form is assigned.

1773 JOB NUMBER

The third group may be referred to as the *Job Number*. It will consist of one or more digits fixed mnemonically with reference to the number of the job in connection with which the form is mostly used.

178 Description of Form

A form may be of different kinds—letter heads ; letter forms for issuing routine letters ; tabular forms with column headings ; tabular forms with row headings ; tabular forms with column headings as well as row headings ; forms such as application forms and requisition forms for use by the public ; and so on.

Again, some forms may have to be printed, some—those for internal use—may be stencilled, while certain other forms may also be maintained in manuscript.

The description of a form will consist of the following items in the sequence shown :

1 Form number ;
2 Name of the form ;
3 Whether the form is to be printed, stencilled or handwritten ;
4 If it is to be printed, the size of type to be used ;
5 The grade of paper to be used ;
6 The colour of paper to be used ; or the colour with which

the edge of the form is to be treated ;

7 The size of the form, if not clear from the first digit of the form number ;

8 Method of filing, if necessary and called for ; and

9 Other pieces of information regarding the matter to be printed, headings, rulings, etc which will vary with the nature of the form.

In case a form is to be ruled, the number of rules to be drawn in a page and the interval between the rules will be given in terms of points—a point being equal to $\frac{1}{72}$ of an inch. In the case of tabular headings, for each heading, the width of the column or the row, as the case may be, will be given in inches within circular brackets wherever necessary. In the case of forms of a complex nature, the entire form will be reproduced on a conveniently reduced scale. Whenever drafts of routine letters are given, the letter head is to be added to them in the usual way, i e in the same style as is indicated for form Q993. In the case of registers, if each page is to be differently paginated it will be described as "Ordinary Pagination". If on the other hand any two opposite pages are to receive the same page number, it will be described as "Folio Pagination".

CHAPTER 18

CORRESPONDENCE, FILES AND RECORDS

181 Introduction

1811 VERTICAL FILE

Filing is a very important phase of work in every office. The general efficiency of a business depends to a great extent upon the efficiency of its filing system. Experience has proved that papers filed horizontally one on top of another in drawers or on shelves are much harder to find than those filed vertically on edge, one back to the other. Thus, there came into use the *Vertical File*.

1812 PROBLEMS OF FILING

The study of the problem of filing correspondence and records has continued until, today, filing equipment and systems have become pretty well standardised. This standardisation includes the various sizes of papers, the types of filing equipment in which they can be placed with the greatest economy of space and the filing methods by which they may be filed quickly and found quickly when needed, so as to satisfy the corollary of the Fourth Law of Library Science, viz Save the Time of the Staff.

1813 MECHANICAL EQUIPMENT

In our country, the financial and other conditions attendant on most of the libraries do not justify the introduction, at present, of any specialised filing equipment which would involve large initial outlay. The usual pad, the work table fitted with a shelf along the farther edge and a vertical file drawer at either side and the record rack are sufficient equipment.

1814 FILE ARRANGEMENT

Regarding the arrangement of files, however, there is no reason why the most up-to-date method should not be used by any library—large or small, rich or poor. It is usual to divide the methods of arranging files into two groups, viz. the alphabetical group and the numerical group. A method that is numerical up to a point and then changes over to the alphabetical and chronological methods is most satisfactory in a library—in fact in any office. The filing method that is given here is of this mixed type.

1815 Filing as a Vocation

But whatever the method of filing adopted, a heavy responsibility rests upon the shoulders of those who do the filing work. The accuracy of this work cannot be checked up at the end of each day as can the accuracy of the book-keeper or the cashier or the typist. A filing error, as a rule, goes unnoticed until that fateful day on which a certain paper is called for and is found missing. The loss of a record is often a most serious matter. It is extremely important, therefore, that all papers be filed with the utmost care and accuracy. The principal object of filing is not filing itself, but the rapid finding of the papers filed. This requires a fairly advanced filing method, the details of which—particularly, file numbering—require to be carefully mastered by a course of training and instruction. In other words, the improved filing methods of today involve the employment of trained operators. Filing has become a definite, and important office vocation. But, in the words of James N McCord, Director of the New York School of Filing, " When it came to the various refinements, the intelligent classification and segregation, the ability to accurately and instantly produce,....there was no source from which properly qualified persons could be secured. Trained stenographers, typists, book-keepers and telephone operators were easily available, but no provision had ever been made for similar instruction for filing and indexing clerks except by library schools whose excellent work is confined to library methods."[19] The library profession may well be proud of this tribute.

182 Filing Method

Let us now turn to the actual filing method. Perhaps it is best to clear, at the outset, the use of the terms involved. The conception of " ultimate file " is developed in the next few pages, for the sake of definiteness and clearness. But let us begin with the ordinary use of the term file.

1821 File Defined

The *New Oxford dictionary* gives the following definitions to the word " file " used as a noun :

1 A string or wire, on which papers and documents are strung for preservation and reference. In recent years extended to various other appliances for holding papers so that they can be easily referred to.
2 A collection of papers placed on a file or merely arranged in order of date or subject for ready reference.

Used as a verb, to file means to place a document in a due position among the records of a court or public office.

1822 Filing Terms

All correspondence should be minutely classified and assigned a *File Mark*. The file mark of a correspondence will consist of two parts, the *File Number* and the *Filing Characteristic*.

The File Number is to be made up successively of the following :

18221 The number of the section of the staff to which it relates. This part of the file number may be referred to as the *Section Number*.

18222 The number representing the factor, or the work, or the job, as the case may be, to which it relates. This part of the file number may be referred to as the *Purport Number*.

18223 The number made up of the Section Number and the Purport Number may be referred to as the *Class Number*.

18224 The number, if any, amplifying the class number. This part of the file number may be referred to as the *Amplifying Number*.

Of these, the Section Number and the Purport Number will consist of Arabic numerals and the Amplifying Number will consist of letters of the Roman alphabet or Arabic numerals or both. The digits in a File Number are to be written from left to right and are to be given place value as in decimal fractions. As for their absolute magnitude, they fall in the following sequence when arranged in the ascending sequence of magnitude : A, B, C,.. Y, Z, 0, 1, 2,..8, 9.

1823 Filing Characteristic

All correspondence which have the same File Number are to be classified among themselves by the *Filing Cha acteristic.* The Filing Characteristic will vary with the File Number. In the majority of cases, it will consist of the name of the correspondent.

1824 Ultimate File

All correspondence having the same File Mark should be fastened by a single tape tag, a pin being used if the number of sheets to be fastened is less than four. It will be called an *Ultimate File.* The correspondence in an Ultimate File are to be arranged chronologically by the date of emanation from or of receipt in the library. If a correspondence is in two or more sheets, they are to be arranged among themselves in their proper sequence, as indicated on them, or if there is no such indication, such that they read continuously, annexures, if any, coming last. The leaves of an ultimate file are to be numbered continuously at the right hand top corner.

The filing characteristic must be chosen so that the papers which get fastened by a single tape tag into an ultimate file satisfy the following conditions :

1 The papers read continuously ; and
2 There is unity of subject-matter.

The Filing Characteristic may have to be omitted if it prevents continuous reading.

1825 Docket Sheet

Each ultimate file must be furnished with a *Docket Sheet.* The Docket Sheet may be a sheet of brown paper. A white label $3 \times 2\frac{1}{2}$ inches is to be pasted near its left hand bottom corner so that the edges of the label are parallel to the corresponding edges of the Docket Sheet and are one inch from them. This label may be referred to as the *Docket Label.* On the Docket Label, the file mark is to be written in lines parallel to the longer edge. The class number is to be in the first line and the filing characteristic in the second line and continued if necessary in the succeeding lines.

Example : 611G
Chandrasekharan (S)
2057

Here 6 is the Section Number. It shows that the file relates to the Circulation Section.

11 is the Purport Number. It shows that it relates to membership.

G is the Amplifying Number. It shows that it relates to a graduate member.

Chandrasekharan (S) 2057 is the Filing Characteristic. It is the name of the member, amplified by his deposit number in order to individualise the different persons having the same name. In this case the name of the member followed by his deposit number is used as the Filing Characteristic.

1826 Definition of Ultimate File

Now we may define an *Ultimate File* as a gathering of a Docket Sheet and one or more sheets of paper containing correspondence, notes, etc characterised by unity of subject and continuity of treatment and arranged chronologically with the Docket Sheet first and fastened together for preservation and ready reference, with the aid of a pin or a tape tag or any other suitable appliance.

1827 Pad of Files

All the ultimate files having the same file number are to be arranged among themselves by the filing characteristic and are to be ordinarily kept in one pad. However, if the number of files belonging to a file number is too many to be put conveniently in one pad, they may be distributed over two or more pads. On the contrary, if the number of ultimate files belonging respectively to two or more consecutive ultimate files is too small to require a separate pad for each file number, a single pad may be used to accommodate all the ultimate files of all such file numbers. A label $3 \times 2\frac{1}{2}$ inches is to be pasted on one of the flaps of the pad just near the point where the flap is stuck to the pad. This label may be referred to as the *Pad Label*. On this label, the inclusive file numbers of all the ultimate files contained in it are to be written in a line or lines parallel to the longer edge of the pad.

1828 Collections of Files

The pads relating to a section are to be arranged vertically in a classified sequence by the file numbers along the farther edge of the work table. If the number of pads is too large to be accommodated in one line, the farther edge of the work table may be fitted with the necessary number of shelves to accommodate all the pads of the section. The collection of files thus formed along the farther edge of the work table may be referred to as the *Current Collection.* Such of the files of the Current Collection as are taken out for disposal on any day are to be kept flat in a separate pad. This flat file pad may be referred to as the *Disposal Pad.* Such of the files as have been finally disposed of are to be sent either to the *Quasi-Current Collection* or to the *Record Collection,* according to the instruction on the subject. A file which is sent to the Quasi-Current Collection is to have its file number, after the alterations, if any, in accordance with instructions, underlined. A file which is sent to the Record Section is to have its file number, after the alterations, if any, in accordance with instructions, both overlined and underlined. The location of the quasi-current collection relating to different sections will be indicated in the respective chapters. But the location of the record collection is the Record Section itself. In case the library is small, and young, and the records are not many in number, it may not be inconvenient to have the record collection also located in the sections concerned.

1829 Change of Collection and Destruction

It requires great discretion to decide when and how long a file should be in the quasi-current collection, when and how long it should be kept in the record collection, and whether it can be destroyed at all and if so, when. The following general principle may be enunciated :

A file is to be taken away from the current collection as soon as it may be reasonably deemed to have been finally disposed of. If it is one that may be required for audit purposes, it should in the first instance be transferred to the quasi-current collection and transferred therefrom to the record collection as soon as the audit is over. Otherwise, it may be transferred directly from the current collection to the record collection. The period for which a file should lie in the record collection will have to be decided for each class of cases, while certain files will have to be treated as permanent records and never destroyed.

183 Enumeration of Files

The eighth part of most of the succeeding chapters is devoted to the files of the section concerned. It will give all the information regarding the files in a tabular form. The following are the headings of the tabular form so far as they may be applicable :

1 The name of the file ; for convenience of reference, each file will be given a name ;
2 The class number ;
3 Method of amplifying the class number, if any ;
4 The filing characteristic ;
5 The time of transfer to the quasi-current collection ;
6 The file number it is to have while lying in the quasi-current collection if different from the original file number ;
7 The time of transfer to the record collection ;
8 The file number it is to have while lying in the record collection if different from the original file number ; and
9 The time of destruction, if not to be preserved permanently.

Class numbers may be amplified by subject device or language device or any other similar device. Subject device consists in putting, after the class number, the number of the main subject of the book or books as given in the scheme of classification in use in the library, to which the file relates. Other devices are to be constructed along analogous lines.

184 Receipt of Mail

As soon as the mail arrives, every inward correspondence gets opened by the librarian and gets his dated initials. They are then sent to the Correspondence Section to be registered.

For each correspondence, the registering clerk writes its File Number above the salutation, if it is not already found in some standard place in the correspondence. He also underlines in pencil the Filing Characteristic, in case it is different from the name of the correspondent. Then he registers the correspondence in the appropriate Inward Correspondence Register. The correspondence and the registers are then sent to the different sections. Along with these, the Outward Correspondence Registers and the files relating to the outward correspondence despatched on the preceding day are also sent to the respective sections.

185 Collection of Papers

As soon as these materials arrive at a section, the head of the section does the following :

1851 He takes charge of the files, relating to his section and returned by the Correspondence Section, and initials against the respective items in the Outward Correspondence Register. In the office copy filed last in each such ultimate file, he examines if the despatcher had stamped the date of despatch. If he had not done so, he brings it to the notice of the despatcher and gets it rectified. If there is inordinate discrepancy between the date of despatch and the date of the office copy as given beneath the initials of the drafting clerk, he brings it to the notice of the librarian.

1852 He rapidly examines if any item in the despatch register relating to his section has the column "Reply Receipt Date" blank. For each such item, he examines if the reply, due date (given in the appropriate column in the despatch register) has been passed. If so, he pulls out the related file from the current collection and places it on the *Disposal Pad.* If the ultimate file is not in the current collection, it is likely to be found in the files just received from the correspondence section or in the *Deferred Disposal Pad.*

1853 He takes charge of the inward correspondence and the enclosures and the accompanying materials, if any, relating to his section and initials against the appropriate items in the Inward Correspondence Register.

1854 He then sends away the Outward Correspondence Register and the Inward Correspondence Register.

1855 Then he pulls out from the current collection the ultimate files relating to each of the inward correspondence received by him and files that correspondence therein. If a letter has no file relating to it, a fresh file is to be started with that letter as the first sheet. As soon as each inward correspondence is thus filed, the related ultimate file is placed on the *Disposal Pad.*

1856 Then, if any outward correspondence needs to be initiated by him on the day, he pulls out the related ultimate file, if any, from the current collection and places it on the *Disposal Pad.* If, however, there is no related file in the current collection, he prepares the necessary Docket Sheet for it and places it on the *Disposal Pad.*

1857 If any matter requires a file from the quasi-current collection or from the record collection, he gets it from the section concerned and places it on the *Disposal Pad.*

1858 In this way he collects all the files that require his attention in the course of the day.

1859 Then he takes one by one each one of the ultimate files in the Disposal Pad and deals with it as shown in the succeeding sections.

186 Letter Drafting

If it requires a letter, the staff-member concerned drafts it. In drafting, the following points are to be remembered : The name and correct address of the addressee is to be written first. In the next line the word " Outside Reference " is to be written and is to be followed by the exact number and date of the reference. In the next line, the word " Subject " is to be written and is to be followed by a succinct but accurate description of the subject. Just above the salutation, the File Number is to be put.

1861 Drafting Principles

The draft reply is to be divided into paragraphs, which are to be numbered, a fresh paragraph being begun for every new statement or fresh argument. The tendency to use unduly long sentences is to be resisted. A draft is to be complete, clear and brief ; complete so as to be in itself sufficiently intelligible without reference to other papers ; clear, that is, free from any ambiguities which may cloud its meaning or necessitate further references which might have been easily avoided ; brief, in order that its reading may occupy the least possible time. A draft is to be written in temperate language and courteously worded. The use of all colloquialisms and abbreviations is to be avoided.

1862 Neatness in Execution

Indiscriminate scribbling on the margins of drafts is to be avoided, as also much writing between the lines. If it be necessary to revise a draft to any great extent, it is better to rewrite it on another sheet of paper than to write between the lines. When a draft has been much cut about, it is to be recopied before being submitted to the librarian.

1863 References

When a letter is in continuation of a series of correspondence, the last of which was received from the person to be addressed, the phrase "With reference to the correspondence ending with your letter" should, as a rule, be employed. On the other hand, if the last letter was one issued by the library, the phrase "In continuation of this office letter" is to be used. Figures and references are, as far as possible, to be embodied in the text and not relegated to appendices or to the margins.

1864 Conventions

At the end of the text and just before the point where the librarian is to put his initials, write the word "Lib". To the left of the word "Lib", put your own initials and below them the current date. Below the current date is to be put the symbol "N R" (meaning "No Reply"), or "S R" (meaning "Short Range Reply"), or "L R" (meaning "Long Range Reply") according as a reply is not obligatory, or a reply is due within two weeks, or a reply is due after two weeks. In case the symbol "S R" is put, if the last date for the reply is exactly a fortnight hence, no date need be added after "S R". If, however, the reply is due earlier, the date on or before which the reply is due is to be entered after "S R" Similarly, if the symbol written is "L R" and if the date for reply is exactly two months hence, no date is to be put after "L R". If, however, the due date for a reply is not exactly two months hence, the due date is to be entered after "L R".

1865 Presentation of File

The sheet of paper on which the reply is drafted is to be added as the last sheet of the related file ; if there be any enclosures, they are to be added to the file after the draft reply. Then the sheet containing the draft reply is to be turned over the Docket Sheet so as to appear first.

1866 Responsibility

The head of the section is not required himself to draft the letter in every case. But he is to satisfy himself that the drafting of his assistants is accurate and complete. All letters emanating from a section are to pass through the head of the section, who will initial them below the word "Lib" in token of his having made himself responsible for them.

When the librarian drafts a letter himself, it is to be understood that the head of the section concerned is as responsible for the correctness of any fact that the librarian may state, as if the letter was drafted by the head of the section himself. Heads of sections are therefore responsible for bringing to the notice of the librarian all relevant facts and papers which the librarian might have accidentally overlooked.

1867 Transmission to Librarian

As soon as the draft reply is complete, in the manner indicated above, its ultimate file is to be placed in the *Transmission Pad* of the section.

187 Routine Letter

If only a routine letter, for which there is a printed or typed form, is required, the staff-member concerned fills up the form and deals with it as in section 186. Generally in such cases, there will be no need for an office copy. If, however, an office copy is necessary, he fills up another copy of the form and uses it as the office copy. The office copy is to be filed first and the fair copy next. If a separate office copy is not made, write near the bottom of the last sheet of the file the endorsement " Replied on " or " Addressed on". The despatcher is to stamp the date of despatch of the fair copy against this endorsement.

188 Reminder

If only a reminder is required, the staff-member concerned fills up a reminder card and deals with it as in section 187. In filling up the reminder card, the file number to be used is the same as the file number of the letter to which it is a reminder, amplified successively by the letter "R" and the Arabic numeral representing the number of the reminder. At the end of the reminder, state in very brief terms the purport of the letter.

Near the left hand end of the office copy of the letter to which the reminder relates, the endorsement "Rem on" is to be put. If there be more than one reminder, the different reminders are to be entered one below another in successive lines. The librarian will put his initials against these entries and that will serve the purpose of office copies for the reminders. The despatch date is to be put against the endorsement as in section 187.

1891 Other Action

If any action other than drafting a letter or writing a reminder is required, the staff-member concerned takes the necessary action and then records at the end of the last letter in the file the action taken and adds his dated initials. Then he deals with it as in section 1867 if it has to go to the librarian or transfers it to the *Preferred Disposal Pad* if the decision is to take it up for disposal at a later date.

18911 "File"

If no action whatever is called for, the staff-member concerned, adds the word "file" near the left hand bottom corner of the last letter in the file and puts his dated initials and then deals with it as in section 1867.

18912 Consultation

If a file requires a previous consultation with the librarian or with any other member of the staff, the staff-member concerned, makes the necessary consultation and takes the further action, called for.

1892 Deferred Disposal

If it is decided that the disposal of the file is to be deferred, the staff-member concerned transfers it to the *Deferred Disposal Pad* after taking such interim action as may be necessary. If ascertainable, he notes down near the left hand bottom corner of the last letter in the file, the date on which the file is to be taken up for disposal.

18921 Arrangement of Deferred Files

The ultimate files in the Deferred Disposal Pad are to be arranged chronologically by the date marked for disposal, the farthest date being kept bottom-most. If two or more ultimate files have the same date mark for disposal, they are to be arranged among themselves by their file marks. The ultimate files which do not mention any definite date for disposal are to be placed in the sequence of their file marks at the top, ie above all the ultimate files which have a definite date marked for disposal.

18922 Transmission to Librarian

Each day the ultimate files in the Deferred Disposal Pad should be systematically examined and disposed of whenever possible. After all the possible ultimate files have been disposed of for the day and transferred to the *Transmission Pad* they are to be rearranged in the Transmission Pad in accordance with their respective file marks and sent to the librarian at the appointed hour of the day, along with the *Transmission Register.*

1893 State of Work Table

The result of this procedure will be that at any time the work table will contain only one Current Collection of Files in the vertical form, one Disposal Pad with the files arranged horizontally, one Deferred Disposal Pad with the files arranged horizontally and at certain moments one Transmission Pad with the files arranged horizontally. The Transmission Pad will be with the librarian or with the Correspondence Section, if it is not on the work table of the section. Each clerk should see that the table is as tidy as possible.

18931 Design on Pads

The Transmission Pad, the Disposal Pad and the Deferred Disposal Pad should all have the number of the section boldly and prominently written in the centre of both the flaps of the file board. In addition, they should have the respective words "Transmission", "Disposal" and "Deferred Disposal" written in clear library hand on the flaps [illegible] the section number. If possible, the colour of the file boards used for the different pads may be different.

1894 Prompt Disposal

It is desirable that each file should be disposed of as promptly and expeditiously as possible. Subject to any special variation necessitated by any particular case, all the routine correspondence of the Circulation Section should be disposed of, on the day on which the inward correspondence is received, while all the other correspondence of that section and all the correspondence of the other sections should be disposed of, within the week in which the inward correspondence is received. It is desirable to have a time scheme for the disposal of each class of files, in as detailed and explicit a form as is feasible.

18941 The Full Route

From the above it can be seen that the routine of correspondence can be pictured as follows : An inward correspondence is first received by the librarian ; it passes through the Correspondence Section to the section to which it relates ; there it gets attached to the appropriate file and then it settles down in the Disposal Pad · from there it goes to the Transmission Pad of the section directly or through the Deferred Disposal Pad ; then in company with the other files in the Transmission Pad, it goes to the librarian ; from the librarian it goes to the Correspondence Section ; if it is to be faircopied by the Correspondence Section, it again goes to the librarian through the fair copy verifier and returns to the Correspondence Section ; thereafter it goes back to its related section for deposit in the current collection of files.

18942 Transmission Register

Whenever a file or any other thing is passed from one section to another, its transfer and retransfer are to be controlled and watched with the aid of a *Transmission Register*. For this purpose each section must maintain the necessary number of transmission registers, with appropriate columns. It may happen that in certain cases, some other registers serve also the purposes of a transmission register. In such cases, separate transmission registers are not necessary.

The Transmission Register for files is to have the following columns:

1 File mark ;
2 Initials of the receiver ; and
3 Date of return to the section.

Each page is to have 15 lines. First put the current date and enter the file marks in the classified sequence. As soon as the Transmission Regis.er comes back, examine if it has received the initials of the receiver. As each file comes back enter the date of receipt. If any file does not return on the due date (usually the next day) take the question up with the concerned person and have it traced out and settled.

18943 Time Scheme

The following time scheme is followed in the Madras University Library in regard to the movement of correspondence :

All inward mails reach the respective sections before 12 noon. All office copies pass through the librarian and reach the correspondence Section before 1 PM All fair copies and routine letters in printed or stencilled forms reach the librarian before 4 PM and reach the Correspondence Section before 5 PM.

1895 Stray Mail

Apart from the main mail of the day, a library is likely to get letters at all odd hours. Such stray letters also will have to be dealt with in the same way as described above. If any particular letter requires urgent attention, it should be made to pass through all the stages immediately. In the case of ordinary letters, it is better to accumulate all of them to a particular hour of the day or even till the next main mail arrives.

1896 Follow-Up-Work

A very important item in dealing with correspondence is to follow up both the inward letters and the outward letters and to watch if the necessary action is taken or if the necessary replies are got.

18961 Inward Correspondence

In the description of the routine of correspondence, provision has been made for these two problems. It will be remembered that in section 1892, the idea of the Deferred Disposal Pad has been developed. This pad is to contain all the inward letters, which are not disposed of then and there, till they are disposed of. Occasionally an inward letter may require disposal only after an indefinitely long time. In such cases it may not be convenient to keep the file itself in the Deferred Disposal Pad. On the contrary, it may be desirable to keep the file in the current sequence but have a remembrancer sheet of paper below all the files of that pad, on which the file mark of such a file is entered with the date on which it should be taken up for disposal. Every day when collecting files for disposal, this remembrancer sheet also should be looked into and the files marked for the day should also be taken out of the current collection.

18962 Outward Correspondence

The method of following up outward correspondence has been indicated in the earlier sections. The method, by which the head of a section will be reminded automatically of the outward letters which require a reminder to be sent, is given in section 1852. The method of sending reminders is developed in section 188.

1897 Cross Reference

It will happen not infrequently that an action initiated with a certain ultimate file has to be followed up with other ultimate files. For example, an indent for Mathematics books will be in file no. 13B. The subject will be pursued in this file by the Book Selection Section until the sanction for the indent is obtained. Further action will have to be taken by the Order Section perhaps in two stages, enquiry and order. For the order in question, the Order Section may have to send one or more enquiries. Each one of these enquiries will form independent files with the file N 22B and their respective filing characteristics. Each of these enquiry files will be pursued until the firms from which the book should be bought are finally settled. Thereafter the orders will form another file with the file N 23B and their respective filing characteristics. The problem is to connect the indent file, the different enquiry files relating to it, and the different order files. This is done by the method of *Cross Reference*. Cross Reference is of two kinds, *Bottom Cross Reference* and *Top Cross Reference*. At the bottom of the last sheet of the indent file mentioned above, a Cross Reference will be entered as follows : " See 22B (*name of the first book*) dated................ " If the indent has given rise to several enquiry files, against all the items which go into one and the same enquiry file, such distinguishing marks as a cross or a tick will be put. That distinguishing mark will be repeated at the bottom and the cross reference will have to be given against it. This will be done for each of the distinguishing marks.

To each Bottom Cross Reference will correspond a Top Cross Reference. The Top Cross Reference will be made at the top of the office copy of the concerned enquiry. It will take the form " See 13B (*expert correspondent*) dated.................".

Similarly the last sheet of each enquiry file will get a Bottom Cross Reference which connects it with the order file in which further action is taken, and each order file will have a Top Cross Reference connecting it with the enquiry file, on which the order is based, or, if there has been no enquiry file at all, with the indent file to which it relates.

This Cross Reference may be not only between the files belonging to the same section but also between files belonging to different sections. It is not necessary to multiply examples here. This Cross Reference Method is:

1 to secure unity in each ultimate file,
2 to eliminate memory, and
3 to bring together automatically all the different files that may be relevant for the disposal of any question.

The occasions which require a Cross Reference will be easily recognised.

Whenever a particular file is sent to the librarian for his consideration, care must be taken to send not only the particular file, but also all the other files which have Cross Reference relation with it and which may be relevant to the subject under consideration.

1898 Extracting

Another complication that usually arises in dealing with correspondence is due to a letter dealing with more than one subject. To avoid this complication, it is necessary that the library should never include in one and the same letter more than one subject. It should also try to persuade the correspondents of the library to follow this principle. One method by which the correspondents can be persuaded is to suggest to them that no letter from them should have reference to more than one letter of the library. However, a library cannot be quite sure of all the correspondents observing this principle. Hence, arises the problem of complex letters. By a *Complex Letter* is meant a letter which deals with more than one subject. The. method of extracting has been developed to meet the case of Complex Letters. The letter in question is assigned to one of the ultimate files to which it relates. Portions of the letter which relate to other ultimate files are extracted in different sheets of paper and those extracts are included in the respective files and treated as independent letters.

This extraction may be done by the Correspondence Section itself before the letters are registered and sent to the different sections. Or, the letter may be registered by the Correspondence Section with the number appropriate to the ultimate file in which the original is to be filed. Then the section that receives the original letter may mark out the portions to be extracted and send it back to the Correspondence Section. Then, the Correspondence Section will make the necessary extracts.

As soon as an extract is signed by the librarian, it should be treated as an inward mail and routed in the usual way.

PART 2

DISTINCTIVE LIBRARY FUNCTIONS

The Way Books and Periodicals Come and Go

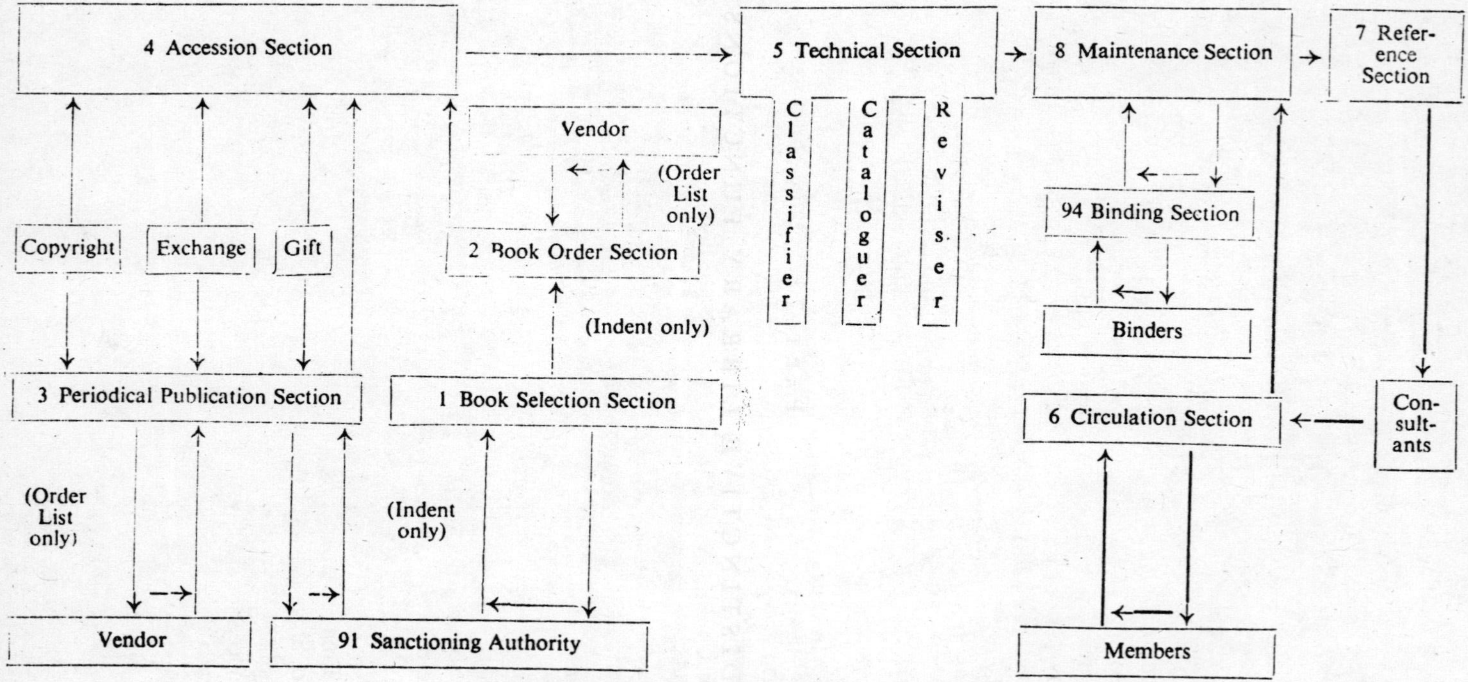

Note the Vital Cycle in Thick Lines at the Right End

CHAPTER 21

BOOK SELECTION SECTION

211 Planning

It may be repeated here that we deal in this book only with the administrative routine connected with book selection. But the theory of book selection is a different matter. It requires a volume by itself. My *Library book selection*[20] deals with it. Reference may also be made here to the foundations of the theory of book selection, which have been indicated in the *Five laws of library science.*[21]

2111 Sources for Selection

The sources for book selection are varied. Suggestions can be got not only from the trade lists and National and State Bibliographies, but also from the bibliographies and reviews occurring in books and periodicals. The suggestions from the reading public form another possible source, although this source is likely to be of uneven merit. The Reference Section, the Shelf Section and the Circulation Section can give much help in this matter.

2112 Experts for Help

It should not be presumed that the entire evaluation of selection can be done by the library itself. It will be a good policy to have the help of experts in different subjects in making the selection. But the whole work of selection should not be shifted to experts. As it is the library that will have access to the greatest number of sources, most of the work should be done by the library, leaving the minimum possible work to be done by the experts.

2113 Financial Responsibility

Finance is an ultimate deciding factor in the selection of books. No library is likely to have unlimited funds to buy everything published—or even to buy all the most worthwhile publications. Hence, the greatest care is to be exercised in spending the sum available for books. To see that the budget is not exceeded on the one hand and that, on the other, no amount is left unappropriated at the end of the financial year, the Book Selection Section should exercise the greatest vigilance possible and work hand in hand with the Book Order Section, the Periodical Publication Section and the Accounts Section. It is also the duty of the Book Selection Section to see that the book fund is distributed in proper proportion among the different subjects in the light of legitimate local demand and that no particular subject usurps far more than what should be its proper share, simply because it happens to be sponsored, for the time being, by an influential person or clique.

2114 Subject Cycles

It will help the symmetrical building up of the stock of the library and add to the systematisation of the work of this section and of the other sections, if the book resources to be added to the library annually in the different subjects are taken up for treatment in systematic cycles, the periodicity for each subject being adjusted from time to time in the light of supply and demand and with a view to spreading the work of the section evenly over the different weeks of the year.

2118 Factors in Planning

The distinctive work of the Book Selection Section is to be planned with reference to the following factors :

1 Sources ;
2 Selection ;
3 Indent ; and
6 Finance.

212 Job Analysis

2121 Sources

The work of the Book Selection Section relating to Sources in general may consist of the following items :

2 Acquiring the sources for book selection by purchase or donation or otherwise, which may be referred to as *Sources Acquiring Work* ; and

8 Arranging the sources of book selection, which may be referred to as *Sources Arranging Work*.

2121:2 *Sources Acquiring Work*

2121:2:1 Sources Acquiring Work is to consist of the following immediate jobs :

1 As and when the names of useful sources for book selection come to notice, jotting down the necessary particulars, which may be referred to as *Sources Noting* ; and
2 As and when specific books of probable interest to the library are brought to notice, jotting down the necessary particulars about them, which may be referred to as *Suggestion Noting.*

2121:2:5 Sources Acquiring Work is to consist of the following weekly job :

2 Sending requisition for sources of book selection, which may be referred to as *Sources Requisitioning.*

2121:8 *Sources Arranging Work*

2121:8:5 Sources Arranging Work is to consist of the following weekly job :

8 Arranging the sources of book selection that are received from time to time in a systematic manner on the sources shelf, which may be referred to as *Sources Shelving.*

2121:8:8 Sources Arranging Work is to consist of the following annual job :

8 Weeding out the out-of-date sources from the sources shelf, which may be referred to as *Sources Weeding.*

2122 SELECTION

The work of the Book Selection Section relating to Selection in general may consist of the following items of work :

1 Selecting from the different sources the items worth consideration by the experts in the different subjects, which may be referred to as *Book Selection Work* ;
2 Writing out book selection cards for the items selected, which may be referred to as *Book Selection Carding Work* ; and
5 Forwarding book selection cards and other references to

the experts for an expression of their opinion or for facilitating the preparation of indent, which may be referred to as *Book Selection Consultation Work*.

2122:1 *Book Selection Work*

2122:1:3 Book Selection Work is to consist of the following casual jobs :

1 Marking in the sources the items that are worth being sent up for consideration by the experts in the different subjects, which may be referred to as *Preliminary Selection* ; and
8 Checking the marked items with the stock in the library, which may be referred to as *Preliminary Checking*.

2122:1:5 Book Selection Work is to consist of the following weekly job :

1 Forwarding the marked sources for the consideration of the librarian, which may be referred to as *Marked Sources Forwarding*.

2122:2 *Book Selection Carding Work*

2122:2:3 Book Selection Carding Work is to consist of the following casual jobs :

1 Writing out book selection card for each of the approved items, which may be referred to as *Book Selection Card Writing* :
5 Tentatively classifying each book selection card, which may be referred to as *Book Selection Card Classifying* ; and
7 Filling up the bibliographical gaps in the book selection cards, which may be referred to as *Book Selection Card Completing*.

2122:2:5 Book Selection Work is to consist of the following weekly jobs :

1 Comparing and verifying the entries in the book selection cards with the sources, which may be referred to as *Book Selection Card Revising* ; and
8 Filing the revised book selection cards in the selected cards tray, which may be referred to as *Book Selection Card Filing*.

2122:5 *Book Selection Consultation Work*

2122:5:4 Book Selection Consultation Work is to consist of the following daily job :

5 When the acquisition of a book has to be urgently considered, sending a reference to the expert concerned and asking for his advice, which may be referred to as *Urgent Book Selection Consulting*.

2122:5:5 Book Selection Consultation Work is to consist of the following weekly jobs :

1 Forwarding the accumulated book selection cards to the experts concerned asking for their recommendations, which may be referred to as *Book Selection Card Forwarding* ;
3 Making a list of the approved items, which may be referred to as *Indent Copying* ; and
8 Sorting the book selection cards returned by the experts and disposing of the cards not recommended, which may be referred to as *Unrecommended Card Filing*.

2123 INDENTS

The work of the Book Selection Section relating to indents in general may consist of the following items of work :

1 Scrutinising the indents for books received from the experts or the authorities concerned which may be referred to as *Indents Scrutinising Work* ; and
3 Getting the necessary sanction for the indents, which may be referred to as *Indents Passing Work*.

2123:1 *Indents Scrutinising Work*

2123:1:5 Indents Scrutinising Work is to consist of the following weekly jobs :

1 Checking the indents received with the stock, the order tray and the bills on hand, which may be referred to as *Indents Checking* ;
23 Preparing book selection cards for such of those items in the checked indent as have not been already carded, which may be referred to as *Supplemental Book Selection Carding* ;

25 Tentatively classifying the supplemental book selection cards, which may be referred to as *Supplemental Book Selection Card Classifying* ;

27 Filling up the bibliographical gaps in the supplemental book selection cards, which may be referred to as *Supplemental Book Selection Card Completing* ;

28 Merging the supplemental book selection cards with the book selection cards already existing in relation to the indents concerned, which may be referred to as *Supplemental Book Selection Card Merging* ;

4 Clearing up doubts and difficulties in consultation with the experts concerned, which may be referred to as *Indents Doubts Clearing* ;

5 Obtaining information about the cost of the items wherever necessary, which may be referred to as *Cost Ascertaining* ; and

6 Estimating the cost of the indents, which may be referred to as *Indents Estimating*.

2123:3 *Indents Passing Work*

2123:3:5 Indents Passing Work is to consist of the following weekly jobs :

1 Preparing the necessary notes for the sanctioning authority, which may be referred to as *Indent Noting* ;

11 Forwarding the indents to the sanctioning authority, which may be referred to as *Indent Forwarding* ;

2 Passing the sanctioned indents on to the Order Section, which may be referred to as *Sanctioned Indent Forwarding* ; and

8 Taking the necessary action on such of the items of the forwarded indents as have not received the sanction of the authority concerned, which may be referred to as *Rejected Items Disposing*.

2126 FINANCE

The work of the Book Selection Section relating to finance in general may consist of the following items of work :

6 Taking the necessary steps to fix the annual allotment for books and periodicals in different subjects, which may be referred to as *Allotment Work* ; and

7 Advising the experts responsible for the preparation of indents for books about the financial position in regard to the different subjects from time to time, which may be referred to as *Allotment Watching Work*.

2126:6 *Allotment Work*

2126:6:8 Allotment Work is to consist of the following annual jobs :

1 Ascertaining from the expert advisers in different subjects if they desire to have any change in the annual allotment to their respective subjects, which may be referred to as *Expert Opinion Obtaining* ;

22 Estimating the cost of the indents awaiting ordering in each subject, which may be referred to as *Arrear Indents Estimating* ;

23 Estimating the cost of outstanding orders for ordinary books in each subject, which may be referred to as *Outstanding Orders Estimating* ;

24 Estimating the probable cost of standing orders of various kinds in each subject, which may be referred to as *Standing Orders Estimating* ;

3 Ascertaining from the Periodical Publication Section the probable cost of the current periodical publications in each subject, which may be referred to as *Periodical Publications Subscription Estimating* ;

6 Ascertaining from the Finance Section the total book fund likely to be sanctioned for the year, which may be referred to as *Budget Ascertaining* ;

7 Ascertaining from the Accounts Section the actual expenditure on books and periodical publications in each subject for the three preceding years, which may be referred to as *Actuals Ascertaining* ;

8 Preparing in the light of the data obtained by the foregoing routines, the schedule of allotment for the different subjects, which may be referred to as *Preliminary to Allotment* ; and

91 Forwarding the schedule of allotment to the sanctioning authority and obtaining the necessary sanction, which may be referred to as *Allotment Sanctioning*.

2126:7 *Allotment Watching Work*

2126:7:7 Allotment Watching Work is to consist of the following quarterly jobs:

The jobs under this section will be similar to the annual jobs 22, 23 and 24 under 2126:6 Allotment Work and in addition the following :

3 Ascertaining from the Periodical Publication Section the annual subscription that will have to be incurred during the current financial year on any new periodical publications that might have been sanctioned in the year, which may be referred to as *New Periodical Publication Cost Ascertaining.*

7 Ascertaining from the Accounts Section the actual expenditure on books during the current financial year, which may be referred to as *Spent Amount Ascertaining.*

8 Advising the experts in the different subjects about the amount remaining unappropriated, which may be referred to as *Allotment Balance Advising.*

2126:7:8 Allotment Watching Work is to consist of the following annual job :

1 Advising the expert in each subject about the annual allotment for the subject, which may be referred to as *Allotment Advising.*

213 **Routine**

2131 SOURCES

2131 : 2 *Sources Acquiring Work*

2131:2:1 *Immediate jobs*

2131:2:11 SOURCES NOTING

The Book Selection Section is likely to come across information regarding sources that may be of use in book selection work at any moment. This may happen either in the course of the section's systematical perusal of the printed materials or in their conversation or correspondence with persons or bodies competent to give advice in the matter. It may even happen in a very unexpected and unusual way while engaged in some other work. As soon as the information is spotted out, note down all the necessary particulars as far as they may be available with regard to the source that should be acquired to aid book selection. It will be convenient to use a

Source Selection Slip with similar headings as the book selection card for noting down the particulars. File all such source slips in the *Source Slips Tray* in a classified sequence on the basis of the subject to which the source relates.

2131:2:12 SUGGESTION NOTING

Books of probable interest to the library are likely to be brought to the notice of the Book Selection Section either by the other sections of the library or by the users of the library or when the Book Selection Section peruses different books and periodicals.

When the suggestion reaches the Book Selection Section, prepare a *Book Selection Card* for it and file it in the *Suggestion Tray*, in the classified sequence.

2131:2:5 *Weekly jobs*

2131:2:52 SOURCES REQUISITIONING

On the appointed day of the week, pick out from the Source Slip Tray the outstanding source slips and send requisition to the appropriate party for the supply of the source.

2131:8 *Sources Arranging*

2131:8:5 *Weekly jobs*

2131:8:58 SOURCES SHELVING

On the appointed day of the week, insert all the sources of book selection received in the course of the week, in the appropriate places in the *Sources Shelf.*

It will be convenient to have the following three characteristics for the classified arrangement of the sources :

1 Subject ;
2 Vendor or publisher, as the case may be ; and
3 The date of the source.

These characteristics may be taken in the sequence given above. A result of this will be that on the Sources Shelf all the source materials relating to a specified subject will be found together. Among the sources relating to a specified subject, all those issued by a specific vendor or publisher will be found together and arranged chronologically in the sequence of the date of issue.

As book selection will have to proceed subject by subject, it can be easily seen that this is the most convenient arrangement for shelving the sources.

2131:8:8 *Annual job*

2131:8:88 SOURCES WEEDING

At the appointed time each year, scrutinise the sources shelf carefully and weed out all unwanted materials.

The sources for book selection accumulate in a library at a very rapid rate. They also grow out of date with equal rapidity. If the weeding out is not done systematically, one is likely to be snowed down by useless rubbish and the Sources Shelf may prove to be an obstruction rather than a help.

2132 SELECTION

2132:1 *Book Selection Work*

2132:1:3 *Casual jobs*

2132:1:31 PRELIMINARY SELECTION

Mark in pencil in the source for book selection each item that in your opinion deserves consideration by the experts who help the library in book selection work. The marking should be done as follows : Guess the main class of the item and put in the left hand margin opposite to the heading of the item the symbol for the main class.

2132:1:38 PRELIMINARY CHECKING

Take each of the marked sources in hand and check the marked items with the library catalogue as well as the book selection cards in the selected cards tray and the order tray. Score out the items that are already represented in the library catalogue or in the selected cards tray.

2132:1:5 *Weekly jobs*

2132:1:51 MARKED SOURCES FORWARDING

On the appointed day of the week, forward to the librarian all the marked sources which have been preliminarily checked.

2132:2 *Book Selection Carding Work*

2132:2:3 *Casual jobs*

2132:2:31 BOOK SELECTION CARD WRITING

As soon as the marked sources are received from the librarian, write out a *Book Selection Card* for each of the items approved by him.

Use the library hand for writing the book selection card. Remember in particular that the book selection card written by you is going to be transformed successively into the indent card, order card and accession card and that it forms a permanent record of the library.

Give in the left hand bottom corner of the book selection card the exact reference to the source from which the book is selected e g P C (meaning *Publisher's circular*) V 38, p 55.

2132:2:35 Book Selection Card Classifying

As far as can be judged by the title, author and review notes, if any, found in the book selection card, classify the book as closely as possible and enter in pencil the class number in the appropriate place in the book selection card. Whenever necessary, consult the technical section.

2132:2:37 Book Selection Card Completing

If the necessary bibliographical details are not to be found in the source, secure them from any other available source and make the book selection card as complete as possible.

2132:2:5 *Weekly jobs*

2132:2:51 Book Selection Card Revising

On the appointed day of the week, take out all the book selection cards written and completed in the week and compare the entries with the sources from which they were taken. Carry out all the corrections found necessary.

2132:2:58 Book Selection Card Filing

As soon as the revising work is over, insert the cards in the *Selected Cards Tray* in the appropriate classified sequence. While inserting a card, if a card is already found for a particular book take away and score out the card which is less full in details.

2132:5 *Book Selection Consultation Work*

2132:5:4 *Daily jobs*

2132:5:45 Urgent Book Selection Consulting

The routine for this job is similar to the routine given in 2132: 5 : 5, except that it will have to be done urgently.

2132:5:5 *Weekly jobs*

2132:5:51 Book Selection Cards Forwarding

On the appointed day of the week, pick out, from the Selected Cards Tray and the Deferred Cards Tray, the book selection cards pertaining to the subject or subjects which fall due to be dealt with in the week in the light of the suggestions contained in the introduction to this chapter and forward them to the experts who help the library in Book Selection Work. In the forwarding letter, mention the number of cards sent, the amount allotted to the subject for expenditure within the year, the amount already spent, the amount still unspent and an estimated cost of the items included in the book selection cards sent. Request the experts to sort the book selection cards into three groups, as "approved", "rejected" and "deferred". If necessary, mention also the date by which the reply is expected. A more satisfactory practice will be to persuade the experts to call at the library and get the work done jointly by the expert and the librarian.

2132:5:53 Indent Copying

Sort the cards in the approved group by the main classes. Separate out the cards that require standing order, prepayment etc. Sort the remaining cards pertaining to a specific main class by the standing vendor with whom the order is to be placed so far as can be ascertained from the Book Order Section. Arrange the cards in each vendor group alphabetically using the heading as the basis. After the arrangement is over, send them to the Correspondence Section for the indents to be typed. It will be an advantage to get five copies to be typed. One copy is to be used as the indent, the second as the order, the third and the fourth as the office copies of the order and the fifth for the file of the reference section.

2132:5:58 Unrecommended Cards Filing

As soon as the cards come back from the experts, file the deferred cards in the appropriate classified sequence in the Selected Cards Tray and file the rejected cards in the appropriate classified sequence in the rejected cards tray. If the expert had not already sorted the cards as desired but had merely noted on the cards his opinion, the cards will have to be sorted out into the three groups as a preliminary step before the unrecommended cards are filed.

It is a matter for consideration whether the finally rejected cards may not be straight away destroyed. But experience shows that it may be helpful to preserve them for some time and pass them on to other libraries which are less organised and seek our help in Book Selection Work. If, however, there is no chance for this, the rejected cards may be destroyed periodically, say, once in a year. As an alternative, the entry on the card may be scored out and the card used for some other purposes, such as for shelf-labels.

2133 INDENTS

2133:1 *Indents Scrutinising Work*

2133:1:5 *Weekly jobs*

2133:1:51 INDENT CHECKING

On the appointed day of the week, check each indent received in the week carefully with the catalogue, the order tray and the bills on hand awaiting payment. Check each item not only with reference to the heading but also with reference to the title, if it is one that is likely to have received a title entry. Check also with reference to the series entry, if the book belongs to a series. Check also the names of translator, editor, etc and in every other possible way to see that no item is unnecessarily duplicated ; in cases of doubt, go to the shelf and examine such of the books as you have reasons to suspect might have been wrongly entered in the indent. If, in your opinion an attempt should be made for securing any item as a donation, put the letter "G" against it. If any item raises issues which cannot be settled without a reference to the expert, put the letter "E" against it. Score out the items which are not wanted. As soon as the checking is over, write the word " Checked " at the left hand bottom corner of the last sheet of the indent, initial and date it.

2133:1:523 SUPPLEMENTAL BOOK SELECTION CARDING, ETC

Supplemental book selection process : the routines for these jobs are similar to the routines of the corresponding jobs given under 2132:2 Book Selection Carding Work.

2133:1:54 Indents Doubts Clearing

On the appointed day of the week, scrutinise the indents checked in the week and refer all the items, against which the letter "E" has been put to the expert concerned setting forth clearly the issues that require to be examined by the expert and asking for a definite decision by him.

2133:1:55 Cost Ascertaining

If against any of the items in the indent, the cost is not given, write to the publisher or vendor, as the case may be, asking for a quotation. In some cases the cost may be estimated and the further work with the indent may be taken on hand. In cases where the cost is likely to be very high or the cost is likely to go beyond the amount allotted for the subject, it is desirable that the cost is previously ascertained before further action is taken.

2133:1:56 Indent Estimating

After all the processes that are mentioned under indents scrutinising work are over, estimate the cost of the indents as closely as possible and write the figure in pencil opposite to the word " Checked " at the bottom of the last sheet of the indent. The estimate should be given both in foreign and local currency to facilitate the work of the ordering section.

2133:3 *Indents Passing Work*

2133:3:5 *Weekly jobs*

2133:3:51 Indent Noting

On the appointed day of the week, for each of the scrutinised indents, prepare an indent note on the *Indent Noting Form*, filling up all the columns as fully as possible, taking care to get the exact amount already spent in the subject and the estimated cost of the outstanding orders from the accounts section and the order section respectively.

As soon as the notes are filled up, forward it to the librarian for his approval and remarks, if any.

2133:3:511 Indent Forwarding

On the appointed day of the week, collect all the indents on which notes have been prepared in the week, including the urgent indents also, if any. Arrange them in the sequence of the subjects and forward them to the Committee Section for inclusion in the papers that are to be sent up to the sanctioning authority during the week or to the librarian, if he is himself the sanctioning authority.

2133:3:52 Sanctioned Indent Forwarding

On the appointed day of the week, take up each of the sanctioned indents received from the Committee Section or the librarian as the case may be and deal with it as follows :

Pick out the four other copies of the indent (see routine 2132:5:53 which provides for five copies of the indents being made at the time of indent copying) in the case of indents copied by the section and score out in them such of the items as have not received the sanction. Score out similarly in the case of indents received in the form of lists from outside. Attach a transmission sheet to one of the copies or the original as the case may be and copy in it relevant extracts from the Indent Noting Sheet. Remember, particularly, to note down the date of sanction and the remarks, if any, of the sanctioning authority and then transmit the four copies of the indent to the Ordering Section.

Along with the copies of the indent or the original as the case may be, transmit also the Book Selection Cards of the sanctioned items.

Note down in the Indent Note Sheet, the date of transmission of the copies to the Order Section and get the dated initials of the head of the Order Section as a token of the section having taken charge of the copies of the Indent and of the related Book Selection Cards.

2133:3:58 Rejected Items Disposing

After the transmission of the copies to the Order Section, pick out the book selection cards of the rejected items and insert them in the proper place in the *Rejected Cards Tray* or *Deferred Cards Tray*, as the case may be. If, however, the instruction of the sanctioning authority is that the item should be brought up definitely at a later meeting, transfer the cards to the *Selected Cards Tray*, with a slip attached to the cards showing the time when they should be sent to the sanctioning authority.

2136 FINANCE

2136:6 *Allotment Work*

2136:6:8 *Annual jobs*

The different jobs of the Allotment Work should be done for each subject separately.

2136:6:81 EXPERT OPINION OBTAINING

At the appointed time each year, write to the experts, helping the library in Book Selection Work in different subjects, seeking their advice as to whether the annual allotment for their respective subjects would require any change. In the letter state the total annual allotment for the preceding year, the amount spent on current periodical publications and the balance available for books and back volumes of periodical publications. Ask also if they would suggest the acquisition of the back volumes of any periodical publication in the ensuing financial year.

2136:6:822 ARREAR INDENTS ESTIMATING

At the appointed time each year, pick out the indents that are either awaiting sanction or having been sanctioned have not yet been transmitted to the Order Section. Estimate which of these indents could be purchased within the financial year and eliminate them. Estimate the cost of the indents that will have to be purchased in the next financial year. This amount may be referred to as *Arrear Indent Cost.*

2136:6:823 OUTSTANDING ORDERS ESTIMATING

Find out from the Order Section the items for which an order had been sent but whose supply could not be expected within the financial year and get an estimate of their cost. This amount may be referred to as *Outstanding Order Cost.*

2136:6:824 STANDING ORDERS ESTIMATING

Find out in consultation with the Order Section, how many volumes are likely to be received in the next financial year under the different standing orders which are current. Estimate their cost. This amount may be referred to as *Standing Order Cost.*

2136:6:83 PERIODICAL PUBLICATIONS SUBSCRIPTION ESTIMATING

Get from the Periodical Publication Section an estimate of the annual subscription for the periodical publications current in each of the subjects. Find out also if there is any probability of any back volumes of periodical publications being acquired and if so get their probable cost.

Ascertain in this way the total amount that is to be spent on periodical publications for each subject in the next financial year. This amount may be referred to as *Periodical Publications Cost*.

2136:6:86 BUDGET ASCERTAINING

Find out from the Finance Section the probable amount that is likely to be available for purchase of books and periodical publications in the next financial year. This amount may be referred to as *Budget Amount*.

2136:6:87 ACTUALS ASCERTAINING

Find out from the Accounts Section the actual expenditure on books and periodical publications in each subject for each of the three preceding financial years. Estimate from these data the average or the normal amount spent on each subject per year. This amount may be referred to as the *Actuals*.

2136:6:88 PRELIMINARY TO ALLOTMENT

In the light of the data obtained by the foregoing routines, prepare a schedule of allotment for the different subjects.

2136:6:891 ALLOTMENT SANCTIONING

Forward the schedule of allotment with the necessary notes to the Committee Section for inclusion in the papers that are to be sent to the sanctioning authority.

2136:7 *Allotment Watching Work*

2136:7:7 *Quarterly jobs*

2136:7:722, 2136:7:723, 2136:7:724

These routines are similar to the corresponding annual routines in "2136:6 Allotment Work".

2136:7:73 NEW PERIODICAL PUBLICATIONS COST ASCERTAINING

Find out from the Periodical Publication Section, if any new periodical publications have been sanctioned during the year and if so how much amount should be set apart for meeting their subscription in the current financial year.

2136:7:77 SPENT AMOUNT ASCERTAINING

Find out from the Accounts Section the amount actually spent on books during the financial year.

2136:7:78 ALLOTMENT BALANCE ADVISING

Find out the total of the amount ascertained by the foregoing routines and subtract it from the annual allotment to the subject. Write to the expert in the subject specifying the amount that is still unappropriated.

2136:7:8 *Annual job*

2136:7:81 ALLOTMENT ADVISING

As soon as the sanction for the schedule of annual allotment is received from the Committee Section, advise the experts in each subject about the amount allotted to the subject for expenditure during the financial year and also the distribution of the amount under different heads such as books, standing orders on books, periodical publications and back volumes of periodical publications.

214 Elimination of Waste

2141 DIVISION OF WORK

If the turnover in the Book Selection Section demands the assignment of several members to it, the distribution of work among the assistants of the section should proceed along the lines of subject specialisation. This will enable each member to acquire an intensive acquaintance with the bibliography of certain subjects or groups of subjects and an intimate knowledge of the resources of the library in those subjects.

2142 RESPONSIBILITY OF HEAD OF SECTION

The head of the section should review the work of the assistants carefully, so that books of a border line nature do not get duplicated by different assistants. This can be done by the scrutiny of the provisional class numbers assigned, as well as by an alphabetical comparison of the different groups of book selection cards. It is desirable that the Annual Allotment Work and the Quarterly Allotment Watching Work should be done by the head of the section himself.

2143 Diaries

Two diaries are necessary for the section.

2144 General Diary

One General Diary on a *daily basis* is to have the following headings :

11 Letters received ;
121 Letters replied ;
122 Letters filed ;
141 Letters drafted ;
142 Routine letters issued ;
15 Reminders sent ;
21 Indents called for ;
22 Indents received ;
31 Book selection cards checked with selected cards tray ;
32 Book selection cards checked with order tray ;
34 Book selection cards checked with bills on hand ;
35 Book selection cards checked with catalogue.

2145 Book Selection Cards Diary

The second diary is to be on a *weekly basis* to show the number of book selection cards written. Its headings must consist of the symbols for the main classes of the classification scheme used or some suitable modification of them.

215 Correlation

Much internal correlation will be necessary to avoid the duplication of the same book by different assistants. Further in the case of books in unfamiliar languages, the assistant who knows the languages will have to give a helping hand in the selection of books in those languages, although the subject of the books may be different from the ones he specialises in.

The following Table of Correlation shows the jobs that bring the section into contact with other sections :

All Sections

2131:2:12 Suggestion Noting.

2 *Book Order Section*

2132:1:38 Preliminary Checking ;
2133:1:51 Indent Checking ;
2133:3:52 Sanctioned Indent Forwarding ;
2136:6:823 Outstanding Orders Estimating ;
2136:7:723 Outstanding Orders Estimating ;
2136:6:824 Standing Orders Estimating ;
2136:7:724 Standing Orders Estimating.

3 *Periodical Publication Section*

2136:6:83 Periodical Publications Subscription Estimating ;
2136:7:73 New Periodical Publications Cost Ascertaining.

4 *Accession Section*

2133:1:51 Indent Checking.

5 *Technical Section*

2132:2:35 Book Selection Card Classifying.

91 *Committee Section*

2133:3:511 Indent Forwarding (Tuesday, 12 noon) ;
2136:6:891 Allotment Sanctioning.

96 *Finance Section*

2136:6:86 Budget Ascertaining.

97 *Accounts Section*

2136:6:87 Actuals Ascertaining ;
2136:7:77 Spent Amount Ascertaining.

216 Illustrative Time Scheme

2165 WEEKLY JOBS

Saturday

2131:8:58 Sources Shelving ;
2133:1:51 Indent Checking.

Sunday

2133:1:51 Indent Checking ;
2133:1:523 Supplemental Book Selection Carding ;
2133:1:525 Supplemental Book Selection Card Classifying ;
2133:1:527 Supplemental Book Selection Cards Completing ;
2133:1:528 Supplemental Book Selection Cards Merging ;
2133:1:54 Indents Doubts Clearing ;
2133:1:55 Cost Ascertaining.

Monday

2132:1:51 Marked Sources Forwarding ;
2132:2:31 Book Selection Card Writing ;
2132:5:53 Indent Copying.

Tuesday

2131:2:52 Sources Requisitioning ;
2133:1:56 Indent Estimating ;
2133:3:51 Indent Noting ;
2133:3:511 Indent Forwarding (12 noon).

Wednesday

2132:2:31 Book Selection Card Writing ;
2132:2:51 Book Selection Card Revising.

Thursday

2132:2:58 Book Selection Card Filing ;
2132:5:51 Book Selection Cards Forwarding ;
2132:5:58 Unrecommended Cards Filing ;
2133:3:52 Sanctioned Indent Forwarding ;
2133:3:58 Rejected Items Disposing.

2167 QUARTERLY JOBS

The last week of each quarter

2136:7:7 The jobs of the Allotment Watching Work.

2163 ANNUAL JOB

January

2131:8:88 Sources Weeding ;
2136:7:81 Allotment Advising.

September—Second week

2136:6:81 Expert Opinion Obtaining ;
2136:6:822 Arrear Indents Estimating.

Third week

2136:6:823 Outstanding Orders Estimating ;
2136:6:824 Standing Orders Estimating.

Fourth week

2136:6:83 Periodical Publications Subscription Estimating.

October—First week

2136:6:86 Budget Ascertaining.

Second week

2136:6:87 Actuals Ascertaining.

November—First week

2136:6:88 Preliminary to Allotment.

December—First week

2136:6:891 Allotment Sanctioning.

217 Forms and Registers

C12 *Book Selection Card.* Printed. 6 pt Bristol board. White. Tray. The text of the form is as follows :

(*Front side*)

Ac N Don N Wl N
Cl N
Auth

Title
Size Coll Ed Yr
Pub Pub price

Series, etc

Review

Reference

(*Back side*)

Vendor

	Date	Initials
Seln		
Apprd		
Order		
Recd		
Paid		
Accnd		
Cut		
Class		
Cat		
Shld		
Bound		
Wl		

Cost Indian
Foreign

Order N

Voucher N

	Cur Yr		Total	
Cum N of Vol in				
Sub				
Lang				
Cum Cost	Rs	nP	Rs	nP
Sub				
Total				

Q12 *Book Selection Consultation Letter Form.* Stencil. 21 lb Printing paper. White. The text of the form is as follows :

Subject : BOOK SELECTION

(*Number*) Book selection cards in (*subject*) are enclosed for your consideration. Please be good enough to sort them into the three groups, "approved", "deferred", and "rejected". The three groups may be separately bundled and sent to me along with a covering letter embodying your recommendation.

The balance available for purchase of books in your subject within the current financial year is Rs ..

Expecting your reply within a week,

S13 *Indent Noting Form.* Stencil. 21 lb Printing paper. White. The text of the form is as follows :

Outside N .. Dated
File N .. Date of receipt
From ..
Subject : Indent for Books

Librarian's Note	*Office Note*	
	N of items recommended	
	N of items already available or on order	
	N of items recommended for duplication	
	Estimated cost of the items not in library	Rs
	Estimated cost of the duplications recommended	Rs
	Total estimated cost	Rs
	Allotment for books	Rs
	Amount already appropriated	Rs
	Balance available	Rs
	Remarks	

Library Committee's decision

Note : If the librarian is the sanctioning authority, the first column should have the heading "Note by Head of Section"; and the bottom line should read "Librarian's decision".

Name	*Class Number*	*Amplifying device*	*Filing characteristic*	*Year of transfer to record sequence after the file is closed*	*Year of destruction after transfer to the record sequence*
Sources	11	Subject Device or/ and Language Device	Correspondent	Year 1	Year 3
Selection	12	Subject Device	Do	Do	Year 5
Indent	13	Do	Do	Do	Year 10
Allotment	16	Do	Do	Do	Do
Outward enquiries	191	Do	Do	Do	Year 3
Inward enquiries	192	Do	Do	Do	Do

Chapter 22

BOOK ORDER SECTION

221 Planning

2211 Far Off Book Market

The work of ordering books in Indian libraries is at present more difficult than it is elsewhere. It is European books and particularly English books that figure most in Indian libraries. Thus, the chief book markets are thousands of miles away—in far off London, New York and other centres in Europe. As a result, Indian libraries are not able to get books on approval to choose between different editions. The task of deciding whether a new edition that is announced is substantially different from the one that the library already possesses becomes extremely difficult. The Book Order Section in Indian libraries has to take a much greater responsibility and put in much more work in checking the indents with the stock than that in European and American libraries.

2212 Indian Publications

In the matter of Indian publications, the situation is even worse. The publishing trade is not yet properly organised in India. Nor is there a bookselling trade, except for school text-books. In most cases, the author himself has to play the role of publisher and bookseller. He lives in out-of-the-way places. As may be expected, he has not developed business methods. Not infrequently, it happens that he does not respond at all to orders. There are instances when the Madras University Library had to send six reminders to an author-cum-publisher-cum-book-seller, before getting a reply. Occasionally it happens that the author had burnt his fingers by venturing to print a work of his and that he had left his place in disgust and migrated to some other place to find some means of living. In all probability, he had left his stock behind, in his deserted house with nobody to look after them ; and there is no one in his old village to redirect his letters to his new address. This picture is by no means an imaginary one. The Madras University Library and the Banaras Hindu University

Library have been experiencing this every now and then. It can be realised how difficult book ordering should be in such circumstances.

Another complicating factor in ordering Indian books is due to there being no conformity to bibliographical standards either in the make-up of the title pages of books or in the preparation of indents by persons specialising in the study of topics usually found only in books in Indian languages published in India. The typographical display of the title page not infrequently places improper emphasis. For example, the name of the patron or some other influential person appears in the boldest and in the biggest type, whereas the name of the author is hidden away in the smallest possible type or is even omitted. Specialists still continue to mention the books only by the title. The idea that the names of authors and publishers are necessary elements in individualising books has not yet become familiar.

There is, at present, a vexatious factor. There is no Net Book System. Some booksellers give a discount slightly greater than what the publisher himself gives. The Central Executive insists on this advantage being taken at any cost. It does not realise that the cost of getting comparative quotation—it has often to be for individual books even—exceeds the probable benefit in most cases. Nor does it realise that a bookseller concerned often delays supply and ultimately even fails to supply.

2213 MULTIVOLUMED BOOKS

Another responsibility of the Book Order Section is that of seeing that the Multivolumed Books are carefully watched and that all the .olumes of a set are acquired as and when published. It is a matter of common knowledge that frequently we come across cases of Multivolumed Books whose volumes are published in different years. Unless a suitable mechanism is devised to deal with such cases, it will lead to the library possessing incomplete sets, to the great annoyance of the readers.

2214 PREPAID BOOKS

Books published serially and books published on Prepaid Subscription basis form other complicating factors which require the greatest vigilance on the part of the Book Order Section.

2215 Standing Vendor

It is a moot point whether it is advantageous for a library to buy its books directly from the publishers or through a Standing Vendor. In the case of Indian books, the question is easily decided in favour of the former alternative. For, India has not yet developed a reliable, painstaking and organised book trade for such books. The vexatious factor mentioned at the end of Section 2212 makes the Standing Vendor System result in extreme delay in the supply of books. Hence, as has already been indicated, the only satisfactory procedure is to deal directly with the publishers or the authors, as the case may be. No doubt, every effort should be made to build and organise a sound booksellers' trade in India, capable of handling all our purchases, Indian or foreign.

The position is, however, different in the case of European and American books. Here, it is an advantage to have a Standing Vendor appointed in India itself or at each important book centre—say, one for London, one for New York, one for Leipzig, one for Paris and so on. On the one hand, these book centres have experienced and competent booksellers of standing, and on the other, it will be difficult for Indian libraries to take all the bibliographical precautions, if they deal directly with the several publishers. There are booksellers in those book centres who are prepared to render us certain amount of bibliographical service.

2216 Terms of Contract

It is necessary that Indian libraries should stipulate certain conditions of a bibliographical nature in appointing a Standing Vendor. He should be asked to undertake the following responsibilities :

1 Every volume should be carefully collated before being supplied. If any defect is discovered at this end, the vendor should take back the defective copy and supply a sound copy at his own cost, including the to and fro freight ;
2 The latest edition of the book is to be supplied, unless there are specific instructions to the contrary ;
3 If the order copy contains a note that a certain edition of a particular book is already in the library, he should find out if the later edition in the market is substantially different from the one in the library. If not, the book should not be supplied,

but an advice should be sent. In cases of doubt, he should state the case and supply the book only after receiving a confirmatory order ;

4 If a book is the reissue of another book under a different title, he should advise the library about it and supply it only after receiving a confirmatory order ;

5 If a book is an off-print from a periodical publication or another book, he should advise the library about it and supply it only after receiving a confirmatory order ;

6 If a book is really a foreign publication, though listed in the trade periodicals of his country by the local representative of the foreign publisher, he should advise the library about it and supply it only after receiving a confirmatory order ;

7 If there is any difference in the name or in the spelling of the name of the author or in the title, he should advise the library about it and make the supply only after receiving a confirmatory order ; and

8 If any book occurs in more than one order or is covered by any of the standing orders, only one copy should be supplied and a second copy should not be supplied without getting a confirmatory order.

In all these cases, if the vendor sends a wrong supply, he should take it back at his own cost.

The experience of the Madras University Library is that a substantial saving is effected in the book fund by the standing vendors undertaking such bibliographical responsibilities. As the trade lists do not generally give frank information on these points, these problems cannot be solved without actually examining the book. This is impracticable for Indian libraries as we are thousands of miles away from the book markets. Hence the responsibility has to be shifted to the standing vendors in the respective book centres. This also shows the futility of appointing Indian booksellers as standing vendors for foreign books, unless they have their own agents in the different book centres of the world, to examine the supply personally before it is shipped.

2217 Out-Of-Print Books

In the matter of Out-Of-Print books, it is best to obtain quotations from different second-hand booksellers and decide the vendor in each case on its merits, rather than appoint a single standing vendor. Very often the catalogues of the second-hand booksellers may obviate even the necessity for enquiry. But these catalogues should not be relied upon, if the amount is considerable. It may be possible to get better terms by obtaining competitive quotations.

2218 Factors in Planning

The distinctive work of the Book Order Section is to be planned with reference to the following factors :

1 Standing vendors ;
2 Enquiries and quotations for unusual individual books ;
3 Books not falling within classes 4 to 8 enumerated below, which may be referred to as *Ordinary Books* ;
4 *Standing Order Books*, which means one of the following :
41 Books belonging to a series whose volumes the library has decided to buy, which may be referred to as *Series Books* ;
42 Books in two or more volumes, all the volumes not being published simultaneously, which may be referred to as *Multivolumed Books* ;
43 Books published in parts or in fascicules, which may be referred to as *Instalment Books* ;
44 Books for which advance payment has to be paid in full or in part before actual publication, which may be referred to as *Subscription Books* ; and
8 Books which can be acquired as donation, which may be referred to as *Gift Books*.

Of these factors, the appointment of standing vendors will have to be done annually, biennially or triennially but not at more frequent intervals. Enquiries will have to be made and quotations will have to be obtained for unusual individual books as and when required, as a casual job. The ordering of ordinary books should be taken up periodically, the periodicity depending upon the quantity of the order. In a big library, it may be convenient to use the week as the period. In what follows, the routine is described on that basis. But if longer periods are practicable in smaller libraries, there will be no difficulty in adopting the routine to any periodicity. The order work for instalment books, subscription books and series books is to be planned on the analogy of the work of the Periodical Publication Section. Hence, in what follows, it is only such items of routine in regard to these books as are different from the routine of the Periodical Publication Section that are elaborated ; and for all other routine, reference is to be made to the routine of the Periodical Publication Section.

22191 Subject Cycles

Thus, the most important part of the routine described in this chapter can be seen to be that which relates to ordinary books. As suggested in section 2114, it will add to the systematisation of the work of this section and of the other sections if the order work for the different subjects are taken up for the weekly order work in systematic cycles, the periodicity for each subject being adjusted from time to time in the light of supply and demand and with a view to spreading the work of the section evenly over the different weeks of the year.

222 Job Analysis

2221 Standing Vendors

2221:8 The work of the Book Order Section relating to Standing Vendors is to consist of the following annual jobs :

1 Calling for the terms on which ordinary books can be supplied to the library by different vendors, which may be referred to as *Calling for Terms of Supply* ;
2 Tabulation of the terms offered by the different vendors, which may be referred to as *Tabulating the Terms of Supply* ; and
5 Fixing the standing vendor or vendors, as the case may be, which may be referred to as *Standing Vendor Appointing*.

2222 Enquiries and Quotations for Unusual Books

2222:5 The work of the Book Order Section relating to Enquiries and Quotations for unusual individual books is to consist of the following weekly jobs :

1 Calling for quotation or for any information in regard to specific book or books, as the case may be, which may be referred to as *Quotation Calling* or *Enquiring* ; and
2 Tabulating the information obtained from the different sources relating to specific books, which may be referred to as *Quotation Tabulating*.

2223 Ordinary Books

2223 The work of the Book Order Section relating to Ordinary Books is to consist of the following items :

1 Tallying and sorting the book selection cards relating to the indent, which may be referred to as *Tallying and Sorting Work* ;
2 Checking the book selection cards with the resources of the library with a view to eliminating duplication, which may be referred to as *Final Checking Work* ;
3 Preparing the order which may be referred to as *Order Preparing Work* ;
4 Consulting the experts concerned about doubtful cases, which may be referred to as *Doubt Clearing Work* ;
5 Issuing the order, which may be referred to as *Ordering Work* ;
6 Carrying out the necessary items of work relating to an order immediately after it is issued, which may be referred to as *Post-Order-Work* ;
7 Receiving the supply relating to an order, which may be referred to as *Book Supply Receiving Work* ; and
8 Dealing with the information received, if any, about the books not supplied, which may be referred to as *Unsupplied Books Disposing Work* ;
82 Ensuring the prompt execution of the orders by the vendors, which may be referred to as *Vigilance Order Work*.

2223:1 *Tallying and Sorting Work*

2223:1:5 Tallying and Sorting Work is to consist of the following weekly jobs :

1 Tallying the indent or the indent copy, as the case may be, received from the Book Selection Section, with the related

book selection cards received from the same section and sorting the latter according to the types of books, which may be referred to as *Preliminary Sorting* ; and

2 Alphabetising the ordinary book order cards relating to all the indents taken up for ordering in the week, which may be referred to as *Order Cards Alphabetising.*

2223:2 *Final Checking Work*

2223:2:5 Final Checking Work is to consist of the following weekly jobs :

23 Checking the alphabetised order cards with the outstanding order tray, which may be referred to as *Checking with Outstanding Order Tray* ;

24 Checking the alphabetised order cards with the standing order cards, which may be referred to as *Checking with Standing Order Cards* ;

4 Checking the alphabetised order cards with the bills on hand, which may be referred to as *Checking with Bills on Hand* ;

495 *Subsidiary job in the Madras University Library* : Getting the alphabetised order cards checked by the exchange section, which may be referred to as *Checking with Exchange List* ;

5 Checking the alphabetised order cards with the library catalogue, which may be referred to as *Checking with Catalogue* ; and

8 In case of doubt, checking the order cards directly with the books on the shelf, which may be referred to as *Checking with Books.*

2223:3 *Order Preparing Work*

2223:3:5 Order Preparing Work is to consist of the following weekly jobs :

11 Sorting the unscored cards from the card checking box and sorting them by vendors, etc. which may be referred to as *Unscored Cards Sorting* ;

118 Picking out the cards of the books which can be got as gifts, which may be referred to as *Gift Cases Picking* ;

12 Estimating the cost of each one of the groups into which the unscored cards have been sorted, which may be referred to as *Order Cost Estimating* ;

13 If the book selection section has transmitted the approved indent in original, getting the order copies typed with the necessary notes, which may be referred to as *Order Copy Making* ;

14 If the book selection section has transmitted only copies of the approved indent, transferring to the copies of the indent the necessary remarks and notes from the related order cards, which may be referred to as *Order Copy Noting* ;

15 Scoring out the rejected items and tallying the unscored items with the unscored cards in the alphabetised order card box of the week, which may be referred to as *Order Copy Completing* ;

5 Consulting the Technical Section, Circulation Section, Reference Section and Maintenance Section for detection of any casual duplications that might have unintentionally crept into the order, which may be referred to as *Inter-sectional Consulting* ; and

6 Finding out if the funds for the subject would admit of the order, which may be referred to as *Finance Diary Consulting.*

2223:4 *Doubt Clearing Work*

2223:4:5 Doubt Clearing Work is to consist of the following weekly jobs :

5 Placing before the experts the issues on which advice is sought, which may be referred to as *Advice Seeking* ; and

8 Taking the necessary action on the receipt of the advice, which may be referred to as *Advice Disposing.*

2223:5 *Ordering Work*

2223:5:5 Ordering Work is to consist of the following weekly jobs :

1 Writing out the formal letter for transmitting the final

order to the vendor, which may be referred to as *Order Writing* ;

24 Scrutinising the order after its return from the librarian, which may be referred to as *Final Scrutiny* ;

28 Filing the order cards in the order tray, which may be referred to as *Order Card Filing* ; and

3 Transmission of the order to the correspondence section for despatch, which may be referred to as *Order Transmitting.*

2223:6 *Post-Order Work*

2223:6:5 Post-Order Work is to consist of the following weekly jobs :

1 Transmitting to the Book Selection Section the original indent, in cases where the original indent had been received, which may be referred to as *Original Indent Transmitting* ;

2 Filing the office copies of the order, which may be referred to as *Order Copy Filing* ;

6 Entering the estimated cost of the order in the finance diary, which may be referred to as *Finance Diary Posting* ;

7 Transmitting to the reference section the third copy of the order, which may be referred to as *Order Copy Transmitting* and

8 Filing the cards scored out during the checking process, which may be referred to as *Scored Cards Filing.*

2223:7 *Book Supply Receiving Work*

2223:7:5 Book Supply Receiving Work is to consist of the following weekly jobs :

1 Reviewing the supply and transmitting it to the accession section, which may be referred to as *Supply Receiving* ;

2 Picking out the order cards from the order tray for each item in the bill, which may be referred to as *Supplied Cards Picking* ;

3 Reconciling the order cards with the bill, which may be referred to as *Order Cards Reconciling* ; and

4 Transmitting the bill and the related reconciled order cards to the Accession Section, which may be referred to as *Bill and Cards Transmitting.*

2223:8 *Unsupplied Books Disposing Work*

2223:8:5 Unsupplied Books Disposing Work is to consist of the following weekly jobs :

1 Picking out from the order tray the cards relating to each item which has not been supplied, but about which some difficulty has been raised by the vendor, which may be referred to as *Unsupplied Cards Picking* ;
2 If the objection raised is such that the order can be confirmed, taking the necessary action along that line, which may be referred to as *Order Confirming* ;
3 If the objection raised is such that the item is to be reordered from some other vendor, taking the necessary action along that line, which may be referred to as *Reordering* ; and
4 If the objection raised is such that the order for the item is to be cancelled, taking the necessary action along that line, which may be referred to as *Order Cancelling*.

2223:82 *Vigilance Order Work*

2233:82:5 Vigilance Order Work is to consist of the following weekly jobs :

1 Noting on the Vigilance Order Copy the estimated earliest possible due week for supply and the final week for full supply, which may be referred to as *Vigilance Order Dating* ;
2 Inserting the Vigilance Order Copy in the Vigilance Order File, which may be referred to as *Vigilance Order Filing* ;
3 Noting in the Vigilance Order Copy the date of supply as and when it arrives, which may be referred to as *Supply Noting* ;
4 Noting in the Vigilance Order Copy any information received about inability to supply, which may be referred to as *Information Noting* ;
5 Keeping track of the supply made on each book order which may be referred to as *Vigilance Follow Up*.

2233:82:8 Vigilance Work is to consist of the following annual job :

6 Destroying the Completed-Supply Order Copies, which may

be referred to as the *Vigilance Order Destroying.*

2224 Standing Orders

The work of the Book Order Section relating to Standing Orders is similar partly to the work relating to ordinary books and partly to the work relating to periodical publications as explained in the routine part of this chapter.

2228 Gift Books

2228:5 The work of the Book Order Section relating to Gift Books is to consist of the following weekly jobs :

1 Writing to the probable donors for the free gift of books, which may be referred to as *Gift Soliciting* ; and
2 As soon as the gift books arrive, sending an acknowledgment to the donor and passing the books on to the accession section, which may be referred to as *Solicited. Gift Accepting.*

223 Routine

2231 Standing Vendors

2231:8 *Annual jobs*

2231:81 Calling for Terms of Supply

At least six months before the expiry of the term of the Standing Vendors, write to different vendors of standing, asking for the terms on which they will agree to be appointed as standing vendors of the library. Mention in the letter of enquiry the approximate amount of annual purchase and the various bibliographical responsibilities which they should undertake, as indicated in the introduction to this chapter. Ask them also to quote the most favourable trade terms. In the case of Foreign Booksellers, it would be a good practice to ask them to send bills in the Currency of Their Country so that the fluctuations in exchange may not unjustly affect either party. In certain countries like Great Britain, there is the net book system. Hence, it may not be possible to get any discount. In other countries discounts may be possible. If the library is a large buyer, it may be possible to make the vendor deliver the books at the library Free of Packing and Freight Charges. It is also necessary to state that the books should be sent by packet post and not by cargo boat, as the latter course would involve much delay.

2231:82 TABULATING THE TERMS OF SUPPLY

As soon as the replies are received from the different vendors, tabulate the terms of supply in a systematic manner and write notes for the consideration of the librarian.

2231:85 STANDING VENDOR APPOINTING

Send the tabulated terms of supply to the librarian at least two months before the expiry of the term of the existing standing vendor and obtain the decision from him. As soon as he selects the Standing Vendor for the next period, communicate the order of appointment promptly. In the communication state explicitly the terms of supply and get from the Standing Vendor a letter of consent to do the service subject to the conditions stipulated.

2232 ENQUIRIES AND QUOTATIONS

2232:5 *Weekly jobs*

2232:51 QUOTATION CALLING OR ENQUIRING

This routine will have to be done in the case of some of the Indian publications and the out-of-print foreign books. For each book or group of books, write to the necessary number of booksellers specifying all the available bibliographical information about the books, asking the bookseller to supplement the bibliographical information in detail along the lines indicated in the introduction to this chapter, and to quote the price. It has to be repeated here that as the Indian book trade has not yet properly evolved, the necessary information may not be obtainable by one letter. The correspondence may have to be continued for some time before a satisfactory result is obtained.

2232:52 QUOTATION TABULATING

As soon as the quotations are received from the different vendors, tabulate them and add the necessary notes for the consideration of the librarian. Take the tabulated statement to the librarian and get his orders as to the further action to be taken.

2233 ORDINARY BOOKS

2233:1 *Tallying and Sorting Work*

2233:1:5 *Weekly jobs*

2233:1:51 PRELIMINARY SORTING

As soon as the indent or the indent copy and the related book selection cards are received from the Book Selection Section, deal with each indent successively as follows :

Pick out the book selection card appropriate to each entry in the indent. Compare them. If the comparison discloses any discrepancy put it aside for rectifying it later in consultation with the Book Selection Section. If there is no discrepancy, put the card in order in the appropriate group, according to the type of book mentioned therein viz ordinary book, instalment book, multivolumed book, subscription book or series book.

After all the items have been so dealt with, put the indent or the indent copy, as the case may be, aside in the Pending Indents File.

Get each of the cards set aside on account of discrepancy disclosed, rectify it with the help of the Book Selection Section and insert it in the appropriate group.

Transfer the cards in the Instalment Group, Multivolumed Group, Subscription Group and Series Group to the appropriate trays to be dealt with in accordance with the routine prescribed for them.

2233:1:52 ORDER CARDS ALPHABETISING

Take out the cards in the Ordinary Books Group relating to the indents which are proposed to be taken up for ordering in the week. Alphabetise them by the heading. Put them in the alphabetised *Card Checking Box*.

2233:2 *Final Checking Work*

In the different jobs of checking work, carefully check each card with reference to each one of the headings that the book is likely to receive, as in routine 2233:2:55.

In case of duplication, score out in pencil across the related order card from the left hand bottom corner to the right hand top corner and transfer the card to behind the "Duplicates" Guide in the box. Similarly, in case any card presents a difficulty which cannot be solved without expert help, transfer it to behind the "Doubtful" Guide in the box. The remaining cards may be referred to as the *Surviving Cards.*

If any peculiarities are brought to notice, note them down in a 3×5 inches slip and pin the slip to the back of the related order card with the side of the slip having the notes away from the back of the order card and the lines in the slip proceeding in the same direction as the lines on the back of the order card. The pin is to be applied at the right hand top corner.

After completion of the checking job with a card, put a pencil mark at the right hand top corner of the card in token of your having completed the checking job.

2233:2:5 *Weekly jobs*

2233:2:523 CHECKING WITH OUTSTANDING ORDER TRAY

Carefully check each of the cards in the Card Checking Box of the week with the cards in the Outstanding Order Tray in which the cards will lie arranged in one alphabetic sequence by their headings.

2233:2:524 CHECKING WITH STANDING ORDER CARDS

Check each of the Surviving Cards in the Card Checking Box with each of the standing order cards awaiting supply.

2233:2:54 CHECKING WITH BILLS ON HAND

Carefully check each entry in each of the bills on hand with the Surviving Cards in the Card Checking Box.

Subsidiary Job in the Madras University Library

2233:2:5495 CHECKING WITH EXCHANGE LIST

Take the Cards Checking Box to the Exchange Section and, with the help of the clerk in charge, scrutinise carefully if any of the books mentioned in the Surviving Cards are likely to arrive by exchange or have already arrived.

2233:2:55 CHECKING WITH CATALOGUE

Carefully check the Surviving Cards in the Card Checking Box, first with the index part of the catalogue. Remember to check it with all the possible entries in the catalogue, e g each one of the headings which the book is likely to receive in accordance with the cataloguing rules.[22]

In the case where the index entry in the catalogue, which has the heading in question, is only a class index entry, check the corresponding order card with the main cards under the class number given in the index card.

In all cases in which the order card has either no heading or has been given a doubtful heading or has any other peculiarities, guess the probable right headings and check them with the index part of the catalogue. Also guess the probable class number of the book and check it with that region of the main part of the catalogue which relates to that class number.

2233:2:58 Checking with Books

If, after these checkings are over, there is still room for doubt in the case of any order card, check it with the books on the shelf.

2233:3 *Order Preparing Work*

2233:3:5 *Weekly jobs*

2233:3:511 Unscored Cards Sorting

Take out all the surviving cards in the alphabetised Order Cards Box, and sort them on the basis of the following characteristics :

Main subject ; and
Vendor

Let the cards falling into the sub-group of a specified vendor in the group of a specified subject be referred to as an *Ultimate Group.*

Alphabetise the cards in each one of the ultimate groups.

2233:3:5118 Gift Cases Picking

Pick out from each of the alphabetised ultimate groups, such order cards as, you think, may be procurable gratis from the publishing body or any other source. Put them in the *Gift Requisition Box,* to be dealt with in accordance with the routine 2238.

2233:3:512 Order Cost Estimating

Estimate the total cost of all the cards in a specified subject and find out if the total does not exceed the balance available to the credit of the subject. If it exceeds, remove the necessary number of cards to the *Deferred Order Cards Tray*. If it does not exceed, see if the necessary margin is left to meet the contingency of having to purchase urgent books in the subject in the remaining part of the year. Only the cards, that are left over after all the necessary eliminations to keep the cost of the order within a reasonable limit, are to be taken for the next routine.

The estimated Cost of the Order is to be entered at the end of the last card in the set.

2233:3:513 Order Copy Making

In the case of those ultimate groups for which the Book Selection Section had furnished the approved indent in original, get four order copies typed. Each entry is to be provided with the necessary consolidated notes in a form which will be intelligible to the vendor, in case the order card has a slip attached to it.

2233:3:514 Order Copy Noting

In the case of such Ultimate Groups for which the Book Selection Section has furnished four copies of the approved indent, transfer to each entry in three of the copies of the approved indent the consolidated notes in a form which will be intelligible to the vendor, in case the order card has a slip attached to it.

2233:3:515 Order Copy Completing

With the aid of the duplicate and the doubtful cards in the alphabetised *Order Cards Box* of the week, score out in all the four copies of the indent the unwanted items. Then, tally carefully the remaining entries in the order copies with the remaining cards and their slips, if any, in the alphabetised Order Cards Box of the week.

2233:3:55 Intersectional Consulting

Pass round a copy of the completed order to each of the Sections that are likely to be of help, viz the Periodical Publication Section, the Accession Section, the Technical Section, the Circulation Section, the Reference Section and the Maintenance Section, for detection of any casual duplications that might have unintentionally crept into the order.

After allowing a reasonable time to each Section, collect from them any helpful remark that they might be able to make and use them for the further improvement of the order.

Subsidiary Rule of the Madras University Library

A copy of the completed order is to be sent also to the Exchange Section.

2233: 3:56 Finance Diary Consulting

Find out from the Finance Diary the amount already appropriated in the subject to which the order relates and the Balance that is available. If the estimated cost of the order exceeds the Balance available, either strike out the necessary number of items or add a note in the order copy, for the information of the vendor, specifying the maximum amount beyond which the cost of the supply should not go and giving him any possible instructions for cutting out items, if necessary.

2233:4 *Doubt Clearing Work*

2233:4:5 *Weekly jobs*

2233:4:55 Advice Seeking

Take all the cards from behind the " Doubtful " Guide and enunciate the difficulties relating to each of them in the form of definite issues and transmit them to the experts concerned for the necessary advice.

2233:4:58 Advice Disposing

As soon as the advice is received from the experts, take the necessary action on each item.

2233:5 *Ordering Work*

2233:5:5 *Weekly jobs*

2233:5:51 Order Writing

For each of the final orders, i e for all the order copies relating to the Ultimate Groups of Order Cards, write out a formal letter transmitting the Order to the Vendor. If the attention of the vendor is to be invited to any special points, remember to state them explicitly. Send them to the librarian.

2233:5:524 Final Scrutiny

After the order letter and the order copies are received from the librarian, examine if his signature and his initials occur in all the necessary places. Remember particularly that all the scored items should have received his initials. Then peruse the order rapidly to give a last chance for detection of unintentional duplication and for any other peculiarities which may require special noting. If any item gets scored out at this stage or if any note is to be added at this stage, bring it to the notice of the librarian and get his approval and also his initials in cases of scoring out.

2233:5:528 Order Card Filing

After the final scrutiny is over, note in each card the number and date of the order and the vendor and put the initials in the appropriate place. Then, alphabetise the order cards.

Insert them in the proper alphabetical sequence in the *Outstanding Order Tray*.

If in the course of the insertion any unintentional duplication is detected, take it to the notice of the librarian and take prompt steps to get the order copy corrected before its despatch either by scoring out or by the addition of notes, as the case may be.

The related card is to be sent to the Unwanted Cards Tray or is to be inserted in the Outstanding Order Tray according to the decision made.

2233:5:53 Order Transmitting

After the filing of the order cards and the consequential action, if any, transmit to the Correspondence Section the office copy and the fair copy of the order letter and the order lists for despatch, specifying the date on which the orders should be despatched.

2233:6 *Post-Order Work*

Note: *The jobs under this work except the fourth are to be taken up after the file relating to the order comes back from the Correspondence Section. But the Finance Diary Posting is to be finished after the final scrutiny of the order and before the order is actually despatched from the Correspondence Section.*

2233:6:5 *Weekly jobs*

2233:6:51 Original Indent Transmitting

As soon as all the items of an original indent received from the Book Selection Section are disposed of, tick in the margin of the original indent against each item finally ordered and put the necessary remarks in the case of the items finally decided 'not to be ordered'. Note on the top of the office copies of the related orders the File Number of the Indent to which they relate. Also put at the bottom of the indent against the different symbols indicating the ordered items, the appropriate File Number of the related Orders. Then, transmit the original indent to the Book Selection Section.

2233:6:52 Order Copy Filing

If the order copy was made in the Order Section, the necessary cross referencing for each copy and the related original indent would have been made in accordance with the routine in 2233:6:51. In such a case, the second copy of the order may be filed straight away, in the Office Copy File in the sequence of the File Mark. The Third copy may be used as Vigilance Order Copy, for Vigilance Order Work. (see section 2223:82).

If, on the other hand, the order copy was made in the Book Selection Section, the necessary cross referencing in the related original indent should be made by getting the original indent from the Book Selection Section and writing down at the bottom the necessary cross references in the manner indicated in routine 2233:6:51; then, the original indent should be transmitted to the Book Selection Section and the office copies of the order are to be filed. This may be called *Vigilance Order File*.

2233:6:56 Finance Diary Posting

On the appointed day each week, enter the estimated cost of the orders issued in the week under the appropriate subject heading in the Financial Diary, which is maintained in common by the book order section, the periodical publication section and the accounts section.

2233:6:57 Order Copy Transmitting

Note in the fourth copy of the order the date of the order and transmit it to the Reference Section for their file.

2233:6:58 SCORED CARDS FILING

On the last day of the week, merge the order cards scored during the different stages of checking and consulting in the tray containing the Rejected Book Selection Cards in one alphabetic sequence.

2233:7 *Book Supply Receiving Work*

2233:7:5 *Weekly jobs*

2233:7:51 SUPPLY RECEIVING

As soon as the supply of books is received from the librarian, peruse the backs as well as the inside of the books rapidly and see if any book has been inadvertently duplicated. Ask the other concerned sections, viz Book Selection Section, Technical Section, Reference Section and Shelf Section, to review them similarly. This reviewing is to be done in a few minutes. It is intended only to detect cases of duplication that might be brought to mind without any serious and prolonged investigation.

2233:7:52 SUPPLIED CARDS PICKING

Pick out all the bills relating to the books reviewed. Arrange the bills by the orders to which they relate. As a result, the bills relating to the same subject will be together and arranged chronologically by the date of order and the different subjects will come in their natural class sequence. For each item of the bill, pick out the related card from the Outstanding Order Tray. If the card corresponding to any item in the bill is not to be found, look for it carefully under any other probable heading under which the card might have been filed. If, in spite of such a search, the card is not to be found, take the office copy of the related order and verify:

1 if the item is in the order ; and
2 if it had not been already supplied.

If both the conditions are satisfied, the card must be found in the Outstanding Order Tray and a careful search must be made.

If, on the other hand, either of the conditions is not satisfied, the book should have been wrongly sent by the vendor or should have been already supplied and paid for. In either case, the supply is not due. Against the items not due, write the words " Not due " in pencil in the concerned bill.

2233:7:53 ORDER CARDS RECONCILING

After all the items in the bill have been disposed of either by picking out the related cards or by writing the words " Not due", compare each card with the related item in the bill. If there is any discrepancy, pick out the letter, if any, received from the vendor explaining such discrepancies. If the explanations given in the vendor's letter are acceptable, make the necessary alterations in the order card. In cases of doubt, consult the librarian before making the alteration in the order card. By a careful perusal of the vendor's letter, see if all the discrepancies raised by him have been fully dealt with by you. If they have been, write a note in pencil at the left hand bottom corner of the vendor's letter to the effect " All discrepancies have been noted and reconciled".

2233:7:54 BILL, BOOKS AND CARDS TRANSMITTING

As soon as the Order Cards Reconciling routine is over, put all the reconciled order cards in a box and transmit it to the Accession Section with the related bills and books.

2233:8 *Unsupplied Books Disposing Work*

2233:8:5 *Weekly jobs*

2233:8:51 UNSUPPLIED CARDS PICKING

Take up all the letters received from vendors about the non-supply of items. Pick out from the Outstanding Order Tray the cards of the items referred to in the letters. Put all such cards in the Unsupplied Cards Box and investigate each case along lines appropriate to it.

2233:8:52 ORDER CONFIRMING

In the case of all the cards in which the investigation shows that the order may be confirmed, advise the vendor accordingly. Insert the related cards in the Outstanding Order Tray. By way of illustration, it may be stated, that cases of this nature may arise on account of:

1 Mis-spelling of the names of authors or titles;
2 Differences in edition ;
3 The edition ordered not being substantially different from the edition in the library ;
4 Difference in price ; and
5 Difference in publisher.

2233:8:53 Reordering

In the case of all the cards in which the investigation shows that the items are to be obtained from some other vendor, cancel the order with the original vendor, and then proceed with the routines given under 2233:5 and 2233:6. By way of illustration, it may be stated that cases of this nature may arise on account of :

1 A book being out of print and hence being obtainable only from second hand book market ;
2 The actual publication of the book being in a country different from that of the vendor and hence being more conveniently purchasable from some other vendor ; and
3 Other similar causes.

2233:8:54 Order Cancelling

In the case of all the cards in which the investigation shows that the order may be cancelled, write a letter to the vendor cancelling the order. Write in pencil the word "Cancelled" at the bottom of the related cards and file them in the *Cancelled Order Tray*.

By way of illustration, it may be stated, that cases of this nature may arise on account of the :

1 Edition offered not being acceptable ;
2 Year of publication not being acceptable ;
3 Price quoted not being acceptable ;
4 Edition offered not being substantially different from the edition in the library ;
5 Book being the same as another book under another title already in the library ;
6 Book being a part of or a reprint from some other book or periodical already in the library ; and
7 Total cost of the supply exceeding any limit that might have

been set when the order was issued ; and
8 Other similar causes.

2233:82 *Vigilance Order Work*

2233:82:5 *Weekly jobs*

2233:82:51 Vigilance Order Dating

Near the right hand top corner of the Vigilance Order Copy, note the Earliest Due Week of Supply as estimated. Note below it the Final Full Supply Week. The Earliest Due Week should be estimated on the basis of the distance of the bookmarket, and of the announced date of publication in the case of a pre-publication order. Note these dates in the second order copy also, put in the Office Copy File.

2233:82:52 Vigilance Order Filing

1 Keep the Vigilance Order Files in a pad or a set of pads to be called *Vigilance Order Pad*.
2 The Vigilance Order Pad will have 60 Week Guides in the form of Card Boards with tabs. In respect of these, follow the analogy of the *Preliminary* given under section 2334:3:46.
3 Each Vigilance Order Copy should be inserted in the proper classified place below the Week Guide of the Earliest Due Week.

2233:82:53 Supply Noting

On the appointed day of the week, before transmitting the bill and the books to the Accession Section as prescribed in Routine 2233:7:54, deal with each Bill as follows :

In the Vigilance Order Copy corresponding to it, enter the Week Number of the Current Week in the Remarks Column against each item, either severally or collectively as may be expedient.

2233:82:54 Information Noting

On the appointed day of the week, which will be after the books received in the Current Week are transmitted to the Accession Section as prescribed in Routine 2233:7:54, enter in the Remarks Column against each appropriate item appropriate remarks based on any letter received from the Vendor, such as:

OP for out of Print,
OS for out of Stock,
PE for Procurable Elsewhere.

This is to be done in unison with the Routine " 2233:8 Unsupplied Books Disposing Work ".

2233:82:55 Vigilance Follow Up

After Supply Noting and Information Noting are finished, on the appointed day of the week, examine each of the Vigilance Order Copies lying below the Week Guide of the Current Week in the Vigilance Order Pad.

1 If the Remarks Column shows that the supply has been completed to the fullest extent available, insert the Vigilance Order Copy in the *Supply Completed Pad*, in its proper classified place.
2 If the Supply is not completed and the Final Full Supply Week has not yet been reached, insert the Vigilance Order Copy to below the Week Guide of the Next Week.
3 If the Supply is not completed and the Final Full Supply Week has been reached, insert it in the *Current Week's Disposal Pad* in the classified sequence.
4 When all the Vigilance Order Copies have been removed from below the Week Guide of the Current Week, shift that Week Guide to the bottom-most position in the Vigilance Order Pad. It will thus become Week Guide for the Corresponding Week of the next year.
5 For each of the Vigilance Order Copies in the *Current Week's Disposal Pad*, send reminder or take any other appropriate action. Note the action taken and the date at the bottom of the Order Copy. If a reminder is sent note the Current Week Number, below the Final Full Supply Week Number. If the week for second or third reminder has come, do similarly.
6 The Waiting Time between two consecutive reminders should be decided according to some convention on the basis of the distance of the book market.
7 After the third reminder, consult the librarian about the

further action to be taken and do as he directs.

8 After action is completed, insert all the Vigilance Order Copies of the Current Week's Disposal Pad in the correct classified place just below the uppermost Week Guide in the Vigilance Order Pad.

2233:82:8 *Annual job*

2233:82:88 VIGILANCE ORDER DESTROYING

On the appointed day of the year, destroy all the Vigilance Order Copies in the Supply Completed Pad.

2234 STANDING ORDERS

The work of the Book Order Section relating to Standing Orders is to consist of weekly jobs similar to those for ordinary books in most respects. The chief difference will consist in :

1 Having the standing order cards in a separate sequence ; and
2 Watching and controlling the regular supply in accordance with the procedure laid down in " Chapter 23, Periodical Publication Section".

22341 *Series Books*

If the publisher is giving his own serial number to the different volumes, the receipt of the volumes can be controlled with the aid of those numbers. Otherwise the volumes should be numbered by the library as and when they are received.

22342 *Multivolumed Books*

The probable number of the remaining volumes and the probable date when they will be published should be ascertained and noted in the related standing order cards to aid the watching of the receipt of these volumes at the proper time.

22343 *Instalment Books*

These books require the greatest care. Here again the periodicity should be ascertained from the publishers and used for watching the systematic receipt of the fascicules. However, it must be remembered that in actual practice, instalment books suffer from great irregularity and even come to an abrupt end on account of financial difficulties. The greatest wariness is necessary in dealing with them. Further, as soon as a particular book is completed, one must carefully watch for the title page and index of the book. The title page and index of a particular book may even be published along with a fascicule of some other book. It will be a good practice to write to the vendor or publisher as soon as a book is completed asking when and in what manner the title page and index will be published.

22344 *Subscription Books*

In the case of a subscription book the library has to advance the cost before the book is printed. Thus, a great risk is undertaken in their cases. Hence, their cases must be closely watched until the account is satisfactorily settled. A subscription book may be of any of the preceding varieties. The number of volumes or fascicules due should be ascertained and a line should be devoted to each one of the fascicules or volumes, as the case may be, in the standing order card and the regular receipt of the parts, watched.

22345 *Trade Announcements*

In the case of standing order books, in addition to taking prompt action as soon as it is discovered that a part or book has not arrived at the scheduled time, trade announcements should be closely watched and, further, it will be a good practice to examine all the standing orders periodically, say once in a quarter, study the files, place the facts before the librarian and take such action as may be called for.

In the Madras University Library, all correspondence relating to standing orders is attended to on Tuesdays.

22346 *Completed Volume*

For each completed volume received in response to a Standing Order, an Accession Card is to be prepared filling up the heading, the title, and such of the process columns on the back of the card as can be filled. This card is to be transmitted to the Accession Section along with the book.

2238 Gift Books

2238:5 *Weekly jobs*

2238:51 Gift Soliciting

In the case of the cards picked out for soliciting gifts in accordance with routine 2233:3:5118 "Gift Cases Picking", write to the probable donors in courteous terms asking for a free gift of the concerned books.

2238:52 Solicited Gift Accepting

As soon as the solicited gift books arrive, send an acknowledgment to the donor in courteous terms. Then put inside the book a slip with the words "Solicited gift book from (*donor*)" and pass the book on to the Accession Section. If it is settled that the solicited donation is refused, include the related book selection card in the week's group of cards awaiting to be ordered. It may be stated here that all unsolicited gift books are to be dealt with by the Accession Section directly.

224 Elimination of Waste

2241 Organisation

If the turnover in the section demands the assignment of several members to it, the distribution of work among the assistants of the section should proceed along the lines of language specialisation. Except in the case of English, specialisation in language may be, generally speaking, equivalent to specialisation in countries. Thus, the specialisation suggested will enable each member of the section to acquire an intensive acquaintance with the trade conditions in certain specified countries. This will also facilitate correspondence in foreign languages.

2242 Bibliographical Flair

The Head of the Book Order Section should develop a bibliographical flair to spot out cases of duplication in the indent as well as in the order list. Every order must be finally scrutinised by him. Invariably the final ordering work also should be done by him. He should particularly verify if all the order copies contain all the notes accumulated in each order card for the information of the vendor. He should also have under his direct control all kinds of standing orders.

2243 Order Tray

The Order Tray is a most vital instrument for avoiding double payment as well as for eschewing unordered books. Hence that tray must be under lock and key in his personal custody. He must be so sure of its accuracy—accuracy in the alphabetisation as well as accuracy in the cards included—that, if a card is not found for a book, he can definitely assert that the book is not due to the library on payment.

2244 Diaries

In addition to filling up the financial diary every week as provided in routine 2233:6:56 and bringing its cumulative total up-to-date from month to month—it will be seen that the financial diary is common to three sections—the head of this section should maintain two other diaries, each on a weekly basis.

2245 General Diary

The first diary is to have the following headings :

11 Letters received;
121 Letters replied;
122 Letters filed;
141 Letters drafted;
142 Routine letters issued;
15 Reminders sent;
21 Indents received;
22 Indents returned;
323 Book order cards checked with outstanding order tray;
327 Book order cards checked with standing order cards;
34 Book order cards checked with bills on hand;
3495 Book order cards checked with exchange list;
35 Book order cards checked with catalogue;
38 Book order cards checked with shelf;
41 Standing orders issued for series books;
42 Standing orders issued for multivolumed books;
43 Standing orders issued for instalment books;

44 Standing orders issued for subscription books;
5 Order cards filed;
7 Ordinary books received from vendor;
71 Series books received from vendor;
72 Multivolumed books received from vendor;
73 Fascicules of instalment books received from vendor;
74 Subscription books received from vendor;
754 Volumes and cards transmitted to the accession section.

2246 Book Order Cards Diary

The second diary is to show the number of book order cards filed in the week according to subjects. Its headings must consist of the symbols for the main divisions of the book classification used or some suitable modification of them.

225 Correlation Table

All Sections

2233:3:55 Intersectional consulting

1 *Book Selection Section*

2233:1:51 Preliminary sorting ;
2233:6:51 Original indent transmitting.

4 *Accession Section*

2233:2:54 Checking with bills on hand ;
2233:2:5495 Checking with exchange list ;
2233:7:54 Bill and cards transmitting (Saturday 1 P M) ;
2238:52 Solicited gift accepting.

5 *Technical Section*

2233:2:55 Checking with catalogue.

7 *Reference Section*

2233:6:57 Order copy transmitting.

8 *Maintenance Section*

2233:2:58 Checking with books.

96 *Finance Section*

2233:3:56	Finance diary consulting ;
2233:6:56	Finance diary posting.

993 *Correspondence Section*

2233:3:513	Order copy making ;
2233:5:53	Order transmitting. (Thursday 3 PM)

226 Illustrative Time Scheme

Weekly Jobs

Saturday

2233:1:51	Preliminary sorting ;
2233:1:52	Order cards alphabetising ;
2233:2:54	Checking with bills on hand ;
2233:2:523	Checking with outstanding order tray ;
2233:2:524	Checking with standing order cards ;
2233:7:51	Supply receiving ;
2233:7:52	Supplied cards picking ;
2233:7:53	Order cards reconciling ;
2233:7:54	Bill and cards transmitting. (1 PM)

Sunday

2233:2:55	Checking with catalogue.

Monday

2233:2:5495	Checking with exchange list ;
2233:2:58	Checking with books ;
2233:3:511	Unscored cards sorting ;
2233:3:5118	Gift cases picking ;
2233:3:512	Order cost estimating ;
2233:4:58	Advice disposing.

Tuesday

2232:51	Quotation calling ;
2232:52	Quotation tabulating :
2233:3:513	Order copy making ,
2233:8	Unsupplied books disposing work.

Wednesday

2233:3:514 Order copy noting ;
2233:3:515 Order copy completing ;
2233:3:55 Intersectional consulting ;
2233:3:56 Finance diary consulting ;
2233:5:51 Order writing.

Thursday

2233:4:55 Advice seeking ;
2233:5:524 Final scrutiny.;
2233:5:528 Order card filing ;
2233:5:53 Order transmitting (3 PM) ;
2233:6:51 Original indent transmitting ;
2233:6:52 Order copy filing ;
2233:6:56 Finance diary posting ;
2233:6:57 Order copy transmitting ;
2233:6:58 Scored cards fiiling.

Annual Jobs

August

2231:81 Calling for terms of supply.

October

2231:85 Standing vendor appointing.

227 Forms and Registers

C 24 *Standing order card.* Manuscript. Bristol board. White. Tray. Front side. 7 lines. Back side 18 lines.

Row headings at the top of the front side :

First line : Series/Heading

Second line : S O Numb .. dated .. Period

Third line : Vendor .. Note

Column headings for the remaining part of the first side and for the back side :

Serial/Vol Numb (1.5 cm). Accession Numb (2 cm). Voucher Numb and date (2.5 cm). Call Number (3 cm). Heading (3 cm). Price (5 cm).

Q22 *Book enquiry form.* Stencil. 21 lb printing paper. White. The text of the form is as follows :

Subject : ENQUIRY ABOUT BOOKS

Please let me know whether you can supply this library with the books mentioned below/in the enclosed list. If so, at what prices ?

Also furnish me with the following information regarding the books :

1 Editions available with the prices.
2 Full name of the author.
3 Full title.
4 Publisher.
5 Date of publication.
6 Series, if any, to which the publication belongs.
7 If it is an off print from a book or a periodical, the name and volume of the book or periodical.
8 If it is an old book published with a new title, the title of the old book.

NB Please do not treat this as an order for supply.

Q231 *Order form to local vendors.* Stencil. 21 lb printing paper. White. The text of the form is as follows :

Subject : BOOK ORDER

Please supply the..........................library with the books in the enclosed list on the terms agreed upon/at their published prices less commission, free of all delivery and packing charges and send a bill in duplicate for payment at an early date.

Q232 *Order form to outside Indian vendors.* Stencil. 21 lb printing paper. White. The text of the form is as follows :

Subject : BOOK ORDER

Please supply the..........................library with the books in the enclosed list mentioned below at their published prices less commission/at the prices quoted by you in your catalogue/in your letter under reference and send a bill in duplicate for payment at an early date. If you want to send the books by railway parcel, the freight should be prepaid and the parcel should be addressed to the Librarian,.................... Library,........................, and not to " self". If you send them by post, please do not send them by VPP.

Q235 *Order form to the standing vendors.* Stencil. 21 lb printing paper. White. The text of the form is as follows :

Subject : Book Order

Please supply the......................Library under the usual conditions with the books in the enclosed lists, viz

Order Numb Dated Remarks.

228 Files

Name	Class number	Amplifying device	Filing characteristic	Year of transfer to record sequence after the file is closed	Year of destruction after transfer to the record sequence
Standing vendors	21	Subject Device or/and Language Device	Vendor	Year 1	Year 5
Standing vendors (second hand books)	218	Do	Do	Do	Do
Enquiries and quotations	22	Subject Device	Heading	Do	Year 3
Ordinary books ordering	23	Do	Vendor and date of order	Do	Year 5
Ordinary books order doubt clearing	234	Do	Heading	Do	Do
Series ordering	241	Do	Series Heading	Do	Do
Multivolumed books ordering	242	Do	Heading	Do	Do
Instalment books ordering	243	Do	Do	Do	Do
Pre-publication ordering	244	Do	Do	Do	Do
Gift books	28	Nil	Donor	Do	Year 3
Outward enquiries	291	Nil	Correspondent	Do	Do
Inward enquiries	292	Nil	Do	Do	Do

CHAPTER 23

PERIODICAL PUBLICATION SECTION

231 Planning

2311 COMPLICATING FACTORS

The work of the Periodical Publication Section assumes great magnitude in libraries of universities, research institutions and other learned bodies. For the definition of the term "Periodical Publication", a reference may be made to the *Classified catalogue code.*[23] As has been stated in the Introduction to Chapter 70 of the same book, "Periodical publications form one of the sources of perplexity" in library work. "Their vagaries may transcend all imagination and anticipation. It looks as if nothing relating to a periodical publication can escape the sport of caprice—publishing society, name, periodicity, *format*, pagination, excrescential attachments to all or stray volumes and, last but not least, span of life and resurrection." A full discussion of the vagaries with illustrations will be found in Part 7 of the same book. While such vagaries are sufficiently baffling to the cataloguer, they nearly break the back of the section, that is entrusted with the task of acquiring the periodical publications. Another complicating factor which leads to this result is that the periodical publications are always published in limited editions. If the non-receipt of a particular number is not brought to the notice of the vendor promptly and a copy claimed from him, there is a great probability for the library not getting it at all. Hence, the greatest amount of vigilance and promptness is necessary in dealing with the acquisition of periodical publications.

2312 CARD SYSTEM

Any method that may work satisfactorily when the number of periodical publications taken by a library is small, may not work when the number increases. The bound book method of keeping the records relating to the Periodical Publication Section breaks down absolutely as the number of periodical publications taken by the library increases beyond a certain limit. We want all the mobility that the card system can give to deal with the periodical publications. Otherwise we cannot secure the necessary economy of energy and economy of time. Again, we must reduce the dependence on memory to a minimum. The bound book method does not help us in this direction as much as we want. It cannot automatically bring to our notice the names of the periodical publications that are due in any particular week or day.

2313 Three Card System

After many experiments, we have devised in the Madras University Library the "Three card system". The routine described in this chapter relates to this system. It is being worked satisfactorily from the year 1930. The amount of saving that has resulted from it can be inferred from the fact that although the number of periodical publications taken in the library has risen from 240 in 1924 to 1,200 in 1934, there has been no increase of staff in the Periodical Publication Section. It still continues single handed. Perhaps, it may be possible to carry on the work without additional staff, until the number reaches about 1,000. In the earlier years when the library was using bound volumes for records, there was tight work even though there were only 240 periodical publications current. But the introduction of the "Three card system" in 1930 has given this phenomenal relief. The "Three card system" secures the maximum turnover with the minimum staff.

In this system, three cards, each 3×5 inches, are maintained for each periodical publication taken in the library. They are called respectively the *Register Card*, the *Check Card* and the *Classified Index Card*. The columns of each of these cards are indicated in Part 7 of this chapter.

The way in which the three cards are operated is explained fully in Part 3 of this chapter.

2314 Register Card

The Register Card is used for recording entries relating to the volume, issue, and the dates of publication and receipt of the periodical publication as and when its issues are received. The voucher number and the date of payment are also noted in this card. The Register Cards are arranged in one alphabetical sequence by the titles of the periodical publications.

2315 Check Card

The Check Card is intended to help the watching of the receipt of the different issues of the publications and to remind us when a particular issue becomes overdue and the need for sending a reminder arises. When a reminder is sent, the issue of reminders is recorded in these cards. Check Cards stand divided into 52 groups according to the week in which the next issue is due. For this purpose, each week is taken to end on an allotted day, say Wednesday. As there may be 5 Wednesdays in some months of the year, there are 5 Week Guides for each month. Thus the total number of Week Guides for the year is 60. But 8 of these will be inoperative. The Week Guides are numbered expressively such as 1.1, 1.2... 1.5,2.1,2.2... 12.4 and 12.5. The Check Cards in each weekly group will lie arranged in one alphabetical sequence by the titles of the periodical publications.

2316 Classified Index Card

The Classified Index Card of a publication shows what volumes of the publication are available in the library. It also shows the cumulative indexes, the supplements and the special volumes, if any, relating to the publication that may be available in the library. As the name indicates, the classified index cards are arranged in a classified sequence by the class numbers of the publications.

2317 Prompt Release

In the matter of handling the new issues that come from time to time, it should be a matter of honour for the Periodical Publication Section that the issues are released for public use in as short a time as possible after the receipt of the mail. It is known that the demand for the dailies, weeklies and fortnightlies is greatest. Hence, the routine in the third part of this chapter provides for dealing with these expeditiously before the long-period ones are taken up.

2318 Factors in Planning

The distinctive work of the Periodical Publication Section is to be planned with reference to the following factors:

1 Standing vendors;

4 Current volumes; and

7 Back volumes.

It will help the symmetrical building up of the periodical publication resources of the library, if the periodical publications taken in the library are divided into the different main subjects and the list relating to each subject is reviewed from time to time in the light of supply and demand both on its own merits and in relation to the lists in the other subjects.

32 Job Analysis

2321 Standing Vendors

The work of the Periodical Publication Section relating to standing vendors, is to consist of jobs similar to those given in section "2221 Standing vendors".

2324 Current Volumes

The work of the Periodical Publication Section relating to the current volumes of the periodical publications taken in the library is to consist of the following items:

1 Choosing, and obtaining the sanction for the acquisition of new publications and reviewing and revising the current list of periodical publications from time to time, which may be referred to as *Periodical Publication Selection Work*;
2 Ordering the sanctioned publications and renewing the order from year to year in the case of continued publications, which may be referred to as *Periodical Publication Ordering Work*;
3 Watching the regular and systematic receipt of the current issues of the publications ordered or otherwise due and making them available for use, which may be referred to as *Periodical Publication Receiving Work*;
4 In the case of the volumes of the publications which have been completed, taking the necessary steps to get the volumes accessioned and made available as a bound volume, which may be referred to as *Completing Work*;
5 Watching the announcement of the publication of cumulative indexes to the periodical publications in the library and taking steps to acquire them, which may be referred to as *Cumulative Index Work*;

6 Taking all such action as the week's supply might require, which may be referred to as *Rounding Off Work*;

7 Calling for and passing the bills for the periodical publications taken in the library, which may be referred to as *Periodical Publication Bill Passing Work*;

8 Placing the loose issues of the periodical received from time to time on the display table in the first instance and later in the shelves, which may be referred to as *Loose Issue Shelving Work*; and

94 Disposing of the unordered and unwanted and wrongly delivered periodical publications, which may be referred to as *Suspense Periodical Publications Work*.

2324:1 *Periodical Publication Selection Work*

2324:1:1 Periodical Publication Selection Work is to consist of the following immediate job:

1 As and when specific periodical publications of probable interest to the library are brought to notice, jotting down the necessary particulars about them, which may be referred to as *Suggestion Noting*.

2324:1:5 Periodical Publication Section Work is to consist of the following weekly jobs:

1 Checking the suggestion slips contained in the Suggestion Slips Box with the list of the periodical publications current in the library, which may be referred to as *Preliminary Checking*;

2 Calling for quotation or for any information in regard to the periodical publication whose acquisition in the library is to be considered, which may be referred to as *Periodical Publication Enquiring*;

3 Checking the suggestion slips with the list of current periodical publications again in the light of the information received as a result of the enquiry, which may be referred to as *Second Checking*;

4 Examining the financial position of the subject concerned in the light of the quotations received, which may be referred

to as *Financial Position Ascertaining*;

5 Sending a reference to the expert concerned asking for advice in regard to the acquisition of the new periodical publication, which may be referred to as *Periodical Publications Consulting*;

6 Preparing the necessary notes for the sanctioning authority, which may be referred to as *Periodical Publication Indent Noting*;

7 Forwarding the indent to the sanctioning authority, which may be referred to as *Indent Forwarding*; and

8 Taking such action as may be necessary on such of the items of the forwarded indents which have not received the sanction of the authority concerned, which may be referred to as *Rejected Items Disposing*.

2324:1:8 Periodical Publication Selection Work is to consist of the following annual jobs :

1 Making a complete list of all the periodical publications current in the year, which may be referred to as *Current List Preparing*;

2 Examining the desirability of continuing the current periodical publications in the ensuing year, which may be referred to as *Current List Reviewing*;

3 Getting information from the co-operating libraries about the extent to which there is unnecessary overlapping in their respective current lists of periodical publications, which may be referred to as *Co-operating Library Consulting*;

4 Examining the financial position in each subject in regard to current periodical publications, which may be referred to as *Financial Position Reviewing*;

5 Seeking the advice of the experts concerned in the revision of the current list, which may be referred to as *Current List Consulting*;

6 Preparing the necessary notes on the current list for the sanctioning authority, which may be referred to as *Current List Noting*; and

7 Forwarding the current list to the sanctioning authority, which may be referred to as *Current List Forwarding*.

2324:2 *Periodical Publication Ordering Work*

2324:2:5 Periodical Publication Ordering Work is to consist of the following weekly jobs :

1 Finally checking the sanctioned indent for periodical publications with the catalogue, which may be referred to as *Periodical Publication Final Checking*;
16 Ascertaining if the finance of the subject will bear the cost of the sanctioned periodical publication, which may be referred to as *Financial Position Deciding*;
2 Preparing the order for each of the periodical publications in the sanctioned list, which may be referred to as *Order Preparing*;
3 Preparing the three cards for regulating the receipt of the current issues of the periodical publications ordered, which may be referred to as *Periodical Publication Carding*;
4 Transmitting the order to the librarian for his signature, which may be referred to as *Periodical Publication Order Transmitting*; and
6 Making the necessary entry in the Financial Diary, which may be referred to as *Financial Diary Posting*.

2324:2:8 Periodical Publication Ordering Work is to consist of the following annual jobs:

1 Making a list of the periodical publications which are to be continued in the ensuing year, which may be referred to as *Renewal Order Listing*;
2 Tallying the renewal order list with the Register Cards Tray, which may be referred to as *Renewal Order List Tallying*;
3 Writing out the renewal order cards, which may be referred to as *Renewal Order Writing*;
4 Tallying the renewal order cards with the renewal order list, which may be referred to as *Renewal Order Tallying*;
5 Verifying the addresses on the renewal order cards, which may be referred to as *Renewal Order Address Verifying*;
6 Sorting the renewal order cards by countries, which may be referred to as *Renewal Order Sorting*;
7 Sending the sorted renewal cards to the librarian for

signature, which may be referred to as *Renewal Order Card Transmitting*;

8 Cancelling the order for the items rejected from the current list, which may be referred to as *Standing Order Cancelling*;

83 Marking the Three Cards of each of the cancelled publications, which may be referred to as *Cancelled Card Marking*:

84 Transferring the Register Cards and the Check Cards of the cancelled publications to the Cancelled Tray, which may be referred to as *Cards Cancelling*; and

96 Posting the estimated annual subscription in the financial diary, which may be referred to as *Financial Diary Annual Posting.*

2324:3 *Periodical Publication Receiving Work*

2324:3:1 Periodical Publication Receiving Work is to consist of the following immediate jobs :

1 Receiving the periodical publication that may come in the form of a V.P. packet, which may be referred to as *V.P. Packet Receiving*; and

2 Returning wrongly delivered periodical publication packets, which may be referred to as *Wrongly Delivered Packet Returning.*

2324:3:4 Periodical Publication Receiving Work is to consist of the following daily jobs:

1 Examining the wrapper of the periodical packets received, which may be referred to as *Wrapper Examining*;

12 Sorting the packets into suitable groups, which may be referred to as *sorting*;

2 Collating the periodical publications received, which may be referred to as *Current Issue Collating*;

3 Alphabetising the collated current issues in each group which may be referred to as *Current Issues Alphabetising*;

4 Registering each of the current numbers in each alphabetised sequence, which may be referred to as *Current Issue Registering*;

5 Cutting and stamping the registered current issues which

may be referred to as *Current Issue Cutting and Stamping*;

56 Perusing the current issues rapidly to detect peculiarities and announcements, if any, which may be referred to as *Current Issue Perusing*;

6 Shifting to behind the appropriate "Week Guide" the Check Card of the periodical publication received, which may be referred to as *Check Card Shifting*;

61 Watching the arrival of the issues of the Dailies, which may be referred to as *Daily Vigilance*;

7 If any loose sheets, plates, maps be found in any of the current issues, fixing them if necessary, which may be referred to as *Loose Sheets Fixing*; and

8 If any correction slips are found in any of the current issues, taking the necessary action in regard to them, which may be referred to as *Correction Slip Disposing.*

2324:3:5 Periodical Publication Receiving Work is to consist of the following weekly job :

1 Watching the arrival of the issues of the periodical publications due in the week which may be referred to as *Weekly Vigilance.*

2324:4 *Periodical Publication Completing Work*

2324:4:5 Periodical Publication Completing Work is to consist of the following weekly jobs :

1 Collecting together all the issues relating to the title page, contents and index received in the week, which may be referred to as *Loose Issues Collecting*;

2 Verifying the volume with the contents page, which may be referred to as *Loose Issues Tallying*;

3 Making up the loose issues into the necessary number of volumes, which may be referred to as *Volume Making Up*;

4 Separating the supplements, if any, which may be referred to as *Supplement Separating.*

5 Writing out special binding instructions, if any, which may be referred to as *Binding Peculiarity Drafting*;

6 Writing out accession cards for the completed volumes, which

may be referred to as *Accession Card Writing*;

7 Transmission of the volumes and the accession cards to the Accession Section, which may be referred to as *Completed Volumes Transmitting*; and

8 Noting the accession number in the Register Cards, which may be referred to as *Accession Number Noting.*

2324:5 *Cumulative Index Work*

2324:5:1 Cumulative Index Work is to consist of the following immediate job :

1 As and when the announcement of a cumulative index comes to notice, noting down the information, which may be referred to as *Cumulative Index Noting.*

2324:5:4 Cumulative Index Work is to consist of daily jobs similar to those of Periodical Publication Receiving Work with the following modifications :

3 Entering the receipt of the cumulative index in the Classified Card, which may be referred to as *Classified Card Entering*, is to take the place of "3 current issues alphabetising".

6 Omit "6 Check Card Shifting".

2324:5:5 Cumulative Index Work is to consist of the following weekly jobs :

1 Checking the cumulative index suggestion slips contained at the beginning of the week's Current Box with the contents of the library, which may be referred to as *Cumulative Index Checking* ;

22 Preparing the order for each of the cumulative indexes to be acquired, which may be referred to as *Cumulative Index Order Preparing*;

23 Transmitting the order to the librarian for his signature, which may be referred to as *Cumulative Order Transmitting*;

26 Noting in the finance diary an estimate of the cost of the cumulative indexes finally ordered, which may be referred to as *Finance Diary Posting*; and

5—8 Similar to the corresponding weekly jobs under "2324:4:5 Weekly jobs of completing work".

2324:6 *Rounding Off Work*

2324:6:5 Rounding Off Work is to consist of the following weekly jobs :

1 Notifying the vendor about the non-receipt of current issues within a reasonable time, after the due date, which may be referred to as *Non-Supply Notifying*;
2 Notifying the vendor about the non-receipt of title page, contents and index, which may be referred to as *TCI Notifying*;
3 Notifying the vendor of the gaps that might have been discovered in the supply in the course of the registering work during the week, which may be referred to as *Gap-in-Supply Notifying*;
4 Notifying the vendor about the defects in the current issues received during the week, which may be referred to as *Defective Supply Notifying*;
5 Acknowledging to the donors the receipt of the current issues of periodical publications supplied gratis, which may by referred to as *Current Issue Acknowledging*;
6 Notifying the vendor of the duplicate issues that might have been inadvertently supplied during the week, which may be referred to as *Duplicate Supply Notifying*;
93 Taking such action as may be necessary on each of the slips found in the week's Current Box, which may be referred to as *Slips Disposing*;
95 Distributing the cards in the week's Current Box after its receipt from the librarian, which may be referred to as *Week's Current Box Distributing*; and
96 Transmitting to the librarian for signature the week's Current Box after all the necessary cards have been written out and inserted, which may be referred to as *Week's Current Box Transmitting*.

2324:7 *Periodical Publication Bill Passing Work*

2324:7:5 Periodical Publications Bill Passing Work is to consist of the following weekly jobs :

12 Calling for bills, in case they are not sent in by the vendors, which may be referred to as *Bills Calling*;

13 Alphabetising the bills by the name of the periodical publication, which may be referred to as *Bills Alphabetising*;
2 Scrutinising the preceding payment for the periodical publication mentioned in the bill, which may be referred to as *Preceding Payment Scrutinising*;
3 Verifying if the claim is in accordance with the accepted subscription rate and if not so, finding out the justification for the change, which may be referred to as *Cost Verifying*;
4 Certifying in each bill the correctness of the claim and the receipt of supply in case of post-payment, which may be referred to as *Bills Certifying*;
5 Revising the certified bills to detect mistakes, if any, which may be referred to as *Bills Revising*;
6 Grouping together such of the verified bills as relate to the same vendor, which may be referred to as *Grouping by Vendors*;
7 Transmitting the bills to the Accounts Section, which may be referred to as *Passed Bills Transmitting*; and
8 On the return of the bills from the Accounts Section after being passed by the librarian, noting down the voucher number in the Register Cards, which may be referred to as *Voucher Number Noting*.

2324:8 *Loose Issue Shelving Work*

2324:8:4 Loose Issue Shelving Work is to consist of the following daily jobs :

1 Arranging the new issues of the periodical publications registered, in a classified sequence, which may be referred to as *New Issues Arranging* ;
2 Placing the new issues on the display table, which may be referred to as *New Issues Displaying*; and
6 Shelving the old issues displayed on the display table, which may be referred to as *Old Issues Shelving*.

2327 BACK VOLUMES

The jobs relating to the ordering and receiving of back volumes of periodical publications are similar in most respects to that of ordering and receiving books.

233 Routine

2331 Standing Vendors

The routine connected with the appointment of Standing Vendors is similar to that given in " 2231 Standing vendors".

23311 Middle Man's Intervention

It is doubtful if the appointment of Standing Vendors is an advantage in the case of periodical publications. The idiosyncrasies of the periodical publications are so many and so sudden and the issues of periodical publications go out of print in such a surprisingly short time, that, except by extraordinary vigilance, the library's collection of periodical publications is liable to become defective and incomplete. Again, the very nature of the content of a periodical publication is such that it loses in value, if its supply is delayed unnecessarily even by one day. Witness for example, the look of disappointment visible in the faces of the eager workers, when, due to some casual hitch in the periodical publication section, there is a few hours' delay in the releasing for public use of the issues that have arrived by the day's mail, or if the weekly foreign mail is delayed by a day, as it occasionally often happens. Therefore, it is desirable that the extra delay likely to be caused by the middleman's intervention should be avoided.

23312 No Standing Vendor

Hence, the work connected with the periodical publications is likely to be much more satisfactory if the library deals with the publishers direct. Even if this might mean some extra cost in administration, that cost is worth the return that we get in the form of satisfaction to the readers. But, it may not mean really extra cost. As the publishers of periodicals allow too small a commission to vendors, a standing vendor is likely to make a small charge on the library over the published price. It is a matter of experience that this charge will nearly balance the extra cost involved in dealing with the publishers directly.

23313 Dailies

It may, perhaps, be not so very objectionable to have standing vendors in the case of dailies, as the agency work for dailies is much more organised and the standing agents get sufficient remuneration for their service from the publishers of the dailies themselves, without having to expect any extra commission or remuneration from the buyers. But, in the case of publications of any other periodicity, a standing vendor may prove to be a fifth wheel.

2334 Current Volumes

2334:1 *Periodical Publication Selecting Work*

2334:1 The routine for the different jobs of this work is similar to the corresponding routine given in sections 2131, 2132 and 2133.

2334:101 *Specimen Copy*

There is, however, one difference. It is desirable that a specimen copy should be obtained from the publishers and perused and sent for the perusal of the expert advisers and of the sanctioning authority, before a decision is made to take a new periodical publication. Very often specimen copies of new periodical publications are usually sent by the publishers gratuitously and they themselves form the sources for selection. Even if specimen copies have not been gratuitously received, in most cases, it may be possible to get them on application. A better credit may be enjoyed if such specimen copies are, after the final selection is over, either paid for in case of selection or returned to the publishers in case of rejection, unless the publisher has definitely instructed that they need not be returned.

2334:102 *Annual Review*

There is yet another difference between book selection work and periodical publication selection work. The latter requires a set of annual jobs, while it is not so in the former case. The annual jobs, enumerated in rule 2324:1:8 of the job analysis part of this chapter, provide for the annual revision of the current list of periodical publications.

2334:103 *Reason for Revision*

That the list needs revision goes without saying. The revision may be necessitated either by the vicissitudes in the periodical publications themselves, or in the appearance of new publications, or by a change in the financial allotment for periodical publications, or by a change in the requirements of the clientele of the library. No library can adopt the policy "once taken, for ever taken" in the case of periodical publications.

2334:104 *Consideration for Librarian's Views*

On the contrary, it is seldom that library committees mostly made of laymen, and even experienced subject specialists realise the full implications of tinkering with the current list of periodical publications now and then. They do not realise how difficult it will be to fill up gaps in a set of periodical publications. They do not take a sufficiently long view of things nor realise that periodical publications have a permanent value and may serve a very useful end in the future, although their use might have gone down a little at the moment. Under these circumstances, the librarian has a very delicate task to perform. He has to give the proper lead to the library committee in the matter and frame the issues to be placed before the library committee and the subject specialist in such a way that hasty and lighthearted decisions may not be easy. The library committees also should realise that the building up of the periodical publication resources of a library requires great forethought, and a sense of values that can be developed only by an intimate knowledge of the users of the library on the one hand and of the publications on the other. The librarian has exceptional opportunities in these directions. Hence, library committees should treat the librarian's views in the matter of revising the current list of periodical publications with great consideration. In fact they should leave the annual revision of periodicals to be done by the librarian in consultation with subject experts. They should restrict their responsibility to seeing that the annual budget provision for periodicals is not exceeded.

23341:105 *Selection Month*

In the case of the publications whose discontinuance is to be decided upon, it is desirable that the discontinuance should have effect only from the beginning of a volume and not in the middle of a volume. However obvious this suggestion may be, it is very often ignored and the result is the ugly presence of incomplete volumes in the shelves of libraries. As more than half the periodical publications begin their volumes in January, it will be a good policy to take up the annual jobs connected with the selecting work some time in August and arrive at the final decision before the end of September.

2334:1:8 *Annual jobs*

2334:1:81 Current List Preparing

In the appointed month of each year, make a complete list of all the periodical publications current in the year. Change sheet whenever the main subject changes. Each item in the list should contain the class number, the title, the stock in library, the periodicity, the annual subscription and remarks.

If the list of the periodical publications taken are not violently changed from year to year, it may be more economical to take stencil copies of the list once in five years. In that case instead of preparing a fresh list, make the necessary corrections in one of the stencil copies.

2334:1:82 Current List Reviewing

Examine each item in the list of periodical publications current in the library. Note down in the remarks column if there is any abnormality. If the Reference Section and the Circulation Section have any definite opinion throwing light on the desirability of continuing it or not, note it down in the remarks column. After each item has been dealt with in that way, take it to the librarian and discuss it with him.

2334:1:83 Co-operating Library Consulting

In the interests of national economy, it is desirable that periodical publications are not unnecessarily duplicated in the different libraries of the same region. Certain periodical publications will have necessarily to be duplicated if they are in frequent demand. In the case of many others, duplication can very well be avoided. For this purpose, the libraries of a region should be in friendly co-operation with one another. Their finances for periodical publications should be regarded as if pooled together as one fund and distributed carefully over as many different periodical publications as possible. There is one danger, however, which must be avoided. None of the co-operating libraries should act independently of the others. The publications assigned to a particular library should not be light-heartedly taken away from it and reassigned to some other library. That will lead to the breaking up of the set in an inconvenient way. Whenever such a reassignment becomes absolutely necessary, the back volumes also should be transferred from the old library to the new one. Remembering these principles in view, consult the co-operating libraries to find out whether the list of periodical publications current in your library requires any amendment.

2334:1:84 Financial Position Reviewing

Examine the financial position of the library as a whole, and also the financial allotment to the different subjects. Examine if the estimated annual subscription to the periodical publications current is within the means of the library as a whole and of each of the subjects. If any readjustment appears to be necessary, prepare the necessary notes for the consideration of the librarian, the expert advisers and the library committee.

2334:1:85 Current List Consulting

If necessary, consult the experts in the different subjects to find out what amendments are desirable in the current list. Word the letter carefully, raising all the points on which advice is sought in the form of definite issues, on which clear and brief replies can be given.

2334:1:86 Current List Noting

After all these processes are over, prepare carefully-worded notes for the consideration of the sanctioning authority.

2334:1:87 Current List Forwarding

At the appointed time, send the current list with its notes to the sanctioning authority through the Committees Section for the necessary approval.

2334:2 *Periodical Publication Ordering Work*

2334:2:5 *Weekly jobs*

2334:2:51 Final Checking

This routine is to be similar to the routine under "2233:2 Final

Checking Work" with the following modifications :

The checking will have to be done only with the catalogue of the library, the Register Card Tray of the Periodical Publication Section and the Classified Card Tray of the same section.

2334:2:516 FINANCIAL POSITION DECIDING

As soon as the final checking is over, examine the financial position of the subject to which the periodical publication relates, in consultation with the Book Selection Section, the Book Order Section, and the Accounts Section. If there is reason to doubt the adequacy of finance, take the instructions of the librarian before proceeding further.

2334:2:52 ORDER PREPARING

For each sanctioned periodical publication for which there is adequate finance, write out an order.

If the decision is to take the periodical publication for an indefinite period, add the following sentence in the order : "This may be treated as a standing order until countermanded."

On the other hand, if the decision is to take it only temporarily say for one or two years, specify explicitly the period for which the supply is to be made.

In many of the periodical publications, the volume periodicity may not agree with calendar years. Hence, it may be advantageous to specify the period for which the supply is to be continued, not by the calendar year but by volume number. Otherwise, there is the risk of the library having incomplete volumes on the shelves. It is seldom that the managing authorities of a library realise this awkwardness. Hence, special care is to be taken in advance in preparing the notes on the indent so that the sanction of the managing body may be got in the appropriate form.

2334:2:53 PERIODICAL PUBLICATION CARDING

As soon as the order copy is written out for a periodical publication, prepare, provisionally in pencil, three cards, viz the Classified Index Card, the Register Card, and the Check Card. Insert them in the appropriate places in their respective trays. If printed or stencil copies of the list of the current periodical publications exist, carry out the interpolation in the copy marked for the year.

2334:2:54 Periodical Publication Order Transmitting

As soon as the periodical publication carding is over, write in the office copy of the order the word, "carded" and initial and date it. Then, transmit it with the file to the librarian for signature.

2334:2:56 Financial Diary Posting

As soon as the librarian has signed the order for a periodical publication, make the necessary entries in the financial diary in the column devoted to the subject to which the publication belongs. It may be repeated here that the financial diary is common to the three sections—Book Order Section, Periodical Publication Section and Accounts Section.

2334:2:8 *Annual jobs*

Although a standing order is recommended to be placed, it is a good practice to review the list of the current periodical publications once in a year and issue renewal orders confirming the standing order or issue cancel orders, according to the decision. From the nature of the case, it is obvious, that this annual work should be made in sufficient time for the renewal order or the cancel order, as the case may be, to reach the publisher before a new volume of the the periodical publication commences. The publishers of learned periodicals are doing a great service at grave financial risk. It is seldom that a learned periodical pays its own way. Hence, it is the duty of all libraries to minimise the risk of the publisher by furnishing him with the necessary information sufficiently in advance to enable him to decide the number of copies to be printed.

2334:2:81 Renewal Order Listing

Take out each card in the Register Cards Tray. Examine the decision on the list of current periodical publications, prepared in connection with the jobs enumerated in rule 2324:1:8 and see if the axe has fallen on it. Examine also if the file relating to the publication has any note that might have been recorded regarding its continuance. Examine also the entries in the Register Card to see if there is anything abnormal about the publication. Pull out the related Classified Card and put it in the classified sequence in the *Renewal Listing Tray* or *Cancel Listing Box*, according as continuation or cancelling is indicated. Place the Register Card back in its original place. After all the cards in the Register Card Tray have been thus disposed of, it follows that the Renewal Listing Tray would have been completed. Prepare an estimate of the annual subscription for the periodical publications in each subject. Discuss with the librarian the cards in the Renewal Listing Tray and the Cancel Listing Box, class by class.

After the necessary transfer of cards is made, have the renewal list typed. Begin a new sheet with every subject. The number of copies to be taken is likely to vary from library to library. It will depend upon the number of persons whose advice is to be sought regarding renewal. In any case, it will be a good plan to have at least five copies made out each year. Once in five years, it will be an advantage to have some fifty copies stencilled. If this is done, the work of typing the list every year may be obviated, because the stencil copies may be used, from year to year with the necessary interpolations and scoring out done annually.

2334:2:82 Renewal Order List Tallying

After the typing of the Renewal Order List or the correcting the Year's Copy of the Stencil List, as the case may be, is over, tally it carefully with the cards in the Renewal Listing Tray. If there is any discrepancy, have it set right. Write the endorsement "Tallied", on the Renewal List and initial and date it.

2334:2:83 Renewal Order Writing

For each of the items in the finally modified renewal list, write out a Renewal Order Card and address it carefully, taking the necessary address from the corresponding card in the Renewal Listing Tray.

2334:2:84 Renewal Order Tallying

After all the renewal cards are written out, and addressed, get them carefully tallied with the finally modified renewal list. As soon as this is over, transfer the classified cards from the Renewal Listing Tray to the Classified Card Tray, taking care to put each card in the appropriate classified place. Put your initials in the renewal order cards as a token of your having tallied them carefully.

2334:2:85 Renewal Order Address Verifying

As soon as the renewal order tallying is over, alphabetise by the title and verify the address in the Renewal Order Cards with the address given in the corresponding Register Card Tray. Put your initials in the left hand bottom corner of the address side of the card as a token of your having verified the address. Ask another person to check the correctness of the order and put his initials in the Renewal Order List in token of his having done so.

2334:2:86 Renewal Order Sorting

As soon as the renewal order address verifying is over, sort the renewal order cards by the countries mentioned in the address. Alphabetise the order cards in each country group, by the address in the card. If there be two or more cards having the same address, consolidate them in one card or one letter, as the case may be.

As soon as the consolidation work is over, get it verified carefully and put your initials in the inside of the consolidated order in token of your having verified it. Then score out and destroy the unwanted renewal order cards.

2334:2:87 Renewal Order Transmitting

Send the sorted renewal order cards and letters along with the finally modified renewal list to the librarian for his signature.

2334:2:88 Standing Order Cancelling

For each of the items in the Cancel Listing Box prepare a cancel order and send it to the librarian for signature along with the files, after carefully tallying the orders with the classified cards in the Cancel Listing Box. Transfer the cards to the *Cancelled Tray*.

2334:2:883 Cancelled Card Marking

Attach a coloured slip to the Register Cards and the Check Cards of the cancelled publications.

2334:2:884 Cards Cancelling

In the course of the receiving work, if you come across a Check Card or a Register Card with a coloured slip attached to it, examine if the current volume is completed. If so, remove it to the Cancelled Tray. The Register Card and Check Card of a publication should be kept together in the Cancelled Tray. They should be arranged alphabetically as the first group in the Cancelled Tray. The Cancelled

Classified Index Cards should be arranged in a classified sequence as a second group after ,the last volume received is posted in them.

2334:2:896 Financial Diary Annual Posting

At the beginning of each financial year, write in the Financial Diary the estimated annual cost of the periodical publications in each subject. The cost is to be estimated in the light of the renewal orders sent and the actual cost paid during the preceding financial year.

2334:3 *Periodical Publication Receiving Work*

2334:3:1 *Immediate jobs*

2334:3:11 V P Packet Receiving

As soon as a V P Packet is presented, examine if its contents are due. If they are due, prepare the Intimation Form for the librarian's signature and send it to him along with the Packet. After it is accepted and comes back to you, remove the Wrapper carefully and treat it as a Bill. Put the contents along with the publications received in the day and deal with them according to the necessary routine.

2334:3:12 Wrongly Delivered Packet Returning

If any packet containing periodical publications has been delivered wrongly in the library either due to wrong address or due to other causes, send it back promptly to the Post Office or the person concerned with the necessary instruction.

2334:3:4 *Daily jobs*

2334:3:411 Wrapper Examining

The periodical publications received in the day by the librarian, will come to you with the Wrapper of each, inserted in the inside. They will come shortly after the mail arrives. As soon as they come, tally each publication with the Wrapper inside it and examine the Wrapper carefully to see whether it is addressed to the library. If there is any discrepancy, put it aside with the Wrapper in its inside in the Doubtful Group of Publications. They may be taken up for disposal at the end of the day

2334:3:412 SORTING

The publications about which everything is normal are to be sorted into suitable groups according to their urgency of demand from readers, as far as it can be ascertained. Each of the succeeding Daily Jobs connected with the Receiving Work as well as the New Issues Displaying Job is to be done group by group in the increasing sequence of urgency. The advantage of this is that the periodicals for which there is usually an immediate demand, will reach the readers' hands as early as possible.

2334:3:42 CURRENT ISSUE COLLATING

Take each of the publications and collate it carefully. Note near the top of the back of the front cover all abnormalities, including missing pages, defective pages, loose sheets, maps, plates, correction slips, etc.

If there is any defect, put it aside in the *Defective Group* of publications. Those without defect are to be put together into the *Sound Group* of publications.

2334:3:43 CURRENT ISSUES ALPHABETISING

Take the publications in the Sound Group in convenient batches and alphabetise them by the title.

2334:3:44 CURRENT ISSUE REGISTERING

Preliminary

01 Pull out the Register Cards Tray and place it on the table.

02 Current Issue Registering is to be done for each Sound Group of Publications, as and when its alphabetisation is completed. Bring each such group to the table as and when it gets formed.

024 Work should also be done on each Defective Group of Publications of the Current Week. Bring each such group to the table along with the last instalment of Sound Group.

Other Steps

03 **Week's Current Box.** The box into which the Register Cards, the Check Cards, the Slips, and the other associated cards of the publications received in the week, are collected from time to time for attention during the Vigilance Work and the Rounding off Work of the Week.

031 Put the Week's Current Box on the table.

04 Registering should be done one publication at a time.

Process of Registering

05 **To register** means to do the following :

051 To enter in the concerned columns in the Register Card in Arabic numerals the Volume and Issue Number, the Current Week Number (and the date also in the Case of a Weekly); and

052 To enter, near the top right hand corner of the front page of the wrapper of the Issue, the class number of the publication as given in the Register Card.

06 As soon as each publication is registered or is found to be either a duplicate or a not-due one, or a defective one, put it Front Cover upwards in the respective groups, one above the other in the sequence in which they are taken up to work with.

07 *Kinds of Peculiarities*

071 The Routine of Registering will vary with the pecularities met with in each publication. The peculiarities are enumerated below and the Routine for each peculiarity is given in the succeeding sections :

072 **Gap-in-Supply Publication.** Publication of which the issue received is later than some earlier issue(s) not yet received.

073 **T C I Received Publication.** Publication whose T C I (Title-Page, Contents and Index) has arrived with the issue received.

0731 **T C I Not Received Publication.** Publication whose T C I is due with the issue received—this will ordinarily be either the last issue of a volume or the first issue of the next volume—but is not found with the issue.

074 **First Arrival Publication.** Publication whose issue has arrived in the library for the first time as a result of ordering or of soliciting gift.

075 **Gift Publication.** Publication being received as a gift. Its Registration Card and Check Card will be of a specified colour—green in the Madras University Library.

076 **Duplicate Publication.** Publication for which a copy of the issue or T C I received has been already registered in the Register Card.

077 **Cancelled Publication.** Publication to be discontinued after

the completion of the current volume. Its Registration Card will have a red slip attached to it.

078 **Not-Due Publication.** Publication for which there is no Registration Card. It is likely to be a Sample Copy or a copy sent by mistake.

0794 **Defective Publication.** Publication lying in the Defective Group of the Current Week.

08 After registering all the publications received at the time,

1 Insert the Register Card Tray in its place; and

2 Remove the Duplicate, the Not-Due, and the Defective Groups to their respective places and insert them in their proper alphabetical places.

2334:3:441 Normal Publication

Register a Normal Publication in the first vacant line in its Register Card. Put its Register Card into the Week's Current Box, in alphabetical sequence. Put the Issue into the *Registered Group* of Issues.

2334:3:442 Gap-in-Supply Publication

Register a Gap-in-Supply Publication in the line appropriate to the Issue, leaving the lines for the earlier unsupplied Issues vacant. Put its Register Card in the Week's Current Box in alphabetical sequence. Put the Issue into the *Registered Group* of Issues.

2334:3:443 T C I Received Publication

1 Register a Publication with the T C I in the last but one line for the current volume if it is its last Issue. If it is the first issue of the next volume, register it in the first line for that volume leaving a line for the T C I.

2 Register the T C I in the last line for the current volume.

3 Put its Register Card in the Week's Current Box in alphabetical sequence.

4 If the T C I and the Issue are not separable, put the whole into the *T C I Group*.

5 If the T C I and the Issue are separable, put the former in the *T C I Group* and the Issue in the *Registered Group* of Issues.

2334:3:4431 T C I Not Received Publication

Register the Issue of a T C I Non-Receipt Publication, leaving the T C I line free. Put the Register Card in the Week's Current Box in alphabetical sequence. Put the Issue in the *Registered Group* of Issues.

2334:3:444 First Arrival Publication

Register a First Arrival Publication in the line appropriate to the Issue which has arrived. Check all the pencil entries in the Register Card with the publication. Rectify them if necessary. Classify the publication, taking the help of the Technical Section if necessary. Write the class number in the Register Card and near the right hand top corner of front cover of the Issue. Put the Register Card in the Week's Current Box in alphabetical sequence. Put the Issue in the *Registered Group* of Issues.

2334:3:445 Gift Publication

The Registration Card for a Gift Publication will be coloured—it is green in the Madras University Library. The work with it will be similar to one or other of the preceding five routines, as the case may be. The routine for a Gift Publication will be similar to that for a purchased publication and will have the additional items given in 2334:6:55.

2334:3:446 Duplicate Publication

Do not register a Duplicate Publication. Put it in the *Duplicate Supply Group* of Issues.

2334:3:447 Cancelled Publication

If the Registration Card has a Red Slip attached to it, its order is cancelled with effect from the next volume.

1 If the Issue belongs to the cancelled volume, it must not be registered. Write the word "Cancelled" near the right hand top corner of the cover. Put it in the *Cancelled Group* of Issues.

2 If the issue belongs to a volume prior to the one cancelled, the routine is similar to one or the other of the 6 routines described in Sections 2334:3:441 to 2334:3:446.

2334:3:448 Not-Due Publication

If there is no Register Card for a publication, it is likely to be a Sample Copy. Put it in the *Not-Due Group* of Issues.

2334:3:4494 Defective Publication

Attach to the Register Card of a Defective Publication a white slip and write on it the Volume and Issue Number of the Publication, its date of receipt, and a statement of the defect found. Take this from the back of the front cover. Put the Register Card in the Week's Current Box in the alphabetical sequence. Put the Issue in the *Defective Supply Group* of Issues.

2334:3:45 Current Issue Cutting and Stamping

As soon as the Registering of each publication is over cut open all the sheets of the publication and put the library stamp on the cover page in a convenient place as near as possible to the right hand top corner. Put the stamp on the first page and the last page and on such of the intermediate pages which are multiples of fifty. Put the stamp on the backs of all the plates. Take care that the stamp is not put on any printed matter in any page.

As soon as the Cutting and Stamping of each issue is over, if there is any loose sheet, plate or map, put the issue aside in the *Loose Sheet Group*. If there is any correction slip, put the issue aside in the *Correction Slip Group*. Put all the other issues in the *Normal Group*.

Note : *In sorting the issues in this manner, use may be made of the notes recorded on the inside of the front cover at the time of collating.*

2334:3:456 Perusing

As the cutting and stamping work is proceeding, peruse each issue rapidly, looking out for any announcement by the publisher either in a separate slip or in some part of the cover pages or at the top of the first page or in the editorial column, if there is one, or in the news column or in the notes column or in any other place. The announcement may relate either to Cumulative Indexes or to changes in the publication itself. Take such action as may be necessary on the announcement, if any is found. If the action required will involve some time and can be postponed to the rounding off day of the week, either put the publication aside for later action or, if possible, note down the name of the publication and the action to be taken in a 3×5 inches slip and put the slip in the Week's Current Box.

2334:3:46 Check Card Shifting

Preliminary

01 After the Perusal of the Issues (described in section 2334:3:456) and the Loose Issue Shelving (described in section 2334:8) for all the Issues in a Registered Group of Issues are over, pull out the Check Card Tray and place it on the Table.

011 The Week Guide of the Current Week will be the First Week Guide in it. Behind it, the Check Cards of the Publications Due in the Current Week will stand in alphabetical sequence.

012 The Check Cards of the publications Due in the successive Later Weeks will stand in alphabetical sequence behind the Week Guide of the respective Later Weeks.

02 **Allotted Day of the Week.** The day of the week allotted to be its last day for the purpose of rounding off the week's work of the Periodical Publication Section.

021 In the Madras University Library Wednesday is the Allotted Day of the Week.

03 **Week Guide.** A card of the size of the Check Card, with a tab projecting from one of its longer edges.

031 **Guide Number in Week Guide.** A number like 11.4, which means the Fourth Week of November, written on the tab of the Week Guide. Fourth Week means the Week in November which ends on the Fourth Allotted Day in that month.

032 Some months will have 5 Allotted Week Days. Therefore, there should be 5 Week Guides for each month. The Week Guide 5 will be in use in certain months and out of use in others.

033 In a month in which the Week Guide 5 is not in use, it will be close to its Week Guide 4 with no Check Cards between them. In that case, the Week Card 5 will be so turned that the Guide Number on it faces the back end of the Check Card Tray.

04 **Next Due Week.** For a Check Card behind the Week Guide of the Current Week, calculate the Next Due Date as follows :

041 If the Period is mentioned in the Check Card as a number of weeks, add that number to the Week Number in the Week Guide of the Current Week.

Example: If 11.4 is the Number of the Current Week and the Period is 1 Week, the Number of the Next Due Week is 11.5, if November has 5 Allotted Days of the Week.

042 If the Period is mentioned in the Check Card as a number

of months, add that number to the Month Number in the Week Guide of the Current Week.

Example 1 If 11.4 is the Number of the Current Week and the Period is 1 Month, the Number of the Next Due Week is 12.4.

2 If 11.4 is the Number of the Current Week and the Period is 3 Months, the Number of the Next Due Week is 2.4—that is the fourth week of the February of the next year.

05 Put the Week's Current Box in a convenient position by the side of the Check Card Tray.

06 Put a Spare Box next to the Week's Current Box.

General

1 For each Register Card in the Week's Current Box, which does not have its Check Card behind it, pull out its Check Card from behind the Week Guide of the Current Week in the Check Card Tray and proceed as described in the succeeding sections.

2 If the Check Card of a Register Card is not found behind the Week Guide of the Current Week, or of the next one or two weeks, calculate its Next Due Week with the aid of the Week of the Last Registration and of its Period. Its Check Card will be behind the Week Guide of that Next Due Week or one of its neighbouring weeks.

8 Unless the day is the Vigilance Day of the Week (see section 2334:3:51 para 01) after all such Register Cards in the Week's Current Box are dealt with in the said way, put the Check Card Tray in its place. Put also the Week's Current Box in its place.

2334:3:461 NORMAL PUBLICATION

For the Register Card of a Normal Publication,

1 Score out in its Check Card the entry, if any, for the Issue registered in the Current Week.

2 If there is no Surviving Unscored Entry in it, insert the Check Card behind the Week Guide of its Next Due Week in the proper alphabetical place and insert its Register Card in the Spare Box in the proper alphabetical place.

3 If there is any Surviving Unscored Entry in it and the date in the Unscored Entry does not indicate any action to be taken in the

Current Week, insert the Check Card behind the Week Guide of the Next Week in the proper alphabetical place, and insert its Register Card in the Spare Box in its proper alphabetical place.

4 If there is any Surviving Unscored Entry in it and the date in an Unscored Entry indicates action to be taken in the Current Week, insert the Check Card behind its Register Card in the Week's Current Box.

2334:3:462 Gap-in-Supply Publication

For the Register Card of a Gap-in-Supply Publication, score out in its Check Card the entry, if any, for the Issue registered in the Current Week. Enter the first two columns in it, insert the Check Card behind its Register Card in the Week's Current Box.

2334:3:463 T C I Received Publication

For the Register Card of a T C I Received Publication,

1 Score out in its Check Card the entry, if any, for the Issue or the T C I registered in the Current Week.

2 If there is no Surviving Unscored Entry in it, insert the Check Card behind the Week Guide of the Next Due Week, in the proper alphabetical place and its Register Card in the Spare Box in its proper alphabetical place.

3 If there is a Surviving Unscored Entry in it, do as prescribed for Normal Publication in section 2334:3:461

2334:3:4631 T C I Not Received Publication

For the Registration Card of a T C I Not Received Publication, enter the first two columns in the Check Card. Insert it behind its Register Card in the Week's Current Box.

2334:3:464 First Arrival Publication

For the Register Card of First Arrival Publications,

1 Carry out in the Check Card any corrections made in its Register Card.

2 Ink the Pencil Entries in its Register Card and Check Card.

3 Insert the Check Card behind the Week Guide of the Next Due Date in its proper alphabetical place.

4 Insert the Register Card in the Spare Box in its proper alphabetical place.

2334:3:465 Gift Publication

For the Register Card of a Gift Publication,

1 Score out in it the entry, if any, for the Issue or T C I registered in the Current Week.

2 Insert the Check Card behind its Register Card in the Week's Current Box.

2334:3:467 Cancelled Publication

For the Register Card of a Cancelled Publication,

1 If the T C I has not yet arrived, do as in Section 2334:3:461.

2 If the T C I has arrived and no Issue is due, attach the Red Slip to the T C I.

3 Put the "Cancelled" stamp on the Register Card and the Check Card.

4 Put them together in the Spare Box, the Register Card being in front of the Check Card.

2334:3:4695 Defective Publication

For the Register Card of a Cancelled Publication,

1 Attach a White Slip to the Check Card and copy in it the entry in the White Slip attached to its Register Card.

2 Insert the Check Card behind its Register Card in the Week's Current Box.

2334:3:4696 Spare Box

After the Check Card Shifting is completed for Current Week, insert each Register Card collected in the Spare Box into the Register Tray in its proper alphabetical place.

2334:3:4698 Daily Vigilance

The Check Cards of the dailies should be kept in a separate group of their own, with only three guide cards viz "Supplied" "Due" and "Overdue." For every daily whose issue has arrived shift as soon as the Check Card shifting is over, if any Check Card still lies behind the due guide of dailies, remind the vendor concerned about the non-supply of the day's issue, either by phone or by post as may be convenient. Then, transfer the cards behind the Due Guide to behind the Overdue Guide and those behind the Supplied Guide to behind the Due Guide.

2334:3:47 Loose Sheets Fixing

Take the publications in the loose sheet group one by one. Take out the loose sheets, plates, maps etc properly fix them in the appropriate places in the appropriate manner, if they deserve to be so treated. Add the issue to the normal group mentioned in routine 2334:345.

2334:3:48 Correction Slip Disposing

Take the publications in the correction slip group one by one. If the corrections to be carried out are not too many, carry out all the corrections indicated. Put the appropriate class number, volume number, issue number, etc on the top most line of the correction slip and put it in the correction slip box in the classified sequence. Add the publication to the normal group referred to in routine 2334:3:45.

If the corrections to be carried out are too many, take the neces-necessary instructions from the librarian as to the procedure to be adopted.

2334:3:5 *Weekly jobs*

2334:3:51 Weekly Vigilance

Definitions and Preliminary

01 **Vigilance day.** The day in the week to be chosen by each library to watch the correct arrival of periodical publications in the library. It is helpful to make the Allotted Day of the Week (See section 2334:3:46 para 02) the Vigilance Day.

011 In the Madras University Library, Wednesday is the Vigilance Day as well as the Allotted Day of the Week.

02 **Period.** 1 The normal (or intended) Number of Weeks between the publication of Two Consecutive Issues of a Periodical, if it is not more than 3 Weeks.

2 The normal (or intended) Number of Months between the publications of Two Consecutive Issues of a Periodical, if it is not less than 1 Month.

03 **Grace Week.** The Number of Weeks to be added to the

Period of a periodical publication to allow for unavoidable delays in publication.

For example, it may be fixed as follows :

For	*Grace Weeks*
Weekly or Fortnightly	1
Monthly	2
Quarterly	4
Larger Periods	8

041 **Week for the First Reminder.** The Last of the Grace Weeks.

042 **Week for the Second Reminder.** The Fourth Week after the First Reminder.

043 **Week for the Third Reminder.** The Fourth Week after the Second Reminder.

044 **Week for Special Action.** The Fourth Week after the Third Reminder. This will mean about three Months after the Grace Weeks are over.

1 Do the Weekly Vigilance job, after the completion of Check Card Shifting on the Vigilance Day of the Week.

2 On that day, retain on the table the Check Card Tray and the Week's Current Box, for the Weekly Vigilance Job.

3 Pull out the Register Tray and keep it on the table.

4 Each of the Check Cards behind the Week Guide of the Current Date will be overdue. It will have an Unscored Entry. It will be one of the following kinds.

40 Whether a Reminder is due or not is indicated by the Grace Weeks considered with the numbers of the week entered in column 2 in the case of an incomplete entry and by the number of Weeks for Reminder in the case of a completed entry.

Reminder Not Due Check Card

41 Check Card not indicating completion of the Weeks for the first, the second, or the third reminder or for special Action, as the case may be.

Reminder Due Check Card

42 Check Card indicating completion of the weeks for the first, the second, or the third reminder, as the case may be.

Special Action Due Check Card

43 Check Card indicating completion of the weeks for special action.

5 Pull out, one by one, each Check Card from behind the Week Guide of the Current Week and deal with it as prescribed in the four succeeding sections.

8 After the completion of the Routines in the four succeeding sections, insert the Register Tray and the Check Card Tray in their respective places and put the Week's Current Box in its place.

2334:3:511 Reminder Not Due Check Card

1 If the Check Card is a Reminder Not Due Card, insert it behind the Week Guide of the Next Week in the proper alphabetical place.

2 If it has a White Slip attached, showing defect in an Issue and if a sound copy of that Issue has been registered in the Current Week, remove the White Slip from it and from its Register Card.

2334:3:512 Reminder Due Check Card

If the Check Card is a Reminder Due Card, pull out its Register Card from the Register Tray. Insert both together (with the Register Card first) in the Week's Current Box in the proper alphabetical place.

2334:3:513 Special Action Check Card

If the Check Card is a Special Action Card, pull out its Register Card from the Register Tray. Insert both together (with the Register Card first) at the end of the Week's Current Box in a Separate Alphabetical Sequence.

2334:3:518 Week Guide Shifting

As the end of the Routine mentioned in the above three sections, there will be no Check Card behind the Week Guide of the Current

Week. Shift it to the last position in the Check Card Tray. It will thus become the Week Guide for the corresponding week of the next year.

2334:4 *Periodical Publication Completing Work*

2334:4:5 *Weekly jobs*

2334:4:51 Loose Issues Collecting

On the appointed day of the week, take each of the items in the TCI group and deal with it as follows: Collect all the loose issues to which the T C I relates. They will ordinarily be on the shelf. If by any chance any loose issue is not found on the shelf, it is likely to have gone on loan to specialists. Send a Registration Slip to the Circulation Section. As soon as the loose issue concerned comes back, put it in the collection.

2334:4:52 Loose Issues Tallying

For each of the volumes whose loose issues have been completely collected, verify with the aid of the contents page, if the volume is complete. If there is any defect in any volume, investigate the matter and set it right. If the defects cannot be set right, take it to the notice of the librarian and get his advice. If correspondence with the publisher or anybody else becomes necessary, tie up the volume and put it in the *T C I Waiting Group*, alphabetically by the title.

2334:4:53 Volume Making Up

Examine the contents page and the completed volume carefully. If there be two or more sequences of pagination, examine if the whole thing should be bound as one volume or in two or three volumes. Even if there be only one sequence of pagination, examine if, on account of unwieldy size or the existence of two or more title pages, it is to be bound in two or more volumes.

At this stage consult the normal Binding Slip for the publication. If your findings agree with the normal instructions in the Binding Slip, separate the completed volume into the necessary number of volumes and tie up each of them. If there is any abnormality, consult the Binding Section, and, if necessary, the Technical Section, and then take it to the notice of the librarian for instructions. Then, carry out his instructions.

2334:4:54 Supplement Separating

Examine if there is any Book or Periodical Supplement with independent pagination. If there.is, deal with it along lines similar to the preceding routine.

2334:4:55 Binding Peculiarities Drafting

If the binding to be done to the completed volume differs in any way from the normal mode of binding the publication, as recorded in the Binding Slip, prepare a Special Slip showing the deviations from the normal binding instruction. Pin this Slip to the bundled volume so as to attract the attention of the other sections that will have to deal with it.

2334:4:56 Accession Card Writing

As soon as the Binding Peculiarities Drafting is over, write out Accession Cards for the volumes made up. The accession number and the collation need not be written out. On the back side of the Accession Card, the Voucher Number can not be written if it is a case of post-payment. In the column "Date of Receipt" enter the date of completing.

2334:4:57 Made-up Volumes Transmitting

Arrange the accessioned volumes in the classified sequence. Arrange the corresponding Accession Cards in the classified sequence and put them in a box. Fill up the Transmission Register. Then, transmit the made-up volumes and the Box of Accession Cards to the Accession Section, along with the Transmission Register. As soon as the Transmission Register comes back, examine if it has received the initials of the Head of the Accession Section, as a token of his having received the materials.

2334:4:58 Accession Number Noting

As soon as the Box of Accession Cards comes from the Accession Section, note the Accession Numbers of the periodical publications in the related register cards. In the concerned Classified Index Card, enter the necessary details about volume number, supplements, and cumulative indexes. Then, transmit the Box of Accession Cards to the Accounts Section.

2334:5 *Cumulative Index Work*

2334:5:1 *Immediate jobs*

2334:5:11 Cumulative Index Noting

You are likely to come across announcements of Cumulative Indexes while perusing current numbers of periodical publications received in the library, as provided in routine "2334:3:456 Perusing". In certain cases you may receive letters from publishers, announcing the issue of Cumulative Indexes. In certain other cases, Cumulative Indexes may come out in regular periods. In all these cases be vigilant to collect the information and note it down in a Selection Slip and put it at the very beginning of the Week's Current Box.

2334:5:4 *Daily jobs*

The daily jobs really relate to the receiving work of the Cumulative Indexes ordered. Hence, they are quite similar to the receiving work of the current issues of periodical publications, with the modification that there will be no current issue alphabetising and that you will have the additional routine of entering the receipt of the Cumulative Index in the Classified Index Card. Again, there will be no Check Card shifting in these cases.

2334:5:5 *Weekly jobs*

The weekly jobs of Cumulative Index Work relate partly to ordering and partly to receiving.

2334:5:51 Cumulative Index Checking

On the appointed day of the week, check each of the Suggestion Slips contained in the Week's Current Box and check them with the resources of the library—directly with the shelf and with the catalogue and the classified index cards. Note down the result of the checking in the Slip.

2334:5:522 Cumulative Index Order Preparing

For each of the Cumulative Indexes, which is not already in the library, prepare a formal order, asking the publisher to send the index with a bill in duplicate as soon as it comes out.

2334:5:523 CUMULATIVE ORDER TRANSMITTING

On the appointed day of the week, send the orders for the Cumulative Indexes for the signature of the librarian.

2334:5:526 FINANCE DIARY POSTING

As soon as the order copies get signed by the librarian, find out the total estimated Cost of the Cumulative Indexes ordered and enter the amount under the proper subject in the Finance Diary.

2334:5:55 *to* 2334:5:58 *Weekly jobs*

The routine for these jobs is exactly similar to that under "2334:4:5 Weekly Jobs of Completing Work."

2334:6 *Rounding Off Work*

2334:6:5 *Weekly jobs*

1 The Purpose of the Rounding Off Work is to take the necessary action on all the defects and peculiarities noticed in receiving and handling the periodical publications and their Register Cards and Check Cards, in the course of the Current Week.

2 It is a convenience to accumulate all such work and the connected correspondence for the whole week, and to have them disposed off on the day after the Vigilance Day.

3 The Rounding Off Work will relate to the :

31 Items accumulated in the Week's Current Box;
36 Publications in the Duplicate Supply Group; and
38 Publications in the Not Due Group.

4 The Items in Week's Current Box will stand sorted into the following groups :

41 The Register Cards, with their respective Check Cards behind them, for all cases in which a Reminder or a Defect Notice or an Acknowledgement is due, arranged all in one alphabetical sequence;
42 The Register Cards, with their respective Check Cards behind them, for all cases in which Special Action is to be taken as a result of failure of supply for 3 months;

43 Slips of the publications, which are to be ordered, arranged in one alphabetical sequence;

44 Slips of the publications, for which any other action may have to be taken, arranged in one alphabetical sequence.

5 The First group mentioned in 41 will consist of cases calling for :

51 Reminder about Non-Supply of Issue;
52 Reminder about Non Supply of T C I;
53 Reminder about Gap-in-Supply;
54 Defect Notice; and
55 Acknowledgment of an Issue of a Gift Publication.

6 The groups mentioned in 4 will stand arranged in the same sequence as the one in which they are mentioned in 4.

2334:6:51 Non-Supply Notifying

For each Check Card indicating Non-Supply, write a Non-Supply Reminder Card finding the particulars about the Issue Due and about the issue last supplied from the corresponding Register Card and address it. Take the address from the Register Card. Fill up the columns in the Check Card. Insert the filled up Reminder Card just behind its Check Card in the Week's Current Box.

2334:6:52 Non-Supply of T C I Notifying

For each of the Check Cards indicating Non-Supply of title page, contents and index, write a T C I Reminder Card and address it. Take the address from the Register Card. Fill up the columns in the Check Card. Insert the filled up Reminder Card just behind its Check Card in the Week's Current Box.

2334:6:53 Gap-in-Supply Notifying

For each Check Card indicating Gap-in-Supply, write a Gap-in-Supply-Card taking the particulars from the corresponding Register Card and address it. Take the address from the Register Card. Fill up the columns in the Check Card. Insert the filled up Gap-in-Supply Card just behind its Check Card in the Week's Current Box.

2334:6:54 Defective Supply Notifying

For each Check Card with White Slip indicating Defective Supply, write a Defective Supply Card and address it. Take the address from the Register Card. Note the date of the Reminder in the White Slips attached to the Check Card. Insert the Defective Supply Card just behind its Check Card in the Week's Current Box.

2334:6:55 Current Issue Acknowledging

For each Check Card indicating acknowledgment for Gift Publication, write an Acknowledgment Card taking the particulars from the corresponding Register Card and address it. Take the address from the Register Card. Insert the filled up Acknowledgment Card behind its Check Card in the Week's Box.

2334:6:56 Duplicate Supply Notifying

For each of the publications found in the Duplicate Group formed in the Current Week, write a letter to the Vendor asking how the Duplicate Copy is to be disposed of.

2334:6:58 Not Due Group

For each of the publications in the Not Due Group, consult the librarian. As instructed by him, either

1 Treat it as a Specimen Copy and take action as in Routine "2334:101; or
2 Do as for Duplicate Supply Notifying; or
3 Take any other action suggested.

2334:6:591 Week's Current Box Transmitting

After all the Slips and the Cards in the Week's Current Box are dealt with, transmit the Week's Current Box for the librarian's signature.

2334:6:592 Special Action Cases

Take instructions from the librarian and act accordingly, in the case of each one of the cases needing Special Action. It may be remembered that their Register Cards and the Check Cards will be at the very end of the Cards in the Week's Current Box. Their publications would have been overdue for 3 months.

2334:6:593 Slips Disposing

For each of the Slips found in the Week's Current Box (See Routine 2334:3:456) take such action as may be necessary. After the action is taken, the Slip may be destroyed.

2334:6:595 Week's Current Box Distributing

As soon as the Week's Current Box comes back from the librarian,

1 Pick out each Check Card. Examine if it has received the librarian's initals and, if not, get his initals. Then, insert it in the Check Card Tray behind the Week Guide of the Current Week, except that those for the Gift Publications, for which an acknowledgment was sent, should be inserted behind the Week Guide of its Next Due Week.

2 Insert the Register Cards in Register Tray in their proper places.

2334:6:596 Week's Current Box Transmitting

Send all the signed Notifying Cards and Acknowledgment Cards to the Correspondence Section for Despatch.

2334:7 *Bills Passing Work*

The Passing of the Bills relating to periodical publications will be a huge task in university libraries, business libraries, libraries of learned societies, and similar libraries, where the number of periodical publications taken is usually large. In other libraries, it may not be so big a problem. Still, the routine set forth here will be applicable in all cases.

It generally happens that payments have to be made In Advance to periodical publications. The bulk of the subscription hence falls due at the close of the calendar year.

In India, which is thousands of miles away from the chief centre of production, it has to be taken up in October. The significance of some of the routines mentioned hereunder, such as 1 and 6, will become apparent in their cases.

But stray bills may be coming in all weeks. That is why the main jobs connected with the passing of Bills in the Periodical Publication Section are described as weekly jobs rather than annual jobs.

2334:7:5 *Weekly jobs*

2334:7:51 Bills Alphabetising

As soon as the Bills of the Week are received from the Correspondence Section, underline in pencil in each Bill the leading word in the name of the periodical publication, under which its Register Card is filed. Then, sort the Bills alphabetically by the title of the periodical publication.

2334:7:52 Preceding Payment Scrutinising

Take each of the Bills in the Alphabetised Group, compare the claim in each with the record of Preceding Payments and see if the claim is due and particularly satisfy yourself that it is not a case of Double Payment. Examine also if the volume for which the claim is now made is the one next to the volume for which payment was last made. If there is any gap, take the necessary action in consultation with the librarian. Check also with the Bills pending in the Accounts Section.

While scrutinising the Preceding Payment, examine also if the periodical publication is being regularly received. If the supply shows any abnormal irregularity, it will be advisable to take the matter to the notice of the librarian and get his previous sanction for proceeding further with the Bill.

2334:7:53 Cost Verifying

While scrutinising the Preceding Payment, find out also if the Cost claimed for the Current Volume is the same or different from the Cost of the Preceding Volume. Refer to the file corresponding to the publication and find out if any Change of Subscription has been recorded in it. If the Cost claimed is different from the Normal Cost, examine if there is any justification for it in the record. Otherwise correspond with the publisher or vendor, as the case may be, and ascertain what the Correct Cost should be.

2334:7:54 Bills Certifying

If a Bill is a case of Advance Payment, write "Adv P" and put your initials in the left hand bottom corner of the Bill after having completed the preceding routine correctly. If it is a case of post-payment, satisfy yourself whether the supply has been satisfactorily received and, if so, add a certificate at the left hand bottom corner to that effect. In either case, it will help future reference, if the particular Subject, to which the Cost of the Periodical Publication should be debited, is indicated in symbols just by the side of your initials, e g assuming that the classification scheme used in the library is Colon Classification, if it is to be debited to Mathematics put "B", if it is to be debited to Commerce, put "X5" and so on. Note, in the appropriate place in the Register Card, the Number and, if necessary, the Year, of the Volume for which the Bill is passed.

2334:7:55 Bills Revising

It is better that this Job of Bills Revising is done by somebody different from the one who had done the preceding routines. Scrutinise and revise the Certified Bills carefully, examining with special care the Preceding Payment and the Correctness of the Cost claimed. Verify also the Total. If it is a case of First Payment, verify if there is proper Sanction. Find out also if the payment relates to any discontinued publications.

It is a matter of experience that a good deal of annoyance and audit trouble can be avoided if the necessary time is devoted to have all the bills carefully revised by a third person before they are finally passed.

2334:7:56 Grouping by Vendors

Take all the Revised Bills and wherever necessary group together the Bills from the same vendor and pin them together, so that they may constitute a Single Voucher.

2334:7:57 Passed Bills Transmitting

After the Grouping by Vendors is over and on the appointed day of the week, transmit all the Revised Bills to the Accounts Section for further action and as soon as the Transmission Register comes back, verify if it has received the initials of the Head of the Accounts Section in token of the Bills having been received by that Section.

2334:7:58 Voucher Number Noting

On the appointed day of the week, take from the Accounts

Section all the Vouchers relating to the Periodical Publication Section passed for payment during the week, and enter the Voucher Number and Date in the appropriate place in the related Register Card. It is this entry which is going to guard you against Double Payment. Hence, this routine must be done very promptly and in any case No Further Set of Bills should be taken up for action before this routine is finished. It is even better to go a step further. No Further Set of Bills should be taken up for action before the Accounts Section has verified the noting down of the Vouchers as provided in Rule 3737:43:55.

2334:8 *Loose Issue Shelving Work*

2334:8:4 *Daily jobs*

Preliminary

01 It will add to the convenience of readers, if the Loose Issue Shelving Work is done in instalments in the decreasing sequence of the urgency of demand from readers. It has been already indicated in the routine relating to "2334:3 Receiving Work" that it is desirable to complete the routine instalment by instalment taken in this sequence.

02 The advantage in this method is as follows : There is usually much demand for the new issues of some periodicals. Hence the readers will be satisfied if these are released for use at the earliest possible moment, instead of holding them over, until the whole set of the periodical publications received in the day are ready for display.

03 A Loose Issue of a Periodical will have to lie, in succession, in Four Places before its volume is completed, bound, and put in its place in the Stack Room. All these four places are best found in the Periodicals Reading Room. They are defined bellow.

Definitions

031 **Current Week's Display Table.** The Periodicals Room Table in which the Issues of the Periodical Publications received in the Current Week are displayed for use by readers. This contains a Label Holder, into which is inserted a strip of card board with the legend "Current Week's Arrivals".

032 **Last Week's Display Table.** The Periodicals Room Table in which Issues of the Periodical Publications were received in the Preceding Week are displayed for use by readers. This contains a Label Holder, into which is inserted a strip of card board with the legend "Last Week's Arrivals."

033 **Earlier Week's Display Table.** The Periodicals Room Table in which the Issues, of the Periodical Publications, received more than Two Weeks earlier, are displayed for use by readers. Its Label Holder will have Subject Guides.

034 **Uncompleted Volume Rack.** Book Rack(s) in or close to the Periodical Room, in which the issues of a volume 'taken out from the Display Table' are kept until it is completed. In the Book Rack, each Periodical Publication has a Shelf Guide. Bay guides also are provided.

035 In each of the above, the Issues are kept arranged in the Classified Sequence.

2334:8:41 New Issues Arranging

As soon as each Instalment of the Periodicals is ready for display, arrange them in a Classified Sequence with the aid of the class number noted at the right hand top corner of the cover of each. In the case of new publications and those that have undergone any change, the issues are to be sent to the Reference Section for perusal and return before being displayed.

2334:8:42 New Issues Displaying

Take the Classified Set of the new Issues to the Current Week's Display Table and insert each in its proper classified place in the galleries of that Table.

2334:8:5 *Weekly jobs*

2334:8:52 Guide Strips Changing

On the Appointed Day of the Week, interchange the Guide Strips of the "Current Week's Display Table" and the "Last Week's Display Table". As a result, the Current Week's Arrivals get transformed into Last Week's Arrivals.

2334:8:53 Removal to Earlier Week's Display Table

1 Collect each Issue lying displayed in the galleries of the Table

now having the Guide Strip "Current Week's Arrivals".

2 Take them to the Earlier Weeks' Display Table. Insert each in its proper classified place in the galleries of that Table. While doing so, collect the earlier issue which it displaces.

3 The galleries of the Table for Current Week's Arrivals would have been completely cleared and made ready to receive the Arrivals of the Current Week.

2334:8:54 Old Issues Shelving

Take the old Issues collected in the preceding routine to the Uncompleted Volumes Rack. Insert each issue into the pile or bundle of its volume. If it is the First Issue of its volume, put it in its proper place in the classified sequence. If it is a New Publication, prepare and insert the Shelf Guide for it.

2334:94 *Suspense Periodical Publications Work*

On the appointed day of the week, take each of the periodical publications accumulated in the Suspense Group in the course of the week. Examine if there is any correspondence relating to it. Find out also if there is any information in the publication itself showing why it had been sent to the library. If it is a Specimen Copy, take the necessary action as in Selecting Work. If it is found to be a case of wrongly sent publication, take the necessary action in consultation with the librarian.

2337 Back Volumes

Back Volumes cost a good deal. Hence, it is only occasionally that they will be bought. When some money is available for Back Volumes, it is not an easy matter to decide, to what publications it should be devoted. The demand from the public on the one hand and the presence of awkward gaps in the stock of the library on the other, should be the two deciding factors. When it is decided to purchase a particular set, it is necessary that Competitive Quotations should be obtained and the purchase should be made from the cheapest market. The routine is similar to the purchase of books including the passing of bills, except that Book Order Cards need not be written, but their purpose may be served by the related files themselves.

234 Elimination of Waste

2341 ORGANISATION

If the turnover in the Section demands the assignment of several members to it, the distribution of work among the assistants of the section should proceed along the lines of language specialisation for all items of work except that of receiving work. But in the case of other items of work the language specialisation suggested will enable each member of the Section to acquire an intensive acquaintance with the trade conditions in certain specified countries.

2343 RELEASE OF PUBLICATIONS

The head of the periodical publication section should strive his best to release the publications for public use as expeditiously as possible. The perusal of the publications for detection of announcements either about changes in the publications or about cumulative indexes should be done personally by the Head of the Section. He should also have under his direct control all work relating to Standing Vendors.

2344 DOUBLE PAYMENT

The Check Card tray is the most vital instrument for controlling the regular receipt of the publications. Hence, the vigilance work should be done by the Head of the Section personally. The Head of the Section should also personally verify the posting of Voucher Numbers in the Register Cards as this is the only means of avoiding Double Payment. He should not distribute any Fresh Bills to his Section until he has verified the Voucher Posting related to the preceding batch of bills. He should also pay particular attention to the proper assembling of Completed Volumes of Periodical Publications.

2346 DIARIES

In addition to filling up the Financial Diary as and when a fresh order is issued and on stated days in the year, he should bring the cumulative total up to date from month to month. He should also maintain two other Diaries.

2347 DIARY 1

The First Diary, which is to be on a weekly basis, is to have the following headings :

11 to 22 Same as for the book order section;
31 Order cards checked;
32 Orders issued;
4 Volumes made up;
45 Binding slips written;
46 Accession cards written;
47 Made up volumes transmitted;
48 Accession numbers noted;
52 Cumulative indexes ordered;
53 Cumulative indexes received;
7 Bills passed;

2348 Diary 2

The Second Diary is to be on a daily basis. It is to show the number of periodical publications received from day to day. Its headings must consist of the symbols for the main divisions of classification system used or some suitable modification of them.

235 Correlation Table

1 *Book Selection Section*

2334:1:54 Financial position ascertaining;
2334:2:516 Financial position deciding;
2334:2:56 Financial diary posting;
2334:2:896 Financial diary annual posting;
2334:5:526 Finance diary posting.

2 *Book Order Section*

2334:1:54 Financial position ascertaining;
2334:2:516 Financial position deciding;
2334:2:56 Financial diary posting;
2334:2:896 Financial diary annual posting;
2334:5:526 Finance diary posting.

4 *Accession Section*

2334:4:55 Binding peculiarities drafting;

2334:4:57 Made up volumes transmitting;
2334:4:58 Accession number noting.

5 *Technical Section*

2334:3:44 Current number registering;
2334:4:55 Binding peculiarities drafting.

7 *Reference Section*

2334:1:85 Current list consulting;
2334:8:41 New issues arranging.

8 *Maintenance Section*

2334:4:55 Binding peculiarities drafting.

91 *Committee Section*

2334:1:57 Indent forwarding;
2334:1:87 Current list forwarding.

96 *Finance Section*

2334:2:56 Financial diary posting;
2334:2:896 Financial diary annual posting;
2334:5:526 Finance diary posting.

97 *Accounts Section*

2334:1:54 Financial position ascertaining;
2334:2:516 Financial position deciding;
2334:4:58 Accession number noting;
2334:7:57 Passed bills transmitting;
2334:7:58 Voucher number noting.

993 *Correspondence Section*

2334:1:54 Periodical publication order transmitting;
2334:2:87 Renewal order transmitting;
2334:6:596 Week's current box transmitting;

995 *Binding Section*

2334:4:52 Loose issues tallying;
2334:4:53 Volume making up;
2334:4:54 Supplement separating;

2334:4:55 Binding peculiarities drafting.

236 Illustrative Time Scheme

Sunday

2334:7 Bills passing work, all the weekly jobs except Passed Bills Transmitting and Voucher Number Noting;

2334:4:5 Completing work, all the weekly jobs except Made Up Volumes Transmitting and Accession Number Noting.

Monday

2334:5:5 Cumulative index work, all the weekly jobs except Order Preparing and Order Transmitting;

2334:1:5 Selecting work, all the weekly jobs except Indent Forwarding;

2334:2:5 Ordering work, all the weekly jobs except Order Transmitting.

Tuesday

2334:1:57 Indent forwarding;

2334:2:54 Periodical publication order transmitting;

2334:4:57 Made up volumes transmitting (11 A M);

2334:5:522 Cumulative index order preparing;

2334:5:523 Cumulative index order transmitting.

Wednesday

2334:3:51 Vigilance, routine of;

2334:6 Rounding off work.

236:8 *Annual jobs*

June and July. 2331 Work relating to the appointment of standing vendors.

August. 2334:1:8 Annual jobs of selecting work.

September. 2334:2:8 Annual jobs of ordering work.

As the daily and the weekly jobs of this section are of a very exacting and relentless nature, no special week is indicated for the annual jobs. They have to be done as pick-up-work and completed in the months against which they are shown.

It may be added here, that there will be no chance to do them in the months of November to February, as the bill passing work will be very heavy in those months. Nor can they be done in March as the completing work will be very heavy in that month.

237 Forms and Registers

C32 *Renewal order card.* Printed. 8 point type. Bristol board. White. The text of the form is as follows :

Reference: This office standing order Numb. . . . dated. . . . .

Kindly renew, on behalf of the . . . . library the subscription to . . . . for volume-year . . and send your bill in duplicate for payment as usual.

C331 *Register card.* Printed. 6 point type. Bristol board. White. Tray. 7 lines in the front page and 14 lines in the back. Gift cases, black border. The text is as follows. Back side, column headings only.

TITLE			PAYMENT	
VENDOR			Vol or year	Voucher N & Date
Cl N	Period in weeks / Grace Weeks	Order N & Date		
			Ann Subs	

Vol & N	Date of pub	Date of rect	Vol & N	Date of pub	Date of rect

C332 *Check card.* Printed. 6 point type. Bristol board. White. Tray. 14 lines on each side. Gift cases, black border. The column headings are as shown below :

Heading											Period / Grace Weeks
Vol of Issue	Due Week	Week of Rem	L's Initials	Vol of Issue	Due Week	Week of Rem	L's Initials	Vol of Issue	Due Week	Week of Rem	L's Initials

C334 *Classified index card.* Printed. 6 point type. Bristol board. White. Tray. Gift cases, black border. The text of the form is as follows:

Cl N Ann Subs per in weeks

Title

Vendor

Publisher

Vol Available

Indexes, etc

Supplements. etc

C34 *Binding peculiarities slip.* Manuscript. Ledger paper. White. Tray. The row headings in the form are as follows:

1 Title.
2 Volume number.
3 Year.
4 Class number.
5 Covering material.
6 Clubbing or splitting peculiarities, if any.
7 Assembling peculiarities, if any.

C361 *T C I Reminder card.* Printed. 8 point type. Bristol board. White. The text of the form is as follows:

I have to inform you that the Title Page, Contents and Index to Vol. . . . of the . . . . have not yet been received here. Kindly despatch them at an early date.

C362 *Non-supply card.* Printed. 8 point type. Bristol board. White. The text of the form is as follows:

I have to inform you that Numb. . . . . of Vol. . of the . . . . was the last part received. Kindly bring the supply up-to-date and send the future parts as issued.

C363 *Gap-in-supply card.* Printed. 8 point type. Bristol board. White. The text of the form is as follows:

I have to inform you that Numb . . . of Vol . . . . of the . . . . has not yet been received though a subsequent part is to hand. Kindly fill up the gap-in-supply at an early date.

Q32 *Standing order form.* Stencil. 21 lb printing paper. White.

The text of the form is as follows:

Subject: PERIODICAL PUBLICATION—ORDER

Please supply to this library the undermentioned periodical publication. The supply is to begin from the first issue of Vol. .. Year .... Each issue is to be supplied promptly as and when published. The title page, contents and index relating to each completed volume should be supplied as soon as they are published.

The non-receipt of an issue, if any, will be notified either immediately on receipt of the later issue or within three months after its due date, when it is known to us.

The cost of a volume is to be recovered by sending a bill in duplicate in advance/after the completion of the volume and the supply of the title page, contents, and index.

This may be treated as a standing order until countermanded.

S31 *Indent forwarding docket form.* Stencil. 21 lb printing paper. White. The text of the form is as follows :

Same as for the book selection section, except for the substitution of the following in the office note part of the docket sheet :

1 Annual allotment for the subject;
2 Estimated cost of the periodical publications already current; and
3 Estimated annual subscription of the periodical publications recommended.

238 **Files**

Name	*Class Number*	*Amplifying device*	*Filing characteristic*	*Year of transfer to record sequence after the file is closed*	*Year of destruction after transfer to the record sequence*
Standing vendors	31	Subject device or/and language device	Vendor	Year 1	Year 5
Sources, enquiries and quotations	32	Subject device	Title	Do	Do
Indent	33	Do	Do	Do	Year 10
Current periodicals	34	Do	Do	Do	Year 5
Finance	36	Do	Correspondent	Do	Year 10
Back volumes	37	Do	Title	Do	Do
Outward enquiries	391	Nil	Correspondent	Do	Year 3
Inward enquiries	392	Nil	Do	Do	Do

Chapter 24

ACCESSION SECTION

241 Planning

2411 Difficulties in Accessioning

Every volume to be included in the stock of the library is to receive a serial number called the Accession Number. The Gift Books are to receive a Donation Number, in addition to the Accession Number. The task of assigning Accession Number and Donation Number to volumes is rendered difficult by one or two factors.

24111 Continuity in Accession Number

In the first place, the apparently trivial matter of maintaining strict continuity in Accession Number causes some trouble. In the routine that is described in the third part of this chapter, the task of assigning Accession Numbers is prescribed to be done at one sitting at a specified time, once in a week. This will minimise the chances for mistakes in the assignment of Accession Numbers and Donation Numbers. When the Accession Numbering Work was spread over several days, we experienced much difficulty. But all that has now been eliminated to a considerable extent.

24112 Definition of Volume

Another difficulty in assigning Accession Numbers and Donation Numbers to volumes centres round the definition of the word "Volume". From this point of view it may be stated that the assignment of the Accession Number is not merely a mechanical process. It requires, on the contrary, much of judgment. Economy in the cost of binding, reduction in the number of undersized volumes difficult to handle, the need for splitting overthick and composite books that may admit of such treatment and several other considerations stand in the way of counting every volume that comes into the library as a separate book solely on the basis that they were stitched or cased and issued separately by the publisher. For example, the schedule of the rate for binding on the one hand

and the nature of the use on the other would justify clubbing together a few successive issues of the calendar of a school or college as a single volume. On the contrary, Van Hise's *Metamorphism*, which is a quarto of 1286 pages and whose weight is unusually great, has to be bound in three volumes, although it was issued as a single volume in the publisher's casing. Thus, it requires a good deal of judgment to decide what exactly a single Accession Number should cover.

24113 Periodical Publications

This problem takes even a more serious turn in the case of Periodical Publications. So it is with *Instalment Books.* In the case of most of the standard books, the problem of assembling and making up a volume is not very difficult as the complete book is properly assembled and cased before it is sold out. In the case of Periodical Publications, on the contrary, we have all kinds of complications arising out of the different sequences of pagination and the existence of more than one title page in the same volume. While many of the Periodical Publications have for each volume a single continuous pagination and issue at the completion of the volume the necessary title page, contents and index, there are cases where the completed volume with continuous pagination is too bulky and hence two or more title pages are issued. In these cases care should be taken to see that the volume is separated as per the title pages and each part accessioned and bound separately. The *Journal of physical chemistry*, the *Journal of the American Chemical Society*, and the *Journal of the Chemical Society of London* are examples of this type. Again there are periodicals which have for each volume two or more sequences of pagination with the corresponding number of title pages, each title page being different from the other. In this case every issue of a volume is to be separated into as many parts as there are title pages, dividing the volume itself into an equal number of separate volumes and accessioning them separately. The *Surgery, gynecology and obstetrics*, has, for example, two sequences of pagination, one for the main periodical and the other for the *International abstract of surgery* and issues two title pages for the two different titles. The *Journal of the Society of Chemical Industry* has at present three sequences of pagination and issues three different titles pages as *Chemistry and industry*, *Transactions of the Society of Chemical Industry* and *British chemical abstracts B: applied chemistry*. Some periodicals include in themselves regular books, parts of which are included in each number of the periodical, the pagination of the book part being different from that of the periodical. A book may be completed in one volume of a periodical or it may be spread over two or more volumes. In such cases, the Completed Book should be separated from the Periodical and accessioned as a separate volume. If the book is not separated thus and accessioned separately, not only the value of it to the ordinary reading public is lost, but the library will be duplicating it, if the library purchases a subsequent separate edition of the book. Examples of this type are found in the *Indian antiquary*, the *Journal of oriental research* (Madras), the *Kalaimagal* and the *Udyanapatrika*.

2412 Help of Other Sections

Hence, accessioning is not a mere mechanical affair and it requires much experience and judgment. The Accession Section will stand much to gain in this matter by indenting upon the experience of the Maintenance Section. In fact, in the Madras University Library, such complicated questions are decided by a Committee consisting of the Heads of the Accession Section, the Periodical Publication Section, the Technical section and the Maintenance Section, before the final approval of the librarian is obtained.

2413 Passing of Bills

It will be found that the task of Passing Bills for the ordinary books acquired by the library is entrusted to the Accession Section and not to the Book Order Section. It is found from experience that the irregularities and defects, discovered in the process of collation and other types of work done by the Accession Section, are so many that it is found to be much more convenient for the Accession Section to pass the bills, instead of transmitting all their findings to the Book Order Section. But it must be remembered that the passing of bills in the case of Periodical Publications is left in the hands of the Section concerned and not entrusted to the Accession Section. Further, in the case of books covered by a Standing Order, the bill requires the countersignature of the Book Order Section. By this countersignature the Book Order Section takes the responsibility for ensuring that there is no Double

Payment. The responsibility of the Accession Section is restricted only to the soundness of the copy.

2414 Copyright and Exchange

In National Libraries with copyright privileges, a Section of the staff will have to be set apart to administer the Copyright Act. Again in many libraries, particularly University Libraries and Libraries of Learned Societies, a section of the staff will have to look after the Exchange of Publications. As these are distinctive library functions, it is found necessary to accommodate them in Part 2. But the numbers available in octave 1 of Part 2 are exhausted already by the more common library functions. Hence it is suggested that the Copyright Section may be numbered 293 and the Exchange Section may be numbered 295.

As Copyright Work is peculiar only to National Libraries, that is, only to one or two libraries in each country, no account is given about that section in this manual. Although Exchange Work is likely to occur in more libraries than Copyright Work, even that is not a very common function in ordinary libraries. Hence, I propose to deal with these questions only in the volume on University Libraries. Their special accession problems are omitted here.

2415 Streams of Volumes

As has been already indicated, the Accession Section is entrusted with the work of including the works received in the library into the Stock Book of the library. The Stock Book is called the Accession Register and it is best maintained in cards. Volumes will come into the library in four distinct streams, viz :

2 Volumes acquired by the Book Order Section;
3 Volumes acquired by the Periodical Publication Section;
8 Volumes received as Unsolicited Gifts; and
95 Volumes received on Exchange.

In Copyright Libraries, there will be a fifth stream added to this, namely the stream of Copyright Copies of Publications.

2416 Weekly Basis

It has been suggested in the preceding chapters, that it will be an advantage to plan the main work of the Book Selection Section, the Book Order Section, and the Periodical Publication Section on a weekly basis, so that the work may be evenly distributed throughout the year. As a consequence of this, the major part of the work of the Accession Section also will have to be planned on a weekly basis.

2418 Factors in Planning

The distinctive work of the Accession Section is to be planned with reference to the following factors:

2 Ordered books ;
4 Accession; and
7 Unsolicited gift books.

242 Job Analysis

2422 Ordered Books

2422 The work of the Accession Section relating to Ordered Books is to consist of the following items :

1 Scrutinising the book supply received in response to orders sent by the Book Order Section, which may be referred to as *Supply Scrutiny Work*;
4 Taking such action as may be necessary on wrong supplies, which may be referred to as *Wrong Supply Work*; and
7 Passing the bills for the Accepted Books, which may be referred to as *Bill Passing Work*.

2422:1 *Supply Scrutiny Work*

2422:1:1 Supply Scrutiny Work of the Accession Section is to consist of the following immediate job :

1 Examining the wrapper of the book packets received, which may be referred to as *Wrapper Examining*.

2422:1:4 Supply Scrutiny Work of the Accession Section is to consist of the following daily jobs :

1 Tallying the Bill with the Books, which may be referred to as *Bill Tallying*; and

2 Tallying the Order Cards with the Books, which may be referred to as *Order Card Tallying.*

2422:4 *Wrong Supply Work*

2422:4:5 Wrong Supply Work of the Accession Section is to consist of the following weekly jobs :

1 Taking the necessary action on books received without Bills, which may be referred to as *Books-Without-Bills Disposing*;
2 Dealing with the Bills, the supply relating to which has not been received, which may be referred to as *Unsupplied-Bills Disposing*;
3 Dealing with cases in which the Book Supply does not agree with the entries in the Order Card in some detail or other, which may be referred to as *Doubtful Supply Disposing*;
4 Dealing with the books found to have defects during the process of collation or during the scrutiny of the books by the Technical Section, which may be referred to as *Defective Supply Disposing*; and
5 Dealing with the books received but not due, which may be referred to as *Not-Due-Books Disposing.*

422:7 *Bill Passing Work*

2422:7:5 Bill Passing Work of the Accession Section is to consist of the following weekly jobs :

1 Verifying if the entries relating to the unaccepted and unsupplied items have all been scored out, in the Bill, which may be referred to as *Bills Verifying*;
2 Verifying the total of the Bill and setting it right if necessary, which may be referred to as *Total Verifying*;
3 Writing out the necessary certificate in the bills, which may be referred to as *Bills Certifying*;
4 Carrying out in the Fair Copies of the Bills all the treatment given to the Duplicate Copies, which may be referred to as *Fair Copy Bill Completing*; and
7 Transmitting the Certified Bills to the Accounts Section for further action, which may be referred to as *Certified Bills Transmitting.*

2424 Accession

The work of the Accession Section relating to Accession is to consist of the following items :

4 Collating all the volumes received for accessioning, which may be referred to as *Collating Work*;
5 Transmitting the accepted volumes to the Technical Section, which may be referred to as *Transmission Work*; and
6 Accessioning the volumes finally approved by the Technical Section, which may be referred to as *Accessioning Work*.

424:4 *Collating Work*

2424:4:5 Collating Work of the Accession Section is to consist of the following weekly jobs :

2 Verifying the Collation of the ordered books with the data given in the Order Card or noting it if it is not already given, which may be referred to as *Ordered Books Collating*;
3 Collating the Completed Periodical Publications and scrutinising whether the volumes have been properly assembled, which may be referred to as *Periodical Publications Collating*; and
8 Collating the Gift Books and noting down the Collation in their Accession Cards, which may be referred to as *Gift Books Collating*.

2424:5 *Transmission Work*

2424:5:5 Transmission Work of the Accession Section is to consist of the following weekly jobs :

1 Arranging the Bills in proper classified sequence, the Bills having the same order number being arranged among themselves chronologically by the date of the order, which may be referred to as *Bills Arranging*;
2 Arranging the Accepted Books relating to the Bills exactly in the sequence in which they appear in the Bills, which may be referred to as *Accepted Books Arranging*;
3 Arranging the Office Copies of the Acknowledgments for the Gift Books by the main classes of the books, which may be

referred to as *Acknowledgments Arranging*;

4 Arranging the Gift Books themselves in the sequence of the arranged Acknowledgments, which may be referred to as *Gift Books Arranging*;

5 Arranging the Accession Cards of the Accepted and Approved Books exactly parallel to the books themselves, which may be referred to as *Accession Cards Arranging*;

6 Sorting the Accession Cards of the Completed Periodical Publications and Instalment Books into two groups, namely the Gift Group and the Purchased Group, which may be referred to as *Periodical Publication and Instalment Book Accession Cards Sorting*;

7 Arranging the cards in each group by the class numbers, which may be referred to as *Periodical Publication and Instalment Book Accession Cards Arranging*;

8 Arranging the Periodical Publications and the Instalment Books themselves exactly parallel to the related Accession Cards, which may be referred to as *Periodical Publications and Instalment Books Arranging*; and

95 Transmitting the Volumes and the related Accession Cards, in the proper sequence, to the Technical Section, which may be referred to as *Collated Volumes Transmitting*.

2424:6 *Accession Work*

2424:6:5 Accessioning Work of the Accession Section is to consist of the following weekly jobs :

1 Arranging the Bills and the Office Copies of the Acknowledgments in the proper sequence, which may be referred to as *Bills Arranging*;

2 Arranging the Accession Cards in the proper sequence, which may be referred to as *Accession Card Arranging*;

3 Arranging the publications in the proper sequence, which may be referred to as *Volumes Arranging*;

4 Writing out the Accession Number in the Bills and in the Office Copies of the Acknowledgments, which may be referred to as *Bills Accession Numbering*;

5 Writing out the Accession Number in the Accession Card relating to the items dealt with in the preceding job, which

may be referred to as *Card Accession Numbering*;

6 Writing out the Accession Number in the volumes themselves which may be referred to as *Volumes Accession Numbering*;

7 Writing out the Donation Numbers in the Office Copies of the Acknowledgments, which may be referred to as *Acknowledgment Donation Numbering*;

8 Writing out the Donation Number in the Accession Cards, which may be referred to as *Card Donation Numbering*;

91 Writing out the Donation Numbers in the volumes themselves, which may be referred to as *Volumes Donation Numbering*;

92 Filling up the headings about date of accessioning in the Accession Cards, which may be referred to as *Accession Date Noting*;

93 Transmitting the Accession Cards to the Book Order Section, Periodical Publication Section, and the Accounts Section for the noting down of the Accession Number and the Voucher Number, which may be referred to as *Accession Cards Circulating*; and

94 Filing the finally tallied Accession Cards in the accession cabinet, which may be referred to as *Accession Card Filing*.

2427 Unsolicited Gift Books

2427:4 The work of the Accession Section relating to Unsolicited Gift Books is to consist of the following daily jobs:

1 Consulting the librarian whether the gift may be accepted, which may be referred to as *Gift Accepting*;

2 Preparing Accession Cards for the Unsolicited Gift Books accepted in the day, which may be referred to as *Donation Card Writing*; and

3 Writing out the Office Copy as well as the Fair Copy of the Acknowledgment for the Gift Books, which may be referred to as *Donation Acknowledging*.

2427:5 The work of the Accession Section relating to Unsolicited Gift Books is to consist of the following weekly jobs:

1 Checking the entries in the Accession Cards with the Gift

Books, which may be referred to as *Donation Card Checking*; and

3 Transmitting the Acknowledgment Letters to the librarian for signature, which may be referred to as *Acknowledgment Transmitting*.

243 **Routine**

2432 Ordered Books

2432:1 *Supply Scrutiny Work*

2432:1:1 *Immediate job*

2432:1:11 Wrapper Examining

As soon as the Bills, the Order Cards and the Books of the day are received from the Book Order Section, rapidly examine the wrappers. Place those that are free from objection in a classified sequence for future reference, if necessary. These wrappers are to be destroyed only at the end of the week. If any wrapper is out of order, have the matter investigated with the Book Order Section and the librarian, if necessary.

2432:1:4 *Daily jobs*

2432:1:41 Bill Tallying

As soon as the Wrapper Examining is over, collect the Bills together and arrange them in the proper classified sequence, the characteristics of classification being, successively Vendor, Subject and Date of Order, the Original Bills and Duplicate Bills forming independent groups. If a Bill is without a Duplicate, prepare a copy and insert it in the Duplicate Group. Put aside the Original Group and work with the Duplicate Group till the Fair Copy Bill Completing Routine (viz 2432:7:54) is reached. Take each Bill in succession and tally each item in the Bill successively as follows:

Pick out the book corresponding to the item, put a tick to the left of the Serial Number of the item in the Bill in token of the book having been picked out and place the books in a sequence parallel to the entries in the Bill. The Group of Books so formed may be referred to as *Bill-Tallied Group*. If any item in the Bill represents two or more volumes, write in pencil to the left of the tick in the margin "2v", "3v", etc as the case may be.

If the Book Order Section has endorsed against any item in the bill as "Not due", place the book relating to that item in the *Not-Due Group* of books and score out the item in the Bill.

If there is any book left over, without entry in any of the Bills, put inside the book as slip with the words "Bill not received" and put the book in the *Bill-Not-Received Group* of books.

If there is any item in the Bill for which the book is not to be found, have the matter investigated. See if the book lies in the Bill-Not-Received Group of books. See if it has been sent by mistake to any other Section, particularly the Periodical Publication Section. Consult the Book Order Section and the librarian. If it is not found anywhere, endorse on the related Order Card "Not received"; put your initials and date. Put it in the *Suspense Box* in the proper alphabetic sequence by the heading.

2432:1:42 Order Card Tallying

Note : *This routine is to be done volume by volume for the books in the Bill-Tallied Group.*

In tallying each book with its Order Card, pay special attention to and compare, the author, title, edition, year, price and special notes, if any, found in the book and its Order Card. If there is any discrepancy, investigate the matter and set it right. If it cannot be easily set right, take it to the notice of the librarian and carry out his instructions.

In case it cannot be set right easily, put inside the book a slip with the word "Discrepancy" and the nature of the Discrepancy written on it and place the book in the *Discrepancy Group*. Note the Discrepancy in the related Order Card in pencil. Initial and date it. Put it in the Suspense Box in the proper alphabetic sequence by the heading.

If the book is acceptable, fill up the heading "Cost" in the Order Card, taking the Amount from the Bill and fill up also the headings in the Order Card relating to "Receipt of the book", putting the current date as the date of receipt.

After the tallying is over, the books must be placed in the *Card-Tallied Group* in exactly the same sequence in which they were found in the Bill-Tallied Group. The Tallied Order Cards hould be arranged and kept in the *Tallied-Card Box* in exactly the same sequence as the books in the Card-Tallied Group.

2432:4 *Wrong Supply Work*

2432:4:5 *Weekly jobs*

2432:4:51 Books Without Bills Disposing

Deal with each of the books in the Bill-Not-Received Group (see 2432:1:41) as follows:

Ascertain from the Book Order Section if the book is due and if so note down in a slip the Order Number, the Date of the Order and the Serial Number of the book in the Order and insert the slip inside the book.

See if the related Bill is in the group of Unsupplied Bills. If not wait for a reasonable time for the receipt of the Bill. After the Bill is got, deal with it in the usual way. If it does not come, write to the vendor asking for the Bill.

2432:4:52 Unsupplied Bills Disposing

You may have to wait for a reasonable time for the book to arrive. If it does not arrive in a reasonable time, write to the vendor about the non-supply of the book. If the number of such items is very small when compared with the total number of items in the Bill, such items may be scored out from the Bill and a Fresh Bill may be called for from the vendor along with the actual supply.

2432:4:53 Doubtful Supply Disposing

Deal with each of the books in the Discrepancy Group (see routine 2432:1:42) as follows :

Write to the vendor bringing the Discrepancy explicitly to his notice. On receipt of the reply, take the necessary action.

2432:4:54 Defective Supply Disposing

Deal with each of the books in the Defective Supply Group (see 2434:4:52) as follows :

Write to the vendor, bringing the defects explicitly to his notice. On receipt of the reply, take the necessary action.

2432:4:55 Not-Due Books Disposing

Deal with each of the books in the Not-Due Group and the Rejected Group (see 2432:1:41) as follows :

Correspond with the person from whom the book was received,

asking him what should be done with it. On receipt of the reply, take the necessary action.

2432:7 *Bill Passing Work*

2432:7:5 *Weekly jobs*

Note: *All the jobs of the Bill Passing Work are to be done at one time on an appointed day of the week.*

2432:7:51 Bills Verifying

Take all the Bills which have been Accession-Numbered. Examine if the entries for the unaccepted and unsupplied, i e unaccessioned items have been scored out. Examine also if all the scored items, have been initialled by the librarian. If there is any irregularity, set it right. Remember particularly to see that the items against which there are no Accession Numbers have been scored out.

2432:7:52 Total Verifying

Verify the total of the amount claimed in each of the Bills. Remember particularly scored items. If the total has to be changed for any reason, score the original total by a single line in ink and write out the correct one beneath or next to it.

2432:7:53 Bills Certifying

After the total is verified, write out in each Bill the necessary certificate to the effect that the supply has been received and brought into the Stock Book. Put your dated initials below the certificate.

2432:7:54 Faircopy Bill Completing

As soon as the Duplicate Copies of the Bills have been finally dealt with completely, take the Faircopies of the corresponding Bills and carry out in them all the alterations, numbering, certifying, etc that have been made in the corresponding Duplicate Copies.

2432:7:57 Certified Bills Transmitting

Collect all the Certified Bills. See if they are in proper sequence. If there is any irregularity in the sequence, set it right. Transmit the Certified Bills to the Accounts Section for further action. As soon as the transmission Register comes back from the Accounts Section, see if the Head of that Section has initialled it in token of his having received the bills.

2434 Accession

2434:4 *Collating Work*

Collate each volume carefully. The following details are to be carefully looked into in Collating Work :

1 *Defects in printing and paper.*

11 Examine if there is any off-setting in any page. Off-setting occurs frequently in Indian-made books. Hence, special vigilance is necessary in their case.

12 Occasionally, a page is blank without being printed. Detect all such cases.

13 Examine each leaf and see if any leaf is torn.

2 *Collation.*

21 Examine if all the formes are included in the copy and if they occur in proper sequence. Not infrequently a forme is missing, or a forme is duplicated, or a forme is misplaced or is stitched upside down.

22 See if all the plates, maps, etc which are not included in the pagination, are found in the copy by referring to the contents page.

23 Some of the Indian books are *Artificial Composite Books.*[24] Sometimes it happens that the publisher issues certain copies without including in them all the constituent works. In such cases, the intention of the Book Order Section or the Indenting Authority should be ascertained and steps must be taken to see that the copy supplied is the proper one.

24 The exact Collation should be noted down in the Accession Card, if it is not already there, and verified and corrected, if necessary, if it has been noted at an earlier stage with the aid of the Source for Book Selection.

3 *Defects in binding.*

31 Examine if the casing is sound.

32 Examine if each forme is properly stitched in.

All the defects discovered are to be taken to the notice of the librarian. If it is decided that the defects are eithér trivial or such that they can be locally rectified without undue extra cost, the necessary rectification should be made and the book is to be accepted. If the defect is declared to be serious, the volume should be put into the *Defective Supply Group*.

The Collation Work will have to be done almost every day in the Accession Section. But it has been here classified as a weekly job with the idea that the Collation Work should be distributed over the different days of the week, according to the nature of the volumes, as shown in the job analysis. Further, in addition to the careful verification of the copies, some extra work may have to be done in the case of the volumes belonging to different categories. In the routine described hereunder for the weekly jobs of this work, it is these special points that are mentioned.

2434:4:5 *Weekly jobs*

2434:4:52 Ordered Books Collating

If for any reason the details of Collation had been omitted in the Book Selection Card, they should now be filled up. If they are given in the card, verify if they are accurate. If not, make the necessary corrections. If the difference between what is noted in the card and what is actually found in the book is significant or very great, have the matter investigated before correcting in the card, and, if necessary, take the matter to the notice of the librarian.

2434:4:53 Periodical Publications Collating

The Periodical Publication Section would have filled only the heading and the title in the Accession Card. The entire Collation and other details are to be filled up by the Accession Section. As the loose issues would have been in circulation for a long time before being assembled into a volume, it is likely to have some leaves damaged or lost. If so, write a descriptive note about such damages near the top on the back of the title page. As has been already indicated in the introduction to this chapter some Periodical Publications may have to be split into different volumes before accessioning, while in the case of others several volumes may have to be clubbed together and treated as a single volume for accessioning and for binding purposes. The binding section is maintaining a *Binding Slip* for each Periodical Publication. Consult the Head of that Section whenever necessary and discuss the matter with the Periodical Publication Section, the Technical Section and the Maintenance Section, if the matter is very complicated. All cases about which an agreed and satisfactory decision cannot be arrived at should be taken to the notice of the librarian.

2434:4:58 Gift Books Collating

In the case of a Solicited Gift Book, the Order Section will transmit to the Accession Section an Accession Card. But it is only the heading and the title that would have been filled up in such cards. All the other details are to be filled up by the Accession Section. In the case of Unsolicited Gift Books, the Accession Card should be completely prepared by the Accession Section.

2434:5 Transmission Work

The routine described hereunder is intended to secure a certain consistent sequence in the Accession Cards. In the group of Accession Cards completed in a week, the following sequence will result from the routine described. The Purchased Books will come first. Among themselves they will be arranged into groups by their Order Numbers. The books belonging to any given Order Number will be arranged among themselves in the sequence in which they occur in the Bill. Next to that, the Gift Books will come. The Gift Books will be found arranged among themselves by their call numbers. Next to the Group of Gift Books, the Periodical Publications will come. They too will be divided into Gift Group and Purchased Group, those in each group arranged among themselves by their call numbers.

2434:5:5 *Weekly jobs*

2434:5:51 Bills Arranging

Take all the Bills dealt with in the course of the week. Examine if they are in proper classified sequence. If there is any irregularity, set it right.

2434:5:52 Accepted Books Arranging

Examine the group of Accepted Books and see that they are in the same sequence as their entries in the Bills.

2434:5:53 Acknowledgements Arranging

Take the Office Copies of all the Acknowledgments for Gift Books sent in the week. Examine if they are in proper classified sequence. If there is any irregularity, set it right. Attach them at the end of the Bills.

2434:5:54 Gift Books Arranging

Arrange the approved Gift Books exactly in the same sequence as their entries in the Acknowledgments and place them next to the Accepted Books Group.

2434:5:55 Accession Cards Arranging

Arrange the Accession Cards of the Accepted and Approved books in sequence exactly parallel to the books themselves and put them in the Transmission Box.

2434:5:56 Periodical Publication and Instalment Book Accession Cards Sporting

Sort the Accession Cards of the completed volumes of Periodical and Instalment Publications received from the Periodical Publication Section, and the Book Order Section respectively into four groups, namely those of (1) Donated Instalment Books, (2) Donated Periodical Publications, (3) Purchased Periodical Publications, and (4) Purchased Instalment Books.

2434:5:57 Periodical Publication and Instalment Book Accession Cards Arranging

Arrange the Accession Cards relating to the volumes in each of the groups mentioned in the preceding routine, by their headings in the case of Instalment Book Cards and by their class numbers in the case of Periodical Publication Cards and put them in the Transmission Box with the Donation Group first and the Purchased Group last.

2434:5:58 Periodical Publications and Instalment Books Arranging

Arrange the Periodical Publications and the Instalment Books among themselves exactly parallel to the related Accession Cards.

2434:5:595 COLLATED VOLUMES TRANSMITTING

Note in the Transmission Register the number of volumes and the number of Accession Cards to be transmitted. Transmit the arranged volumes and the Transmission Box with its cards to the Technical Section. As soon as the Transmission Register comes back from the Technical Section examine, if it has received the initials of the Head of that Section in token of his having received the materials.

2434:6 *Accessioning Work*

2434:6:5 *Weekly jobs*

Note : *All the jobs of the Accessioning Work are to be done at one time on an appointed day of the week.*

2434:6:51 BILL ARRANGING

Scrutinise the Duplicate Copies of the Bills, and the Office Copies of the Acknowledgments for Gift Books. If there is any irregularity, set it right. If any entry in the bill represents two or more volumes, note in the margin of that entry "2v", "3v", etc as the case may be, if it has not been already so noted.

2434:6:52 ACCESSION CARD ARRANGING

Tally the Accession Cards with the Bills and the Office Copies of the Acknowledgments and secure that their sequence is exactly parallel to the sequence in which their entries occur in the Bills and in the Office Copies of the Acknowledgments.

At the end of the Accession Cards relating to books, put the Accession Cards of the week relating to Periodical Publications and Instalment Books, putting the cards of the Gift Group first and the Purchased Group next.

A result of this will be that the Accession Cards of the week will fall in the following sequence. First the Accession Cards of the Purchased Books in the Bill sequence; next, the Accession Cards of the Donated Books in the Acknowledgment sequence; next the Accession Cards of the Donated Instalment Books and Periodical Publications in the classified sequence; and lastly the Accession

Cards of the Purchased Periodical Publications and Instalment Books in the classified sequence.

2434:6:53 Volumes Arranging

Arrange the volumes exactly in the same sequence as the Accession Cards. While doing so, see also if all the publications are there.

2434:6:54 Bills Accession Numbering

Write down in ink the Accession Number in strict serial sequence against each item in the office copies of the Bills and the Acknowledgments.

Remember that the first Accession Number to be used is the one next to the last Accession Number given on the preceding occasion when accessioning was done.

Remember also, that, if the margin of any entry contains a note like "2v", "3v", etc the appropriate number of Accession Numbers are to be given to that entry.

2434:6:55 Card Accession Numbering

After the Bill Accession Numbering is over, take out the Accession Cards of the different items successively, put down in ink the correct Accession Number or Numbers in the appropriate place in each Accession Card and replace the card in its original place.

After the Accession Cards relating to all the books have been dealt with, continue Accession Numbering the Accession Cards relating to the Instalment Books and Periodical Publications.

2434:6:56 Volumes Accession Numbering

After the Card Accession Numbering is over, write out the correct Accession Number in each of the respective volumes. The Accession Number is to be written in ink, as near the centre as possible on the back of the title page, i e above the Call Number, leaving the necessary space for the Donation Number in the case of Gift Volumes.

If there is no title page, it is to be written at the top of the first page.

2434:6:57 Acknowledgment Donation Numbering

After the Volumes Accession Numbering is over, give serial

Donation Numbers to the office copies of the Acknowledgments, the Donation Number being written just below the Accession Number.

Remember that the first Donation Number to be used is the one next to the last Donation Number given on the preceding occasion when Donation Numbering Work was done.

Remember also that, if any entry has received two or more Accession Numbers, it is to be given an equal number of Donation Numbers.

2434:6:58 Card Donation Numbering

After the Acknowledgment Donation Numbering is over, take out the Accession Cards of the different items successively, put out the Accession Cards of the different items successively, put down in ink the correct Donation Number in the proper place and replace the card in its original place.

After the Accession Cards relating to all Donated Books have been dealt with, continue Donation Numbering to the Accession Cards relating to Gift Periodical Publications.

2434:6:59 Volumes Donation Numbering

After the Card Donation Numbering is over, write out the correct Donation Number in each of the respective volumes. The Donation Number is to be written in ink, just below the Accession Number on the back of the title page of the volume, or at the top of the first page, as the case may be.

2434:6:592 Accession Date Noting

After the Noting of Accession Numbers and Donation Numbers are over, fill up the columns about the date, etc of accessioning in all the Accession Cards. As soon as this is over, the Volumes and the Accession Cards are to be left in charge of the Technical Section. But the bills and the office copies of the Acknowledgment letters should be taken away by the Accession Section, the former for Bills work and the latter for Filing.

2434:6:593 Accession Card Circulating

As soon as the accession card box of the week is received from the Maintenance Section after being tallied with the shelf register cards, pass it round to the Book Order Section, the Accounts Section and the Periodical Publication Section, to enable them to note down the Accession Number and the Voucher Number in the Standing Order Cards of the Book Order Section, in the Register Cards of the Periodical Publication Section and in the Accession Cards themselves.

2434:6:594 Accession Card Filing

On the appointed day of the week, as soon as the Accession Cards come back to the Accession Section from circulation, examine if all the Accession Cards have come back and if they are in strict numerical sequence without any gaps. If there is any discrepancy, investigate the matter and have it set right. After all the defects are set right, file the Accession Cards in the proper numerical sequence in the *Accession Cabinet*.

2437 Unsolicited Gift Books

2437:4 *Daily jobs*

2437:41 Gift Accepting

In the case of every unsolicited Gift Book, discuss with the librarian whether it is to be accepted and take such action as may be necessary.

2437:42 Donation Card Writing

For each accepted unsolicited Gift Book received in the day, write out an Accession Card, remembering to use the card lined with the proper colour in accordance with the convention of the library.

2437:43 Donation Acknowledging

Fill up an Acknowledgment Card for each book. Write out also the heading and the title of the book and the name and address of the donor in a 3×5 inches slip of paper. This slip will be treated as the Office Copy for the Acknowledgment. This slip will receive the Accession Number and the Donation Number, when the accessioning work is done. If the books are too many, a consolidated list will do.

437:5 *Weekly jobs*

2437:51 Donation Card Checking

On the appointed day of the week, as soon as the Collation

of the Gift Books of the week is over, complete all the entries that may be found incomplete in the Accession Cards of each of the Gift Books. Further, check the Acknowledgment Cards with the Gift Books of the week and the related Accession Cards.

2437:53 Acknowledgment Transmitting

Send for the librarian's signature all the Acknowledgment Cards which have been checked and found correct. Send also the office copies, although they are in the form of slips, so that the office copies may get the despatch date in the Correspondence Section. This despatch date will be of use for future reference.

244 Elimination of Waste

2441 Organisation

If the turnover in the section demands the assignment of several members to it, it may be an advantage to specialise them in different items of work, such as, accessioning, bill passing, gift books, exchange, and so on.

2443 Prompt Release of Books

The Head of the Section should strive his best to release the books for public use as expeditiously as possible. He should carefully revise the bills passed and countersign the certificate in the bills.

2444 Revision of Accession Numbers

The work of assigning Accession Numbers and Donation Numbers is a ticklish job. Outsiders may think that it is a very mechanical process requiring only an ability to write consecutive integers in the proper sequence. But it is not really so simple. As has already been indicated in the introduction to this chapter, a good deal of judgment and consultation with various other Sections are necessary to decide what constitutes a volume for accessioning. Apart from this, it is a matter of experience that, occasionally, woeful mistakes occur in assigning Accession Numbers either by the leaving of gaps or by the repetition of a number by oversight—very often due to exhaustion. Indeed, assigning integral numbers, each number running to five or six digits, is a very exhausting job. Hence, it is the duty of the Head of the Accession Section to check the continuity of the Accession Numbers and the Donation Numbers and revise the entry of those numbers at the proper juncture in all places both in the books and in the records.

2448 Diary

The Accession Section is to maintain one diary on a weekly basis. Its headings are to be as follows :

11 to 15 same as for the book order section ;
21 Books without bills ;
22 Unsupplied bills ;
23 Doubtful supplies ;
24 Defective supplies ;
25 Not-due books ;
27 Bills passed ;
42 Ordered books accessioned ;
428 Gift books accessioned ;
43 Periodical publications accessioned ;
44 Last accession number assigned ;
447 Last donation number assigned ;
494 Accession cards filed.

245 Correlation table

2 *Book Order Section*

2432:1:41 Bill tallying;
2432:4:55 Not-due books disposing;
2434:6:593 Accession card circulating.

3 *Periodical Publication Section*

2434:4:53 Periodical publications collating;
2434:6:593 Accession card circulating.

5 *Technical Section*

2434:5:595 Collated volumes transmitting (Books—Monday 5 PM) ;
Periodical publications—Saturday 12 noon ;

2434:6:5 Accessioning work (Thursday 4 P M).

8 *Maintenance Section*

2434:6:593 Accession card circulating.

97 *Accounts Section*

2432:7:57 Certified bills transmitting (Saturday 5 P M) ;
2434:6:593 Accession card circulating.

993 *Correspondence Section*

2432:4:5 Wrong supply work;
2437:53 Acknowledgment transmitting.

246 Illustrative Time Scheme

246:4 *Daily jobs*

2432:1:41 Bill tallying;
2432:1:42 Order card tallying;
2438:41 Gift accepting;
2437:42 Donation card writing;
2437:43 Donation acknowledging.

246:5 *Weekly jobs*

Saturday

2434:5 Transmission work (Periodical publications 12 noon);
2432:7:5 All the weekly jobs of bill passing work;

Saturday

2432:7:57 Certified bills transmitting (5 P M) ;
2434:4:52 Ordered books collating.

Sunday

2434:4:52 Ordered books collating;
2434:4:58 Gift books collating.

Monday

2438:51 Donation card checking;
2434:5 Transmission work (Books, 5 P M).

Tuesday

2432:4:5 Wrong supply work;
2437:53 Acknowledgment transmitting.

Wednesday

2434:4:53 Periodical publications collating.

Thursday

2434:6:594 Accession card filing;
2434:6:5 Accessioning work (4 P M).

247 Forms and Registers

The only register of this Section is the *Accession Register*. Its number may be fixed as C4. It is made up of accession cards filed in cabinets. Accession Card is the name assumed by C12 Book Selection Card, when it reaches the accession cabinet with all the entries duly made in it. The following colour scheme may be adopted for the cards: Donated books, black border. Purchased periodical publications, red border. Donated periodical publications, left half of the border, red and the right half of the border, black.

C47 *Acknowledgment card.* Printed. 11 point type. Bristol board. White. The text of the form is as follows :

I acknowledge, with thanks, the receipt of the undermentioned publications kindly presented to this library.

248 Files

Name	*Class Number*	*Amplifying device*	*Filing characteristic*	*Year of transfer to record sequence after the file is closed.*	*Year of destruction after transfer to the record sequence.*
Wrong supply	44	Nil	Vendor	Year 1	Year 5
Books without bills	441	Subject Device	Heading	Do	Do
Bills without supply	442	Do	Do	Do	Do
Doubtful supply	443	Do	Do	Do	Do
Unsound supply	444	Do	Do	Do	Do
Not-due supply	445	Do	Do	Do	Do
Errors in bill	447	Do	Vendor	Do	Do
Unsolicited gift books	47	Nil	Donor	Do	Year 10
Outwar enquiries	491	Do	Correspondent	Do	Year 3
Inwar enquiries	492	Do	Do	Do	Do

CHAPTER 25

TECHNICAL SECTION

251 Planning

2511 SCOPE OF THE CHAPTER

The major items of the work of the Technical Section are classification and cataloguing. These pieces of work are of a highly technical nature. But this chapter does not deal with the technique either of classification or of cataloguing. On the other hand, it deals only with the routine connected with these two processes. It also gives an account of all the routine that has to be performed to make the volumes fit for public use, and to bring the catalogue cabinet up to date.

2512 ACCURACY

Accuracy is the very essence of a library catalogue and of all the marks that are made by the Technical Section either in the book or in any of the library records. Hence, the routine described in this chapter provides for an elaborate system of checking and counterchecking. In fact, the checking is further continued by the Maintenance Section, as will be seen in chapter 28. It is our experience that the time spent on so much of checking is well spent. It is our painful experience that, in spite of so much checking, an occasional slip creeps through and acts as a hindrance at some future time—sometimes, years later. Hence, it would be very unwise to stint in providing the necessary time to complete the checking processes in a leisurely and thorough manner.

2513 NUMBER OF SETS OF CATALOGUE

Except in very small libraries, it is found to be certainly convenient and even necessary to have a separate set of the catalogue for the use of the classifier and the cataloguer. It is not convenient for the cataloguer and the classifier to use the public catalogue, on account of its distance and its constant use by others.

Again, if the library is sufficiently big, it may be convenient to have another set of the catalogue in the librarian's room. However much one would like to avoid it, serious workers, who visit the library, raise problems in reference work, while conversing with the librarian. Psychologically, it would be more effective, if a set of the catalogue is available near at hand in the librarian's room and the problems raised are solved then and there. Even otherwise, to enable the librarian to think out the symmetrical and systematic building up of the stock of the library, it is desirable that a separate set of the catalogue is at his elbow.

For these reasons, it will be a good policy to type out two copies of the catalogue, as soon as the chief cataloguer writes out the cards for the public catalogue. While the public catalogue, which has to bear much wear and tear, should be in specially made tough catalogue cards, the additional catalogues need not be prepared in such costly cards. On the other hand, since it is only one or two persons that are likely to handle these sets—the classifier and the cataloguer in the case of one set and the librarian in the case of the other—it is sufficient if the copying is done on slips cut out of 30lb ledger paper. This is found to be satisfactory. The labour of preparing two copies is not much more than that of preparing one, as the second copy may well be a carbon copy.

In large library systems with several branches, it may be necessary to have many sets of the catalogue. That problem has been fully discussed in the *Classified catalogue code.*[25]

2514 Correction of Call Number

As will be seen in that part of the introduction to chapter 28, which relates to correction collection, the call numbers of books will require systematic revision from time to time, in the light of the experience gained in serving the books to the readers and in consequence of the realignment and the reorientation of the divisions of knowledge, brought about now and then in the learned world. Hence, correction work has been marked out as an independent factor in the work of this section.

2518 Factors in Planning

The distinctive work of the Technical Section is to be planned with reference to the following factors:

1 Classification;

2 Cataloguing;
3 Preparation of the volumes for public use;
4 Correction of call numbers and catalogue entries;
5 Binding;
6 Classification and cataloguing codes; and
7 Catalogue cabinet.

The periodicity of the work of this section should be similar to the periodicity of the work of the sections dealt with in the preceding chapters. Hence, it follows that the work of the Technical Section also should be planned on a weekly basis, so that the work may be evenly distributed throughout the year. As a consequence of this, the major part of the work of this section will consist of of weekly jobs.

252 Job Analysis

2521 Classification

2521 The work of the Technical Section relating to Classification is to consist of the following items:

1 Making a preliminary survey of the volumes received from the accession section, which may be referred to as *Preliminary Work*;
2 Assigning call numbers to the volumes, which may be referred to as *Call Numbering Work*;
4 Detecting duplication, defects, etc. in the volumes, which may be referred to as *Detection Work*; and
8 Checking the assigned call numbers, which may be referred to as *Checking Work*.

2521:1 *Preliminary Work*

2521:1:5 Preliminary Work relating to Classification is to consist of the following weekly jobs:

4 Tallying the volumes and the accession cards as soon as they arrive from the Accession Section, which may be referred to as *Tallying*; and
5 Sorting the volumes by their main classes, which may be

referred to as *Preliminary Sorting.*

2521:2 *Call Numbering Work*

2521:2:5 Call Numbering Work relating to Classification is to consist of the following weekly jobs:

1 Assigning call numbers to the volumes that present no difficulty, which may be referred to as *Normal Volumes Call Numbering*;
2 Assigning call numbers to such of the volumes in the deferred group as are manageable without consulting the librarian, though not so easy as the normal volumes, which may be referred to as *Deferred Volumes Call Numbering*;
3 Discussing with the librarian the volumes which are difficult to classify, which may be referred to as *Classification Consulting*;
4 Assigning call numbers to the difficult volumes, which may be referred to as *Difficult Volumes Call Numbering*;
5 Noting down the sources from which data are taken for constructing class numbers, which may be referred to as *Sources Noting*; and
6 Noting down the new classes opened as a result of the discussion with the librarian, which may be referred to as *New Classes Noting.*

2521:4 *Detection Work*

2521:4:1 Detection Work of the Technical Section is to consist of the following immediate job:

4 Informing the Accession Section about the detection made, which may be referred to as *Detection Notifying.*

2521:8 *Checking Work*

2521:8:5 Checking Work relating to Classification is to consist of the following weekly jobs:

1 Checking the call number assigned to each volume, which may be referred to as *Call Number Checking*;
2 Checking the cross references indicated for each volume, which

may be referred to as *Cross Reference Checking*; and

6 Checking the placing of the new classes that arose in classifying the volume, which may be referred to as *New Placing Checking*.

2522 CATALOGUING

2522 The work of the Technical Section relating to Cataloguing is to consist of the following items:

1 Sorting the volumes according to cataloguing peculiarities, which may be referred to as *Preliminary Work*;
2 Writing out the necessary fresh catalogue cards, which may be referred to as *Fresh Card Writing Work*;
3 Making the necessary entries in the catalogue cards already existing, which may be referred to as *Card Consolidation Work*;
4 Dealing with the volumes that raise difficulties in cataloguing, which may be referred to as *Refractory Cases Work*;
5 Checking the catalogue cards, which may be referred to as *Checking Work*; and
6 Typing catalogue slip, which may be referred to as *Typing Work*.

2522:1 *Preliminary Work*

2522:1:5 Preliminary Work relating to Cataloguing is to consist of the following weekly job:

1 Sorting the volumes on the basis of their cataloguing peculiarities, which may be referred to as *Sorting*.

522:2 *Fresh Card Writing Work*

2522:2:5 Fresh Card Writing Work relating to Cataloguing is to consist of the following weekly by-jobs:

1 *Main Card Writing*;
2 *Cross Reference Cards Writing*;
3 *Index Cards Writing*;
4 *Back of Main Card Writing*; and
8 *Shelf Register Card Writing*.

2522:3 *Card Consolidation Work*

2522:3:5 The Card Consolidation Work relating to Cataloguing is to consist of the following weekly jobs:

1 Picking out the cards for consolidation from the catalogue cabinet, which may be referred to as *Consolidation Cards Picking*; and
3 Making the necessary entries in the consolidation cards, which may be referred to as *Consolidating*.

2522:4 *Refractory Cases Work*

2522:4:5 The Refractory Cases Work relating to Cataloguing is to consist of the following weekly jobs:

1 Consulting the librarian about the refractory cases, which may be referred to as *Refractory Cases Consulting* ;
5 Noting down the sources from which data are taken to aid cataloguing work, which may be referred to as *Sources Noting*; and
6 Noting down the amendments to the Catalogue Code that may arise out of the discussion with the librarian, which may be referred to as *Amendments Noting*.

2522:5 *Checking Work*

2522:5:5 The Checking Work relating to Cataloguing is to consist of the following weekly jobs:

2 Checking the fresh cards written, which may be referred to as *Fresh Cards Checking*;
3 Checking the alterations made in consolidated cards, which may be referred to as *Consolidated Cards Checking*; and
6 Checking the amendments to the Catalogue Code, which may be referred to as *Amendments Checking*.

2522:6 *Typing Work*

2522:6:5 The Typing Work relating to Cataloguing is to consist of the following weekly jobs:

1 Copying the fresh catalogue cards written, which may be

referred to as *Fresh Slips Typing* ;

2 Picking out from the cabinets the slips that require consolidation, which may be referred to as *Consolidation Slips Picking*;

3 Carrying out the necessary alterations in consolidated slips, which may be referred to as *Slips Consolidating*; and

6 Checking the slips freshly typed and consolidated, which may be referred to as *Slips Checking*.

2523 PREPARATION OF THE VOLUMES

2523 The work of the Technical Section relating to the Preparation of the Volumes for public use may consist of the following items:

1 Noting the accession number or the call number as the case may be, in the concerned cards, which may be referred to as *Card Numbering Work*;

2 Making the volumes fit for use by cutting open, stamping, fixing the date label, tag, etc which may be referred to as *Preparation Work* ;

3 Noting the call number and the accession number in the different parts of the volumes, which may be referred to as *Volumes Numbering Work*; and

8 Sorting the prepared volumes into sequences and arranging them, which may referred to as *Prepared Volumes Arranging Work*.

2523:1 *Card Numbering Work*

523:1:5 The Card Numbering Work relating to the Preparation of the Volumes for public use is to consist of the following weekly jobs:

1 Noting the accession number in the main and the shelf register cards, which may be referred to as *Accession Number Noting* ;

2 Noting the call number in the accession cards, which may be referred to as *Call Number Noting*; and

6 Writing out the book card for each volume, which may be referred to as *Book Carding*.

2523:2 *Preparation Work*

2523:2:5 The Preparation Work relating to the Preparation of the Volumes for public use is to consist of the following weekly jobs:

1 Cutting open the pages of the volumes and easing their backs, which may be referred to as *Cutting Open*;
2 Putting the library stamp in the appropriate places in the volumes, which may be referred to as *Stamping*;
3 Fixing the tags to the backs of the volumes, which may be referred to as *Tagging*;
5 Fixing the book pocket to the volumes, which may be referred to as *Pocket Fixing*; and
6 Fixing the date labels to the volumes, if needed, which may be referred to as *Date Labelling*.

2523:3 *Volumes Numbering Works*

2523:3:5 The Volumes Numbering Work relating to the Preparation of the Volumes for public use is to consist of the following weekly jobs:

1 Writing the call number on the jackets of the volumes, which may be referred to as *Jacket Numbering* ;
2 Writing the call number and the accession number on a leaf in the inside of the book, which may be referred to as *Inside Numbering*;
3 Writing the call number on the tags on the backs of the volumes, which may be referred to as *Tag Numbering* ; and
6 Writing the call number and the accession number in the date labels of the volumes, which may be referred to as *Date Label Numbering*.

2523:8 *Prepared Volumes Arranging Works*

2523:8:5 The Prepared Volumes Arranging Work relating to the Preparation of Volumes for public use is to consist of the following weekly jobs:

1 Sorting the prepared volumes by their sequences, which may be referred to as *Sorting*;
2 Arranging the volumes in each sequence by their call numbers, which may be referred to as *Arranging*; and

6 Inserting the book-tickets in the book pockets or disposing them in any other appropriate way, which may be referred to as *Book-ticket Disposing*.

2524 Correction of Call Numbers and Catalogue Entries

2524 The work of the Technical Section relating to Correction of Call Numbers and Catalogue Entries may consist of the following items:

1 Collecting the volumes to be corrected and their main cards and their first impression main slips, which may be referred to as *Preliminary Work*;
2 Reclassifying the volumes, which may be referred to as *Reclassification Work*;
3 Carrying out the corrections in the first impression slips, which may be referred to as *First Impression Slips Work*;
4 Carrying out the corrections in all the other cards and slips, which may be referred to as *Correction Completing Work*; and
5 Reinserting the corrected main cards and the first impression slips, which may be referred to as *Reinsertion Work*.

2524:1 *Preliminary Work*

2524:1:5 The Preliminary Work relating to the Correction of Call Numbers and Catalogue Entries is to consist of the following weekly jobs:

1 Notifying the Maintenance Section of the volumes that are proposed to be taken up for correction, which may be referred to as *Maintenance Section Notifying*;
2 Taking charge of the volumes, which may be referred to as *Correction Volumes Accepting*; and
3 Picking out the main cards and the first impression main slips of each of the volumes, which may be referred to as *Main Card Picking*.

2524:2 *Reclassification Work*

2524:2:5 The Reclassification Work relating to the Correction of Call Numbers and Catalogue Entries is to consist of the following weekly jobs:

1 Reclassifying each volume and writing out on the back of the title page the new call number, which may be referred to as *Call Number Revising*;
2 Checking the new call number, which may be referred to as *New Call Number Checking*;
3 Correcting in the main card and in the main slip of the first impression, which may be referred to as *Main Card Correcting*; and
8 Transmitting the corrected volumes to the Maintenance Section for the further stage of work to be done by them, which may be referred to as *Corrected Volumes Transmitting*.

2524:3 *First Impression Slips Work*

2524:3:5 The First Impression Slips Work relating to the Correction of Call Numbers and Catalogue Entries is to consist of the following weekly jobs:

1 Picking out all the first impression slips, other than the main ones, relating to each of the corrected volumes, which may be referred to as *First Impression Slips Picking*;
2 Carrying out the necessary corrections in all the first impression slips, which may be referred to as *First Impression Slips Correcting*; and
3 Sorting and arranging the corrected first impression slips, which may be referred to as *First Impression Slips Arranging*.

2524:4 *Correction Completing Work*

2524:4:5 The Correction Completing Work relating to the Correction of Call Numbers and Catalogue Entries is to consist of the following weekly jobs:

1 *Cards Correcting*;
2 *Second Impression Slips Correcting*; and
3 *Language Slips Correcting*.

2524:5 *Reinsertion Work*

2524:5:5 The Reinsertion Work relating to the Correction of

Call Numbers and Catalogue Entries is to consist of the following weekly jobs:

1 *Main Cards Reinserting*; and
2 *First Impression Slips Reinserting.*

2525 Binding

2525:5 The Binding Work relating to the Technical Section is to consist of the following weekly job:

1 Examining the call numbers of the volumes selected for binding to see if they require any revision, which may be referred to as *Call Number Examining.*

2525:6 The Binding Work relating to the Technical Section is to consist of the following monthly jobs:

2 Preparing the instruction for tooling, which may be referred to as *Binding Slip Preparing*;
5 Transmitting the volumes and the slips to the Binding Section which may be referred to as *Binding Books Transmitting.*

2526 Classification and Catalogue Codes

2526:5 The work of the Technical Section relating to Classification and Catalogue Codes is to consist of the following weekly jobs:

1 Carrying out the amendments arrived at in the course of the week in the Classification or Catalogue Code, as the case may be, which may be referred to as *Code Correcting*; and
2 Bringing the monthly statement of corrections up to date, which may be referred to as *Monthly Amendment Statement Filling.*

2526:6 The work of the Technical Section relating to Classification and Catalogue Codes is to consist of the following monthly job:

3 Transmitting the monthly statement of corrections to the

Staff Council, which may be referred to as *Code Corrections Transmitting*.

2527 Catalogue Cabinet

2527 The work of the Technical Section relating to the Catalogue Cabinet is to consist of the following items :

1 Sorting all the cards written in the week, which may be referred to as *Sorting Work*;
2 Discussing the cards with the librarian, which may be referred to as *Reviewing Work*;
3 Transmitting the accession cards and the shelf register cards to the Maintenance Section, which may be referred to as *Accession Cards Transmitting Work*;
4 Inserting the catalogue cards in the public catalogue cabinets, which may be referred to as *Card Inserting Work*; and
5 Inserting the catalogue slips in the appropriate cabinets, which may be referred to as *Slip Inserting Work*.

2527:1 *Sorting Work*

2527:1:5 Sorting Work relating to the Catalogue Cabinet is to consist of the following weekly jobs:

1 Sorting and arranging the catalogue cards, written in the week, in the proper sequence, which may be referred to as *Catalogue Cards Sorting*;
2 Arranging the shelf register cards, written in the week, in the proper sequence, which may be referred to as *Shelf Register Cards Arranging*;
3 Tallying the accession numbers in the main cards and the shelf register cards, which may be referred to as *Accession Number Tallying*; and
8 Making a count of the volumes treated and the cards written, which may be referred to as *Technical Section Counting*.

2527:2 *Reviewing Work*

2527:2:5 Reviewing Work relating to the Catalogue Cabinet is to consist of the following weekly jobs:

1 Discussing the arranged cards with the librarian, which may

be referred to as *Catalogue Cards Discussing*;

2 Carrying out the corrections suggested by the librarian, which may be referred to as *Correction Carrying Out*; and

5 Notifying the other Sections concerned of any suggestions that might have arisen in the course of the discussion with the librarian, which may be referred to as *Suggestions Transmitting*.

2527:3 *Accession Cards Transmitting Work*

2527:3:5 Accession Cards Transmitting Work relating to the Technical Section is to consist of the following weekly jobs:

1 Coupling each shelf register card with its appropriate accession card, which may be referred to as *Shelf Register Card Coupling*;

3 Checking the accession number in the shelf register card, which may be referred to as *Shelf Register Card Checking*; and

8 Transmitting the coupled cards to the Maintenance Section, which may be referred to as *Coupled Cards Transmitting*.

2527:4 *Card Inserting Work*

2527:4:5 Card Inserting Work relating to the Technical Section consists of the following weekly job:

1 Inserting the catalogue cards in the public catalogue cabinet, which may be referred to as *Card Inserting*.

2527:4:8 Card Inserting Work relating to the Technical Section to consists of the following annual jobs:

1 Redistributing the cards in the cabinet, so as to eliminate congestion in the trays, which may be referred to as *Cabinet Easing*; and

2 Making the necessary alterations in the guide cards, which may be referred to as *Guide Card Changing*.

2527:5 *Slip Inserting Work*

2527:5:5 Slips Inserting Work relating to the Technical Section is to consist of the following weekly jobs:

1 Sorting and arranging the slips in the proper sequence, which may be referred to as *Slips Arranging*; and
2 Inserting the slips in the appropriate cabinets in the proper sequence, which may be referred to as *Slips Inserting*.

2527:5:8 The Slips Inserting Work relating to the Technical Section is to consist of annual jobs similar to the annual jobs of the Card Inserting Work (see 2527:4:8).

253 Routine

2531 Classification

2531:1 *Preliminary Work*

2531:1:5 *Weekly jobs*

2531:1:54 Tallying

As soon as the volumes and the accession cards arrive from the Accession Section on the appointed day of the week, tally the volumes and the accession cards rapidly. If there is any discrepancy, get it settled with the Accession Section.

2531:1:55 Preliminary Sorting

As soon as the tallying is over, sort the volumes rapidly by their main classes. Unless the book is of a very elusive nature the main class can be readily fixed by a perusal of the title and the contents page and, if necessary, by turning through the pages rapidly.

While sorting, place on the title page of each volume a *Process Slip*.

Definition. By a Process Slip is meant a slip 5" × 3"—even a waste slip with one blank side will do. On this slip, the various notes indicated in the succeeding routines will have to be noted by the classifier for the guidance of the cataloguer. Ultimately these process slips will have to be used for preparing the monthly statement of amendments to the classification code and the cataloguing code, and destroyed thereafter.

Draw a vertical line dividing the length of the slip exactly into two parts. Reserve the left hand side for noting cross references. Divide the right hand half into three compartments by two horizontal lines. Use the first compartment to indicate class index entries, not requiring consolidation, the second to indicate cross reference index entries, and the third to indicate such of the series index entries or other book index entries or main entries or class index entries, as require consolidation of cards.[26]

2531:2 *Call Numbering Work*

2531:2:5 *Weekly jobs*

2531:2:51 Normal Volumes Call Numbering

As soon as the sorting is over, decide the class number of the volumes one by one. If any volume is elusive and requires detailed study, or appears to call for the creation of a new class either by interpolation or by one of the Devices,[27] put it aside temporarily in the group of deferred volumes. In the case of the normal volumes, fix the call number and write it on the leading line of the process slip. Remember to amplify the call number by the appropriate Collection Symbol wherever necessary (see introduction to Chapter 28.) Examine the main slips representing the books already in the library having the same ultimate class as the book on hand and see if the assigning of the class number is consistent with the old placings. At the same time, if there is already any catalogue slip with the same ultimate class and the same book number as the volume on hand, add the appropriate digit as the accession part[28] of the book number.

If there is any lack of consistency, it is better to bring the related books and compare them with the volume on hand and decide the class number.

As soon as you arrive at the most satisfactory Call Number for the book, write the call number along with the Collection Number, if any, at the verso of the title page, just half an inch below its central line, or if that place happens to be printed over, put it as near that place as possible. If the book has no title page, write his number at the top of the first page, leaving space for at least two lines between the top edge of the book and the call number.

Fill up the process slip as fully as possible.

As the call numbering of the normal volumes proceeds, pass them on by instalments to the cataloguer through the reviser.

Remember that all the books brought for perusing should be

returned promptly to the replacing shelf. Otherwise, you may be probably depriving some reader of the use of those books.

2531:2:52 Deferred Volumes Call Numbering

After the Call Numbering has been done for all the normal volumes, study the deferred volumes. Make up your mind as to the best way of placing them. If you are satisfied with your placing of any such volume, proceed with it further as for normal volumes.

But remember to add a note in the process slip showing the peculiarities of the volume to which the special attention of the librarian should be drawn when the final reviewing work is done by him (see rule 2537:2:51). In such cases, the consultation with the librarian stands postponed to the stage of finally reviewing the classification and cataloguing work.

2531:2:53 Classification Consulting

If, however, you are not satisfied with your placing, or if you think that a new class is to be opened either by interpolation or by the aid of any device, take all such volumes to the librarian at the appointed hour on the appointed day of the week. Discuss them with him before proceeding further.

2531:2:54 Difficult Volumes Call Numbering

After the discussion with the librarian is over, proceed to give them call numbers, in the light of the decision arrived at with the librarian, in the same manner as for normal volumes. But remember to write out, in the proper place in the process slip, the new classes opened, if any. If any new rule is framed, note it in the monthly statement.

2531:2:55 Sources Noting

If you have to make use of any source, outside the volume classified and outside the common reference books, in fixing the class number or the book number of the volume, note down in a 5″×3″ slip, the call number of the volume in the leading line, the call number of the source in the second line, the heading of the source in the third line, its short title in the fourth line, and the exact page reference in the last line. File all such source slips then and there in the *Source Slips Tray* in a classified sequence.

The time spent in writing and filing such source slips is well spent. It will save, in the future, many difficulties and much time in referring to the source. It is our experience that a neglect of this apparently trivial detail would lead in the long run to much waste of time and sometimes even to inconsistency in classification and cataloguing work.

2531:2:56 NEW CLASSES NOTING

On the appointed day of the week, immediately after the process slips are removed from the volumes, but just before handing the volumes over to the Maintenance Section, take out all the process slips in which new classes are entered and note down in pencil all the new classes in your interleaved copy of the classification code. Similarly note down all the amendments to the cataloguing rules in your interleaved copy of the cataloguing code.

File all such process slips for use in the preparation of the monthly statement of amendments to the classification code and the cataloguing code. All the other process slips may be destroyed immediately.

2531:4 *Detection Work*

2531:4:1 *Immediate jobs*

2531:4:14 DETECTION NOTIFYING

In the course of the Classification Work, be as vigilant as possible to detect any possible unintended duplication of volumes. As soon as you spot out such a duplication, take the book and the related accession card to the Accession Section and explain the matter to that section. Leave the volume and the card, if necessary, in their hands and proceed with your work. Do similarly, if you happen to detect any defect in the volumes.

2531:8 *Checking Work*

2531:8:5 *Weekly jobs*

2531:8:51 CALL NUMBER CHECKING

The reviser should check the call numbers assigned by the classifier to the volumes, before they reach the cataloguer or at any rate before the cataloguer writes out the call numbers in the different cards.

To eliminate unnecessary waste of time on the part of the cataloguer, it may be a good policy for the cataloguer to write out the catalogue cards without the call number, until the reviser has made sufficient progress with his work, and to come back to such cards and fill in the call numbers after the revising work is over.

If the reviser does not agree with the placing of any volume, he should discuss it with the classifier. If an agreement cannot be arrived at between them, the matter should be referred to the librarian.

2531:8:52 Cross Reference Checking

The reviser should check the correctness of the class number to which cross reference is made, the appropriateness of the cross reference in the light of the policy and practice of the library, and the accuracy of the reference.

2531:8:53 New Placings Checking

The reviser should pay special attention to the new classes opened either in consultation with the librarian or independently by the classifier. All such new placings should be critically examined with the aid of the related source slips and in the light of all the mnemonic and other features of the classification code. If you do not agree, discuss it with the classifier. If there is any difference of opinion, it must be referred to the librarian.

2532 Cataloguing

2532:1 *Preliminary Work*

2532:1:5 *Weekly jobs*

2532:1:51 Sorting

As the classified volumes arrive from the classifier through the reviser, sort them out according to their cataloguing difficulties. It is possible to recognise the following groups for this purpose:

1 Volumes which are in familiar languages and whose process slips do not indicate consolidation of cards, which may be

referred to as *Fresh Cards Group*;

2 Volumes which are in familiar languages and whose process slips indicate consolidation of cards, and periodical publications, which may be referred to as *Consoliddtion Group*;

3 Volumes in unfamiliar languages which do not require consolidation, which may be referred to as *Linguistic Fresh Card Group* ;

4 Volumes in unfamiliar languages, which require consolidation, which may be referred to as *Linguistic Consolidation Group*; and

5 Volumes which present unusual cataloguing peculiarities and which would probably involve amendments to the cataloguing code, which may be referred to as *Refractory Group.*

Apart from the volumes themselves, the process slips will indicate definitely the cases of consolidation. The necessary information will be found in the lowest compartment in the right half of the process slip.

It will be convenient to deal with the volumes in these groups one after another in the sequence given. But, if so inclined, cataloguers may, by way of variation, choose a few volumes alternately from these groups.

2532:2 *Fresh Card Writing Work*

2532:2:5 *Weekly jobs*

2532:2:51 MAIN CARD WRITING

First write the main card in accordance with the rules of the Catalogue Code.

2532:2:52 CROSS REFERENCE CARDS WRITING

Write out a cross reference card for each one of the cross reference entries indicated in the process slip.

2532:2:53 INDEX CARDS WRITING

Write out the index card for each one of the headings in accordance with the Catalogue Code, except that a fresh card is not to be written, if the heading has been indicated in the process slip, as one requiring consolidation of cards.[29]

2532:2:54 BACK OF MAIN CARD WRITING

Arrange the cross reference cards in a classified sequence and the index cards according to the type of the entry.

Copy on the back of the main card the cross references in the classified sequence and the headings of the index cards in the proper part in accordance with the Catalogue Code.[30]

2532:2:58 SHELF REGISTER CARD WRITING

Write out the shelf register card for each volume.

It is desirable that no deviation should be made from the principle, "one card, one volume" in writing out the shelf register cards.

All the cards written for a volume are to be placed along with the process slip on the title page and the volumes are thereafter to be transmitted to the reviser in instalments.

2532:3 *Cards Consolidation Work*

2532:3:5 *Weekly jobs*

2532:3:51 CONSOLIDATION CARDS PICKING

With the aid of the process slips found in the volumes of the consolidation group, pick out from the public catalogue the cards in which consolidation work is to be done. Arrange such cards in successive groups, all the cards relating to the same volume forming a group.

2532:3:53 CONSOLIDATING

Having written out the fresh cards necessary for each volume, write out the consolidated entries or make the necessary alterations in the already existing cards, as the case may be, in accordance with the rules of the Catalogue Code. As the work with a volume gets completed, pass it on to the reviser in the usual way with the cards and the process slip placed on the title page.

2532:4 *Refractory Cases Work*

2532:4:5 *Weekly jobs*

2532:4:51 REFRACTORY CASES CONSULTING

Study the peculiarities about each of the volumes in the refractory group. Make up your mind as to the best way of dealing with them and as to the amendments to the Catalogue Code, if any, which they suggest. Then, take them to the librarian and discuss them with him. After getting his final decision, write out the necessary catalogue cards and pass them on with the books to the reviser in the usual way.

2532:4:55 SOURCES NOTING

If the data for cataloguing had been taken from any source outside the book—this is likely to happen frequently in the case of periodical publications—prepare a source slip as indicated in rule 2531:2:55 and file it in the source slips tray.

2532:4:56 AMENDMENTS NOTING

If any amendments to the Catalogue Code are arrived at in the course of the week, note down all such amendments in your interleaved copy of the Catalogue Code. Put them also in the monthly statement of amendments.

2532:5 *Checking Work*

2532:55 *Weekly jobs*

2532:5:52 FRESH CARDS CHECKING

As the catalogued volumes are received from the cataloguer, the reviser is to check each of the cards on the title page of each volume. He is to pay special attention to the accuracy of the work—in the call number, in punctuation, in the use of capitals, and with regard to strict conformity to the Catalogue Code. He is also to examine if all the cards indicated in the process slip have been written out. He is also to tally the notes on the back of the main card with the other cards.

2532:5:53 CONSOLIDATED CARDS CHECKING

If the volume contains any consolidated card, the reviser is to examine with care if the consolidation work has been done in the proper style in accordance with the Catalogue Code.

2532:5:56 AMENDMENTS CHECKING

If any card discloses any deviation from the Catalogue Code, the reviser should examine if it had been done deliberately on account of the refractory nature of the volume; and if so, he should examine critically each amendment to the rule and satisfy himself if the amendment is properly worded, if it is not in conflict with any of the existing rules and if it is in conformity with the mnemonic features and the general spirit of the Catalogue Code. If he feels any doubt in the case of any of the amendments, he should discuss it with the cataloguer and if difference of opinion persists even after the discussion, he should refer the matter to the librarian.

As the checking work progresses, the checked volumes should be passed on to the typist in instalments for the typing work.

2532:6 *Typing Work*

2532:6:5 *Weekly jobs*

2532:6:51 FRESH SLIPS TYPING

Make the necessary number—two copies have already been suggested for ordinary libraries—of typescript copies of all the fresh cards except the shelf register cards. In the case of the main slip, remember to type the accession number of the volume at the bottom line, taking the accession number from the back of the title page of the volumes, as the accession number will not be found at this stage in either the main card or the shelf register card. It will be put in only at a later stage (see rule 2533:1:51).

Subsidiary Rule of the Madras University Library

If any volume is in any language other than the favoured language and further if it is neither a periodical publication nor a book belonging to the class "literature", type out an extra copy of the main card with the name of the language of the volume typed and underlined near the right hand top corner.

Such slips are grouped by languages and the slips in each language are arranged in a classified sequence.

This is found to be very convenient in watching the building up of the resources of the library in the different languages and particularly in connection with the consultation work with the experts at the book selection stage.

It has been found convenient to have the catalogue slips in pieces of four. Let us refer to each unit of four as a sheet. As the typing of the slips is over, the sheet should not be cut into slips.

The work of the reviser will be greatly facilitated if the sheets are left as they are on the title pages of the related volumes, unless a sheet relates to more than one volume, in which case it must be suitably cut.

2532:6:52 Consolidation Slips Picking

As soon as the fresh slips typing is over, for each consolidated card, as indicated in the process slips, pick out the related slips of the first as well as the second impression and place them in the *Consolidated Slips Box.*

2532:6:53 Slips Consolidating

Take the slips in the Consolidated Slips Box, carry out the necessary alterations and place the slips back in the Consolidated Slips Box; and put the box by the side of the volumes.

2532:6:56 Slips Checking

The reviser is to compare the fresh slips typed and also the consolidated slips with the related cards and carry out all the corrections. He is also to verify the accession numbers typed in the main slips with reference to the accession numbers written at the back of the title pages of the volumes.

After the checking and the necessary corrections are over, he should cut the catalogue sheets into slips and, without separating the first impression and the second impression slips from one another, arrange the slips in two collections. The first collection is to contain all the main slips, cross reference slips and language slips. The second collection is to contain all the index slips. In each collection, the slips relating to a volume are to be kept together. The two collections are to be put in the *Unsorted Slips Box.*

2533 Preparation of the Volumes

2533:1 *Card Numbering Work*

2533:1:5 *Weekly jobs*

2533:1:51 Accession Number Noting

As soon as the slips checking is over, proceed with each volume as follows:

Write out in the main card and the shelf register card the accession number of the volume, taking the accession number from the back of the title page of the volume.

2533:1:52 CALL NUMBER NOTING

Note the call number of the volume in its accession card, taking the call number from the back of the title page of the volume. After the call number is noted in the accession card, put it back in its place and turn it through a right angle in its own plane in the clockwise direction.

Then take out the bunch of cards on the title page of the volume and put it in the Unsorted Cards Box. The bunches for the successive volumes are to be put in successive sequences.

After the call number noting is done for all the volumes, examine if any accession card is lying in the box, without being turned through a right angle. If there is any such card, it means that the volume relating to it has not been dealt with. Trace out that volume, do the needful for it and bring it up to this stage.

2533:1:56 BOOK TICKET

Then, prepare a book ticket for the volume, taking the call number from the back of the title page and the short heading and the short title from the appropriate book index card. File all such book tickets in a classified sequence in the book tickets tray.

At this stage, pass on the volumes in instalments to the peon entrusted with the preparation work.

2533:2 *Preparation Work*

2533:2:5 *Weekly jobs*

Note: *In the case of the volumes which are proposed to be sent to the binder straightaway before being made available for use, no job of this work other than stamping need be done at this stage.*

2533:2:51 CUTTING OPEN

Take each volume and cut open the pages. Remember that in certain formats, the bottom edge may have to be cut open. After all the sheets are cut open, ease the back of the volume by opening it somewhere in the middle and placing it on a flat table and gently running your thumb from the top to the bottom along the inner margin and then working your way to the two covers, turning a few leaves at a time and similarly pressing. As the glue at the back of the volume is likely to have hardened, this easing work is to be done in a very careful and gentle way, so that the back of the book does not break.

The cutting open should be done only with a cutting bone. The temptation to use the finger or a pencil for this job should be strictly resisted. Such a practice will lead either to the blurring of the edge or to the sheets being torn irregularly sometimes even affecting the printed matter. It goes without saying that this cutting open work should be done for every sheet without exception, as otherwise it is likely to be cut open carelessly by the reader who comes across it. It may also happen that this discovery is made by the reader some years later. The impression, produced by finding a book not cut in a library for years, is damaging to the reputation of the library in several ways.

2533:2:52 Stamping

As soon as the cutting open is over, put the library stamp in the conventional places in the book.

Each library is to develop a convention for stamping. One possible convention is this : The top of the verso of the title page, the top of the first chapter or introduction, as the case may be, the bottom of the last page of the text, the bottom of the last page of the volume, the bottom of the last page of the first chapter which ends after the middle of the volume, each plate, map and any other sheet not included in pagination. In all cases, particular care should be taken to see that the library stamp does not fall upon any printed matter. Again, the stamp should be put in proper alignment. Putting it in a slovenly and slanting position produces a jarring effect on the mind.

2533:2:53 Tagging

After the stamping is over, stick up a tag on the back of the volume. If there is a jacket, it should be removed temporarily for this purpose and replaced after the tagging is over. The tag should be applied exactly one inch above the bottom of the book. It will be convenient to have a piece of metal, half an inch wide and bent at right angles with each of the arms exactly one inch long, to mark out the position for applying the tag.

If the volume is too thin to have the tag on its back, fix it on the front cover close to the back and adjacent to the position it should have had on the back.

2533:2:55 Pocket Fixing

If book-pocket is in use, fix it near right-hand bottom corner of the inside of the front cover of the volume.

2533:2:56 Date Labelling

Fix the date label to the volume. The date label is to be gummed only along the left edge and fixed on the very first page after the cover, whether that page is an end paper or the half title page or the title page or, as it occasionally happens in the case of Indian books, the contents page or the first page of the text. Care must be taken to fix the date label so that its edges are exactly parallel to the edges of the volume. Again, if the size of the date label is smaller than the size of the volume, the date label should be fixed symmetrically except that the pasting done should be only along the left edge of the page. If the size of the date label is bigger than that of the volume, the date label should be reduced to the size of the page.

The jobs involved in the preparation work may perhaps be best done one after the other. As soon as all the jobs are over, the volumes are to be passed on to the next stage, viz volumes numbering work.

2533:3 *Volumes Numbering Work*

Note: *It will be convenient to take the call numbers and the accession numbers for the numbering work, mentioned hereunder, from the accession cards. It will be very inconvenient to take these numbers from the back of the title page as it involves turning through the pages, carrying the numbers in one's head during this process. Remember to copy the sequence symbols also.*

2533:3:5 *Weekly jobs*

2533:3:51 Jacket Numbering

If the volume has a jacket, write the call number in ink on the jacket at a place corresponding approximately to the position of the tag, or as near it as possible, if that position is not blank. If the colour of the jacket does not admit of writing with black ink, use red ink or paste a tag on the jacket and write on it.

The presence of the jacket on the book has got a pleasing effect. One feels like reading a new book, only if the book has a jacket on. Of course, the jacket will wear out after the book passes through the hands of half a dozen readers. But, till then, the jacket will act as a symbol of freshness in the minds of the readers. Further, when the books come to the shelf, the presence of the jacket is in many cases an index that it is a recent addition and the Reference Section finds it a good help in spotting out new additions for helping the readers. That is why the labour of writing the call number on this ephemeral jacket is advocated. The jacket may also be preserved by covering it with a transparent material.

2533:3:52 Inside Numbering

Write in pencil the accession number and the call number on a conventional page somewhere in the inside of the volume.

A convenient convention may be as follows:

1 The end of that chapter which ends earliest after the fiftieth page, provided it is not the last page of the volume;
2 If such a page is not available in any volume, the bottom margin of the verso of the middle sheet of the volume. The volume is likely to be a pamphlet in most of such cases.

2533:3:53 Tag Numbering

Write the call number alone in ink on the tag on the back or on the cover of the volume, the class number and the book number being written in different lines, one below the other. Prudence will require that these numbers should be written at the centre of the tag, leaving the maximum possible margin all round so that later corrections may be carried out in that tag itself.

2533:3:56 Date Label Numbering

Write out in ink the accession number and the call number in the appropriate places in the date label.

2533:8 *Prepared Volumes Arranging Work*

2533:8:5 *Weekly jobs*

2533:8:51 Sorting

As soon as the volumes numbering work is over, sort the prepared volumes by their collections. The sequence to which a given volume belongs will be indicated by the presence of an appropriate conventional symbol in association with call number (see Introduction to Chapter 28 for the meaning and significance of the word collection). Remember to form a separate collection of all the volumes that are to be sent straight away to the binder before being made available for public use.

Take away all the process slips from the volumes and put them in the process slips box in the classified sequence, ignoring the collection number.

2533:8:52 Arranging

Arrange the volumes in each collection by their call numbers. The volumes will be in this sequence until the Maintenance Section takes charge of them.

2533:8:56 Book Ticket Disposing

Insert the appropriate book tickets in the book pockets of the different volumes. Immediately after the insertion, compare the accession number and the call number in the book ticket with the accession number and the call number in the date label, or if there is no date label, with that on the back of the title page. If, however, a book ticket is not found in a book, it would mean that the book is to be sent to the bindery before being sent to the shelf. Insert the book cards of such books in the *Binding Sequence Book Tickets Tray* in the classified sequence. These book tickets will be transferred to the Maintenance Section and the Maintenance Section will insert them in the book pockets of the related volumes, when the volumes come back from the bindery.

2534 Correction of Call Numbers and Catalogue Entries

2534:1 *Preliminary Work*

2534:1:5 *Weekly jobs*

2534:1:51 Maintenance Section Notifying

On the appointed day of the week, collect all the volumes whose call numbers and catalogue entries require to be corrected in the course of the week. Place the volumes on the shelf register cabinet, as the last piece of work in the day.

2534:1:52 Correction Volumes Accepting

On the next day, by about 12 noon, the Maintenance Section would have transferred the shelf register cards of the selected books from their normal places to the correction collection. On getting intimation from the Maintenance Section that this routine is over, take charge of the volumes from the Maintenance Section.

2534:1:53 Main Card Picking

For each of the volumes brought up for correction, pick out the main card from the public catalogue cabinet and also the first impression main slip from the classifier's set of the catalogue. Couple the main card and the main slip of each volume and place all such coupled cards and slips in the *Correction Box* in the classified sequence.

2534:2 *Reclassification Work*

2534:2:5 *Weekly jobs*

2534:2:51 Call Number Revising

Take out each volume and after a careful perusal of the same, if it is necessary to alter the call number, make the alteration in the call number written on the back of the title page. Do like this for each of the volumes.

2534:2:52 New Call Number Checking

After all the volumes have been reclassified or as they are being reclassified, whichever is convenient, get the new call numbers checked by some other member.

2534:2:53 MAIN CARD CORRECTING

After the checking of the new call number is over, carry out the corrections in the main card and the main slip of each volume. As soon as this is over, rearrange the coupled main cards and slips in the classified sequence according to the new call numbers.

2534:2:58 CORRECTED VOLUMES TRANSMITTING

As soon as the revision of the call number is over, fill up the correction diary and transmit the volumes to the Maintenance Section. Enter in the Transmission Register the number of volumes so transmitted and, as soon as it comes back, examine if it has received the initials of the head of the Maintenance Section in token of his having received the volumes.

2534:3 *First Impression Slips Work*

2534:3:5 *Weekly jobs*

2534:3:51 FIRST IMPRESSION SLIPS PICKING

With the aid of the entries on the back of the main card, pick out all the first impression slips other than the main ones, relating to each of the corrected volumes. All the slips relating to a volume are to be kept together behind the main card, in the *Slips Correction Box*.

2534:3:52 FIRST IMPRESSION SLIPS CORRECTING

Carry out all the necessary corrections in the first impression slips.

2534:3:53 FIRST IMPRESSION SLIPS ARRANGING

Collect together all the first impression slips including the main slips. Sort them and arrange them in the proper sequence, i e the main slips and the cross reference slips in the classified sequence and the index slips in the alphabetic sequence.

2534:4 *Correction Completing Work*

2534:4:5 *Weekly jobs*

2534:4:51 CARDS CORRECTING

Take the Slips Correction Box to the public catalogue cabinet and carry out the corrections in all the cards corresponding to the slips in the Slips Correction Box.

2534:4:52 Second Impression Slips Correcting

Take the Slips Correction Box to the second impression slips cabinet and carry out the corrections in the second impression slips corresponding to the slips in the Slips Correction Box.

2534:4:53 Language Slips Correcting

Take the Slips Correction Box to the language slips cabinet and carry out the corrections in the language slips relating to the main slips in the Slips Correction Box.

2534:5 *Reinsertion Work*

2534:5:5 *Weekly jobs*

2534:5:51 Main Cards Reinserting

After all the corrections are over, reinsert all the corrected main cards in the classified part of the public catalogue cabinet in their proper places.

2534:5:52 First Impression Slips Reinserting

After the main cards are reinserted, reinsert all the corrected first impression slips in their proper places in the first impression slips cabinet.

2535 Binding

2535:5 *Weekly job*

2535:51 Call Number Examining

Examine each of the volumes picked out by the Maintenance Section for binding in the course of the week and transmitted to the Technical Section for scrutiny of call number. Verify the call number in accordance with the routine set down under "2531:2 Call Numbering Work". If there is need for correction, go through all the routines set down under "2534 Correction of Call Numbers and Catalogue Entries"

2535:6 *Monthly jobs*

2535:62 Binding Slip Preparing

For each volume awaiting to be bound, prepare a binding slip. Put down in succession the different items to be tooled on the back the book, viz the short title, the surname of the author, or other heading, the volume number in the case of multivolumed books, the volume number and the year in the case of periodical publications, and the call number. Place the slips in sequence in the *Binding Slips Box*.

2535:65 BINDING BOOKS TRANSMITTING

On the appointed day of the month, transmit the volumes and the binding slips to the Binding Section.

2536 CLASSIFICATION AND CATALOGUE CODES

2536:5 *Weekly jobs*

2536:51 CODE CORRECTING

On the appointed day of the week, with the help of the process slips in the Process Slips Box (see routine 2533:8:51), verify the alterations, made in the Classification and Catalogue Codes in the interleaved copies of your section and carry out the corrections, in pencil, in the interleaved copies of the librarian.

2536:52 MONTHLY AMENDMENT STATEMENT FILLING

Make a list of all such amendments in the book of monthly statement of corrections.

2536:6 *Monthly jobs*

2536:63 CODE CORRECTIONS TRANSMITTING

Transmit the monthly statement of corrections to the Staff Council both for discussion and for the information of the other Sections. After the meeting of the Staff Council, hand over the monthly statement to the Secretary of the Staff Council, who will circulate it to the concerned sections for incorporation in the interleaved copies of the respective Sections.

2537 CATALOGUE CABINET

2537:1 *Sorting Work*

2537:1:5 *Weekly jobs*

2537:1:51 CATALOGUE CARDS SORTING

Take out all the catalogue cards in the Unsorted Cards Box

and sort and arrange them in accordance with the rules bearing on the subject.[31] Remember that no account need be taken of the collection numbers in this sorting. Place the sorted cards in the arranged sequence in the Sorted Cards Box.

2537:1:52 Shelf Register Cards Arranging

Arrange the shelf register cards in the Unsorted Cards Box in the classified sequence overlooking the collection numbers if any.

2537:1:53 Accession Number Tallying

Take each one of the shelf register cards in the proper sequence. Compare the accession number written on it with the accession number written on the related main card. If there is any discrepancy, get it set right by a reference to the back of the title page of the related volume. After tallying the accession numbers, file the shelf register cards in the classified sequence in the Sorted Cards Box behind all the catalogue cards.

2537:1:58 Technical Section Counting

As soon as the accession number tallying is over, count the number of volumes catalogued in different subjects and the cards written; and post the figures in the diaries concerned.

2537:2 *Reviewing Work*

2537:2:5 *Weekly jobs*

2537:2:51 Catalogue Cards Discussing

Take the Sorted Cards Box and the Process Slips Box to the librarian at the appointed hour on the appointed day of the week for the final reviewing work. Remember to bring to the special notice of the librarian such of the points as you might have noted in the process slip as requiring discussion. Note down the results of the discussion, particularly if any alterations are to be made, either mentally or, if they are too many or too difficult, in the related process slips.

2537:2:52 Correction Carrying Out

After the discussion with the librarian is over, carry out all the corrections, arrived at in the course of the discussion, in all the necessary places; examine in particular whether any of the following require correction—back of the title page, the interior of the book, the date label, the tag, the jacket, the shelf register card, the accession card, the book card and the different catalogue cards. It is not meant that a correction will necessarily arise in all these cases. One should remember these cases and satisfy oneself whether any of them require correction or not.

2537:2:55 Suggestion Transmitting

In the discussion with the librarian, various points may arise affecting the other Sections, e.g. the Book Selection Section may have to be asked to take steps to acquire some related volumes, such as those belonging to a multivolumed series or a publisher's series or even independent volumes. The Periodical Publication Section may have to be advised about the idiosyncrasies of the periodical publications. The Accession Section may have to be advised about special points in accessioning work. The attention of the Reference Section may have to be invited to certain volumes. The Binding Section may have to be given certain special instructions.

Transmit all such suggestions to the Sections concerned, orally or in writing, according to the nature of the suggestion.

2537:3 *Accession Cards Transmitting Work*

2537:3:5 *Weekly jobs*

2537:3:51 Shelf Register Cards Coupling

After the final reviewing work is over, pass the Catalogue Cards Box on to the next stage, namely Card Inserting Work, after removing all the shelf register cards from it. Couple each shelf register card, with its related accession card, placing the shelf register card behind the accession card.

2537:3:53 Shelf Register Card Checking

While coupling the shelf register card with the accession card, tally the accession number in the shelf register card with that in the accession card. If they do not agree, refer to the related volume and make the necessary corrections in the shelf register card or the accession card, as the case may be, and examine also the accession number in the related main card and if it requires any correction, carry it out.

After the accession numbers are reconciled, arrange the coupled accession cards and shelf register cards in the sequence of the accession numbers in the Transmission Box.

2537:3:58 COUPLED CARDS TRANSMITTING

After the checking of the shelf register cards is over, examine if each accession card has a shelf register card coupled with it. While doing so, examine also if the accession cards are all there in the proper sequence, from the first to the last number due to be in the batch. If there is any discrepancy, investigate and set it right. Then, hand over the Transmission Box containing the coupled cards to the head of the Maintenance Section.

2537:4 *Cards Inserting Work*

2537:4:5 *Weekly job*

2537:4:51 CARD INSERTING

Take the Sorted Cards Box, which will now contain only the catalogue cards, to the catalogue cabinet. Insert the cards in the proper places in the cabinet.

If in the course of insertion any discrepancy is brought to notice, get it set right. Here are some of the types of discrepancies that may be discovered:

1 Two main cards may have exactly the same call number; in that case the book number will have to be amplified or corrected in the accession part of the book number in the new main card and the consequential alteration made in all necessary places.

2 A class index card or a cross reference index card may happen to be a mere duplicate of an already existing card; in that case, the new card may have to be discarded.

3 A class index card or a book index card may be such that it can be consolidated with an already existing card; in that case, the necessary consolidation may have to be made.

2537:4:8 *Annual jobs*

2537:4:81 CABINET EASING

Periodically—say, once in a year—examine whether there is too much congestion in any of the trays of the public catalogue cabinet.

If there is, redistribute the cards allowing sufficient space in each tray for at least a year's growth. In distributing the cards, it will be convenient, if as far as practicable, each tray is made to contain a definite set of cards, say a particular class or a particular alphabet and so on. In other words, do not split between two consecutive trays a set of cards which are more conveniently kept together.

When such redistribution takes place, remember to change the tray labels appropriately. There can be nothing more annoying than a tray being adorned by an old label, which no longer describes correctly the contents of the tray.

2537:4:82 Guide Card Changing

It will be a good practice to review the guide cards in the public catalogue cabinet once in a year. New guide cards might be necessary or experience might have shown that the existing guide cards require to be changed.

2537:5 *Slip Inserting Work*

2537:5:5 *Weekly jobs*

2537:5:51 Slips Arranging

Take out all the slips lying in the Unsorted Slips Box without separating the slips of the first impression from those of the second impression. In other words, treat the two slips together as one unit. Arrange them in the proper sequence. After the arrangement is over, take out all the second impression slips and arrange them separately in the same sequence as the first impression slips.

2537:5:52 Slips Inserting

Insert the first impression slips in the first impression cabinet, i.e. the cabinet of the Technical Section. Insert also the second impression slips in the second impression cabinet, i e the cabinet of the librarian. Remember all the points mentioned under routine 2537:4:51 while inserting the slips.

2537:5:8 *Annual jobs*

Carry out for the first impression cabinet and for the

second impression cabinet all the routines mentioned under 2537:4:81.

Elimination of Waste

2541 Organisation

If the turnover in the section demands the assignment of several members to it, it may be an advantage to specialise them in different items of work such as classification, cataloguing, typing the catalogue slips, preparing the volumes for public use and revision. In large libraries where several members are assigned to each of these items of work, it may be an advantage to have the different classifiers specialise in different subjects and the different cataloguers specialise in different languages. The revising staff may be divided into two groups, one for revising the classification and the other for revising the catalogue entries. The members of these two groups should be made to specialise in the same way as classifiers and cataloguers.

2542 Head of the Section

The Head of the Section should personally attend to all amendments to the Classification Code and the Catalogue Code. He should also review the catalogue cards every week. He should develop the necessary flair to detect mistakes in classification as well as inaccuracy in cataloguing at sight.

2543 Eye for Detection of Mistakes

The call numbers and the accession numbers of each volume have to be written in many places—in the volumes, in the catalogue cards, shelf register cards and accession cards. Absolute accuracy is necessary in copying them out. Even the slightest mistake will give much trouble at any moment later on. Hence, the Head of the Section should develop a very keen eye to detect mistakes even of the slightest nature in the copying of call numbers.

2544 Punctual Release of Books

It must be a matter of honour to the Technical Section to release the publications for public use in strict conformity with the time-table. Occasionally elusive books may turn up. In such cases, the Technical Section should put int he necessary extra work and strive to release the volumes punctually at the appointed hour.

2545 Three Diaries

The Technical Section is to maintain three diaries on a weekly basis.

2546 Volumes Diary

The first diary may be called the *Volumes Diary*. Its column headings are to be the symbols for the main divisions of the classification scheme used, or any modification of the same, and in addition "Total number of volumes". In each week the number of volumes finally dealt with by the section is to be noted in this diary.

2547 Type of Cards Diary

The second diary may be called the *Type of Cards Diary*. Its headings are to be 1 shelf register cards, 2 main cards, 3 cross reference main cards, 4 index cards, 5 cross reference index cards, 6 total, 7 the number of periodical publication cards consolidated, 8 the number of other cards consolidated, and 9 the total number of cards consolidated.

2548 Correction Diary

The third diary may be called the *Correction Diary*. Its column headings are to be similar to those of the Volumes Diary.

255 Correlation table

1 *Book Selection Section*

2537:2:55 Suggestion transmitting.

3 *Periodical Publication Section*

2535:62 Binding slip preparing;
2537:2:55 Suggestion transmitting.

4 *Accession Section*

2531:1:54 Tallying;

2531:4:14 Detection notifying;
2535:62 Binding slip preparing;
2537:2:55 Suggestion transmitting.

6 *Circulation Section*

2533:2:55 Pocket fixing;
2533:2:56 Date label numbering.

7 *Reference Section*

2537:2:55 Suggestion transmitting.

8 *Maintenance Section*

2533:2:53 Tagging;
2533:3:51 Jacket numbering;
2533:3:53 Tag numbering;
2533:8:5 All the weekly jobs of prepared volumes arranging work (Wednesday 4 P M);
2534:1:51 Shelf section notifying;
2534:1:52 Correction volumes accepting;
2534:2:58 Corrected volumes transmitting (Wednesday 12 noon);
2535:62 Binding slip preparing.

93 *Staff Council*

2536:61 Code corrections transmitting.

995 *Binding Section*

2535:62 Binding slip preparing;
2535:65 Binding books transmitting;
2537:2:55 Suggestion transmitting.

256:5 *Weekly jobs*

Saturday

2531:1:5 All the weekly jobs of preliminary work (Periodical publications, 12 noon);
2531:2:5 All the weekly jobs of call numbering work (Periodical publications);
2532:1:51 Sorting (Books);
2532:2:5 All the weekly jobs of fresh card writing work (Books);

2534:1:5 All the weekly jobs of preliminary work;
2534:2:5 All the weekly jobs of reclassification work.

Sunday

2531:8:5 All the weekly jobs of checking work (Periodical publications);
2532:2:5 All the weekly jobs of fresh card writing work (Books);
2531:2:54 Difficult volumes call numbering;
2532:4:51 Refractory cases consulting;
2532:6:5 All the weekly jobs of typing work.

Monday

2532:6:5 All the weekly jobs of typing work;
2531:1:5 All the weekly jobs of preliminary work (Books, 5 PM);
2532:3 All the weekly jobs of refractory cases work, except, 2532:4:51;
2532:5:5 All the weekly jobs of checking work (Cataloguing).

Tuesday

2532:6:5 All the weekly jobs of typing work;
2531:2:5 All the weekly jobs of call numbering work (Books) except;
2531:2:54 Difficult volumes call numbering;
2537:2:5 All the weekly jobs of reviewing work;
2533 All the items of work in the involved preparation of the volumes for public use;
2536:51 Code correcting;
2537:1:5 All the weekly jobs of sorting work.

Wednesday

2532:1:51 Sorting (Periodical publications);
2532:2:5 All the weekly jobs of fresh card writing work (Periodical publications);
2532:3:5 All the weekly jobs of card consolidation work;
2533:8 Prepared volumes arranging work (12 noon);
2535:51 Call number examining;
2531:2:5 All the weekly jobs of call numbering work;

2537:3:5 All the weekly jobs of accession cards transmitting work (11 A M);
2537:4:51 Card inserting;
2537:5 All the weekly jobs of slip inserting work.

Thursday

2531:8:5 All the weekly jobs of checking work (Classification);
2534:3:4 All the weekly jobs of first impression slips work;
2534:4:5 All the weekly jobs of correction completing work;
2534:5:5 All the weekly jobs of reinsertion work.

Monthly jobs

Penultimate Tuesday

2535:6 Binding books transmitting.

Last Wednesday

2536:61 Code correction transmitting.

Annual jobs

June

2537:4:8 All the annual jobs of card inserting work.

July

2537:5:8 All the annual jobs of slip inserting work.

257 Forms and Registers

The Technical Section has no forms and registers except the catalogue cards. It is a matter of opinion whether the catalogue cards and pads are to be considered merely as stationery or as forms. But as they are to be specially ruled, I am inclined to call them forms. The description of these forms is given in books on cataloguing. It is enough if we assign numbers to them here.

The white cards may be given the number C51.

The cross reference cards, usually coloured, may be given the number C52.

The guide cards may be given the number C53.

The catalogue pad may be given the number S51.

258 Files

As this section has no correspondence, it has no files to keep, except the files relating to "2591 Outward enquiries" and "2592 Inward enquiries" for which the details are similar to the correspondence files in the other sections.

CHAPTER 26

CIRCULATION SECTION

261 Planning

2611 PARAMOUNT PURPOSE OF THE LIBRARY

In the *Five laws of library science*,[32] it has been stated "That in libraries books are collected for **Use**, kept for **Use** and served for **Use**. The endless technical processes and routine—getting suggestions from experts, acquiring by purchase or gift, accessioning, classifying, cataloguing, shelf-registering, shelving, charging and discharging—all these are carried on only **For Use**. To fulfil this paramount mission of the First Law to the fullest extent, the Library Staff should not only remind themselves of that mission constantly, not only acquire the scholarship and professional training necessary, but also develop certain attitudes and interests which are equally indispensable."

26111 CONTACT WITH READERS

While thus a library exists to get the books used by readers, it is only two Sections of the library staff that normally come in contact with the readers, viz the Reference Section and the Circulation Section. Of these the Reference Section is in charge of the academic side of bringing readers and books together. The Circulation Section, on the other hand, is in complete charge of the mechanics of the use of the books by the readers. At least some of the readers may use the resources of the library without coming into contact with the Reference Section. But no reader can escape coming into relation with the Circulation Section, at least twice on every occasion he visits the library. Thus, it is the performance and attitude of the Circulation Section that largely makes or mars the reputation of a library, in one respect.

26112 COURTEOUS SENTINEL

The counter is the Rubicon and the Circulation Section forms in a sense, the sentinels who watch and regulate the ingress and the egress of the users of the library. While the Circulation Section should have all the circumspection, the loyalty and the precision of a sentinel, it should remember that it is not in the employ of the military department, but of the humane library department. The Circulation Section should know how to be courteous without being lax, to be strict without being offensive, and to be friendly without being chatty.

26113 Extreme Vigilance

The responsibility of the Circulation Section is particularly heavy in open access libraries. It is to be remembered that in an open access library, things are to be so arranged that nobody can come in or go out except with the consent and surveillance of the Circulation Section and that no book or material can get out of the library without the permission or the connivance of the Circulation Section. For, an open access library implies *extreme vigilance* at the entrance and the exit and *extreme freedom* in the inside of the library for all readers.

2612 Counter Equipment

While the Circulation Section should take up all the responsibilities for the safety of the resources of the library, the library authorities should not stint, or cause any delay, in getting the counter arrangement, particularly the wicket-gate arrangement, as perfect and efficient as necessary. Any breakdown in the counter equipment should be immediately set right, without the interference of any red-tape procedure.

2613 Variety of Functions

In addition to playing the role of sentinels, the Circulation Section have to maintain all the records relating to each one of the thousands of users of the library. It is the Circulation Section that should admit users as members, and deal with the withdrawal of membership; it is the Circulation Section that should keep all the records relating to loan of books; it is the Circulation Section that should remind members about overdue books; it is the Circulation Section that should collect the dues from the members; it is the Circulation Section that should take charge of the volumes returned after consultation by users; and it is the Circulation Section that is to manage the entire work of interlibrary loan.

2614 Theory of Issue Method

The main work entrusted to the Circulation Section is the issue work. It is not proposed to deal with the theory or the history of issue methods in this manual. For the general foundations of the theory of issue methods, a reference may be made to my *Five laws of library science.*[33] However, the result of the discussion in the *Five laws* may be summarised here for ready reference as follows:

Lightning speed and absolute accuracy should characterise the work of the Circulation Section. Speed is imposed by the Fourth Law. To secure speed and accuracy, the library profession has devoted a good deal of thought during the last three generations and has continuously improved the issue methods. A detailed history of this attempt of the library profession will throw much light on the earnestness of the library profession in satisfying the laws of library science.

2615 "Reader's Ticket, Book Ticket" Method

In this chapter we go into the routine related to "Reader's Ticket, Book Ticket" method of issuing. In this method, each volume in the library has a small Book Ticket in the form of a pocket, put inside the pocket formed at the bottom of the date label by folding it over and pasting down the edges. This ticket gives the call number of the book, the accession number, its author and its title. Each borrower is provided with as many reader's tickets as the number of volumes he is entitled to have on loan at a time. This ticket is of a size that it can be inserted into the book ticket. The book has a date label pasted on the very first page. Issuing the book will consist of stamping the due date on the date label, putting a reader's ticket in the book ticket of the book, and putting this out of the pocket in the date label. The coupled book ticket and reader's ticket will be filed in the sequence of the call numbers, in the "*Charged Tray*" behind the date guide, showing the date not later than which the book is to be returned to the library. This Charged Tray will furnish all the information that a charging system may be expected to give.

When the book is returned, the call number of the book and the due date stamp on its date label help the Discharging Staff to locate the related book ticket in the Charged Tray. Then the coupled book ticket and reader's ticket are taken out. The book ticket is inserted in the pocket in the date label of the book and the ticket is handed over to the borrower.

The full details of this system and the various subsidiary functions necessarily to be performed by the Circulation Section are fully dealt with in this chapter.

2616 Periodicity

From the nature of the work, it can be seen that most of the jobs of the Circulation Section are of the "immediate" type. What is left over, will have to be rounded off on a daily basis. In this matter, the work of the Circulation Section differs from the work of the other Sections, as the week is a more convenient unit of time for them.

2617 Conscience Box

Near the entrance wicket-gate, there should be a Conscience Box—a locked box with a small slit in its lid as we have in temples to collect offerings—into which the members who have delayed the return of books beyond the due date may drop their overdue charges. It should have glass sides. After practising the Victorian method of formally collecting the overdue charges with formal notice, issue of formal receipt and maintenance of separate accounts, libraries have learnt that ;

1 the game is not worth the candle, and
2 a splendid opportunity for the development of civic conscience is thereby being lost.

The Conscience Box Method is now adopted even for the collection of bus-fares in America. Our libraries should straightaway begin with trust in this manner. Trust will beget trust.

26171 Not a Source of Revenue

It must be borne in mind that Overdue Charge is not to be taken as a source of revenue for the library. Its purpose is only to act as a delicate help in chastening the conscience of the reader to make him respect the Rules of the Library. This purpose is achieved better if the Overdue Charge is deposited voluntarily without the formalities of demanding and receipting as in revenue collection. A gentle and polite suggestion of the amount due as overdue charge may be necessary in some cases. The majority of the members will do the needful without even that suggestion. No doubt, an exceptional person may occasionally abuse this freedom and trust. It is enough if he is watched and helped out of the abuse. All the other normal persons need not be subjected to the vulgarity of demand and receipting.

26172 Game Not Worth the Candle

The cost of collection, 5 naye paise, as overdue charge exceeds that value, if overdue-registering, demanding, receipting in duplicate, etc are to be gone through involving the time of the Circulation Section, the Librarian, the Accounts Section, the Central Office, and later on, the Audit. The Library Authorities and the Audit Authorities should rationalise this affair and agree to the introduction of the Conscience Box Method on grounds of real economy and valuable promotion of civic sense among readers.

2618 Factors in Planning

The distinctive work of the Circulation Section is to be planned with reference to the following factors:

1 The users of the resources of the library;
2 The resources of the library; and
3 The co-operating libraries.

2611 Users

The users of the library fall into the following classes :

1 Persons entitled to borrow the resources of the library for study outside the library premises, who may be referred to as *Members*;
2 Persons entitled to the use of the resources of the library within the library premises only, who may be referred to as *Consultants*;
3 Persons entitled to the use of the resources of the library even within the library premises only on special permit, who may be referred to as *Special Permit Holders*;
4 Groups of persons using the resources of the library

co-operatively in groups, who may be referred to as *Study Groups*;

5 Persons not entitled to any use of the library, who may be referred to as *Ineligibles*; and

6 Persons not yet assigned to any of the other classes, who may be referred to as *Enquirers*.

26111 Members

The members of the library fall into the following classes:

1 Ordinary members;
2 Contingent members; and
3 Members with special privileges.

261111 *Ordinary Members*

Ordinary members are members who are not contingent members or members with special privileges.

261112 *Contingent Members*

Contingent members are members whose membership is contingent on certain definite factors, such as:

1 Residence;
2 Relationship to other persons or institutions; and
3 Time limit.

261112i Membership dependent upon residence within prescribed limits may be referred to as *Geographically Contingent Membership*.

2611125 Membership, which would expire as soon as the relationship to certain persons or institutions ceases, may be referred to as *Relationally Contingent Membership*.

2611126 Membership, which would expire at the end of a definite period of time, may be referred to as *Chronologically Contingent Membership*.

261113 *Members with Special Privileges*

Members with special privileges are members who are entitled to special privileges in accordance with the rules.

Subsidiary Rules of the Madras University Library

The following are the special privileges in accordance with the rules of the library:

1 Privilege to borrow more than three volumes at a time, which may be referred to as *Extra Volumes Privilege*;
2 Privilege to borrow bound volumes of periodicals, which may be referred to as *Periodicals Privilege*;
3 Privilege to borrow loose numbers and bound volumes of periodical and more than three volumes at a time, which may be referred to as *Department Privilege*, as this privilege is allowed only to the research departments of the University;
4 Privilege to get books delivered at the residence, which may be referred to as *Home Delivery Privilege*;
5 Privilege to borrow from the library occasionally without deposit, which may be referred to as *Government Privilege*, as the privilege is allowed only to government departments; and
6 Exemption from the educational or other qualifications, which may be referred to as *Research Privilege*, as this privilege is allowed only to those who are certified to be engaged in research or advanced study.

2612 Resources

From the point of view of the Circulation Section, the resources of the library fall into the following classes:

31 Volumes returned at the counter by the users;
33 Oft used reference books kept at the counter, books kept in the text-book reading room, and issued on demand for use within the library premises;
34 Bespoken books;
4 Volumes lost or damaged by the users; and
5 Volumes not in library but to be borrowed from some co-operating library.

2615 Co-operating Libraries

Co-operating libraries are libraries, public or private, which have the privilege of interlibrary loan with the library and they may be looked upon as:

1 Libraries which have the privilege of borrowing, in which connection they may be referred to as *Borrowing Libraries*; and
2 Libraries which have the privilege of lending, in which connection they may be referred to as *Lending Libraries.*

262 Job Analysis

2621 Users

The work of the Circulation Section relating to users in general may consist of the following items:

1 Work relating to the entrance of users into the library, which may be referred to as *Entrance Work*;
2 Work relating to the exit of users from the library, which may be referred to as *Exit Work*;
3 Work relating to the charged tickets tray, which may be referred to as *Charged Tray Work*; and
4 Work relating to the unclaimed property left in the library, which may be referred to as *Counter Unclaimed Property Work*.

2621:1 *Entrance Work*

2621:1:1 Entrance Work is to consist of the following immediate jobs:

1 Scrutiny of the gate register, which may be referred to as *Gate Register Scrutiny*;
2 Taking charge of the private property, if any, of the users, which may be referred to as *Counter Custody*;
31 Discharging the library books returned by the members or their agents, which may be referred to as *Discharging*;
33 Noting down oral requests for renewals, which may be referred to as *Renewal Noting*;
4 Overdue collection, which may be referred to as *Overdue Receiving*;
5 Releasing the entrance gate so as to allow the user to open

it and enter the library, which may be referred to as *Entrance Gate Releasing*; and

8 Answering queries, which may be referred to as *Query Answering*.

2621:1:2 Entrance Work is to consist of the following hourly job:

6 Noting down the hours, in the gate register, which may be referred to as *Gate Register Timing*.

2621:1:3 Entrance Work is to consist of the following casual jobs:

1 Renewing the sheets in the gate register, which may be referred to as *Gate Register Renewal*.

2621:1:4 Entrance Work is to consist of the following daily jobs:

11 Filing the used-up gate register sheets, which may be referred to as *Gate Register Filing*;

12 Putting up the gate register sheets for the next day, which may be referred to as *Gate Register Putting Up*; and

6 Changing the date of the stamp with which the current date is stamped, which may be referred to as *Current Date Changing*.

2621:2 *Exit Work*

2621:2:1 Exit Work is to consist of the following immediate jobs:

1 Vigilance, which may be referred to as *Counter Vigilance*;

31 Receiving the books returned after consultation, which may be referred to as *Consultation Discharging*;

32 Receiving the books required by the members or their agents on loan and the related tickets, which may be referred to as *Preliminary to Charging*;

33 Charging the loan books, which may be referred to as *Charging*;

4 Receiving bespeaking cards for books not found on the

shelves, at the moment, which may be referred to as *Bespeaking Card Receiving*;

5 Releasing the exit gate so as to enable the user to open it and go out of the library, which may be referred to as *Exit Gate Releasing*;

6 Handing over the charged books to the user, which may be referred to as *Loan Issuing*; and

7 Returning deposited private property, which may be referred to as *Counter Custody Discharging.*

2621:2:3 Exit Work is to consist of the following casual jobs:

8 Noting down a count of the books lent and consulted, which may be referred to as *Issue Counting*; and

83 Arranging the charged cards, which may be referred to as *Charged Cards Arranging.*

2621:2:4 Exit Work is to consist of the following daily jobs:

6 Changing the date in the date stamp, so as to show the date of the " due day " of the books lent out, which may be referred to as *Due Date Changing*;

81 Preparing and putting up the counting sheets, which may be referred to as *Counting Sheet Preparing*; and

88 Totalling the issues, which may be referred to as *Issue Totalling.*

2621:3 *Charged Tray Work*

2621:3:3 Charged Tray Work is to consist of the following casual jobs:

1 Closing up charged cards, which may be referred to as *Charged Tray Closing Up*; and

4 Bespeaking books, which may be referred to as *Bespeaking.*

2621:3:4 Charged Tray Work is to consist of the following daily jobs:

14 Detecting abuse of tickets, which may be referred to as

Ticket Detecting;

31 *Charged Tickets Filing*;

32 Disposing of the written requests for renewal, which may be referred to as *Renewal Request Disposing*;

33 Renewal work, which may be referred to as *Renewing*;

36 Changing the guides, which may be referred to as *Guide Changing*;

41 Recording overdue cases, which may be referred to as *Overduing*; and

45 Issuing overdue notice, which may be referred to as *Overdue Noticing*.

2621:3:5 Charged Tray Work is to consist of the following weekly job:

14 Sending a report to the librarian on the result of detecting abuse of tickets, which may be referred to as *Detected Ticket Reporting*.

2621:4 *Counter Unclaimed Property Work*

2621:4:4 Counter Unclaimed Property Work is to consist of the following daily job:

7 Handing over the property to the stores section, which may be referred to as *Unclaimed Property Transmission*.

26211 MEMBERS

The work of the Circulation Section relating to the members in general may consist of the following items:

12 Admitting persons as members, which may be referred to as *Admission Work*;

13 Changing tickets of members, which may be referred to as *Change of Ticket Work*;

14 Work relating to loss of tickets by members, which may be referred to as *Lost Ticket Work*;

3 Work relating to withdrawal of members, which may be referred to as *Withdrawal Work*; and

4 Work relating to the dues from members, which may be

referred to as *Dues Collection Work.*

26211:12 *Admission Work*

26211:12:1 Admission Work is to consist of the following immediate jobs:

1 Giving the intending member the application card and a copy of the rules, which may be referred to as *Preliminary to Admission*;
2 Scrutinising the application card and passing it to the librarian for orders, which may be referred to as *Admission Scrutiny*;
31 Receiving the deposit money, if any, and preparing the receipt therefor, which may be referred to as *Deposit Receipting*; and
32 Preparing the reader's tickets, which may be referred to as *Ticketing.*

26211:12:4 Admission Work is to consist of the following daily jobs:

4 Preparing the overdue register sheets, which may be referred to as *Overdue Sheeting*;
6 Handing over the deposit collection and the application cards to the cashier, which may be referred to as *Deposit Forwarding*; and
8 Preparing and filing the docket sheets, which may be referred to as *Membership Docketing.*

26211:12:5 Admission Work is to consist of the following weekly jobs:

2 Filing the application cards, which may be referred to as *Application Card Filing*; and
4 Filing overdue register sheets, which may be referred to as *Overdue Sheet Filing.*

26211:13 *Change of Ticket Work*

26211:13:1 Change of Ticket Work is to consist of the following immediate jobs:

1 Scrutiny of the conditions justifying the change of tickets, which may be referred to as *Justification of Change of Ticket*;
2 Cancelling old tickets, which may be referred to as *Ticket Cancelling*;
3 Preparing fresh tickets, which may be referred to as *Renewal of Tickets*; and
8 Noting down a count of the number of cases of renewals, which may be referred to as *Tickets Renewal Counting*.

26211:13:5 Change of Ticket Work is to consist of the following weekly job:

7 Remitting to the stores section through the cashier and the accountant all the tickets cancelled in the course of the week, which may be referred to as *Cancelled Tickets Remitting*.

26211:13:8 Change of Ticket Work is to consist of the following annual job:

5 Inviting the attention of the chronologically contingent members to the expiry of their tickets, which may be referred to as *Expiry of Tickets Reminding*.

26211:14 *Lost Ticket Work*

26211:14:1 Lost Ticket Work is to consist of the following immediate jobs:

1 Receiving the necessary fees and issuing duplicate tickets to the member who has lost his tickets and has fulfilled all the necessary conditions, which may be referred to as *Duplicate Ticketing*; and
8 Keeping account of the duplicate tickets issued, which may be referred to as *Duplicate Ticket Issue Counting*.

26211:14:4 Lost Ticket Work is to consist of the following daily jobs:

3 Furnishing the member concerned with an account of the procedure to be followed, which may be referred to as *Proce-*

dure Advising;

4 Noting the fact of the loss in the overdue register and preparing an observation slip, which may be referred to as *Preliminary to Detecting*;

5 Sending to the member concerned, a copy of the draft form of the indemnity bond, which may be referred to as *Bond Form Forwarding*; and

6 Receiving the indemnity bond from the member, after the lapse of the waiting period, which may be referred to as *Bond Receiving.*

26211:3 *Withdrawal Work*

26211:3:1 Withdrawal Work is to consist of the following immediate job:

1 Receiving from the member, who desires to withdraw his membership, a notice of withdrawal in writing, which may be referred to as *Withdrawal Notice Receiving.*

26211:3:4 Withdrawal Work is to consist of the following daily jobs:

1 Withdrawing the files of the members who have given notice of withdrawals, scrutinising them and taking the necessary action, which may be referred to as *Withdrawal Files Scrutiny*; and

2 Scrutinising the files, the application card and the overdue register to find out if the withdrawal may be allowed, which may be referred to as *Preliminary to Refunding.*

26211:3:5 Withdrawal Work is to consist of the following weekly jobs:

16 Notifying the cashier about the amount that will be required for the refund on the next day, which may be referred to as *Withdrawal Notifying*;

31 Obtaining from the cashier the amount requisite for the day's refund, which may be referred to as *Refund Cash Receiving*;

32 Collecting the tickets of the members and cancelling them, which may be referred to as *Ticket Cancelling*;

35 Refunding the deposit money to the member, which may be referred to as *Deposit Refunding*;

6 Sending to the cashier the files relating to the withdrawals effected, which may be referred to as *Withdrawal Files Forwarding*; and

7 Remitting to the stores section through the cashier and the accountant all the tickets cancelled, which may be referred to as *Cancelled Tickets Remitting*.

26211:4 *Dues Collection Work*

26211:4:1 Dues Collection Work is to consist of the following immediate jobs:

1 Finding out the amount due, which may be referred to as *Dues Fixing*;

2 Receiving the dues and preparing the receipt therefor, which may be referred to as *Dues Receipting*; and

3 Returning the ticket in case any ticket is retained in the *Kept Tickets Tray* against the dues, which may be referred to as *Ticket Returning*.

26211:4:3 Dues Collection Work is to consist of the following casual job:

4 Noting down the receipt of the amount in the overdue register, which may be referred to as *Receipt Posting*.

26211:4:4 Dues Collection Work is to consist of the following daily job:

6 Handing over the dues collection of the day to the cashier, which may be referred to as *Dues Collection Forwarding*.

26211:4:7 Dues Collection Work is to consist of the following quarterly jobs:

1 Preparing a quarterly statement of the outstanding dues

and submitting it to the librarian for consideration, which may be referred to as *Dues List Preparing*; and

5 Sending demand statements in the case of the first instances and reminders in the case of the others, which may be referred to as *Dues Demanding*.

2622 Resources

262231 Returned Volumes

The work of the Circulation Section relating to the volumes returned from loan and consultation is to consist of the following items :

4 Picking out worn-out volumes needing mending or rebinding, which may be referred to as *Counter Worn Out Volumes Work*;

5 Setting right the defects, if any, in the marks in the volumes, designed to facilitate counter work, which may be referred to as *Counter Reconditioning Work*; and

8 Forwarding the volumes to the temporary replacing shelf provided by the Maintenance Section or to other appropriate places, which may be referred to as *Returned Volumes Forwarding Work*.

262231:4 *Counter Worn-Out Volumes Work*

262231:4:3 Counter Worn-Out Volumes Work is to consist of the following casual jobs:

1 Examining the condition of the volumes in the temporary replacing table and sorting them into different groups in accordance with the soundness of their condition, which may be referred to as *Returned Volumes Sorting* ; and

2 Carrying out minor mendings to the volumes that require such treatment immediately, which may be referred to as *Minor Mending*.

262231:4:4 Counter Worn-Out Volumes Work is to consist of the following daily job:

8 Forwarding the worn-out volumes to the Maintenance Section

for the necessary treatment, which may be referred to as *Worn-Out Volumes Forwarding*.

262231:5 *Counter Reconditioning Work*

262231:5:3 Counter Reconditioning Work is to consist of the following casual jobs:

3 Renewing the tag in the back, if it is worn out, which may be referred to as *Tagging*;
4 Renewing the book ticket, if it is worn out, which may be referred to as *Book Ticketing*;
5 Renewing the book pocket, if it is separate and is worn out, which may be referred to as *Pocket Fixing*; and
6 Pasting a date label if there is none or if the old one has been completely filled up, which may be referred to as *Date Labelling*.

262231:8 *Returned Volumes Forwarding Work*

262231:8:3 Returned Volumes Forwarding Work is to consist of the following casual jobs:

1 Further sorting of the volumes grouped as fit to be sent to the shelf, in accordance with their respective sequences, which may be referred to as *Sound Volumes Sorting*; and
8 Forwarding the groups of volumes to the appropriate places, which may be referred to as *Sound Volumes Forwarding*.

262233 Books of the Counter Sequence

262233:1 The work of the Circulation Section in regard to the books of the counter sequence is to consist of the following immediate job:

1 Issuing the volumes required by the users, which may be referred to as *Counter Sequence Issuing*.

262234 Bespoken Books

The work of the Circulation Section in regard to the bespoken books may consist of the following items:

1 Picking out the bespeaking cards of the books that become available from day to day and sending them to the users concerned, which may be referred to as *Bespeaking Card Disposal Work*; and

8 Maintaining the bespoken books in the proper sequence, which may be referred to as *Bespoken Books Sequence Work*.

262234:1 *Bespeaking Cards Disposal Work*

262234:1:4 Bespeaking Cards Disposal Work is to consist of the following daily jobs:

1 *Bespeaking Cards Picking*; and

3 *Bespeaking Cards Forwarding*.

262234:8 *Bespoken Books Collection Work*

262234:8:4 Bespoken Books Collection Work is to consist of the following daily jobs:

1 Releasing the books not claimed within the prescribed period, which may be referred to as *Bespoken Books Releasing* ; and

6 Changing the guides separating the bespoken books into different daily groups, which may be referred to as *Bespoken Guide Changing*.

26224 Lost Or Damaged Books

The work of the Circulation Section in regard to the books lost or damaged by users is to consist of the following items:

4 Receiving a special deposit from the user concerned to cover the cost of repairing or replacing the book, as the case may be, which may be referred to as *Special Deposit Receiving Work*;

8 Taking steps to have the repair or the replacing, as the case may be, effected, which may be referred to as *Special Deposit Advice Work*; and

97 Refunding to the user his special deposit or any balance that may be left thereof after the repair or the replacing of the book, as the case may be, is over, which may be

referred to as *Special Deposit Refunding Work.*

26224:4 *Special Deposit Receiving Work*

26224:4:4 Special Deposit Receiving Work is to consist of the following daily jobs:

1 Estimating, by reference to the Binding Section, or the Accession Section or the trade lists, as the case may be, the amount of special deposit to be claimed from the user responsible for the damage or loss, which may be referred to as *Special Deposit Estimating*;
2 Advising the user concerned about the amount to be paid as special deposit, which may be referred to as *Special Deposit Claiming*;
4 Collecting the special deposit from the user concerned, which may be referred to as *Special Deposit Collecting*; and
8 Notifying the Maintenance Section of the damage or loss, as the case may be, which may be referred to as *Maintenance Section Notifying.*

26224:8 *Special Deposit Advice Work*

26224:8:1 Special Deposit Advice Work is to consist of the following immediate jobs:

2 Ascertaining from the user concerned whether he himself proposes to repair or replace the book, as the case may be, or whether he desires that the library should do it, which may be referred to as *Preliminary to Maintenance Section Advising* ; and
8 Advising the Maintenance Section about the action taken on damagedor lost books and about the further action, if any, which that section should take in the matter, which may be referred to as *Maintenance Section Advising.*

26224:97 *Special Deposit Refunding Work*

26224:97:1 Special Deposit Refunding Work is to consist of the following immediate jobs:

8 Receiving the repaired book or fresh copy of the lost or

irreparable book, in case the user made himself responsible to get it and forwarding it to the Maintenance Section, which may be referred to as *Fresh Copy Forwarding*; and

97 Returning to the user his special deposit, which may be referred to as *Special Deposit Returning*.

26224:97:3 Special Deposit Refunding Work is to consist of the following casual jobs:

1 Getting a certificate from the Maintenance Section that the matter, for which special deposit was received, had been set right, which may be referred to as *Preliminary to Special Deposit Returning*;

2 Notifying the user concerned about the readiness of the library, to return whatever balance remains of the special deposit, which may be referred to as *Special Deposit Return Notifying*; and

5 If the user concerned does not call to take back what is due to him, forwarding the amount due to him, which may be referred to as *Special Deposit Returning*.

26225 Books from the Co-operating Libraries

The work of the Circulation Section in regard to the books from co-operating libraries is to consist of the following items:

1 Borrowing from a co-operating library, the book, not in library but required by a user, which may be referred to as *Borrowing Work*; and

2 Returning the borrowed books when no longer required or before the due date, whichever is earlier, to the library concerned, which may be referred to as *Borrowed Book Returning Work*.

26225:1 *Borrowing Work*

26225:1:3 Borrowing Work is to consist of the following casual jobs:

1 Finding out by enquiry in which library the book is available, which may be referred to as *Locating the Book to be Borrowed*;

2 Requisitioning the book from the library having it, which may be referred to as *Requisitioning from Co-operating Library*;

3 Notifying the user concerned about the arrival of the book in the library, which may be referred to as *Borrowed Book Notifying*; and

17 Noting down in the overdue register of the user, the amount incurred, if any, as expenditure in borrowing the book, which may be referred to as *Borrowing Expenditure Noting*.

26225:2 *Borrowed Book Returning Work*

26225:2:3 Borrowed Book Returning Work is to consist of the following casual jobs:

1 Getting the book from the user in time before the date on which it is due to be returned to the co-operating library, which may be referred to as *Borrowed Book Collecting*;

2 Asking for an extension of the loan period of the book if it is wanted for a longer period, which may be referred to as *Loan Period Extending*;

3 Returning the borrowed book to the library from which it was borrowed, which may be referred to as *Borrowed Book Returning*;

7 Noting down in the overdue register of the user the amount, if any, incurred as expenditure in returning the borrowed book to the library concerned, which may be referred to as *Returning Expenditure Noting*; and

76 Sending a bill to the user for the amount, if any, incurred as expenditure in connection with the whole process of securing the book for his use from a co-operating library, which may be referred to as *Billing Borrowed Book Expenditure*.

2625 CO-OPERATING LIBRARIES

2625:8 The work of the Circulation Section relating to the co-operating libraries may consist of the following annual job:

1 Renewing the understanding with them in the matter of interlibrary loan, which may be referred to as *Co-operation Renewal*.

263 Routine

2631 Users

2631:1 *Entrance Work*

2631:1:1 *Immediate jobs*

2631:1:11 Gate Register Scrutiny

Request the user to fill all the columns in the gate register. Examine if it is done properly. If not, ask the user to complete it.

Subsidiary Routine of the Madras University Library

Scrutinise the educational qualification column with special care. If the user does not possess either the necessary qualification or a special permit, inform him politely that he is not entitled to use the library. If, however, he wants special permission, send him to the librarian.

In some libraries, the rules specify that entering the name in the gate register implies agreement to abide by the rules. In such cases, the gate register becomes a necessity. Occasionally, the library may find it necessary to know whether a particular person called at the library on a particular day and, if so, in what part of the day. In such cases, the gate register will be of help. Another direction in which the gate register will be of use is that of building up the statistics of users. But, if statistics is the only purpose in view, the entrance gate may be fitted with an automatic counting device and the user may be saved the bother of filling up a line of the register.

In the Madras University Library, which is not open to the general public, the register is of use in restricting admission into the library to those who are entitled to it.

The users are not allowed to bring their sticks and umbrellas inside the library. They have to deposit them at the counter before entering the library and get tokens in exchange. Occasionally, it happens that a user loses the token while inside the library. In such a case, the number of his token can be found out and his property identified, if the number of the token is noted in the gate register. The frequency of cases of this type in the Madras University Library is about 1 in 500, which means that at least two or three cases of this type occur every day.

2631:1:12 COUNTER CUSTODY

Take charge of the stick or umbrella of the user. Give the correct token in exchange and request him to enter the token number in the gate register. Take charge of other private property such as books, cycle lamps, cycle pumps, boxes and other receptacles, before the user enters the library.

2631:1:131 DISCHARGING

If the user brings library books for return, deal with each book as follows :

IF THE BOOK IS NOT OVERDUE

From the due date and the call number in the date label in the book, pick out the Book Ticket and the Reader's Ticket coupled with it, from behind the Due Date Guide in the Charged Tickets Tray. Insert the Book Ticket in the pocket at the bottom of the date slip. If the date label contains any special notes about the plates, maps, etc in the book, rapidly examine if they are all intact. See also if there is any evidence of any fresh damage to the book. If things are normal, place the book on the Temporary Replacing Shelf.

If there is any damage, send the book to the librarian along with a note and with the member's file and request the person concerned also to see the librarian.

If the Book Ticket has a coloured slip attached to it, place the book in the Bespoken Books Collection (see rule 263234:8) instead of on the Temporary Replacing Shelf.

Hand over the Reader's Ticket to the person who returned the book, asking him to see if it is the correct ticket in some such fashion as follows: "Mr. V S Krishnaswami, is it right", or "Is this your ticket" or "Please see if this ticket is correct".

Subsidiary Routine of the Madras University Library

If the ticket is uncovered or white or yellow, do not hand over the ticket to the person returning the book, but return it to the person in the section in charge of such tickets.

2631:1:133 Renewal Noting

If a member or his representative orally asks for the renewal of a book, ask for the due date and author and title of the book. Locate the Charged Coupled Book Ticket. If it is not bespoken, tell him that the book will be renewed.

If the book is due on that day itself, renew it in accordance with routine 2631:3:433.

If the book is due on a later date, attach a white slip to the Coupled Book Ticket.

If the book is overdue, collect the overdue charge due in accordance with rule 2631:1:14 relating to overdue books, before telling him that the book will be renewed.

It is desirable that renewal noting should be done in the presence of the person asking for it.

2631:1:14 Overdue Receiving

If the Book Is Overdue

Before releasing the Book Ticket, inform the person, returning the book, about the overdue charge. If he pays the amount, release the Book Ticket, ask the member to get in and tell him that the ticket will be returned along with the overdue charge receipt.

Rest as in rule 26311:4.

If he is unable to pay the amount immediately, prepare a slip showing the amount due, initial and date it and clip it to the Reader's Ticket and file it in the *Kept Tickets Tray* or charge it if renewal is sought.

Post the date of return in the Overdue Register and note the due date, the name of the member and the call number of each overdue book returned or renewed, in a slip of paper for the information of the accountant.

Rest as for books not overdue.

Old Overdue Charge

If a person wants to pay old overdue charge, pick out the tickets of the member concerned from the Kept Tickets Tray. Find out the total amount due on all his tickets. Tally the amount with that shown in the Overdue Register, collect the amount and deal with the case as in rule 26311:4.

2631:1:15 ENTRANCE GATE RELEASING

The entrance gate is to be released to enable the user to enter, only after all the routines described till now have been completed, so far as they may be applicable to him. Further, before a user is let in, business should not be started with the next one. The users should be attended to strictly in the sequence in which they come. If any user tries to come before his turn he should be politely requested to observe the rule of the queue.

2631:1:18 QUERY ANSWERING

If a user wants information which can be given off hand and in a few words, give him the information. If, on the other hand, the query requires a long investigation before answer, admit him into the library and send him to the Reference Section.

2631:1:2 *Hourly job*

2631:1:26 GATE REGISTER TIMING

Note down in the gate register each hour after the opening of the library, e.g. at 8 A M, at the end of the last line filled up by the users, put down 8 A M and so on.

2631:1:3 *Casual job*

2631:1:31 GATE REGISTER RENEWAL

As soon as a gate register sheet is filled up, insert another gate register sheet, number the pages serially in continuation of the last number in the previous sheet and put the date stamp of the day at the right hand top corner of each side.

2631:1:4 *Daily job*

2631:1:411 GATE REGISTER FILING

At the end of each day, file all the filled up gate register sheets in the proper sequence in the gate register binder.

2631:1:412 GATE REGISTER PUTTING UP

Just before closing time, insert a fresh gate register sheet in the gate register pad at the counter. Number the sides of the sheet serially, beginning with "1", and put the date stamp of the next day at the right hand top corner of each side.

2631:1:46 Current Date Changing

Just before closing time, change the date of the stamp with which the current date is stamped, so as to show the date of the next day.

2631:2 *Exit Work*

2631:2:1 *Immediate job*

2631:2:11 Counter Vigilance

When a user desires to go out, ask him to return at the counter all the books he has used. Carefully examine if the user is carrying away any volume of the library either forgetfully or surreptitiously. If so, collect the volume or volumes from him before releasing the exit gate.

2631:2:131 Consultation Discharging

As a user returns the books consulted, rapidly examine each book to see if it has suffered any fresh damage. If it has, send the user to the librarian with the book. If it has not, place the book aside but near at hand until you are ready for Issue Counting. The damaged book also should be placed there as soon as it is returned from the librarian.

2631:2:132 Preliminary to Charging

When a user presents his ticket and a book, see if the owner of the ticket himself presents it. If doubtful, ask him politely if he is himself the owner of the ticket. If he is not the owner of the ticket, ask for a letter of authorisation. If there are reasons to suspect that it is a case of sublending, send him to the librarian. At the same time send also the book and the file of the member concerned with a note explaining the ground for the suspicion. The book is to be issued only if the librarian directs it to be issued.

When a book whose loan is restricted to members with a special privilege is presented, examine if the colour of the ticket permits the loan (see rule 26311:12:132).

2631:2:133 Charging

If the loan is admissible, put the due date stamp in the date label of the book in the earliest unoccupied line. Tally the Book Ticket with the book. Insert the Reader's Ticket in the Book

Ticket. Place the Coupled Book Ticket in the *First Temporary Charging Tray.*

Subsidiary Routine of the Madras University Library

IF THE PERIOD OF LOAN IS THE WHOLE TERM

In the case of violet tickets, care must be taken to put the date of the last working day of the term as due date. These Coupled Book Tickets should be inserted in the Department Charging Tray. If, however, the material issued is a loose number of a periodical, the first fortnightly due date alone is to be put.

IF THE PERIOD IS SUBNORMAL

If a book has to be lent to less than the normal one fortnight, write the correct due date on the date slip. Mark the Loan Counting Sheet. Insert the Coupled Book Ticket at the proper place behind the correct due date.

MOFUSSIL MEMBER

If a mofussil member or his messenger happens to call at the library and desires to take books on loan, get his ticket or tickets from the concerned person in the section and do the charging as usual. Further, in addition to the first fortnightly due date, put down in pencil the second fortnightly due date also. The Coupled Book Ticket should be inserted in the proper place behind the date guide of the second fortnight.

HOME DELIVERY MEMBERS

If a home delivery member or his messenger calls at the library and desires to take books on loan, get the necessary ticket or tickets from the concerned person in the section and do the charging work as usual.

2631:2:14 BESPEAKING CARD RECEIVING

Whenever a person desires to bespeak a book, give him the bespeaking card. Ask him to enter the call number, author and title of the book and his own address in the proper places and to affix the proper postage stamp in the proper place. In token of your having satisfied yourself that the person has filled up the necessary particulars correctly and affixed the stamp, initial the card at the left hand bottom corner and stamp the date of the day just near the left hand top corner. Then place the card in the *Temporary Bespeaking Box*. If there is already a card with the same call number, put the figure 2 or 3, etc as the case may be; after the date stamp.

2631:2:15 Exit Gate Releasing

The exit gate is to be released to enable the user to leave the library, only after all the routines described till now have been completed, so far as they may be applicable to him. Further, before a user is let out and routines 2631:2:16 and 2631:2:17 are finished, business should not be started with any other user. The users should be attended to strictly in the sequence in which they come. If any user tries to come before his turn he should be politely requested to observe the rule of the queue. Remember the vigilance job 2631:2:11.

2631:2:16 Loan Issuing

As soon as the user crosses the exit gate, hand over his loan book or books to him.

2631:2:17 Counter Custody Discharging

In return for the token given by the user, give him the stick or the umbrella, as the case may be. Give him also the other materials he might have left at the counter while entering the library. Perhaps this job is better done at the entrance gate. It is a good practice to ask each user whether he had left any of his things at the counter for custody, while his loan books are being handed over or, if he is not borrowing any book, as he crosses the exit gate.

2631:2:3 *Casual jobs*

2631:2:38 Issue Counting

For each book discharged after consultation and accumulated near at hand, put a mark on the Consultation Counting Sheet against the name of its subject and put it on the table reserved for the books to be sent to the Replacing Shelf. For each Coupled Book Ticket, kept in the First Temporary Charging Tray, put a mark on the Loan Counting Sheet against the name of its subject.

Subsidiary Routine in the Madras University Library

For every book lent to a Department of Research, put a mark against the item "department". For every book sent to the mofussil or to a Government department, put a mark against the item "mofussil" or "Government", as the case may be. For every book lent to a co-operating library, put a mark against the appropriate item.

For each one of the four books against a given item, put a vertical stroke. For the fifth book against the same item, put a horizontal stroke across the middle of the four vertical strokes. Repeat similarly for every succeeding groups of five issues. This mode of marking will facilitate adding up at the end of the day. If, however, five or multiples of five strokes have to be put against the same item at one and the same moment, enter the figure, 5, 10, 15 ....as the case may be, instead of putting strokes.

2631:2:383 CHARGED CARDS ARRANGING

After the issue counting is finished, place each coupled book card in the *Second Temporary Charged Tray* in the place appropriate to its call number.

2631:2:4 *Daily jobs*

2631:2:46 DUE DATE CHANGING

Just before closing time, change the date of the stamp with which the due date is to be stamped, so as to show the date on which the books lent on the next day will fall due.

2631:2:481 COUNTING SHEET PREPARING

Write on the top of a quarter sheet of paper "consultation". Stamp next to it the date of the next day. Write along the left edge the symbols for the subjects into which the issue should be classified. This will serve as the *Consultation Counting Sheet*. Do similarly for the *Loan Counting Sheet*. This is to be done as one of the first jobs just before closing time.

Subsidiary Rules of the Madras University Library

After the subject symbols are over, add successively "Departments of research", "Mofussil", "Government", "Interlibrary loan", "New members", "Change of tickets" and "Lost tickets reported". These headings will be of use in keeping account of the respective operations. Enter near the right hand bottom corner, the dates of the two successive fortnights from the day. These dates will be of use in entering the due dates for mofussil loans (see rule 2631:2:133).

2631:2:488 Issue Totalling

As one of the first items of work in the morning, count the issues marked in the Counting Sheets of the preceding day and post the figures in the issue diary.

2631:3 *Charged Tray Work*

2631:3:3 *Casual jobs*

2631:3:31 Charged Tray Closing Up

The charged coupled book cards are to be carefully closed up so as to stand erect and with comfortable tightness.

2631:3:34 Bespeaking

Take each of the cards out of the Temporary Bespeaking Box at the exit counter.

Locate in the charged tray, the Book Ticket with the call number mentioned in the Bespeaking Card and attach a red slip to it, unless it has one already. If the Book Ticket is not found in the Charged Tray but the book is in the Bespoken Collection, attach the red slip to its Book Ticket. If the book is not traceable at all, ask the Reference Section to investigate it. Arrange the bespeaking cards in the *Bespeaking Cards Box* by the call numbers of the books bespoken. If there be two or more bespeaking cards for one and the same book, arrange them among themselves in the sequence of the dates stamped above the call number. If there be two or more bespeaking cards for one and the same book and with one and the same date stamped, arrange them among themselves in the sequence of the digits entered after the date stamp, putting in correctly such digits if they do not exist already.

2631:3:4 *Daily jobs*

2631:3:414 Ticket Detecting

As early as possible in the morning, examine the Reader's Tickets charged on the preceding day to find out with the help of the observation slips (see 26311:14:44), if any of the tickets, reported by the members to have been lost, stands charged. If any abuse of tickets is detected, report it to the librarian.

2631:3:431 Charged Tickets Filing

At the end of the day, the Due Date Guide for the issues of the day is to be placed in the Charged Tray and all the Charged Book Tickets in the Second Temporary Charged Tray are to be transferred behind it.

2631:3:432 Renewal Request Disposing

For all the letters received in the day asking for renewals, locate in the Charged Tray the Coupled Book Tickets corresponding to the books for which renewal has been asked. If it can be renewed, attach a white slip to it. If it has such a slip, already, write "R" at the right of the lowest horizontal dash on it. If the book has been bespoken, i e has a coloured slip attached to it or has been already renewed for the maximum number of times allowed under the rules, i e if the horizontal dashes on the white slip attached to it have been crossed by a vertical line, write a letter to the member concerned, saying that the book cannot be renewed and should be returned on the due date.

2631:3:433 Renewing

Pick out all the Coupled Book Tickets with white slips attached and standing behind the date guide of the day, provided that, if the white slip has a horizontal dash, the last such dash is followed by the letter "R", and transfer them to the temporary charging tray after putting a horizontal dash on the white slips attached to the Coupled Book Tickets. When the last possible renewal is made, instead of putting a horizontal dash on the white slip, put a vertical stroke across the earlier horizontal dashes.

Subsidiary Rules of the Madras University Library

In the Madras University Library, in addition to renewals on request, there is also the system of automatic renewals for those who are entitled to have loan for two or more fortnights. The following is the routine connected with them. In the case of white tickets standing behind the date guide of the day, attach a white slip, mark a vertical line and transfer it to the Temporary Charging Tray.

If, after these automatic renewals, a renewal has to be made on request, write "R" after the strokes representing automatic renewals, as soon as the request is received and is admitted. When the renewal date comes, proceed in the usual way with the system of horizontal dashes.

In the case of white tickets, the maximum number of renewals allowed being three, two horizontal dashes crossed by a vertical stroke in the second sequence will indicate that no further renewal can be allowed.

2631:3:436 Guide Changing

Behind the Overdue Amount Guide showing the highest amount, insert the guide showing the next higher amount and release the old guide. Do similarly in the case of each one of the guides, if there is any undischarged book card behind it. Lastly insert the five naye paise guide behind the due date guide bearing the date of the day, if there is any undischarged book card behind it. All the date guides and Overdue Amount Guides, behind which no book card is left, are to be removed and put in the sequence order in the *Unused Guides Tray.*

Note: This rule is stated for definiteness, on the basis of the library rule levying a fine of five naye paise per volume per day on overdue books.

2631:3:441 Overduing

As early as possible in the morning, transfer all the Coupled Book Tickets standing charged behind the five naye paise guide to a tray and alphabetise them by the names of the members. For each such card, make an entry under the following headings in the overdue register of the member concerned : Call Number ; and Due Date.

Then, rearrange the book cards by call number and retransfer them to the Charged Tray behind the five naye paise guide. This is not needed if the Conscience Box Method is used.

2631:3:445 Overdue Noticing

Before beginning the Guide Changing Work, prepare Overdue

Notice Cards for each member whose tickets stand charged behind the five naye paise guide. Write down the address of the member, taking the correct address. Enter in the body of the card the names of the books, whose Book Tickets stand coupled with his tickets behind the five naye paise guide, initial it, and send the cards to the librarian for signature. Issue similarly second overdue notices for the Coupled Book Tickets, that stand charged behind the 50 naye paise guide. Issue similarly third overdue notices in the case of the Coupled Book Tickets, standing charged behind the one rupee guide. The third overdue notices are to be sent by registered post. In the case of the Coupled Book Tickets that stand charged behind the Rs 1.50 guide, send a messenger to collect the books from the members. If the member is a student or is employed, address the head of the institution concerned to collect the books from the party concerned and send them to the library ; or send a special messenger, in case there is no response.

Note: In speaking of the overdue amount guides, the practice of levying an overdue charge of five naye paise per volume per day has been assumed for making the instruction definite.

2631:3:5 *Weekly job*

2631:3:514 DETECTED TICKET REPORTING

Once in a week, send a written report to the librarian showing the consolidated result of the Lost Ticket Detecting Job. If no abuse was detected on any day of the week, send a *nil* report.

2631:4 *Counter Unclaimed Property Work*

2631:4:4 *Daily job*

2631:4:47 COUNTER UNCLAIMED PROPERTY FORWARDING

Examine if any property taken by the Circulation Section for safe custody remains unclaimed at the end of the day. Find out the ownership either by the marks on the property or by the token issued if it can be traced from the gate register. Write out a note of your findings along with a description of the property and any other information you are able to guess or remember about it, on a piece of paper. On the next morning forward the property and the note to the Stores Section through the librarian.

26311 MEMBERS

26311:12 *Admission Work*

26311:12:1 *Immediate jobs*

26311:12:11 PRELIMINARY TO ADMISSION

Hand over the application card and a copy of the Rules of the Library to the person intending to become a member. Inform him to the necessary extent, how the form is to be filled up and request him to read the Rules carefully.

26311:12:12 ADMISSION SCRUTINY

As soon as the application card is received from him, examine carefully if all the items have been duly filled up. Verify the accuracy of the statements and signatures contained in it whenever necessary. If there is any discrepancy, get it rectified by the applicant. As soon as you are satisfied that everything is in order, initial it near the point where the librarian is to write down the "admit" order and pass the card on to the librarian.

If convenient, the intending member may be requested to see the librarian personally with the application card.

Subsidiary Rules of the Madras University Library

If the applicant is an undergraduate or an unregistered graduate, verify if he is recommended by a competent person as provided in the Rules of the Library. If he has certified himself as a registered graduate or a member of any of the authorities of the University or a teacher of the University or of a college of the University, verify the accuracy of the statement. If the applicant is an undergraduate, find out from him the year in which he is normally to appear for the degree examination and note it at the right hand top corner of the application card.

26311:12:131 DEPOSIT RECEIPTING

As soon as the application card is received from the librarian with the order "admit", receive the deposit amount from the intending member. Tell him that the receipt and the tickets will be ready shortly. Direct him to go to the stack-room to acquaint himself with the arrangement of books and to select the books.

If the intending member is new to the library, he may also be asked to inform the Reference Librarian on duty in the stack-room that he is new to the library. Prepare the receipt for the amount.

If the Rules of the Library do not provide for a deposit, this routine will not arise.

26311:12:132 TICKETING

Prepare the necessary number of tickets of the proper colour in accordance with the Rules and send the tickets and the receipt book to the librarian. As soon as the receipt book comes back from the librarian, see if it has received the signature of the librarian and if the tickets have received his stamp. If they are in order, keep the receipt and the tickets in readiness to be handed over to the member at the earliest opportunity.

The number of the ticket will be written in the first line, the surname of the member in the second line and the forenames within brackets in the third line. The address of the member should be written after these. The accompanying picture shows the two sides of Reader's Ticket and a Book Ticket with the Reader's Ticket inserted in the latter.

It may be explicitly stated here that assuming for definiteness that a member is given three Reader's Tickets at any time the number of library books in his possession plus the number of free tickets he has, should be equal to three. If he has three books, he will have no free tickets. If he has two books he will have one free ticket. If he has one book, he will have two tickets. If he has no book, he will have all the three tickets with him.

The following is a model colour scheme for tickets :

Children's Ticket	Red
Fiction Ticket	Yellow
Ordinary Ticket	Green

Usually, even an ordinary book can be taken on a yellow ticket. But no fiction can be taken on a green ticket. If there are other privileges, like loan of periodicals, other suitable colours may be used to indicate such privileges.

Each ticket should be given its Ticket Number. The Ticket Number should be expressive. This is illustrated by the following

interpretation of Ticket Number : 906D58.12.3
Here

906=Expires in June 1959.
D58=Member's main interest is in Aeronautics.
12=Twelfth member admitted in June 1958.
3=Third ticket of the member.

The interval between the issue of a Reader's Ticket and its expiry has been taken to be one year in the above example. But it can be of any duration as fixed by the Rules of the Library.

Book Ticket	Coupled Ticket-Pair
2:8 N59 5374 .... RANGANATHAN (S R) Library administration	2:8 N59 5374 906D62.12.3 YOGESHWAR (T R) RANGANATHAN (S R) Library administration

Note: The dots on the Book Ticket and Coupled Ticket-Pair will be printed in white on the coloured ticket.

Reader's Ticket (Back)	Reader's Ticket (Front)
Not transferable Crest VIKRAM UNIVERSITY LIBRARY Ujjain	906D62.12.3 YOGESHWAR (T R) BINOD MILLS UJJAIN A P S 14 Dec 1957

Interpretation of ticket number:
906=Expires in June 1959.
D62=Member's main interest is Machine Tools:
12=Twelfth member admitted in December 1957;
3=Third ticket of the member.

Subsidiary Rules of the Madras University Library

26311:12:13201 The following is the colour scheme for the tickets :

Brown	for undergraduates.
Green	for graduates.
Red	for those who have the periodicals privilege.
Violet	for the departments of research.
White	for mofussil members.
Yellow	for those who have the home delivery privilege.
Uncovered	straw-board for those who have government privilege.

26311:12:13202 The following is the number of tickets to be issued :

20 for teachers.
6 for research students.
3 for all the others.

The colour scheme may be varied in any convenient manner to suit the special circumstances of each library. In public libraries, it is usual to give each member two tickets of one colour and one ticket of another colour, with the understanding that only non-fiction books can be borrowed on the two tickets of the first colour and any book, including a fiction, on the ticket of the second colour. This is devised to restrict the number of fiction books on loan with any reader at a time to one. Similarly, a college or school library can regulate the issue of text-books or any class of books which are in great demand.

26311:12:4 *Daily jobs*

26311:12:44 OVERDUE SHEETING

Towards the close of the day, but before forwarding the deposit to the cashier, take the admission cards of all the members admitted in the course of the day and arrange them in the sequence of the admission numbers. For each card prepare an Overdue Sheet, remembering particularly to enter after the name, the year of expiry of membership in the case of chronologically contingent members and alphabetise them. After membership docketing is over, insert all the Overdue Sheets of the day in the proper alphabetical sequence in the weekly *Overdue Sheets Pad.*

26311:12:46 Deposit Forwarding

At the end of the day, forward to the cashier all the admission cards received in the day, the deposit receipt book, and the cash collected as deposit. If any portion of the amount collected as deposit has been used in the course of the day for the refunding of deposit, the connected withdrawal papers are to be sent in the place of the amount (see routine 6311:3:97). When the receipt book comes back, see if the cashier has initialled and dated at the back of the last of the used counterfoils as a token of his having received the amount. If not, get it done.

26311:12:48 Membership Docketing

As soon as the Overdue Sheets have been alphabetised, but before they are inserted in the Weekly Overdue Sheets Pad, prepare a Docket Sheet for each member as follows : Write in the label of the Docket Sheet, the following items in successive lines :

1 Number of the file ;
2 Name of the member ;
3 Ticket number ; and
4 Admission number.

Insert all the docket sheets in the proper place among the files of the section.

26311:12:5 *Weekly jobs*

26311:12:52 Application Card Filing

As soon as the application cards of the week are received from the Account Section, alphabetise them and tally them with the overdue sheets in the Weekly Overdue Sheets Pad. If there is any discrepancy, get it set right by a reference to the Account Section and by other means. As soon as the tallying is found to be perfect, rearrange the admission cards in the sequence of the deposit numbers and insert them in the Admission Cards Cabinet in the same sequence.

26311:12:54 Overdue Sheet Filing

As soon as the admission card filing is over, insert, in the proper alphabetic sequence, the overdue sheets lying in the Weekly Overdue Sheets Pad, in the overdue register, which should be of the loose leaf pattern. If the Conscience Box Method is used this will serve only as Alphabetical List of Members and for noting special deposits, if any.

26311:13 *Change of Ticket Work*

Readers' Tickets may have to be changed for one or other of the following reasons :

1 Reissue of tickets, if necessary, in the case of chronologically contingent membership, on the expiry of the tickets ;
2 Change of class of membership, i e changing the colour of the ticket ; and
3 Ticket being worn-out by use or other causes.

Subsidiary Rules of the Madras University Library

26311:1301 All brown tickets and all red tickets which have a digit at the right hand bottom corner are chronologically contingent tickets and are to be changed in July, in the case of brown tickets, and in September, in the case of red tickets, of the year whose last digit is entered at the right hand bottom corner of the tickets.

26311:1302 Change of class of membership may occur in the following cases :

1 Undergraduate members becoming graduate ;
2 Graduate members getting periodicals privilege ;
3 Graduate members becoming mofussil members and *vice versa* ; and
4 Graduate members becoming home delivery members and *vice versa*.

26311:13:1 *Immediate jobs*

26311:13:11 Justification of Change of Ticket

Receive the ticket that requires changing and examine its condition carefully, if it is to be changed on account of its being worn-out or otherwise spoiled ; if the change is to be made for other reasons, study the file of the member concerned. After satisfying yourself that the change is justified, prepare a note to that effect and send it to the librarian for orders.

26311:13:12 TICKET CANCELLING

After the order for change is received, deface the old tickets with the "Cancelled" stamp.

26311:13:13 RENEWAL OF TICKETS

Prepare fresh tickets in the place of the cancelled ones as provided in rule 26311:12:132. Send the file, the cancelled tickets, and the fresh tickets to the librarian. As soon as they come back from the librarian, see if the cancelled tickets have received his initials and the fresh tickets have received his stamp. If they are in order, keep the tickets in the kept tickets tray, to be handed over to the member at the earliest opportunity. Note the necessary information in the Overdue Register.

26311:13:18 TICKETS RENEWAL COUNTING

For each of the cancelled tickets, as well as the fresh tickets issued, put a stroke on the Loan Counting Sheet against the appropriate item and file the cancelled tickets in the cancelled tickets tray in the alphabetic sequence.

26311:13:5 *Weekly jobs*

26311:13:57 CANCELLED TICKETS REMITTING

Same as in rule 26311:3:57.

26311:13:8 *Annual jobs*

26311:13:85 EXPIRY OF TICKETS REMINDING

On the appointed day or week in the month, send letters to the members holding tickets which expire that month, requesting them to return the expired tickets and, if necessary and permissible, take such fresh tickets as they may be entitled to.

Subsidiary Rules of the Madras University Library

26311:13:8501 The cases that require expiry-of-ticket reminding in any year are those whose file numbers end with *B* or *R* followed by the last digit of the year. Such files will be found together.

26311:13:8502 In the case of brown tickets, such letters should be addressed early in July ; and in the case of red tickets, early in October.

26311:14 *Lost Ticket Work*

26311:14:1 *Immediate jobs*

26311:14:11 DUPLICATE TICKETING

As soon as a member who has been advised to call at the library for receiving duplicate tickets arrives, collect the duplicate ticket fees from him in accordance with rule 26311:4:11 and prepare and issue the duplicate tickets to him in accordance with rule 26311:12:132, except that the word " duplicate " should be written in red ink across the ticket.

26311:14:18 DUPLICATE TICKET ISSUE COUNTING

For every duplicate ticket issued, put a stroke against the proper item in the Loan Counting Sheet.

26311:14:4 *Daily jobs*

26311:14:43 PROCEDURE ADVISING

In the case of each notice of loss of ticket received in the day, send to the member concerned a copy of the Rules regarding loss of tickets and the procedure that should be adopted ; or, if the notice of loss of ticket is defective in any particular, write to him asking for proper notice.

26311:14:44 PRELIMINARY TO DETECTING

As soon as the procedure advising process is over, prepare an *Observation Slip* in the following manner. Examine the *Observation Slips Box* to see if there is already a slip for the member. If there is one, the number of the ticket now lost is to be added as an additional item. If there is no slip for the member, prepare a fresh slip giving the ticket number in the first line, the name of the member in the second line and the date of notice of loss of ticket in the third line. Insert the filled-up slip in the observation slips box in the proper numerical sequece. If a lost ticket is traced, destroy the related observation slip.

Additional Jobs of the Madras University Library

The experience with cases of lost tickets in the Madras University Library is of some interest. For some years, the following practice was adopted. Whenever a member notified loss of tickets, he was asked to report at the end of three months the result of his endeavour to trace them out. If, at the end of that period, he was unable to trace them out, duplicate tickets were given without any charge. It was found that this privilege was abused in several ways. After taking the duplicate tickets, the old tickets were also presented. The tickets reported to be lost were sometimes presented by the relatives of the members, the relatives stating that the member gave them the tickets for their use. Some members reported loss of tickets repeatedly almost every year. While the tickets of some members were locked up in the library against money due from them, they used to come months later with the story that the tickets were lost. Due to one cause or other, notice of lost tickets came to be received almost every week.

Then, it was felt that something should be done to help the formation of a higher sense of responsibility in the matter of library tickets. As a result, it became the practice to charge a fee for the issue of duplicate tickets and to ask the members to execute an indemnity bond.

26311:14:45 Bond Form Forwarding

After the expiry of, three months in the case of reissue of ticket and six months in the case of withdrawal of deposit, from the date of notice of loss of ticket, and on receipt of information from the member that he is unable to trace the lost ticket, forward to him a copy of the appropriate draft form of the indemnity bond, filling up in the draft all the items that need filling up, along with a covering letter asking the member to send the bond executed on proper stamped paper—25nP paper if the number of tickets lost is one or two, and 50nP paper if the number of tickets lost is three.

26311:14:46 Bond Receiving

As soon as the indemnity bond is received, scrutinise it carefully and see if it is in order by a reference to the concerned files. Prepare a note to the librarian and obtain his sanction for the issue of a duplicate ticket or refund of deposit as the case may be. As soon as the sanction is received, write a letter to the member concerned asking him to call at the library on a specified date with the duplicate ticket fees at the rate of 25nP per ticket in the case of reissue of tickets, or asking him to bring his other tickets, if any, or books borrowed on them, in the case of withdrawal of deposit.

26311:3 *Withdrawal Work*

Withdrawal work requires some careful planning particularly if the rules require the members to deposit caution money. It would be convenient if the rules provide that a week's notice should be given for all withdrawals. It adds to economy, if a further convention is established that the refund of deposit will be made only on a particular day of the week. Supposing that Tuesday is the refund day, all the cases, of which notice has been received on any day in the week ending with the preceding Monday, may be attended to on that day.

26311:3:1 *Immediate job*

26311:3:11 WITHDRAWAL NOTICE RECEIVING

If any member desires to withdraw his deposit, ask him to give a request in writing. While receiving the letter of request, inform him of the day and time when he should call at the library for getting the refund of his deposit and ask him also if he would return his tickets. If he returns them, keep them in the kept tickets tray. Note in the withdrawal notice the day and time fixed for refund ; note also if the tickets have been received.

26311:3:4 *Daily jobs*

26311:3:41 WITHDRAWAL FILES SCRUTINY

In the case of each withdrawal notice received in the day, proceed as follows : Pick out the file of the member concerned and study it to find whether the withdrawal may be allowed. Examine also the overdue register and note if any amount is due from him. Next compare the signature in the notice with the signature in the member's admission card. If the signature is alright, if there is no complication in the matter, if the member has not been informed in person about the date of withdrawal in accordance with rule 26311:3:11, and if the member has not asked for the deposit to be sent by post, write a postcard informing him about the day and time on which he should call at the library to receive the refund of his deposit. If his tickets have not been received already, state in the letter that he should bring the tickets with him. Further, mention also that, in case he is unable to come in person, he should send an authorisation letter, specifying the name of the person whom he sends to receive the money. If there is any complication in the matter, the necessary correspondence must be started and continued until the complication is removed.

The files of all persons whose deposits can be refunded without further correspondence are to be placed in the deferred disposal pad in the alphabetic sequence by the name of the member.

26311:3:5 *Weekly jobs*

26311:3:516 WITHDRAWAL NOTIFYING

Find out from the Deferred Disposal Pad the number of files which require refund. This will be equal to the total number of withdrawal files in the pad *minus* the number of files in which only a transfer has been asked for. Then, send a note to the cashier about the amount that will be required for refund of deposit on the next day.

26311:3:52 PRELIMINARY TO REFUNDING

On the day preceding refund day, for each withdrawal file found in the deferred disposal pad, pick out the admission card and the overdue sheet and pin them to the file. Study each case carefully and add a note in a slip of paper attached to the file on the following points :

1 whether the tickets have been received ;
2 whether it is a case of indemnity bond ;
3 whether anything is due from him ; and
4 whether refund or transfer, as the case may be, may be allowed.

26311:3:531 REFUND CASH RECEIVING

On the morning of the withdrawal day, obtain from the cashier the amount required for the day's refund, taking into account any deposit amount that might have been received from members after the deposit forwarding work of the preceding day.

26311:3:532 Ticket Cancelling

As soon as the member concerned arrives on the refund day, collect the tickets of the member either from him or from the Kept Tickets Tray or from the member of the Section concerned, as the case may be, and stamp them with the " Cancelled " stamp.

26311:3:535 Deposit Refunding

Take the file of the member concerned. Study the note left in the last slip attached to the file and in its light, add a note in the admission card in the appropriate place, stating if the refund may be made either in full or after deducting any sum due. Then forward the file, and the cancelled tickets to the librarian for sanction of refund. When they come back from the librarian, examine whether the cancelled tickets have received his initials and if the necessary sanction has been accorded. If everything is in order, ask the member or his agent, as the case may be, to sign at the appropriate place in the admission card in token of his having received the amount. If the signature is correct, hand over the entire deposit amount or the deposit amount less any amount due from him, as the case may be. For the dues deducted, give the usual receipt.

If the refund is to be made by post, the necessary money order form or cheque, as the case may be, should be forwarded to the librarian along with the files and the cancelled tickets, for his signature and as soon as they come back from the librarian, and after the necessary scrutiny, the amount should be transmitted by post. Add a note in the place of the signature of the member in the admission card to the effect that the amount has been transmitted by money order or cheque, as the case may be, and put your dated initials.

If the withdrawal notice has asked for a transfer of the amount and not refund, it is not necessary to get the signature of the member or his agent in the admission card ; it is enough if a note is added in that place to the effect that the amount has been transferred in favour of so and so, mentioning his deposit number. Add your dated initials.

All the cancelled tickets should be inserted in the Cancelled Tickets Tray in the alphabetic sequence of the names of the members.

26311:3:56 Withdrawal Files Forwarding

At the end of the withdrawal day, collect all the files relating to the withdrawals effected in the course of the day, count them, note the number against the proper item in the Loan Counting Sheet and then forward the admission cards and the overdue register sheets to the cashier, along with any money that was drawn in the morning from him but was not disbursed. The Transmission Register advising the amount should be got back from the cashier with his signature and date.

26311:3:57 Cancelled Tickets Remitting

At the end of the withdrawal day, collect all the cancelled tickets and fill up the appropriate columns in the Cancelled Tickets Forwarding Book. Make up the total for the week, initial in the proper place and transmit the cancelled tickets to the cashier, with the instruction, that, after the cashier had verified the cancelled tickets relating to withdrawals, the cancelled tickets and the Cancelled Tickets Note Book may be transmitted to the Stores Section through the Account Section. When the Cancelled Tickets Note Book is received from the Stores Section, examine if it has received the initials of the store-keeper, and if not, get his initials.

26311:4 *Dues Collection Work*

Dues may accrue from members in the following ways :

1 As overdue charge on overdue books (see rule 2631:3:436) ;
2 As fee for duplicate tickets (see rule 26311:14:11) ;
3 As freight incurred on behalf of the member (see rule 26325:2:376) ;
4 As special deposit to cover lost or damaged books (see rule 26324:4:4) ; and
5 Subscription.

26311:4:1 *Immediate jobs*

26311:4:11 Dues Fixing

As soon as a member offers to pay his dues, find out the amount due from him by a reference to 1 the kept tickets tray ; 2 the overdue register ; and 3 the files, in the case of special deposit and duplicate ticket fees, and if otherwise necessary.

26311:4:12 Dues Receipting

Collect from the member the amount due from him and inform him that the receipt for the amount will be ready by the time he leaves the library. Prepare the receipt, noting the amount against each item in the receipt book both in the counterfoil and in the original, initial it, and send it to the head of the section for counter-signature. Then, send the receipt book to the librarian for signature. When the receipt book comes back, if everything is in order, tear off the original and hand it over to the exit gate for delivery to the member concerned.

If the overdue charge is to be deposited by the member in the Conscience Box, it will not be included in the receipt book.

Subsidiary Rule of the Madras University Library

If the amount due is as subscription for home delivery service, the counter-signature of the home delivery clerk also should be obtained. Unless the party himself is present in the library, this receipt should be handed over to the home delivery clerk for transmission to the member concerned.

26311:4:13 Ticket Returning

If any of the tickets have been withheld for overdue charge, and if the related overdue charge has been paid, release the related tickets from the kept tickets tray and hand them over to the exit gate along with the receipt for delivery to the member concerned.

26311:4:3 *Casual jobs*

26311:4:34 Receipt Posting

For every receipt prepared, enter the receipt number and the date of collection in the overdue register against the appropriate item, such as overdue charge, freight, duplicate ticket fee, special deposit, subscription, etc.

26311:4:4 *Daily jobs*

26311:4:46 Dues Collection Forwarding

At the appointed hour of the day, total the collection from the time the collection was last forwarded to the cashier, with the aid of the counterfoils in the receipt book. If the Conscience Box Method of collecting overdue charges is used, the amount in the

Conscience Box will be added once in a week to the cash to be sent to the Central Office by the Account Section in accordance with the routine described in Section 3734:56. Verify the cash and transmit the amount to the cashier with the receipt book having noted the amount on the back of the last filled up counterfoil. When the receipt book comes back, examine if the cashier has put his initials with date on the back of the last counterfoil as a token of his having received the correct amount.

6311:4:7 *Quarterly jobs*

6311:4:71 DUES LIST PREPARING

Once in a quarter, prepare an alphabetical list of all the outstanding dues. Get it verified by another member of the Section.

6311:4:75 DUES REMINDING

Prepare a demand letter for each member whose name appears in the quarterly dues list. If the dues are only old arrears, instead of preparing a demand letter, it is enough if a reminder letter is prepared. After these letters have been checked with the quarterly dues list, send them for the signature of the librarian. When they come back from the librarian, and if they are in order, despatch them.

If the amount due is very small, say less than 25nP, or if it is recent dues, or if the member is one who frequents the library, the demand letter need not be posted, but may be kept at the entrance gate and handed over to the member concerned, when he calls at the library.

2632 **Resources**

263231 RETURNED VOLUMES

263231:4 *Counter Worn-out Volumes Work*

263231:4:3 *Casual jobs*

263231:4:31 RETURNED VOLUMES SORTING

From time to time, examine the condition of the volumes returned at the counter either by the members or their agents at the entrance gate or by the users at the exit gate. Sort them into different groups in accordance with the soundness of their condition as follows :

1 Those that are sound and may be sent to the shelf ;
2 Those that require immediate minor mending ;
3 Those that require more careful mending by the Maintenance Section ; and
5 Those that require rebinding.

263231:4:32 MINOR MENDING

In the case of the volumes that require immediate minor mending, such as fixing a loose sheet or plate, carry out the necessary mending and place them in the group of sound volumes.

263231:4:4 *Daily jobs*

263231:4:48 WORN-OUT VOLUMES FORWARDING

Towards the end of the day, before the members of the Maintenance Section go home, transmit to that Section all the volumes that require either rebinding or prolonged mending by the Maintenance Section itself.

263231:5 *Counter Reconditioning Work*

The different jobs of counter reconditioning work are to be done as pick-up work at odd moments. The Circulation Section should never engage itself in these jobs when a reader requires attention. At the same time, it is a matter of experience that the Circulation Section does have many odd moments when it does not have to attend to readers. Hence, it should be a matter of honour for the Circulation Section to complete all the jobs of Counter Reconditioning Work themselves and not pass them on to other Sections on the pretext of their not having sufficient leisure to attend to them.

263231:5:3 *Casual jobs*

263231:5:33 TAGGING

If any of the volumes in the group of sound volumes has lost or damaged its tag, apply a new tag and write down the call number on the tag in ink, the call number and the book number being written in different lines one below the other. Prudence will require that these numbers should be written at the centre of the tag, leaving the maximum possible margin all round so that later corrections may be carried out in that tag itself.

263231:5:34 BOOK CARDING

If the book ticket of any of the volumes is worn-out, prepare a fresh book ticket. After the new book ticket is verified with the old book ticket or with the book itself by some other member of the Section, insert the new book ticket in the book pocket and destroy the worn-out one.

263231:5:36 DATE LABELLING

If the pocket in the date label in any of the volumes is worn-out or if the date label has been completely filled up, paste another date label over the old one. The pasting is to be done only along the left hand edge of the date label. If the old date label is smaller in size than the new date label, the new date label is to be cut to the same size.

Sometimes it may happen that a volume presented by a member is without a date label. In such a case, the presumption is that the volume is not to be lent out.

After the date label is pasted, write down the accession number and the call number of the book in the appropriate places on the new date label.

It is a moot point whether the old date label is to be retained or torn away. The practice in the Madras University Library is to retain the old date labels, since they give a full picture of the extent to which the volume has been borrowed.

263231:8 *Returned Volumes Forwarding Work*

263231:8:3 *Casual jobs*

263231:8:31 SOUND VOLUMES SORTING

As soon as the number of volumes accumulated in the group of sound volumes grows to a suitable extent, sort the volumes according to their respective locations. For example, the following groups may be recognised :

3 Loose numbers of periodicals ;
6 Books kept in the counter collection ;
7 Reference books kept in the reading room collection ;
81 Books kept in the closed access collections ; and
82 Other volumes.

263231:8:38 SOUND VOLUMES FORWARDING

As soon as the sorting of the sound volumes is over, retain the volumes of the counter sequence in the counter itself and send away all the other volumes to their appropriate places. The loose numbers of periodicals are to be sent to the person in charge of the periodicals room. The reference books belonging to the reading room sequence are to be inserted in their places by a member of the Circulation Section. Books belonging to the closed access collections are to be handed over personally to the head of the Reference Section. All the other volumes are to be sent to the *Replacing Shelf.*

By a replacing shelf is meant shelf space, preferably at the very entrance to the stack room, where all the books intended for reshelving by the Maintenance Section are to be kept in a classified sequence. Another alternative is to use the window sills of the windows facing the several gangways as the Replacing Shelf. Each window sill is to receive the books in the subjects accommodated in the book racks in the cross gangway facing it. Of course, the window sills should be lined with timber. The Reference Section are to take charge of these volumes as and when they are transmitted by the Circulation Section and insert them in the proper classified sequence in the Replacing Shelf. As readers come into the stack room, the Reference Section should invite the attention of the readers to the books lying in the Replacing Shelf.

In the Madras University Library, the books in the Replacing Shelf are sent to their normal places by the Maintenance Section between 11 A M and 12 noon each day. At all other hours, the books that are accumulated there are given full chance to be taken away by readers. Thus, the most popular books frequently go back from the Replacing Shelf to the readers. As a result of this, the amount of reshelving work of the Maintenance Section is somewhat reduced.

263233 BOOKS OF THE COUNTER COLLECTION

263233:1 *Immediate job*

263233:11 COUNTER COLLECTION ISSUING

Books in the Counter Collection are usually in great demand.

Hence, to fulfil the Second Law of Library Science in the form " Books for all", it is desirable that the Circulation Section regulates their use by a carefully thought-out scheme of rationing, such as giving only one volume at a time, fixing a time limit for use and so on. All rationing is bound to give rise to bitterness and complaint, unless tactfully managed. Hence, it i. desirable that a sincere appeal should be made to the civic sense of the users and every attempt should be made to regulate the use with the consent of all concerned.

Text Book Collection

In a University or College or School Library, instead of Counter Collection, a Text Book Collection of several volumes should be maintained, without open access, in a special Text Book Reading Room. Its Time-Rationed issue should be operated at its own counter. It is desirable to inform each reader, when his turn will come for the book bespoken by him.

263234 Bespoken Books

263234:1 *Bespeaking Cards Disposal Work*

263234:1:4 *Daily jobs*

263234:1:41 Bespeaking Cards Picking

Towards the end of the day but in good time to catch the last mail of the day, for each of the volumes added in the course of the day to the Bespoken Books Collection (viz the zeroth collection), pick out the related appropriate bespeaking card from the Bespeaking Cards Tray. If there be two or more bespeaking cards for the same volume, the card presented earliest as indicated by the date stamp, bare or amplified, in it, is to be picked out and a red slip is to be placed with the Book Ticket of the book. When the book is issued, this red slip will be attached to the Coupled Book Ticket and Reader's Ticket.

Remember, however, that preference should be given to such bespeaking cards as have asked the volumes only for consultation purposes.

Tally the volume with the entries in the bespeaking card. If it is alright, place the volume back in its original place in the

Bespoken Volumes Collection and place the bespeaking card in the Transmission Box.

263234:1:43 BESPEAKING CARDS FORWARDING

After all the bespeaking cards of the day have been thus picked out and placed in the Transmission Box, put your dated initials just beneath the word " librarian " in each card in token of your having taken up the responsibility in the matter. Get the signature of the librarian. After the Transmission Box comes back from the librarian, despatch the bespeaking cards.

263234:8 *Bespoken Books Collection Work*

The following practice is followed in the Madras University Library in maintaining the Bespoken Books Collection :

The bespoken books are to be kept arranged near the entrance gate in five collections, viz:

0 Zeroth collection consisting of the books whose bespeaking cards have not yet been forwarded ;
1 First collection consisting of the books whose bespeaking cards were forwarded on the day ;
2 Second collection consisting of the books whose bespeaking cards were forwarded one day earlier ;
3 Third collection consisting of the books whose bespeaking cards were forwarded two days earlier ; and
4 Fourth collection consisting of books whose bespeaking cards were forwarded three days earlier.

The books in each of the collections are to be kept in the sequence of their call numbers. The collections are to be separated by guides. A guide is just a strip of card board 6 inches by 2 inches, with the Collection Number written prominently at both ends. As soon as the bespeaking cards are forwarded to the librarian, release all the books behind the Collection Guide numbered 4. Examine if they have been bespoken by others, and if so, transfer them to the Zeroth Collection to be newly formed thereafter. If they have not been bespoken by others, place them in the Temporary Replacing Table. Then, shift the Collection Guides in the appropriate manner, i e shift guide '4' to the place of guide '3' ; guide '3' to the place of guide '2' ; guide '2' to the place of guide '1' ; guide '1' to the place of guide '0' and place guide '0' so as to cover the books, whose bespeaking cards are to be forwarded on the next day.

263234:8:4 *Daily jobs*

263234:8:41 Bespoken Books Releasing

As stated above, as soon as the bespeaking cards of the day are sent to the librarian for signature, release the bespoken books in the Fourth Collection and deal with them in the manner suggested above.

263234:8:46 Bespoken Guide Changing

After the books of the Fourth Collection are released, change the bespoken guides in the manner indicated above.

26324 Lost or Damaged Books

26324:4 *Special Deposit Receiving Work*

The jobs of the Special Deposit Receiving Work will have to be done as Immediate Jobs in case the user concerned is on the spot and desires to have the question settled immediately. Otherwise, they are best done on a daily basis.

26324:4:4 *Daily jobs*

26324:4:41 Special Deposit Estimating

Occasionally it happens that a reader loses a volume of the library or damages it. It is obvious that in the former case he should be asked to supply the library with a fresh copy. In the latter case, the treatment to be given will depend upon the extent of damage. The volume may either be repaired locally or the damage may be so serious that the user has to be asked to furnish the library with a fresh copy. Which of the alternative course is to be adopted has to be determined in consultation with the librarian.

If the decision is to get a fresh copy from the user, find out the published price of the book from the Accession Section or from the trade lists, as the case may be. If the book is a rare one, it may be necessary to estimate the current price of the book from second-hand catalogues. If the decision is to have the book repaired locally, get from the Binding Section the estimated cost of the repair. In any case, make a liberal estimate so as to avoid the contingency of recovering excess amount from the user at a later stage. It is always easier to refund the balance rather than recover the excess.

26324:4:42 Special Deposit Claiming

As soon as the estimated cost is obtained, inform the user concerned in person, if he is present in the library, or by letter, about the amount and ask him to pay the amount as Special Deposit immediately.

26324:4:44 Special Deposit Collecting

As soon as the user brings the Special Deposit, receive the amount and prepare and give him a receipt for the amount. The amount is to be transmitted to the Finance Section at the end of the day along with the miscellaneous collections.

As soon as the Special Deposit receipting is over, pick out the related coupled reader's ticket and book ticket. Place the Book Ticket in the *Lost Volumes Collection* and return the Reader's Ticket to the user. If it is a case of damaged volume, it may happen that the user is not a member. In that case, simply transfer the book card to the lost volumes sequence.

There is the question, how long overdue charges should be allowed to accrue in the case of lost or damaged volumes :

1 Overdue charge may be made to accrue till the fresh copy arrives ;
2 The levy of the overdue charge may be stopped with effect from the date on which Special Deposit is paid by the user ; and
3 The levy of overdue charge may be stopped with effect from the date on which the notice of loss is given.

The adoption of the first alternative is rather too hard in Indian libraries, as it often happens that a fresh copy of the book has to be procured from foreign countries. It takes not less than six weeks for the fresh copy to arrive.

A more humane alternative seems to be the adoption of the

second one. But there is a curious abuse of this alternative by certain unscrupulous members. In this alternative, it is open to a member, who wants to retain a book for a long time after the due date, to report loss of the book, pay the Special Deposit and produce the old copy after he no longer requires it, with the story that he has recovered it somehow. Some members succumb to the temptation to do this, especially in the case of books of topical importance and particularly text-books which are of great importance in connection with examinations. I wonder whether this abuse may not be guarded against by providing that in case the user returns the old library copy, he should pay the overdue charge till the date of return. Of course in this case we have no means of distinguishing genuine loss and recovery from pretended loss and recovery.

The third alternative is not desirable. Because Special Deposits are not easily forthcoming unless the overdue charge is made to accrue until the date of payment of Special Deposit, the library has to wait indefinitely long to get the Special Deposit.

26324:4:48 Maintenance Section Notifying

As soon as the Circulation Section hears of the loss or damage of a volume, the Maintenance Section must be informed about it in writing, so that it can transfer the related shelf register card to the damaged and lost sequence. It will be a good policy to send the damaged copy also to the custody of the Maintenance Section.

26324:8 *Special Deposit Advice Work*

6324:8:1 *Immediate jobs*

6324:8:12 Preliminary Maintenance Section Advising

As soon as the special deposit for lost or damaged volume is received, ascertain from the user concerned whether he himself proposes to repair or replace the volume or whether he desires the library to do it. The user should be asked to state his choice in writing.

26324:8:18 Maintenance Section Advising

As soon as the choice of the user is ascertained, inform the Maintenance Section in writing about the further action, if any, that that Section should take in the matter, remembering to note down at the bottom of the letter received from the user an endorsement showing the advice sent to the Maintenance Section. The dated initials of the head of the Maintenance Section should be obtained in token of his having received the advice.

26324:97 *Special Deposit Refunding Work*

26324:97:1 *Immediate jobs*

26324:97:18 Fresh Copy Forwarding

In case the user made himself responsible to repair the damaged volume or to supply a fresh copy of the lost or irreparably damaged volume, receive the fresh volume from the user and forward it to the Maintenance Section with a slip inserted in it showing the nature of the case.

26324:97:197 Special Deposit Returning

Ascertain from the Maintenance Section if the volume given by the user is acceptable. Their advice should be got in writing. If it is acceptable, return to the user the special deposit he had made for the volume. Obtain the necessary amount from the cashier and after giving the amount to the user, obtain a proper receipt from him for the amount. The receipt is to be sent to the Accounts Section. Note down the fact that the special deposit affair has been closed, against the entry of the special deposit in the overdue register of the user, if he is a member, or in the file, if he is not a member.

26324:97:3 *Casual jobs*

If the user had authorised the library to repair the damaged volume or to buy a fresh copy of the lost volume, the following casual jobs are to be done in connection with the special deposit refunding work.

26324:97:31 Preliminary to Special Deposit Returning

As soon as the damaged volume has been repaired or a fresh copy of the lost volume has been obtained, get a certificate from the Maintenance Section that the matter has been set right and find out the balance of the special deposit to be refunded to the user or the excess amount to be recovered from him.

26324:97:32 SPECIAL DEPOSIT BALANCE RETURN NOTIFYING

Inform the user concerned about the amount due to him or the amount due from him and ask him to settle the account as early as possible.

26324:97:35 SPECIAL DEPOSIT RETURNING

As soon as the user concerned calls at the library, refund to him the balance of the special deposit if any, or collect from him the excess amount due. If, however, the user does not call at the library, remit the balance due to him by money order. If any excess amount is due from him, remind him about it and take every possible step to collect it as early as possible.

If it is a case of damaged volume having been replaced by a fresh copy, get the damaged volume from the Maintenance Section. Write an endorsement on its title page as follows and initial and date it :

" This copy has been replaced by a fresh copy by Mr.... Hence, this copy is given away to Mr.....This is no longer the property of this library.

Librarian

(*Name of the Library*) "

Get the signature of the librarian and hand over the volume to the user concerned after taking the necessary receipt from him.

26325 BOOKS FROM THE CO-OPERATING LIBRARIES

26325:1 *Borrowing Work*

26325:1:3 *Casual jobs*

26325:1:31 LOCATING THE BOOK TO BE BORROWED

If it is decided that a volume not in the library is to be obtained from some Co-operating Library for a user, find out by enquiry in which library the volume in question is available.

In these days, it is not possible to expect any library to have a printed catalogue. Even if there is a printed catalogue, it is likely to be out of date. Hence, one has to guess, with the aid of previous experience, the names of libraries that are likely to have the volume and write to them asking if the volume is available with them.

26325:1:32 REQUISITIONING FROM CO-OPERATING LIBRARY

As soon as it is ascertained which Co-operating Library has got the volume required and is prepared to lend it, apply to that Co-operating Library asking for a loan of the volume in question. In doing so, remember the rules concerning interlibrary loan and the principles governing them, which are set forth later in this chapter under "2635 Co-operating Libraries".

26325:1:33 BORROWED BOOK NOTIFYING

As soon as the requisitioned volume arrives at the library, inform the user, on whose behalf it was got, about its arrival. While informing him, state also the date before which the volume is to be returned to the Co-operating Library.

26325:1:37 BORROWING EXPENDITURE NOTING

As soon as the requisitioned volume arrives at the library, if any sum has been paid for packing and transport charges of the book, note the amount in the overdue register of the user concerned.

26325:2 *Borrowed Book Returning Work*

26325:2:3 *Casual jobs*

26325:2:31 BORROWED BOOK COLLECTING

Collect the borrowed volume from the user in time before the date on which it is due to be returned to the Co-operating Library.

26325:2:32 LOAN PERIOD EXTENDING

If, however, the user desires to have the period of loan of the volume extended, write to the Co-operating Library, a week or more before the due date according to the distance of the library concerned, asking for an extension of the period of loan. If the Co-operating Library declines to give the extension, collect the volume from the user immediately.

26325:2:33 BORROWED BOOK FORWARDING

As soon as the volume is collected from the user, send it by registered post, with acknowledgment due, to the concerned Co-operating Library.

26325:2:37 FORWARDING EXPENDITURE NOTING

Note down in the overdue register of the user the amount, if any, incurred as expenditure in returning the borrowed book to the Co-operating Library concerned.

26325:2:376 BILLING BORROWED BOOK EXPENDITURE

As soon as the borrowed volume is returned to the Co-operating Library, make a consolidated statement of the total expenditure in getting and returning the borrowed volume and send the bill to the user concerned. Watch the matter and take the necessary steps to collect the amount as early as possible.

2635 CO-OPERATING LIBRARIES

The exacting nature of the Second Law of Library Science, viz. " Books for all " is such that no library, however rich, can ever find the necessary finance to be absolutely self-contained. Interlibrary loan is a matter of necessity in any country. The general question of interlibrary loan has been fully discussed in my *Five laws of library science.*[34]

The highly evolved stage to which interlibrary loan has reached in Denmark and Germany is also described in the same book.[35]

In giving effect to the policy of interlibrary loan, however, care must be taken to see that the interests of the local clientele of the library are not allowed to suffer in any way. To secure this end, I am giving here a set of draft rules for regulating interlibrary loan.

26351 CONDITIONS OF INTERLIBRARY LOAN

1 PROHIBITED CATEGORIES

No application for interlibrary loan is to be made in the following cases :

11 Books costing less than three rupees unless they are technical or specialist publications or they are more than five years old ;

Note : " Specialist publications " is to be so interpreted as to cover most literature that would not be included in the normal stock of an average library.

12 Text-books and quasi text-books, required continuously for examination purposes ;
13 Fiction and quick reference books ;
14 Books of which the indenting library has a copy ; and
15 Loose numbers of periodicals.

2 Rights of the Lending Library

21 Loan of a book may be deferred :
211 In the case of a recent addition, to such time as the local demand may justify ; and
212 In the case of a book for which there is an unusual temporary demand, to such time as may be necessary.
22 Loan of a book may be subjected to special conditions.
Note : Special conditions may relate, for example, to 1 period of loan ; 2 non-removal of the book from the premises of the borrowing library ; and so on.

23 The loan of any book may be refused without assigning any reasons.
Note : The book may be in a bad condition. The copy may happen to be a unique or a rare one. The book may be a giant volume, which it is not desirable to subject to transport. The book may contain too many plates, which again, it is not desirable to subject to transport.

3 Obligations of the Borrowing Library

31 Every application for interlibrary loan is to contain a certificate that the indenting library does not possess a copy of the book. This certificate should be signed by the Head of the indenting library.
32 The borrowing library is to pay the to and fro transport and other incidental charges.
33 The borrowing library is to make good any loss or damage that may happen to the book, from the moment it leaves the lending library till the moment it comes back to it.
34 If a volume of a set is lost or damaged, the borrowing library

is liable to replace the whole set.

35 The borrowing library is to fulfil the conditions, if any, imposed by the lending library with regard to the use of any book lent.

36 While returning the book, the borrowing library is to forward a statement showing the number of different readers who used the book while it was in its possession.

2635:8 *Annual job*

2635:81 CO-OPERATION RENEWAL

At the appointed time each year, write to the co-operating libraries renewing the understanding with them in the matter of interlibrary loan. This kind of annual re-examination of the arrangement for interlibrary loan is desirable from the point of view of all concerned.

264 Elimination of Waste

2641 ORGANISATION

If the turnover in the section demands the assignment of several members to it, it may be an advantage to specialise them in different items of work such as entrance gate work, exit gate work and correspondence work. Further, if the library works for long hours and on all days in fulfilment of the First Law of Library Science, it is obvious that the Circulation Staff will have to work in several shifts. This would mean that the same work will have to be carried through by different persons at different times. This implies that the organisation of the Circulation Work should be quite thorough, so that the change of hands may be effected as imperceptibly and quickly as possible. The beehive analogy referred to in section 155 is applicable almost in all its entirety to the work of this section.

2642 HEAD OF THE SECTION

The Head of the Section should see to it that the beehive spirit is maintained at as high a level as possible among the members of his section.

He should review and test-audit the charging and discharging processes and apparatus at frequent intervals to see that the machinery is being worked efficiently and accurately. He should develop the necessary acumen to detect mistakes in charging and discharging work and to solve them expeditiously.

The rate of ingress of readers in the library is a factor which is entirely outside the control of the library staff. It is seldom uniform. The Head of the Section should have the acuteness to study the vagaries in the rate of ingress and distribute his assistants in the most helpful manner. He should invariably be at the counter at moments of extraordinary rush and control and direct the handling of the traffic in a quiet and unperturbed manner. He should personally check, at the end of the day, the tickets in the charged tray.

2643 Money Matters

It is also desirable that the Head of the Section should have direct touch with all money matters. He should personally check, every day, the posting of overdue cases in the overdue register, the posting of overdue receipts and all other miscellaneous receipts in the overdue register. In the Madras University Library, he is also obliged to have intimate control of the selection and despatch of books to, and receipt of books from, the home delivery members.

2644 Diaries

The Counter Section is to maintain four diaries on a daily basis.

2645 Diary 1

The first diary may be called the *Issue Diary*. Its columns are to be the symbols for the main divisions of the classification scheme used or any modification of the same and, in addition, the following headings :

1 Total.
2 Total consultation.
3 Total loan.
4 Total number of readers.
51 Receipt of interlibrary loan.
52 Issue of interlibrary loan.
6 Total issue to research departments. (Special in the Madras University Library.)

2646 Diary 2

The second diary may be called the *Routine Diary*. Its headings are to be as follows :

1 *General Correspondence*

11 Authorisation letters received.
12 Authorisation letters disposed.
13 Other letters received.
14 Other letters disposed.
15 Letters originated.
16 Reminders sent.

2 *Home Delivery*

21 Letters received.
22 Letters disposed.
23 Books received.
24 Books sent.
25 Members served.
26 Subscription expiry cases.

3 *Mofussil Loan*

31 Letters received.
32 Letters disposed.
33 Books Received.
34 Books Sent.
35 Members Served.
36 Members from whom books were received.

4 *Renewal and Bespeaking*

41 Renewal Requests Received.
42 Renewals done.
43 Renewals rejected.
44 Bespeaking requests received.
45 Bespeaking cards sent.
46 Bespeaking cards untraced.

6 *Overdue Cards*

61 First reminder sent.
62 Second reminder sent.

63 Third reminder sent.
64 Registered reminder sent.

7 *Miscellaneous*

73 Special permit given.
74 Change of ticket made.

(Classes 2 and 3 are peculiar to the Madras University Library.)

2647 Diary 3

The third diary may be called the *Finance Diary*. Its headings are to be as follows :

1 *Admission*

11 Graduates.
12 Students.
13 Exemption cases.
14 Mofussil.
15 Home delivery.
16 Total.

(These items are peculiar to the Madras University Library.)

3 *Withdrawal*

31 Withdrawal notices received.
31 Withdrawals effected.

4 *Loss of Tickets or Books*

41 Books lost.
42 Books damaged.
43 Books replaced.
44 Tickets lost.
45 Lost tickets detected.
46 Duplicates issued.

6 *Finance*

61 Fine cases.
62 Miscellaneous collection cases.
63 Special deposit cases.
64 Duplicate ticket fee cases.
65 Subscription cases.
7 Hands off duty.

2648 Diary 4

The fourth diary may be called the *Hourly Statistics Diary*. This diary should have a separate column for each hour the library is open and in addition a sufficient number of columns for the totals at suitable intervals, say one at 10 A M, another at 3 P M, another at 6 P M, another at 8 P M, and another for the grand total. In addition, it may be advisable to have special columns to note the actual number of readers in the library at some important moments. For example, in the Madras University Library, we note down the number of readers in the library at 5 30 P M, 6 30 P M, 7 30 P M and at 8 P M

265 Correlation Table

3 *Periodical Publications Section*

263231:8:38 Sound Volumes Forwarding.

4 *Accession Section*

26324:4:41 Special Deposit Estimating.

7 *Reference Section*

2631:3:34 Bespeaking ;
26311:12:131 Deposit Receipting ;
263231:8:38 Sound Volumes Forwarding.

8 *Maintenance Section*

263231:4:48 Worn-out Volumes Forwarding ;
263231:8:38 Sound Volumes Forwarding ;
26324:4:48 Shelf Section Notifying ;
26324:8:18 Shelf Section Advising ;
26324:97:31 Preliminary to Special Deposit Returning.

96 *Finance Section*

26311:3:516 Withdrawal Notifying ;
26311:3:531 Refund Cash Receiving ;
26311:3:56 Withdrawal Files Forwarding ;
26311:3:57 Cancelled Tickets Remitting ;
26311:4:46 Dues Collection Forwarding ;
26311:12:46 Deposit Forwarding.

97 *Accounts Section*

2631:1:14 Fine Receiving ;
26311:3:535 Deposit Refunding ;
26311:4:34 Receipt Posting.

995 *Binding Section*

26324:4:41 Special Deposit Estimating.

997 *Stores Section*

2631:4:47 Counter Unclaimed Property Forwarding ;
26311:3:57 Cancelled Tickets Remitting.

266 **Illustrative Time Scheme**

DAILY JOBS

2631:2:488 Issue Totalling ;
2631:2:481 Counting Sheet Preparing ;
263234:8:4 All the daily jobs of bespoken books sequence work ;
2631:3:441 Overduing ;
2631:3:433 Renewing ;
2631:3:432 Renewal Request Disposing ;
2631:3:414 Ticket Detecting ;
2631:4:47 Counter Unclaimed Property Forwarding ;
26311:14:4 All the daily jobs of lost ticket work ;
26311:3:41 Withdrawal Files Scrutinising ;
26311:3:52 Preliminary Refunding ;
26311:12:44 Overdue Sheeting ;
26311:12:47 Membership Docketing ;
263234:1:41 Bespoken Cards Picking ;
263234:1:43 Bespoken Cards Forwarding ;
26311:12:46 Deposit Forwarding ;
26311:4:46 Dues Collection Forwarding ;
2631:3:445 Over Noticing ;
263231:4:48 Worn-out Volumes Forwarding ;
2631:3:436 Guide Changing ;
2631:3:431 Charged Ticket Filing ;
2631:1:46 Current Date Changing ;
2631:2:46 Due Date Changing ;
2631:1:411 Gate Register Filing.

2631:1:412	Gate Register Putting Up.

Weekly Jobs

Saturday

2631:3:514	Detected Ticket Reporting.

Monday

26311:3:516	Withdrawal Notifying.

Tuesday

26311:3:5	All the weekly jobs of withdrawal work except
26311:3:516	Withdrawal Notifying ;
26311:13:57	Cancelled Tickets Remitting.

Thursday

26311:12:52	Application Card Filing ;
26311:12:54	Overdue Sheet Filing.

Quarterly Jobs

First Month—First Week

26311:4:71	Dues List Preparing.

First Month—Second Week

26311:4:75	Dues Demanding.

Annual Jobs

July and September

26311:13:85	Expiry of Tickets Reminding.

December

2635:81	Co-operation Renewal Work.

267 Forms and Registers

A61 *Reader's ticket*. Printed. 6 point type. Bristol Board, lined on one side with calico. 6×4×.3 cm. Colour scheme. The name of the library and its coat of arms or emblem are to be printed on the lined side. The unlined side is to have the row headings : Ticket Number ; Name of Member ; and his address.

A62 *Book ticket*. Manuscript. Manilla. In the form of a pocket to hold a Reader's Ticket. Front fold 4×4.5 cm. Back fold 7.5×4.5 cm. The name of the library is to be printed in display type on the back of the back fold. The exposed portion of the front of the back fold is to contain the Class Number in the first or leading line, the Book Number in the second line, and the Accession Number in the third line. The folded flap is to contain the heading, the title and the series, if any, in successive lines.

C612 *Bespeaking card*. Printed. 8 point type. Bristol board. White.

The text of the form is as follows :

(*Name of the library*)

Call number
Author
Title

N B 1 The book will not be issued unless this card is produced.
2 Write your address on the other side and affix the necessary postage stamp.
3 This can be used for registering one volume only.

In reply please quote N 6234 dated....

Dear Sir,

The above mentioned book is now available in the library. Kindly arrange to take it on loan within two days.

C614 *Overdue notice card*. Printed. 8 point type. Bristol board. White. The text of the form is as follows :

(*Name of the library*)

In reply please quote N 611....dated....

Dear Sir,

The undermentioned book/books due from you on .... has/have not yet been returned. Kindly return them/it immediately along with the overdue charges.

N B I prefer the words "overdue charges" to "fine", as the word "fine" appears to irritate some members.

C62. *Application card.* Printed. 8 point type. Bristol board. White. Tray. The text of the form is as follows on the front side :

(*Name of the library*)

Admn N Ticket N Wtdl N

Name in block letters

Residence

College/Office address

I herewith deposit........rupees and I agree to abide by the rules of the Library.

Date Signature

(*Not to be filled by the applicant*)

L

Date of notice O N

Received the refund of my deposit amount.,

Date Signature

The text of the form on the back side will depend upon the nature of the library. It will contain the declaration by the member about his eligibility for membership or the recommendation of the guarantor. In the Madras University Library, the text of the back side is as follows :

Mr is a

student of the class of the college / graduate of the Madras University

and may be permitted to borrow books from the University Library.

Date Principal, Professor, college / Member of the Senate, the Academic Council, the Board of Studies in

I am a Member of the Senate / Registered graduate / Teacher in College of the Madras University.

Date Signature

C64 *Lost ticket observation slip*. Stencil. Ledger paper. Box. The row headings are to be as follows :

Name of the member
N of the ticket lost
Date of notice
Date of report of the endeavour to trace the lost ticket
Date of issue of duplicate
Date of withdrawal
Remarks

C67 *Dues demand card*. Printed. 8 point type. Bristol board. White.

The text of the form is as follows :

(*Name of the library*)

In reply please quote N 611.... dated....

Dear Sir,

A sum of Rs .... is due from you as per rule .... of the rules of the library. Kindly arrange to remit the amount immediately.

Special to the Madras University Library

C68 *Home delivery advice slip*. Printed. 6 point type. 21 lb printing paper. White. Cabinet.

The text of the form is as follows :

(*Name of the library*)

Date

Name

Address

N of vol received
N of vol to be returned

N of vol returned

Signature

***N B** Any communication intended for the Library may be written overleaf.*

O61. *Date label.* Printed. 10 point type. 16 lb. printing paper. White. 19×11.5 cm.

4 cm. of the bottom should be turned over. This turned portion should be pasted along all the edges so as to form a pocket with a mouth 6.5 cm wide. This is to hold the Book Ticket when the book is in the library. The space above the turned flap should have 15 horizontal rulings and 3 vertical rulings equally spaced.

The flap should be printed as follows :

(*Name of the library*)

C N

Ac N

Date of release for loan

This book should be returned on or before the date last marked below. An overdue charge of 5 naye paise will be levied for each day the book is kept beyond that date.

Special to the Madras University Library

O651 *Mofussil loan forwarding address slip.* Printed. Display type. 16 lb printing paper. White. The text of the form is as follows :

Books with care
Railway Parcel

To

(*Name of the library*)

O655 *Mofussil loan return address slip.* Printed. Display type. 16 lb. printing paper. White. The text of the form is as follows :

Books with care
Railway Parcel

To

The Librarian
(*Name of the library*)
(*Station*)

Sender.

Q61 *Deposit receipt book.* Printed. 11 Point type. 21 lb printing paper. White. To be bound in booklets of 50. Each sheet is to consist of a receipt form and its counterfoil. The boundary line between the receipt form and the counterfoil is to be perforated. The text of the receipt form is as follows :

(*Name of the library*)

Ser N

Received from .... the sum of Rs .... being the deposit for loan of books from the library, as per rule .... of the library rules.

Date

Chief of Circulation Section. Librarian

Q64 *Overdue register*. Printed. 8 point type. Ledger paper. White. Loose leaf binder.

The number of rules below the column headings is to be 10 on each side.

Row headings near the top are to be as follows :

(*Name of the library*)

Address Name

Deposit N N and nature of tickets.

Below that the following column headings are to be printed :

Call N (4 cm) ; Due date (2.5 cm) ; Return date (2.5 cm) ; Days overdue (1.5 cm) ; Overdue charge Rs nP (2.5 cm) ; Date of collection (2.5 cm) ; Receipt N (2.5 cm) ; Remarks (2.5 cm).

Q66 *Miscellaneous receipt book*. Printed. 8 point type. 21 lb printing paper. White. To be bound in booklets of 50. Each sheet is to consist of a receipt form and its counterfoil. The boundary line between the receipt form and the counterfoil is to be perforated. The text of the receipt form is as follows :

(*Name of the library*)

Ser N

Received from .... the sum of Rs ....
as per details given below :

Rs nP

Subscription for quarter ending
Special deposit
Delivery charges
Fee for .... duplicate ticket

Overdue charge on a book due on
Date
Chief of Circulation Section
Circulation clerk   Librarian

S61 *Gate register*. Printed. Display type. 21 lb printing paper. White. To turn on the longer edge. The number of horizontal lines below the column headings in each side is to be 15 and are to be numbered 1 to 15. The columns are to be parallel to the shorter side.

The column headings are to be:

Ser N (2.5 cm) ; Name in block letters (7.5 cm) ; Full address (.15 cm) ; Qualifications (4 cm) ; Token N (1.5 cm) ; Remarks (4 cm).

The text of the form above the column headings is to be as follows :

PLEASE WRITE LEGIBLY (*Name of the library*)

Enter your name and address in token of your agreeing to abide by the rules of the library.

268 **Files**

The outward and the inward enquiry files are to be numbered 691 and 692 respectively and dealt with in the usual way. The other files peculiar to the Section are shown in the usual tabular form on the next page.

268 Files

Name	*Class N*	*Amplifying device*	*Filing characteristic*	*Year of transfer to record sequence after the file is closed*	*Year of destruction after transfer to the record sequence*
User	61	Nil	Rules	Year 1	Permanent
Member	611	Ticket device	Member	Do	Year 3
Consultant	612	Nil	Consultant	Do	Do
Special Permit	613	Nil	Special permit holder	Do	Do
Study group	614	Subject device	Leader	Do	Year 5
Ineligible	615	Nil	Correspondent	Do	Year 3
Enquirer	618	Nil	Enquirer	Do	Do
Bespeaking cards	6234	Nil	Nil	Do	Year 1
Interlibrary borrowing	625	Subject device	Heading	Do	Year 3
Lending libraries	652	Nil	Library	Do	Year 5

N B 1 Members' files are to be closed after they withdraw from membership. The withdrawn members' files are to be arranged alphabetically, ignoring the amplifying device, and kept in the quasi-current sequence till the audit is over. After the audit is over, the files of all withdrawn members are to be kept in the record sequence alphabetically in three annual groups, till destruction.

2 The general users' files which are numbered '61' will mostly consist of the files relating to the rules of the library. The files relating to specific rules are to be individualised by the short title of the rules.

269 Rules of the Library

The theory of the rules regulating the use of the resources of the library by the public is expounded in my *Five laws of library science.*[36]

The details of the rules are bound to vary according to the nature of the library. Variation may be expected particularly in regard to :

1 hours of opening ;
2 admission into the library ; and
3 the privilege of borrowing.

Subject to the necessary modification in these matters, the following may be taken as a set of model rules.

Model Rules for a Library

1 *Hours of Opening*

11 The hours, when the .... library will be open to the public, shall be fixed by the Library Committee, from time to time.

12 The Library Committee has decided as follows for the time being.

The library shall be open to the public on all days from (7 A M to 9 P M).

N.B. *The loan counter shall be closed half an hour before the closing of the library.*

2 *Admission to the Library*

21 No person, who is not of sound mind, nor cleanly in person, nor properly dressed, shall be admitted into the library.

Note: The decision of the librarian, or of his deputy during his absence, in regard to these matters shall be final.

[*The rules may provide for admission by special permit in the case of specified classes of persons, such as non-tax payers, strangers, etc.*]

22 A person desirous of using the library shall enter his name and address legibly in the gate register which is kept for the purpose. Such entry shall be taken as an acknowledgment that the person agrees to conform to the rules of the library.

221 Sticks, umbrellas, boxes and other receptacles and such other articles as are prohibited by the Circulation Staff shall be left at the entrance.

222 Dogs and other animals shall not be admitted.

241 Silence shall be strictly observed in the library.

242 Spitting and smoking are strictly prohibited.

243 Sleeping is strictly prohibited.

251 No person shall write upon, damage, or make any mark upon any book, manuscript or map belonging to the library.

252 No tracing or mechanical reproduction shall be made without express permission from the librarian.

253 The readers shall be responsible for any damage or injury done to the books or other property belonging to the library, and shall be required to replace such books or other property damaged or injured or to pay the value thereof. If one book of a set is injured, the whole set is liable to be replaced.

254 Before leaving the library the reader shall leave on the reading table any books which he had taken for consultation or return to the Circulation Staff, if so instructed.

26 Cases of incivility, or other failure in the service, should be reported immediately to the librarian, or his deputy during his absence.

3 *Loan Privilege*

31 The following are entitled to take out books on loan on their enrolling themselves as Members. Forms of enrolment can be had free of cost at the counter.

Each library will have to decide its own conditions in this matter

[The Second Law of library science would plead for the most generous framing of this rule.]

32 Each member shall make a cash deposit of Rs...and he shall be given as many member's tickets as the number of volumes, he is entitled to remove from the library at one time. A book will be lent to a member only in exchange for one of his tickets, which will be handed back to the member when he returns the book, unless it is returned after due date, in which case the ticket will be handed back only after the overdue charge is paid.

33 A week's notice shall be given before a deposit is withdrawn. No deposit shall be repaid until all the books and dues outstanding against the member and all his member's tickets have been duly returned.

34 A member who has lost a ticket shall make a written report of the same to the librarian.

35 Three months' time shall elapse after the date of such notice, before a duplicate can be issued. During this period, the member shall attempt to trace and recover the ticket if possible and send a second report at the end of the period, stating the result of his endeavours.

36 If the ticket has not been traced, the member shall give an indemnity bond in the prescribed form and pay a fee of......for each duplicate ticket required.

37 After the receipt of the indemnity bond and the fee, the duplicate ticket will be issued.

38 If a member, who has lost one or more of his tickets, applies for the withdrawal of deposit amount, no action will be taken on such application till the expiry of six months after the report of loss of ticket. If the ticket is not recovered by the member before the end of that period, he shall give an indemnity bond in the prescribed form in respect of the lost tickets. After the receipt of the indemnity bond, the application for withdrawal will be dealt with in the usual way.

4 *Conditions of Loan*

41 Each member may have out on loan not more than (three) separate volumes at one time and must make his own arrangements for the conveyance of books to and from the library, except that in the case of invalid or lady members books may be delivered once a week at their residences on payment of an advance quarterly subscription of......

42 Before leaving the counter, the member shall satisfy himself as to whether the book lent to him is in sound condition and, if not, he shall immediately bring the matter to the notice of the librarian or his deputy in his absence ; otherwise he is liable to be held responsible for the replacement of the book by a sound copy. If one book of a set is injured or lost the whole set shall be liable to be replaced, the value being immediately remitted to the library for return after the set is actually replaced.

43 Periodical publications, dictionaries, works which might be difficult to replace and such other works as may be declared reference books by the librarian shall not be lent out.

44 Members are not allowed to sub-lend the books of the library.

45 All books on loan shall be returned at the expiration of a fortnight from the date of issue. Books which are temporarily in special demand may be lent for such shorter period as may be necessary or may be temporarily declared reference books under rule 43. Loans may at any time be terminated by order of the librarian.

46 If a book is not returned at the library when due, an overdue charge of five naye paise per volume per day shall be levied.

47 Loan may be renewed for a further period of one fortnight provided :

1 The renewal application reaches the librarian not less than three and not more than six clear days before the date on which the book is due ;
2 No other reader has applied for the book in the meantime ; and
3 Not more than three consecutive renewals shall be allowed for the same book without its production in the library for inspection.

In case condition 2 is not satisfied, the librarian shall cause a letter to that effect to be posted to the member concerned, and the books shall be returned on the due date.

48 A member against whom any overdue or other charge is outstanding shall not be allowed to borrow books or withdraw his deposit until he has paid the amount due.

5 *General*

51 The librarian may refuse, under special circumstances, admission into the library to any person or the use of any book without assigning any reason therefor.

52 The Library Committee may refuse, under special circumstances, any application for the privilege of loan of books without assigning any reason therefor.

53 The Library Committee may grant special loans on such conditions as it may prescribe.

54 Any infringement of the rules will render the privilege of admission to and of borrowing books from the library liable to forfeiture.

6 *Additional Rules for a University Library*

61 A Teacher of the University is entitled to have 20 Reader's Tickets.

62 A Teacher's Ticket will allow periodicals being borrowed against it.

63 The Due Date for a volume taken against a Reader's Ticket is the last day of the term during which it is borrowed—viz the day before the commencement of the Puja Holidays, the Winter Holidays, and the Summer Holidays respectively.

64 A Department of Research may take on loan for an indefinite period not more than 500 of such volumes as may be agreed upon between the Head of the Department and the Librarian.

641 This will be called Permanent Loan.

642 Permanent Loan will be controlled by exchange of letters specifying the volumes and not by Reader's Tickets.

643 The volumes on Permanent Loan shall ordinarily be taken out and returned, preferably, once in a year—say within the first month of an academic year.

65 A volume taken out either for a whole term or on permanent loan may be re-called by the librarian at any time after one month of its being taken out, if it is required for use by others.

66 No cash deposit need be paid by a teacher or a department of the University.

67 The University shall debit to the account of a teacher any sum due from him to the library under Rule 253.

CHAPTER 27

REFERENCE SECTION

271 Planning

2711 New Terms

"Reference Service" and "Reference Staff" are new phrases which have not yet found their way into dictionaries.

2712 Old Meaning

They stand for concepts which are being developed only in our own lifetime. According to James I Wyer,[37] "The theory of what passed for reference work a half-century ago was : Provide the books and keep out of the way of readers as much as possible." "Make the books easily available in reading rooms so that the time of the librarian and assistants may be economised for other labour." But a great change has come over the phrase, reference work, since the Great War. The library profession cannot yet be said to have completely explored the full possibilities and ramifications of reference service. The exploration is being actively pursued, and every year, new attitudes are being developed under the urge of the spirit of humanism.

2713 New Meaning

The basic notions about reference service and reference staff that follow immediately from the Laws of Library Science, are indicated in my *Five laws.*[38] It may be stated here that the main conclusion is just the opposite of the old outlook described in Wyer's book. The present attitude is that reference service means "the provision of human beings as canvassing agents for books. Their business should be to interpret the books to the readers". This view of reference service is fully explained in my *Reference service and bibliography.*[39] It is further required that the time of the staff spent in routine work should be minimised, so that the greatest number of hands may be spared for reference service for the longest time possible.

27131 Theory and Practice

Separate treatises are now being written on this new view of reference service. Wyer's book is a good example of such a treatise. Volume 9 of the Madras Library Association Publication Series is on this subject.[39] A full account of the theory and practice of reference service will be developed in that volume. This chapter interests itself only in the routine aspect of reference work.

2714 Minimise Routine

By its very nature, reference service is that function which has got the least routine. It has to be out and out academic and personal in its nature. Administrative routine cannot figure in it. I hold that it should not be allowed to enter it, lest it should corrupt, and detract from, the proper academic attitude. There appears to be a *Fascination of Administrative Routine*, even as there is the Fascination of the Precipice. Due, perhaps, to historical causes, India is suffering from a hypertrophy of administrative functions. Administration has forgotten its proper place. It has usurped the highest place and entrenched itself with all the cunning that it is capable of. Academic work and academic service have been driven to wait in its ante-chambers. This has resulted in the people engaged in academic work developing an inferiority complex. The result is that men, born and appointed for academic work and academic service, appear to be ashamed of their work as an inferior one ; and, the more ambitious ones try to create opportunities to grasp and unwind red-tape, to write business letters, to order people about, to put on an administrative air and thereby to gain what passes for prestige and dignity. This is a sign of the degeneracy of the times. It is unfortunate. Every effort should be made to resist this tendency.

2717 Vital Function

In any case, the reference staff of a library should have the strength of mind to resist the *Fascination of Administrative Routine and Prestige*. The organisation of the Reference Section of a library should be such that the temptation of administrative prestige is kept as much out of its sight and scent as possible. It should not be saddled with any correspondence work. All its correspondence should be relegated to some other Section, preferably the Circulation Section, as they maintain the files relating to all the users of the library. Thus, the routine of the Reference Section should be confined only to the filing of the results of their bibliographical research. Their full energy and time should be spent in understanding the readers on the one hand and the resources of the library on the other, so that they may efficiently discharge the vital function of establishing contact between the right reader and the right book, at the right time and in the right manner.

2718 Factors in Planning

The distinctive work of the Reference Section is to be planned with reference to the following factors :

2 Replacing shelf ;
3 Initiation of new readers ;
4 Vigilance ;
6 Ready reference ;
7 Long range reference ;
8 Shelf study ; and
85 Reference cabinet.

272 Job Analysis

2722 Replacing Shelf

The work of the Reference Section relating to the Replacing Shelf admits of no analysis into periodical jobs. It is to consist of the casual job of arranging the books accumulated in the replacing shelf, in a classified sequence, which may be referred to as *Replacing Shelf Arranging*.

2723 Initiation of New Readers

The work of the Reference Section relating to Initiation of Readers admits of no analysis into periodical jobs. It is to consist of the Immediate Job of initiating newcomers in the use of the library apparatus, as and when they come.

2724 Vigilance

The work of the Reference Section relating to Vigilance admits of no analysis into periodical jobs, except perhaps that mention may be made of the Daily Job of noting down the names of the users of the library whose civic sense is low.

2726 Ready Reference

The work of the Reference Section relating to Ready Reference admits of no analysis. It has to consist of the single Immediate Job of helping the reader in finding out the information he seeks.

2727 Long Range Reference

The work of the Reference Section relating to Long Range Reference admits of no analysis. It has to consist of the Casual Job of tracing out the information or the sources for the information, which is required by any reader and which requires prolonged search and study and cannot be furnished immediately from ready reference books.

2728 Shelf Study

The work of the Reference Section relating to Shelf Study admits of no analysis. It has to consist of the Casual Job of systematically building up intimate acquaintance with the resources of the library, whenever there is no reader to be attended to.

27285 Reference Cabinet

27285:3 The work of the Reference Section relating to Reference Cabinet is to consist of the following casual jobs :

1 Writing out in reference slips, the references traced, which may be referred to as *Reference Slips Writing* ;
2 Arranging the slips in groups by the topics to which they relate, which may be referred to as *Reference Slips Grouping* ;
3 Providing each group with a suitable guide card, which may be referred to as *Reference Slips Guiding* ;
5 Classifying the reference slip guides by the topics which they represent, which may be referred to as *Reference Guide Classifying* ;
7 Filing the guided groups of reference slips in the reference cabinet, which may be referred to as *Reference Slips Filing* ; and
8 Reviewing the slips in the reference cabinet and their grouping and arrangement, which may be referred to as *Reference Cabinet Reviewing*.

273 Routine

2732 Replacing Shelf Arranging

From time to time the Circulation Section will send to the Replacing Shelf, the volumes returned from loan and consultation. Arrange them in a classified sequence, as a pick-up-work. If they are not properly arranged, it will be difficult to find those books without waste of time, when there is a demand for them. Unless a book is with a reader or under repair, it should be readily found by, and for, any reader. Otherwise, both the Second Law and the Third Law would be violated. A chaotic sequence in the Replacing Shelf would lead to such a violation. If it is remembered that the volumes in the Replacing Shelf are to be sent to their proper places only once in a day, it can be realised how many volumes will accumulate in the Replacing Shelf in the course of the day and how important the Replacing Shelf Arranging Job is.

2733 Initiation of New Readers

As soon as a new reader is come across, receive him in a courteous manner and, without in any way appearing to be officious, take him round the stack room, explain the classified arrangement of books ; in the course of doing so, find out what subject or subjects he is interested in. Spend more time in the region containing books relating to his subjects and explain to him the detailed classification of those subjects. Then, take him to the catalogue cabinet and explain to him in brief terms, by means of concrete examples relating to the books in which he is interested, the structure of the catalogue, its various parts, and in particular, the use of the cross reference cards. As the next step, explain to him the formalities to be gone through in taking books for consultation and returning them and in borrowing books from the library for home reading. Without explicitly referring to them, try to instil into the reader as high a civic sense as possible in his relation to the library, and also inspire in him a feeling of confidence and friendliness.

2734 Vigilance

Readers who are accustomed to the library may not require your attention or assistance on every occasion. But unfortunately some of the readers might have a hardened civic conscience which induces them to have recourse to various types of malpractices in order to have some advantage over their brother readers. For example, some may deliberately misplace the books so that they alone may know their location and not anybody else. Some may fall a victim to the temptation to extract pages from books, if they are left all alone. Some may even be carried along by the devil to the extent of hiding small books in their pockets and so on. Fortunately such criminally minded readers are few ; but, as one thief is sufficient to annoy a small community, even one such reader is sufficient to bring the open access system into disrepute. Further, the confirmed criminals are the most difficult to detect. Hence, the need for keeping a watchful eye over the readers in the stack room. As the Reference Section is the only section that is permanently stationed in the stack room, this dirty job has to fall on its shoulders. But take care that you do not offend or annoy innocent readers in your enthusiasm to detect the elusive criminals. Make a note of the " doubtfuls " in the black book and circulate it confidentially among the other members of the staff.

2736 Ready Reference

As soon as a reader asks for any piece of Ready Information, i e information that can be easily obtained from ready reference books, direct him to those books. If the reader is a very busy person—not a busy-body—you may occasionally go to the extent of actually finding out the information for him. But much discretion should be used in going to this full length, lest the readers should be tempted to shirk their own duties and responsibilities in helping themselves.

If any unusual type of information is spotted out in the course of this work, note it down in a *Reference Slip*.

2737 Long Range Reference

You may get requisitions for Long Range Reference either by letter or in person from various readers. By Long Range Reference is meant Reference Service which cannot be done in a short time with the aid of ready reference books, but requires prolonged investigation and search.

Long Range Reference Service includes bibliographical service or the preparation of special bibliographies for the use of readers, either on demand or in anticipation.

Naturally this piece of work cannot be done either as Immediate Jobs or even as jobs of definite periodicity. It will have to be done as a pick-up-work. As soon as the information is gathered, furnish it to the reader in person if the reader happens to call at the library or to the Circulation Section for transmission to the reader by post. Here again your business should be more often to locate the services for the information sought and leave it for the reader himself to make use of the sources suggested by you.

The reference cabinet should be invariably looked into before any long range reference service is undertaken. It is probable that the same or a similar piece of topic had already been fully worked out and that the related reference slips are filed in it. They may require only to be supplemented and brought up-to-date.

2738 SHELF STUDY

The Shelf Study also is to be done as a pick-up-work. It consists of utilising the spare hours in building up an intimate acquaintance with the resources of the library. This is a very important aspect of Reference Service. It is the systematic shelf study that helps the Reference Section to build up the capital, so to speak, from which it can draw for Ready Reference service and Long Range Reference Service.

27385 REFERENCE CABINET

27385:3 *Casual jobs*

27385:31 REFERENCE SLIPS WRITING

As and when a new piece of information is spotted out, whether in the process of Ready Reference Service or Long Range Reference Service, or Shelf Study, write out a *Reference Slip*. A Reference Slip should contain in sequence, the call number of the volume used, its heading, its title, and the exact page of reference.

27385:32 REFERENCE SLIPS GROUPING

As soon as a few slips get accumulated, group the Reference Slips according to the topics to which they relate and put them in the *Reference Slip Box*.

27385:33 REFERENCE SLIPS GUIDING

When a suitable opportunity occurs, study the Reference Slips grouped in the Reference Slip Box and insert suitable guides, putting a guide card having the name of the topic to which the group of slips relates.

27385:35 REFERENCE GUIDE CLASSIFYING

Then, assign proper class numbers to the *Reference Slip Guides*, i e to the topics which they represent. Write this class number at the left hand top corner of each of the Reference Slips in the group.

27385:37 REFERENCE SLIPS FILING

Pick out the different groups of Reference Slips along with their guides and file each group in the proper classified sequence in the Reference Cabinet.

27385:38 REFERENCE CABINET REVIEWING

Periodically, say once in six months, or whenever a suitable opportunity occurs, examine the contents of the Reference Cabinet. Some groups of slips may require to be brought up-to-date, some may have to be discarded, while perhaps, in some cases, some reclassification may be necessary. All the necessary things should be done to the Reference Cabinet periodically in this manner, as the Reference Cabinet is a great time-saving device for the Reference Section. Work once done can be used for ever. It even converts Long Range Service into Ready Reference Service. The Reference Section should devote sufficient thought and energy to review the Reference Cabinet from time to time and keep it in a trim condition.

274 Elimination of Waste

2741 ORGANISATION

If the turnover in the Section demands the assignment of several members to it, the distribution of work among the members of the Section should proceed along the lines of subject specialisation. In this arrangement each member of the Section will get a good opportunity to pick up a sufficiently intimate knowledge of certain subjects.

2742 General Competence

This does not mean, however, that a particular member is to ignore all the subjects except his special ones. The exigencies of the work in the Reference Section would demand that any member should render help to any reader on any subject so far as Ready Reference Service or general help to readers is concerned.

2743 Sense of Honour

It can be seen, from the introduction to this chapter and from the description contained in the routine part of this chapter, that Reference Service is not clerical work. It is academic in its nature. Hence, it is not possible to have quantitative measures for its out-turn. The proper utilisation of the time of the Reference Section has therefore to depend entirely upon their devotion to duty and sense of honour. The Head of the Reference Section should set an example to his assistants and stimulate in them an inherent urge to play up.

2747 Diary 1

Perhaps, the section may maintain a diary on a Daily Basis with the following headings :

3 Number of readers initiated.
4 Number of vigilance cases.
61 Number of readers helped with ready reference.
62 Number of items of ready reference.
66 Number of bespoken books traced.
71 Number of readers helped with long range reference.
72 Number of items of long range reference.
8 Number of bays of shelf study.
85 Number of reference slips written.
851 Number of reference guides written.
857 Number of reference slips filed.

2748 Diary 2

A second diary, showing the number of occasions readers were helped in different subjects, may be maintained on a daily basis, with the main divisions of the classification scheme used or suitable modifications of them as headings.

275 Correlation

As this Section has not got any elaborate routine to be done, it does not admit of any correlation table. It may be stated in general terms, however,

1 That the Reference Section will have to help the Book Selection Section as often as possible in the choice of books, particularly with reference to the demand from readers and the gaps in the collection in the library ;

2 That they will have to help the Book Order Section on the weekly order day in detecting cases of unconscious duplication with the aid of their intimate acquaintance with the resources of the library ;

3 That they will have to help the Periodical Publication Section also in a similar manner and help them further in bringing to their notice the appearance of new periodicals, the publication of cumulative indexes and other surprise items relating to periodical publications, which they might come to know of in the course of their reference work and shelf study ;

5 That they will have to bring to the notice of the Technical Section, errors in classification and cataloguing, which they have a great opportunity to detect in the course of their daily duty, and also discuss with the Technical Section the reaction which the classification produces on the readers, and thereby help the improvement of the classification system ;

6 That they will have to be in constant touch with the Circulation Section so that they can frequently compare notes about the readers in the library for facilitating their vigilance work and for understanding the readers, with a view to finding out the best way in which they can serve them with the resources of the library ; they should also help in tracing out uncharged bespoken books ;

8 That they will have to discuss with the Maintenance Section the shelf-rearrangement desirable as a means of publicity and that they should find out from the Maintenance Section the regions which are not sufficiently popular and try to popularise them ; they should also issue and receive

back the volumes in the Closed Collections ;

95 That they should work hand in hand with the Publicity Section for the fulfilment of the Third Law of Library Science " Every Book Its Reader " ; and

995 That they should help the Binding Section freely and bring to their notice any incongruity in the way in which periodical publications have been assembled and bound, so that the most serviceable and uniform method of assembling and binding may be evolved in the library.

276 Time Scheme

It can be seen from the routine part of this chapter that the jobs of this section are either Immediate Jobs or Casual Jobs. Hence, this section does not admit of a time scheme. But the section should remember one point. The task of bringing the reference cabinet up-to-date from time to time and reviewing the cabinet periodically should not be allowed to be crowded out.

277 Forms and Registers

This section has no correspondence to do and no records to keep, except the Reference Slips. The specification for the Reference Slip is as follows :

C7 *Reference slip*. Manuscript. Ledger paper. Cabinet.

The headings have been given in routine " 27385:31 Reference Slips Writing ".

278 Files

As this section has no correspondence, it has no files to keep, except the files relating to " 791 Outward enquiries " and " 792 Inward enquiries " for which the details are similar to the correspondence files in other sections. It may be stated that the enquiries here refer, *not* to enquiries from readers, *but* to enquiries relating to the work of the reference section from outside libraries and members of the library profession.

CHAPTER 28

MAINTENANCE SECTION

281 Planning

2811 ART OF SHELF ARRANGEMENT

The Maintenance Section is to be in complete charge of the shelves. It should arrange the books in the shelves so as to fulfil the Fourth Law of Library Science, viz " Save the time of the reader". Reference books like encyclopaedias, dictionaries, current year-books and directories and recent additions should be located in a prominent place and as near the reading room as possible. The selection of the works for this group has to be determined and has to be varied from time to time by careful observation and experimentation. A list of the recent additions for a period of at least six months may be kept in the same place. Latest issues of periodicals should be exhibited on the tables with adequate table guides for each subject. The arrangement of books in the stack room itself requires special consideration. The arrangement cannot be permanent in the changing library world. It will have to be judiciously varied and readjusted from time to time. Several factors will have to be examined from time to time for this purpose. One would very much like to have the books and periodicals arranged in the sequence in which the subjects occur in the schedule of classification for the mere satisfaction of having them arranged in strict accordance with the schedule sequence. But the theoretical or psychological sequence of the subjects found in the schedules of classification is seldom strictly parallel to the popular sequence. Nor is the popular sequence a permanent one. It does and must change with time.

2812 VARIATION OF ARRANGEMENT

Hence, the rigid arrangement by the schedule of classification only results in wasting the time and energy, not only of the reading public but also of the Reference Section. In an arrangement like this, a majority of readers may have to waste their time and energy in walking unnecessarily great distances to get at their books.

The Reference Section also is affected in the same way, as its movements are dependent on the movements of the readers. It is quite necessary to break the schedule sequence and judiciously repermute the subjects on the shelves. To give an example, literature, as the most popular subject attracting the greatest number of readers, may be located as near the entrance as possible, irrespective of its proper place in accordance with the schedule of classification. Other subjects may be arranged at distances from the entrance varying inversely with their popularity. Any one arrangement should not be considered as final (merely on the ground of unwillingness to undertake additional labour). Its utility must be constantly tested by experience in the light of the statistics of issue. Any reshuffling of subjects found to be necessary should be immediately carried out even at the cost of additional labour and time, as *the convenience* of the readers is *the convenience* of the library. The collection of the popular books may be called the *Main Collection*, as it has been done in the Madras University Library, to distinguish it from the other collections that are to follow.

2813 Multiplication of Collections

In every subject, we have three groups of volumes. One group consisting of standard books and current treatises, a second consisting of periodicals and serials and a third, of books of archaic interest and hence of comparatively infrequent demand. In an ordinary library, the popularity of these three groups is likely to be in a descending sequence of magnitude. If the volumes of the second and third groups are allowed to be in the Main Collection, they will be obstructive rather than helpful and make the readers traverse unnecessarily long distances between the various main subjects or classes, nay even between the various sub-classes of one and the same main class. To walk to and fro along rows of chemistry periodicals before getting a text-book in chemistry or to run the eyes through volumes of budget estimates before locating a book on public finance may prove to be a regular ordeal for a large class of readers. Hence, the volumes belonging to the second and the third groups should be separated and located quite apart from the Main Collection. They are called the *Secondary* and the *Tertiary Collections* in the Madras University Library. It is not enough if the volumes are merely separated ; but their location should be indicated by putting near the call number a suitable symbol, in the volumes and in all the connected records wherever the call number appears. This symbol will indicate that such volumes are kept in a place different from their normal position in the Main Collection. This symbol is quite necessary also to facilitate the reshelving of the books returned at the counter from time to time. In the case of subjects, and whole divisions of subjects, periodical sets and serial publications which, by their very nature, are to be located only in the Secondary Collection, the Secondary Collection symbol may be omitted and taken as understood.

28131 Closed Collection

Again, certain types of books, if they are put in the way of the readers, are likely to be adversely affected by their being mal-handled by a few black sheep to such an extent that they are of no use to others who really want them. In this category we may include Fine Arts books, books full of art plates and books of pornographic interest. Such books may be kept in a non-open-access or Closed Collection (not necessarily in closed shelves). By a Closed Collection is meant that readers will not normally be allowed to have direct or open access to the shelves forming it, but will obtain their books in most cases by the old application slip system. This restriction may be waived in the case of certain classes of responsible readers. This Closed Collection gives us control over the use of these books. None of the Fine Arts books will retain good plates if they are placed in the open access shelves. Similarly all pages savouring of obscenity are systematically purloined (to satisfy the morbid curiosity of the black sheep) from otherwise scientific treatises. A monumental example of this in the Madras University Library is Havelock Ellis' *Psychology of sex*. Previous to its withdrawal from circulation, it was in so much demand that it was treated as a reference book and kept on the Circulation Counter. Every other reader would ask for "Ellis". Such books also should be taken over to the Closed Sequence. Such a Closed Collection is called a *Special Collection* in the Madras University Library and their call numbers are put between two horizontal parallel lines to indicate their location.

Again in a large growing library of national importance, it may not be desirable to weed out the out-of-date editions and books.

At the same time, it would be uneconomical to put them in the Main Collection. They may have to be kept in a collection of their own, till their transfer to the dormitory library. It is usual to allot to them the far off and the inaccessible parts of the library. It is called the *Tertiary Collection* in the Madras University Library.

28132 Abnormal Size Collection

To come to the actual arrangement of books on the shelves, it is quite necessary to see that the shelves present an aesthetic appearance. This presentable appearance is of extreme importance in an open access library ; for, the first thing that creates a good impression in a reader is the trim condition of the shelves with sufficient direction guides, stack guides and shelf guides. It is a most unsightly thing in a library to see on the shelves giants, pygmies and weaklings, all in a conglomeration minus the respect due to their ordinal arrangement. Hence, all volumes which, on account of their size and weight, preclude easy handling should be kept in a separate collection—called the *Oversize Collection* in the Madras University Library—and in such a manner that their potential energy is at a minimum. For example, the bottom most plank throughout the book-racks may be used for this collection. A suitable method invented by the Madras University Library to indicate their location is to overline their call numbers. Pamphlets and miniature volumes may be kept in a Closed Collection—called the *Undersize Collection* in the Madras University Library—and their location is indicated similarly by the underlining of their book numbers. If this is not done, such volumes invariably get themselves lost, either amidst other volumes or in the pockets of the book vandals.

28134 Temporary Collections

The abovementioned sequences by no means exhaust the sequences that should be maintained in a growing library. While these sequences are of a permanent nature, need is felt for the formation of certain Temporary Collections.

28135 Correction Collections

If the library makes any attempt whatever to keep itself abreast of the times, there will be constant need to revise the class numbers assigned to the books in stock, in the light of the experience gained in serving the books to the readers and in consequence of the realignment and reorientation of the divisions of knowledge brought about now and then in the ever-turbulent universe of knowledge.

For example, it is by no means easy to determine the most helpful placing of books of psycho-therapeutical interest. It is possible to find a place for them in psychology as well as in medicine. In such a case, it is desirable to experiment with either placing and arrive at a decision in the light of the experience gained. Such experimentation necessarily implies revision of class members.

As an illustration of the operation of the second cause for correction, one may cite the example of X-Rays. When they were first discovered in association with the conduction of electricity through gases, Dewey accommodated them in electricity. But it soon came to be realised that they constituted a class of radiation. This realisation naturally brought in its train the need for changing the class number of the books on X-Rays from the number in the basic class " Electricity " to the number in the basic class " Radiation".

Another example is that of Humanism in metaphysics—Humanism is itself being developed just now by Irving Babbit, Paul Elmer More and Ernest Seilliere. Books pertaining to this school of metaphysics came to be published only three decades ago. When the first few volumes came out it was hardly possible to appraise them correctly. It was very difficult to fix their correct " View Number " as their point of view appeared to be very elusive ; with the result, different books received different point of view numbers. But quite recently, when a sufficient number of books of that nature had arrived in the library, they were all assembled together and re-examined in relation to one another. Further, some of the latest books contained some definite marks of crystallisation. With the aid of these data, the Madras University Library has recently decided to give them the " View Number, 9 " and to amplify the digit '9' by the Subject Device, using for the amplifying number 'Y' Social Sciences. This is to say, the class number of those books has come to be fixed as R39(Y). So long as human knowledge progresses, this kind of correction must also go on.

When groups of books are segregated from the stock and assembled for this kind of re-examination and re-christening, they have always a tendency to stay long, away from the stack room. Special steps have to be taken to call for them at systematic intervals, in order to prevent their staying away altogether. The Madras University Library has found it helpful to regard this temporary group as a Temporary Collection. It has called it the *Correction Collection*. In practice, this Correction Collection is divided into several subcollections depending upon the Section that takes the responsibility for the correction—say the Technical Section, the Reference Section, etc.

28136 Binding Collection

Another factor that calls for a Temporary Collection is one of necessary occurrence in a popular library, which gets its books well-used and well-thumbed. As the books get worn-out by such legitimate use, it falls to the lot of the Maintenance Section to play the role of the family doctor to such books. At the right time, the Maintenance Section is to send such books to the hospital on medical leave. The process of relieving them, keeping them in mind when they are patients in the bindery, and reclaiming them promptly when their treatment is over, is best regulated by looking upon them as forming a Temporary Collection—the *Binding Collection*. Here again, it is likely that more than one monthly batch will be in the hospital simultaneously. It may also be wise to have their call numbers re-examined and reshaped before they are sent away to the bindery, as they are likely to have their call numbers marked permanently on their back in glittering letters of gold when they come back hale and healthy from their sojourn in the bindery. These considerations are enough to show that the Binding Collection should have a number of Sub-Collections.

28137 Topical Collection

Apart from finding for every reader his book and for every book its reader, the Reference Section has also to satisfy the Fourth Law, viz "Save the Time of the Reader". In certain situations, the Reference Section can achieve maximum result in this matter, if and only if the co-operation of the Maintenance Section is forthcoming. This co-operation, the Maintenance Section can and should easily offer. One of the vital reasons for maintaining the shelf register in cards on the basis of *one volume—one card*, is the extreme mobility that it gives to the arrangement of books. The Maintenance

Section should exploit this mobility for the benefit of the readers, by freely forming *Special Temporary Collections* to meet the special demands that may arise from time to time. A few concrete examples will make this clear. When a special course of lectures on educational experiments was being delivered to a large class of teachers, the syllabus of the lectures was perused in advance and in consultation with the lecturer all the books in the library that had a bearing on the course of lectures were assembled together and put in a special cupboard as a Special Temporary Collection dubbed *Educational Experiments Lecture Collection*. The *Principle of Parallel Movement* enabled the Maintenance Section to form such a collection and have easy control over it, thus enabling the Reference Section to serve the teachers attending the lectures with the least loss of time. Apart from the saving of time, the psychological effect was felt to be much more vital.

Every class of library, which wants to function up, will find occasion to form such *Topical Collections* from time to time. Local festivals, local celebrations and any other important local event will give the occasion to the library to form such Temporary Topical Collections. The discussion of a Bill or any momentous resolution that may come up before a Legislative Council will give the occasion for a Legislative Council Library to form such Temporary Topical Collections from time to time. The rush of enquirers and the pressure of time in a Legislative Council library would make the work of the librarian inefficient, if not impossible, if such Temporary Topical Collections are not intelligently sensed and formed in advance ; and, their formation would be impossible even if they are sensed, but for the extraordinary power which is given to him by this wonderful invention, by the library profession, of this extremely mobile shelf-register-in-cards, and the equally facile *Principle of Parallel Movement*. Perhaps, the value of the freedom to form such Temporary Topical Collections at pleasure will be most appreciated in business libraries, whose patrons know best the value of time and indeed look upon time as money and money as time.

2814 List of Collections

It may perhaps be better at this stage to give a complete list of the Collections maintained in the Madras University Library, to bring out the vastness of the complexity of the problem.

28141 Permanent Collections

28142 *With Open Access*

1 Counter Collection. No symbol. Books in constant use which are kept at the counter.

2 Reference Collection.. No symbol. Contains reference books, such as encyclopaedias, dictionaries, etc.

3 International Mind Alcove Collection. Symbol "I M A" Call number on the tag in red ink. Books supplied by the Carnegie Endowment for International Peace, assembled permanently in the reading room to attract the attention of the public.

4 Main Collection. No symbol.

5 Secondary Collection. Symbol : "*"

28143 *Without Open Access*

6 Language Collection. Several sub-collections, one for each language. Books in the Indian languages in all subjects with the exception of Philology, Religion and Indian Philosophy and books on Literature in the European languages other than English, are assigned to these groups of collections. No symbol necessary as the language number will indicate the collection.

7 Special Collection. Symbol: Underlining and overlining the call number.

8 Undersized Collection. Symbol : Underlining the call number.

9 Oversized Collection. Symbol : Overlining the call number.

10 Worn-out Collection. Symbol : Encircling the call number.

11 Tertiary Collection. Symbol : Putting 'T' above the call number.

28144 *With No Access*

12 Duplicate Collection. No symbol necessary.

Departmental Collection

13 General Departmental Collection, or Gen D

14 Sanskrit Department Collection, or 15D

15 Islamic Department Collection, or 2D

16 Tamil Department Collection, or 31D
17 Malayalam Department Collection, or 32D
18 Kanarese Department Collection, or 33D
19 Telugu Department Collection, or 35D
20 Mathematics Department Collection, or BD
21 Bio-Chemistry Department Collection, or ED
22 Botany Department Collection, or ID
23 Zoology Department Collection, or KD
24 Music Department Collection, or N8D
25 Philosophy Department Collection, or RD
26 Geography Department Collection, or UD
27 History Department Collection, or VD
28 Economics Department Collection, or XD

28145 Temporary Collections

29 RA Collection, or recent additions. Symbol : stamping the date of release from the Collection at a conventional place on the date label.

30 BT Collection, or books picked out for binding and lying in the Technical Section for correction.

31 BB Collection, or books lying in the Binding Section, being prepared for binding.

32 B (*month*) or the Collection of books lying in the bindery, the month indicating the month, in which it was sent out of the library, e g B (July), B (August), etc.

33 BC Collection, or the Collection of books sent to the binder for correction, that is, for rectification of the mistakes made in binding or in tooling.

34 B Sp Collection, or the Collection of books sent for urgent binding, apart from the monthly batches.

35 CR Collection, or the Collection of books lying with the reference section for correction of call number.

36 CT Collection, or the Collection of books lying in the T Section for correction of call number.

37 BL Collection, or the Collection of books lost or damaged by readers and pending their being replaced.

38 Topical Collections to be formed from time to time. Symbol : the date of release being stamped and encircled in red ink in a conventional place in the date label.

From our experience in the Madras University Library, the readers of this book may be assured that this bewildering number of Collections is by no means to be attributed to the "fascination of fuss", which a new profession like the library profession may be suspected to be prone to. On the other hand, the enormous difficulties, misfits and confusion experienced by us were eliminated only after the discovery of the need for and the bold adoption of such a multiplication of collections.

2815 Principal of Parallel Movement

Having been obliged to disturb the schedule sequence and to arrange the books in so many collections, it is a great responsibility for the Maintenance Section to maintain correct sequence in the shelves and to see that every book is in its correct place. The mechanical apparatus invented by the library profession to secure this is what is known as the *Shelf Register*. It is made up of cards of standard size viz 5×3 inches written on the principle—one title, one card—with the call number in the leading line. These shelf register cards are kept *absolutely parallel* to the books on the shelves, which means that they are to be arranged in 40 or more collections. What is more, except when the books leave their proper place on the shelves to get into the hands of a reader, every movement of the books should be controlled and imitated by an exactly parallel movement among the shelf register cards. The discovery of this *Principle of Parallel Movement* has turned out to be the panacea of most of the ills in the maintenance of the books in the library and brought in its train the inevitable genesis of the Maintenance Section. The shelf register cabinet is the hub of the stock in the library and correspondingly the Maintenance Section is the hub of the staff of the library.

2816 Accession and Shelf Registers

The second duty of the Maintenance Section is to maintain the Shelf Register, as it is in charge of the entire stock of the library. The Accession Register records the books and periodicals in the numerical sequence in which they are accessioned and is in fact made up of the accession cards. The Shelf Register gives the call number on the left hand top corner, the accession number below and, below these, the heading, the title and the series. These cards are arranged according to the call numbers in collections exactly parallel to the collections of books in the stack room and elsewhere. The accession cards are the rigid records for the stock of the library and the shelf register cards are the controlling switches of the stock. The accession cards are permanent in their arrangement and are not disturbed. The shelf register cards are mobile and are moved according to the reallocation of the books to the various collections from time to time.

The Accession Register and the Shelf Register are the only two records available for the purpose of periodical stock-taking. The Accession Register is quite unfit for this purpose as the stock-taker will have to run constantly here and there and up and down for checking successive entries in it. The Shelf Register, with its arrangement exactly parallel to the books, is the most suitable and convenient record that can be used to check the stock. Hence, the Shelf Register is to be regarded as virtually the stock register. As such, greatest care should be taken by the Maintenance Section in maintaining its complicated arrangement in so many collections, taking care to insert the cards in their appropriate collections. The shelf register cards of books which change their collections periodically, and otherwise, should simultaneously be transferred to the respective new collections. Otherwise books which are found missing in one collection will be found in a different collection. Periodically, say once in a year, or after each stock-taking, whichever is earlier, the arrangement of the shelf register cards should be checked to rectify casual misplacements.

2817 Shelf Study

Lastly, the head of the Maintenance Section in particular and his assistants in general should devote their moments of slack work to studying the contents of the shelves so as to develop a fair knowledge of their contents, as this knowledge is of vital importance to the efficiency of their work, particularly in their relation to the other Sections of the staff.

2818 Factors in Planning

The distinctive work of the Maintenance Section is to be planned with reference to the following factors :

1 Used volumes ;

2 New volumes ;
3 Stack room ;
4 Correction of call numbers ;
5 Binding ;
6 Topical collections ;
7 Reference study ; and
8 Shelf register cabinet.

282 Job Analysis

2821 Used Volumes

The Work of the Maintenance Section relating to used volumes is to consist of the following items :

1 Replacing the used volumes in their respective shelves, which may be referred to as *New Volumes Replacing Work* ;
4 Purchasing copies of the volumes lost by users on behalf of the users concerned, which may be referred to as *Lost Volumes Work* ; and
5 Getting damaged volumes bound on behalf of the users concerned, which may be referred to as *Damaged Volumes Work*.

2821:1 *Used Volumes Replacing Work*

2821:1:4 The Used Volumes Replacing Work of the Maintenance Section is to consist of the following daily jobs :

1 Sorting the volumes returned from the counter according to their sequences, which may be referred to as *Returned Volumes Sorting* ;
2 Arranging the sorted volumes in the classified order, which may be referred to as *Returned Volumes Arranging* ; and
3 Placing the arranged volumes in their appropriate places in the shelves, which may be referred to as *Returned Volumes Shelving*.

2821:4 *Lost Volumes Work*

2821:4:4 The Lost Volumes Work of the Maintenance Section is to consist of the following daily job :

8 Transferring the related shelf register card to the lost volume sequence, which may be referred to as *Lost Volumes Card Transferring*.

2821:4:5 The Lost Volumes Work of the Maintenance Section is to consist of the following weekly jobs :

1 Ascertaining if the volume is in print, and if so, finding out information about the publisher, price, etc. which may be referred to as *Lost Volume Data Ascertaining* ;
2 If the book is not in print, calling for quotation from second-hand booksellers, which may be referred to as *Lost Volume Quotation Calling* ;
3 Issuing the order for a copy of the volume, which may be referred to as *Lost Volume Ordering* ;
4 Receiving and dealing with the volume as soon as it comes from the vendor, which may be referred to as *Replaced Volume Receiving* ;
5 Writing out accession number, call number, etc. in the volume and preparing the volume for public use, which may be referred to as *Replaced Volume Preparing* ;
6 Advising the circulation section about the receipt of the volume and about the cost incurred in obtaining the fresh copy, which may be referred to as *Circulation Section Advising* ; and
8 Retransferring the related shelf register card from the lost volumes sequence to its normal place, which may be referred to as *Lost Volume Card Retransferring*.

2821:5 *Damaged Volumes Work*

2821:5:4 The Damaged Volumes Work of the Maintenance Section is to consist of the following daily job :

8 Transferring the related shelf register card to the lost volume sequence, which may be referred to as *Damaged Volume Card Transferring*.

2821:5:5 The Damaged Volumes Work of the Maintenance Section is to consist of the following weekly jobs :

.51 Forwarding the damaged volume to the Binding Section

to get it bound, which may be referred to as *Damaged Volume Forwarding* ;

56 Ascertaining from the binding section the cost of binding, which may be referred to as *Binding Cost Ascertaining* ;

6 Advising the Maintenance Section about the receipt of the bound volume and about the cost incurred in rebinding it, which may be referred to as *Maintenance Section Advising*; and

8 Retransferring the related shelf register card from the lost volume sequence to its normal place, which may be referred to as *Damaged Volume Card Retransferring.*

2822 New Volumes

The work of the Maintenance Section relating to New Volumes is to consist of the following items :

1 Tallying the accession cards and shelf register cards relating to the new volumes, which may be referred to as *New Volumes Tallying Work* ;

3 Taking charge of the new volumes of the week from the Technical Section and the Publicity Section and putting them on the shelves, which may be referred to as *New Volumes Shelving Work* ; and

5 Releasing the volumes in the recent additions shelf for loan, which may be referred to as *New Volumes Releasing Work.*

2822:1 *New Volumes Tallying Work*

2822:1:5 The New Volumes Tallying Work of the Maintenance Section is to consist of the following weekly jobs :

1 Reconciling the entries in the accession cards and the shelf register cards, which may be referred to as *Cards Reconciling* ;

2 Transmitting the accession cards to the Accession Section, which may be referred to as *Accession Cards Transmitting.*

2822:3 *New Volumes Shelving Work*

2822:3:5 The New Volumes Shelving Work of the Maintenance Section is to consist of the following weekly jobs :

16 Sorting the shelf register cards by their collections, which

may be referred to as *Shelf Register Cards Sorting* ;

17 Arranging the sorted cards in each collection, which may be referred to as *Shelf Register Cards Arranging* ;

21 Tallying the volumes with the shelf register cards which may be referred to as *New Volumes Tallying* ;

22 Verifying the entries in the book cards, which may be referred to as *Book Card Verifying* ; and

3 Shelving the volumes in the appropriate places, which may be referred to as *New Volumes Shelving.*

2822:5 *New Volumes Releasing Work*

2822:5:5 The New Volumes Releasing Work of the Maintenance Section is to consist of the following weekly jobs :

1 Picking out from the recent additions shelf the volumes that are to be released, which may be referred to as *New Volumes Picking* ;

2 Checking the call numbers and the accession numbers on the tag, the date label and the inside of the volume, which may be referred to as *Released New Volumes Checking* ;

3 Shelving the volumes in the appropriate places, which may be referred to as *Released New Volumes Shelving* ; and

8 Transferring the related shelf register cards from the recent additions sequence to the appropriate places, which may be referred to as *Released New Volumes Card Transferring.*

2823 Stack Room

The Work of the Maintenance Section relating to the Stack Room may consist of the following items :

1 Checking the stock of the library, which may be referred to as *Checking Work* ;

3 Rearranging the volumes, which may be referred to as *Re-arranging Work* ; and

5 Scrutinising and rectifying the guides in the stack room, which may be referred to as *Guiding Work.*

2823:1 *Checking Work*

2823:1:5 The Checking Work of the Maintenance Section

relating to the stock of the library is to consist of the following weekly jobs :

1 Checking the shelf register cards with the issue tray, which may be referred to as *Charged Tray Checking* ;
2 Checking the shelf register cards with the books on the shelves, which may be referred to as *Shelf Checking* ;
3 Investigating the volumes not accounted for, which may be referred to as *Investigating* ; and
4 Reporting to the librarian the result of the investigation, which may be referred to as *Inventory Reporting*.

2823:3 *Rearranging Work*

2823:3:4 The Rearranging Work of the Maintenance Section is to consist of the following daily jobs :

2 Tidying up the volumes on the shelves, which may be referred to as *Shelf Tidying* ; and
3 Rectifying the order of the books on the shelves, which may be referred to as *Shelf Rectifying*.

2823:3:8 The Rearranging Work of the Maintenance Section is to consist of the following annual jobs :

1 Redistributing the volumes in the shelves at points where there is congestion, which may be referred to as *Shelf Easing* ;
2 Rearranging the position of the classes and collections in the light of the suggestions of the Reference Section and the Publicity Section, which may be referred to as *Shelf Rearranging* ; and
8 Carrying out the consequential rearrangement in the shelf register cabinet, which may be referred to as *Cards Rearranging*.

2823:5 *Guiding Work*

2823:5:4 The Guiding Work of the Maintenance Section is to consist of the following daily job :

3 Scrutinising the tags on the backs of the volumes and renewing

them whenever necessary, which may be referred to as *Tag Scrutinising*.

2823:5:6 The Guiding Work of the Maintenance Section is to consist of the following monthly job :

1 Scrutinising and making the necessary changes in the shelf guides, which may be referred to as *Shelf Guides Scrutinising*.

2823:5:8 The Guiding Work of the Maintenance Section is to consist of the following annual jobs :

1 *Bay Guide Scrutinising* ;
2 *Tier Guide Scrutinising* ; and
3 *Guide Plan Scrutinising*.

2824 CORRECTION OF CALL NUMBERS

The Correction Work of the Maintenance Section may consist of the following items :

1 Transmitting to the Technical Section the volumes that require correction, which may be referred to as *Correction Transmitting Work* ;
2 Carrying out the corrections indicated by the Technical Section, which may be referred to as *Correcting Work* ; and
8 Reinserting the corrected shelf register cards, which may be referred to as *Correction Reinserting Work*.

2824:1 *Correction Transmitting Work*

2824:1:4 The Correction Transmitting Work of the Maintenance Section is to consist of the following daily jobs :

1 Collecting together the volumes whose call numbers require correction and arranging them by their collections and call numbers, which may be referred to as *Correction Collection Arranging* ;
2 Transferring the shelf register cards relating to the volumes of the Correction Collection, which may be referred to as *Correction Collection Card Transferring* ; and

3 Transmitting the volumes to the Technical Section, which may be referred to as *Correction Collection Transmitting.*

2824:2 *Correcting Work*

2824:2:5 The Correcting Work of the Maintenance Section is to consist of the following weekly jobs :

1 Carrying out the corrections in the call number of the shelf register card, which may be referred to as *Card Correcting* ;
2 Carrying out the corrections in the call numbers entered in the different parts of the volume, which may be referred to as *Volume Correcting* ; and
3 Shelving the corrected volumes in the appropriate places, which may be referred to as *Corrected Volumes Shelving.*

2824:8 *Reinserting Work*

2824:8:5 The Reinserting Work of the Maintenance Section of call numbers is to consist of the following weekly jobs :

4 Correcting the call numbers in the related accession cards, which may be referred to as *Accession Card Correcting* ;
6 Sorting the shelf register cards into the collections, which may be referred to as *Corrected Cards Sorting* ;
7 Arranging the shelf register cards in each collection by their call numbers, which may be referred to as *Corrected Cards Arranging* ; and
8 Inserting the arranged shelf register cards in their appropriate places, which may be referred to as *Corrected Cards Re-inserting.*

2825 BINDING WORK

The work of the Maintenance Section relating to Binding may consist of the following items :

1 Transmitting the volumes collected for binding to the Technical Section for scrutiny of call number and correction, if any, which may be referred to as *Binding Transmitting Work* ;
2 Carrying out the corrections, if any, made by the Technical Section, which may be referred to as *Binding Correcting Work* ;

5 Tallying the binding list with the related shelf register cards, which may be referred to as *Binding List Tallying Work* ; and
8 Reinserting the shelf register cards after the volumes come back from the Binding Section, which may be referred to as *Binding Reinserting Work*.

2825:1 *Binding Transmitting Work*

2825:1:4 The Binding Transmitting Work of the Maintenance Section is to consist of the following daily jobs :

1 Picking and collecting the volumes that require binding, which may be referred to as *Worn-out Volumes Picking* ; and
4 Collating the volumes collected for binding, which may be referred to as *Worn-out Volumes Collating*.

2825:1:5 The Binding Transmitting Work of the Maintenance Section is to consist of the following weekly jobs :

2 Transferring the shelf register cards of the collated worn-out volumes, which may be referred to as *Worn-out Volumes Card Transferring* ;
3 Removing the book cards from the volumes, which may be referred to as *Book Card Removing* ; and
5 Transmitting the volumes to the Technical Section, which may be referred to as *Worn-out Volumes Transmitting*.

2825:2 *Binding Correcting Work*

2825:2:5 The Binding Correcting Work of the Maintenance Section is to consist of the following weekly jobs :

1 Correcting the call numbers in the shelf register cards, which may be referred to as *Card Correcting* ;
2 Correcting the call numbers in the volumes, which may be referred to as *Volume Correcting* ; and
5 Retransmitting the corrected volumes to the Technical Section, which may be referred to as *Corrected Worn-out Volumes Retransmitting*.

2825:2:6 The Binding Correcting Work of the Maintenance

Section is to consist of the following monthly jobs :

4 Correcting the call numbers in the related accession cards, which may be referred to as *Accession Card Correcting* ; and
8 Rearranging the shelf register cards in the binding sequence of the month by their new call numbers, which may be referred to as *Binding Cards Rearranging*.

2825:5 *Binding List Tallying Work*

2825:5:6 The Binding List Tallying Work of the Maintenance Section is to be done as a monthly job.

2825:8 *Binding Reinserting Work*

2825:8:6 The Binding Reinserting Work of the Maintenance Section is to consist of the following monthly jobs :

1 As soon as the binding list is received from the Binding Section after the volumes are returned from the binder, scrutinising the list, which may be referred to as *Binding List Scrutinising* ;
21 Tallying the bound volumes returned by the Binding Section with the shelf register cards, which may be referred to as *Bound Volumes Tallying* ;
22 Inserting the book cards in the volumes, which may be referred to as *Book Card Inserting* ;
26 Transmitting to the Circulation Section, the bespoken volumes, which may be referred to as *Bespoken Volumes Transmitting* ;
31 Sorting the bound volumes returned by the Binding Section, which may be referred to as *Bound Volumes Sorting* ;
32 Arranging the sorted volumes, which may be referred to as *Bound Volumes Arranging* ;
33 Placing the arranged bound volumes on the shelves, which may be referred to as *Bound Volumes Shelving* ;

Note : *The three processes of* sorting, arranging, *and* shelving the bound volumes *may be referred to as* Reshelving.

4 Investigating the volumes relating to the undischarged shelf register cards of the binding sequence, which may be referred

to as *Undischarged Cards Investigating* ; and

8 Reinserting the shelf register cards of the volumes which have been sent for shelving, which may be referred to as *Binding Sequence Cards Reinserting*.

2826 Topical Collections

The Work of the Maintenance Section relating to topical sequences may consist of the following items :

1 Collecting together the volumes for the topical sequence, which may be referred to as *Topical Collection Collecting Work* ;

2 Shelving the collected volumes in the appropriate place, which may be referred to as *Topical Collection Shelving Work* ; and

8 Releasing the volumes from the topical sequence, which may be referred to as *Topical Collection Releasing Work*.

2826:1 *Collecting Work*

2826:1:3 The Topical Collection Collecting Work of the Maintenance Section is to consist of the following casual jobs :

1 Picking out the volumes which deserve to be placed in the topical sequence, which may be referred to as *Topical Volumes Picking* ;

2 Transferring the shelf register cards, which may be referred to as *Topical Sequence Cards Transferring* ; and

3 Stamping on the date labels of the volumes the date of release from the topical sequence, which may be referred to as *Release Date Marking*.

2826:2 *Shelving Work*

2826:2:3 The Topical Collections Shelving Work of the Maintenance Section relating to topical sequences is to consist of the following casual jobs :

1 Writing the main guide for the topical sequence, which may be referred to as *Main Guide Writing* ;

2 Putting the volumes in the proper sequence on the shelves

in the topical sequence, which may be referred to as *Topical Volumes Shelving* ; and

4 Writing and inserting the necessary shelf guides, which may be referred to as *Topical Collections Guiding*.

2826:8 *Releasing Work*

2826:8:3 The Topical Collection Releasing Work of the Maintenance Section is to consist of the following casual jobs :

1 Tallying the volumes in the released topical collection with the shelf register cards, which may be referred to as *Released Volumes Tallying* ;

3 Redistributing the volumes to their normal places, which may be referred to as *Released Volumes Shelving* ; and

8 Reinserting the shelf register cards of the released topical collection in their normal places, which may be referred to as *Topical Sequence Cards Reinserting*.

2827 REFERENCE STUDY

2827:3 The work of the Maintenance Section relating to Reference Study is to consist of the following casual jobs :

1 Pursuing and investigating the long range reference problems transferred by the Reference Section, which may be referred to as *Reference Investigating* ;

7 Transmitting the results of the investigation to the Reference Section, which may be referred to as *Reference Section Advising* ; and

8 Picking up acquaintance with the volumes in the shelves at odd hours, which may be referred to as *Shelf Studying*.

2828 SHELF REGISTER CABINET

2828:5 The work of the Maintenance Section relating to the shelf register cabinet is to consist of the following weekly job :

8 Inserting the shelf register cards in the shelf register cabinet, which may be referred to as *Shelf Register Cards Inserting*.

2828:8 The work of the Maintenance Section relating to the

shelf register cabinet is to consist of the following annual jobs :

1 Redistributing the shelf register cards so as to relieve any congestion that might have developed in any region, which may be referred to as *Cabinet Easing* ; and

4 Scrutinising and making the necessary changes in the tray guides, which may be referred to as *Tray Guide Changing*.

283 **Routine**

2831 Used Volumes

2831:1 *Used Volumes Replacing Work*

2831:1:4 *Daily jobs*

2831:1:41 Returned Volumes Sorting

At the appointed hour of the day, sort the volumes returned from the counter and lying in the replacing shelf, according to their collections.

2831:1:42 Returned Volumes Arranging

Arrange the volumes in each collection, taking the collections one after another. Place the arranged volumes on the trolley. As soon as the trolley is full, the next routine is to be done and after its completion, the arrangement of the remaining volumes is to be resumed.

2831:1:43 Returned Volumes Shelving

As soon as the trolley is filled up, push the trolley to the related shelves and insert the volumes in the appropriate places. When the volumes are inserted, care must be taken to see that the classified sequence is accurately maintained and that the shelves are left in a tidy condition, the volumes standing upright and not leaning about in a slovenly manner.

It would be conducive to economy of labour if the replacing of used volumes is done only once a day. Till then, the volumes returned from the counter may be kept in the temporary shelf, referred to as the *Replacing Shelf*. The users of the library can have access to this shelf. In fact, this temporary shelf may be those in the first two or three days in the stack room, so that the users' attention is easily drawn to them and the Reference Section may also look into them now and then as need arises. Many of the volumes in the Replacing Shelf will generally go back to the readers. It is our experience in the Madras University Library that about 50 per cent of the volumes get recirculated while on the Replacing Shelf. This involves a proportionate saving in the labour of replacing. The window sills against the cross-gangways in the stack room may be used as Replacing Shelves, if they are timber-lined.

2831:4 *Lost Volumes Work*

2831:4:4 *Daily job*

2831:4:48 Lost Volume Card Transferring

As soon as intimation is received from the Circulation Section about the loss of a volume by a user, transfer the related shelf register card to the lost volumes collection.

2831:4:5 *Weekly jobs*

2831:4:51 Lost Volume Data Ascertaining

As soon as intimation is received from the Circulation Section that the user, who had lost a volume, had made a special deposit to cover the cost of the volume and that he had requested that the library might get a fresh copy, find out from the accesssion card the necessary bibliographical data about the volume lost—publisher, price, format and edition.

2831:4:52 Lost Volume Quotation Calling

Then, find out from the trade bibliographical catalogue like the *Reference catalogue*, whether the volume is still in print. If it is not in print, write to second-hand booksellers, calling for quotations for a second-hand copy.

2831:4:53 Lost Volume Ordering

As soon as it is discovered that the volume is in print or as the quotation received is found to be acceptable, order for a copy of the volume.

2831:4:54 REPLACED VOLUME RECEIVING

As soon as the copy of the volume comes from the vendor, collate it carefully and verify if its collation and its other bibliographical peculiarities agree with what is recorded in the related accession card, getting the accession card from the Accession Section. Pass the concerned bill and send it to the Accounts Section for payment.

2831:4:55 REPLACED VOLUME PREPARING

If the volume is acceptable, enter in all the necessary places of the book, the accession number and the call number. Paste a book pocket, a date label, and a tag. Write the accession number and the call number in the date label and the call number on the tag. If the edition got is different, the book number may have to be changed in consultation with the Technical Section. In that case, advise the Technical Section about the change, so that they may carry out the correction in the catalogue and its copies ; carry out the correction in the shelf register card and the accession card.

2831:4:56 CIRCULATION SECTION ADVISING

As soon as the preparation of the volume is over, inform the Circulation Section that the lost volume has been replaced. Further, find out from the Accounts Section the actual cost incurred in replacing the volume and communicate it to the Circulation Section. Then, get the related book card from the Circulation Section and insert it in the book pocket after making the corrections, if any.

2831:4:58 LOST VOLUME CARD RETRANSFERRING

After advising the Circulation Section, pick out the related shelf register card from the lost volume collection and place it in its normal place. Then, send the volume to the shelf.

2831:5 *Damaged Volumes Work*

2831:5:4 *Daily job*

2831:5:48 DAMAGED VOLUME CARD TRANSFERRING

As soon as intimation is received from the Circulation Section about the volume damaged by a user, transfer the related shelf register card to the lost volume collection.

2831:5:5 *Weekly jobs*

2831:5:551 DAMAGFD VOLUME FORWARDING

As soon as the damaged volume is reveived from the Circulation Section, if it is only to be repaired, send it to the Binding Section after consulting the Technical Section for the change of call number, if any. If not, place the book in the damaged volumes collection and proceed with all the necessary routines as if the volume had been lost.

2831:5:556 BINDING COST ASCERTAINING

As soon as the volume comes back from the Binding Section properly repaired, go through all the processes for receiving a bound volume. Find out from the Binding Section the cost incurred in repairing the volume.

2831:5:56 COUNTER SECTION ADVISING

Advise the Circulation Section about the receipt of the repaired volume and about the cost incurred in rebinding it. If it is a case of the volume having been damaged and a fresh copy having been obtained, send the damaged copy to the Circulation Section so that they may return it to the user concerned. Obtain the related book card from the Circulation Section and insert it in the book pocket of the repaired copy or the fresh copy, as the case may be, after making the corrections, if any.

2831:5:58 DAMAGED VOLUME CARD RETRANSFERRING

After advising the Circulation Section, pick out the related shelf register card from the lost volume collection and place it in its normal place. Then, send the volume to the shelf.

2832 NEW VOLUMES

2832:1 *New Volumes Tallying Work*

2832:1:5 *Weekly jobs*

2832:1:51 CARDS RECONCILING

At the appointed hour on the appointed day of the week (see rule 2537:3:58), get from the Technical Section the *Transmission Box*. This box will contain the accession cards coupled with the related shelf register cards arranged in the accession sequence (see rule 2537:3:53).

Compare each accession card with its related shelf register card carefully. Note in particular if they agree on the following points : 1 accession number ; 2 donation number, if any ; 3 call number ; 4 heading; 5 short title; and 6 series, if any. Examine if there is any discontinuity in the accession numbers and the donation numbers. If there is any discrepancy, get it rectified by the Technical Section. As the cards are reconciled, place the accession cards in the *Transmission Box* in the accession sequence and the related shelf register cards in the *Shelf Register Cards Box* in the accession sequence.

2832:1:52 ACCESSION CARDS TRANSMITTING

After the shelving of the new volumes is over, fill up the columns entitled " shelving " in the related accession cards ; then, hand over the *Transmission Box* containing the accession cards to the head of the Accession Section and when the transmission register comes back, examine if it contains the initials of the head of the Accession Section, as a token of his having received the *Transmission Box* with its contents.

2832:3 *New Volumes Shelving Work*

2832:3:5 *Weekly jobs*

2832:3:516 SHELF REGISTER CARDS SORTING

As soon as the cards reconciling is over, sort the shelf register cards by their collection numbers.

2832:3:517 SHELF REGISTER CARDS ARRANGING

Arrange the cards in each of the collections by their call numbers and put the cards in the arranged sequence in the *Shelf Register Cards Box.*

2832:3:521 TALLYING

Take the Shelf Register Cards Box to the place where the Technical Section has kept the volumes of the week. These volumes will be found properly arranged. Tally the volumes with the cards. While tallying, verify the numbers on the back of the title page. If there is any discrepancy get it set right by the Technical Section. If the discrepancy affects also the accession card, get it corrected.

2832:3:522 BOOK CARD VERIFYING

As soon as the tallying is over, take the Book Card Tray from the Technical Section. Verify each card with its related Shelf Register Card and insert it in the book pocket of the appropriate volume. While inserting, verify whether the accession number and the call number in the book card agrees with those on the date label in the volume.

If any volume is without a book pocket, it means that it will have to go directly to the binder before being placed on the shelf. Leave the book cards of such volumes in the Book Card Tray. Also separate the shelf register cards of such volumes from those of the others and form them into a separate Binding Collection. Move the related volumes also to the Binding Collection. As soon as the process is over for all the volumes, take the book cards tray and merge them in the proper classified sequence in the *Maintenance Section Tray* containing the book cards of the volumes selected for binding.

2832:3:53 NEW VOLUMES SHELVING

As soon as the book card verifying is over, shelve the new volumes in the appropriate places.

Subsidiary Rules of the Madras University Library

Deal with the volumes intended for the binder in accordance with the rules in "2835 Binding".

In co-operation with the Publicity Section and the Technical Section, put the release date stamp at the proper place in the date label of all the other volumes. After this process is over, shelve them in the recent additions shelf.

Send the volumes belonging to the closed collections to their permanent places.

2832:5 *New Volumes Releasing Work*

2832:5:5 *Weekly jobs*

2832:5:51 PICKING

As one of the last jobs on the appointed day of the week, pick out from the recent additions shelf the volumes whose release date stamp denotes the next day. This work will be facilitated by a reference to the recent additions list containing the names of the volumes to be released in the week. Assemble all these volumes in a classified sequence and tick off for each volume its entry in the recent additions list. If any entry in the list is left unticked, investigate and find out the volume. If there is any difficulty, report to the librarian.

2832:5:52 Released Volumes Checking

Check the call numbers on the tag of each volume with the recent additions list. Verify the accession number and the call number written on the inside of the volume with those written on the date label. If there is any discrepancy, get it set right by the Technical Section. One of the advantages of checking the numbers in the inside of the volume at this stage is that it gives an opportunity to look into the volume and detect any mutilations that had already been made by the readers while the volume had been in the recent additions shelf.

2832:5:53 Released Volumes Shelving

After the released volumes are checked, find out from the Circulation Section if any of the volumes had been bespoken. Leave all such volumes with the Circulation Section and shelve the remaining volumes in their proper places.

2832:5:58 Released Volumes Card Transferring

With the aid of the ticked copy of the recent additions referred to in rule 2832:5:51, pick out the shelf register cards of the released volumes from the Recent Additions Collection and transfer them to their appropriate permanent places.

2833 Stack Room

2833:1 *Checking Work*

It is a moot point as to when the checking of the volumes in the library should be done. It is my experience that doing the entire checking at high pressure in a few weeks results in much dislocation in the work of the library. The dislocation will increase with the size of the library. The modern spirit of library service has lead the library profession to give up the old practice of closing down the library for checking purposes. The routine suggested here will show that the checking can be done effectively without in any way interfering with the main purpose of the library, viz " service to the readers", and without in any way dislocating the smooth running of the routine of the library from day to day. In fact, it is proposed here that the checking work should be woven into the texture of the weekly routine of the library.

Each library is to decide the number of hours it can set apart for the checking work each week. This is to be decided taking into consideration the number of volumes in the library, the number of members on the staff, and the number of checking cycles that must be completed in a year. Again the number of checking cycles need not be the same for all the collections in the library. It is obvious that the open access collections should be checked more often than the closed collections.

Having arrived at the number of volumes that should be checked each week, it can be easily calculated, how many days in the week will have to be devoted to this routine. My own experience is that in a library whose size is in the neighbourhood of 1,00,000 volumes, it is sufficient if one day is devoted every week to this routine. About 4,000 volumes can be checked in this way each week. Hence in what follows, the checking work is described as a weekly job.

2833:1:5 *Weekly jobs*

2833:1:51 Charged Tray Checking

At the beginning of the appointed day of the week, take out the shelf register card trays corresponding to the weekly quota of checking. Take them to the counter. Inform the person in charge of the charged tray, of the range of call numbers included in the quota. Ask him to read out from the charged tray such of the call numbers in the range of the quota as stand charged. As he reads out the number, turn the related shelf register card in its position in the tray through a right angle in its own plane such that the call number end goes up i e in the clock-wise direction and leave it there. At the end of this process, it follows that all the shelf register cards which are standing in the turned position correspond to the books which are on loan.

2833:1:52 Shelf Checking

As the charged tray checking is going on, ask a member of the Section to rectify the sequence of the volumes on the shelves in the region corresponding to the shelf register tray that is being checked. Also ask him to pick out from the replacing shelf all the volumes belonging to the region of the quota of the day and shelve them in their proper places.

As soon as the Charged Tray Checking is over, take the shelf register cards tray to the appropriate shelves. Ask another member to go on reading the call numbers on the backs of the volumes in the shelf. It will be learnt from experience that the reading of the book number alone is practically sufficient in most cases. This fact will result in reducing the time taken for checking, considerably. As he goes on reading them, go on tallying the shelf register cards. If you come across any turned card, bring it to its normal position. An alternative method may be to bring such turned cards to their normal positions just before the tray is inserted in the cabinet. But if you come across a card whose call number is not read out, i.e. for which there is no volume in the shelf and at the same time the card is in its normal position, pick out that card and put it in the *Investigation Box*.

As soon as the quota of cards is finished, put the tray of the shelf register cards back in its cabinet.

2833:1:53 Investigating

After the shelf checking is over, investigate the volumes corresponding to the shelf register cards accumulated in the Investigation Box. The volumes may be lying in the replacing shelf, or they may be in the hands of the readers, or they may have been misplaced in any other shelves, or they might have been lost or the related charged cards might have been slightly misplaced in the charged tray. Put the shelf register cards of the volumes traced out, back in the shelf register cabinet.

2833:1:54 Inventory Reporting

As soon as the investigation is over, take all the cards still remaining for investigation to the librarian and give him a report of the result of the checking work.

2833:3 *Rearranging Work*

2833:3:4 *Daily jobs*

In open access libraries, slight and unintentional misplacement of books is likely to happen frequently, not to mention the wilful, but occasional, misplacement by selfish readers at moments when their civic conscience happens to be at its lowest ebb. Further, as the books on the shelves are handled by the users, they are likely to fall into a slovenly and slanting condition now and then. At the same time if such disturbances are allowed to accumulate from day to day, the result will be almost chaotic. Apart from the difficulty of the Reference Section in promptly picking out the volumes required, it will have a very bad psychological effect on the readers themselves. As a result, the main objective of the library, viz to attract and serve the readers in increasing numbers, will be frustrated. Hence, the daily jobs of rearranging work are very essential. If the library is big, the whole stack room should be divided into convenient zones and each zone assigned to a definite person. It may be difficult to find a sufficient number of hands in the Maintenance Section.

This difficulty has been in a way met in the Madras University Library as follows :

The members of all Sections other than the Maintenance Section, Reference Section, and the Circulation Section, i e the Sections which do not have to deal primarily with the stack room and the readers, are used for this purpose each day. The zones are distributed among them. They are divided into two batches. One batch goes to the stack room and attends to the daily jobs of the rearranging work between 11 and 12 each day, when the Reference Section is weakest—in fact, has only one member. The idea is that in addition to their doing the daily job of rearranging work, they will also do the necessary vigilance work when the readers come to their regions. It is our experience that the least number of readers visit the library at that interval and hence one member of the Reference Section is sufficient to serve them in purely reference matters.

The second batch is asked to do the daily job of rearranging work between 5 and 6 P M in the evenings. During this hour, the Reference Section is strongest. In spite of it, the rush of readers during that interval is so great, that the presence of the members of the other Sections in the stack room for doing the daily jobs of rearranging work is a source of great relief to the Reference Section so far as the vigilance work goes. In this sense, every member of every Section other than the Reference Section and the Circulation Section works as a member of the Maintenance Section one hour in the day. The chief advantage to these members in associating themselves with this work is that it gives them the only opportunity to come into active touch with that most sacred event, viz the establishment of contact between the reader and the books under the guidance of the library staff, which constitutes the library proper. It must be remembered that, otherwise, these members always work behind the screen at office desks and however much they may handle books, they miss the real library atmosphere.

The permanent members of the Maintenance Section are entrusted with the task of rapidly rectifying the shelves once in a week, i e setting right any disarrangements that might have escaped the notice of the members of the other Sections doing the rectifying work. In other words, although the members of the other Sections help the Maintenance Section in this matter, it is the Maintenance Section that has got the entire responsibility. It must be a matter of honour to every member of the Maintenance Section to be able to say " Come in at any time and you will find the volumes in my zone in a perfect condition".

2833:3:42 Shelf Tidying

At the appointed hour of the day, rapidly walk through your zone and tidy up the volumes which are lying in a slovenly manner.

2833:3:43 Shelf Rectifying

After the shelf tidying is over, examine the volumes in your zone carefully and if there is derangement in the sequences of the books, set it right. Divide the number of bays in your zone into convenient daily quota, so that your zone is completely covered over once in a week.

2833:3:8 *Annual jobs*

2833:3:81 Shelf Easing

In the appointed month of the year—it is best to choose the

slackest month—go round the stack room. See whether there is too much congestion. If so, remove the congestion by redistributing the volumes. It would be a proper plan to make a preliminary survey and note down all the regions that require easing. Then, plan on paper how the volumes are to be redistributed. After obtaining the approval of the librarian, the easing is to be done.

2833:3:82 Shelf Rearranging

Combine with the shelf easing job the annual shelf rearranging job also. The Reference and the Publicity Sections will have some suggestions to make about the rearrangement to satisfy the Third Law[40] viz " Every book its reader", or to satisfy the Fourth Law[41] viz " Save the time of the reader".

The Maintenance Section itself might have developed some ideas about the rearrangement in the course of its year's work. In the light of these suggestions, draw up a plan of rearrangement on paper and discuss it with the librarian. Take it to the Staff Council, if he suggests it. After the plan of rearrangement receives the final approval, carry out the rearrangement. This would surely involve a great movement of books. Book trollies will have to be plying from end to end continuously for some days. Hence it is desirable that this work should be undertaken in the slackest month so that there may be the least mutual obstruction between the readers and the staff.

2833:3:88 Cards Rearranging

As the rearranging of books is going on, if any deviation from the previously settled plan is rendered expedient, correct the plan also accordingly then and there. When the rearrangement work is finished, with the help of the corrected plan, rearrange the shelf register cards in the cabinet exactly parallel to the books in accordance with the *Principle of Parallel Movement* (see section 2815).

2833:5 *Guiding Work*

2833:5:4 *Daily jobs*

2833:5:43 Tag Scrutinising

On the appointed hour each day, examine the tags on the backs of books systematically. If any tag is worn-out, replace it by a fresh one and write out the call number carefully. It will be a good policy to place all the volumes, for which the tags have been renewed, on the trolley and ask some other member of the staff to verify the correctness of the call number on the tag. This verification must be done on the same day. After the verification is over, replace the volumes in their proper places. This job should be so distributed that the entire stack room is covered at least once in six months.

2833:5:6 *Monthly jobs*

2833:5:61 Shelf Guides Scrutinising

Once in a month, in the appointed week, walk through the gangways, carefully examining the shelf guides. If any shelf guide is in wrong position, shift it to the right position.

There is nothing more annoying than having a shelf guide against books which do not relate to the guide. It should be a matter of honour for the Maintenance Section that the shelf guides are always in the right position.

If any shelf guide is worn-out, replace it by a fresh one.

2833:5:8 *Annual jobs*

The annual jobs of Guiding Work are to be done immediately after the annual rearranging work is over. The volumes are likely to have changed places as a result of the rearrangement. If the bay guides, tier guides, and the guide plan are not promptly set right, it is obvious that they will be misleading.

2833:5:81 Bay Guide Scrutinising

The bay guide may either require a simple transfer to some other bay or it may have to be rewritten. Do whatever is necessary.

2833:5:82 Tier Guide Scrutinising

The tier guides also should be scrutinised as the bay guides. That is, they will have to be either rewritten or merely transferred. Use stencils for writing these guides. Writing with Indian ink on white background will give satisfaction.

2833:5:83 Guide Plan Scrutinising

The Guide Plan should be entirely rewritten once in a year, as soon as the rearranging work is over.

2834 Correction of Call Numbers

The volumes for correction will be spotted out at any time by the Technical Section, the Maintenance Section or the Reference Section. Further, it is convenient to have the volumes picked out on any day transmitted to the Technical Section on the same day, so that the volumes may be with that section for the maximum period to enable the classifier to meditate upon the new situation created and arrive at the proper placing in consultation with the librarian. Hence, the first piece of work connected with correction, viz Transmitting Work, is to be performed on a daily basis.

But once the volumes are corrected by the Technical Section there is no need to continue this daily basis any longer. On the other hand, it is much better that all later work connected with correction is given the same periodicity as most of the other pieces of work in a library, viz the week. Hence, it will be found that except for the first work, all other works relating to this factor are analysed as weekly jobs.

2834:1 *Correction Transmitting Work*

2834:1:4 *Daily jobs*

2834:1:41 Correction Collection Arranging

As the first thing each morning, examine the volumes accumulated on the correction shelf. Find out also whether the Circulation Section or the Reference Section or the Technical Section has spotted out any other volumes for correction. Bring all such volumes together and arrange them in a classified sequence on the shelf register cabinet.

2834:1:42 Correction Collection Card Transferring

For each of the volumes in the Correction Collection, transfer the shelf register card from its normal position to the Correction Collection.

2834:1:43 Correction Collection Transmitting

After the card transferring is over for all the volumes, count the number of volumes and transmit them to the Technical Section. When the *Transmission Register* comes back, examine if the head of the Technical Section has initialled it in token of his having received the volumes.

2834:2 *Correcting Work*

2834:2:5 *Weekly jobs*

2834:2:51 CARD CORRECTING

On the appointed day of the week, the corrected volumes will be received from the Technical Section.

Each volume will have its call number corrected only on the back of the title page. Arrange the volumes in the sequence of the old call number found on the back of the volume. Pick out, in sequence, the shelf register card for each volume from the correction collection of the week. Correct the call number in it and put it in a box after the correction is over. If any card does not have the corresponding volume, shift that card to behind the " not-returned " guide.

2834:2:52 VOLUME CORRECTING

After the shelf register cards of all the volumes have been thus corrected, take each volume in sequence and correct the call number in the tag on the back of the volume, in the book card, in the date label and in the inside of the volume. If the volume corrected is a periodical publication send it to the Periodical Publication Section so that they may embody the corrected class number in all their three cards. Get the volume back in time for shelving.

2834:2:53 CORRECTED VOLUMES SHELVING

After all the volumes have been corrected, rapidly compare the call numbers written in the different parts of the books with the shelf register cards to see if any casual mistakes have crept in. If there is any mistake, rectify it. When the comparison is being finished, place the volumes in different collections, according to the collection number found in the call number. After all the volumes have been thus dealt with, arrange the volumes in each sequence by their call numbers. Transfer them to a trolley and put them in the proper places on the shelves.

2834:8 *Correction Reinserting Work*

2834:8:5 *Weekly jobs*

2834:8:54 ACCESSION CARD CORRECTING

Take the corrected Shelf Register Cards Box. Rearrange them

in the sequence of their accession numbers. Take it to the accession cabinet. Carry out the necessary correction in the call numbers of the related accession cards.

2834:8:56 Corrected Cards Sorting

After the accession card correcting is over, sort the corrected shelf register cards lying in the box by their sequences.

2834:8:57 Corrected Cards Arranging

After the sorting of the corrected cards is over, arrange the cards in each collection by their call numbers.

2834:8:58 Corrected Cards Reinserting

After the arrangement of the corrected cards is over, reinsert the cards in their appropriate places in the shelf register cabinet.

2835 Binding

2835:1 *Binding Transmitting Work*

835:1:4 *Daily jobs*

2835:1:41 Worn-Out Volumes Picking

Have the stack room divided into convenient zones, for the daily picking up of the worn-out volumes. Pick out each day the worn-out volumes found in the zone allotted for the day. Find out also if the Circulation Section or the Reference Section have set apart any worn-out volume. Bring them to the worn-out volumes shelf.

2835:1:44 Worn-Out Volumes Collating

Collate carefully each of the volumes lying in the worn-out shelf. If any leaves are missing, note it down near the top of the back of the title page. If too many leaves are missing or if the paper is too brittle, consult the librarian whether it is worthwhile rebinding the volume. If the decision is against rebinding them, transfer the volumes to the Condemned Collection, and carry out the necessary routine for change of collection.

2835:1:5 *Weekly jobs*

2835:1:52 Worn-Out Volumes Card Transferring

Take the volumes finally decided to be bound, to the shelf register cabinet. Pick out the shelf register card relating to each volume and transfer it to the Binding Collection of the month.

2835:1:53 Book Card Removing

After the card transferring is over, take out the book cards of the volumes and insert them in the classified sequence in the Book Cards Tray.

2835:1:55 Worn-Out Volumes Transmitting

After the book card removing is over, count the number of volumes and enter the number in the Transmission Register and transfer the volumes to the Technical Section. When the Transmission Register comes back, see if it has received the dated initials of the head of the Technical Section in token of his having received the volumes.

2835:2 *Binding Correcting Work*

2835:2:5 *Weekly jobs*

The routines for " 1 Card Correcting " and " 2 Volume Correcting " are similar to the routines " 2834:2:51 " and " 2834:2:52", respectively.

2835:2:55 Corrected Worn-Out Volumes Retransmitting

After all the necessary correction is over, retransmit the corrected volumes to the Technical Section in the usual way.

2835:2:6 *Monthly jobs*

2835:2:64 Accession Card Correcting

This routine is similar to that for 2834:8:54. Fill up also the date of binding.

2835:2:68 Card Rearranging

Arrange the shelf register cards of the Binding Collection of the month by their call numbers. Remember that the shelf register cards of the new volumes that need to be bound before being released for use is also to be inserted in this sequence each week.

2835:5 *Binding List Tallying Work*

2835:5:6 *Monthly jobs*

2835:5:61 TALLYING

As soon as the binding order list of the volumes of the Binding Collection of the month is received from the Binding Section on the appointed day, tally the list with the shelf register cards of the Binding Sequence of the month. If there is any discrepancy, get it set right by the Technical Section.

2835:8 *Binding Reinserting Work*

2835:8:6 *Monthly jobs*

2835:8:61 BINDING LIST SCRUTINISING

As soon as the binding list of the volumes returned from the binder is received from the Binding Section, transfer the shelf register cards of the unticked items to behind the not-returned guide.

2835:8:621 BOUND VOLUMES TALLYING

When the Binding Section transfers the bound volumes, tally the bound volumes with the shelf register cards in the related Binding Collection. While tallying, scrutinise the tooling as carefully as possible. As it is not unusual for the binders to apply a wrong cover to the book, it is better to examine the title page also. If there is any difficulty, return the volumes to the Binding Section for the necessary correction. Transfer the related shelf register cards to behind the not-returned guide.

2835:8:622 BOOK CARD INSERTING

As soon as the tallying is over, pick out for each volume its book card from the Book Cards Tray and insert it in the book pocket of the volume.

2835:8:626 BESPOKEN VOLUMES TRANSMITTING

As soon as the book card inserting is over, obtain from the Circulation Section the Bespoken Cards Box. Pick out each of the bound volumes for which there is a bespeaking card and send them, along with the box, to the Circulation Section.

2835:8:63 Reshelving

The routines " 31 Sorting", " 32 Arranging", and " 33 Shelving " are to be done as provided under " 2831 Used Volumes".

2835:8:64 Undischarged Cards Investigating

Discuss with the Binding Section the volumes relating to the shelf register cards of the Binding Collection which are lying behind the not-returned guide. If there is anything out of the way, bring it to the notice of the librarian.

2835:8:68 Binding Sequence Cards Reinserting

For all the volumes returned from the binder, accepted and reshelved, transfer the related shelf register cards from the Binding Collection to its appropriate place in the Shelf Register Cabinet.

2836 Topical Sequences

2836:1 *Topical Collection Collecting Work*

2836:1:3 *Casual jobs*

2836:1:31 Topical Volumes Picking

Consult the Publicity Section and the Reference Section about the Topical Collections to be formed, the volumes to be included in the collection and the period for which the collection is to be maintained. In the light of the suggestions received, pick out the volumes and assemble them on the shelf register cabinet.

2836:1:32 Topical Collection Cards Transferring

For each of the volumes, transfer the related shelf register card from its permanent place to the appropriate Topical Collection.

2836:1:33 Release Date Marking

After the card transferring is over, stamp on the date labels of the volumes the date of release from the Topical Collection. Enclose the date in red ink.

2836:2 *Topical Collection Shelving Work*

2836:2:3 *Casual jobs*

2836:2:31 MAIN GUIDE WRITING

Write out a suitable display guide for the Topical Collection. It is desirable to make it as ornamental and as attractive as possible, as one of the objects of the formation of the Topical Collection is in fulfilment of the Third Law. "Every Book its Reader".[42]

2836:2:32 TOPICAL VOLUMES SHELVING

Put the volumes selected for the Topical Collection in a classified sequence in the appropriate shelves set apart for them.

2836:2:34 TOPICAL COLLECTION GUIDING

Write out and insert the necessary shelf guides in the Topical Collection Shelves.

2836:8 *Topical Collection Releasing Work*

2836:8:3 *Casual jobs*

2836:8:31 RELEASED VOLUMES TALLYING

On the day appointed for releasing the volumes of a Topical Collection, transfer the shelf register cards of the collection to a box. Tally the volumes with them. If any volume is not to be found, trace it out. If it cannot be traced out, bring it to the notice of the librarian for further action.

2836:8:33 RELEASED VOLUMES SHELVING

After the tallying is over, transfer the released volumes to the trolley and have them reshelved in their proper places.

2836:8:38 TOPICAL COLLECTION CARDS REINSERTING

Reinsert the shelf register cards of the volumes of the released Topical Collection in their appropriate places in the shelf register cabinet.

2837 Reference Study

2837:3 *Casual jobs*

2837:31 Reference Investigating

As and when long range reference problems are transferred by the Reference Section, pursue the investigation as diligently as possible as a pick-up-work, i e at hours when you are free from the necessary routines of the Section. It will be a good practice to note down in the standard 5″ by 3″ slips your findings as the investigation proceeds. Collect all such slips and arrange them in a classified sequence in the *Reference Box*.

2837:37 Reference Section Advising

As soon as you feel that you have completed all that is possible in investigating the problem transferred by the Reference Section, transfer the Reference Box to the Reference Section and, if necessary, have a short discussion with that Section to clear abstruse points.

2837:38 Shelf Studying

As a pick-up-work whenever you have no work on hand, make a systematic study of such of the volumes on the shelves as you think will repay study. If you come across any topic in any volume, where it can be least expected, write out a cross reference card in consultation with the Technical Section or, if you have no time, bring it to the notice of the Technical Section and ask them to prepare the necessary cross reference cards.

2838 Shelf Register Cabinet

2838:5 *Weekly job*

2838:58 Shelf Register Cards Inserting

On the appointed day of the week, insert the shelf register cards of the new volumes catalogued in the week in the appropriate places in the shelf register cabinet. Remember in particular the cards belonging to the Binding Collection.

2838:58 *Annual jobs*

2838:81 Cabinet Easing

Once in a year or whenever the need arises, redistribute the shelf register cards in the trays of the shelf register cabinet so as to relieve congestion, if any, and so as to provide space for the year's growth.

2838:84 Tray-Guide Changing

Whenever a redistribution is made in the shelf register cabinet, the tray guides also should be immediately examined and rectified, if necessary.

284 Elimination of Waste

2841 Organisation

If the turnover in the Section demands the assignment of several members to it, the distribution of work among the assistants of the section should proceed along the lines of sequence specialisation. This will enable each member to acquire an intensive acquaintance with the work connected with certain sequences and an intimate knowledge of the resources of the library in these sequences.

2842 Head of the Section

The Head of the Section should review the work of the assistants carefully every day. He must infuse a high sense of responsibility in the assistants. For, the maintenance of the books in proper order on the shelves has to depend entirely on the sense of duty and the sense of honour of the assistants. Any shoddy work in the maintenance of shelf sequence will, by imperceptible degrees, lead to ultimate chaos, while it is by no means easy to detect the misplacements at each step. In addition to infusing the right spirit in his assistants, the Head of the Section should develop the necessary flair to spot out casual misplacements. He should go round the stack room systematically to find out the type of misplacements that occur and devise remedies for them.

2842 Shelf Register Card

Another arduous task of the Head of the Maintenance Section is the maintenance of the shelf register cards in a sequence which is strictly parallel to the sequence of the books on the shelves. This highly complicated task should be done by the Head of the Section himself. The tallying of the accession cards, the shelf register cards and the books received from the Technical Section from week to week will have to be done co-operatively by the Head of the Section and some of his assistants.

It is also the duty of the Head of the Maintenance Section to see to the cleanliness of the stack room and the reading room. He should devise a well thought-out time scheme for dusting and enforce it. The problem of insects is very serious in tropical countries. There are many bookworms which are anxious to make books an article of diet. One of the effective ways of saving the books from the ravages of these insects is, not to allow the books to lie in the shelves undisturbed for too long a period—particularly the books in dark corners—as the silverfish which are so fond of books are equally fond of darkness and can thrive only in dark corners, undisturbed by human hands. Hence, the Head of the Maintenance Section should see that the books in all such places get dusted and cleaned at frequent intervals. The frequency with which a region is cleaned may vary inversely as the popularity of the region. For example, if the main collection to which the public have open access is cleaned up once in three months, it may be necessary to clean up the closed collections, such as the undersized sequence, once in a fortnight.

2844 Diaries

Two diaries are to be maintained by this Section, one on a daily basis and the other on a weekly basis.

2845 Daily Diary

The diary on daily basis is to have the following headings :

1 Number of volumes replaced in each collection, with a separate column for each collection.
2 Total number of volumes replaced.
3 Number of bays rectified.
4 Number of tags renewed.
5 Number of book cards renewed.
6 Number of volumes transmitted for correction of call numbers.
7 Number of worn-out volumes picked.
8 Number of worn-out volumes collated.

2846 Weekly Diary

The diary on weekly basis is to have the following headings :

1 Number of letters received.
2 Number of letters disposed.
3 Number of letters originated.
4 Number of letters filed.
5 Number of lost books ordered.
6 Number of lost books received.
7 Number of damaged volumes sent for repair.
8 Number of damaged volumes repaired.
9 Number of shelf register cards tallied.
10 Number of new volumes shelved.
11 Number of new volumes released.
12 Number of bays checked.
13 Number of volumes for which collection symbols were marked.
14 Number of shelf guides prepared.
15 Number of volumes corrected.
16 Number of worn-out volumes transmitted.
17 Number of binding items tallied.
18 Number of topical collections formed.
19 Number of reference topics pursued.

285 Correlation Table

As has been already stated in the introduction, in a sense the Maintenance Section is the hub of the staff of the library. Much of the work of the library has to turn upon the Maintenance Section. Much depends upon its vigilance and much depends upon its friendly co-operation with the other Sections.

2851 Relation to Book Selection, Book Order and Periodical Publication Sections

In the course of their shelf study, the members of the Maintenance Section are likely to come across incomplete sets of books and periodicals. They may bring these to the notice respectively of the Book Selection Section and the Periodical Publication Section, so that they might take the necessary action to complete such sets. The intimate knowledge that the Maintenance Section acquires in their daily work with the titles in the library can be placed at the disposal of the Book Order Section whenever an order is sent out. A perusal of the order copy by the Maintenance Section may detect many tricky titles, which might have been too elusive to the book order section. In the Madras University Library, this practice is resulting now and then, in the avoidance of duplication in the stock.

2854 Relation to Accession Section

It has been already stated in Chapter "24 Accession Section" that the assignment of the accession number is not merely a mechanical process, and that the Maintenance Section can contribute much towards deciding what exactly a single accession number should cover.

2855 Relation to Technical Section

While tallying the shelf register cards and the accession cards, the Maintenance Section is likely to come across casual errors of omission and commission. These, they may immediately bring to the notice of the Technical Section, so that the errors may be rectified before the catalogue cards are inserted in the cabinet and the volumes sent to the shelves.

Books which are taken by the Technical Section for correction of call numbers are likely to stay long in the Section in the absence of immediate demand for these. In such cases, the Maintenance Section, by maintaining the correction collection of shelf register cards, may remind the Technical Section of such delays so that it might expedite the correction. The correction collection of the shelf register cards is also useful in restoring volumes which have inadvertently strayed to the stack room from the correction collection in the Technical Section. Before this kind of control by the Maintenance Section was introduced, many difficulties were experienced in the Madras University Library in rounding up evading volumes. Sometimes, the process used involved inordinate loss of time.

2857 Relation to Reference Section

Coming to the Reference Section, it will be seen that the Maintenance Section has to work shoulder to shoulder with this Section.

The reference librarians are the men on the spot that have to attend to the immediate needs of the readers. Their time is not at their disposal. Reference questions that could be tackled on the spot without much expenditure of time are done by them. But special bibliographies and reference questions which require long and protracted search may have to be handed over to the Maintenance Section.

The Reference Section fulfils the Second Law of Library Science, viz " Every Reader His Book", by itself. But the Third Law, viz " Every Book Its Reader " has to be fulfilled by it only jointly with the Maintenance Section. The Maintenance Section in the course of its shelf study should note all the valuable materials found in the nooks and corners of the library and bring them to the notice of the Reference Section to be used by it in fulfilment of the Third Law. Here are some recent experiences of the Madras University Library. The Maintenance Section had located a substantial article on the psychology of nail-biting in V 2 of the *Smith College studies in social work*. Similarly, it had unearthed an article on finger-print detection in the January 1934 issue of the *Analyst*, a periodical in chemistry, least suggestive of such a topic. Again in the course of systematic shelf study, it found in *Bulletin* 46 of the Pusa Agricultural Institute, a substantial account of the modern methods of bee-keeping in India. These out of the way references were promptly brought to the notice of the Reference Section, who really play the part of canvassing agents for the books of the library. This resulted in securing for the volumes concerned a new but interested class of readers—a real fulfilment of the Third Law. Such remote references will go on accumulating in the experience of the Maintenance Section. It is the duty of the Maintenance Section to note down all such references, ask the Technical Section to prepare cross reference cards and inform the Reference Section of these discoveries.

That the Maintenance Section should work hand in hand with the Reference Section in order to satisfy the Fourth Law, viz " Save the Time of the Reader " has been already discussed in the introduction to this chapter.

2858 Relation to Circulation Section

The Maintenance Section needs the co-operation of the

Circulation Section in withholding from circulation, books that require mending or binding. Otherwise, books which are in constant circulation will not have the opportunity of being mended or bound sufficiently early, i e before the damage goes beyond the limit of recovery. The Circulation Section should send to the Maintenance Section such of those books as are lent out and which are required by the other Sections for correction, etc so that the shelf register cards of those books may be moved appropriately before the books go to the different sections.

28591 The Table

Apart from these general statements, the following correlation table lists the rules that describe the routine which brings the Maintenance Section into contact with the other sections :

3 *Periodical Publication Section*

2834:2:52 Volume correcting.

4 *Accession Section*

2831:4:51 Data ascertaining ;
2832:1:52 Accession cards transmitting ;
2834:8:54 Accession cards correcting ;
2835:2:64 Accession cards correcting.

5 *Technical Section*

2831:4:55 Replaced volumes receiving ;
2831:5:551 Damaged volume forwarding ;
2832:1:51 Cards reconciling ;
2832:3:521 Tallying ;
2832:3:522 Book card verifying ;
2832:3:53 New volumes shelving ;
2834:1:41 Correction sequence arranging ;
2834:1:43 Correction sequence transmitting ;
2834:2:51 Card correcting ;
2835:1:55 Worn-out volumes transmitting ;
2835:2:55 Corrected worn-out volumes retransmitting ;
2835:5:61 Tallying ;
2837:38 Shelf studying.

6 *Circulation Section*

2831:1:41 Returned volumes sorting ;
2831:4:48 Lost volume card transferring ;
2831:4:51 Data ascertaining ;
2831:4:56 Counter section advising ;
2831:5:48 Damaged volume card transferring ;
2831:5:551 Damaged volume forwarding ;
2831:5:56 Counter section advising ;
2832:5:58 Released volumes shelving ;
2833:1:51 Charged tray checking ;
2834:1:41 Correction sequence arranging ;
2835:1:41 Worn-out volumes picking ;
2835:8:626 Bespoken volumes transmitting.

7 *Reference Section*

2833:3:82 Rearranging ;
2834:1:41 Correction sequence arranging ;
2835:1:41 Worn-out volumes picking ;
2836:1:31 Topical volumes picking ;
2837:31 Reference investigating ;
2837:37 Reference section advising.

93 *Staff Council*

2833:3:82 Rearranging.

95 *Publicity Section*

2832:3:53 New volumes shelving ;
2833:3:82 Rearranging ;
2836:1:31 Topical volumes picking.

97 *Accounts Section*

2831:4:54 Replaced Volume Receiving.

995 *Binding Section*

2831:5:551 Damaged volumes forwarding ;
2831:5:556 Binding cost ascertaining ;
2835:8:61 Binding list scrutinising ;
2835:8:621 Bound volumes tallying ;
2835:8:64 Undischarged cards investigating.

286 Illustrative Time Scheme

DAILY JOBS

2831:1:4	All the jobs of replacing work (11 AM) except that a second replacing is to be done at 5 PM on Thursday ;
2831:4:48	Lost volume card transferring ;
2831:5:48	Damaged volume cards transferring ;
2833:3:42	Shelf tidying ;
2833:3:43	Shelf rectifying ;
2834:1:4	All the jobs of correction volumes transmitting work (11 AM) ;
2835:1:4	All the daily jobs of binding volumes transmitting work.

WEEKLY JOBS

Saturday

2831:4:54	Receiving ;
2831:4:55	Replaced volumes preparing ;
2831:4:56	Counter section advising ;
2831:4:58	Lost volume card retransferring ;
2833:1:5	All the jobs of checking work.

Sunday

2831:5:5	All the jobs of damaged volumes work ;
2833:1:5	All the jobs of checking.

Monday

2831:4:51	Data ascertaining ;
2831:4:52	Quotation calling ;
2831:4:53	Ordering ;
2831:5	All the weekly jobs of damaged volumes work.

Tuesday

2832:5:5	All the jobs of new volumes releasing work (5 PM) ;
2835:2:5	All the jobs of correcting work (4 PM).

Wednesday

2832:1:5	All the jobs of tallying work ;
2832:3:516	Shelf register cards sorting ;

2832:3:517 Shelf register cards arranging ;
2832:3:521 Tallying (5 P M) ;
2832:3:522 Book card verifying ;
2838:58 Shelf register cards inserting.

Thursday

2834:2:5 All the jobs of correcting work ;
2834:8:5 All the jobs of reinserting work ;
2835:1:5 All the weekly jobs of transmitting work.

Monthly Jobs

First Saturday

2833:5:61 Shelf guides scrutinising.

Penultimate Tuesday

2835:5:61 Binding list tallying.

First Thursday

2835:8:8 All the monthly jobs of reinserting work.

Thursday following Last Tuesday

2835:2:68 Corrected cards sorting.

Annual Jobs

July

2833:3:8 All the annual jobs of rearranging work ;
2833:5:8 All the annual jobs of guiding work;
2838:8 All the annual jobs of shelf register cabinet.

287 Forms and Registers

C8 *Shelf register card.* Printed. 8 point type. Bristol board. White. Cabinet.

The text of the form is as follows :

C N
Ac N
Author
Title
Series, etc

Wl N
Don N

Name	*Class number*	*Amplifying device*	*Filing characteristic*	*Year of transfer to record sequence after the file is closed*	*Year of destruction after transfer to the record sequence*
Lost or damaged volumes	81	Nil	Heading	After stock taking	Year 3
Stock verification	83	Last digit of the year	Correspondent	Year 1	Year 10*
Topical sequences	86	Subject Device	Do	Do	Year 3
Outward enquiries	891	Nil	Do	Do	Do
Inward enquiries	892	Nil	Do	Do	Do

* The sanctions for the writing off of volumes are, however, to be preserved permanently.

Part 3

GENERAL OFFICE FUNCTIONS

CHAPTER 31

COMMITTEE SECTION

311 Planning

3111 PARENT ORGANISATION

The management of most of the types of libraries is usually vested in committees. Such committees derive their powers from a larger parent body, which manages the larger organisation of which the library forms a part. This larger organisation may be a Local Body or the executive of a university or a college council or a trust board or any other corporate body. For the sake of brevity and because the majority of libraries are public libraries managed by Local Bodies, I shall refer to the larger parent organisation as the Local Body in what follows.

3113 FUNCTIONS OF THE LIBRARY COMMITTEE

The sphere of action of the Library Committee of a Local body is bounded on one side by the sphere of the parent body and on the other by the sphere of the permanent executive. The boundary line between the functions of a Local Body and its Library Committee is usually clearly drawn by the legislature. It may be further amplified by the bye-laws and standing orders of the Local Body itself. The exact position of the boundary line is not however the same in all cases. Some Library Committees are given only advisory powers. That practice, however, is not very common now. In most cases, the entire power of levying the library rate, of borrowing money, of managing real property, if any, and of passing the library budget, is vested in the Local Body itself. The Library Committee is given freedom only to spend the library revenue in any manner it likes, subject to the provisions in the budget. The location of branch libraries, the framing of Library Rules, the appointment of the library staff, the policy of book selection and all such internal matters connected with the library are, however, vested solely in the Library Committee. In a few cases, the boundary line leaves a larger sphere for the Library Committee. Even the power of raising a loan and levying a rate is vested in the Library Committee. Some of the libraries had been given land grants for their upkeep. The management of all such real property is usually vested in the Library Committee itself. The function of the Local Body ends with the appointment of the Library Committee, the approving of the library budget and the reviewing of the annual report.

3114 Permanent Executive

But such a clear understanding is non-existent, in respect of to the boundary line between the functions of the Library Committee and those of the Library Executive. Nor is it possible to draw this line in any definite manner by rules and regulations. It must be left to some broad commonsense principles. The true sphere of usefulness of the Committees is in deliberation and in the enunciation and direction of policy generally. If this commonsense principle is forgotten, it would immediately lead to an incursion upon the proper sphere of the Permanent Executive. This is likely to happen particularly, if the Committee contains members, among whom, not unnaturally, there may be, for some time until experience tells, some distrust of the Executive and a feeling that their will can find its way only, if they keep their hands firmly on the wheel itself, even in small matters—a feeling probably helped by the fact that, until then, some of them may not have had experience of management on a large scale. Yet the relentless march of functions, the growing complexity of administration, and the ever-widening sphere of duties, bring with them increasing necessity for using the specialist and for recognising that he, and almost he alone, holds the key to problem after problem and that he must be used.

3115 Sub-Committees

Apart from keeping clear of the functions that are more appropriate to the Local Body and to the Permanent Executive, one has to consider what would be the most convenient way for the Library Committee to discharge its own legitimate functions. Should the Library Committee deal with all the questions directly ? Or is it better to have them dealt with entirely or at least investigated in the first instance by suitable Sub-Committees ? The English Act provides that any Library Committee to which any powers are delegated may, subject to any direction of the Local Body, delegate all or any of these powers to a Sub-Committee consisting either in whole, or in part, of members of the Library Committee. This provision amounts to a gentle hint that it would be more conducive to efficient business if a Library Committee functions through standing Sub-Committees. It is desirable to provide for these things in the scheme by which the Local Body adopts the Library Act. The number of Sub-Committees ranges from one to twelve in England and America. But the average number is four. The most popular, among the numerous branches of this committee family, are those concerned with finances; with administration (i e staff, rules, etc) ; and with buildings and grounds.

3116 Local Advisory Committee

Apart from this internal organisation, the Library Committee should also have a Local Advisory Committee attached to each one of its branches and delivery stations. In particular, each panchayat area should have a Local Committee to advise the Library Committee of the District Board. There can be no question of delegation of powers to such a Local Committee. But none the less they form an important limb of the library polity of a state and it is desirable that they should be explicitly provided for in the Library Act itself.

It is possible to continue the Theory of Library Committee in this strain. But it would take us far beyond the limits of this book. Its proper place is in a volume on library legislation and organisation.[13] We are concerned here only with the routine, preliminary and subsequent to the committee's work.

3118 Factors in Planning

The distinctive work of the Committee Section is to be planned with reference to the following factors :

3 Preparation of business ;
5 Disposal of decisions ; and
6 Sub-Committees.

It may be convenient to have a meeting of the committee once in a month. But routine business may be done also in circulation. Probably circulation work may be done once in a week. The job analysis and routine given hereunder refer to the monthly meetings. In the case of circulation work, they may require a slight modification. For example, there will be no preliminary agenda. On the other hand there will be only one agenda.

312 Job Analysis

3123 Preparation of Business

The work of the Committee Section relating to the preparation of business is to consist of the following items :

1 Drafting and circulating the preliminary agenda, which may be referred to as *Preliminary Agenda Work* ; and
2 Drafting the final agenda, which may be referred to as *Final Agenda Work.*

3123:1 *Preliminary Agenda Work*

3123:1:6 The preliminary agenda work is to consist of the following monthly jobs :

1 Collecting from the different sections all the papers that require consideration at a meeting of the committee, which may be referred to as *Meeting Papers Collecting* ;
2 Scrutinising the papers received from the different sections for consideration at a meeting of the committee, which may be referred to as *Meeting Papers Scrutinising* ;
3 Requesting the sections concerned to furnish the necessary additional information, if any such is required, which may be referred to as *Meeting Papers Completing* ;
4 Arranging the meeting papers in a classified sequence and numbering them, which may be referred to as *Meeting Papers Numbering* ;
5 Writing out the agenda, including the time, date, and place of meeting, which may be referred to as *Agenda Writing*; and
6 Circulating the agenda with the related papers, which may be referred to as *Agenda Circulating.*

3123:2 *Final Agenda Work*

3123:2:6 The final agenda work is to consist of the following monthly jobs :

1 Examining the papers received after circulation and gathering any additional data that might have been called for by the committee in circulation, which may be referred to as *Additional Data Collecting* ;
2 Adding any additional urgent matter that may have to be put before the meeting, which may be referred to as *Agenda Supplementing* ;
3 Sending a reminder to the members of the committee about the time and place of the meeting, which may be referred to as *Meeting Reminding* ; and
4 Sending to the meeting all the papers likely to be required directly or indirectly at the meeting, which may be referred to as *Meeting Papers Putting Up.*

3125 Disposal of Decisions

The work of the Committee Section relating to disposal of decisions is to consist of the following items :

1 Drafting the minutes of the meeting, which may be referred to as *Minutes Work* ; and
2 Redistributing the papers to the sections concerned, which may be referred to as *Redistribution Work.*

3125:1 *Minutes Work*

3125:1:6 The minutes work is to consist of the following monthly jobs :

1 Collecting together all the papers considered by the meeting and verifying if they are alright, which may be referred to as *Meeting Papers Verifying* ;
2 Writing out the minutes of the meeting, which may be referred to as *Minutes Writing* ; and
3 Circulating the draft minutes to the members of the committee for confirmation, which may be referred to as *Minutes Circulating.*

3125:2 *Redistribution Work*

3125:2:6 The redistribution work is to consist of the following monthly jobs :

1 Copying in the docket sheets of the different papers the relevant extracts from the minutes of the meeting, which may be referred to as *Minutes Extracting* ; and
2 Redistributing the papers to the sections concerned, which may be referred to as *Meeting Papers Redistributing*.

3126 SUB-COMMITTEES

The work of the Committee Section relating to Sub-Committees will be similar to its work relating to the Committee itself.

313 Routine

3133 PREPARATION OF BUSINESS

3133:1 *Preliminary Agenda Work*

3133:1:6 *Monthly jobs*

3133:1:61 MEETING PAPERS COLLECTING

On the appointed day of the month, collect from the different Sections all the papers that they might have marked for consideration by the Committee. While doing so, instruct them to send all the related files and other materials. As soon as all the papers are received, sort them roughly and take them to the librarian and get his instructions regarding their inclusion in the agenda.

3133:1:62 MEETING PAPERS SCRUTINISING

In the case of each one of the items to be included in the agenda, study the notes put down by the Section in the docket sheet and see if they contain, in brief terms, the salient facts that should be placed before the Committee. Examine also if the files contain all the relevant papers. If any book or periodical publication should be sent to the Committee as specimen, see if it has been put up by the section concerned.

3133:1:63 MEETING PAPERS COMPLETING

If, in the course of scrutinising the meeting papers, you come across any defect in the notes prepared or any incompleteness in the papers or materials put up, inform the Section concerned about it and get the papers completed. Then, send them to the librarian, so that he may add his notes.

3133:1:64 Meeting Papers Numbering

After the meeting papers are completed, arrange them in a classified sequence and number the papers in each class serially.

3133:1:65 Agenda Writing

As soon as the arrangement of the papers is over, write out the preliminary agenda. After getting its approval by the librarian, get it faircopied. Arrange all the meeting papers on a pad and place the agenda paper at the very top. Remember that the agenda should contain definite information as to the place, date, and time of meeting. Some libraries regard this itself as meeting notice. Another practice is to send a separate meeting notice.

3133:1:66 Agenda Circulating

Put the file of papers in a box and send it round to the members of the Committee.

3133:2 *Final Agenda Work*

3133:2:6 *Monthly jobs*

3133:2:61 Additional Data Collecting

As soon as the papers come back from circulation, see if the circulation card has received the initials of each member and examine the files and the agenda paper. If any member of the Committee has asked for any additional data or has made any remarks, consult the librarian about them and collect the necessary data or take such other action as may be decided upon.

3133:2:62 Agenda Supplementing

If any urgent matter has cropped up after the circulation of the preliminary agenda and before the meeting day, take the permission of the librarian and add it as supplementary item in the final agenda. While doing so, get all the necessary papers relating to those items in the same way as described under routine "3133:1 Preliminary agenda work".

3133:2:63 Meeting Reminding

On the day just preceding the meeting day, send a reminder card to all the Members of the Committee, specifying the time and place of the meeting.

3133:2:64 Meeting Papers Putting Up

At least half an hour before the meeting, take all the papers that are to be considered by the Committee. In consultation with the librarian have the papers arranged in a sequence parallel to the sequences of the items in the agenda. If any specimen materials are to be considered by the Committee, have them also arranged in another parallel collection. It is desirable to place on the meeting table a copy of the Rules of the Library and any other laws and regulations that have a bearing on the management of the library. There is nothing more annoying than the librarian having to call for such materials in the middle of the meeting. For the same reason, care must also be taken to anticipate intelligently all the files that are likely to be of use to the Committee in discussing and disposing of the different items in the agenda.

3135 Disposal of Decisions

3135:1 *Minutes Work*

3135:1:6 *Monthly jobs*

3135:1:61 Meeting Papers Verifying

As soon as the meeting of the Committee is over, collect all the papers on the meeting table. Sort them into different collections and arrange the papers in the different collections properly. Tally them with the office copy of the agenda and see if all the copies and materials are found. If there is anything missing, take it to the notice of the librarian and get it rectified.

3135:1:62 Minutes Writing

After all the papers are thus collected, write out the minutes of the meeting, either from the draft of the minutes given by the librarian or to his dictation. Get the draft minutes faircopied.

Much time can be gained if two copies of agenda are prepared before the meeting, leaving half margin. In that case, a rough draft of the minutes may be written by the librarian, during the meeting itself, in one of the copies. After receiving the approval of the librarian, the draft may be faircopied or typed in the other copy.

3135:1:63 MINUTES CIRCULATING

Circulate the faircopy of the draft minutes to the Members of the Committee for their approval. If the work is properly organised, it must be possible for the minutes to start in circulation within an hour after the meeting. As soon as the draft minutes come back, examine if they have been approved as they are. If any amendments are suggested by any Member, take them to the librarian and carry out his instructions.

3135:2 *Redistribution Work*

3135:2:6 *Monthly jobs*

3135:2:61 MINUTES EXTRACTING

In the docket sheet of each item, extract, from the approved minutes, the resolution relating to the item. After the extracting work is done for each one of the items, send the papers in the proper classified sequence to the librarian for his initials below the extracts. As soon as the papers come back, see if the librarian has put his initials under each one of the extracts. If not, get the matter set right.

3135:2:62 MEETING PAPERS REDISTRIBUTING

After the librarian has initialled the extract from the minutes in each one of the docket sheets of the papers placed before the meeting, distribute the papers to the Sections concerned to enable them to take the necessary action. Send also other materials, if any.

3136 SUB-COMMITTEES

Meetings of Sub-Committees will have to be attended to in the same way as meetings of Committee except that the resolution of a Sub-Committee may be sent on to the Committee directly without being redistributed to the Sections, if possible.

314 Elimination of Waste

3141 Head of the Section

The Head of the Committee Section must take care to see that the circulation papers as well as the meeting papers of the Committee and the Sub-Committees are prepared properly and promptly, and that there is no delay in redistributing the papers to the different Sections. It is always a delicate matter to ensure the safety of the papers that go out in circulation. He must therefore have proper control over the incoming and outgoing of papers and set right all defects then and there, without any lapse of time.

3142 Diary

He may have to maintain one diary on a weekly basis with the following headings :

1 Date of circulation ;
2 Number of papers sent up ;
3 Number of books and other materials circulated ; and
4 Date of redistribution of papers.

315 Correlation

It is obvious that the Committee Section will have something or other to do with each one of the Sections of the library. But it is not possible to give a definite Correlation Table here.

316 Time Scheme

It would be a good practice to have the meeting papers started one week before the date of the meeting. As has been already indicated, the meeting papers ought to be redistributed to the Sections concerned within a day after the meeting.

The monthly meeting may be fixed for a definite day in the first week, subject to sparing adjustment to suit the convenience of the members. The weekly circulation work may be done on a particular day every week, say Wednesdays.

317 Forms and Registers

S31 *Minutes Book*. Ledger paper. Bound. 250 pages. Pages to be machine numbered. 30 lines per page.

Name	*Class number*	*Amplifying device*	*Filing characteristic*	*Year of transfer to record sequence after the file is closed*	*Year of destruction after transfer to the record sequence*
Constitution	912	Nil	Correspondent	Year 1	Year 10
Meetings and proceedings	913	Nil	Month and week of origination to be shown in Arabic numerals, the month number and week number being separated by a colon	Do	Do
Sub-committee	916	Subject device	Convener	Do	Do
Outward enquiries	9191	Nil	Correspondent	Do	Year 3
Inward enquiries	9192	Nil	Do	Do	Do

CHAPTER 32

STAFF SECTION

321 Planning

3211 MAIN BUSINESS

The main business of the Staff Section is to maintain all the records about the creation of posts, the appointment of persons thereto, and their service conditions. The Section has also to maintain the papers relating to each one of the persons in the service of the library and the history of their services. All these matters will be governed by local official practice, rules and regulations. Hence, it is only the barest minimum of information, regarding the routine of the work of this section, that will be found in this chapter.

3212 CADRE REGISTER

The part " 328 Files " of this chapter gives the different files that should be maintained by the Staff Section. If any cadre has more than one post, the class number of the post is to be got by augmenting the cadre number by the addition of the Arabic numerals 1, 2, 3, etc respectively for the first, second, third, etc posts. The amplifying device is to consist of the letter *b* followed by suitable sub-divisions. In association with these files, the section should also maintain a register, which may be numbered S921 and called *Cadre Register*.

Three sets of documents are to be maintained by this Section for each person in the service of the library, viz,

3 Service register ;
4 File of permanent papers ; and
5 File of temporary papers.

3213 SERVICE REGISTER

The service register, whose number may be fixed as S923, is to be maintained with the pages and columns in conformity with local practice. This will give the history of the service of the incumbent concerned. The service registers are to be arranged alphabetically by the names of the incumbents. Detailed instructions for the maintenance of such registers are usually given in the registers themselves.

3214 Permanent Papers

By "924 Permanent papers" is meant all documents, other than those relating to casual and compensation leave, bearing upon the service of an incumbent. As a result of the provision made in the part "328 Files", it can be seen that the files of permanent papers are to be kept strictly in the alphabetical sequence by the name of the incumbent. The chief type of paper that will involve some routine is the application for leave other than casual or compensation leave.

The file of permanent papers is to contain all the papers relating to leave other than casual leave and compensation leave, the appointment order, the transfer order, and any other papers that might be marked for this file by the librarian.

3215 Temporary Papers

By "9925 Temporary papers" is meant papers of an ephemeral nature such as applications for casual and compensation leave, applications for or explanations of late attendance, and so on. There should be a separate file of temporary papers for each incumbent for each casual-leave-year. The first paper in each file is to consist of a tabular statement, which may be referred to as the *Casual Leave Register*.

3218 Factors in Planning

The distinctive work of the Staff Section is to be planned with reference to the following factors :

1 Cadre of appointments ;
2 Incumbents ;
4 Casual and compensation leave ; and
7 Pay bill.

322 Job Analysis

3221 Cadre of Appointments

The work of the Staff Section relating to cadre of appointments is to consist of the following items :

1 Work relating to the creation or abolition of posts, which may be referred to as *Cadre Modifying Work* ; and
2 Recruiting of persons to vacant posts, which may be referred to as *Recruiting Work*.

3221:1 *Cadre Modifying Work*

3221:1:3 The cadre modifying work is to consist of the following casual jobs :

1 Obtaining the necessary sanction for creation or abolition of posts, which may be referred to as *Strength of Staff Changing* ;
2 Obtaining the necessary sanction for change in scale of pay, which may be referred to as *Scale of Pay Changing* ; and
7 Carrying out the necessary changes in the cadre register, which may be referred to as *Cadre Register Modifying*.

3221:2 *Recruiting Work*

3221:2:3 The recruiting work is to consist of the following casual jobs :

1 Calling for applications, which may be referred to as *Advertising* ;
2 Sorting and arranging the applications, which may be referred to as *Applications Sorting* ;
3 Informing candidates about the time and place of interview, which may be referred to as *Notifying Applicants* ;
4 Tabulating the results of the interview and communicating the recommendation to the authorities concerned, which may be referred to as *Interview Result Communicating* ;
5 Communicating the order to the selected candidate, which may be referred to as *Appointing* ; and
7 Making the necessary entries in the cadre register, which may be referred to as *Cadre Register Posting*.

3222 INCUMBENTS

The work of the Staff Section relating to incumbents is

to consist of the following items :

1 Dealing with cases of confirmation, which may be referred to as *Confirming Work* ;
2 Maintaining the service register, which may be referred to as *Service Register Work* ;
3 Dealing with the applications for regular leave, which may be referred to as *Regular Leave Work* ; and
6 Dealing with cases of retirement, which may be referred to as *Retirement Work.*

3222:1 Confirming Work

3222:1:3 The confirming work is to consist of the following casual jobs :

1 Writing to the authorities concerned for the confirmation of incumbents as and when occasion arises for the same, which may be referred to as *Confirmation Recommending* ;
2 Obtaining the certificate of physical fitness, which may be referred to as *Medical Certificate Requisitioning* ; and
6 Obtaining age exemption, if necessary, which may be referred to as *Age Exemption Obtaining.*

3222:2 *Service Register Work*

3222:2:3 The service register work is to consist of the following casual job :

1 Opening the service register, which may be referred to as *Service Register Opening.*

3222:2:8 The service register work is to consist of the following annual job :

1 Bringing the service register up-to-date, which may be referred to as *Service Register Posting.*

3222:3 *Regular Leave Work*

3222:3:3 The regular leave work is to consist of the following casual jobs :

2 Bringing the leave account of the incumbent up-to-date, which may be referred to as *Leave Account Working* ;

4 Noting the necessary endorsement on the application for regular leave, which may be referred to as *Regular Leave Application Noting* ;

5 Communicating the order on the leave application to the incumbent concerned, which may be referred to as *Leave Order Communicating* ;

71 Entering the information about the leave in the leave register, which may be referred to as *Leave Register Entering* ; and

72 Making the necessary entries in the leave register as soon as the incumbent returns from leave, which may be referred to as *Leave Return Noting*.

3222:6 *Retirement Work*

3222:6:3 The retirement work is to consist of the following casual jobs :

1 Noting on the application for retirement the necessary endorsement, which may be referred to as *Retirement Application Noting* ;

2 Communicating the order on the retirement application to the incumbent concerned, which may be referred to as *Retirement Order Communicating* ;

4 Closing the service register, which may be referred to as *Service Register Closing* ; and

7 Making the necessary entries in the cadre register, which may be referred to as *Cadre Register Filling*.

3224 CASUAL AND COMPENSATION LEAVE

3224:4 The work of the Staff Section relating to casual and compensation leave is to consist of the following daily jobs :

1 Obtaining from the head of the section, in which the incumbent works, the necessary endorsement on the application for casual or compensation leave, which may be referred to as *Endorsement Obtaining* ;

2 Obtaining the librarian's orders, which may be referred to as *Order Obtaining* ;

3 Communicating the order to the incumbent concerned and to the head of the section concerned, which may be referred to as *Sanction Communicating* ; and

4 Filling up the columns of the casual leave register, which may be referred to as *Casual Leave Register Entering*.

3227 Pay Bill

3227:6 The work of the Staff Section relating to pay bill is to consist of the following monthly job :

7 Revising the pay bill prepared by the accounts section, which may be referred to as *Pay Bill Revising*.

323 **Routine**

3231 Cadre of Appointments

3231:1 *Cadre Modifying Work*

3231:1:3 *Casual jobs*

3231:1:31 Strength of Staff Changing

As and when need arises for creating or abolishing a post or for transforming a post from one category to another, write out a note setting forth all the factors that contribute to the change contemplated. After getting the approval of the librarian, write a formal letter to the authorities concerned for the necessary sanction, embodying the ideas contained in the approved note. Transmit the letter to the authorities concerned along with a proposition statement in accordance with the rules on the subject and obtain the sanction.

3231:1:32 Scale of Pay Changing

Whenever the scale of pay of a post needs revision, proceed in the same way as in the strength of staff changing.

3231:1:37 Cadre Register Modifying

As soon as the sanction of the authorities concerned is received for any change in the strength of the staff or in the scale of pay of any post, make the consequential changes in the cadre register.

If a new post is created, open a new page for it. If the scale of pay is changed for any post, indicate it in the page devoted to that post.

3231:2 *Recruiting Work*

3231:2:3 *Casual jobs*

3231:2:31 ADVERTISING

If any vacancy occurs in the staff either due to creation of a new post, or to some one going out on regular leave, or to retirement of any incumbent, call for applications either by advertisement or by any other method in accordance with the convention or rules bearing on the subject. In the notification calling for applications, state clearly the name of the post, the salary, the period of vacancy, the qualifications required, and the last date for the receipt of applications.

3231:2:32 APPLICATIONS SORTING

On the day succeeding the last date for the receipt of applications, consult the librarian regarding the principle that must be followed in sorting the applications. Sort the applications into the groups suggested by the librarian and arrange the applications in each group alphabetically and number the applications according to the scheme approved by the librarian.

3231:2:33 NOTIFYING APPLICANTS

Take the applications to the librarian and discuss with him as to which applicants should be called for an interview. Write to the applicants selected by the librarian for interview asking them to call at the library at a specified date and time.

3231:2:34 INTERVIEW RESULT COMMUNICATING

Just before the interview, prepare a tabular statement with the columns suggested by the librarian to enable him to note down the results of the interview. As soon as the interview is over, get the interview notes from the librarian and ascertain from him the final recommendation. Write out a letter setting forth the recommendations of the librarian and communicate to the Sanctioning Authority.

3231:2:35 Appointing

As soon as the sanction for appointment is received from the Sanctioning Authority, communicate the order to the selected candidate, setting forth in clear terms the conditions of his service and specifying the date and time when he should join duty.

3231:2:37 Cadre Register Posting

As soon as a newly appointed incumbent joins duty, make the necessary entries in the page allotted to the post to which he is appointed.

3232 Incumbents

3232:1 *Confirming Work*

3232:1:3 *Casual jobs*

3232:1:31 Confirmation Recommending

In accordance with the rules and conventions regarding the confirmation of incumbents appointed on probation, prepare a note to the Sanctioning Authority for considering the question of confirmation of incumbents. The note is to contain information regarding the following :

1 Name ;
2 Qualifications ;
3 Date of recruitment ;
4 History of service up to the date of confirmation ; and
5 Recommendations of the heads of the sections in which the incumbent had been working.

Take the note to the librarian and get his recommendation. Write a letter to the Sanctioning Authority embodying the approved items in the note.

3232:1:32 Medical Certificate Requisitioning

As soon as the order of confirmation is received from the Sanctioning Authority, send a requisition to the approved Medical Authority to examine the incumbent and declare whether he is fit for appointment in the library. The certificate of medical fitness is to be attached to the first pay bill of the incumbent after confirmation.

3232:1:36 AGE EXEMPTION OBTAINING

If the incumbent's age is above the maximum age prescribed for appointment, write about it along with the proposal for confirmation and obtain the necessary age exemption from the authorities concerned. This exemption certificate also should be attached to the first pay bill of the incumbent after confirmation.

3232:2 *Service Register Work*

3232:2:3 *Casual jobs*

3232:2:31 SERVICE REGISTER OPENING

As soon as an incumbent is confirmed in the service of the library, open a Service Register for him. The routine connected with the opening of Service Registers will be found described in the Service Register itself; or you will have to follow the local practice, rules and regulations.

It is not unusual to open Service Registers even in the case of probationers and temporary incumbents.

3232:2:8 *Annual jobs*

3232:2:81 SERVICE REGISTER POSTING

At the appointed time each year, say in the first week of April, make the necessary entries in the Service Register of each incumbent up-to-date in accordance with the instructions for maintaining the Service Registers and get the signature of the librarian and of the incumbent.

3232:3 *Regular Leave Work*

3232:3:3 *Casual jobs*

Note : By regular leave is meant leave other than casual and compensation leave. It may be leave on full salary or on partial or no salary, with or without medical certificate.

3232:3:32 LEAVE ACCOUNT WORKING

As soon as an application for regular leave is received from an incumbent, bring the leave account of the incumbent, given at the end of his service register, up-to-date.

3232:3:34 Regular Leave Application Noting

Attach an endorsement sheet to the leave application and note on the endorsement sheet about:

1 the last occasion on which the incumbent was on leave and the nature of the leave he then had ;
2 the total amount of leave standing to his credit, under different heads ;
3 the acting arrangements that will have to be made ; and
4 any other relevant factors.

The note is to be written in consultation with the head of the section to which the incumbent belongs. Put up also the Service Register of the incumbent. Send the whole file to the Sanctioning Authority.

3232:3:35 Leave Order Communicating

As soon as the sanction for the leave is got, communicate the sanction to the incumbent concerned and also send an appointment order to the person selected to act in his place or in the chain. Send the sanction order to the Section on Elimination of Waste, for incorporation in the Staff Order Book and return. On the evening of the day preceding the date of commencement of leave, the incumbent should be asked to hand over charge to his substitute or, the Head of his Section if the substitute has not yet reported himself. After getting the certificate from the Head of the Section to the effect that he has handed over charge in the proper way, he is to be given a relief order. In the case of Heads of Sections, a similar procedure is to be followed, substituting the word "Assistant Librarian" in the place of "Head of the Section".

3232:3:71 Cadre Register Entering

After the leave order comes back from the Elimination of Waste Section, make the necessary entries in the Cadre Register. Enter in the page allotted to the post the details about the acting incumbent. Enter in the Leave Register the details about the person going out on leave.

3232:3:72 LEAVE RETURN NOTING

As soon as the incumbent returns from leave, make the necessary entries in the Leave Register, as well as the page allotted to the post in the Cadre Register.

3232:6 *Retirement Work*

3232:6:3 *Casual job*

The routine connected with Retirement Work will depend largely on local practice. What is given here is merely illustrative.

3232:6:31 RETIREMENT APPLICATION NOTING

Six months before the time for retirement by superannuation arises for an incumbent, obtain an application from him for retirement. It may happen that an incumbent may have to retire earlier due to some reason or other. As soon as an application for retirement is received, obtain the necessary information about the pension to which he is eligible and write out the endorsement setting forth the salient features in his service and the pension to which he will be eligible. Send the application with the endorsement to the Sanctioning Authority.

3232:6:32 RETIREMENT ORDER COMMUNICATING

As soon as the sanction for the retirement is received, communicate it to the incumbent concerned as well as to the Assistant Librarian for incorporation in the Staff Order Book and return.

On the date of retirement, the incumbent should be relieved in the same manner as provided in routine 3232:3:32.

3232:6:34 SERVICE REGISTER CLOSING

On the date on which an incumbent retires, close his Service Register in accordance with the rules on the subject and deal with it as provided in the rules.

3232:6:37 CADRE REGISTER FILLING

On the date of retirement of an incumbent, make the necessary entries in the Cadre Register, both in the page allotted to the post and also in the page allotted to pensioners.

3234 CASUAL AND COMPENSATION LEAVE

3234:4 *Daily jobs*

3234:41 ENDORSEMENT OBTAINING

As soon as an application for casual or compensation leave is received, the Head of the Staff Section is to attach it to the temporary file of the incumbent and send it to the Head of the Section to which the incumbent belongs. The Head of the Section should note on it :

1 the amount of leave for which the incumbent is eligible ;
2 whether the incumbent has finished all the items of work which should be finished by him at the time ;
3 whether the Head of the Section recommends the leave ; and
4 what arrangements the Head of the Section proposes for carrying on the work of the incumbent during his absence.

If the arrangement involves the co-operation of any other member of the same Section, or of any other Section, the consent of the member or the Head of the Section concerned, should also be recorded in the application. Then, the file is to be got back in the Staff Section.

3234:42 ORDER OBTAINING

Then, send the file to the librarian for sanction.

3234:43 SANCTION COMMUNICATING

As soon as the order of the librarian is received, send the file to the Head of the Section to which the incumbent belongs. The Head of the Section notes the order of the librarian and communicates the order to the incumbent concerned. Then, he will retransmit the file to the Staff Section.

3234:44 CASUAL LEAVE REGISTER ENTERING

Each day the Head of the Staff Section will enter, in the Attendance Register, the word "L" against the name of the incumbent under the respective dates on which casual or compensation leave has been availed of.

On the day the incumbent returns from leave, make the necessary entries in the Casual Leave Register of the incumbent concerned.

Occasionally it happens that a person who goes out on casual leave falls ill and takes regular leave. In such cases, the casual leave will have to be converted into regular leave. It is for this reason that it has been suggested that the Casual Leave Register is to be filled up only after return from leave.

3237 PAY BILL

3237:6 *Monthly job*

3237:67 PAY BILL REVISING

In the last week of each month, check the Pay Bill prepared by the Accounts Section. Use the Cadre Register, the Leave Register and the files of the incumbents to verify the data and the figures given in the Pay Bill. If there is any discrepancy, get it rectified by the Accounts Section. Put your dated initials next to that of the accountant in token of your having satisfied yourself about the accuracy of the Pay Bill.

324 Elimination of Waste

The postings in the Cadre Register, the Leave Register and the Service Registers should be carefully checked and maintained up-to-date.

325 Correlation Table

All Sections

3232:1:32 Confirmation Recommending ;
3232:3:31 Regular Leave Application Noting ;
3232:3:32 Leave Order Communicating ;
3234:41 Endorsement Obtaining ;
3234:43 Sanction Communicating.

97 *Accounts Section*

3237:67 Pay Bill Revising.

326 Illustrative Time Scheme

Most of the jobs of this section are of a casual nature, as they will arise only occasionally. But the jobs relating to casual and compensation leave are of a daily nature. The routine connected with them is to be done in the following sequence:

DAILY JOBS

3234:44 Casual Leave Register Entering (11-30 A M) ;
3234:41 Endorsement Obtaining ;
3234:42 Order Obtaining (1 P M) ; and
3234:43 Order Communicating.

MONTHLY JOB

3237:67 Pay Bill Revising (last week).

ANNUAL JOB

3232:2:81 Service Register Posting (first week of April).

327 Forms and Registers

S921 *Cadre Register*. Manuscript. 30 lb ledger paper. White. Bound book. 20 lines. Folio pagination.

Three pages for each post with the following text :

(*a*) *First line* : Date of effect ; Name of the post ; Scale of pay ; Sanction number and date ; File number.
(*b*) *Column headings* :
1 Name of incumbent (5 cm) ;
2 Nature of tenure (permanent, acting, etc) (2.5 cm) ;
3 Pay (2.5 cm) ;
4 Date of commencement of the pay (2.5 cm) ;
5 Due date of next increment (2.5 cm) ;
6 Date of termination or change of pay (2.5 cm) ;
7 Reason for termination or change of pay (leave, increment, change of scale, promotion, retirement, ceasing of acting period, etc) (5 cm) ;
8 Sanction for (7) (7.5 cm) ; and
9 Remarks.

Whenever there is change of name or scale of pay, the details are to be entered in red ink in the earliest vacant line, in the same style as the first line.

S923 *Service Register*. Printed. Text depending on local practice, rules and regulations. One register for each permanent incumbent.

S924 *Leave Register*. Manuscript. 21 lb printing paper. White. Stitched book. 20 lines. Folio pagination. Number of pages depends on the strength of the staff and the leave rules—say roughly twice as many pages as there are members on the staff.

The column headings are to be as follows :

1 Name of the incumbent (5 cm) ;
2 Pay at the commencement of the leave (2.5 cm) ;
3 Leave pay (2.5 cm) ;
5 Sanction order (5 cm) ;
6 Date of commencement (2.5 cm) ;
7 Due date of termination (2.5 cm) ;
8 Actual date of termination (2.5 cm) ;
9 Name of acting incumbent (5 cm) ;
10 Pay of acting incumbent (2.5 cm) ;
11 Date of commencement of acting (2.5 cm) ; and
12 Remarks.

Note : In respect of category 8, the leave is extended, write the word " extended " in red ink in this column and begin a fresh line for the extended leave.

Name	*Class number*	*Amplifying device*	*Filing characteristic*	*Year of transfer to record sequence after the file is closed*	*Year of destruction after transfer to record sequence*
Cadre	921	Subject device	Correspondent	Year 10	Permanent
Librarian	9211	Do	Do	Do	Do
Assistant librarian	9212	Do	Do	Do	Do
Upper division assistants	9213	Do	Do	Do	Do
Lower division assistants	9214	Do	Do	Do	Do
Junior assistants	9215	Do	Do	Do	Do
Temporary assistants	9216	Do	Do	Do	Do
Muchi, attenders, etc	9217	Do	Do	Do	Do
Peons	9218	Do	Do	Do	Do
Permanent papers	924	Nil	Incumbent	Do	Year after retirement 5
Temporary papers	925	Nil	Do	Year 1	Year 3
Outward enquiries	9291	Nil	Correspondent	Do	Do
Inward enquiries	9292	Nil	Do	Do	Do

CHAPTER 33

STAFF COUNCIL

331 Need

The need for and the utility of the Staff Council have been indicated already in Chapter 15. A fuller discussion of the same is also to be found in my *Five laws of library science.*[44]

333 Routine

The routine connected with the Staff Council is similar to the routine connected with the Library Committee.

It may be necessary to write out staff orders in the light of the decisions arrived at by the Staff Council, on such matters as require staff orders.

335 Correlation

It goes without saying that the Staff Council is the most vital instrument for bringing about the most effective correlation between the work of the different Sections. As such, it can be seen that the Section in charge of the affairs of the Staff Council will have to deal with each of the other Sections of the library, both in arranging the business for the Staff Council and in giving effect to the decisions of the Staff Council.

336 Time Scheme

Each Section may have its own meeting in the penultimate or any other definite week of each month. The Staff Council may meet in the last week of the month. The Secretaries of the different Sections may communicate to the Secretary of the Staff Council such items, as their respective Sections would like to bring up before the Staff Council, in good time for inclusion in the agenda of the Staff Council.

337 Forms and Registers

The minutes book of the Staff Council is to be similar to that of the Library Committee. Its number is to be S93. The numbers of the minutes books of the different Sections are to be got by amplifying S93 by the addition of the number of the Section concerned.

338 Files

The agenda and the draft minutes of the Staff Council are to be numbered 93 and 935, respectively and amplified by the number of the month of the meeting. They may be destroyed at the end of the year.

CHAPTER 34

ELIMINATION OF WASTE

341 Planning

3411 AGENCY FOR SUPERVISION

The overall Elimination of Waste Work will have to be done entirely by the librarian himself in small libraries. On the other hand, in large libraries an independent Section of the staff will have to be put in charge of the sole task of supervising the regular and correct performance of the routine in the various sections of the library and to deal with such topics as the annual report of the library, which cannot be assigned to any other single Section. It is not unusual to assign this overseeing business to the Correspondence Section for the reason that practically all correspondence has to pass through the hands of that Section. But in medium-size libraries, it may be advantageous for the librarian to share the overseeing work with the assistant librarian, or with the Manager of the general administrative staff as distinguished from the staff entrusted with the distinctive library functions. In such a division of labour, the librarian may keep in his hands the supervision of the correct performance of all the technical duties, such as classification, cataloguing, preparation of bibliographies, and so on. The assistant librarian or the manager may be asked to supervise the administrative routine connected with all duties.

3412 ASSISTANT LIBRARIAN

With the requirements of a medium-size library in view and having relegated the librarian's share of supervision to the chapter " 391 Librarian", this chapter will deal only with the supervision of administrative routine. The person in charge of it shall be referred to as the Assistant Librarian.

3418 FACTORS IN PLANNING

The distinctive overall work of Elimination of Waste is to be planned with reference to the following factors :

1 Annual report ;
2 Staff ;
3 Staff order book ;
4 Diaries ;
5 Junction moments ;
6 Progress report ;
7 Accounts ; and
8 Inspection.

342 Job Analysis

Annual Report

3421:8 The work on Elimination of Waste relating to Annual Report is to consist of the following annual jobs :

1 Giving notice to the different Sections about the date on which data for the Annual Report should be ready, which may be referred to as *Notifying the Sections* ;
2 Framing the skeleton of the Annual Report, which may be referred to as *Skeleton Framing* ;
3 Getting from the different Sections the necessary data, which may be referred to as *Data Collecting* ;
4 Making a preliminary draft of the Annual Report, which may be referred to as *Report Drafting* ;
5 Discussing the preliminary report with the librarian and taking his instructions, which may be referred to as *Report Consulting*;
6 Making the final draft of the Annual Report, which may be referred to as *Report Completing* ;
7 Forwarding the Annual Report to the authorities concerned for consideration, adoption and review, which may be referred to as *Report Forwarding* ; and
8 Taking the necessary action on the resolution of the authorities concerned on the Annual Report, which may be referred to as *Report Review Disposing*.

3422 Staff

The work on Elimination of Waste relating to Staff is to consist of the following items :

1 Distributing the work among the different Sections, which may be referred to as *Distribution Work* ;
2 Assignment of staff to different Sections, which may be referred to as *Assignment Work* ;
5 Enforcing proper discipline among the Staff, which may be referred to as *Discipline Work* ; and
6 Drafting the time-table for the Staff and amending it from time to time, which may be referred to as *Time-Table Work.*

3422:1 *Distribution Work*

3422:1:3 The Distribution Work is to consist of the following casual jobs :

1 Consulting the librarian and Staff Council in regard to Distribution of Work, which may be referred to as *Distribution Consulting* ;
2 Informing the Heads of Sections about the Distribution decided upon, which may be referred to as *Distribution Communicating* ; and
3 Watching the suitability of the Distribution of Work and reporting to the librarian from time to time, which may be referred to as *Distribution Reporting.*

3422:2 *Assignment Work*

3422:2:3 The Assignment Work is to consist of the following casual jobs :

1 Consulting the librarian and the Staff Council in regard to Assignment of Work, which may be referred to as *Assignment Consulting* ;
2 Informing the staff about the assignment of work decided upon, which may be referred to as *Assignment Communicating* ;
3 Watching the suitability of the assignment of work and reporting to the librarian from time to time, which may be referred to as *Assignment Reporting* ; and
4 Making temporary reassignment at times of pressure which may be referred to as *Assignment Adjusting.*

3422:5 *Discipline Work*

3422:5:1 The Discipline Work is to consist of the following immediate jobs :

1 Regulating and controlling the movement of peons, which may be referred to as *Peons' Movement Regulating* ;
2 Getting the late coming of the members of the staff recorded, which may be referred to as *Late Attendance Watching* ; and
4 Bringing all abnormal occurrences to the notice of the librarian, which may be referred to as *Abnormalities Intimating.*

3422:5:4 The Discipline Work is to consist of the following daily jobs :

1 Examining the Attendance Register, which may be referred to as *Attendance Register Scrutinising* ;
2 Getting the sanctioned casual and compensation leave entered in the Attendance Register by the Head of the Staff Section, which may be referred to as *Attendance Register Completing* ; and
3 Informing the librarian of the absence of members of staff without leave, which may be referred to as *Absence Intimating.*

3422:5:5 The Discipline Work is to consist of the following weekly jobs :

1 Obtaining from the members of the staff who had come late or had absented themselves without permission in the course of the week, which may be referred to as *Explanation Obtaining* ;
2 Forwarding to the librarian the explanations obtained for late coming and absence without permission, which may be referred to as *Explanation Forwarding* ; and
3 Transmitting to the Staff Section the explanations of the staff, after they are returned from the librarian, which may be referred to as *Explanations Transmitting.*

3422:5:6 The Discipline Work is to consist of the following monthly jobs :

1 Writing out the Attendance Register, which may be referred to as *Attendance Regist., Writing* :
2 Marking the leave arrangement in the Attendance Register, which may be referred to as *Attendance Register Amending* ; and
3 Rectifying the address of the members of the staff, which may be referred to as *Address Rectifying.*

3422:6 *Time-Table Work*

3422:6:3 The Time-Table Work is to consist of the following casual jobs :

1 Obtaining from the Heads of Sections the draft time-table for the respective Sections, which may be referred to as *Section Time-Table Obtaining* ;
5 Reconciling the time-tables of the different Sections, which may be referred to as *Time-Tables Reconciling* ; and
6 Watching the due observance of the time-table by the different Sections and reporting to the librarian deviations, if any, which may be referred to as *Deviation Intimating.*

3423 STAFF ORDER BOOK

3423:3 The work on Elimination of Waste relating to Staff Order Book is to consist of the following casual jobs :

1 Writing or causing to be written the necessary orders from time to time, which may be referred to as *Staff Order Writing* ;
2 Circulating the Staff Order Book to the members of the staff concerned, which may be referred to as *Staff Order Circulating* ; and
3 Circulating the Staff Order Book to new recruits, which may be referred to as *New Recruits Instructing.*

3424 DIARIES

3424:4 The work on Elimination of Waste relating to Diaries is to consist of the following daily jobs :

1 Scrutinising the Diaries of the different Sections, which may be referred to as *Diaries Scrutinising* ; and

2 Informing the librarian of abnormalities, if any, which may be referred to as *Diary Abnormalities Intimating.*

3424:5 The work on Elimination of Waste relating to Diaries is to consist of the following weekly job :

1 Scrutinising the weekly cumulative totals in the Diaries, which may be referred to as *Weekly Totals Scrutinising.*

3424:6 The work on Elimination of Waste relating to Diaries is to consist of the following monthly job :

1 Scrutinising the monthly totals and the monthly postings of the Diaries, which may be referred to as *Monthly Total Scrutinising.*

3424:8 The work on Elimination of Waste relating to Diaries is to consist of the following annual job :

1 Scrutinising the annual totals and the annual posting of Diaries, which may be referred to as *Annual Postings Scrutinising.*

3425 Junction Moments

3425:1 The work on Elimination of Waste relating to Junction Moments is to consist of the following immediate job :

1 Watching the proper finishing off of Junction Moment Work and reporting to the librarian about it, which may be referred to as *Junction Moment Reporting.*

3426 Progress Report

3426:5 The work on Elimination of Waste relating to Progress Report is to consist of the following weekly job :

1 Obtaining from the Heads of Sections their weekly Progress Reports and examining them, which may be referred to as *Weekly Progress Scrutinising.*

3426:6 The work on Elimination of Waste relating to Progress

Report is to consist of the following monthly job :

1 Informing the librarian about the defects observed in the Weekly Progress Reports, which may be referred to as *Progress Reporting*.

3427 Accounts

3427:5 The work on Elimination of Waste relating to Accounts is to consist of the following weekly jobs :

1 Examining if the Finance Diaries have been properly filled up, which may be referred to as *Financial Diary Scrutinising* ; and
7 Examining if the expenditure under the different heads is within the limits of the budget, which may be referred to as *Progress of Expenditure Watching*.

3428 Inspection

3428:7 The work on Elimination of Waste relating to Inspection is to consist of the following quarterly jobs :

1 Inspecting the maintenance of the records and the general duties of the different Sections, which may be referred to as *Inspecting* ; and
2 Reporting to the librarian the results of the inspection, which may be referred to as *Inspection Reporting*.

343 Routine

3431 Annual Report

3431:8 *Annual jobs*

From the nature of the subject, the Annual Report is to be put in charge of the Assistant Librarian. The data for it will have to be obtained from different Sections and properly edited. For definiteness, the calendar year has been assumed to be the year for the Annual Report.

3431:81 Notifying the Sections

Early in December, inform all the Sections of the library that the data for the Annual Report should be furnished by a specified date. It is desirable that the data sought from the different Sections should be such as can be expressed as definite quantities. Wherever possible regular tabular forms may be furnished. This does not mean, however, that there should be no general narration. All such narration can be furnished as remarks in the briefest terms possible.

3431:82 SKELETON FRAMING

Within two weeks after informing the Sections, frame the skeleton for the Annual Report in consultation with the librarian. It will be a good plan to make the skeleton conform as closely as possible to the analysis contained in the administration manual. Communicate to the different Sections the relevant portions of the skeleton to enable them to fit in the information, collected by them, into the frame.

3431:83 DATA COLLECTING

In the first week of January, obtain from the different Sections the data collected by them for the Annual Report. Examine if every part of the skeleton has been filled up with the necessary data. If, in assembling the data, any gap is discovered, obtain from the Sections concerned the information necessary to fill up the gap.

3431:84 REPORT DRAFTING

Weave the data into the Annual Report in a readable form. Provide an introduction, summarising the salient features of the year's work and indicating the outstanding developments planned for the ensuing year. Tabular statements which would go far beyond one page, may, if otherwise admissible, be relegated to the appendix.

3431:85 REPORT CONSULTING

Present the draft Annual Report to the librarian and within a week after that, discuss it with him. Note down the instructions that he gives.

3431:86 REPORT COMPLETING

Revise the draft Annual Report in the light of the instructions given by the librarian. If any additional data are required, get them from the Sections concerned. If any part of the Annual

Report requires redrafting, get it redrafted. Send the final Annual Report to the librarian for approval and signature. After it is approved, send it to the Correspondence Section. Ask the Correspondence Section to make four copies of the report. One copy is to serve as the office copy. One copy is to serve as the press copy. One copy is for the librarian's file. And, the fourth copy is for transmission to the Authorities concerned.

3431:87 REPORT FORWARDING

As soon as the faircopying of the report is over, send it with a forwarding letter to the reviewing Authorities.

3431:88 REPORT REVIEW DISPOSING

When the review of the Authorities concerned reaches the library, take such action as the review may call for, in consultation with the librarian.

3432 STAFF

3432:1 *Distribution Work*

3432:1:3 *Casual jobs*

3432:1:31 DISTRIBUTION CONSULTING

Whenever deemed necessary, bring up, for the consideration of the librarian, proposals for the redistribution of work among the different sections. Proposals for a redistribution should be definite and should contain in brief terms the reasons for the redistribution suggested. If the librarian gives his general approval to the proposal, put it before the Staff Council, to get the views of the different Sections, and work out the details.

3432:1:32 DISTRIBUTION COMMUNICATING

As soon as a redistribution of work gets the approval of the Staff Council and the librarian, embody it in the Staff Order Book and communicate it to the Sections concerned.

3432:1:33 DISTRIBUTION REPORTING

Watch the progress of work in the different Sections. Examine if the current Distribution of Work is satisfactory and if better results can be obtained by any redistribution. Redistribution may be easily called for, whenever there is change of hands. Make a report to the librarian whenever a readjustment is necessary.

3432:2 *Assignment Work*

3432:2:3 *Casual jobs*

3432:2:31 Assignment Consulting

Whenever necessary and particularly when a new hand is recruited either in acting arrangement or otherwise, discuss with the librarian and the Staff Council the best way in which the members of the staff can be assigned to the different Sections. It is also desirable that the staff are reassigned to different Sections periodically so as to give a chance for every member to acquaint himself with the work in the different Sections. It must be remembered, however, that this reshuffling should be done with great care, so that the advantages of specialisation are not lost to the library.

3432:2:32 Assignment Communicating

As soon as the approval of the librarian is obtained for any assignment, incorporate it in the Staff Order and communicate it to the concerned members of the staff.

3432:2:33 Assignment Reporting

Watch the progress of the work in the different Sections and the appropriateness of the work assigned to the different members of the staff. Discuss the matter with the Heads of Sections and whenever the Head of a Section reports misfits and you agree with him, work out the best way of eliminating the defect and send a report to the librarian.

3432:2:34 Assignment Adjusting

It will happen now and then that, in spite of all the care to distribute the work evenly throughout the hours of the day, the days of the week and the weeks of the year, occasions arise when there is unusual crowding of work at particular moments or stretches of time. Such occasions may be due to causes beyond the control of the library such as an unusual rush of readers or an unusually large number of absentees among the staff. It may also be inevitable in certain parts of the year, in consequence of the peculiar nature of certain items of work. Whenever congestion of work arises, it may be necessary to take a suitable member of the staff from a Section which has got light work and assign him temporarily to the Section where there is pressure. In consultation with the Heads of Sections, proposals for such temporary readjustments should be taken to the librarian and given effect to after his approval. Similarly assign pick-up-work whenever necessary.

3432:5 *Discipline Work*

3432:5:1 *Immediate jobs*

3432:5:11 Peons' Movement Regulating

Management of peons is one of the most difficult and delicate tasks of the assistant librarian. Partly due to their low cultural level, some of them may not be able to take an intelligent view of their work or their duties or their obligations. Again, great care will be necessary to draft a suitable time-table for the peons so that the work of any Section may not suffer due to paucity of peons' service. Whenever peons have to be sent out for outdoor work, great care and tact is necessary to secure that they do not loiter away for an unduly long time on the pretext of some difficulty in finishing their outdoor work. A proper detailed time scheme should be drawn up and strictly enforced. Lack of firmness in enforcing the time scheme will greatly corrode and undermine discipline.

3432:5:12 Late Attendance Watching

If any particular member of the staff comes to the library after the time scheduled for him, see that he notes down the correct time of his arrival in the Attendance Register. Note in your diary the names of such persons and the dates on which they come late, for use in connection with obtaining explanations from them at the end of the week. Punctuality in a public library is of great importance. Every effort should be made to secure that every member of the staff reaches the library and begins his work at the proper time.

3432:5:14 Abnormalities Intimating

Keep a general watchful eye over the library and whenever

any Abnormal Occurrence comes to your notice, inform the librarian about it and take such action as may be necessary. Points, which require such watching, are lack of civility to the readers on the part of the staff, ugly broil among the peons, unnecessary indulgence in talk either among the staff or between the staff and the readers, petty thefts and so on, which, though trivial and not easily noticeable, will affect the reputation of the library in the long run.

3432:5:4 *Daily jobs*

3432:5:41 Attendance Register Scrutinising

Immediately after the expiry of the hour when the majority of the staff are scheduled to arrive at the library, take the Attendance Register and scrutinise it carefully. If any member of the staff, that had already come, had failed to enter in the Attendance Register, get it entered by him and politely suggest to him that the register should be entered by him as the first thing after arrival at the library.

3432:5:42 Attendance Register Completing

Send the Attendance Register to the Staff Section and ask them to enter the casual and compensation leave granted and availed of by the staff for the day.

Put a conventional mark in the attendance register against the names of those who are having their weekly holidays.

3432:5:43 Absence Intimating

If, after the entries in the Attendance Register are completed, there is still any blank space, allow a reasonable time for the member concerned to arrive—say, half an hour. Thereafter, send an Absentee Statement to the librarian.

3432:5:5 *Weekly jobs*

3432:5:51 Explanation Obtaining

On the appointed day of the week, with the help of the notes of late attendance marked in your diary, the Absentee Statements sent to the librarian and the Attendance Register, prepare a list of persons whose explanation for late attendance or absence without permission is to be got. Get the explanations of the persons concerned.

3432:5:52 Explanation Forwarding

If there is any further information necessary to make the explanation complete, get it and send all the explanations to the librarian for his orders.

3432:5:53 Explanation Transmitting

As soon as the explanations come back from the librarian with his orders, send them to the Staff Section, along with the Absentee Statements of the week, for the necessary action.

3432:5:6 *Monthly jobs*

3432:5:61 Attendance Register Writing

In the last week of each month, write out the Attendance Register for the succeeding month. It would be a good plan to enter the names of the staff, Section by Section. It is a matter of experience in libraries that the Sections which have to deal with the public and have to work on all days get their weekly holidays on different days. The members of such Sections do not take the public holidays even. On the contrary, the members of the Administrative Sections take their weekly holidays on the same day and enjoy also all the public holidays. Hence, it will be a good plan to have the names of the members of the staff, written Section by Section.

3432:5:62 Attendance Register Amending

Whenever a member of the staff is granted regular leave, i e leave other than casual and compensation leave, note the information against the name of the incumbent in the Attendance Register and enter the name of the acting incumbent just below the name of the person in whose place he acts. Make the necessary changes on the return of the incumbent from leave. Similarly, whenever a member of the staff is transferred from one Section to another, the necessary alterations will have to be made in the Attendance Register.

3432:5:63 Address Rectifying

It is a good practice to have, in the Attendance Register, the correct private address of every member of the staff. In times of emergency, it may be necessary to send urgent communications to the members at their residence. The Attendance Register is the best place where the addresses may be recorded ; it goes without saying that the addresses must be correct and up-to-date, if the purpose is to be served. Hence, it is suggested that the assistant librarian should circulate the Attendance Register to the members of the staff on the first of every month, and ask them to verify their respective addresses and correct them if necessary.

3432:6 *Time-Table Work*

3432:6:3 *Casual jobs*

3432:6:31 Section Time-Table Obtaining

Whenever a readjustment is made in the work of a Section, obtain from the Head of that Section the new Time-Table and the new scheme of distribution of work among the members.

3432:6:35 Time-Table Reconciling

Study the Time-Table of the different Sections in relation to one another, particularly with special reference to Junction Moments and in consultation with the Heads of Sections, get the time-tables of the different Sections properly articulated. It will be a good practice to have three copies of all the approved time-tables and schemes of distribution of work—one for the section, one for the assistant librarian and one for the librarian.

3432:6:36 Deviation Intimating

Watch the working of the Time-Tables of the different sections and, if in the actual working, any deviations are found to be necessary or admissible, inform the librarian about them and get the alterations made with his approval.

3433 Staff Order Book

3433:3 *Casual jobs*

3433:31 Staff Order Writing

The assistant librarian should see that every important decision by the Staff Council or by the librarian regarding the staff and their work is recorded in the form of an order in the Staff Order Book. For example, the granting of regular leave to the members of the staff and the appointment of acting incumbents, the scheme of distribution of work among the different Sections, the assignment of members to the different Sections are matters of routine occurrence, which should be incorporated in the Staff Order Book. The orders may be numbered serially for each year.

3433:32 STAFF ORDER CIRCULATING

As soon as a Staff Order is written out and signed by the librarian, circulate it promptly to the members concerned and get their initials in token of their having read the order.

3433:33 NEW RECRUITS INSTRUCTING

Whenever a new person is appointed in the library, the assistant librarian should give him the Staff Order Book and instruct him to read the relevant staff orders to enable him to acquaint himself with the important conventions and practices of the library.

3434 DIARIES

3434:4 *Daily jobs*

3434:41 DIARIES SCRUTINISING

As one of the first items of work each day, examine the Diaries of the different Sections. See if all the columns are properly filled up. If there is any defect, ask the Head of the Section concerned to rectify it.

3434:42 DIARY ABNORMALITIES INTIMATING

As soon as the Diaries Scrutinising is over, send a report to the librarian that the Diaries have all been filled up and also state in the report, if anything abnormal is brought out by the entries in the Diaries, to enable the librarian to take the necessary action.

3434:5 *Weekly job*

3434:51 WEEKLY TOTALS SCRUTINISING

On the Saturday of every week, examine if the weekly cumulative totals have been entered in all the diaries. If they have not been done, ask the Head of the Section concerned to complete it.

3434:6 *Monthly job*

3434:61 MONTHLY TOTAL SCRUTINISING

In a similar manner, on the second day of every month, examine if the monthly totals have been entered in the Diaries and carried forward to the Diaries of the next month. If there is any defect, get it rectified by the Head of the Section concerned.

3434:8 *Annual job*

3434:81 ANNUAL POSTING SCRUTINISING

In the first week of January each year, examine if the annual posting of all the Diaries have been done and if the yearly Diaries have been properly filled up. If there is any defect, get it set right by the Head of the Section concerned.

3435 JUNCTION MOMENTS

3435:1 *Immediate job*

3435:11 JUNCTION MOMENT REPORTING

It should be one of the most vital functions of the assistant librarian to watch the proper finishing off of Junction Moment Work and report to the librarian about it promptly as soon as the work is over. The importance of Junction Moment Work has been fully discussed in Chapter 16 of this book. The smooth running of the library will be very much disturbed, if the Junction Moment Work does not pass off without a hitch. It is therefore necessary that these Junction Moments should be carefully watched and the necessary adjustments made on such occasions, so that the work may be carried on without a hitch. If there is any unusual hitch, take the aid of the librarian to resolve the hitch.

3436 PROGRESS REPORT

3436:5 *Weekly job*

3436:51 WEEKLY PROGRESS SCRUTINISING

Every Saturday, get from the Heads of Sections a Progress Report about the work of their Sections in the preceding week. For each Section, a suitable form of report should be designed in the light of the time-table. The form should consist of a series of questions to which the answer should be either in the form of 'yes' or 'no' or in the form of quantitative information. In addition to special questions, the form for each section is likely to contain the following common questions :

1 Have the reminders due in the week for outward correspondence been issued ? If not, how many are outstanding ?
2 Have all the letters received in the previous week been disposed of ? If not, how many are outstanding ?
3 Are there any letters that have been awaiting disposal for a month or more ? If so, how many ?
4 Has the weekly totalling of the diary been finished ?
5 Have all the routines of the week been rounded off ?

Against each question there should be space for a brief explanation of the Head of the Section in case of deviation of normal progress of work.

After the scrutiny of the Progress Reports, the assistant librarian should have a talk with the Heads of Sections concerned and see that the work of the Sections are all brought up-to-date and that all arrears are completed.

3436:6 *Monthly job*

3436:61 Progress Reporting

On the Sunday following the first Saturday of each month, the assistant librarian should make a report to the librarian about the outstanding defects observed in the work of the different sections along with the explanations of the Heads of Sections concerned. He should also discuss with the librarian the defects and find out the causes for the defects. If the causes are traceable to faulty organisation, he must get the necessary instructions from the librarian to have the fault removed. If the defects are due to lack of vigilance on the part of the staff, he should carry out such disciplinary action as the librarian would prescribe.

3437 Accounts

3437:5 *Weekly job*

3437:51 Financial Diaries Scrutinising

On the Saturday of each week, the assistant librarian should examine carefully if the columns in the Financial Diaries are properly posted. There should be two Financial Diaries. One Diary is to be common to three Sections, viz Book Order Section, Periodical Publication Section and Accounts Section. The purpose of this Diary is to give in a succinct form the amount appropriated or spent on books and periodical publications in different subjects. The purpose of the Second Diary is to give in a succinct form the amount appropriated or spent under the different headings and sub-headings shown in the budget. The prompt filling up of these Diaries is very important, lest the expenditure or the commitment to expenditure should unconsciously go beyond the budget limits.

3437:57 Progress of Expenditure Watching

Apart from seeing that the columns in the Financial Diaries are properly filled up, the assistant librarian should carefully examine the correct figures both under commitment and under actual expenditure under the different headings and sub-headings. He should see that the matter is comfortably within the budget limits. At the same time, as the end of the year is approached, he should watch if the entire sanctioned amount is spent. Whenever the assistant librarian finds uneven progress or any other abnormality, he should invite the attention of the librarian to the same, so that he may examine the situation and set it right.

3438 Inspection

3438:7 *Quarterly jobs*

3438:71 Inspecting

The assistant librarian should inspect each Section at least once in a quarter. Among other things, he should examine the following points :

1 If all the files of the Section are properly maintained ;
2 In particular, if the necessary cross references are made in the files ;
3 If the files are kept in the proper classified sequence ;
4 If all the registers of the Section are kept up-to-date and maintained in a good condition ; and
5 If the materials in charge of the Section are kept in a tidy condition.

It would be a good plan for the assistant librarian to spread the inspection of the different sections over the different weeks of the quarter.

3438:72 Inspection Reporting

As soon as the inspection of all the Sections is over, for the quarter, the assistant librarian should send a report about his findings to the librarian. The report should state in clear terms the defects found and the remedies suggested.

A few days after sending the report to the librarian, he should discuss them with the librarian and take such action as may be decided upon in the discussion.

345 Correlation Table

From the nature of its work, the work of the overall Elimination of Waste Section is out and out correlated with the work of every Section. Hence, practically every job will have to be put down against every Section, except the following, which have relation only to the Sections against which they are noted.

2 *Book Order Section*

3437:51 Financial diaries scrutinising ;
3437:57 Progress of expenditure watching.

3 *Periodical Publications Section*

3437:51 Financial diaries scrutinising ;
3437:57 Progress of expenditure watching.

92 *Staff Section*

3432:5:42 Attendance register completing.

97 *Accounts Section*

3437:51 Financial diaries scrutinising ;
3437:57 Progress of expenditure watching.

346 Illustrative Time Scheme

Most of the jobs being of a casual nature, will not figure in this scheme.

Daily Jobs

3432:5:4 All the daily jobs of discipline work ;

3434:4 All the daily jobs relating to the diaries of the sections.

Weekly Jobs

Saturday

3432:5 Discipline work (All the weekly jobs) ;
3436:61 Weekly progress scrutinising ;
3437:5 All the weekly jobs relating to accounts.

Sunday

3434:51 Weekly totals scrutinising.

Monthly Jobs

First Sunday

3436:61 Progress reporting.

Second Sunday

3434:61 Monthly total scrutinising.

Quarterly Jobs

First Thursday

3438:7 Inspection reporting.
The inspecting work may be spread over different weeks.

Annuals Jobs

The time scheme is indicated in the routine part of this chapter, which deals with the annual report, viz routine 3431.

347 Forms and Registers

Q94 *Staff Order Book*. 20 lb printing paper. White. Stitched 96 pages.

S94 *Attendance Register*. Printed. 10 p type. 30 lb ledger paper. White. Bound. Number of pages to depend on the number of members on the staff, so that the register may be completed in five years. Folio pagination. 30 lines per page. But every odd line to begin only from the fourth column, so that in the first three columns, there are only 15 lines. From the fourth column onwards, the odd lines are to be used for noting the time and the even lines for the initials of the members of the staff. The column headings are to be as follows :

Serial number (1.5 cm). Name (5 cm). Designation (2.5 cm). For the next 16 columns, the headings are to be written in manuscript and should show the day of the week and the date (1.5 cm). Each of these columns is to be sub-divided into two sub-columns, one for the morning and the other for the evening. Each month will be spread over two pages. The last column is to be entitled "Remarks".

The following words may be printed in block letters above the column headings :

First line : . . . . Library.

Second line : Attendance Register for the Month of . . . . , 195

Name	*Class number*	*Amplifying device*	*Filing characteristic*	*Year of transfer to record sequence after the file is closed*	*Year of destruction after transfer to the record sequence*
Annual report	941	The last digit of the year to which the report relates	Correspondent	Year 2	Year* 10
Distribution schedule	9422	Section number	Nil	Year 1	Year 1
Assignment schedule	9423	Do	Nil	Do	Do
Time-table	9426	Do	Nil	Do	Do
Progress report	946	Do	Nil	Do	Year 3
Inspection report	948	Do	Nil	Do	Do
Outward enquiries	9491	Nil	Correspondent	Do	Do
Inward enquiries	9492	Nil	Do	Do	Do

* A clean copy of the annual report, as finally adopted, is to be kept permanently in the record section, though the other papers of the file are destroyed.

CHAPTER 35

PUBLICITY SECTION

351 Not A Routine Affair

Publicity, to be effective, should strive to escape becoming a routine affair. Novelty of method is so necessary that it is futile to reduce publicity to routine. Still, each library will have to choose some modes of publicity which admit of repetition at stated intervals. It is only such modes of publicity that will admit of job analysis and routine.

352 Modes of Publicity

Here are a few examples of such modes of publicity :

1 The list of recent additions may be :

11 published in the local dailies ;

12 circulated to important local centres like colleges, schools, hostels, clubs and other learned associations ; and

13 may be put up prominently on the notice-board of the library.

These Jobs may be repeated every week.

2 The statistics of issue may be published in the local dailies once in a month.

3 A general article setting forth the services, which the library is prepared to render to the public, may be featured in the dailies, say once in a quarter.

4 A short account of the library and its work may be inserted every year in the local directories and in the calendars of the local educational and other institutions.

5 Whenever any local festival or fair is conducted or any other celebration made, the library may participate in such celebrations in a suitable manner, distributing leaflets and conducting exhibitions. Naturally these will involve only casual jobs.

6 The Publicity Section may interest itself in the organisation of study groups to pursue particular topics in close association

with the library. The organisation of such groups will involve much routine work, to regulate the hours of meeting of such study groups and to procure for them all the necessary facilities.

7 The Publicity Section may also keep itself in touch with the different learned bodies and business associations of the locality. Their book needs may be studied and the necessary action taken to get the resources of the library used by such bodies.

8 The Publicity Section may have to arrange for library talks, story hours, and other similar extension work, so as to stimulate the interest of the public in the resources of the library. For this, it will have to work out a well co-ordinated programme, secure lecturers, send notifications to the public, keep the magic lantern, etc in proper working order and so on.

In all these jobs, the Publicity Section will have to work in close co-operation with the Reference Section, the Maintenance Section and the Technical Section.

9 The Publicity Section may also have to make street surveys and institution surveys to find out who have not come under the influence of the library. Then, the Section will have to devise methods for persuading those persons to become patrons of the library.

353 Routine

Each library will have to work out its own publicity programme, analyse each factor into items of work and jobs and write out the routine for each job. The forms and registers as well as the files to be kept will vary therefore from library to library and, in the same library, from time to time. The time-table also will have to vary similarly.

354 Books on Publicity

There are excellent books on library publicity work. McColvin's book[45] is adapted to English conditions. Similarly Cannon's book[46] deals with American conditions. The principles of library publicity have also been discussed in my *Five laws of library science*, in relation to the Third Law, viz " Every Book its Reader".[47]

355 Salesmanship in Libraries

I have also discussed the same question from another point of view, in a lecture[48] on "Salesmanship in libraries" delivered at the All-India Library Conference held in Calcutta in September 1933.

In that lecture I started with the definition of salesmanship as follows: "Salesmanship is the art of building up the appreciation of the value or the desirability of a service, idea, or ideal, so that it is accepted and satisfaction follows its adoption." According to the New English Dictionary, "A library is a public institution or establishment charged with the care of a collection of books and the duty of making them accessible to those who require the use of them." I made out a case that this dictionary definition, which was written at the close of the nineteenth century, fell far short of the modern ideas of librarianship, and suggested that another function should be added to it. The definition proposed by me was as follows: "A library is a public institution or establishment charged with the care of a collection of books, the duty of making them accessible to those who require the use of them and the task of converting every person in its neighbourhood into a habitual library goer and reader of books." When this enlarged view of librarianship is adopted, the necessity for all conceivable methods of publicity and salesmanship will be easily granted. This has led to the appointment of full-timed publicity officers in certain libraries.[49]

CHAPTER 36

FINANCE SECTION

361 Planning

3611 FINANCIAL POWER

Whatever be the nature of the library, Library Committees are rarely invested with financial powers. The task of finding money, investing funds, managing property, preparing and getting the sanction for the budget and all other matters relating to the finances of the library usually fall to the share of the Central Executive of the major organisation of which the library is a department. But nevertheless, there is some amount of financial work that falls to the share of the library.

3612 DATA FOR BUDGET

The Finance Section of the library will have to do the initial work in the framing of the library budget. The finance department of the Central Executive will supply such items as income expected from different sources, insurance charges, electric current charges and other items, of which they have the necessary information. The library will have to provide the necessary figures under miscellaneous receipts and under the different heads of expenditure for which the Central Executive has not furnished figures. Other figures required in the budget, such as the actuals for the part of the year that had elapsed at the time of the preparation of the budget, the revised allotment for the year and the actuals for the preceding year will have also to be furnished by the library to the possible extent.

3613 REAPPROPRIATION

Again, whenever the progress of expenditure in the course of the year indicates the need for reappropriation from one head to another, the necessary action will have to be taken by the Finance Section of the library sufficiently early to prevent any possible deadlock in the work of the library.

3614 Charge of Cash

The Finance Section of the library should also be in charge of all the cash that comes into the library. For example, the daily miscellaneous receipts collected by the Circulation Section should be taken charge of by the cashier of the Finance Section and handed over at stated intervals to the Accounts Section, for transmission to the Central Executive or for such other legitimate disposal as may become necessary.

3615 Reader's Deposit

If the rules of the library provide for the receipt of deposits from members, the cashier should take charge of the daily collection of deposits from the Circulation Section and remit the same to the bank from time to time. Similarly, he must draw the necessary amount from the bank and furnish it to the Circulation Section to make refunds of deposit. Further, it is usual, for the sake of convenience, to leave the investment of the readers' deposit in the hands of the library. If so, the Finance Section will have to be in charge of this work.

3616 Permanent Advance

Lastly, the cash received as permanent advance and as periodical reimbursements of the same should be kept by the cashier and the necessary cash paid to the Accounts Section or the Circulation Section, as the case may be, for making payments, for the bills passed for payment and for certain types of recurrent petty advance cash payments, which have received the necessary sanction.

3617 Finance Rules

The work of the Finance Section will have to depend largely on the Public Finance Code in force in the locality or on the financial rules framed by the larger organisation, of which the library is a department. Further, the subject of the sources of library finance and the principles regulating the proportion in which the library finance is to be distributed under different heads belong more appropriately to a book on library organisation. Hence, this chapter deals only with the routine connected with the work of the Finance Section.

3618 Factors in Planning

The distinctive work of the Finance Section is to be planned with reference to the following factors :

1 Budget ;
2 Pay amount ;
4 Miscellaneous receipts ;
5 Members' deposit ; and
8 Petty cash.

362 Job Analysis

3621 Budget

The work of the Finance Section relating to Budget is to consist of the following items :

1 Drafting the annual budget, which may be referred to as *Budget Drafting Work* ;
4 Watching the progress of expenditure, which may be referred to as *Expenditure Watching Work* ;
5 Taking the necessary action for reappropriation whenever it becomes necessary, which may be referred to as *Reappropriation Work*.

3621:1 *Budget Drafting Work*

3621:1:8 The Budget Drafting Work is to consist of the following annual jobs :

1 Asking the Central Executive to furnish such figures as it can for the preliminary drafting of the budget, which may be referred to as *Central Executive Notifying* ;
2 Asking the different Sections of the library to supply the necessary figures which come within their purview, for the preliminary drafting of the budget, which may be referred to as *Section Notifying* ;
3 Making a rough draft of the budget, which may be referred to as *Preliminary Drafting* ;
5 Discussing the preliminary draft with the librarian, which may be referred to as *Consulting* ;
6 Making the final draft of the budget in the light of the discussion with the librarian, which may be referred to as *Budget Drafting* ;

7 Transmitting the draft budget along with the other necessary documents to the Central Executive, which may be referred to as *Draft Budget Transmitting* ; and
8 Communicating the necessary extracts from the sanctioned budget to the different sections, which may be referred to as *Budget Figure Communicating.*

3621:4 *Expenditure Watching Work*

3621:4:6 The Expenditure Watching Work is to consist of the following monthly jobs :

1 Scrutinising the finance diaries, which may be referred to as *Finance Diary Scrutinising* ; and
4 Reviewing, with the head of the Accounts Section and the librarian, the abnormalities that may be disclosed by the finance diaries, which may be referred to as *Finance Diary Reviewing.*

3621:5 *Reappropriation Work*

3621:5:6 The Reappropriation Work is to consist of the following monthly jobs :

1 Consulting the librarian about the need for reappropriation that may be indicated by the finance diaries, which may be referred to as *Reappropriation Consulting* ;
5 Applying for such reappropriation as the librarian may approve, which may be referred to as *Reappropriation Seeking* ; and
8 Advising the section concerned about the sanction of reappropriation, which may be referred to as *Reappropriation Sanction Communicating.*

3622 Pay Amount

3622:6 The work of the Finance Section relating to Pay Amount is to consist of the following monthly jobs :

1 Taking charge of the undisbursed pay from the Accounts Section, which may be referred to as *Undisbursed Pay Receiving* ; and
2 Handing over to the accountant the undisbursed pay as and

when he needs them for disbursement, which may be referred to as *Undisbursed Pay Returning*.

3624 MISCELLANEOUS RECEIPTS

3624:4 The work of the Finance Section relating to Miscellaneous Receipts is to consist of the following daily job :

6 Collecting from the Circulation Section the miscellaneous receipts of the day, which may be referred to as *Miscellaneous Receipts Collecting*.

3624:5 The work of the Finance Section relating to Miscellaneous Receipts is to consist of the following weekly jobs :

6 Paying to the Circulation Section such amount as may be required by them for return of special deposit, which may be referred to as *Special Deposit Returning* ;

73 Paying to the Accounts Section such amount as may be necessary to meet expenditure from special deposits, which may be referred to as *Special Deposit Expenditure Meeting* ; and

77 Paying to the Accounts Section the amount of the miscellaneous receipts which has to be transmitted to the Central Executive, which may be referred to as *Miscellaneous Receipts Transmitting*.

3625 MEMBERS' DEPOSIT

3625:4 The work of the Finance Section relating to Member's Deposit is to consist of the following daily job :

6 Collecting from the Circulation Section the amount received as member's deposit in the course of the day, which may be referred to as *Deposit Amount Collecting*.

3625:5 The work of the Finance Section relating to Member's Deposit is to consist of the following weekly jobs :

3 Remitting to the bank the cash balance of the deposit account, which may be referred to as *Deposit Amount Remitting* ;

4 *This job is peculiar to the Madras University Library* : Notifying the Bank about the amount that may have to be withdrawn on the succeeding day, which may be referred to as *Withdrawal Notifying* ;
5 Withdrawing from the Bank the amount necessary for return of deposit, which may be referred to as *Withdrawing* ;
6 Handing over to the Circulation Section the amount necessary to meet withdrawals of membership on the day, which may be referred to as *Withdrawal Amount Transmitting* ; and
7 Collecting from the Circulation Section the admission cards, the cancelled tickets and the overdue register sheets of the members who have withdrawn and transmitting the same to the Accounts Section for further action, which may be referred to as *Withdrawal Documents Transmitting*.

3625:6 The work of the Finance Section relating to Member's Deposit is to consist of the following monthly jobs :

51 Obtaining the necessary sanction for investing or reinvesting the cash balance of the deposit account in fixed deposits or securities, which may be referred to as *Investment Sanction Obtaining* ;
55 Making the investment or reinvestment of the cash balance of the deposit account in fixed deposits or securities as per sanction, which may be referred to as *Deposit Amount Investing* ;
56 Scrutinising the bonds received and entering the investments in the investment register, which may be referred to as *Investment Register Posting* ;
58 Putting the bonds in double lock, which may be referred to as *Bond Custody* ;
61 Collecting interest on investments, which may be referred to as *Interest Collecting* ;
66 Making the necessary entries about the interest in the Investment Register, which may be referred to as *Interest Posting* ; and
67 Handing over the interest collected to the Accounts Section for transmission to the Central Executive, which may be referred to as *Interest Transmitting*.

3628 Petty Cash

3628:1 The work of the Finance Section relating to Petty Cash is to consist of the following immediate job :

1 Paying the necessary amount to meet the V P's which have been passed for acceptance by the librarian, which may be referred to as *V P Disbursing*.

3628:4 The work of the Finance Section relating to Petty Cash is to consist of the following daily job :

6 Handing over the necessary amount to the Accounts Section or the Circulation Section, as the case may be, for meeting approved recurring expenditure, which may be referred to as *Daily Disbursing*.

3628:5 The work of the Finance Section relating to Petty Cash is to consist of the following weekly jobs :

6 Receiving the replacement of permanent advance, which may be referred to as *Replacement Receiving* ;

76 Handing over to the Accounts Section the estimated cash necessary to meet the weekly bills, which may be referred to as *Weekly Disbursing* ;

77 Getting back from the Accounts Section the balance that might be left over after disbursement, which may be referred to as *Balance Receiving* ; and

78 Producing for inspection by the librarian the cash balance of the week, which may be referred to as *Cash Balance Verifying*.

363 **Routine**

3631 Budget

3631:1 *Budget Drafting Work*

3631:1:8 *Annual jobs*

3631:1:81 Central Executive Notifying

In good time before the date on which the Draft Budget should be sent up, write to the Central Executive asking them to furnish such figures as they can—particularly on the receipt side—for use in drafting the Budget.

3631:1:82 SECTION NOTIFYING

At the same time, cause a Staff Order to be issued asking the different Sections of the library to furnish the necessary figures before a specified date for the Drafting of the Budget. The Book Selection Section must furnish the amount allotted for books. The Periodicals Publication Section should give the cost of current periodical publications and of back volumes likely to be purchased in the course of the ensuing year. The Staff Section should furnish the cadre register to enable the Finance Section to work out the pay of the staff. The Accounts Section should give the annual expenditure for the preceding financial year as well as for the expired portion of the current financial year under the different budget heads. The Correspondence Section should give information about the amount to be allotted for postage. The Printing and Binding Sections should give the figures for printing and binding charges respectively. The Building and Equipment Section should find out from the different sections the extra furniture necessary and give an estimated cost of the furniture required. In particular, it should remember to ask the Technical Section whether any catalogue cabinet is necessary, the Maintenance Section whether any book rack is necessary, the Staff Section whether the office cycle requires any expensive repair or replacement, and the Correspondence Section whether the typewriter or the duplicator requires any expensive repair or replacement. The Stores Section should estimate the cost of the stationery and other articles that may have to be purchased in the year.

3631:1:83 PRELIMINARY DRAFTING

With the aid of the data obtained from the Central Executive and from the various sections of the library, work out the Budget carefully in accordance with the rules on the subject.

3631:1:85 CONSULTING

When the figures are still in pencil, prepare notes for discussion with the librarian. Take the preliminary draft and the notes to the librarian and take his instructions on the different points that require consideration. While discussing with him, take down the necessary notes.

3631:1:86 BUDGET DRAFTING

With the aid of the notes taken while consulting the librarian, make the necessary alterations in the preliminary Draft of the Budget. Work out also all the other statements and tables which the Financial Rules may require. Write out a letter to the Central Executive forwarding the Draft Budget. Send the whole thing to the librarian for approval.

3631:1:87 DRAFT BUDGET TRANSMITTING

After the office copy of the Draft Budget and the connected papers get the approval of the librarian, send them to the Correspondence Section for the usual processes of faircopying, etc and transmission to the Central Executive.

3631:1:88 BUDGET FIGURE COMMUNICATING

As soon as the sanctioned budget is received from the Central Executive, make the necessary extracts and send them to the concerned sections for their respective files.

3631:4 *Expenditure Watching Work*

3631:4:6 *Monthly jobs*

3631:4:61 FINANCE DIARY SCRUTINISING

In the first week of every month, scrutinise the Finance Diary, which is common to the Book Order Section, the Periodical Publication Section and the Accounts Section. See if all the entries have been duly filled up and the cumulative totals worked out. If there is any discrepancy, get it rectified by the section concerned. If the scrutiny reveals any abnormality, under any of the budget heads, make a note of all such abnormalities.

3631:4:64 FINANCE DIARY REVIEWING

At the appointed time each month, go to the librarian with the Finance Diaries and the notes prepared about the abnormal features in it. Invite the Head of the Accounts Section also to be present at the meeting. Discuss with the librarian the progress of expenditure and take instructions from him as to what should be done either to regulate the progress of expenditure more satisfactorily or to meet any abnormalities that might have developed. After the consultation is over, take such action as might have been indicated by the discussion.

3631:5 *Reappropriation Work*

3631:5:6 *Monthly jobs*

3631:5:61 Reappropriation Consulting

In the second week of each month, examine if any reappropriation was suggested by the Financial Diary Reviewing Job done in the preceding week. Then, discuss with the librarian in what shape the reappropriation proposal should be made. The circumstances calling for and allowing reappropriation will depend largely on the local Financial Rules and Practice.

3631:5:65 Reappropriation Seeking

If the librarian has decided that any reappropriation should be sought, prepare the necessary reappropriation statement in accordance with the Financial Rules, and a letter of requisition to forward the same. Send it to the librarian and the Correspondence Section in the usual way and see that it is despatched to the Central Executive in good time for the sanction for the reappropriation to be obtained before it is too late.

3631:5:68 Reappropriation Sanction Communicating

As soon as the sanction for the reappropriation sought is received, communicate the information to the Section concerned so that the Section may proceed with its work in the light of the information. Even if the sanction is refused, the information should be communicated.

3632 Pay Amount

3632:6 *Monthly jobs*

3632:61 Undisbursed Pay Receiving

On the evening of the pay disbursement day, ask the Accounts Section if there is any undisbursed pay left over. If there is, take charge of it and acknowledge it in the Transmission Register of the Accounts Section. Keep this amount quite apart from the other cash of the library. Put, in the receptacle containing the amount, a slip giving the amount of undisbursed pay and the date. Either on the receptacle or in the slip, write the words "Undisbursed pay".

3632:62 Undisbursed Pay Returning

As soon as the Head of the Accounts Section says that the persons whose pay has been kept in your custody have called at the library for it, hand over the necessary amount from the undisbursed pay receptacle and get the necessary acknowledgment from the Head of the Accounts Section in the Transmission Register. This will have to be done as often as necessary until the whole of the undisbursed pay is returned.

3634 Miscellaneous Receipts

3634:4 *Daily job*

3634:46 Miscellaneous Receipts Collecting

Just before the end of the day, obtain from the Circulation Section the amount collected by them as miscellaneous receipts. Verify the total amount due by adding up the amount in the various counterfoils commencing from the one after the one on the back of which you had put your initials on the last occasion and ending with the last of the used up counterfoils. If the amount is correct, put your dated initials under total amount written by the Circulation Section on the back of the last of the used up counterfoils. If there is any discrepancy, get it rectified by talking to the head of the Circulation Section. Keep this cash in a separate receptacle labelled " Miscellaneous receipts".

3634:5 *Weekly jobs*

3634:56 Special Deposit Returning

When the Circulation Section asks for the whole or the balance, as the case may be, of any Special Deposit made by a user against a lost or damaged book, for refund to the user concerned, send the amount to the Circulation Section and get the initials of the head of the Circulation Section in the Transmission Register as a token of his having received the amount.

3634:573 Special Deposit Expenditure Meeting

If the whole or part of a Special Deposit is required by the Accounts Section for paying any of the charges incurred in getting the lost copy replaced or the damaged copy set right or replaced, send the necessary amount to the Accounts Section and get the dated initials of the Head of the Accounts Section in token of his having received the amount.

3634:577 Miscellaneous Receipt Transmitting

On the appointed day of each week, find out from the Accounts Section the amount of the miscellaneous receipts that is to be transmitted to the Central Executive and hand over the amount to the Head of the Accounts Section and get his dated initials in the Transmission Register in token of his having received the amount.

3635 Members' Deposit

3635:4 *Daily job*

3635:46 Deposit Amount Collecting

Similar to 3634:46.

3635:5 *Weekly jobs*

3635:53 Deposit Amount Remitting

From time to time according to the exigencies, remit to the Bank the cash balance in the Deposit Account. Fill up the form for remitting the amount and its counterfoil with care. Enter the amount in the Transmission Register and get the dated initials of the peon who is sent to the Bank with the money. As soon as he comes back, verify if the counterfoil has received the signature of the Bank authority or, if there is any pass book, if the necessary entries have been made in the pass book. If there is any discrepancy, make the necessary investigation and get the matter set right. If the peon does not return within a reasonable time, inform the librarian about it and take the necessary action to set the matter right.

3635:54 Withdrawal Notifying

As has been stated in the job analysis, this job is peculiar to the

Madras University Library. On the day preceding the withdrawal day, inform the Bank about the amount that is proposed to be withdrawn on the succeeding day, if the amount exceeds Rs 100. The information should be given by a formal letter signed by the librarian.

3635:55 Withdrawing

On the withdrawal day, prepare the withdrawal form for the necessary amount in consultation with the Circulation Section and get the signature of the librarian. Send the pass book and the signed withdrawal form to the Bank through the peon after getting his dated initials in the Transmission Register. As soon as the peon comes back, take charge of the cash. If there is any discrepancy in the amount received or in the pass book or if the return of the peon is unusually delayed, report the matter to the librarian and take the necessary action to get the matter set right.

3635:56 Withdrawal Amount Transmitting

On receipt of the requisition from the Head of the Circulation Section for the amount required for making refund of deposit, send the amount to the Head of the Circulation Section and get his dated initials in the Transmission Register in token of his having received the amount.

3635:57 Withdrawal Documents Transmitting

At the end of the withdrawal day, get back from the Circulation Section the balance of cash, if any, and the admission cards, the cancelled tickets and the overdue register sheets of the members to whom deposit was refunded on the day. Verify if the total of the amount refunded as shown by the withdrawn admission cards and of the cash that is received back from the Circulation Section equals the amount which the Circulation Section should account for. If there is any discrepancy, get the matter set right with the aid of the Head of the Circulation Section. As soon as things are made normal, transmit the admission cards and the overdue register sheets to the Head of the Accounts Section for further action.

3635:6 *Monthly jobs*

3635:651 Investment Sanction Obtaining

As and when the cash balance in the deposit account either

in office custody or in Bank custody exceeds the amount that should be normally held for meeting withdrawals, bring it to the notice of the librarian and ascertain from him how much amount should be deposited in fixed deposits or in securities. Having ascertained, by a study of the money market and by correspondence with the Banks, the most favourable form of investment which is permissible by the Financial Rules, prepare a letter to the Central Executive seeking sanction for the investment. In the letter state the circumstances of the case clearly, the amount that is to be invested or reinvested, and the form and the period of investment. Send the letter of request to the Central Executive in the usual way through the librarian and the Correspondence Section.

3635:655 Deposit Amount Investing

As soon as the sanction for the investment or reinvestment is received from the Central Executive, take the necessary action. Either send the amount or the discharged deposit receipt or security in case of reinvestment, to the Bank with a covering letter asking for the issue of the necessary deposit receipt or security. The amount or documents sent should be entered in the Transmission Register and the dated initials of the messenger should be taken.

3635:656 Investment Register Posting

As soon as the messenger returns, scrutinise the bond, i e deposit receipt or security as the case may be, and see if it is alright. If there is any discrepancy, bring it to the notice of the librarian and get into touch with the Bank and get the matter rectified. If the messenger does not return within a reasonable time, inform the librarian about it and take the necessary action.

As soon as the bonds are found to be in order, make the necessary entries in the Investment Register. As soon as all the columns in the Investment Register are filled up, get the initials of the librarian in the Register.

3635:658 Bond Custody

Place the bonds in safe custody in the presence of the librarian. It is desirable to put these bonds under double lock, one of the keys being with the librarian.

3635:661 Interest Collecting

On the appointed day when an interest falls due, send a requisition to the Bank for payment of interest. The several formalities connected with this will depend upon the instructions of the Bank. It may be an advantage to get the requisition signed by the librarian a day earlier. If the messenger does not come back in time, inform the librarian and take the necessary action.

3635:666 Interest Posting

Make the necessary entries in the Investment Register about the interest received and get the initials of the librarian.

3635:667 Interest Transmitting

As soon as the messenger brings the amount, verify if it is in order. If there is any discrepancy, get it rectified by a reference to the Bank. As soon as it is alright, transmit the amount to the Accounts Section with the request that the amount may be sent to the Central Executive. The dated initials of the Head of the Accounts Section should be obtained in the Transmission Register in token of his having received the amount.

3638 Petty Cash

3638:1 *Immediate job*

3638:11 V P Disbursing

As soon as any V P article has been passed for payment by the librarian, make the necessary payment to the postman. Take charge of the V P article and transmit it to the librarian. Leave instructions to the Section concerned that the cover of the V.P. article on which the value is entered should be preserved and used as the voucher.

3638:4 *Daily job*

3638:46 Daily Disbursing

At the commencement of each day, if any Section, which is entitled to incur approved recurring expenditure, asks for money, see if the amount is in accordance with the sanctioned schedule or, if it is special, satisfy yourself that the demand is legitimate. Then, send the cash to the Section concerned and take the dated initials of the Head of that Section as a token of his having received the amount.

3638:5 *Weekly jobs*

3638:56 Replacement Receiving

As soon as the replacement amount of the permanent advance is received from the Accounts Section, take charge of it and put your dated initials in the Transmission Register of the Accounts Section.

3638:576 Weekly Disbursing

On the payment day, ascertain from the Head of the Accounts Section the estimated amount that will be required in the course of the day to pay petty bills. Hand over the necessary amount to him and take his dated initials in the Transmission Register.

3638:577 Balance Receiving

At the end of the day, find out if any balance is left over with the Accounts Section and if so take charge of it after putting your dated initials in the Transmission Register of the Accounts Section.

3638:578 Cash Balance Verifying

As soon as the Accounts Section reports that the accounts of the week are ready for review by the librarian, verify if the cash balance agrees with what the books of the Accounts Section show. If there is any discrepancy, get the matter investigated with the aid of the Head of the Accounts Section and set the matter right. As soon as the tallying is over and the accounts are passed by the librarian, produce the cash before the librarian and get his dated initials in the account books.

364 Oversight

The Head of the Finance Section should be very careful in dealing with cash. The cash in the different accounts, viz miscellaneous receipt, deposit amount, and petty cash amount, are to be kept separately in different receptacles. Whenever money is handed over to ány Section or to the peon, he must get the dated initials of the Head of that Section or the peon as the case may be, in the Transmission Register. He should also pay special attention to investments, reinvestments and the drawing of interest on investments. Another very important duty of the Head of the Finance Section is to watch the progress of expenditure as shown in the Finance Diary and see that the budget limit is not exceeded at all.

365 Correlation Table

All Sections

3631:1:82	Section notifying ;
3631:1:88	Budget figure communicating ;
3431:5:68	Reappropriation sanction communicating.

2 *Book Order Section*

3631:4:61	Finance diary scrutinising ;
3638:11	V P disbursing.

3 *Periodical Publication Section*

3631:4:61	Finance diary scrutinising ;
3638:11	V P disbursing.

6 *Circulation Section*

3634:46	Miscellaneous receipts collecting ;
3635:56	Special deposit returning ;
3635:46	Deposit amount collecting ;
3635:54	Withdrawal notifying ;
3635:55	Withdrawing ;
3635:56	Withdrawal amount transmitting ;
3635:57	Withdrawal documents transmitting ;
3638:11	V P disbursing ;
3638:46	Daily disbursing.

8 *Maintenance Section*

3638:11	V P disbursing.

97 *Accounts Section*

3631:4:6	All the jobs of expenditure watching work ;
3632	All the jobs relating to pay amount ;
3634:573	Special deposit expenditure meeting ;
3634:577	Miscellaneous receipts transmitting ;
3635:57	Withdrawal documents transmitting ;

3635:667 Interest transmitting ;
3638:46 Daily disbursing ;
3638:5 All the weekly jobs relating to petty cash.

998 *Correspondence Section*

3631:1:87 Draft budget transmitting.

366 **Illustrative Time Scheme**

Daily Jobs

3638:46 Daily disbursing ;
3634:46 Miscellaneous receipts collecting ;
3635:46 Deposit amount collecting.

Weekly Jobs

Monday

3635:54 Withdrawal notifying.

Tuesday

3635:53 Deposit amount remitting ;
3635:55 Withdrawing ;
3635:56 Withdrawal amount transmitting ;
3635:57 Withdrawal documents transmitting.

Wednesday

3634:573 Special deposit expenditure meeting ;
3634:577 Miscellaneous receipts transmitting ;
3638:576 Weekly disbursing ;
3638:577 Balance receiving ;
3638:578 Cash balance verifying.

Monthly Jobs

First Working Day

3632:61 Undisbursed pay receiving.

First Saturday

3631:4:61 Finance diary scrutinising.

First Monday

3635:651 Investment sanction obtaining.

Second Sunday

3631:4:64 Finance diary reviewing ;
3631:5:61 Reappropriation consulting.

Second Monday

3631:5:65 Reappropriation seeking.

ANNUAL JOBS

April

3631:88 Budget figure communicating.

October (last week)

3631:1:81 Central executive notifying ;
3631:1:82 Section notifying.

November (third week)

3631:1:83 Preliminary drafting.

November (last week)

3631:1:85 Consulting.

December (first week)

3631:86 Budget drafting ;
3631:87 Draft budget transmitting.

367 Forms and Registers

S96 *Investment register*. Manuscript. 21 lb paper. White. Folio pagination. Stitched. The column headings are to be as follows : Serial number (1.5 cm) ; Date of investment (2.5 cm) ; Particulars (5 cm) ; Face value (2.5 cm) ; Date of maturity (2.5 cm) ; Date of recovering (2.5 cm) ; Rate of interest (2.5 cm) ; L's initials (1.5 cm) ; Date of recovery of interest (2.5 cm) ; Amount (2.5 cm) ; L's initials (1.5 cm) ; Remarks.

368 Files

Name	*Class number*	*Amplifying device*	*Filing characteristic*	*Year of transfer to record sequence after the file is closed*	*Year of destruction after transfer to the record sequence*
Budget	961	Last digit of year	Nil	Year 2	Permanent
Reappropriation	9615	Do	Correspondent	Do	Year 10
Budget correspondence	9618	Do	Do	Do	Do
Remittance	9653	Nil	Nil	Year 1	Year 1
Withdrawal notifying	9654	Nil	Nil	Do	Do
Withdrawing	9655	Nil	Nil	Do	Do
Investment	9656	Nil	Date of maturity	Do	Year 10
Outward enquiries	9691	Nil	Correspondent	Do	Year 3
Inward enquiries	9692	Nil	Do	Do	Do

CHAPTER 37

ACCOUNTS SECTION

371 Planning

3711 BOOK-KEEPING

The maintenance of the accounts of libraries is likely to be regulated largely by local practice, as recorded in the Public Accounts Code in force or in special codes framed on the basis of the Public Accounts Code. Further, the statutory obligation to maintain the accounts is likely to be vested in the Accounts Section of the Central Executive of the larger organisation of which the library is a department. However, a fair amount of book-keeping will have to be done by the Accounts Section of the libraries also. It is desirable that the library should furnish to the Central Executive the rough basic figures for the balance-sheet, as obtainable from the account books maintained in the library.

3712 PAY BILL

The pay bills for the staff will have to be prepared and presented every month. The acquittance roll will have to be prepared by the library.

3713 MISCELLANEOUS RECEIPTS

The detailed account of the miscellaneous receipts such as overdue charges, special deposits for lost or damaged books, fees for duplicate tickets, and other petty cash receipts will have to be maintained by the Accounts Section. The Circulation Section, which receives the amount, will have to be furnished with approved receipt books and the accounts should be written up from day to day with the aid of the counterfoils in the receipt books. The Accounts Section will have to arrange for the remittance of the accumulated receipts at stated intervals to the Central Executive and obtain a receipt for them.

3714 READER'S DEPOSIT

If the rules of the library provide for receiving deposits from readers, the deposit account will have to be written from day to day and the necessary action taken for remitting the cash to the Bank and for withdrawing cash from the Bank, whenever it is required for returning deposits.

3715 Purchase Bills

Again, all the bills for the supplies made to the library will have to be checked, certified and passed for payment, by the library. This process is full of details and requires careful and systematic work. The amount spent on books and periodicals should be allocated to the different subjects from week to week. These allocation records of expenditure must be scrupulously maintained, so that the available balance for any subject is always known. This piece of work cannot be shifted to the shoulders of the Central Executive. It is purely internal to the library and the Accounts Section of the library is the most convenient agency for doing it. Another troublesome detail connected with payment of bills is the watching of the receipt of acknowledgments and securing them whenever they do not come promptly. As the library is having regular correspondence with the parties, the library is the suitable agency to get the acknowledgments, which are so necessary for audit.

3716 Permanent Advance

Lastly, it is usual for the Central Executive to deposit a certain amount with the librarian as permanent advance to make petty cash payments. This necessitates the maintenance of a permanent advance cash book, in which petty cash payments are entered, as and when they are made. The cancelled bills are to be sent to the Central Executive from time to time and sums corresponding with disbursements are to be obtained to maintain the permanent advance at its original amount.

3717 Audit

It is the duty of the Accounts Section to submit all the necessary account books to the audit from time to time and take all the action that may be necessary to satisfy the legitimate demands of audit. Just before the annual audit, the Accounts Section should notify the other Sections about the approximate date of audit and ask them to mobilise all their records which may have to be produced for audit. While it may be expected that no special preparation would be necessary to face the audit if the daily and weekly routines are properly performed, it is a matter of experience that it would be wiser to have the accounts reviewed carefully by the Accounts Section itself just before audit, so that any casual error or defect may be rectified before detection by the audit.

3718 Factors in Planning

The distinctive work of the Accounts Section is to be planned with reference to the following factors :

1 Balance-sheet ;
2 Pay bills ;
4 Miscellaneous receipts ;
5 Members' deposit ;
7 Bills ; and
8 Petty cash.

It has been suggested in the earlier chapters that it would be convenient if most of the jobs in a library are carried out on a weekly basis. In particular, it has been suggested that book orders may be issued every week. As a result of this, book supply may be expected every week. Thus, bills for books will have to be passed every week. Except, perhaps, in the case of pay bills, which may have to be prepared on a monthly basis, most of the other items of work of the Accounts Section are best done on a weekly basis.

372 Job Analysis

3721 Balance Sheet

3721:5 The work of the Accounts Section relating to Balance-Sheet is to consist of the following weekly jobs :

4 *Miscellaneous Receipts Account Totalling* ;
5 *Deposit Account Totalling* ; and
7 *Contingent Account Totalling.*

3721:8 The work of the Accounts Section relating to Balance-Sheet is to consist of the following annual jobs :

2 *Acquittance Roll Totalling* ;
4 *Miscellaneous Receipts Account Totalling* ;
5 *Deposit Account Totalling* ;
7 *Contingent Account Totalling* ;
8 Furnishing data for the balance-sheet, which may be referred to as *Balance-Sheet Data Furnishing* ; and
91 Reviewing the balance-sheet with a view to regulating future work, which may be referred to as *Balance-Sheet Reviewing.*

3722 Pay Bills

3722:6 The work of the Accounts Section relating to Pay Bills is to consist of the following monthly jobs :

1 Preparing the monthly pay bill and the necessary absentee statement, and increment certificates, which may be referred to as *Pay Bill Drafting* ;
2 Transmitting the draft pay bill to the Staff Section for the necessary scrutiny, which may be referred to as *Draft Pay Bill Transmitting* ;
3 Faircopying the draft pay bill approved by the Staff Section, which may be referred to as *Pay Bill Faircopying* ;
4 Transmitting the faircopied pay bill to the librarian for signature, which may be referred to as *Pay Bill Faircopy Transmitting* ;
5 Presenting the pay bill to the authority concerned for payment, which may be referred to as *Pay Bill Presenting* ;
6 Obtaining from the authority concerned the cash required for the disbursement of pay, which may be referred to as *Pay Amount Receiving* ;
72 *Acquittance Roll Writing* ;
76 Disbursing the pay to the members of the staff, which may be referred to as *Pay Disbursing* ; and
8 Scrutinising and completing the acquittance roll and getting the librarian's signature, which may be referred to as *Acquittance Roll Completing.*

3724 Miscellaneous Receipts

3724:4 The work of the Accounts Section relating to Miscellaneous Receipts is to consist of the following daily jobs :

46 Checking the charged overdue tickets and making the necessary entries in the overdue tickets diary, which may be referred to as *Overdue Checking* ;

47 Verifying if all the miscellaneous receipts have been posted in the overdue register, which may be referred to as *Receipt Posting Checking* ; and

7 Writing out the miscellaneous account book, which may be referred to as *Miscellaneous Account Writing.*

3724:5 The work of the Accounts Section relating to Miscellaneous Receipts is to consist of the following weekly jobs :

6 Writing the necessary letter and forwarding the miscellaneous receipts of the week to the authority concerned, which may be referred to as *Miscellaneous Receipts Forwarding* ;

6J Posting the receipt of the acknowledgment for the miscellaneous receipt amount forwarded and of payments made out of special deposits, which may be referred to as *Acknowledgment Posting* ; and

7 Closing the week's account in the miscellaneous account book, which may be referred to as *Miscellaneous Receipts Account Closing.*

3725 MEMBERS' DEPOSIT

3725:4 The work of the Accounts Section relating to Member's Deposit is to consist of the following daily job :

6 Writing out the deposit account book, which may be referred to as *Deposit Account Writing.*

3725:5 The work of the Accounts Section relating to Member's Deposit is to consist of the following weekly jobs :

7 Closing the week's account in the deposit account book, which may be referred to as *Deposit Account Closing* ; and

75 Posting the receipt of the acknowledgment for the deposit amounts returned by money order, which may be referred to as *Acknowledgment Posting.*

3727 Bills

The work of the Accounts Section relating to Bills may consist of the following items :

1 Registering the bills received and following up the different stages, which may be referred to as *Bills Register Work* ;

2 Passing the bills received from the different sections for payment and preparing them for the librarian's order, which may be referred to as *Bills Passing Work* ;

31 Work relating to bills which are marked for payment by the central executive, which may be referred to as *Direct Payment Work* ;

32 Work relating to bills marked for payment within the locality, which may be referred to as *Local Payment Work* ;

33 Work relating to bills marked for payment within the country, which may be referred to as *Inland Payment Work* ;

35 Work relating to bills marked for payment outside the country, which may be referred to as *Foreign Payment Work* ;

43 Posting the voucher number in the passed bills, which may be referred to as *Voucher Number Posting Work* ;

44 Revising the passed bills and transmitting them to the librarian for signature, which may be referred to as *Bills Revising Work* ;

46 Obtaining from the cashier the necessary amount, which may be referred to as *Cash Receiving Work* ;

47 Making the payment by transmitting the amount by post or messenger, which may be referred to as *Remittance Work* ;

5 Receiving the acknowledgments for the payments made and taking the necessary action in the cases where acknowledgments are not received, which may be referred to as *Acknowledgment Work* ;

6 Allocating the amount in the different bills to the different heads, to which they relate, which may be referred to as *Allocation Work* ; and

7 Watching the progress of expenditure and taking the necessary action from time to time to secure conformity to the budget, which may be referred to as *Expenditure Watching Work*.

3727:1 *Bills Register Work*

3727:1:4 The Bills Register Work is to consist of the following daily jobs :

3 Coupling each bill with its duplicate, if any, and registering it, which may be referred to as *Bills Registering* ; and
5 Distributing all the bills registered in the course of the day to the sections concerned, which may be referred to as *Bills Distributing.*

3727:1:5 The Bills Register Work is to consist of the following weekly jobs :

1 Noting in the appropriate column of the register the details about payment, which may be referred to as *Payment Details Noting* ;
2 Noting the date of advice of payment, which may be referred to as *Advice Date Noting* ; and
6 Communicating to the sections concerned and the librarian a list of the bills which are in arrears for two weeks or more, which may be referred to as *Bills-in-Arrears Listing.*

3727:2 *Bills Passing Work*

3727:2:5 The Bills Passing Work is to consist of the following weekly jobs :

1 Verifying the total of the bills received from the different sections as fit for payment, which may be referred to as *Total Verifying* ;
2 In case any bill is without a duplicate, preparing a duplicate copy for it, which may be referred to as *Duplicate Copy Preparing* ;
31 Stamping the faircopy of the bill with the " Pay-order stamp", which may be referred to as *Faircopy Stamping* ;
32 Writing out the pay order in the faircopy as well as the office copy of the bills, which may be referred to as *Pay-Order Writing* ;
4 Arranging the bills, on which the pay order has been written, in the conventional sequence, which may be referred to as

Bills Arranging ; and

7 Making the necessary entries in the contingent register, which may be referred to as *Contingent Register Writing*.

3727:31 *Direct Payment Work*

3727:31:5 The Direct Payment Work is to consist of the following weekly jobs :

1 Writing out a requisition letter• to the central executive, asking for direct payment to the parties concerned, in the case of the bills marked for direct payment, which may be referred to as *Direct Payment Advising* ; and

2 As soon as the bills come back from the librarian after signature, collecting the bills for direct payment and attaching them to the direct payment advice letter and transmitting the whole thing to the Correspondence Section for further action, which may be referred to as *Direct Payment Forwarding*.

3727:32 *Local Payment Work*

3727:32:5 The Local Payment Work is to consist of the following weekly job :

1 Writing out a letter forwarding cash in the case of bills marked for payment within the locality, which may be referred to as *Local Payment Advising*.

3727:33 *Inland Payment Work*

3727:33:5 The Inland Payment Work is to consist of the following weekly job :

1 Writing out the money order in the case of bills marked for payment within the country, which may be referred to as *Inland Money Order Writing*.

3727:35 *Foreign Payment Work*

3727:35:5 The Foreign Payment Work is to consist of the following weekly jobs :

1 Finding out the equivalent in local currency of the amount

to be paid in foreign countries, which may be referred to as *Equivalent Finding* ;

2 Writing the foreign money order in the case of petty bills marked for payment outside the country, which may be referred to as *Foreign Money Order Writing* ;

3 Writing out a letter of advice to each of the parties to whom money order is sent, which may be referred to as *Foreign Money Order Advising* ;

5 Writing a requisition for foreign drafts in the case of heavy bills marked for payment outside the country, which may be referred to as *Draft Requisitioning* ;

61 Writing out covering letters for forwarding the drafts, which may be referred to as *Draft Advising* ;

63 On receipt of the draft advising letters from the librarian after signature, attaching the drafts to the respective letters of advice and transmitting them to the Correspondence Section for despatch, which may be referred to as *Draft Forwarding* ; and

7 Posting the cost, in local currency, of the foreign money orders or drafts, as the case may be, in the contingent register, which may be referred to as *Equivalent Posting.*

3727:43 *Voucher Number Posting Work*

3727:43:5 The Voucher Number Posting Work is to consist of the following weekly jobs :

1 Posting the voucher number in the passed bills before transmitting the same to the librarian for signature, which may be referred to as *Voucher Numbering* ; and

5 Posting the voucher number in the records of the different sections which passed the bills for payment, which may be referred to as *Voucher Number Posting.*

3727:44 *Bills Revising Work*

3727:44:5 The Bills Revising Work is to consist of the following weekly jobs :

1 Verifying if there is proper sanction for each bill, which may be referred to as *Sanction Verifying* ;

2 Verifying the totals, which may be referred to as *Total Verifying* ;
3 Verifying the certificates of the sections concerned, which may be referred to as *Certificate Verifying* ;
4 Verifying the accuracy of the entries in the contingent register, the forwarding letters, etc which may be referred to as *Entries Verifying* ;
5 Verifying the entries in the bills register at the different stages, which may be referred to as *Bills Register Verifying* ; and
6 Verifying if the payment is within the limits of the sanctioned budget, which may be referred to as *Progress of Expenditure Verifying.*

3727:46 *Cash Receiving Work*

3727.46:5 The Cash Receiving Work is to consist of the following weekly jobs :

1 Estimating the total amount required for payment of the bills from the permanent advance, which may be referred to as *Estimating* ; and
6 Obtaining from the cashier the estimated amount required, which may be referred to as *Cash Receiving.*

3727:47 *Remittance Work*

3727:47:5 The Remittance Work is to consist of the following weekly jobs :

21 Entrusting to the delivery peon the necessary cash and the concerned forwarding letters for payment, which may be referred to as *Local Payment Transmitting* ;
24 Watching the return of the delivery peon and verifying if he had made the payment properly, which may be referred to as *Local Payment Watching* ;
31 Entrusting to the peon doing postal work the necessary cash and the concerned money order forms, for remitting to the post office, which may be referred to as *Money Order Forwarding*;
34 Watching the return of the peon doing postal work, tallying the postal receipts and getting back the balance of cash,

if any, which may be referred to as *Money Order Remittance Watching* ;

35 Transmitting the money order advice letters to the Correspondence Section for despatch, which may be referred to as *Money Order Advice Transmitting* ;

38 Filing the money order receipts in the sequence of the voucher numbers, which may be referred to as *Money Order Receipts Filing* ; and

6 Remitting to the cashier the balance of cash, if any, which may be referred to as *Cash Balance Returning.*

3727:5 *Acknowledgment Work*

3727:5:4 The Acknowledgment Work is to consist of the following daily jobs :

1 Registering the receipt of the acknowledgments in the bills register, which may be referred to as *Acknowledgments Registering* ; and

2 Temporarily filing the acknowledgments, which may be referred to as *Acknowledgments Temporary Filing.*

3727:5:5 The Acknowledgment Work is to consist of the following weekly jobs :

1 Transmitting to the librarian the acknowledgments received in the week for his scrutiny, which may be referred to as *Acknowledgments Transmitting* ;

2 Permanently filing the acknowledgments for payments made out of permanent advance, which may be referred to as *Permanent Advance Acknowledgments Filing* ; and

5 Transmitting to the Central Executive the acknowledgments for payments by drafts, which may be referred to as *Draft Acknowledgments Transmitting.*

3727:5:6 The Acknowledgment Work is to consist of the following monthly jobs :

2 Sending reminders to such of the inland payees whose acknowledgments have not been received, which may be referred

to as *Inland Acknowledgments Reminding*; and

5 Sending reminders to such of the foreign payees whose acknowledgments have not been received, which may be referred to as *Foreign Acknowledgments Reminding*.

3727:6 *Allocation Work*

3727:6:5 The Allocation Work is to consist of the following weekly jobs :

1 Allocating the amount of each voucher to the different budget heads, which may be referred to as *Budget Head Allocating*; and

2 Allocating the amount in the vouchers relating to books and periodical publications to the different subjects, which may be referred to as *Book Fund Allocating*.

3727:7 *Expenditure Watching Work*

3727:7:5 The Expenditure Watching Work is to consist of the following weekly job :

1 Posting in the finance diaries the amount spent under the different budget heads and on different subjects during the week, which may be referred to as *Finance Diary Posting*.

3727:7:6 The Expenditure Watching Work is to consist of the following monthly job :

1 Verifying the cumulative total under the different headings of the finance diaries, which may be referred to as *Cumulative Total Verifying*.

3727:7:7 The Expenditure Watching Work is to consist of the following quarterly job :

4 Reviewing the progress of expenditure with the head of the Finance Section and the librarian and taking such action as may be necessary, which may be referred to as *Progress of Expenditure Reviewing*.

3728 Petty Cash

3728 The work of the Accounts Section relating to petty cash may consist of the following items :

7 Maintaining the petty cash account book, which may be referred to as *Petty Cash Account Work* ; and
8 Obtaining replacement of the petty cash disbursed, which may be referred to as *Replacement Work*.

3728:7 *Petty Cash Account Work*

3728:7:5 The Petty Cash Account Work is to consist of the following weekly jobs :

6 Writing out the petty cash account book, which may be referred to as *Petty Cash Account Writing* ; and
7 Closing the week's account in the petty cash account book, which may be referred to as *Petty Cash Account Closing*.

3728:8 *Replacement Work*

3728:8:5 The Replacement Work is to consist of the following weekly jobs :

1 Transmitting to the central executive the vouchers for the amount disbursed out of the permanent advance and applying for replacement of an equal amount, which may be referred to as *Replacement Requisitioning* ;
2 Acknowledging the receipt of the replacement amount, which may be referred to as *Replacement Acknowledging* ; and
6 Sending the replacement amount to the cashier, which may be referred to as *Replacement Cash Handing Over*.

3728:8:8 The Replacement Work is to consist of the following annual job :

1 Sending the annual acknowledgment of permanent advance to the central executive, which may be referred to as *Permanent Advance Acknowledging*.

373 **Routine**

3731 Balance Sheet

3731:5 *Weekly jobs*

3731:54 Miscellaneous Receipts Account Totalling

On the appointed day of the week, total up all the columns in the miscellaneous account book. The total of the totals of the columns and the total of the totals of the rows should be the same figure. If they do not tally, find out the mistake and rectify it. The totals of the columns are to be made in pencil in the first instance and inked only after the tallying is over.

3731:55 Deposit Account Totalling

On the appointed day of the week, total up all the columns of the deposit account book. The total in the credit side should tally with the total on the debit side. If they do not tally find out the mistake and rectify it.

3731:57 Contingent Account Totalling

On the appointed day of the week, total the columns in such of the pages of the contingent register as have been completely filled up. The total of the totals of the columns and the total of the totals of the rows should be the same figure. If they do not tally, find out the mistake and rectify it. The totals of the columns are to be made in pencil in the first instance and inked only after the tallying is over. Post the totals of the different columns in the *Main Financial Diary* and enter also the cumulative totals. The cumulation of the total should be carried through for the whole of the financial year.

3731:8 *Annual jobs*

3731:82 Acquittance Roll Totalling

Total the columns in the Acquittance Roll and verify if it agrees with the figure in the Main Financial Diary. If there is any discrepancy, investigate the matter and set it right.

3731:84 Miscellaneous Receipts Account Totalling

Verify the total of the columns of the Miscellaneous Receipts

Account Book. If there is any discrepancy investigate the matter and get it set right.

3731:85 Deposit Account Totalling

Similar to 3731:84

3731:87 Contingent Account Totalling

Similar to 3731:84

3731:88 Balance Sheet Data Furnishing

With the help of the totals obtained by the preceding routines, work out the rough Balance Sheet and transmit it to the Central Executive to facilitate their working out the Balance Sheet. If there is any discrepancy between the figures furnished by you and those arrived at by the Central Executive, investigate the matter and get it set right.

3731:91 Balance Sheet Reviewing

As soon as the Balance Sheet is finally worked out and received from the Central Executive, study its main features and prepare notes on such points as require discussion with the librarian. Discuss the Balance Sheet with the librarian and take down notes of the discussion. Take such action as may be called for by the notes, so that the finances of the library may be regulated in the future year in conformity with the suggestions arrived at in the discussion.

3732 Pay Bills

3732:6 *Monthly jobs*

3732:61 Pay Bill Drafting

On the appointed day of the month, prepare the Pay Bill and the necessary absentee statements, increment certificates and other documents in accordance with the rules on the subject. The data for the Pay Bill are to be taken from the attendance register, the staff order book, the Pay Bill of the preceding month and the office copies of the increment certificates of the corresponding months of the preceding year. Put the figures provisionally in pencil.

3732:62 Draft Pay Bill Transmitting

Transmit the pencil copy of the draft Pay Bill to the Staff Section for the necessary scrutiny. The Staff Section will verify them with reference to the cadre register maintained by them.

3732:63 Pay Bill Faircopying

As soon as the draft Pay Bill comes back from the Staff Section, examine the alterations suggested by that Section. If there is any difficulty in accepting the alterations, discuss it with the Staff Section. As soon as the final draft is arrived at, faircopy the Pay Bill and its enclosures.

3732:64 Pay Bill Faircopy Transmitting

As soon as the faircopying is over, transmit the office copy as well as the faircopy to the librarian for signature. Remember to send the office copies of the increment certificates of the corresponding months of the preceding year in case any increment certificate is included in the faircopies. If any newly created post is entered in the Pay Bill, send to the librarian the letter communicating the sanction for the new place. Do similarly in the case of absentees whose leave commenced in the course of the month.

3732:65 Pay Bill Presenting

On the appointed day, present the faircopy of the Pay Bill and its enclosures to the authorities concerned and get a token therefor. At the same time file all the office copies in the proper place.

3732:66 Pay Amount Receiving

On the appointed day, return the token to the authorities concerned, and get the pay amount. Verify the cash carefully as soon as it is received.

3732:72 Acquittance Roll Writing

In good time before the pay amount is expected to arrive, write out the Acquittance Roll carefully in accordance with the instructions on the subject.

3732:76 Pay Disbursing

At the time appointed for the disbursement of pay, take the signature of each payee in the Acquittance Roll and pay the amount due to him. Attend to the different payees in the sequence in which they arrive. If anybody has not turned up, send for him. If he does not come, hand over the balance of pay to the Finance Section for safe custody, and take the dated initials of the Head of that Section in the Transmission Register in token of his having received the amount.

As soon as the payees concerned turn up, get the necessary amount from the Finance Section and disburse it in the usual way. This must be done until the whole pay amount is disbursed.

3732:78 Acquittance Roll Completing

As soon as the payments are made to all the payees, scrutinise the Acquittance Roll carefully. If there is any defect, get it set right. Then, take the Acquittance Roll to the librarian and get his signature in token of the Acquittance Roll for the month having been completed.

3734 Miscellaneous Receipts

3734:4 *Daily jobs*

3734:446 Overdue Checking

As one of the first jobs each day, post in the *Overdue Tickets Diary* the number of charged overdue tickets behind each overdue guide. Verify if the overdue has been collected, or the ticket is held up against the amount due in the Kept Tickets Tray and if the amount due is entered in the Overdue Register, in all the cases in which an overdue ticket had been released since the last occasion when the Overdue Checking was done. The number of cases can be determined as follows : Suppose the number of overdue tickets behind the 20 naye paise guide is three today and that the number of overdue tickets behind the 15 naye paise guide was five on the preceding day ; then, you should expect that two of the tickets due to be behind the 20 naye paise guide should have been discharged since the Overdue Checking was done on the preceding day. In the same way the total number of overdue tickets discharged can be calculated for all the overdue guides.

In the case of the 5 naye paise guide, the number of tickets, that were behind the overdue guide at the time of the closing of the library on the preceding day, will have to be ascertained from the senior member of the Reference Section who was on duty at the closing time. Further, for each of the tickets lying behind the 5 naye paise guide, verify if the necessary entries have been made in the Overdue Register.

If there is any discrepancy, get it set right by talking to the Head of the Circulation Section and if the discrepancy is serious, make a report of the same to the librarian.

The overdue checking is to be done daily without break. Hence, if any day happens to be a holiday with the Accounts Section, the Head of the Accounts Section should hand over the Overdue Tickets Diary to the Head of the Reference Section on the preceding day and arrange with him for the checking to be done by the Reference Section on such holidays.

This routine will not be necessary if Conscience Box is used.

3734:447 Receipt Posting Checking

As soon as the Overdue Checking is over, take up the Miscellaneous Receipt Book and verify if every receipt of the preceding day has been posted in the Overdue Register. If the preceding day was a holiday with the Accounts Section, this verification should be done for all the days since the last verification was done. If two or more persons have the same name, see if it had been individualised by putting the deposit number of the person after his name. If not, talk to the Head of the Circulation Section and get the matter set right. If there is any other discrepancy, get it set right by talking to the Head of the Circulation Section.

This routine will not be necessary if Conscience Box is used.

3734:47 Miscellaneous Account Writing

As soon as the Receipt Posting Checking is over, take the Miscellaneous Receipt Book with you to your seat and write out the Miscellaneous Account Book for the preceding day (or days in case the preceding day or days were holidays for the Accounts Section) with the aid of the counterfoils of the Miscellaneous Receipt Book. It may be stated here that the writing of the account should on no account be postponed beyond the scheduled time. The account book is to be written expeditiously and the Miscellaneous Receipt Book is to be sent back to the Circulation Section as promptly as possible, as that Section may require it at any moment.

If any payment is made out of special deposit, enter it in red ink in the Miscellaneous Account Book on the very day on which the payment is made. The librarian will initial against this entry and this will serve as the office copy of the forwarding letter, if any.

This routine will cover only special deposits, etc but not overdue charges, if Conscience Box is used.

3734:5 *Weekly jobs*

3734:56 Miscellaneous Receipts Forwarding

At the appointed time on the appointed day of the week, as soon as the Totalling of the Miscellaneous Account Book is over, find out the amount that should be remitted to the Central Executive from the miscellaneous receipts of the week. Remember that all the amount of this account, except the special deposits received from the users against lost or damaged books, is to be so remitted. Make the entry of remittance in the Miscellaneous Account Book in red ink. The librarian will initial against this red ink entry and this will serve as the office copy of the forwarding letter. Prepare the necessary forwarding letter. Get it signed by the librarian and despatched by the Correspondence Section. Get the amount from the Finance Section and transmit it to the Central Executive, having taken the dated initials of the messenger in the delivery book. As soon as the messenger comes back, see if the representative of the Central Executive has signed in the delivery book in token of his having received the amount. If there is any discrepancy or if the peon does not return within a reasonable time, investigate the matter and set it right.

3734:565 Acknowledgment Posting

As soon as the Acknowledgment for the miscellaneous receipt amount forwarded is received from the Central Executive or as soon as the Acknowledgment for the payment made out of the special deposit is received from the party concerned, make a note of its receipt against the corresponding entry in the Miscellaneous Account Book, and file the receipt in the chronological sequence in the *Miscellaneous Account Acknowledgment File*. If the Acknowledgment is not received within a reasonable time, remind the party concerned periodically, until the Acknowledgment is received. If there is any discrepancy, it must be rectified by corresponding with the party concerned before the Acknowledgment is filed.

3734:57 Miscellaneous Receipts Account Closing

After the forwarding of the miscellaneous receipts amount to the Central Executive is over, close the miscellaneous account in the Miscellaneous Account Book and take it to the librarian at the appointed time along with the other account books for his review and initials. The counterfoils of the Miscellaneous Receipt Book, the Vouchers of Payments made out of special deposit and the Acknowledgment Receipts are to be produced before the librarian at the time of review.

3735 Members' Deposit

3735:4 *Daily job*

3735:46 Deposit Account Writing

As soon as the miscellaneous account writing is over, get the Deposit Receipt Book from the Circulation Section and write out the Deposit Account of the preceding day (or days in case the preceding day or days were holidays for the Accounts Section) with the aid of the counterfoils of the Deposit Receipt Book and the application cards of the withdrawn members. It may be stated here that the writing of the account book should on no account be postponed beyond the scheduled time. Again, the receipt side is to be written out first expeditiously and the Deposit Receipt Book is to be sent back to the Circulation Section as promptly as possible, as that Section may require it at any moment. After the debit side is written out, the withdrawal number is to be posted in each concerned application card and the related Overdue Register Sheet.

Find out from the Finance Section the amount remitted to the Bank or received from the Bank from out of the Deposit Account and make the necessary entries in the Deposit Account Book. This can be done with the aid of the Bank Pass Book, the counterfoils of the remittance forms and the withdrawal forms.

If any investment is made or withdrawn, remember to ascertain from the Finance Section and enter it in the Deposit Account Book. If any interest on investment is received and remitted to the Central Executive, remember to enter this item also in the Deposit Account Book. The forwarding of the interest amount and the watching of the receipt of the acknowledgment should be done on lines similar to the forwarding of miscellaneous receipts amount (see routines 3734:56 and 3734:565).

3735:5 *Weekly jobs*

3735:57 Deposit Account Closing

On the appointed day of the week, close the week's account in the Deposit Account Book and take it along with the other account books, at the appointed hour, to the librarian for his review and initials. The counterfoils of the Deposit Receipt Book, the remittance forms and the withdrawal forms and the Bank Pass Book are to be produced before the librarian at the time of review.

At the same time, the Transmission Registers relating to the issue of tickets and receipt of cancelled tickets at the Stores Section are also to be produced before the librarian for review.

The Application Cards and the Overdue Register Sheets of the members who have withdrawn in the course of the week are also to be produced before the librarian for review. In case the deposit has been refunded to the agent of a member and not directly to the member, and in case the deposit is transferred to somebody else's account the letter of authorisation is to be pinned to the related application card. Similarly, if the deposit is remitted by money order, the authorisation letter for the same and the postal receipt for the money order are to be pinned to the related application card.

After the review of the account by the librarian is over, the application cards (with the enclosures pinned to them, if any), and the Overdue Register Sheets of the withdrawn members are to be filed in their respective collections in the sequence of their withdrawal numbers. These two collections are to be kept by the Accounts Section in the quasi-current sequence of files, till the audit is over. Thereafter, they are to be transferred to the record collection, where each collection will be kept in a single alphabetic sequence of its own.

If Conscience Box is used, Personal Sheets will take the place of Overdue Register Sheets.

3735:575 ACKNOWLEDGMENT POSTING

Similar to routine 3734:565 except that the postal acknowledgment is to be pinned to the related withdrawn application card.

3737 BILLS

3737:1 *Bills Register Work*

3737:1:4 *Daily jobs*

3737:1:43 BILLS REGISTERING

As soon as the bills are received from the librarian, couple each bill with its duplicate, if any. Sort the bills into groups by the sections to which they relate. Arrange the bills in each group into sub-groups according to the probable form of payment as indicated in rule 3737:2:54. Arrange the bills in each sub-group in the ascending sequence of the amount of the bill. Then, take the bills group by group in the sequence of their Section Numbers, and register them in the *Bills Register*. Post the number, which a bill receives in the Bills Register, at the right hand top corner of the bill as well as its duplicate.

3737:1:45 BILLS DISTRIBUTING

Send the registered bills to the Sections concerned along with the Bills Register. As soon as the Bills Register comes back, examine if the Head of each Section has initialled against the items relating to his Section. If not, get it done.

3737:1:5 *Weekly jobs*

3737:1:51 PAYMENT DETAILS NOTING

On the appointed day of the week, as soon as Voucher Numbering is over for all the bills of the day, fill up, for each bill, the columns headed " Voucher N", " Amount paid " and " Requisition date", in the Bills Register. In the case of Direct Payment Bills, draw a line across all the succeeding columns. In the case of Pre-Payment Bills paid out of the Permanent Advance, write " P P" in the column " Requisition date " and draw a line across all the succeeding columns. In the case of Post-Payment Bills, paid out of the Permanent Advance, write "P A" in the column "Requisition date".

3737:1:52 ADVICE DATE NOTING

After the Payment Details Noting, fill up the column entitled "Advice date" in the case of all local payments, inland payments, and foreign money order payments. In the case of draft payments, fill up this column on the day, on which the drafts are actually forwarded.

3737:1:56 BILLS-IN-ARREARS LISTING

On the appointed day each week, scrutinise the Bills Register to find out if any bill registered three weeks or more earlier remains unattended to by the Section concerned. Such bills may be referred to as *Bills in Arrears*. If the column entitled " Voucher number " is not filled against an entry of the bill, it may be taken as not attended to. Make a list of all such bills in each Section and inform the Head of the Section concerned about it.

Further, if any bill has been in arrears for one month or more, bring it to the notice of the librarian.

3737:2 *Bills Passing Work*

Each one of the jobs of this work except Bills Arranging will have to be done for each bill, that has been passed for payment by the Section concerned and sent to the Accounts Section for further action, before the next job is taken up.

3737:2:5 *Weekly jobs*

3737:2:51 TOTAL VERIFYING

Verify the total of the bill. All the bills from the same party are to be pinned together in the sequence of their respective order numbers and regarded as a single consolidated bill. If a bill is in two or more sheets, pin them in the proper sequence. If each sheet has an independent total which is not carried forward from sheet to sheet, write, on the back of the last sheet of the bill, the total of each sheet in proper sequence and total up these totals. Get the posting of the figures and the grand total verified by another person. This will have to be done both for the original and for the duplicate copy of the bill.

3737:2:52 Duplicate Copy Preparing

If any bill is without a duplicate, prepare a duplicate copy for it.

3737:2:531 Faircopy Stamping

In a convenient place on the faircopy of the bill, put the "Pay-Order" stamp. If the bill is in two or more sheets put at the bottom of each sheet other than the last of the faircopy as well as the office copy, the stamp "Included in Voucher Number . . ."

3737:2:532 Pay-Order Writing

Write the amount in words in the imprint of the "Pay-Order" stamp and put your initials in the proper place. Write the Pay-Order, inclusive of remittance charges, if any, at the end of the office copy of the bill and add the word " Librarian " thereafter and put your dated initials beneath that word.

3737:2:54 Bills Arranging

Put the faircopy of each bill behind its duplicate. We shall refer to this as the *Coupled Bill*. Arrange the Coupled Bills, on which the Pay-Order has been written, in the following manner. First sort the Coupled Bills into the following groups :

1 *Direct Payment Cases* ; i e heavy inland bills (e g exceeding Rs 20) which are to be transmitted to the Central Executive for payment direct to the parties concerned ;
2 *Draft Cases* ; i e heavy foreign bills for which payment has to be made by foreign drafts ;
3 *Pre-Payment Cases* ; i e petty bills for which cash had to be paid at the time of supply or service ;
4 *Local Payment Cases* ; i e petty bills for supply or services already made or rendered by parties within the locality ;
5 *Inland Payment Cases* ; i e petty bills for supplies or services already made or rendered by parties within the country and for which payment has to be made by inland money order ; and
6 *Foreign Payment Cases* ; i e petty bills for supplies or services already made or rendered by parties outside the country and for which payment has to be made by foreign money order.

In the case of the second and the sixth group, further sub-divide the bills into sub-groups by the countries of payments, into the necessary number of sub-groups.

In each group or sub-group, as the case may be, arrange the bills in the ascending sequence of the amount passed for payment.

3737:2:57 Contingent Register Writing

Enter the bills in the Contingent Register in the sequence in which they have been arranged. In the case of foreign payments, enter the amount in foreign currency in the remarks column. Its equivalent in local currency will have to be entered only at a later stage. At the right hand end of the remarks column of each entry, put conventional symbols to enable later reference easy.

The practice in the Madras University Library is as follows :

Nature of payment	*Symbol*
Direct payment cases	R
Draft cases	D
Cash pre-payment cases	C

The other cases do not have any symbol.

3737:31 *Direct Payment Work*

3737:31:5 *Weekly jobs*

3737:31:51 Direct Payment Advising

For the Direct Payment cases, fill up the *Direct Payment Requisition Form*, requesting the Central Executive to make direct payments to the parties concerned in the case of the enclosed passed bills. Get it despatched by the Correspondence Section in the No Reply Despatch Register.

3737:31:52 Direct Payment Forwarding

As soon as the bills come back from the librarian after signature, collect all the bills for Direct Payment. Separate the office copies from the faircopies. Keep the office copies for office file, and attach the faircopies to the requisition letter and transmit the whole thing to the Correspondence Section for inclusion in the cover being sent on the day to the Central Executive.

3737:32 *Local Payment Work*

3737:32:5 *Weekly job*

3737:32:51 Local Payment Advising

In the case of Petty Bills for which cash has to be paid to parties residing within the locality, fill up a *Cash Forwarding Form.* Put the register number of the bill near the centre of the top edge of the receipt part of the form and the Voucher Number of the bill at the right hand top corner of the same. Get it despatched by the Correspondence Section int he No Reply Despatch Register.

3737:33 *Inland Payment Work*

3737:33:5 *Weekly job*

3737:33:51 *Inland Money Order Writing*

In the case of Inland Petty Bills which have to be paid within the country by money order, write out an inland money order form. Mention in the coupon the outside number and the outside date of the bill to which the payment refers. Stamp the date of issue of the money order and write out the words "Librarian/. . Library" below the point where the librarian is to put his signature. If these details are not given in the coupon, it will be very difficult for the party at the other end to identify the money order as the one that was received from the library.

Further, in the portion of the money order form which will come back to the library as the acknowledgment, write out the register number of the bill to the left of the address of the remitter, that is, before the word " Librarian". This number will be of help in relating the money order acknowledgment to the proper voucher.

3737:35 *Foreign Payment Work*

3737:35:5 *Weekly jobs*

3737:35:51 Equivalent Finding

For each Foreign Petty Bill for which payment has to be made by foreign money order, find out the current rate of exchange from the financial news columns of the latest issue of the local daily. Work out the sterling equivalent of the amount of the bill. Remember to follow the instructions in the postal guide for the issue of sterling money orders to foreign countries. To give an example, in the case of money orders to the United States of America, a sum of 4 d will have to be added to the sterling equivalent. For all practical purposes, therefore, it is the exchange equivalent plus 4 d that should be taken as the equivalent.

3737:35:52 Foreign Money Order Writing

As soon as the equivalent is found out, write out the foreign money order form. It may be stated here that foreign money order forms have no coupon, nor do they have provision for the transmission of the acknowledgment of the payee to the remitter.

3737:35:53 Foreign Money Order Advising

As soon as the foreign money order writing is over, fill up the *Foreign Money Order Advice Form*. Put the register number of the bill near the centre of the top edge of the receipt part of the form and the voucher number of the bill at the right hand top corner of the same. Get it despatched by the Correspondence Section in the No Reply Despatch Register.

3737:35:55 Draft Requisitioning

For all the Heavy Foreign Bills for which payment has to be made by foreign drafts, fill up a *Draft Requisition Form*. If the request is for two or more drafts, give a tabular statement of the drafts required on the back of the form, the tabular statement having the following columns :

1 Voucher number ;
2 Amount ; and
3 In favour of.

Get it despatched by the Correspondence Section in the No Reply Despatch Register.

3737:35:561 Draft Advising

As soon as the requisitioned drafts are received, examine if the drafts are in proper form, if the amount is correct, if the name of the payee is correct, and if there is no unattested correction. If the amount is heavy and if the draft is not already crossed, cross it. If there is any discrepancy, get the matter set right by a reference to the Draft Issuing Authority. As soon as the draft is made normal, fill up the *Draft Forwarding Form.* Put the register number of the bill near the centre of the top edge of the receipt part of the form and the voucher number of the bill at the right hand top corner of the same. Get it despatched by the Correspondence Section in the No Reply Despatch Register.

3737:35:563 DRAFT FORWARDING

As soon as the Draft Forwarding Form comes back from the librarian after signature, attach the appropriate draft to it and hand it over to the Correspondence Section for transmission to the post office.

3737:35:57 EQUIVALENT POSTING

For each foreign money order or draft sent, post the cost in local currency in the appropriate column and line in the Contingent Register. If a number of drafts for one and the same Country had been received in the same consignment, the Draft Issuing Authority might not have given the equivalent in local currency for each draft separately. In such a case, you will have to work out the cost of each draft. In any case, you will have to work out the equivalent of each draft to verify the accuracy of the charges made by the Draft Issuing Authority. If there is any discrepancy, get the matter set right by addressing the Draft Issuing Authority.

3737:43 *Voucher Number Posting Work*

3737:43:5 *Weekly jobs*

3737:43:51 VOUCHER NUMBERING

Write out the Voucher Number in the faircopy as well as the office copy of each of the bills which have been passed for payment and entered in the Contingent Register. The Voucher Number is to be taken from the Contingent Register and this job is to be done immediately after the Contingent Register is written and before the bills are transmitted to the librarian for signature and passing. The Voucher Number should also be entered in the imprint of the stamp "Included in Voucher Number . . .", found at the bottom of the different sheets of any bill, which is in two or more sheets.

3737:43:55 Voucher Number Posting

On the appointed day of the week, post the Voucher Numbers in the related records in the possession of the Sections which passed the bill. For example, the following are some of the records that may have to be so dealt with :

For every bill relating to a Standing Order and passed by the Book Order Section, the Head of that Section would have already posted the Voucher Number in the related Standing Order Card. Verify if the Voucher Number has been correctly posted.

For every bill relating to a Periodical Publication, the Head of the Periodical Publication Section would have posted the Voucher Number in the related Register Card. Verify if the Voucher Number has been correctly posted.

For every bill passed by the Accession Section, the Voucher Number and the date are to be entered in the Accession Card of each book included in the bill. It is this job that is to be done first. The two preceding ones are to be done last, so that the sections concerned with them may have time to post the Voucher Number.

For every bill passed by the Circulation Section, enter the Voucher Number against the related entry in the concerned Overdue Register Sheets or the Personal Sheets, as the case may be.

For every bill for Service Stamps passed for payment, verify if the receipt of stamps has been entered in the Stamp Account Register and enter the Voucher Number.

For every bill passed by the Printing Section, note the Voucher Number and date against the appropriate item in the *Printing Register*.

For every bill passed by the Binding Section, note the Voucher Number and the date against the appropriate item in the *Binding Register*.

For every bill passed by the Building and Equipment Section, note the Voucher Number and date against the appropriate item in the *Equipment Order Book* and verify also if the article has been entered in the Stock Register, whenever necessary.

For every bill passed by the Stores Section, verify if the receipt of the stores has been entered in the appropriate Stock Book and enter the Voucher Number against the entry of the receipt of the article.

3737:44 *Bills Revising Work*

The person who revises the bills is to carry out each one of the following jobs for each of the bills. He should do all the jobs, except a small part of the fifth one, for a bill, before passing on to the next bill. He should initial in the proper place in the imprint of the Pay-Order Stamp in the faircopy in token of his having satisfied himself that everything is in order and also below the word " Librarian " in the office copy of the bill and in the money order forwarding and draft forwarding letters and in all other necessary places in token of having satisfied himself that everything is in order.

3737:44:5 *Weekly jobs*

3737:44:51 SANCTION VERIFYING

Verify if there is proper sanction for the order and the supply covered by the bill. For this, you will have to ask the Section concerned to produce the necessary files. If there is any difficulty, discuss it with the librarian. In particular, satisfy yourself that payment had not already been made for the supply or service in question, by referring to the related records in the possession of the concerned Section, as indicated in rule " 3737:43:55 Voucher Number Posting".

3737:44:52 TOTAL VERIFYING

Verify the total of each bill carefully. If there is any alteration, see if it has been attested by the appropriate authority.

3737:44:53 CERTIFICATE VERIFYING

Verify if the Section concerned has entered the necessary certificate that the service or supply has been rendered or made satisfactorily.

3737:44:54 ENTRIES VERIFYING

Verify the accuracy of the entries in the Contingent Register, the forwarding letters, the money order forms, the requisition letters, etc. In the case of foreign money orders, verify if the sterling equivalent has been based on the proper rate of exchange and has been calculated correctly. Verify also if the Account Section and the Heads of the Sections concerned have put their initials in the appropriate places in each bill or in each sheet, as the case may be. Verify also if the Voucher Number is correctly posted in all the sheets of the bill.

3737:44:55 Bills Register Verifying

Verify the entries in the Bills Register ; particularly see if the Voucher Number and the amount passed for payment are correctly posted.

In direct payment and draft cases, see if the date of despatch of the requisition for direct payment or draft, as the case may be, is entered correctly in the appropriate column. Further, if it is a case of direct payment, see if a line is drawn across the remaining columns against the entry and if the word " Direct payment " is written.

In pre-payment cases, see if the word " P P" is entered in the column " Date of requisition " and a line is drawn right along the remaining part of the line of the entry.

Put your initials in the appropriate places for all the above cases.

In the case of post-payment of petty bills, see if the word "P A" is entered in the requisition column and if the date of advice of payment is entered in the appropriate column. Put your initials in the necessary places. In the case of payment by foreign drafts, the bills register verifying will require the following additional job :

At the time when the draft advising is done (see rule 3737:35:561), verify the correctness of the draft, the accuracy of the entries in the draft forwarding letter. If there is any discrepancy, get it set right. If it is made normal, verify if the advice date is entered in the appropriate place in the bills register and put your initials in the proper place in the register.

3737:44:56 Progress of Expenditure Verifying

Before finally passing the bill to the librarian, examine if the payment involved is within the limits of the Sanctioned Budget. If there is any difficulty, consult the librarian.

3737:46 *Cash Receiving Work*

3737:46:5 *Weekly jobs*

3737:46:51 ESTIMATING

Among the bills to be paid from the Permanent Advance, the payment would have been made for some already. In the case of those for which payment is yet to be made, estimate the total amount required for payment in the day. In the case of foreign money orders, work out the correct equivalent on the basis of the current exchange rate, which is announced from time to time by the Post Office.

3737:46:56 CASH RECEIVING

Obtain from the cashier the necessary amount and put your dated initials in the Transmission Register of the Finance Section in token of your having received the money.

3737:48 *Remittance Work*

3737:47:5 *Weekly jobs*

3737:47:521 LOCAL PAYMENT TRANSMITTING

In the case of Local Payment, entrust to the delivery peon the necessary cash and the concerned forwarding letters. Take the dated initials of the peon in the Transmission Register in token of his having received the amount. Note in it the time at which he is started on delivery work.

3737:47:524 LOCAL PAYMENT WATCHING

Watch the return of the delivery peon and as soon as he comes, note the time of his return. By a reference to the delivery book brought by him, see if he has made the payment correctly. If the peon does not return within a reasonable time, inform the librarian and investigate the matter. If there is evidence of any wrong payment, take the necessary action and get the matter set right.

3737:47:531 MONEY ORDER FORWARDING

For all Money Order cases, entrust the peon doing postal work with the necessary cash and the money order forms for remitting to the Post Office. Take his dated initials in the Transmission Register in token of his having taken charge of the amount. Note also the time at which he has started.

3737:47:534 MONEY ORDER REMITTANCE WATCHING

As soon as the peon doing postal work returns from the Post Office, note the time of his arrival in the Transmission Register. Tally the postal receipts with the bills and get back the balance of cash, if any. Note down the balance of cash received in the Transmission Register. If the peon does not return within a reasonable time or if there is any discrepancy in the money order receipts, investigate the matter and set it right.

3737:47:535 MONEY ORDER ADVICE TRANSMITTING

In the case of Foreign Money Orders, transmit the money order advice letters to the Correspondence Section for further action.

3737:47:538 MONEY ORDER RECEIPTS FILING

Enter in red ink on each of the Money Order Receipts the number of the Voucher to which it relates. Also note the Money Order Receipt Number in the office copy of the Voucher concerned. The Money Order Receipt Number may be put as a denominator to the Voucher Number.

Arrange the Money Order Receipts in the sequence of the Voucher Numbers and pin them up. After production before the librarian at the account reviewing time, these receipts will have to be merged in one group in the proper Voucher Number sequence in the File of Money Order Receipts.

3737:47:56 CASH BALANCE RETURNING

If there is any cash left over, after the payment of the day is completed, remit it to the cashier and take his dated initials in the Transmission Register in token of his having received the amount.

3737:5 *Acknowledgment Work*

3737:5:4 *Daily jobs*

3737:5:41 ACKNOWLEDGMENTS REGISTERING

As soon as the Acknowledgments received in the day arrive

from the librarian, sort them by the Bill Register Numbers noted in them. If any Acknowledgment is without a Bill Register Number, it may be kept last. Then, enter the date of receipt of the Acknowledgment in the appropriate column, against the entry of the appropriate bill in the Bills Register. In the case of items which do not have a Bill Register Number in them, trace out the number and then proceed in the usual way.

3737:5:42 Acknowledgments Temporary Filing

Then, sort the Acknowledgments into two groups :

1 Acknowledgments for Drafts, which will have to be transmitted to the Central Executive for custody ; and
2 Acknowledgments for Petty Cash Payments, which will have to be retained in the library.

Arrange the Acknowledgments in each group by their Voucher Numbers having put the Voucher Number and the Bill Register Number in case they are not already found in the Acknowledgments. Pin the Draft Acknowledgments together and keep them for further action. Pin the Petty Cash Acknowledgments together and keep them in that condition, until they are ready for being permanently filed.

3737:5:5 *Weekly jobs*

3737:5:51 Acknowledgments Transmitting

On the appointed day of the week, fill up an *Acknowledgment Forwarding Form* for all the Draft Acknowledgments of the week. Send the Draft Acknowledgments as well as the Petty Cash Acknowledgments to the librarian along with the Contingent Register. This is to be done at the same time as the bills are transmitted for passing.

3737:5:52 Permanent Advance Acknowledgments Filing

As soon as the Acknowledgments come back from the librarian, merge the Petty Cash Acknowledgments in the *Petty Cash Acknowledgments File* in the sequence of their Voucher Numbers.

3737:5:55 Draft Acknowledgments Transmitting

Transmit to the Correspondence Section the Draft Acknowledgments and the forwarding letter for despatch to the Central Executive.

3737:5:6 *Monthly jobs*

3737:5:62 Inland Acknowledgments Reminding

On the appointed day of the month, find out from the Contingent Register the cases of Local and Inland Payments made one month or more earlier, for which the Acknowledgments have not yet come to hand. Send reminders to the parties concerned for Acknowledgments.

The convention in the Madras University Library is that the items in the Contingent Register, which have no letter or figure against them in the " remarks " column and the tick against which in the " remarks " column has been crossed only once, are those for which Inland Acknowledgments have not yet been received.

For all these cases, if the party says that he has not received the amount, investigate the matter. If it is a case of money order, write to the Postal Authorities, stating the amount, receipt number and date and the name of the Post Office, where the money order was handed in. Pursue the matter until it is satisfactorily settled.

3737:5:65 Foreign Acknowledgments Reminding

Do similarly in the case of foreign money orders, except that the Acknowledgment is deemed due only if it has been delayed by three months. Further the reminding will have to be done also in the case of Vouchers which have the letter "D" against their entries in the Contingent Register. In both classes of cases, the amount in foreign currency will be found enteredi n the remarks column.

If it is a case of addressing the Postal Authorities to investigate the payment of a foreign money order, the necessary fee will have to be paid to the Postal Authorities on demand.

3737:6 *Allocation Work*

3737:6:5 *Weekly jobs*

3737:6:51 Budget Head Allocating

On the appointed day of the week, if any bill passed for payment in the week has covered more than one Budget Head or Sub-Head, work out the exact amount that should be allocated to each Budget

Head or Sub-Head, as the case may be. In the case of payments by drafts, work out the figures provisionally. They are to be corrected after the exact cost of the drafts is known.

3737:6:52 Book Fund Allocating

As soon as the Budget Head Allocating is over, if any bill for books and periodical publications passed for payment in the week refers to more than one subject, work out the exact amount that should be allocated to each subject. In the case of payments by drafts, it is enough if the work is done after the exact cost of the draft is known.

3737:7 *Expenditure Watching Work*

3737:7:5 *Weekly job*

3737:7:51 Finance Diary Posting

As soon as the Allocation Work is over, post the figures in the *Main Finance Diary* as well as the *Subsidiary Finance Diary*. If any bill is to be paid by a foreign draft, the approximate cost of the bill may be posted in pencil provisionally in the main heading in the Main Finance Diary and corrected and inked as well as posted under the Sub-Heads after the cost of the draft is learnt from the Draft Issuing Authorities.

In the case of the Subsidiary Finance Diary, it is enough if the posting is made after the cost of the drafts is known in the case of payments by drafts.

Remember to work out the Cumulative Totals of the different columns in the last week of the month.

3737:7:6 *Monthly job*

3737:7:61 Cumulative Total Verifying

On the appointed day of each month, verify the accuracy of the Cumulative Totals in the Finance Diaries of the Section.

3737.7:7 *Quarterly job*

3737:7:74 Progress of Expenditure Reviewing

Same as the routine given under rule "3631:4:64 Finance Diary Reviewing."

3738 PETTY CASH

3738:7 *Petty Cash Account Work*

3738:7:5 *Weekly jobs*

3738:7:56 PETTY CASH ACCOUNT WRITING

On the appointed day of the week, soon after the payments are made, and the Miscellaneous Receipts and Deposit Account Books are written out, collect together all the Vouchers, which were paid out of the petty cash during the week or since the last account closing day, as the case may be. Put the " Paid " stamp on each Voucher and fill up the headings. Separate the Pre-Payment Vouchers from the Post-Payment Vouchers. Arrange the Pre-Payment Vouchers by the dates of payment. If there be two or more Vouchers belonging to the same date, arrange them among themselves by their Voucher Numbers. Arrange the Post-Payment Vouchers by their Voucher Numbers and place them at the end of the Pre-payment Vouchers. Then, write out the debit side of the *Petty Cash Account Book*, date by date and voucher by voucher Apply the " Cancelled " stamp to each Voucher.

On the credit side, first enter the opening balance which should be the same as the closing balance on the last account closing day. If any replacement of Permanent Advance was made in the course of the week, enter it in the next line against the words " By replacement of voucher numbers . . . .". Then total up the two figures. The total should be equal to the Permanent Advance.

3738:7:57 PETTY CASH ACCOUNT CLOSING

After the Petty Cash Account Writing is over, add up the debit side and enter the total at the debit side. Write on the first vacant line on the credit side the words " Amount spent " and enter against it the total on the debit side. Then, strike the balance. Then, calculate the total amount spent since the last requisition for replacement of permanent advance and enter the figure in the next line. Then, add up the last two lines. The total should give the Permanent Advance. If there is any discrepancy, investigate the matter and set it right. As soon as the account is closed, on the appointed day of the week, take the account book and the " Paid " Vouchers to the librarian for review and signature. The review of this account is to be done at the same time as the review of the other accounts.

3738:8 *Replacement Work*

3738:8:5 *Weekly jobs*

3738:8:51 Replacement Requisitioning

If on any account closing day, the balance of Permanent Advance goes below a conventional figure, proceed to ask for replacement as follows : Collect all the Vouchers paid out of the Permanent Advance since the last requisition for replacement. Arrange these Vouchers in the sequence of their Voucher Numbers. Enter the Voucher Numbers and the amounts on the back of the *Replacement Requisition Form.* Find the total This must agree with the corresponding figure given on the credit side of the account of that day. If there is any discrepancy, get it set right. Then, fill up the front side of the requisition form, classifying the amount spent according to the Budget Heads. Attach the Vouchers to the Replacement Requisition Letter. Get it despatched by the Correspondence Section and send it to the librarian for signature. This is best done at the same time as the weekly review of accounts is done. After the librarian sends it back, send it to the Correspondence Section for transmission to the Central Executive, along with the other letters of the day.

3738:8:52 Replacement Acknowledging

As soon as the Replacement Account comes from the Central Executive, fill up the Acknowledgment Form, get the signature of the librarian and send it to the Correspondence Section for despatch.

3738:8:56 Replacement Cash Handing Over

Send the Replacement Amount, having cashed the cheque if the payment had been by cheque, to the Finance Section and get the dated initials of the Head of that Section in the Transmission Register as a token of his having received the amount.

3738:8:8 *Annual job*

3738:8:81 Permanent Advance Acknowledging

On the 1 April, write out a letter to the Central Executive

acknowledging the full amount of Permanent Advance. Get the signature of the librarian and send it to the Correspondence Section for despatch.

374 Elimination of Waste

3741 ORGANISATION

If the turnover in the section demands the assignment of several members to it, the specialisation of the assistants of the section may be made by the different accounts. It should be a matter of prestige for the Head of the Accounts Section that no opportunity is given for the Audit to pick holes in the work of the Section. The greatest possible care and vigilance should be exercised by him to see that the Financial and Account Rules are faithfully observed and that the accounts are accurately written out according to the time schedule. He should personally do the revision work and the progress of expenditure watching work. He should also make himself personally responsible for all the work connected with the balance-sheet.

3744 DIARIES

Four diaries are to be maintained by this Section.

3745 DIARY 1

The First Diary, which may be called the *Main Finance Diary*, is to be maintained on a weekly basis. Its column headings should be the detailed headings in the Budget. If necessary and called for, some of the ultimate headings of the Budget may be further sub-divided. For example, if "Stationery, printing and binding" forms an ultimate budget head, it may be convenient to divide it into "stationery", "printing" and "binding". The first line of the diary below the column headings may be devoted to the entry of the Sanctioned Budget Figures. The upper half of the diary is to be used for recording the actual amount spent. The lower half of the diary is to be used for recording the amount appropriated. The diary should be sent round to the different Sections to get the lower half filled up from week to week.

3746 DIARY 2

The Second Diary, which may be called the *Subsidiary Finance*

Diary, is also to be maintained on a weekly basis. Its column headings are to be the symbols for the different subjects to which the amount spent on books and periodical publications is to be allocated. It is to consist of three parts. The first part is for recording the amount appropriated by the Book Order Section. The second part is for entering the amount actually spent. The third part is for recording the amount appropriated by the Periodical Publication Section. In other respects, this diary is similar to the Main Finance Diary.

3747 DIARY 3

The Third Diary, which may be called the *Overdue Tickets Diary*, is to be maintained on a daily basis. Its column headings are to be 5, 10, 15 naye paise, etc assuming that the overdue charge per volume per day is 5 naye paise. The figures put in any column against each date are the number of overdue tickets lying in the Charged Tray, behind the overdue guide showing the overdue charge indicated at the column headings.

This diary is not necessary if the Conscience Box is used.

3748 DIARY 4

The Fourth Diary, which may be called the *Routine Diary*, is to be maintained on a daily basis. Its column headings are to be as follows :

11 to 15 Same as for book order section.
4 Miscellaneous postings checked.
71 Bills registered.
721 Certified bills received.
722 Number of bills passed.
723 Number of vouchers.
725 Number of drafts despatched.
732 Standing order bills checked.
733 Periodical publication bills checked.
734 Accession cards posted.
736 Counter bills checked.
738 Other bills checked.
76 Bills allocated.
775 Acknowledgments checked.

776 Acknowledgments filed.
777 Reminder for acknowledgments.

375 Correlation Table

2 Book Order Section

3737:1:45 Bills distributing ;
3737:1:56 Bills-in-arrears listing ;
3737:43:55 Voucher number posting ;
3737:44:51 Sanction verifying ;
3737:44:53 Certificate verifying.

3 Periodical Publication Section

3737:1:45 Bills distributing ;
3737:1:56 Bills-in-arrears listing ;
3737:43:55 Voucher number posting ;
3737:44:51 Sanction verifying ;
3737:44:53 Certificate verifying.

4 Accession Section

3737:1:45 Bills distributing ;
3737:1:56 Bills-in-arrears listing ;
3737:43:55 Voucher number posting ;
3737:44:53 Certificate verifying.

6 Circulation Section

3734:446 Overdue checking ;
3734:447 Receipt posting checking ;
3734:47 Miscellaneous account writing ;
3735:76 Deposit account writing ;
3737:43:55 Voucher number posting ;
3737:44:53 Certificate verifying.

8 Maintenance Section

3737:1:45 Bills distributing ;
3737:1:56 Bills-in-arrears listing ;
3737:44:51 Sanction verifying ;
3737:44:53 Certificate verifying.

92 *Staff Section*

3732:62 Draft pay bill transmitting.

94 *Elimination of Waste Section*

3732:61 Pay bill drafting.

96 *Finance Section*

3732:676 Pay disbursing ;
3735:56 Miscellaneous receipts forwarding ;
3737:46:56 Cash receiving ;
3737:46:56 Cash balance remitting ;
3737:7:51 Finance diary posting ;
3737:7:74 Progress of expenditure reviewing ;
3738:8:56 Replacement handing over.

993 *Correspondence Section*

3734:56 Miscellaneous receipts forwarding ;
3737:31:51 Direct payment advising ;
3737:32:51 Local payment advising ;
3737:35:53 Foreign money order advising ;
3737:35:55 Draft requisitioning ;
3737:35:563 Draft forwarding ;
3737:43:55 Voucher number posting ;
3737:44:53 Certificate verifying.

994 *Printing Section*

3737:1:45 Bills distributing ;
3737:1:56 Bills-in-arrears listing ;
3737:43:55 Voucher number posting ;
3737:44:51 Sanction verifying ;
3737:44:53 Certificate verifying.

995 *Binding Section*

3737:1:45 Bills distributing ;
3737:1:56 Bills-in-arrears listing ;
3737:43:55 Voucher number posting ;
3737:44:51 Sanction verifying ;
3737:44:53 Certificate verifying.

966 *Building and Equipment Section*

3737:1:45 Bills distributing ;
3737:1:56 Bills-in-arrears listing ;
3737:43:55 Voucher number posting ;
3737:44:51 Sanction verifying ;
3737:44:53 Certificate verifying.

997 *Stores Section*

3737:1:45 Bills distributing ;
3737:1:56 Bills-in-arrears listing ;
3737:43:55 Voucher number posting ;
3737:44:51 Sanction verifying ;
3737:44:53 Certificate verifying.

376 Illustrative Time Scheme

Daily Jobs

3734:4 All the daily jobs relating to miscellaneous receipts ;
3735:46 Deposit account writing ;
3737:1:4 All the daily jobs of bills register work ;
3737:5:4 All the daily jobs of acknowledgment work.

Weekly Jobs

Saturday

3737:43:55 Voucher number posting.

Sunday

3737:1:56 Bills-in-arrears listing ;
3737:2:51 Total verifying.

Monday

3737:2 All the jobs of bills passing work ;
3737:31 All the jobs of direct payment work ;
3737:32:51 Local payment advising ;
3737:33:51 Inland money order writing ;
3737:35 All the jobs of foreign payment work except
5737:35:561 Draft advising ;
3737:35:563 Draft forwarding and

3737:35:57 Equivalent posting ;
3737:43:51 Voucher numbering ;
3737:5:55 Draft acknowledgments transmitting ;
3737:1:51 Payment details noting ;
3737:1:52 Advice date noting (except draft cases).

Tuesday

3737:44 All the jobs of bills revising work ;
3737:43:55 Voucher number posting.

Wednesday

3737:5:51 Acknowledgments transmitting ;
3737:46 All the jobs of cash receiving work ;
3737:47 All the jobs of remittance work ;
3734:5 All the weekly jobs relating to miscellaneous receipts ;
3735:5 All the weekly jobs relating to members' deposit ;
3738:7 All the jobs of petty cash account work ;
3731:54 Miscellaneous receipt account totalling ;
3731:55 Deposit account totalling ;
3738:8:51 Replacement requisitioning ;
3737:5:52 Permanent advance acknowledgments filing.

Thursday

3737:35:561 Draft advising ;
3737:35:563 Draft forwarding ;
3737:35:57 Equivalent posting ;
3737:43:55 Voucher number posting ;
3737:6 All the jobs of allocation work ;
3737:7:51 Finance diary posting ;
3737:1:52 Advice date noting (draft cases only).

Monthly Jobs

These relate to the pay bill. Their time scheme is to be fixed according to local practice.

First Tuesday

3737:7:61 Cumulative total verifying.

Second Tuesday

3737:5:6 All the monthly jobs of acknowledgment work.

Quarterly Jobs

First Tuesday

3737:7:74 Progress of expenditure reviewing.

Annual Jobs

1 *April*

3738:8:81 Permanent advance acknowledging.

April

3731:8 All the annual jobs relating to balance-sheet.

377 Forms and Registers

Q974 *Miscellaneous receipt forwarding form.* Stencil. 21 lb printing paper. White. The text of the form is as follows :

In reply please quote N 974 dated . . .

Sir,

Subject : MISCELLANEOUS RECEIPTS

I forward herewith a sum of Rs . . per details given below and to request you to be so good as to credit the amount to the library account. Kindly acknowledge receipt.

	Rs.	nP
1. Overdue collections		
2. Subscriptions		
3. Miscellaneous		
Total		

Q9771 *Direct payment requisition form.* Stencil. 21 lb printing paper. White. The text of the form is as follows :

In reply please quote N 9771 dated . .

Subject : DIRECT PAYMENT

Sir,

I forward herewith vouchers N__________________ for payment direct to the party (parties) concerned.

Details

Rs nP

(The relevant budget heads are to be detailed here)

Total

Q9772 *Draft requisition form.* Stencil. 21 lb printing paper. White. The text of the form is as follows :

In reply please quote N 9772 dated ....

Subject : DRAFT REQUISITIONING

I forward herewith vouchers N . . . and request that you will be so good as to obtain drafts for the amounts in favour of those specified on the reverse and send them to me at an early date for transmission. Kindly let me know the equivalents of the drafts in local currency separately and also the rates of exchange.

Q97723 *Draft forwarding form.* Printed. 21 lb printing paper. White. The form is to be perforated along a line midway between the two shorter edges. On the right of the perforated line, the text is to be as follows :

In reply please quote N 9772 dated ..

This refers to your bill N .. dated ..

Dear Sir,

Subject : PAYMENT FOR SUPPLY

I forward herewith a draft for____________________ ______________in full satisfaction of your Bill N____________ dated the____________________subject to post audit and readjustment. Kindly send a stamped receipt for the amount in the form annexed, immediately after the receipt of the draft.

Yours faithfully,

Librarian

On the left of the perforated line, the text is to be as follows :

N__________ Reg N________ Voucher N________

Received from the librarian .. the sum of ..

in payment of ....

Station___________________

Date__________________ Signature

N B This payment is made subject to audit at the close of the financial year.

A receipt stamp is to be affixed in case the amount exceeds the limit exempted by the Stamp Act.

Q97725 *Acknowledgment forwarding form.* Stencil. 21 lb printing paper. White. The text of the form is as follows :

In reply please quote N 9772 dated ..
Sir,

Subject : ACKNOWLEDGMENTS

I forward herewith for retention in your office__________ receipts in support of vouchers N__________of this library.

Q9774 *Cash forwarding form.* Printed. 21 lb printing paper. White. The form is to be perforated along a line midway between the two shorter edges. On the right of the perforated line, the text of the form is as follows :

In reply please quote N 9774 dated ..
This refers to your Bill N .. dated ..

Sir,

Subject : PAYMENT FOR SUPPLY

I forward herewith a sum of Rs________in payment of your Bill N________dated________subject to post audit and readjustment and to request that you will be good enough to furnish me by return of post with an acknowledgment of the receipt of the amount in the form annexed.

Yours faithfully,
Librarian

On the left of the perforated line, the text is to be as follows :

N________ Reg N________, Voucher N____

Received from the librarian ________ the sum of Rupees________in payment of________.

Station________

Date________ Signature

NB A receipt stamp should be affixed in case the amount exceeds Rs 20 but no stamp need be affixed if the bill presented for payment was duly stamped.

This payment is made subject to audit at the close of the financial year.

Q9775 *Foreign money order advice form.* Printed. 21 lb printing paper. White. The form is to be perforated along a line midway between the two shorter edges. On the right of the perforated line, the text is to be as follows :

In reply please quote N 9775 dated ..
This refers to your Bill N .. dated ..
Dear Sir,

Subject : PAYMENT ROR SUPPLY

A money order for £__________ sterling equivalent for __________ has been sent in payment of your Bill N________dated ________ subject to post audit and readjustment. Kindly furnish me by return post with an acknowledgment of the receipt of the amount in the form annexed. Please note that the amount acknowledged should be in the same denomination as that claimed in your bill.

I wish to add for your information that my name as entered in the money order is____________

Yours faithfully,
Librarian

On the left of the perforated line the text is to be as follows :

N________ Reg N__________ Voucher N________
Received from the librarian____________ the sum of______ ______ in payment of________________.
Station__________
Date__________ Signature

N B A receipt stamp is to be affixed in case the amount exceeds the limit exempted by the Stamp Act.

This payment is made subject to audit at the close of the financial year.

Q9777 *Foreign acknowledgment reminding form.* Stencil. 21 lb printing paper. White. The text of the form is as follows :

In reply please quote N 9777 dated ..
Dear Sir,

Subject : ACKNOWLEDGMENT

I bring to your notice that an acknwoledgment of the amount of the $\frac{\text{draft}}{\text{money order}}$ for____________ $\frac{\text{forwarded with}}{\text{advised in}}$ this office letter N________ .dated___ _________ has not yet been received. I shall be obliged if you can kindly expedite the despatch of the same as it is required here for audit.

Q978 *Replacement requisition form.* Stencil. 21 lb printing paper. White. The text of the form is as follows :

In reply please quote N 978 dated ..

Sir,

Subject : REPLACEMENT REQUISITION

I forward herewith vouchers N____________________ ____ amounting to Rs_________ and to request that you will be so good as to draw a cheque for the amount in my favour and send it to me at an early date for replacement.

Rs nP

Details

(The relevant budget heads are to be detailed here)

Total

S972 Pay bill.
S973 Increment certificate.
S974 Absentee statement.
S975 Acquittance roll.

These four forms are to be in accordance with local practice.

S9771 *Bills register.* Printed. 10 point type. 21 lb printing paper. White. Bound book. Folio pagination. 30 lines. The text above the column headings is to be :

" Register showing the bills received in the .. library .. and disposed of during the year .. "

The column headings are to be as follows :

Serial N (1.5 cm) ; Date of receipt (2.5 cm) ; Outside N (1.5 cm) ; Outside date (1.5 cm) ; From whom (5 cm) ; For what (5 cm) ; Amount (2.5 cm) ; Section N (1.5 cm) ; Voucher N (1.5 cm) ; Amount paid (2.5 cm) ; Requisition date (2.5 cm); Reviser's initials (.5 cm) ; Payment advice date (2.5 cm) ; Reviser's initials (.5 cm) ; Acknowledgment receipt date (2.5 cm) ; Acknowledgments transmission date (2.5 cm) ; Reviser's initials (.5 cm) ; Remarks.

S9772 *Miscellaneous account register.* Printed. 10 point type.

Ledger paper. White. Bound book. Folio pagination. 30 lines. The text above the column headings is to be :

" .. Library, .. Miscellaneous Receipt Account for the year .."

The column headings are to be as follows :

Date (2.5 cm) ; Receipt N (1.5 cm) ; From whom (10 cm) ; Subscription (2.5 cm) ; Overdue charges (2.5 cm) ; Duplicate ticket fee (2.5 cm) ; Special deposit (2.5 cm) ; Other receipts (2.5 cm) ; Total of weekly collections (2.5 cm) ; Total (2.5 cm) ; Remarks.

S9773 *Deposit account book*. Printed. 10 point type. Ledger paper. White. Bound book. Folio pagination. 20 lines. The text above the column headings on the left side is to be :

" ... Library.

Credit "

The column headings are to be as follows :

Month (2.5 cm) ; Date (1.5 cm) ; Deposit N (2.5 cm) ; From whom (9 cm) ; Cash Rs (2.5 cm) ; Bank Rs nP (4 cm).

The text above the column headings on the right side is to be " Deposit Account for the year ..

Debit "

The column headings are to be as follows :

Month (2.5 cm) ; Date (2.5 cm) ; Refund N (2.5 cm) ; Deposit N (2.5 cm) ; To whom (9 cm) ; Cash Rs nP (2.5 cm); Bank Rs nP (4 cm).

S9774 *Contingent register*. Printed. 10 point type. Ledger paper. White. Bound book. Folio pagination. 20 lines. The text above the column headings is to be :

" Register of contingent charges of the .. library .. for the year .."

The column headings are to be as follows :

Date (2.5 cm) ; To whom (5 cm) ; Voucher N (1.5 cm) ; Then, a column of 1.5 cm for each of the budget heads and the necessary subdivisions of the same, e g books, periodicals, manuscripts, stationery, printing, binding, postage, furniture, electric current, other charges ; Other charges ; Total ; And finally, a column for " Remarks".

S9778 *Permanent advance account book*. Printed. 10 point type. Ledger paper. White. Bound book. Folio pagination. 20 lines.

The text above the column headings on the left side is to be: " .... Library.

Credit "

The column headings are to be as follows :

Month (2.5 cm) ; Date (1.5 cm) ; Particulars (13 cm) ; Rs nP (2.5 cm).

The text above the column headings on the right side is to be: " Permanent Advance Account for the year..

Debit "

The column headings are to be as follows :

Month (2.5 cm); Date (1.5 cm); Voucher N (1.5 cm); Particulars (11.5 cm) ; Rs nP (2.5 cm).

Name	*Class number*	*Amplifying device*	*Filing characteristic*	*Year of transfer to record sequence after the file is closed*	*Year of destruction after transfer to the record sequence*
Balance-sheet	971	Last digit of year	Correspondent	Year 2	Year 3
Pay bill	972	Nil	Nil	Do	Year 10
Miscellaneous receipt	974	Nil	Correspondent	Year 1	Year 3
Deposit account	975	Nil	Do	Do	Do
Voucher	977	Nil	Nil	Do	Permanent
Direct payment	9771	Nil	Correspondent	Do	Year 3
Draft payment	9772	Nil	Do	Do	Do
Local payment	9774	Nil	Do	Do	Do
Money order payment	9775	Nil	Do	Do	Do
Money order receipts	9776	Nil	Nil	Do	Do
Acknowledgments	9777	Nil	Nil.	Do	Do
Permanent advance	978	Nil	Correspondent	Do	Do
Outward enquiries	9791	Nil	Do	Do	Do
Inward enquiries	9792	Nil	Do	Do	Do

CHAPTER 38

RECORDS SECTION

381 Time for Transfer

Completed registers and files are to be transferred to the Records Section from time to time. The time when the files are to be transferred are indicated in the part "8 Files" of the several chapters of the book. The registers are to be transferred one year after their completion.

382 Preparation of the Records

As has been already indicated in Chapter 18 "Correspondence, Files and Records", the number of the file marked on its docket label is to be first amended, if necessary and provided for, and then both underlined and overlined, as a mark of its having been admitted to the Records Collection. In the case of a bound register, a label is to be applied to its back, at a height of one inch from the bottom. On this label, the number of the register is to be written and both underlined and overlined. Beneath the number, the name of the register is to be written. If the register is in loose leaves, the leaves are to be tied up between two card boards cut to their size ; and, a label, similar to the docket label, is to be applied and written over. If the register is in cards, the cards are to be put in a tray and a properly written label is to be inserted in the label holder. Wherever possible, the inclusive dates are to be added to the various labels referred to in this paragraph.

383 Arrangement of the Records

The records are to be arranged in two sequences in the following sequence : The register sequence and the files sequence. In each sequence, the registers or the files, as the case may be, are to be arranged in the sequence of their respective register numbers or file marks. The registers or files, having the same numbers, or marks are to be arranged among themselves chronologically.

384 Issue of the Records

Whenever a record is required for use by any Section, the Head of that Section will send a requisition with the counter-signature of the assistant librarian. The requisition will be in a 3×5 inches slip, with the following headings :

Record number.
Section.
Date of requisition.
Date of probable return.
Head of the section.
Assistant librarian.
Date of issue.
Head of the section.
Date of reminder.
Date of return.
Record keeper.

The headings indicated for the slip show clearly what the Head of the Records Section is to do. Before issue, the date of probable return is to be marked in pencil just below the docket label of the file ; and if a register, at the right hand top corner of its first page. The number of the borrowing section is to be entered as the numerator of the date. After the issue of the record, the slip is to be filed in the *Issue Box* by the date of probable return. As soon as the record comes back, the requisition slip is to be traced out from the Issue Box, with the aid of the date of probable return, and returned to the Section after the necessary entries. Each day, a reminder is to be sent to the Section concerned for the record that has been overdue by one day, one week or one month. If a record is overdue by more than one month, it must be got back personally and reissued, if necessary. If this is not practicable for any unavoidable reason, the matter is to be reported to the librarian and his instructions are to be taken.

385 Destruction of Records

The period of destruction for the different files has been indicated in part " 8 Files " of the several chapters. In the case of registers, it may be stated that the accession register and the shelf register will never come to the Records Section, as they have to be perpetually current. In the case of the other registers, which will all be transferred to the Records Section on completion, they may be destroyed after ten years, unless they are marked for being kept permanently. It is suggested that the service registers, the cadre register, the acquittance roll, the deposit account book and the contingent register may be kept permanently. The application cards of all withdrawn members may also be kept permanently in one alphabetical sequence.

Further, the used up diaries and transmission registers may be destroyed after three years, except that the monthly and annual abstracts of statistics may be kept permanently.

386 Time Scheme

In June, the records, which should be destroyed in the year, should be collected and formed into a special sequence. The assistant librarian will scrutinise them carefully and give a report to the librarian, who will then pass orders for destruction. All the metallic pieces and tags attached to files are to be removed and such of the docket sheets as are in good condition are to be taken for use in other files. Then, the records ordered to be destroyed are to be cut to pieces and burnt in the kiln maintained for the purpose.

387 Form

The *Issue Form* of the section may be numbered C98 and the files of the section may have 98 for the file number and the correspondent's name for the filing characteristic.

CHAPTER 391

LIBRARIAN

3911 Creative Work

Part I contains many indications regarding the function of the librarian. His main province should be that of creative work in all matters connected with the technique of library work and service, and the organisation and management of the library.

3912 Personal Touch with Readers

His second chief business should be to get himself into personal touch with the reading public. If the librarian has to be definitely assigned to one section or other of the library, I should suggest that he should assign himself to the Reference Section more than anything else. For it is this section that would give the greatest opportunity for coming into personal contact with the readers of the library. Or in other words, it is this section that is in charge of the most vital social business of the library. If it is remembered that everything that is done in a library is to serve the readers, the importance of the librarian knowing each reader personally and knowing his bibliographical wants and reading interests will be easily realised.

3913 Accession and Shelf-Registers

The custody of the shelf register cards and the accession cards is the third duty of the librarian ; and it is a sacred duty. The cabinets containing them should be in his personal custody. It is preferable to have the shelf register cabinet in his room itself. Neither the shelf register cabinet nor the accession register cabinet should be allowed to be operated upon except in his immediate presence.

3914 Solution of Difficulties

He has also to solve all the puzzles that may arise in classification and cataloguing, from time to time.

3915 Routine Work

But, let it not be understood that the librarian will have no routine to do. A cursory search in the various chapters will bring out quite a long string of jobs in which the librarian has to take a personal part. Most of the jobs will have to go to him for consideration and solution, when they reach a breaking point due to one cause or another. Apart from these contingencies, my experience is that, in medium sized libraries, regular, systematic, unavoidable routine of a definitely repetitive nature takes away more than twenty hours of the librarian's time in a week—this is to say, nearly two-thirds of his scheduled official time. The following Illustrative Time Scheme will throw light on this estimate.

3916 **Illustrative Time Scheme**

Daily. Inward correspondence opening (¼ h) (11 A M); Circulation Section correspondence and urgent correspondence of other sections (½ h) (1 P M); Routine letters of the Circulation Section (¼ h) (4 P M); Round of visit to the different parts of the library (⅓ h).

Total 1⅓ h per day, or per week 8 h

Special work on different days of the week

Saturday. Heavy inward correspondence brought by foreign mail (½ h); Perusal and rapid picking up of acquaintance with new books and periodicals (2 h); Sanctioning of indents for stationery and forms (¼ h) (2 P M); Scrutiny of the diaries of the sections (¼ h) (3 P M). Total 3 h

Sunday. Refractory cases in classification and cataloguing (3 h) (2 30 P M). Total 3 h

Tuesday. Meeting of Staff Council or Sections of Staff (½ h) (10 30 A M); Review of the catalogue cards of the week (2 h) (11 30 A M); The ordinary correspondence of the week, other than those of the Circulation Section (1 h) (1 30 P M); Sanctioning refund of deposit (½ h). Total 4 h

Wednesday. Passing of bills (½ h) (11 A M); Routine letters of the Periodical Publication Section (½ h) (3 P M); Reviewing the weekly accounts (½ h) (3 30 P M); Scrutinising and passing

orders for books and periodicals (1 h) (4 P M) ;
Scrutiny and custody of accession cards and shelf
register cards (1 h) (5 P M). Total 3½ h

Total for the week 21½ h

Thus, the only time that is left for the vital work of meeting the readers and discussing their book needs with them is a little less than 18½ hours in the week.

3917 Delight of Service

Although routine and administration necessarily usurp, thus, a large slice of the librarian's official time, and although some more of his time will be consumed by committee work and liaison work on behalf of the library, no librarian, true to his profession, should succumb to the temptation of the red-tape and forget his duty to the first three Laws of Library Science. So far from augmenting the time given to routine, he should try to cut it down and give himself up as long as possible for direct service to readers. I am sure that, once the pleasures of service are really tasted, the tendency will be to throw to the wind the official schedule of 40 hours per week and stay on at the personal service of readers as long as physical fitness would permit. Even here, what is physical fitness ? My own impression is that the more the librarian spends his time with the books and the readers, the greater will be his chances for keeping fit. Losing oneself in the service of readers is the best form of insuring one's health. Overstaying with readers in the library may look like a task, until one gets into the full swing of enthusiasm for the work. But once one gets into the swing, the mind will easily transcend the limitations of time. Nay, it will find its delight only in one setting, and that is, the setting provided by a library full of books and full of readers feeling fully at home in the confidence that personal help will be forthcoming whenever necessary.

CHAPTER 392

LIBRARY PROFESSION

3921 Function of the Section

In the interest of professional solidarity in the country and in the interest of the furtherance of library technique, it is necessary that the staff of every library should cultivate a sense of professional loyalty, which would make them share their progress and research with the brother members of the profession. Although there will not be any routine to justify the formation of a Section, a separate chapter has been devoted to this subject in order to emphasise this vital question. This subject is sure to have files related to it. That at least is another justification for having a separate number and chapter for this subject.

3923 Areas of Work

The files relating to this subject may be grouped under three heads :

1 Those that would bring the staff of the library into contact with the profession outside the library ; they may be subdivided into those relating to
    2 Professional associations ;
    6 Professional publications ; and
    8 Professional conferences.

2 Those that would bring outside persons into contact with the library for professional purposes ; they may be subdivided into those relating to
    2 Visits by persons already in the profession ;
    6 Fresh men who want to learn work by observation or apprenticeship ; and
    8 Formal *library training classes.*

3 Those that relate to general movements for *interlibrary co-operation* ; they may be sub-divided into those relating to
    2 Standardisation of practice ;
    6 Interlending of resources ; and
    8 Interlending of staff.

3925 File Numbers

The file numbers for the above mentioned nine categories may be fixed respectively as follows :

99212, 99216, 99218 ;
99222, 99226, 99228 ;
99232, 99236, 99238.

3926 Life of the Files

These files may be destroyed ten years after their final disposal.

3927 Contact and Research

The librarian should encourage the members of the staff to take as intimate an interest as possible in professional matters. He should also endeavour to prevent them from falling into the rule-of-thumb rut. The meetings of the Staff Council will give ample opportunities to suggest research problems and to stimulate the staff to pursue them. He should also secure adequate publicity in professional circles for the achievements of the members of the staff. Correspondence with the leading personalities in the profession in the different countries of the world should be a regular feature of the library. The atmosphere among the library staff should be such that, when a conference is announced, the sections vie with one another in offering professional papers. Contributions to professional periodicals should also be a regular feature of the library.

CHAPTER 393

CORRESPONDENCE SECTION

3931 Planning

39311 CHIEF MAIL OF THE DAY

The routine described here relates to the inward correspondence received by the chief mail in the day, the outward correspondence to be sent out at the end of the day and the faircopying which is to feed the day's despatch of outward correspondence. In most of the libraries, it will be possible to single out certain mail hours as the main ones in this manner. In the Madras University Library, for example, the heaviest inward mail for the day is received at 10 AM while the heaviest outward mail is despatched at 6 PM Hence, most of the jobs relating to the Correspondence Section have to be looked upon as daily jobs.

39312 URGENT MAIL

However, letters are likely to come into a library at all odd hours. While the letters which appear to be urgent should be registered and sent to the Sections concerned immediately, it would be an advantage to accumulate all other stray letters, to be dealt with ata particular hour, all together. In a similar way, while urgent letters should be faircopied and despatched immediately, it will be conducive to economy to deal with all the ordinary letters on a daily basis.

39313 DAILY JOBS

Thus, since the only immediate jobs of the Correspondence Section will be those relating to urgent correspondence and since the routine relating to them will be exactly similar to the routine relating to the ordinary correspondence, except that they will have to be attended to immediately, the job analysis given in the second part of this chapter has not classified the jobs into immediate, hourly, etc except in the case of a few weekly jobs.

39318 FACTORS IN PLANNING

The distinctive work of the Correspondence Section is to be

planned with reference to the following factors :

1 Inward correspondence ;
2 Outward correspondence ; and
4 Faircopying.

393181 Inward Correspondence

From the point of view of the Correspondence Section, the inward correspondence falls into the following classes :

1 Correspondence not falling into divisions 2, 4, 6, 7 or 8, which may be referred to as *General Inward Correspondence* ;
2 Indents for books and letters forwarding them, which may be referred to as *Indents* ;
4 Proofs, and printed and bound materials, and letters forwarding them, which may be referred to as *Press Materials* ;
6 Letters relating to the Circulation Section, which may be referred to as *Readers' Letters* ;
7 Bills and receipts, and letters forwarding them, which may be referred to as *Bills and Receipts* ; and
8 Letters addressed or delivered to the library by mistake, which may be referred to as *Misdelivered Letters*.

393182 Outward Correspondence

From the point of view of the Correspondence Section, the outward correspondence falls into the following classes :

1 Letters, packets, etc regarding which either
 11 no reply or action can become due, by its very nature ;
 12 no reply or action is regarded necessary by the sections concerned ; or
 13 the reply or action expected is one that is planned to be watched by the sections concerned by a special device, at the section itself, such as overdue notices from the Circulation Section, part-not-received notices of the Periodical Publication Section, payment forwarding letters of the Accounts Section, printing and binding orders and so on, which may be referred to as *No-Reply Correspondence* and will be marked "N R" by the sections concerned ;

2 Letters, packets, etc other than N R, regarding which the reply or action is expected within two weeks which may be referred to as *Short Range Correspondence* and will be marked "S R" by the sections concerned. Thc symbol "S R" will be amplified by the sections concerned by the date before which the reply is due, if the period allowed is less than two weeks ; and
3 Letters, packets, etc other than N R, regarding which the reply or action is expected within three months, which may be referred to as *Long Range Correspondence*, and will be marked "L R" by the sections concerned. The symbol "L R" will be amplified by the sections concerned by the date before which the reply is due, if the period allowed is less than three months.

393184 Faircopying

From the point of view of the Correspondence Section, the materials for faircopying fall into the following classes :

1 Inward correspondence the purport of which falls within the purview of two or more sections and at the same time does not admit of being dealt with by the overseeing section, which may be referred to as *Composite Letters* ;
2 Draft letters, of which the number of copies to be made is not sufficiently great to justify mechanical duplication, which may be referred to as *Simple Draft Letters* ;
3 Draft letters, of which the number of copies to be made is sufficiently great to justify mechanical duplication, which may be referred to as *Circular Draft Letters* ;
4 Forms which are to be mechanically duplicated and not printed, which may be referred to as *Unprinted Forms* ; and
5 Long lists of books, periodicals, etc. which may have to be enclosures to letters or which may be required for office reference, which may be referred to as *Lists*.

3932 Job Analysis

39321 Inward Correspondence

The work of the Correspondence Section relating to inward

correspondence is to consist of the following jobs :

1 Sorting the inward correspondence into the classes enumerated in rule 393181, which may be referred to as *Inward Correspondence Sorting* ;

2 Further classification of the materials in each class, except class 8, which may be referred to as *Inward Correspondence Classifying* ;

3 Registering each correspondence in the appropriate inward correspondence register, which may be referred to as *Registering* ;

51 Entering the date of receipt of reply against the corresponding item in the appropriate outward correspondence register, which may be referred to as *Inward Correspondence Cross Referring* ;

52 Forwarding the inward correspondence to the sections concerned, which may be referred to as *Inward Correspondence Forwarding* ;

521 Verifying if the register concerned has been properly initialled by the person concerned, which may be referred to as *Inward Correspondence Acknowledgment Verifying* ;

6 Preparing the arrear list of inward correspondence, which may be referred to as *Arrear Listing* ; and

8 Taking the appropriate action about the misdelivered correspondence, which may be referred to as *Misdelivered Correspondence Disposing.*

39322 Outward Correspondence

The work of the Correspondence Section relating to outward correspondence is to consist of the following jobs :

1 Sorting the outward correspondence into the classes enumerated in rule 393182, which may be referred to as *Outward Correspondence Sorting* ;

2 Arranging the materials in each class in the sequence of the file number, which may be referred to as *Outward Correspondence Arranging* ;

31 Entering each correspondence in the appropriate despatch register, which may be referred to as *Despatching* ;

32 Addressing the envelope for each and inserting it therein, which may be referred to as *Addressing* ;
41 Affixing the stamp to the letters and the articles, which may be referred to as *Postage Stamp Affixing* ;
411 Posting the postage amount in the despatch registers, which may be referred to as *Stamp Noting* ;
42 Forwarding the stamped letters and articles to the post office, which may be referred to as *Forwarding to Post Office* ;
421 Verifying if the postal receipt has been duly received in the case of registered letters and articles, which may be referred to as *Postal Forwarding Verifying* ;
43 Entering in the delivery book and forwarding the letters and articles by messenger, which may be referred to as *Forwarding by Messenger* ;
431 Verifying if the letters and articles forwarded by the messenger have been duly acknowledged in the delivery book, which may be referred to as *Delivery Book Verifying* ;
51 Entering the date of despatch of reply against the corresponding item in the inward correspondence register, which may be referred to as *Outward Correspondence Cross Referring* ;
52 Forwarding the despatched files to the sections concerned, which may be referred to as *Despatched Files Forwarding* ;
521 Verifying if the despatched files concerned have been duly acknowledged by the sections concerned, which may be referred to as *Despatched Files Acknowledgment Verifying* ;
7 Totalling up the stamp account and posting the daily cumulative total, which may be referred to as *Stamp Totalling* ;
71 Bringing the stamp account book up-to-date, which may be referred to as *Stamp Accounting* ;
75 Preparing the order for stamps, which may be referred to as *Stamp Ordering* ; and
76 Receiving the stamps and storing them, which may be referred to as *Stamp Receiving.*

39324 FAIRCOPYING

The work of the Correspondence Section relating to faircopying is to consist of the following weekly jobs :

2 *Machine Trimming* ; and
3 *Duplicator Trimming.*

393241 Composite Letters

The work of the Correspondence Section relating to composite letters is to consist of the following jobs :

1 Extracting the marked portions, which may be referred to as *Extracting* ;
2 Comparing the extract with the original, which may be referred to as *Extract Comparing* ; and
3 Forwarding it to the librarian for signature, which may be referred to as *Extract Forwarding.*

393242 Simple Draft Letters

The work of the Correspondence Section relating to simple draft letters is to consist of the following jobs :

1 *Fair Copying* ;
2 Comparing the faircopy with the original, which may be referred to as *Faircopy Comparing* ; and
3 Forwarding to the librarian for signature, which may be referred to as *Faircopy Forwarding.*

393243 Circular Draft Letters

The work of the Correspondence Section relating to circular draft letters is to consist of the following jobs :

1 *Stencil Cutting* ;
2 Comparing the cut stencil with the original, which may be referred to as *Stencil Comparing* ;
3 Forwarding the cut stencil to the librarian for signature, which may be referred to as *Stencil Forwarding* ;
4 Taking copies from the cut stencil, which may be referred to as *Duplicating* ;
5 Forwarding the copies to the despatcher, which may be referred to as *Circular Letter Copies Forwarding* ;
6 Filing the used stencil, which may be referred to as *Cut Stencil Filing* ; and

7 Cleaning the duplicator, which may be referred to as *Duplicator Cleaning*.

393244 Unprinted Forms

The work of the Correspondence Section relating to unprinted forms is to consist of the following jobs :

Similar to the analysis of 393243 with the following exceptions :

3 Stencil forwarding may not be necessary in all cases.

5 The forms are to be forwarded to the storekeeper or to the sections concerned, instead of to the despatcher.

393245 Lists

The work of the Correspondence Section relating to lists is to consist of the following jobs :

If the lists are to be typed, the analysis is similar to the analysis of 393242. If the lists are to be mechanically duplicated, the analysis is similar to the analysis of 393243 with the following exception :

5 The copies of the lists are not to be sent to the despatcher in all cases ; they may have to be sent to the sections concerned.

3933 Routine

39331 Inward Correspondence

39331:1 Inward Correspondence Sorting

As soon as the mail is received from the librarian, pick out each letter and examine if it has received the signature of the sender and the stamp of the librarian. If it has not, put it aside in the Group of Unstamped Letters.

The Stamped Letters are to be sorted into the various groups mentioned in rule 39311, namely, general correspondence, indents, press materials, counter letters, bills and receipts, and misdelivered materials ; and further, all items marked urgent are to be formed into a separate group.

Send the Group of Unstamped Letters to the librarian. As soon as they are received, distribute them to the appropriate groups. Send the Unsigned Letters to the Senders in the usual way.

Note: *The next four routines are to be first finished for the readers' letters and other correspondence marked urgent, before they are done for the other groups.*

39331:2 Inward Correspondence Classifying

This routine is to be done group by group

As soon as the sorting is over, pick out each letter and peruse it rapidly, underlining in pencil any reference that may exist either to enclosed papers or to accompanying articles. Examine if the enclosure or the accompanying material, as the case may be, has been duly received and note the result in the margin and put your initials against it. If there is any discrepancy, investigate the matter and, if unsolved, report the matter to the librarian. In case the Filing Characteristic of the letter is different from the name of the correspondent, underline also the word or words representing the Filing Characteristic.

Again, if the correspondent has not given the Class Number of the File as a reference, with the aid of the purport of the letter and the classified schedule of files, fix the Class Number of the letter as fully as possible and write it in red ink, just above the salutation " Sir " or " Dear Sir", etc as the case may be.

If any letter consists of loose sheets, fasten them together by a pin, or a tape-tag if the number of sheets is greater than three.

As soon as these processes are over, arrange the letters in each group in a classified sequence i e in accordance with the File Numbers.

39331:3 Registering

It is convenient to have different registers for registering the general correspondence, indents, press materials, counter letters *and* bills and receipts. *The symbols for these registers may be taken as* I C G, I C I, I C P, I C C, *and* I C B, *respectively.*

Before commencing the Registering Work for the day with any Register, put the stamp of the current date at the end of the first vacant line in it.

Pick out each letter in sequence and make the necessary entries in the appropriate Inward Correspondence Register. Whenever a date is to be entered by hand, it is enough if the number of the date and month are entered in sequence, separated by a dot. Further, if a letter is marked urgent, its entry is to be made in red ink.

As soon as a letter is registered, put your initials in some vacant place as close to the librarian's stamp as possible.

Subsidiary Rule of the Madras University Library

The press materials and the bills and receipts are to be handed over to the Sections concerned, who will register them and deal with the other routines relating to them.

39331:51 Inward Correspondence Cross Referring

As soon as the Inward Correspondence Registering is over, for each item in the register that is in response to a communication from the library, pick out the appropriate Despatch Register and against the entry of that communication, put, in the column "Reply received date", the stamp of the current date.

39331:52 Inward Correspondence Forwarding

As soon as the Cross Referring is over with an Inward Correspondence Register, send it along with the letters and their respective enclosures and accompanying materials to the Sections concerned.

39331:521 Inward Correspondence Acknowledgment Verifying

As soon as the Inward Correspondence Register comes back from the Sections, verify if each item has received the initial of the concerned clerk as a token of his having received the materials transmitted to him. If any item has not received it, investigate the matter and get it initialled. If unsolved, report to the librarian.

39331:6 Inward Correspondence Arrear Listing

On the first Saturday of each month, as soon as the Inward Correspondence Cross Referring is over, examine each register and prepare a list of papers lying unattended to by the different Sections for more than one month.

A paper is deemed to be lying unattended to in a Section, if the column "Disposal date" is left unfilled.

Send the list to the Sections concerned and get their explanations.

The list is then to be sent with the explanations to the librarian, through the assistant librarian.

Further, in the case of entries made in red ink, i e urgent items, the arrear listing is to be done every Saturday for all items that have been lying unattended to for more than one week.

Pin together all the pages in which the " Disposal date " column has been filled up in all the lines.

39332 Outward Correspondence

39332:1 Outward Correspondence Sorting

As soon as the letters to be despatched are received from the librarian along with their respective files, pick out each letter and its related file and examine if it has received the signature of the librarian and in case it has enclosures, if they have received his signature. If not, put it aside into the Group of Unsigned Letters.

The signed letters along with their files are to be sorted into the various groups mentioned in rule 39312, namely, No Reply Correspondence or N R, Short Range Correspondence or S R, and Long Range Correspondence or L R Send the group of unsigned letters to the librarian. As soon as they are received from him duly signed, distribute them to the appropriate groups.

39332:2 Outward Correspondence Arranging

Note: *This routine is to be done group by group.*

As soon as the sorting is over, pick out each letter and its associated file and peruse it rapidly. If there is any reference to enclosures, pick out the enclosure and pin it with the letter or fasten it with a tag if the total number of sheets exceeds three. Also examine if the File Number, the Outside Reference Number and the Subject are properly mentioned in appropriate places. If there is any defect, get it rectified with the aid of the Head of the Section concerned. As soon as these processes are over, arrange the letters together with their related files in each group in a classified sequence, i e in the sequence of the file numbers.

39332:31 Despatching

Note: *It is convenient to have different registers for despatching the* N R correspondence, *the* S R correspondence, *and the* L R correspondence. *The symbols for these registers may be taken as* N R D, S R D, *and* L R D, *respectively.*

Before commencing the despatching work of the day with a Despatch Register, put the stamp of the current date at the end of the first vacant line in it. Pick out each letter in sequence and make the necessary entries in the appropriate Despatch Register. If what is despatched is a packet, enter the word "Packet" in the "remarks column". Whenever a date is to be entered by hand, it is enough if the numbers of the date and the month are entered in sequence and separated by a dot.

As soon as the letter is despatched, put the stamp of the current date in the appropriate place in the faircopy as well as in the office copy, which should be pinned to the related file.

As soon as the stamping is over, put the faircopy in the proper order in the *Despatched Faircopy Tray* and the related file in the *Despatched File Tray.*

39332:32 Addressing

As soon as the Despatching Work is over, pick out each letter and pick out a cover of suitable size to hold the correspondence and write the correct address on the cover. The address may be found in the faircopy. If, however, it is not fully given there, it may have to be taken from the Inward Correspondence from the Party, which will be found in the related file, or from the " Address book " in the case of parties to whom letters emanate from the library frequently, or by getting the information from the Head of the Section concerned. If the letter is to go by Registered Post, write "Registered" at the top of the cover; if it is to be Insured, write at the top " Insured for Rs . . . " (Put in the correct figure after the word " Rs "), and prepare the Acknowledgment Slip. Put your initials at the left hand bottom corner of the cover. Write the class numbers of the files of the letters to be put into a cover, at the left hand top corner of the cover. Then, insert the correspondence in the cover, and put it in the *Addressed Tray.*

If two or more letters are to be sent to the same addressee, put all of them in one cover.

If any material is to accompany the letter, get the material properly packed and addressed. At the top of the address slip of the accompanying material, put the appropriate phrase, such as, "Book post",

" Packet post ", " Registered post ", or " Registered packet post Insured for Rs . . . ", etc as the case may be. Place all such accompanying articles in proper sequence by the side of the addressed tray.

39332:41 Stamp Affixing

As soon as the addressing is over, in the case of all the correspondence of the day, pick out each letter and packet one by one and deal with it as follows :

If it is to be sent by Post, affix the necessary and sufficient postage stamp, weighing the letter or article, as the case may be, whenever necessary and put it in the *Stamped Tray.*

39332:411 Stamp Noting

As soon as the stamp is affixed on letters and packets, enter the stamp amount in the "Stamp" column of the Despatch Register in the case of each letter or article, as the case may be, lying in the Stamped Tray. If a letter or packet is to be sent by Registered Post, enter its weight in its "remarks" column. If a Postal Acknowledgment is due, add in the "remarks" column the word "A D".

Subsidiary Rule of the Madras University Library

For all places within our commonwealth, use service stamps and for all places outside our commonwealth, use ordinary stamps. Care must be taken to enter the stamp amount in the appropriate column—private stamp column or service stamp column, as the case may be.

39332:42 Forwarding to Post Office

As soon as the Postage Stamp Noting Process is over, sort the letters and packets into two groups as Ordinary Post and Registered Post and put them into appropriate bags.

Send them to the Post Office through the peon, giving him the necessary instructions. Note down in the *Transmission Register* the time at which he is started and take his initials.

Subsidiary rule of the Madras University Library

All registered letters and articles are to reach the Post Office before 4 P M Hence, they should be dealt with first.

39332:421 Postal Forwarding Verifying

As soon as the peon returns from the Post Office, note down his time of return in the Transmission Register, collect from him the Postal Receipts for all registered letters and articles and attach them to the appropriate files or, if there is no file, forward them to the Sections concerned. If the Postal Receipt is not received, get it properly settled.

If his return is unduly late, inform the Head of the Section in charge of the peons.

39332:43 Forwarding By Messenger

If a letter or packet is not to be posted, but is to be sent through a messenger, make the necessary entries in the Delivery Book. If necessary and called for, write on the cover the words "The bearer waits for reply". If the cover contains any money or any other valuable, note that also at the top of the cover. Put all such letters and articles in the Messenger Forwarding Bag. As soon as a sufficient number of letters have accumulated in the Messenger Forwarding Bag, start the messenger, handing over to him the Bag containing the letters and articles and the Delivery Book and giving him the necessary instructions.

If any valuable is to be sent by a messenger, note it in the Transmission Register and take his initials. Note down also the time at which the messenger is started.

39332:431 Delivery Book Verifying

As soon as the messenger returns, note down the time of his return in the Transmission Register. Examine the Delivery Book and verify if it has received the initials or signature of the respective addresses or their agents. If there is any discrepancy, bring it to the notice of the librarian. If his return is unreasonably late, report to the Head of the Section in charge of the peons.

39332:51 Outward Correspondence Cross Referring

At the end of the day or earlier if an opportunity presents itself, for each item, entered in the Despatch Register, which is in response to an inward correspondence, and for each File which has come from the librarian with the remark " file", take out the appropriate Inward Correspondence Register and put the stamp of the current date in the appropriate column against the entry of the corresponding inward correspondence.

If the outward correspondence is a reminder, trace out in the Despatch Register the entry of the item for which it is a reminder and put the stamp of the current date in the " Reply received date " column. All the files, whose work has been properly rounded off, are to be placed in the *Distribution Tray.*

Pin together all the pages in which the " Reply received date " column has been filled up in all the lines.

39332:52 Despatched Files Forwarding

As one of the first items each day, pick out all the files lying in the Distribution Tray and send them to the respective Sections along with the Despatch Register.

39332:521 Despatched File Acknowledgment Verifying

As soon as the Despatch Register comes back, verify if the Head of the concerned Section has put his initials against the appropriate entries in token of his having received the Despatched Files. If not, get the matter set right by speaking to the Head of the Section.

39332:7 Stamp Totalling

As one of the first items each day, total up the figures in the Postage Stamp Columns of the Despatch Registers for the preceding day and enter also the cumulative total for the week. The day's total is to be entered at the last line of the " cumulative total " column and the cumulative total for the week, in the line below it, the two figures being separated by a single horizontal red line.

39332:71 Stamp Accounting

As one of the first items of work on the first day of the week, close the weekly total columns for the Stamp Amount in the Despatch Registers. Put two horizontal red lines below the cumulative total of the week. Then, fill up the Stamp Account Register and see if the total value of the Stamps on Hand agrees with the balance that should be on hand. If there is any discrepancy, investigate the matter and report to the librarian and take such other action as may be necessary to get it set right.

39332:75 Stamp Ordering

On the appointed day of the week, in which the Stamp on Hand goes below the minimum prescribed, find out from the different Sections if any Section anticipates any abnormal consumption of Postage Stamps in the week. In the light of the information received, prepare the indent for Postage Stamps. After getting the sanction of the librarian, prepare an Order for the Stamp and send it to the Treasury with the necessary cash obtained from the cashier. The amount and the time are to be written in the Transmission Register and the initials of the peon going to the Treasury to purchase the stamps are to be got in it.

39332:76 Stamp Receiving

As soon as the Stamps are received from the Treasury, enter the time of return of the peon in the Transmission Register and check the Stamps with the bill and the order. If there is any discrepancy, investigate the matter and have it set right. Write the necessary certificate on the bill and send it to the Accounts Section. Distribute the stamps into the receptacles in the Stamp Box. It will facilitate the daily and weekly Stamp Verification Work and otherwise make the work systematic and tidy, if the stamp sheets are cut into pieces, each having a definite number of stamps to the value of, say, 25, 50 naye paise, etc according to convenience, before they are deposited in the Stamp Box. The Stamp Box is to be so designed as to have exactly fitting compartments for each denomination of stamp. If the peon does not return within a reasonable time, inform the Head of the Section in charge of the peons.

39334 Faircopying

39334:2 Machine Trimming

On the appointed day each week, examine the typewriting machine. Clean it rapidly. If the ribbon requires changing, change it. If any part requires oiling, have it oiled. Do every other thing necessary to get the machine in an efficient working condition.

39334:3 Duplicator Trimming

On the appointed day each week, examine the duplicator machine. Clean it rapidly. If any part requires oiling, have it oiled. Do every other thing necessary to get the machine in an efficient working condition.

393341 Composite Letters

393341:1 Extracting

As early as possible in the day, type out the portion marked out to be extracted from the composite letters by the different Sections. The style of typing the extract should be as follows:

Outside reference N . . . dated . . .
Library reference N . . . dated . . .
Extracted from letter N . . . dated . . . from . . .
filed in file N . . . on (date).

[*Extract*]

(True extract)

Librarian

393341:2 Extract Comparing

Compare the Extract Copy with the Original and put your initial and date near the word " Librarian ".

393341:3 Extract Forwarding

As soon as the comparing is over, send the Extract Copy with the Original to the librarian for signature.

Note: When it comes back from the librarian with his signature, deal with it as if it were an Inward Correspondence.

393342 Simple Draft Letters

393342:1 Faircopying

Before commencing the faircopying, examine each draft letter carefully. Satisfy yourself in particular if it has received the initials of the librarian, and if the File Number, the Outside Reference Number and the Subject are properly mentioned in appropriate places. Examine also if the Despatch Instruction regarding the class of the correspondence as N R, S R and L R has been furnished by the Section concerned. If any of these things is not in order, get it set right by the Section concerned.

As soon as a draft letter is found to be in order, take the specified number of copies in letter head of suitable size. If a draft letter exceeds the largest size letter head, use blank sheets of paper as continuation sheets. If there is any enclosure to be faircopied, have it done. At the bottom of the letter, type your initials and the date as well as the symbol N R, S R or L R as the case may be, indicating the Despatch Register to which the letter relates.

393342:2 Faircopy Comparing

Similar to 393341:2.

393342:3 Faircopy Forwarding

Similar to 393341:3.

393343 Circular Draft Letters

393343:1 Stencil Cutting

Similar to 393342:1 except that at the bottom line, the number of copies to be taken should be indicated before the initials of the typist.

393343:2 Cut Stencil Comparing

Similar to 393341:2.

393343:3 Cut Stencil Forwarding

Similar to 393341:3.

393343:4 Duplicating

As soon as the Cut Stencil comes back from the librarian with his signature, take out the specified number of copies, as shown in the bottom most line before the initials of the typist.

393343:5 Circular Letter Copies Forwarding

As soon as the specified number of copies are taken, send them to the despatcher along with the original files.

393343:6 Cut Stencil Filing

As soon as the copies and the related files are forwarded to the despatcher, take out the Cut Stencil from the duplicator machine and file it in the appropriate classified sequence according to the File Number along with the earlier cut stencils for future use, if necessary.

393343:7 Duplicator Cleaning

As soon as the cut stencil is filed away, clean the duplicator so that it may be fit for use on the next occasion.

3934 Elimination of Waste

39341 Organisation

If the turnover in the section demands the assignment of several members to it, the first division of functions among the staff may be into 1 Faircopying ; and 2 Registering and despatching.

When the work grows still more, further specialisation may have to be by the correspondence of groups of sections of the library, the sections of the library being divided into convenient groups for this purpose.

39347 Head of the Section

The Head of the Section should do the preliminary sorting of the inward and outward correspondence. He should see that the greatest economy possible is effected in despatch work. That is to say, he should see that all the correspondence to one particular individual or party are despatched in one cover. He should personally see to the handing over of the correspondence to the peon who goes to the post office. He should also verify the total of the stamp account. Wherever private stamps, and not service stamps, are used, he should personally verify the correctness of the stamps affixed.

He should see that the time scheme is rigorously maintained. In particular, he should see that the inward correspondence reaches the Heads of the Sections concerned at the scheduled time and that all letters received for despatch in the day are finished before the close of the day. He should also see that all the despatched files are maintained in their proper sequence and handed over to the Heads of the Sections concerned early on the next day. He should see that the cross reference work is done without any omission.

39348 DIARY

The section may have to maintain one diary on a daily basis. Its headings are to be as follows :

11 Numb of letters received.
12 Numb of materials accompanying letters received.
13 Numb of extracts prepared from letters.
14 Numb of cases in which materials, that should have accompanied, did not accompany.
15 Numb of wrongly delivered letters or materials disposed of.
21 Numb of letters and articles despatched by ordinary post.
22 Numb of letters and articles despatched by messenger.
23 Numb of letters and articles despatched by registered post.
24 Total number of letters and articles despatched.
25 Numb of entries made in all the despatch registers taken together.
251 Numb of entries made in the No Reply Despatch register.
252 Numb of entries made in the Short Range Despatch register.
253 Numb of entries made in the Long Range Despatch register.
32 Numb of ordinary letters faircopied.
33 Numb of circular letters stencilled.
34 Numb of forms stencilled.
35 Numb of lists faircopied.
6 Total amount of stamps spent.
61 Amount of service stamps spent.
62 Amount of private stamps spent.

3935 Correlation Table

From its very nature, the work of this section is related to those of all the other sections. In fact, this section has hardly any independent work, i e except in relation to other sections. Hence, no Correlation Table is necessary.

3936 Illustrative Time Scheme

DAILY JOBS

3931 The routines relating to inward correspondence, in the order in which they are mentioned in the jobs analysis part and the routine part.

3932:52 Despatched files forwarding ;
3932:521 (11 30 A M) Circulation Section and (12 noon) other sections; Despatched files acknowledgments verifying (1 P M) ;
39334 All the daily routines relating to outward correspondence, except the two already listed, in the order in which they are mentioned in the job analysis part and the routine part (4 30 P M).

WEEKLY JOBS

Saturday

39332:71 Stamp accounting ;
39334:2 Machine trimming ;
39334:3 Duplicator trimming ;
39331:6 Urgent inward correspondence arrear listing.

It may be added that :

Heavy inward mail will have to be registered on Saturdays ;

Book indent copies will have to be typed on Mondays and routine letters of the Accounts Section will also have to be despatched on Mondays ;

Many letters of several sections will have to be typed on Tuesdays ;

Order copies, and library committee papers will have to be typed on Wednesdays ;

Heavy foreign mail will have to be despatched on Thursdays.

MONTHLY JOBS

First Saturdays. 99331:6 Inward correspondence arrear listing.

It may be added that the binding list will have to be faircopied on the Saturday and Sunday preceding the last Tuesday.

3937 Forms and Registers

It may be stated at the outset that the following style of printing the letter heads is economical:

Coat of Arms	To	From The Librarian, . . . Library. (*Station*)

In reply please quote N .. dated ..
This refers to your N .. dated ..

Sir,

Subject :

The same style is to be adopted also to routine letter forms, whose text is printed or stencilled.

The matter is to be parallel to the longer edge in the case of cards and quarto sizes and parallel to the shorter edge in the case of folio size.

C993 *Card letter head.*
C9938 *Small envelope.*
Q993 *Quarto letter head.*
Q9937 *Endorsement form.*
Q9938 *Medium envelope.*
S993 *Folio letter head.*

The following are to be the inward correspondence registers :

S99311 *ICG* or *Inward correspondence* (*General*).
S99312 *ICI* or *Indents register.*
S99316 *ICC* or *Inward correspondence* (*Counter*).

and any other further modifications of these as may be warranted by the turnover in the library.

The specification for the registers ICG and ICC is as follows :

Printed. 10 point type. 21 lb printing paper. White. Bound. 30 lines. Folio pagination.

The column headings are to be as follows :

Left side.

Line N (1.5 cm) ; Outside N (2.5 cm) ; Outside date (2.5 cm) ; Filing characteristic or purport (7.5 cm) ; Correspondent (7.5 cm).

Right side.

Line N (1.5 cm) ; Class N (2.5 cm) ; Date reference to despatch register (1.5 cm) ; Initials (1.5 cm) ; Final disposal (6.5 cm) to be sub-divided as Date (2.5 cm) ; Nature (4 cm) ; If deferred, disposal due date (1.5 cm) ; Interim disposal (1.5 cm) to be sub-divided as Nature (2.5 cm), Date (1.5 cm) ; Remarks.

The specification for S99312 Indents Register is to be as follows :

Printed. 10 point type. 21 lb printing paper. White. Bound.

20 lines. Folio pagination.

The column headings are to be as follows :

Left side.

Line N (1.5 cm) ; Outside N (1.5 cm) ; Outside date (1.5 cm) ; Date of receipt (2.5 cm) ; Class N (2.5 cm) ; Initials (1.5 cm) ; Carding date (1.5 cm) ; Preliminary checking date (1.5 cm) ; N of items (1.5 cm) ; Estimated cost (2.5 cm) ; Transmission for sanction date (2.5 cm) ; Sanction receipt date (2.5 cm).

Right side.

Line N (1.5 cm) ; Quotations calling date (1.5 cm) ; Quotations receiving date (1.5 cm) ; Final checking date (1.5 cm) ; Date of order (5 cm) to be sub-divided as First (1.5 cm), Second (1.5 cm), Third (1.5 cm) and Final (1.5 cm) ; Supply date (2.5 cm) to be sub-divided as First (1.5 cm) and Final (1.5 cm) ; Supply due date (1.5 cm) ; Final disposal date (1.5 cm) ; Remarks.

The following are to be the outward correspondence registers :

S99321 *NRD* or *No reply despatch register.*

S99322 *SRD* or *Short range despatch register.*

S99323 *LRD* or *Long range despatch register* and any other further modifications of these as may be warranted by the turnover in the library.

The outward correspondence registers of the section are to have the following specification :

Printed. 10 point type. 21 lb printing paper. White. Bound. 30 lines. Folio pagination.

The column headings of the registers are to be as follows :

Left side.

Line N (1.5 cm) ; Private stamp (4 cm) to be sub-divided as Each Item (2 cm), DCT—(meaning " daily cumulative total")—(2 cm) ; and each sub-heading to be sub-divided into Rs nP ; Service stamp (4 cm) to be sub-divided as DCT (2 cm) and Each Item (2 cm) and each sub-heading to be sub-divided as Rs nP ; Country if foreign (2.5 cm) ; Filing characteristic or purport (7.5 cm).

Right side.

Line N (1.5 cm) ; Addressee (7.5 cm) ; Class N (2.5 cm) ; Date of receipt of file in the section (1.5 cm) ; Initials (1.5 cm) ; Reply due date (1.5 cm) ; Reply receipt date (2.5 cm) ; Remarks.

S9936 *Stamp account register*. Printed. 10 point type. Ledger paper. White. Bound. 20 lines.

The text above the column headings is to be " . . .Library, Stamp Account for (*month*), (*year*)".

The first column heading is " Details " (1.5 cm) ; there should be five other column headings at the rate of one for the date of each of the stamp account closing days of the month. They are, for example, Saturdays in the Madras University Library. Each of these five columns is to be sub-divided into four columns equally spaced. The heading for the first column is " N " which stands for the number of stamps on hand. The other three columns are to be headed " Rs nP".

The row headings are to be as follows :

Opening balance ; By purchase ; Total ; Week's use ; Closing balance ; Stock in hand ; 3 nP ; 5 nP ; 10 nP ; 15 nP ; 20 nP ; 25 nP ; 50 nP ; Rs 1 ; etc.

Thus, one page will be sufficient for one month.

S9937 *Endorsement form.*

S9938 *Big envelope.*

3938 **Files**

As this section has no correspondence of its own, it has no files to keep, except the files relating to "99391 Outward enquiries " and "99392 Inward enquiries", for which the details are similar to the correspondence files in the other sections.

CHAPTER 394

PRINTING SECTION

3941 Materials to be Printed

The arguments against the printed catalogue have been set forth in my *Five laws of library science*[50] and *Classified catalogue code.*[51] If it is remembered that the pest of a printed catalogue is being successfully eliminated by the library profession, it can be realised that there is very little printing to be done in a library. The only things to be printed are the forms and the registers. It is best that the library gets them done by the printer appointed by the Central Executive, without wasting any time and energy over the selection of printers and the settlement of rates.

3942 Co-operative Library Supplies

Perhaps, a more economical plan will be for all the libraries in the country to agree to get their forms and registers made and supplied by a central agency, official or non-official. Such a large scale production would ensure, on the one hand, simplified and standardised practice leading to national economy and, on the other, it may be cheaper as well, for individual libraries. But, I wonder how long it would take for India to get to that stage of co-operative library supplies. At present, the only alternative available is the former one.

3943 Periodicity

The printing work to be done is to be ascertained from the Stores Section. The two Sections should co-operate with each other fully and try to reduce the number of occasions for printing to the minimum possible—once in a year is the ideal to be aimed at.

3944 Preliminary to Order

Before printing a fresh stock of forms and registers, the Printing Section should get a certificate from the Stores Section that the forms and registers have been discussed with the Sections concerned and the Staff Council and that the necessary amendments and alterations have been made. They should also verify if the necessary sanction of the librarian has been obtained by the Stores Section for the printing as well as the number of copies desired to be printed. Then, the cost of printing is to be estimated and it should be verified, whether it is within the budget allotment.

3945 Printing Order

When all these conditions are satisfied, the printing order may be drafted and sent to the librarian for approval and signature and then to the Correspondence Section for faircopying and despatch in the usual way. The office copy should contain a certificate that the cost of the order is within the budget allotment. Whenever possible a specimen printed form may be sent. Otherwise, detailed instructions should be given in the order about the format, the type, the rulings, etc. Remember that the number of the form is to be printed at the left hand bottom corner.

3946 Stationery Indent

The indent for the required stationery should be made on the weekly indents day.

3947 Register

The printing work is to be controlled and regulated by means of the *Printing Register*. Its specification is as follows :

S994 *Printing register*. Manuscript. 21 lb printing paper. White. Stitched. Folio pagination. 30 lines per page. The column headings are to be as follows :

Serial N (.5 cm) ; Name of form or register (4 cm) ; Form number (.5 cm) ; Quantity (1.5 cm) ; L's initials (.5 cm) ; Date of order (2.5 cm) ; Date of receipt of proof (2.5 cm) ; Date of despatch of proof (2.5 cm) ; Date of receipt of revised proof (2.5 cm) , Date of strike order (2.5 cm) ; L's initials (.5 cm) ; Date of receipt of supply (2.5 cm) ; Date of transmission to the stores section (2.5 cm) ; Initials of head of stores section (.5 cm) ; Date of receipt of bill (2.5 cm) ; Date of passing (2.5 cm) ; Amount (2.5 cm) ; Initials of the head of the section (.5 cm) ; Remarks.

3948 Files

The files of the section are to have 994 for the class number and the name of the form, in the case of specific forms and the name of the correspondent in the case of general files, for the Filing Characteristic.

Chapter 395

BINDING SECTION

3951 Planning

39511 Contract

It is a matter of policy whether a library should have its own bindery or whether it should get its volumes bound by outsiders on contract. I feel that few Indian libraries of today have reached the position when they can manage a bindery. While owning a bindery will add greatly to convenience, a library can think of it only at a much later stage, i e after it has organised itself along other lines so as to make the service to the public prompt and efficient. I believe it will take some years for our libraries to reach that stage.

39512 Detailed Specification

Hence, I have drafted this chapter on the assumption that the binding is to be done by outsiders. But a word of warning may be given. Unlike printing, binding is a very vital affair for the library. Hence, it must have a voice in all matters connected with the binders. The standard of binding in India appears to be very poor at present. I found that reinforced library binding was quite unknown in Madras thirty years ago. Even such things as split boards, and French joints were absolutely unknown to the binding trade. We could not even get the necessary materials in the local market. We could not get, for example, mill boards in sufficient quantity, as the binding trade was using only inferior straw boards. We could not get, again, unbleached tape for sewing. Buckram or any other unbleached linen as covering material was not available. It took us some time to teach the workmen the correct way of binding. During World War II, what had been gained has been lost. We are still in a bad position.

Hence, it is necessary that the most detailed specification for library binding should be included in the tender forms. It would be even a good policy to ask the tenderers to meet the librarian in person and take the necessary instructions regarding the full implications of the various terms in the specification, before they quote. This preliminary talk will save a good deal of misunderstanding and difficulty at later stages. Unlike what was suggested about the appointment of printers, the library should take the lead and should be given the primary voice in the appointment of binders.

It may be stated here that it is not the purpose of this manual to go into the details of library binding, to discuss the merits and demerits of the various styles of forwarding and finishing, or to examine the kind of covering materials that will satisfy the demands of the hard use of a library volume on the one hand and of economy—ultimate economy—on the other. For such details one should refer to the books on library binding.[52]

39513 Mending Work

Even though it may be premature for many of the Indian libraries to have their own bindery, I think at least a few libraries can provide for a mending department and a tooling department. A stitch in time saves nine. The Circulation Section and the Maintenance Section can pick out volumes from time to time which require a little repair. If the repair can be done then and there, the life of the binding and hence of the book can perhaps be prolonged to a remarkable extent. In practice, the absence of the mending department drives the volumes to an untimely end.

39514 Tooling Call Number

If the library equips itself with the tooling implements and if one or two members of the staff acquire the necessary skill, the call numbers can be straight away tooled on the back and the bother of affixing the tags, writing on them and replacing them from time to time will be saved.

39515 Bind After Accessioning

Another matter of policy is whether a book should be sent to the binder after the publisher's case is worn-out or even at the beginning, before it is released for circulation. Personally I am of the opinion that the life of a book will be considerably lengthened if the latter course is adopted. In any case, books in paper covers should not be released for use before being bound.

It will be very difficult to decide to what degree the publisher's case should be worn-out before the book is sent to the binder.

In actual practice, various considerations will prevail, so that the book is not withdrawn from circulation until the exposed back also is very much damaged.

39516 Books with Poor Paper

At the same time, I do not think that every book will deserve the costly library binding. In the case of books of passing interest, particularly ordinary fiction in public libraries and several of the Indian books, which are printed on very bad paper, it may be cheaper to buy additional copies than to have them bound in the library style. Further, the paper is likely to perish very rapidly. Hence, there is no point in making the binding extra strong in their cases.

39517 Buy Books in Sheets

If the policy of the library is to have all the worthwhile books bound before circulation, it will be more economical to buy the books in sheets, i e uncased. The library will thus be saving the cost of the publisher's case.

39518 Factors in Planning

The distinctive work of the binding section is to be planned with reference to the following factors :

1 Standing binders ;
2 Volumes for binding ;
3 Bound volumes ;
4 Corrections ;
5 Mending ; and
6 Bills.

3952 Job Analysis

39521 Standing Binders

39521:8 The work of the Binding Section relating to standing binders is to consist of the following annual jobs :

1 *Tender Calling* ;
2 *Tender Tabulating* ; and
3 Tabulating the terms offered by the different binders and

fixing the standing binder or binders, which may be referred to as *Standing Binder Appointing*.

39522 Volumes for Binding

39522:6 The work of the Binding Section relating to the volumes for binding is to consist of the following monthly jobs :

1 Tallying the volumes with the binding slips and arranging them, which may be referred to as *Tallying* ;
2 Scrutinising the volumes from the point of view of their binding peculiarities and preparing them, which may be referred to as *Preparing* ;
3 Transmitting the binding slips to the Correspondence Section for faircopying, which may be referred to as *Slips Transmitting* ;
4 Correcting the typed sheets and noting down the nature of the covering materials, which may be referred to as *List Correcting*;
5 Transmitting the volumes to the binder, which may be referred to as *Volumes Transmitting* ; and
8 Transmitting copies of the lists to the other sections, which may be referred to as *List Transmitting*.

39523 Bound Volumes

39523:6 The work of the Binding Section relating to the bound volumes is to consist of the following monthly jobs :

1 Tallying the bound volumes returned by the binder with the order list, which may be referred to as *Tallying* ;
2 Verifying the correctness of the tooling on the bound volumes, which may be referred to as *Tooling Verifying* ;
4 *Collating* ; and
8 Transmitting the checked list to the Maintenance Section, which may be referred to as *Checked List Transmitting*.

39524 Correction

39524:6 The work of the Binding Section relating to correction is to consist of the following monthly jobs :

1 Discussing with the librarian the defects found in examining

the bound volumes, which may be referred to as *Consulting* ;

23 Transmitting the slips for the volumes requiring correction to the Correspondence Section, which may be referred to as *Correction Slips Transmitting* ;

24 Correcting the list received from the Correspondence Section, which may be referred to as *Correction List Correcting* ;

25 Transmitting the volumes to the binder for correction, which may be referred to as *Correction Volumes Transmitting* ;

28 Transmitting copies of the correction list to the other sections, which may be referred to as *Correction List Transmitting* ;

31 *Corrected Volumes Tallying* ;

32 *Correction Verifying* ; and

38 *Checked Correction List Transmitting.*

39525 Mending

The job analysis for mending is similar to that for binding.

39527 Bills

39527:6 The work of the Binding Section relating to bills is to consist of the following monthly jobs :

1 Tallying the bill with the checked order copy, which may be referred to as *Tallying* ;

2 Verifying the description of the volume found in the bill, which may be referred to as *Data Verifying* ;

3 Verifying the amount claimed in the bill for each volume, which may be referred to as *Rate Verifying* ;

7 Passing the bill for payment after the necessary certification, which may be referred to as *Bill Passing* ; and

8 Transmitting the volumes, for which the bill has been passed, to the shelf section for shelving, which may be referred to as *Bound Volumes Transmitting.*

3953 Routine

39531 Standing Binders

39531:8 *Annual jobs*

The routine connected with the Appointment of Standing Binders is similar to those given under "2231 Standing Vendors".

39532 Volumes for Binding

39532:6 *Monthly jobs*

39532:61 Tallying

On the appointed day of the month, as soon as the Binding Slips of the volumes set apart for binding arrive from the Technical Section, tally the Binding Slips with the volumes. The Binding Slips will have indication of the items which require to be tooled on the back of the volume. Scrutinise them carefully and carry out any corrections that may be called for. Verify in particular the correctness of the spelling and of the call numbers. If there are too many casual mistakes or if there is any fundamental error in principle, discuss them with the Technical Section so that such mistakes may not recur in future.

39532:62 Preparing

As soon as the tallying is over, examine each volume carefully and see if they have any defects. In particular look for the following :

1 Is the pagination continuous ?
2 Are the advertisements included in the pagination ? Are they to be retained ? Or, can they be discarded ?
3 Are the cover sheets of the different issues included in the pagination ? Are they to be retained ? Or, can they be discarded ?
4 Is there a separate title page and contents page for the volume? Or, is it necessary to retain the title pages and the contents page of the individual issues ?
5 Is there any Book Supplement or Periodical Supplement ? If so, do the Supplements have their own pagination ? Are the Supplements to be separately bound as distinctive volumes ? Or, are they to be bound with the main volume ?
6 If there be more than one pagination in each number, assemble the sheets in the proper sequence in each sequence of pagination ;
7 See if any pages are missing ;

8 See if there are any plates or folded maps ; if there are, write the necessary special instructions in the Binding Slip within brackets ;

9 Examine if the style of binding and tooling indicated in the Binding Slips are in conformity with the treatment given to the other volumes of the set, in the case of multivolumed books and periodical publications. If there is any discrepancy, discuss the matter with the Technical Section and the Maintenance Section. If an agreement can not be arrived at, take it to the librarian for his decision ; and

10 Examine if there is any Binding Instruction given in the volume by the publisher himself. If it differs from what is given in the Binding Slip, discuss it with the librarian.

39532:63 Slips Transmitting

As soon as the preparing job is over, arrange the Binding Slips in the Transmission Box in the proper classified sequence. It may add to convenience if the books, pamphlets and periodical publications are arranged in three distinct groups and the slips also are arranged in parallel groups. Then, send the Transmission Box to the Correspondence Section for faircopying, on the appointed day of the month. Ask for four copies of the list—one faircopy, one office copy, one copy for the Reference Section and one copy for the Technical Section.

39532:64 List Correcting

As soon as the typed sheets of the Binding Order arrive from the Correspondence Section, on the appointed day of the month, compare the typed matter with the Binding Slips carefully. Remember in particular to examine if the small letters in the call numbers are underlined. This is necessary to invite the attention of the binder that he should use the italics for the lower case. Otherwise the lower case letters will not show forth properly in tooling. As soon as the correcting of the list is over, note down against each item the Covering Material to be used. In deciding the Covering Material, take into consideration,

1 The material used in the earlier volumes of the same set ;
2 The weight of the volume ;

3 The frequency with which it is likely to be handled ;
4 The condition of the paper ; and
5 The value of the book.

After the correction of the list is over, pick out the Binding Slips relating to multivolumed and periodical publications and file them, in a classified sequence in the *Normal Binding Slips Tray.* The other slips may be destroyed.

39532:65 Volumes Transmitting

As soon as the List Correcting is over, on the appointed day of the month, tally the number of volumes with the total number in the lists and hand over the volumes to the binder. Ask him to do the necessary collation in the library premises. This will save a good deal of further correspondence and misunderstanding. After he finishes the collation, ask him to put in the last page of each volume its serial number as found in the list and after getting the Binding Order signed by the librarian and despatched by the Correspondence Section in the usual way, give him the Binding Order and take the necessary receipt from him. It would be a good policy to use one copy of the Binding Order List as the Binding Order and another copy of the same as an Acknowledgment of the Binder.

39532:68 List Transmitting

As soon as the volumes are transmitted to the binder, send a copy of the list to the Maintenance Section for tallying with the Shelf Register Cards of the Binding Sequence and prompt return. Send the other two copies for the files of the Reference Section and the Technical Section respectively. Remember to fill up the columns in the Binding Register.

39533 Bound Volumes

39533:6 *Monthly jobs*

39533:61 Tallying

As soon as the bound volumes arrive from the bindery, on the appointed day of the month, tally the volumes with the office copy of the related order list. It will add to the convenience of all concerned if the binder is instructed to return the volumes packed exactly in the sequence in which they appear in the Binding Order Lists. As each item of the list is tallied, put a pencil tick against the item in the left hand margin. Place the volume back in the shelf in the appropriate classified sequence. Then, the result will be that the sequence of the volumes will be parallel to the entries in the lists. As soon as all the volumes have been dealt with in this way, write the word "Tallied" and put your dated initials at the end of the last sheet near the left hand bottom corner in token of your having tallied the volumes. If any item of the lists remains unreturned, correspond with the binder and get the matter set right.

39533:62 Tooling Verifying

After the Tallying is over, examine the Tooling on the back of the book. Pay special attention to the correctness in spelling and call number and particularly to the lower case letters in the class numbers. In the case of periodical publications, pay special attention to volume number and year. For each of the items for which the tooling has been verified and found to be correct, put a cross on the tick of the related entry in the list. If the tooling is wrong in any of the volumes, transfer the volumes to the *Objection Group*. As soon as the tooling is verified in this manner, write the words " Tooling verified " and put your dated initials at the end of the last sheet in token of your having verified the tooling.

39533:64 Collating

Collate each volume returned from the binder carefully. If there is any new defect, i e defect not noted to have been in existence at the time the volume was sent to the binder, note it on a slip of paper and put it inside the volume and transfer the volume to the Objection Group. Also put a cross against the related entry in the Order List. Put your dated initials at the end of the last page of the volume in token of your having collated it.

39533:68 Checked List Transmitting

As soon as the Collation is over, transmit the Checked Order List to the Maintenance Section for perusal and return. This will give an opportunity for the Maintenance Section to know what volumes have not came back and what volumes are held in objection. This piece of information will be of help to the Maintenance Section in answering the queries they receive frequently from the Reference Section on behalf of readers who ask for the volumes.

It may also be seen from rule 2835:8:61 that the Maintenance Section would have separated the related shelf register cards into three groups, namely Returned Group, Objection Group, and Not Returned Group.

39534 CORRECTION

39534:6 *Monthly jobs*

39534:61 CONSULTING

As soon as the Checked List comes back from the Maintenance Section, take the list as well as the volumes in the Objection Group to the librarian. Discuss each case with him as to what further action is to be taken.

The routine for all the other jobs relating to the factor "Correction" is similar to those of the corresponding jobs under the factor "39532 Volumes for binding", except that :61 is to be changed to :611.

39535 MENDING

The routine for Mending is similar to the routine for Binding.

39538 BILLS

39537:6 *Monthly jobs*

39537:61 TALLYING

If the bill is not forthcoming within a reasonable time after the receipt of the bound volumes, call for the bill. As soon as the Binding Bill is received, tally it with the related Checked Order Copy of the Binding List item by item. As soon as an item is checked, put a pencil tick in the left hand margin against the item in the bill. If there is any discrepancy, have it investigated. Items under objection are to be scored out and the librarian's initials taken against them. If necessary, write to the binder and settle the matter. As soon as all the items have been tallied, put your dated initials near the left hand bottom corner of the last sheet in the bill.

39537:62 Data Verifying

As soon as the Tallying is over, verify with the bound volumes the data given in the bill regarding 1 the size, 2 the number of pages, 3 loose maps, etc, 4 covering material and the style of binding. If there is any discrepancy, make the necessary correction in the Duplicate Copy of the Bill and put a pencil cross against the item at the left hand margin of the bill to invite the attention of the librarian to it at a later stage.

39537:63 Rate Verifying

After the Data Verifying is over, examine if the amount claimed for each volume is in agreement with the accepted rate. If there is any discrepancy, make the necessary correction in pencil in the Duplicate Copy of the Bill and put a cross to invite the attention of the librarian to it at a later stage.

39537:64 Bill Passing

As soon as the Rate Verifying is over, take the bills to the librarian and discuss with him all the cases in which discrepancies have been found, i e each of the items against which a cross has been put in the margin in the Duplicate Copy of the Bill. Carry out his instructions. Then, write a certificate near the left hand bottom corner of the Last Sheet of the Bill to the effect that the work has been done in accordance with the specifications and that the amounts claimed is in accordance with the accepted rate. Put your dated initials in the certificate. Then, pass the bill to the Accounts Section for further action.

39537:68 Bound Volumes Transmitting

As soon as the Bill Passing is over, arrange the volumes in proper classified sequence and transmit them to the Maintenance Section. Note down in the Transmission Register the number of volumes thus transmitted and, when the Transmission Register comes back, see if it has received the dated initials of the Head of the Maintenance Section in token of his having received the volumes.

3954 Elimination of Waste

39541 Head of the Section

The Head of the Binding Section should devote sufficient attention to the style of binding and the assembling of the volume, so that uniformity and convenience are secured to the maximum possible degree. He should also personally verify the accuracy of the data given and the charges claimed in the bills. He should make it a point to visit the bindery, just before the covering material is applied, as this is the only stage when the soundness of the binding materials used and the mode of stitching can be tested. For this purpose, he should instruct the binders to intimate to the librarian the date on which the covering material is to be applied and to proceed with the covering work only after his inspection.

39548 Diary

The section is to have a diary on a daily basis, with the following headings :

1 Numb of volumes prepared for binding;
2 Numb of volumes collated;.
3 Numb of volumes found defective in collation;
4 Numb of volumes for which tooling was scrutinised;
5 Numb of volumes found defective in tooling;
6 Numb of volumes whose sizes were checked in the bill;
7 Numb of volumes whose sizes had to be corrected in the bill.

3955 Correlation Table

This section will have to be in constant touch with the accession section, periodical publication section, reference section and maintenance section to decide the assembling peculiarities of volumes and the style of binding. Apart from this general remark, the following table may be given :

5 *Technical Section*

39532:61 Tallying ;
39532:68 List transmitting;
39534:628 Correction list transmitting.

7 *Maintenance Section*

39532:68 List transmitting ;
39534:628 Correction list transmitting.

8 *Maintenance Section*

39532:68 List transmitting ;
39533:68 Checked list transmitting ;
39534:628 Correction list transmitting ;
39534:638 Checked correction list transmitting ;
39537:68 Bound volumes transmitting.

97 *Accounts Section*

39537:64 Bill passing.

993 *Correspondence Section*

39532:63 Slips transmitting ;
39534:623 Correction slips transmitting.

3956 Illustrative Time Scheme

Daily Jobs

The work with the bound volumes returned from binding will have to be done on a daily basis at the rate of a few volumes per day.

Monthly Jobs

The work before sending the volumes to the bindery is to be done once a month as follows :

The week preceding the Saturday preceding the last Tuesday	39532:62 Preparing;
Saturday preceding last Tuesday	39532:63 Slips transmitting;
Monday preceding last Tuesday	39532:64 List correcting;
Last Tuesday	39532:65 Volumes transmitting and 39532:68 List transmitting.

The jobs relating to correction are also to follow the same Time Scheme as those relating to the volumes for binding.

3957 Forms and Registers

S995 *Binding register*. Manuscript. 21 lb printing paper. White. Stitched. 20 lines. Entries relating to correction order are to be in red ink. The column headings are to be as follows :

Serial N (.5 cm) ; Date of order (1.5 cm) ; N of volumes (1.5 cm) ; Date of request for inspection (1.5 cm) ; Date of inspection (1.5 cm) ; Date of return (1.5 cm) ; N of defective volumes (1.5 cm) ; N of volumes accepted (1.5 cm) ; Date of completion of scrutiny (1.5 cm) ; Date of receipt of bill (1.5 cm) ; Date of passing of bill (1.5 cm) ; Date of transmission of bound volumes to the shelf section (1.5 cm).

3958 **Files**

Name	*Class number*	*Amplifying device*	*Filing characteristic*	*Year of transfer to record sequence after the file is closed*	*Year of destruction after transfer to the record sequence*
Standing vendor	9951	Nil	Correspondent	Year 1	Year 3
Binding order	9952	Number of the month	Nil	Do	Do
Correction order	9954	Do	Nil	Do	Do
Outward enquiries	99591	Nil	Correspondent	Do	Do
Inward enquiries	99592	Nil	Do	Do	Do

3959 Specification for Reinforced Library Binding

1 *Collation.* All books received by the contractor are to be examined and collated and any found to be imperfect or seriously damaged are to be returned unbound to the librarian. Torn leaves and plates are to be neatly repaired.

11 A periodical shall not be held to have been collated properly nor to be perfect, unless all the parts of a volume are bound in correct sequence of pagination and the usual title and contents pages and indexes are inserted in the proper places. Unless each imperfect and damaged book is reported upon to the librarian and unless the librarian has instructed the contractor to proceed with the work on such books, the bill will not be paid for any such books bound or repaired.

12 Wrappers and advertisements in periodicals and books are to be bound in, if the contractor is instructed to do so ; otherwise, they are not to be bound in.

2 *Sewing.* Books printed on paper of good quality are to be sewn one sheet on (except where thinness of paper makes it necessary to sew two sheets on) with unbleached thread of suitable thickness over unbleached linen tapes. Books printed in soft, spongy or brittle paper are to have the sections lined at inner and outer folds with strips of thin but tough paper before they are sewn. All sections broken at the back are to be lined with tough paper or linen strips, and where necessary neatly overcast on modern methods of cross stitching before being sewn to the tapes. The first and last sections of all books are to be enclosed at back in linen strips. All separate leaves, plates, maps, plans, etc are to be mounted on guards of linen or tough thin paper and to be sewn in. Pasting on is not to be permitted. Double plates are to be guarded at the fold. No charge is to be made for the first dozen plates so guarded in each book. For books up to post octavo ($6\frac{1}{4}'' \times 3\frac{7}{8}''$) three tapes, one-quarter inch in width, are to be used. For books of crown octavo ($7\frac{1}{2}'' \times 5''$) four tapes, one-quarter inch in width, are to be used. For books of larger sizes the number of tapes and their width is to be increased in proportion. Two of the tapes are to be placed within one inch of the head and tail of each book.

21 Straight-line machine stitching will not be accepted.

22 Books printed on calendared or heavily loaded art paper are to be reported to the librarian and a quotation sent to him for

lining each leaf of such books with a linen hinge on a throw-up guard.

23 All folded maps and illustrations are to be mounted on jaconet or thin linen of good quality and to be charged for separately.

3 *End-papers.* End-papers are to be of good tough opaque paper of approved mild colour, with at least one plain white leaf between each of them and the printed matter. The end-papers are to be made with strong linen of cloth joints and to be sewn on as a section.

4 *Cutting edges.* Unless otherwise instructed the contractor is to cut edges of books accurately and to take care to leave margins as wide as possible. Unless other instructions are given, the edges are to be sprinkled or tinted with a colour harmonising with the colour of the materials used for covering.

5 *Forwarding.* Unless otherwise directed, all books should have French joints and tight or close flexible backs with the covering material attached directly to the back. Tapes are to be firmly inserted between split boards. Books bound in quarter leather or in cloth or in buckram are to have the boards slightly rounded at corners and the covering material is to be neatly folded and not mitred.

51 Leather is not to be unduly pared down or unduly stretched in covering. The covering material of back is to extend over boards to at least one-sixth of the width of the book. All books should open up freely and lie flat.

6 *Lettering.* Lettering is to be impressed in best gold directly on to the material which covers the book. The lettering is to be of good size and easily readable ; small lettering will not be accepted except on very thin books. No extra charge will be allowed up to and including fifty letters or/and figures.

7 *Sizes.* The size of a book is to be determined by the measurement of the board, the square of which must not exceed one-eighth of an inch in books up to crown octavo, and proportionately for larger sizes. Extra charges for thickness is to be allowed only when the thickness of the volume exceeds one half the width of its boards. No extra charge is to be made for two or more volumes bound in one, unless the thickness of such a volume exceeds one half the width of the boards. In submitting the bills for work done, the measurement of the board should be given in inches in addition to the conventional mode of specifying the size.

81 *Alternative suggestions.* When the preceding instructions are

obviously inapplicable to any book or for any reason undesirable, the contractor is to submit suggestions for binding such a book with estimate of cost.

82 *General.* The whole of the work in binding is to be carried out with due regard to the fact that the books will be subjected to hard wear and tear and that the binding is to be permanent. Special instructions, if any, given with reference to particular volumes sent for binding should be faithfully carried out.

91 Materials

911 *Thread.* To be of best unbleached linen of suitable thickness.

912 *Tapes.* To be of best unbleached linen, of close strong texture and of the specified width.

913 *Glue.* To be best quality flexible glue mixed with copper sulphate to keep off insects.

914 *Boards.* To be good quality mill boards.

915 *Leathers.* The contractor must guarantee and produce, when required, the guarantee of the firm supplying the leather, that all skins used:

1 have been tanned in sumach or oak bark or similar vegetable stuff or a mixture of them ;
2 are free from sulphuric or other deleterious acids ;
3 have been dyed with colours that are fast with respect to light as well as moisture ; and
4 are genuine as described.

916 *Buckram.* To be linen buckram of best quality.

917 *Cloth.* To be good quality art canvas or imperial morocco cloth of fast colour and finish.

918 *Gold.* To be best English gold.

92 *Sizes and styles.* All combinations of the following :

921 *Style.*

9211 Half morocco and calico.
9212 Half morocco and marble.
9213 Half calico and marble.
9214 Full buckram.
9215 Half buckram and calico.

9216 Half buckram and marble.
922 *Size.*
9221 Pott.
9222 Foolscap.
9223 Post.
9224 Crown.
9225 Demy.
9226 Medium.
9227 Royal.
9228 Imperial.
923 *Folds.*
9231 Broadside.
9232 Folio.
9233 Quarto.
9234 Octavo.
9235 Duodecimo.
924 *Number of pages.*
9241 Pamphlets, i e volumes having 100 pages or less.
9242 Volumes having more than 100 pages.
92421 For first 500 pages.
92422 For every additional 500 pages or part thereof.

The following table of sizes in inches of printing paper may be of use. The pages of cut books will be a little smaller than the sizes given below. *

Size	*Broadside*	*Folio*	*4to*	*8vo*	*16mo*
Pott	15½ × 12½	12½ × 7¾	7¾ × 6¼	6¼ × 4	4 × 3
Foolscap	17 × 13½	13½ × 8½	8½ × 6¾	6¾ × 4¼	4½ × 3⅛
Post	20 × 16	16 × 10	10 × 8	8 × 5	5 × 4
Crown	20 × 15	15 × 10	10 × 7½	7½ × 5	5 × 3¾
Demy	22½ × 17½	17½ × 11¼	11¼ × 8¾	8¾ × 5⅝	5½ × 4¼
Medium	24 × 19	19 × 12	12 × 9½	9½ × 6	6 × 4¾
Royal	25 × 20	20 × 12½	12½ × 10	10 × 6¼	6¼ × 5
Double Pott	25 × 15½	15½ × 12½	12½ × 7¾	7¾ × 6¼	6¼ × 4
Double Foolscap	27 × 17	17 × 13½	13½ × 8½	8½ × 6¾	6¾ × 4¾
Super Royal	27½ × 20½	20½ × 13¾	13¾ × 10¼	10¼ × 7	7 × 5
Double Crown	30 × 20	20 × 15	15 × 10	10 × 7½	7½ × 5
Imperial	30 × 22	22 × 15	15 × 11	11 × 7½	7½ × 5½
Double Post	32 × 20	20 × 16	16 × 10	10 × 8	8 × 5

* Cockerell (Douglas) : *Some notes on book binding*. 1929. p 91.

CHAPTER 396

BUILDING AND EQUIPMENT SECTION

3961 Planning

39611 EXCLUDED FIELD

It is not the aim of this chapter to deal with the design of library buildings or library furniture—to discuss for example the location of the library building ; the number, the shape, the size, the location and the orientation of the different rooms of the library ; the number, the size, the treatment and the distribution of the doors and the windows ; the nature and the shape of the roof ; the ventilation, the lighting arrangement and the air conditioning of the building ; the counter fittings ; the stack room furniture, the reading room furniture and the office furniture. Such details would form the subject-matter of a book on library architecture ; they may also find a place in a book on library organisation. Some of the basic principles that should be borne in mind in dealing with such matters have been developed in my *Five laws of library science.*[53] Specifications and drawings are given in my book *Library building, fittings and furniture.*[54] The problem of insurance will also come only in the book on library organisation.

3962 The Four Enemies

In this chapter, we are concerned only with the daily routine connected with the ordinary upkeep of the library building and its furniture, as distinct from the design and engineering aspects of construction and repair. It is usual to speak of the four enemies of libraries, viz Fire, Water, Vermin and Humans.

39621 THE HUMAN ENEMY

Of these, precautions will have to be taken by almost every Section of the library against the unscrupulous humans who descend to the level of book-thieves and book-vandals.

Reference has already been made of the special responsibility in this matter, both of the Reference Section and of the Circulation Section. While they will have to deal with the book-thieves and book-vandals, who gain admission into the library in the garb of polite readers, it is the duty of the Building Section to guard the library against the onslaught of the burglarious variety of the human enemies of libraries. The routine described later on for the closing and the opening of the library deals with this matter.

39622 The Vermin

With regard to the vermin, it is the Maintenance Section that will have to guard against the ravages of the members of the natural group " insecta". But it is the business of the Building Section to guard the library from the mischief of the rodents, the rats, the bats, the bandicoots, the squirrels, and so on. The action to be taken by this Section with regard to this matter is given in the routine describing the closing and the opening of the library.

39623 Water

The damage due to water may be of two kinds. The damage that the water in the atmosphere does is very subtle. It is particularly so, if the humidity of the atmosphere is very high. The harm done by humidity can be easily seen on the covers of books during the monsoon season. While it is the duty of the Maintenance Section to clean books individually and scrub away the fungus growth, the Building Section should minimise the humidity of the air in the stack room by taking some precautions, such as placing buckets of coal in different parts of the room or by taking such other remedial steps as may be prescribed. Further, in places of high humidity, wooden shelves should be preferred to steel shelves, both on account of the immediate injury due to sweating and on account of the ultimate injury due to rusting, that is sure to develop in the long run, whatever be the extraordinary claims made by the makers regarding the anti-corrosive treatment given to their so called " stainless steel". A more direct form of injury that water can do to a library occurs during the monsoon season, when roofs begin to leak. In places which are accustomed to have torrential rains for some days in the year, it is highly desirable that the roof should not be of the flat type. On the other hand, the traditional gable roof, so common in such areas, will be more dependable. However, this is not a matter which concerns the Building Section, unless the library's advice had been taken at the time of the construction of the library building. All that we are concerned with here, is, what action the Building Section should take when there is actual leakage. In co-operation with the Maintenance Section, it must remove all the books of the library from the spot where there is leakage. Books which have been wetted inadvertently should be promptly dried. For this purpose, it would be a wise plan to have a drying verandah in that part of the library building which is inaccessible to the readers. Having attended to the immediate needs in this way, the Building Section should notify the Central Executive about the leakages and request them to make the necessary repair promptly.

39624 Fire

Lastly, we come to the first mentioned enemy of the library, viz fire. The following gives a description of the steps that the Building Section should take as a precaution against fire.

39625 Precautions Against Fire

1 Before the library closes for the night, the Head of the Section is to go round the library and see that no naked lights are in use and that there is no accumulation of waste paper, rags, etc in any Section ; if there is any, it should be removed to the waste paper room.

2 No lamps or candles are to be used without glass shades.

3 For sealing purposes, the services of only the muchi should be utilised. A covered-in lamp is to be used for melting wax. Otherwise, a match should not be struck in the office, except for the purpose of lighting a lamp as in sub-paragraph 2 above. The splinter is to be completely put out before being thrown away.

4 All waste paper, rags, etc should be daily collected and deposited in the rubbish bin that is kept outside the library.

5 For use in times of emergency, the library is to have a sufficient number of fire extinguishers and fire buckets, and they are to be distributed over the various parts of the library. The fire buckets are to be filled up with sand or dry earth. In case the insurance company insists upon the buckets being filled up with water, water should be replenished at least once in a week. It would be convenient to have a time scheme by which a definite number of buckets are replenished with water each day of the week, in such a way

that all the buckets get their turn once in every week.

39626 Outbreak of Fire

1 Immediately on an outbreak of fire, alarm should at once be given by telephone to the fire brigade. For the purpose of calling up the fire brigade, quote the prescribed number printed on the outer sheet of the *Telephone directory* or in some other place. Mention the location of the library as clearly and definitely as possible. If the librarian is not present on the spot, send word to him.

2 Pending the arrival of the fire engines, every endeavour should be made to confine the fire, by using the extinguisher and the sand in the buckets to the best advantage by the members of the office. As draughts of fire will tend to increase the fire, all doors and windows, which it is not necessary to use for ingress or egress, should be closed ; and, beginning as near the seat of fire as possible, all inflammable materials should be collected and removed to a place of safety as rapidly as possible.

3 Fire caused by ignited oil should be at once smothered by means of the sand in the buckets kept for the purpose. All movements should be carried out with the greatest possible silence and rapidity and special care must be taken not to crowd the passages or staircases.

39627 Fire Drill

It will be a good practice to have a fire drill once in a month. Each member should be allotted a specific duty and place. As soon as the alarm signal is given, the members of the staff should expeditiously rush to their allotted posts and begin their respective duties, subject to such special instructions as may be given by the librarian or, in his absence, by his deputy.

3963 Routine

The routine of the Building Section has to be of a daily nature. It may be as follows :

39631 Opening Routine

Before opening the main gate, go round the building and see if there is anything abnormal. Ask the nightwatch about his observations in the night. Check his work. See if the lock of the main gate is intact and untampered with. Then, examine if the doors and the windows are in the proper bolted position. Then, ask the peon to open them and report to you anything abnormal that he might notice. Ask him to report also all cases of broken panels, broken bolts, hooks, etc. Then, walk through the different parts of the buildings in accordance with a systematic plan, examining if there is any defect anywhere in the electric installation. Examine also if there is evidence of damage done by rats, bats, squirrels and other similar creatures. Examine also if there is any sign of white ants anywhere. If there had been rain on the preceding day, examine if there are signs of leakage anywhere. Examine if the counter wicket gates are in a sound condition and if they work properly. Examine if all the electric switches are in good working condition. As you go round, if any defects are observed, make an accurate note of the same in your diary. Soon after this process is over, take the necessary action about each of the defects noticed. If anything serious is noticed, send word to the librarian immediately. Fill up the columns relating to opening in the diary of the section. Wind up the clocks and the time pieces on the due days and set them right whenever necessary. See if the sweepers and cleaners do their routine.

39632 Closing Routine

Examine if there is no person in any room or part of the building before it is closed. Ask a peon to go round and close and fix the bolts of all the doors and windows in a systematic manner. Inspect each of the doors and windows and examine if they have been securely bolted. Examine if any inflammable material is lying about loosely anywhere and if it does, have it removed. Put the bait in the rat traps and distribute the traps in the parts of the library, which are known to be frequented by rats. Rats are cunning creatures. It is our experience that we have to change the bait from time to time and also change the places where the traps are placed from time to time. In spite of all the ingenuity that man is capable of, the rodents are uncanny enough to thwart all his efforts, evade his traps and take its toll from some other part of the library. If the building could be designed rat-proof, a good deal of this bother will be avoided.

Take the diary of the section with you and turn the fans and lights off individually after satisfying yourself that nobody is left behind in any part of the library. Then, turn off the sub-main switches. Then, turn off the main switch. Then, ask the peon to lock the main door securely. Pull it and see if it is properly locked. Ask the night watchman also to satisfy himself that it is properly locked. Then, seal it up. Then, enter the columns relating to closing, in the section's diary. Send the key and the diary to the person who is to have custody of the same during the night.

39633 FURNITURE ROUTINE

The ordering and repair of furniture should be done as far as possible as an annual job. The routine set forth in the next chapter for the ordering of stores is to be followed for furniture also, so far as it may be applicable.

3964 Elimination of Waste

The Closing and Opening Diary is to be on a daily basis in the form of a quarto note-book—as it has to be carried out of the building every day—with the following column headings, each column being 4 inch in width :

Morning

Date ;
Is the lock in the main gate intact ;
Hour of opening ;
Opened by peon ;
Supervised by clerk ;
Is the main off ;
Is the safe intact ;
Are the bolts and doors intact ;
Any of the readers' property left such as cycle, umbrella, pen, book, sticks, etc ;
Are the sub-mains off ;
Bulbs blind ;
Electric lines out of order ;
Fans out of order ;
Rats caught ;
Places damaged by rats ;

Places damaged by rain ;
Disinfectant used ;
Abnormalities reported to librarian, if any ;
Remarks.

Night

Is a rat trap placed in the affected places ;
Rat bait ;
Are all doors bolted ;
Any readers' property left such as cycle, umbrella, pen, books, sticks, etc ;
Are all lights and fans off ;
Is the sub-main off ;
Is the main off ;
Is the main gate closed ;
By whom closed (*peon*) ;
By whom checked (*peon*) ;
By whom supervised (*clerk*) ;
Hours of closing ;
Abnormalities, if any, reported to librarian ;
Remarks.

3967 Registers

The Building and Equipment Section will have to maintain a stock register for the furniture of the library. It is desirable that the register is kept in two note books.

The first note book may contain the class number, description, cost and location of each piece of furniture. This may be called the *Furniture Register*.

The second note book may give a separate page for each one of the rooms of the library building and give in that page a list of the furniture in that room in the order of their class numbers. This may be called the *Furniture Location Register*.

3968 Files

Apart from the enquiry files, which should be treated in the usual way, the distinctive files of the section are to be numbered 996. The parts of the buildings or the furniture dealt with are to be used as the filing characteristic.

CHAPTER 397

STORES SECTION

3971 Planning

39711 SCOPE OF THE SECTION

The Stores Section is to be in charge of stationery, forms and registers, and stray articles other than furniture, required for the use of the library. Of these, stationery, forms, and registers would figure most in a library. Stray articles may include among other things electric bulbs, other lighting equigments, match box, spare parts and implements relating to cycles, typewriting machines, wicket gate fittings, etc.

39712 PURCHASE OF STORES

Except in the case of purchases to be made occasionally out of petty cash, it is not desirable for the library to go in for large purchases directly. It is much better to save time and energy by leaving such large purchases to the Central Executive. The business of the Stores Section should merely be that of preparing the indent for such articles, sending the indent to the Central Executive and taking charge of the articles when they arrive.

39713 ISSUE OF STORES

The issue of the articles, is to be regulated and controlled by a combined Stock and Issue Register. In the case of each article, the following "constants" are to be fixed from experience and suitably changed at intervals in the light of further experience :

1 Maximum to which the stock should be brought up periodically—say, once in a year, the period being determined for each article ;
2 The Minimum below which the stock should not go, ie when the stock reaches that figure, steps should be taken for replenishment ;
3 The Annual Consumption ;
4 The Quantum of Issue.

39714 Determination of Quantum

It will add to convenience and economy of time, if articles are issued only in a definite number of Quanta. The Quantum for each article is to be determined according to its nature ; for example, catalogue cards are to be issued only in Quanta of 100. The Indenting Section should ask only for 100 cards or multiples of 100 cards. It should not ask for fractions of a Quantum. The Quantum for writing paper may be 25 sheets ; and so on.

39715 Stock and Issue Register

In the light of these figures and in the light of the frequency of issue, each article is to be given a certain number of pages in the Stock and Issue Register so that the pages allotted to all the articles are finished off, more or less at the same time.

39716 Time Scheme for Issue Stores

Apart from this standardisation of the Quantum of issue, it is desirable that the issue is controlled and standardised from the point of view of time also. It is slovenly and annoying for a Section to ask for supply of stationery and forms at all odd hours, or just at the moment when the stock has been fully exhausted. On the other hand, it will add to the convenience of all concerned, if the indents are made and the articles are issued by the Stores Section on a definite periodical basis.

In the Madras University Library, this is done once in a week as per the following programme :

1 The Stores Section distributes the indent forms to the different Sections at 11 A M on Saturdays.
2 The Stores Section collects the indents from the different Sections between 12 30 and 1 P M on the same day.
3 The Stores Section distributes the supply to the different Sections between 2 and 3 P M on the succeeding day.

The Sections are expected to anticipate the week's requirements and prepare their indents as closely as possible to the actual need. Over-indenting is to be avoided as carefully as under-indenting.

39717 Housing of the Stores

Another important factor in the organisation of the work of the

Stores Section relates to the storing of the articles. In the case of forms and registers, receptacles of suitable size and shape are necessary. The forms and registers are to be arranged strictly in the sequence of their Numbers as shown in the schedule given hereunder. Similarly, the stationery and other articles also should be arranged in some conventional sequence in receptacles of proper shape and size. The Store Room should be kept scrupulously clean and tidy. If the Quantum Principle of distribution is adopted, and if the articles themselves are packed in Quanta, the tidiness of the storing arrangement will be easily secured. Further, the Quarterly Verification of the Stock will be greatly facilitated.

397171 Schedule of Forms and Registers

Number	*Name*	*Printed or otherwise*
	Abnormally small size	
A61	Readers' ticket	Printed
A62	Book card	Manuscript
A63	Book pocket	
	Card size	
C12	Book selection card	Printed
C23	Book-order follow-up card	Printed
C24	Standing order card	Manuscript
C32	Renewal order card	Printed
C331	Register card	Printed
C332	Check card	Printed
C334	Classified index card	Printed
C34	Binding peculiarities slip	Manuscript
C361	T C I Reminder card	Printed
C362	Non-supply card	Printed
C363	Gap-in-supply card	Printed
C4	Accession register (C12 in cabinet)	Printed
C47	Acknowledgment card	Printed

Number	Name	Printed or otherwise
C51	Catalogue card (White)	Ruled
C52	Cross reference card (Coloured)	Ruled
C53	Guide card	Tabbed
C612	Bespeaking card	Printed
C614	Overdue notice card	Printed
C62	Application card	Printed
C64	Lost ticket observation slip	Stencilled
C67	Dues demand card	Printed
C68	Home delivery advice slip	Printed
C7	Reference slip	Manuscript
C8	Shelf register card	Printed
C98	Issue form	Stencilled
C993	Card letter head	Printed
C9938	Small envelope	Printed
C995	Binding slip	Manuscript
C9971	Indent slip	Stencilled
C9973	Monthly supplies indent slip	Stencilled
C9975	Indent consolidating form	Stencilled
	Octavo size	
O61	Date label	Printed
O651	Mofussil loan forwarding slip	Printed
O655	Mofussil loan return address slip	Printed
	Quarto size	
Q12	Book selection consultation letter form	Stencilled
Q22	Book enquiry form	Stencilled
Q231	Order form to local vendors	Stencilled
Q232	Order form to outside inland vendors	Stencilled
Q235	Order form to standing vendors	Stencilled
Q32	Standing order form	Stencilled

Number	Name	Printed or otherwise
Q61	Deposit receipt book	Printed
Q64	Overdue register	Printed
Q66	Miscellaneous receipt book	Printed
Q94	Staff order book	Stitched
Q974	Miscellaneous receipt forwarding form	Stencilled
Q9771	Direct payment requisition form	Stencilled
Q9772	Draft requisition form	Stencilled
Q97723	Draft forwarding form	Printed
Q97725	Acknowledgments forwarding form	Stencilled
Q9774	Cash forwarding form	Printed
Q9775	Foreign money order advice form	Printed
Q9777	Foreign acknowledgment reminding form	Stencilled
Q978	Replacement requisition form	Stencilled
Q993	Quarto letter head	Printed
Q9937	Quarto endorsement form	Printed
Q9938	Medium envelope	Printed
	Super size	
S13	Indent noting form	Stencilled
S31	Indent forwarding docket form	Stencilled
S51	Catalogue pad	Ruled
S61	Gate register	Printed
S91	Minutes book	Ruled
S921	Cadre register	Manuscript
S922	Service register	Printed
S923	Leave register	Manuscript
S93	Minutes book	Ruled
S94	Attendance register	Printed
S96	Investment register	Manuscript
S972	Pay bill	Printed

Number	Name	Printed or otherwise
S973	Increment certificate	Printed
S974	Absentee statement	Printed
S975	Acquittance roll	Printed
S9771	Bills register	Printed
S9772	Miscellaneous account register	Printed
S9773	Deposit account book	Printed
S9774	Contingent register	Printed
S9778	Permanent advance account book	Printed
S993	Folio letter head	Printed
S99311	Inward correspondence register (General)	Printed
S99312	Indents register	Printed
S99316	Inward correspondence register (Counter)	Printed
S99321	No reply despatch register	Printed
S99322	Short range despatch register	Printed
S99323	Long range despatch register	Printed
S9936	Stamp account register	Printed
S9937	Folio endorsement form	Printed
S9938	Big envelope	Printed
S994	Printing register	Manuscript
S995	Binding register	Manuscript
S996	Opening and closing register	Manuscript
S997	Stock and issue register	Printed

397172 Schedule of Stationery

Straw board.
Packing paper (60 lb)
Brown cartridge paper (46 lb)
Bristol boards, 4 sheets thick
Ledger paper 68.5×43 cm (for printing)
Paper (white) 21 lb 60.5×43 cm (for printing)
Paper (white) 16 lb 68.5×43 cm
Section paper
Manifolding paper

Carbon paper
Impression paper
Stencil paper
Drying book
Blotting paper
Flat file boards
Hinged file boards
Bound file books
Black ink
Red ink
Rubber stamp ink
Stamping pad
Stencil (Alphabet and Arabic numerals)
Ruler
Paper weights
Drawing pin
Tape tag
Pin
Gem clip
Paper clip (steel)
Twine
Thread
Gum bottle
Sealing wax
Sponge
Dater
Calling bell
Typewriter
Pencil (black lead)
Pencil (blue lead)
Pencil (red lead)
Pencil (phono) required for writing call numbers also
Penholder
Nibs
Ink bottle
Ink stand
Eraser
Eraser, ink (black)
Eraser, ink (red)
Stencil ink
Punch plier
Needle
Inch tape
Foot-rule
Knife
Scissors
Paper cutter
Dhungry cloth
Umbrella
Wheat flour
Copper sulphate
Phenyle
Soap
Match box
Lantern
Kerosene oil
Typewriter ribbon
Typewriter eraser
Typewriter oil
Benzine oil
Typewriter metal polish
Typewriter brush
Long cloth
Duplicating machine
Duplicator ink
Duplicator obliterine
Roneo pen
Stencil plate
Candle stand
Candle
Electric bulb
Lamp black
Cycle, with its tools
Rubber solution
Cycle oil
Valve tube

Pump connection
Metal polish
Grease
Polishing wax
Sand paper
Tonk's shelf plates and other similar fittings
Nail puller
Hammer and other tools

39718 Factors in Planning

The work of the Stores Section is to be planned with reference to the following factors :

2 Supplies ;
4 Forms and registers ;
6 Distribution ; and
8 Storing.

It is desirable that the requirements for a year are carefully anticipated and that supplies are acquired once in a year. It is pestering to send indents in driblets on all odd occasions. On the other hand, the distribution of supplies to the staff is best done on a weekly basis. It is not desirable to inconvenience the Sections by giving more than what is necessary for a week and asking them to form a subsidiary store ; nor is it desirable to make them indent for articles too frequently. It would be convenient for all concerned if the whole work of weekly distribution is done at a definite time on a definite day in the week.

3972 Job Analysis

39722 Supplies

The work of the Stores Section relating to supplies is to consist of the following items :

1 *Indent Work* ;
2 *Acquisition Work* ; and
3 *Receiving Work.*

39722:1 *Indents Work*

39722:1:5 The indents work of the Stores Section is to consist of the following weekly job :

1 Getting the sanction of the librarian for the purchase of petty articles such as soap, kerosene oil, flour and so on, which may be referred to as *Petty Articles Requisitioning*.

99722:1:8 The indents work of the Stores Section is to consist of the following annual jobs :

1 Preparing a tabular statement of the annual consumption of the different articles for the three preceding years, which may be referred to as *Consumption Rate Estimating* ;
2 Asking the different sections of the library to state if their requirements for the ensuing year is likely to be very different from the average consumption and if so, in what way and by how much, which may be referred to as *Section Notifying* ;
3 Making a rough draft of the quantity required, which may be referred to as *Preliminary Drafting* ;
4 Discussing the preliminary draft with the librarian, which may be referred to as *Consulting* ; and
6 Making the final draft of the indent in the light of the discussion with the librarian, which may be referred to as *Indent Drafting*.

39722:2 *Acquisition Work*

39722:2:5 The acquisition work of the Stores Section is to consist of the following weekly job :

1 In the case of petty articles to be purchased out of petty cash, making the necessary purchases, which may be referred to as *Petty Articles Purchasing*.

39722:2:8 The acquisition work of the Stores Section is to consist of the following annual job :

1 Transmitting the final indent to the Central Executive, which may be referred to as *Indent Transmitting*.

39722:3 *Receiving Work*

The receiving work is similar both in the case of the general annual indents and the weekly indents for petty articles. Hence, in what follows, it is described merely as an annual job.

39722:3:8 The receiving work of the Stores Section is to consist of the following annual jobs :

1 Calling for bills in case they are not sent in by the suppliers (including the Central Executive), which may be referred to as *Bills Calling* ;
2 Verifying if the claim in the bills is in accordance with the accepted quotation, which may be referred to as *Cost Verifying*;
3 Certifying the bills and passing them for payment, which may be referred to as *Bills Certifying* ;
4 Revising the certified bills to detect mistakes, if any, which may be referred to as *Bills Revising* ;
5 Grouping together such of the verified bills as relate to the same supplier, which may be referred to as *Grouping by Suppliers* ;
7 Transmitting the verified bills to the Accounts Section, which may be referred to as *Passed Bills Transmitting* ; and
8 On the return of the bills from the Accounts Section, after being passed by the librarian, noting down the voucher number in the stock and issue register, which may be referred to as *Voucher Number Noting.*

39724 FORMS AND REGISTERS

The work relating to forms and registers is best done on an annual basis, i e it is desirable that the forms and registers are printed all at one time. If, in spite of all possible precautions, the stock on hand of any particular form or register gets depleted, it will have to be printed in the middle of the year, as a casual job. The routine relating to such casual jobs is similar to the routine for annual printing. Hence, the jobs relating to forms and registers are described here as annual jobs.

39724:8 The work of the Stores Section relating to forms and registers is to consist of the following annual jobs :

1 Preparing a tabular statement of the annual consumption of the different forms and registers for the three preceding years, which may be referred to as *Consumption Rate Estimating* ;
2 Asking the different sections of the library to state if their

requirements for the ensuing year are likely to be very different from the average consumption and if so, in what way and by how much, which may be referred to as *Section Notifying* ;

3 Making a rough draft of the quantity required, which may be referred to as *Preliminary Drafting* ;

4 Discussing the preliminary draft with the librarian, which may be referred to as *Consulting* ;

6 Making the final draft of the indent in the light of the discussion with the librarian, which may be referred to as *Indent Drafting*;

7 Finding out from the different sections if the design of any form requires alteration, which may be referred to as *Form Design Consulting* ; and

8 Requesting the printing section to get the approved forms and registers printed, which may be referred to as *Printing Section Requesting*.

39726 DISTRIBUTION

39726:5 The work of the Stores Section relating to distribution is to consist of the following weekly jobs :

11 Distributing the indent forms to the different sections, which may be referred to as *Indent Form Distributing* ;

12 Collecting the indents from the different sections, which may be referred to as *Indents Collecting* ;

13 Adding the regular monthly supplies indent, whenever necessary, which may be referred to as *Monthly Supplies Indenting* ;

14 Obtaining the sanction of the librarian for the indents, which may be referred to as *Sanction Obtaining* ;

15 Consolidating the sanctioned indents, which may be referred to as *Indents Consolidating* ;

21 Entering the issues in the stock and issue register, which may be referred to as *Issue Entering* ;

22 Collecting the stores in accordance with the consolidated indent, which may be referred to as *Stores Collecting* ;

31 Distributing the articles to the sections in accordance with the sanctioned indents, which may be referred to as *Stores Distributing* ;

32 Verifying if the initials of the heads of sections or of the

concerned members of the staff have been received in the stock and issue register, which may be referred to as *Acknowledgment Verifying* ;

4 Indenting for fresh supplies in the case of such articles of the stock as have gone below the minimum prescribed, which may be referred to as *Casual Indenting* ; and

8 Filing the indents after the distribution of the stores, which may be referred to as *Distributed Indents Filing.*

39728 STORING

39728:7 The work of the Stores Section relating to storing is to consist of the following quarterly jobs :

1 Verifying the arithmetical accuracy of the entries in the stock and issue register, which may be referred to as *Stock and Issue Register Verifying* ;

2 Tidying up the articles in the store, which may be referred to as *Stores Tidying Up* ;

31 Verifying the stock in the stores, which may be referred to as *Stock Verifying* ; and

32 Sending the stock and issue register to the librarian for review, which may be referred to as *Stores Reviewing.*

39728:8 The work of the Stores Section relating to storing is to consist of the following annual job :

1 Verifying the stock of the stores of the library at the appointed time each year, which may be referred to as *Annual Stock Verifying.*

3973 **Routine**

39732 SUPPLIES

39732:1 *Indents Work*

39732:1:5 *Weekly job*

39732:1:51 PETTY ARTICLES REQUISITIONING

As has already been stated in the introduction to this chapter, it is desirable that very few articles are left over for casual purchase. Whenever the need arises for such casual purchase, prepare a requisition stating the time and quantity of last purchase, the quantity on hand, the quantity required and the estimated cost. Get the sanction of the librarian.

39732:1:8 *Annual jobs*

39732:1:81 CONSUMPTION RATE ESTIMATING

In the appointed month each year, make a tabular statement of the Annual Consumption of the different articles, excluding forms and registers, for the three preceding years. It may be an advantage to have three copies of this statement prepared.

39732:1:82 SECTION NOTIFYING

Circulate the tabular statement of annual consumption to the different Sections, along with the tabular statement of the Annual Consumption of forms and registers. Request the sections to intimate to you before a specified date any remarks that they would like to make on the quantity of materials that should be indented for use in the ensuing year.

39732:1:83 PRELIMINARY DRAFTING

In the appointed month, as soon as the remarks of the different sections are received, make a rough draft of the Annual Indent. In preparing the draft, it may be remembered that both over-indenting and under-indenting should be avoided. There should be only one indent for the whole year. At the same time, it is not proper to evade careful thinking and estimating by asking for more quantity than would be actually necessary. Remember also to include in the indent any new article that is likely to be required in the course of the year and to exclude from the indent, articles usually included in the Annual Indent but not required for the ensuing year. It is desirable that an estimate of the cost of the indent is made at this stage so that the indent may be adjusted to be within the budget allotment.

39732:1:84 CONSULTING

Discuss the preliminary draft of the indent with the librarian along with the remarks received from the different sections. Take down notes of the directions that might be given by the librarian.

39732:1:86 Indent Drafting

After consulting the librarian, prepare the final draft of the Annual Indent in the light of the discussion and get his approval. Then, get the indent faircopied by the Correspondence Section.

39732:2 *Acquisition Work*

39732:2:5 *Weekly job*

39732:2:51 Petty Articles Purchasing

For the petty articles for the purchase of which the sanction of the librarian has been received in the week, get the amount required from the Finance Section and make the purchase at the cheapest possible rate consistent with quality. Ask the peon sent for the purchase to get a cash bill for the purchases made. Quotations are to be obtained, wherever necessary.

39732:2:8 *Annual job*

39732:2:81 Indent Transmitting

Scrutinise carefully the faircopy of the indent. Write a letter of transmission to the Central Executive and pass it on with the faircopied indent to the librarian and the Correspondence Section in the usual way, for transmission to the Central Executive.

39732:3 *Receiving Work*

39732:3:8 *Annual jobs*

39732:3:81 Bills Calling

If the supplier has not sent the Bill along with the supply, call for the Bill. Even if the supply is made by the Central Executive, request the Central Executive to send the Bill so that the necessary book adjustments may be made in proper time.

39732:3:82 Cost Verifying

When the Bills arrive, verify if the claim in the Bills is in accordance with the accepted rate. If there is any discrepancy, investigate the matter and set it right.

39732:3:83 Bills Certifying

Examine if the quantity and quality mentioned in the Bills is in accordance with the supply. Enter the quantity in the Stock and Issue Register and write the usual Certificate in the Bill about the correctness of the supply and its inclusion in the Stock and Issue Register.

39732:3:84 Bills Revising

Take the Certified Bills and peruse them carefully to see if there is any mistake by oversight or any mistake in totalling. If there is any mistake, get it rectified.

39732:3:85 Grouping by Suppliers

Group together such of the Verified Bills as belong to the same supplier. Different Bills in the same group are to be arranged among themselves by the date of order.

39732:3:87 Passed Bills Transmitting

As soon as the preceding routine is over, transmit the Bills to the Accounts Section for further action.

39732:3:88 Voucher Number Noting

As soon as the bills come back from the Accounts Section after being passed by the librarian, note down the Voucher Number against each item in the Stock and Issue Register. This is very important, as this is the only means by which Double Payment can be avoided.

39734 Forms and Registers

39734:8 *Annual jobs*

The routine of all the annual jobs relating to Forms and Registers is similar to the corresponding annual jobs relating to " 39732:1 Indents Work " except for the following :

39734:87 Form Design Consulting

Whenever a form has to be printed, it should be carefully considered in consultation with the Sections concerned, whether the design of the form requires any alteration in the light of past experience.

In this connection, a reference may be made to Chapter 17. If any change of design is suggested, it must be discussed with the librarian and the form should be altered in accordance with his directions.

39734:88 Printing Section Requesting

After the alterations in design are decided upon, and the quantity of forms required is ascertained, and as soon as the annual supply of stationery is received, request the Printing Section to get the necessary forms printed.

39736 Distribution

39736:5 *Weekly jobs*

39736:511 Indent Form Distributing

At the appointed hour, on the appointed day of the week, give each Section an Indent Form and tell them that the Indent for the week's supply should be ready at a specified hour. The Section should also be reminded that the Indent should be carefully prepared so as to cover exactly the requirements for the week and that the articles required should be entered strictly in the sequence of the numbers assigned to them. Further the indent for any article should be only in the form of an integral multiple of the Quantum of Issue fixed for the article.

39736:512 Indents Collecting

At the appointed hour on the same day, collect from the different Sections their respective Indents. Examine if each Indent has got the several columns duly filled up and if it is in accordance with the Sanctioned Schedule, if any.

39736:513 Monthly Supplies Indenting

In the case of regular monthly supplies to the different members of the staff, prepare the Indent yourself.

39736:514 Sanction Obtaining

Arrange the different Indents in the sequence of section numbers. Place the Monthly Supplies Indent and the Indent for Readers' Tickets at the very end. Send the whole lot to the librarian for his sanction.

39736:515 Indents Consolidating

As soon as the Indents come back with the librarian's sanction, consolidate all the Indents in the *Indents Consolidating Form* and send the same to the librarian for his review. The articles are to be entered in this form strictly in the sequence of the numbers assigned to them.

39736:521 Issue Entering

As soon as the Consolidated Indent comes back from the librarian, enter the issues to the different Sections of the different articles in the appropriate pages of the Stock and Issue Register. When entering the same, remember that the Balance on hand of each article should be carefully calculated and entered in the appropriate column of the register.

39736:522 Stores Collecting

After the Issue Entering is over, proceed to the Stores Room with the consolidated indent. Collect the stores required in accordance with the Consolidated Indents. Assemble the collected stores and tick off the items in the Consolidated Indent, verifying if the quantity is alright.

39736:531 Stores Distributing

Then, distribute the articles to the different Sections in accordance with their Sanctioned Indents. As soon as an article is given to a person, get his initials in the appropriate column in the page of the Stock and Issue Register devoted to the article. Request the person to verify, if the figure in the Balance Column is accurate, i e ask him to see if there is any arithmetical error in calculating the Balance.

39736:532 Acknowledgments Verifying

As soon as the Distribution of the Stores is over, examine each of the pages and see if the initials of the persons concerned have been received in token of their having received the articles of supply and verified the correctness of the Balance in the Stock and Issue Register.

39736:54 Casual Indenting

While verifying the acknowledgments, the Head of the Section should also examine, if the quantity on hand of any article has gone below the minimum prescribed. If so, he should take action to get a fresh supply of the article.

39736:58 Distributed Indents Filing

As the last job of distribution, file the Sanctioned Indents and the related Consolidated Indent in the proper chronological sequence in the *Sanctioned Indents File.*

39738 Storing

39738:7 *Quarterly jobs*

39738:71 Stock and Issue Register Verifying

At the appointed time of each quarter, verify the arithmetical accuracy of the entries in the Stock and Issue Register.

39738:72 Stores Tidying Up

Once in a quarter, scrutinise the condition of the Store Room and tidy up the stores so that they lie in a trim and well packed condition in their respective receptacles.

39738:731 Stock Verifying

While tidying up the stores, it may be a good plan to Verify the Stock and enter the Quarterly Certificate of Stock Verification.

39738:732 Stores Reviewing

As the last of the quarterly jobs relating to storing, take the Stock and Issue Register to the librarian for review. He may test-audit the register and also verify some of the stock at random. Then, he will put his dated initials against the different items.

39738:8 *Annual job*

39738:81 Annual Stock Verifying

It will be a good plan to have the entire stores carefully checked once in a year before the year's supply is received. The process of Annual Verification of Stock is similar to the quarterly jobs described above.

3974 Elimination of Waste

The Head of the Stores Section should see that slovenliness of every nature is avoided both in dealing with the stores and in entering the Stock and Issue Register. Receptacles for the different articles should be properly designed so that each receptacle takes a definite number of Quanta of the articles. If it is so designed, it will be easier to ensure tidiness. The Head of the Section should personally see about the accuracy of the figures entered in the Stock and Issue Register. He should also personally prepare the Annual Indent.

3975 Correlation

From the nature of the case, it is obvious that this section will have to do with every other Section of the library, directly, every week, in distributing the stores. At the time of preparing the indent, it should discuss with the Heads of the different Sections, in the most cordial terms possible, their annual requirements and get out of them their best possible help so that the Annual Indent may be as close as possible to the actual needs.

3976 Illustrative Time Scheme

Weekly Jobs

Saturday

39736:511 Indent form distributing (11 A M) ;
39736:512 Indents collecting (1 P M) ;
39736:513 Monthly supplies indenting (1 P M) ;
39736:514 Sanction obtaining (1 30 P M) ;
39736:515 Indents consolidating (2 30 P M) ;
39736:521 Issue entering (3 30 P M).

Sunday

39736:522 Stores collecting (1 P M) ;
39736:531 Stores distributing (2 P M) ;
39736:532 Acknowledgments verifying (3 30 P M) ;
39736:54 Casual indenting (4 P M) ;
39736:58 Distributed indents filing (5 P M).

Quarterly Jobs

The quarterly jobs relating to the storing are to be done in the first week of each quarter.

Annual Jobs

April

39732:1 Annual jobs of indents work ;
39732:1:81 Indent transmitting ;
39734 All the annual jobs of the work relating to Forms and Registers.

June

39738:81 Annual stock verifying.

July

39732:3 All the jobs of receiving work.

3977 Forms and Registers

C9971 *Indent slip*. Stencil. Ledger paper. White.

The column headings are to be as follows :

Article (7.5 cm); Quantity on hand (1.5 cm); Quantity required (1.5 cm) ; Remarks.

The text above the column headings is to be :

Number and name of the section ; initial of the head of the section ; date ; L's sanction and initials.

C9972 *Monthly supplies indent slip*. Stencil. Ledger paper. White.

The row headings are to be :

Month ;

Article ;

Successive names of persons or sections ;

Total ;

L's sanction and initials.

C9975 *Indent consolidating form*. Stencil. Ledger paper. White.

The column headings are to be as follows :

Number of form or article (2.5 cm) ; The numbers of each of the different indenting sections, and lastly, total (1.5 cm for each of these columns).

S997 *Stock and issue register.* Printed. 10 point type. 21 lb printing paper. Bound book. 30 lines.

The column headings are to be as follows :

Date (2.5 cm) ; From whom received or to whom issued (5 cm) ; Receipts (2.5 cm); Issue (2.5 cm); Balance (2.5 cm); Initials of receiver (1.5 cm) ; Remarks.

3978 Files

Name	*Class number*	*Amplifying device*	*Filing characteristic*	*Year of transfer to record sequence after the file is closed*	*Year of destruction after transfer to the record sequence*
Indent	9972	Last digit of the year to which the indent relates	Correspondent	Year 1	Year 3
Forms	9974	N of the form	Do	Do	Do
Distribution	9976	N of the article	Do	Do	Do
Sanctioned indents	9977			Year 1	Year 1
Stock verification	9978	Last digit of the year to which the verification refers	Correspondent	Do	Do
Outward correspondence	99791	Nil	Do	Do	Do
Inward correspondence	99792	Nil	Do	Do	Do

CHAPTER 398

STATISTICAL SECTION

3981 Function of Statistics

In all spheres of human activity, statistics have been recognised as a fundamental instrument in planning and control. Intensive statistical surveillance is a recognised method of providing an adequate check on current performance and a basis for long range planning. The business of the Statistical Section is to supply the administration with basic information, to keep it posted on current developments and to collate data for periodical review of its operations.

3982 Statistical Sources

The material required by the Statistical Section is obtained from the diaries of the different Sections of the library. The proper use of statistics demands an intimate knowledge of how the figures are arrived at. Hence, the Statistical Section should discuss the headings of the diaries with the Head of the Section concerned and get them suitably formulated and amended whenever necessary, so as to provide for the collection of useful and productive data by the sections.

3983 Statistical Abstracts

The monthly and the annual abstracts and totals of the diaries of the different Sections are to be made and maintained by the Statistical Section.

3984 Statistical Presentation

When the data are all in hand, the subsequent processes include editing and tabulating. Editing consists in reviewing the figures which will be used in tabulation and translating and presenting them into such terms as will be useful in further study.

3985 Correlation Study

The planning of the tables includes the provision for finding the correlations between the various items in the diaries.

3986 Statistical Inference

Lastly, come, the analysis of the data and the drawing of inferences for the improvement of administration. The statistical assistant should extract from the tables such inferences as will, when related to one another, throw light on the progress of the work in the library, indicate what sections are functioning satisfactorily, what leakages are taking place, and what economy may be effected, without impairing efficiency. He should bring to the notice of the librarian the long-period changes and the short-term fluctuations.

3987 Statistical Diagram

The representation of statistics in diagrammatic form is a proper method of recording the fluctuating facts. They indicate clearly and concisely the results obtained. The Publicity Section may use them merely as pictures and illustrations. But, the Statistical Section should so devise the graphs and diagrams as to make clear the truth and meaning underlying the tabulated data extracted from the diaries of the Sections and to lay bare the tendencies and changes.[55]

3988 Librametry

Though library statistics have been collected for years, statistical methods have not yet come to be applied in libraries to the extent that is possible. From the little experience we had gained in the Madras University Library, it can be stated that there is much scope for scientifically handling the vast amount of crude data that are being built up from day to day by every library. The study of these crude data by the approved methods of statistical analysis will eliminate the play of vague feelings and preconceived notions, and reduce the chances for unreliable conclusions. It will bring to the surface and reveal tendencies and factors, which lie hidden at great depths behind the crude data. It will furnish correct, quantitative, reliable conclusions and, what is more helpful, a measure of their reliability. A specimen of such a statistical examination of a library problem is the *Colon* v. *Decimal Classification ; A statistical study of their notation.*[56]

In my address to the Aslib Conference at Leamington Spa in

September 1948, I coined the term "Librametry" to denote the statistical study of Library Science and Service. It is described in my *Five laws of library science.*[57] Librametry is yet a young discipline. Its development and application will increase the efficiency of library administration.

EPILOGUE

It is only within limits that such detailed instructions and technique can be of use. They are not intended to be literally followed by all and at all times.

Such detailed instructions and technique are certainly necessary for the beginner ; and they will continue to be helpful until he gets into the full swing of enthusiasm for his work. But the moment he feels the thrill of delight and his whole personality gets merged in the work and begins to express itself in it—rules and methods are not for him. He will then have transcended them all ; and yet his work will be far better than that of the routine worker who blindly, though faithfully, follows all the rules.

Adapted from Vatsyayana

शास्त्राणां विषयस्तावद्यावन्मन्दरसा नराः ।

[रसास्वादे] प्रवृत्ते तु नैव शास्त्रं न च क्रमः ॥

वात्स्यायनः

BIBLIOGRAPHY

Note : 1 The reference after the serial number is to the number of the section in this book, where the reference occurs.

2 The following contractions are used :

C C	Ranganathan (S R). *Colon classification.* Ed 5. V 1, Basic classification. 1957. (Madras Library Association, publication series, 22.)
C C C	Ranganathan (S R). *Classified catalogue code with additional rules for dictionary catalogue.* Ed 4. 1958. (Madras Library Association, publication series, 24.)
Five Laws	Ranganathan (S R). *Five laws of library science.* Ed 2. 1957. (Madras Library Association, publication series, 23.)

1. Sec 012. *Five Laws.* Chap 7.
2. Sec 022. Ranganathan (S R). *Library man-power analysis* (0). (Abgila).
3. Sec 022. Ramabhadran (S). *Library man-power analysis* (Abgila and Annals).
4. Sec 07. CC. Chap 6 of the Rules.
5. Sec 08. Aurobindo. *Mother.* 1928.
6. Sec 111. Ranganathan (S R). *Prolegomena to library classification.* Ed 2. 1957. Chap 13 to 18. Sec 221, 231. Chap 24 to 28. Sec 621, 631, 662, 678.
7. Sec 1143. Headicar (B M). *Manual of library organisation.* (Library Association series of library manuals, 7). 1935. 9.
8. Sec 115. *Five Laws.* Chap 7.
9. Sec 1234. CC. Rule 6503.
10. Sec 1362. CCC. Rule 0713.
11. Sec 138. *Five Laws.* Sec 68.
12. Sec 14411. Dawe (Grosvenor). *Melvil Dewey etc.* 1932. 183.
13. Sec 145. *Bulletin of the Taylor Society.* 1924. 203.
14. Sec 146. Whitehead (Alfred North). *Adventures of ideas.* 1933. 102.
15. Sec 1463. Jacks (L P). *Revolt against mechanism.* (Hibbert lectures, 1933.) 1934. 75 to 76.
16. Sec 1531. *Five Laws.* Sec 754.
17. Sec 155. *Five Laws.* Sec 756.

18. Sec 155. Maeterlinck (Maurice). *Life of the bee* ; tr by Alfred Sutro. 1927. Chap 3. Sec 54.
19. Sec 1815. McCord (James N). *Text book of filing*. 1929. VII.
20. Sec 211. Ranganathan (S R). *Library book selection*. 1952 (Indian Library Association, English series, 5).
21. Sec 211. *Five Laws*. Book selection and Second Law, Sec 461 to 464. Book selection and Third Law, Sec 58. Book selection and Fourth Law, Sec 684
22. Sec 2233:2:55. CCC. Rule and its subdivisions.
23. Sec 231. CCC. Rule 1332.
24. Sec 2434:4. CCC. Rule 1334.
25. Sec 2513. CCC. Rule 0706.
26. Sec 2531:1:55. CCC. Rule 1534.
27. Sec 2531:2:51. CC. Rules 683 to 692.
28. Sec 2531:2:51. CC. Rule 034.
29. Sec 2532:2:53. CCC. Rule 1535.
30. Sec 2532:2:54. CCC. Rule 516.
31. Sec 2537:1:51. CCC. Chap 06.
32. Sec 261. *Five Laws*. Issue methods and Fourth Law, Sec 67. Issue methods and Fifth Law, Sec 74 to 742.
33. Sec 2614. *Five Laws*. Sec 174.
34. Sec 2635. *Five Laws*. Sec 444 and 827.
35. Sec 2635. *Five Laws*. Denmark 3441. Germany 3513.
36. Sec 269. *Five Laws*. Sec 48 to 4871 and 7451.
37. Sec 2712. Wyer (James I). *Reference work*. 1930. 3.
38. Sec 2713. *Five Laws*. Reference service and First Law, Sec 172 to 18. Reference service and Third Law, Sec 54 to 544. Reference service and Fourth Law, Sec 66 to 665.
39. Sec 2713 and 27131. Ranganathan (S R) and Sundaram (C). *Reference service and bibliography*. V I. 1940. (Madras Library Association, publication series, 9.) Parts 1 to 3.
40. Sec 2833:3:82. *Five Laws*. Sec 523.
41. Sec 2833:3:82. *Five Laws*.
42. Sec 2836:2:31. *Five Laws*. Sec 576.
43. Sec 3116. *Five Laws*. Sec 42 Headicar (B M). *Manual of library organisation*. 1935. (Library Association series of library manuals, 7).
44. Sec 331. *Five Laws*. Sec 754.

45. Sec 354. McColvin (Lionel R). *Library extension work and publicity*. 1927.
46. Sec 354. Cannon (C L). *Publicity for small libraries*. 1929. (American Library Association manual, 31).
47. Sec 354. *Five Laws*. Sec 56 to 578.
48. Sec 355. Ranganathan (S R). *Salesmanship in libraries*. (Modern librarian, 4, 1934, 97 to 101) ; and summary in (Library Association record, series 4, 1, 1934, 215).
49. Sec 355. Peterson (Milfred Othmer). *Library publicity methods*. (Proceedings of the Library Service Section of the First All Asian Educational Conference, 1930, ed by S R Ranganathan, 1930).
50. Sec 3941. *Five Laws*. Sec 722.
51. Sec 3941. CCC. Rule 0703.
52. Sec 39512. Cockerell (Douglas). *Some notes on book-binding*. 1929. Methews (William F). *Book binding*. 1929.
53. Sec 3961. *Five Laws*. Sec 16, 712 to 72.
54. Sec 3961. Ranganathan (S R), Sarma (R R), and Seshachalam (C). *Library building, fittings and furniture*. 1959.
55. Sec 3987. Karston (Karl G). *Charts and graphs*. 1925.
56. Sec 3988. Ranganathan (S R). *Colon vs Decimal Classification* : A statistical study of their notation. (South Indian teacher, 7, 1934, 588 to 592). Also in Ranganathan (S R). *Prolegomena to library classification*. Ed 2. 1957. Sec 567.
57. Sec 3988. *Five Laws*. Sec 86.

INDEX

Note : 1 The reference is to the number of the chapter or the section as the case may be.

2 A number with one or two colons is that of a section on Routine.

3 Reference is not given to sections on Job Analysis. It can be got by replacing in the number for the section on Routine, the digit 3 occurring as the third significant digit by the digit 2.

For example, the section number for "Abnormalities Intimating" is given as 3432:5:14 in the index. This is the number for the Routine of that Job. The section for Job Analysis of it is the number 3422:5:14.

Again, the section number for "Acquisition of Petty Articles" is 39732:2 in the index. This section describes the Routine of the Job. Its section in Job Analysis is 39722:2. The digit 9 is not significant, when it comes as the second digit in the number of a section.

Abnormal size collection 28132
Abnormalities intimating 3432:5:14
Absence intimating 3432:5:43
Absentee statement 3732:61
Accepted books arranging 2434:5:52
Accepting
  Correction volumes 2534:1:52
  Gift 2437:41
  Solicited gift 2238:52
Accession 2434
Accession cabinet 2434:6:594
Accession card
  and book selection card 2132:2:31
  Arranging 2434:5:55
    Book 2434:5:55
    For accessioning 2434:6:52
  Circulation 2434:6:593
    Correcting
      Binding 2835:2:64
    Correction work 2834:8:54
  Filing 2434:6:594
  Periodical publications 2334:4:56
  Specification 217
  Transmitting 2832:1:52
  Transmitting work 2537:3
  Voucher number posting 3737:43:55
Accession date noting 2434:5:592
Accession number noting
  Periodical publication 2334:4:58
  Technical section 2533:1:51
Accession number tallying 2537:1:53
Accession numbering
  Bills 2434:6:54
  Cards 2434:6:55
  Volumes 2434:6:56
Accession register
  Specification 247
  vs shelf register 2816
Accession section 24
Accessioning work 2434:6
Account closing
  Deposit 3735:57
  Miscellaneous receipt 3734:57
  Petty cash 3738:7:57
Account writing
  Deposit 3735:46
  Miscellaneous receipt 3734:47
  Petty cash 3738:7:56
Accounts
  and assistant librarian 3437
  Audit of 3717
Accounts section 37
Accuracy of work 137
  Circulation section 2614
Acknowledging
  Current issue 2334:6:58

Acknowledging—*contd*
  Donation 2437:43
Acknowledgment
  Arranging 2434:5:53
  Donation numbering 2434:6:57
  File 378
  Forwarding form 3737:5:51
  Specification 377
  Posting
    Deposit return 3735:575
    Miscellaneous receipt 3734:565
  Registering 3737:5:41
  Reminding
    Foreign cases 3737:5:65
    Indian cases 3737:5:62
  Temporary filing 3737:5:42
  Transmitting
    For gift books 2437:53
    For payments 3737:5:51
  Verifying 39736:532
  Work 3737:5
Acquiring work
  Petty articles 39732:2
  Sources 2131:2
Acquittance roll
  Completing 3732:78
  Specification 377
  Totalling 3731:82
  Writing 3732:72
Actuals ascertaining 2136:6:87
Ad hoc committee 15
Additional data collecting 3133:2:61
Address book 39332:32
Address rectifying 3432:5:63
Addressing of envelopes 39332:32
Adjustment, Mutual 14
Administration, Scientific 12
Administrative routine, Fascination of 2714
Admission
  Card cabinet 26311:12:52
  Preliminary to 26311:12:11
  Restriction 2631:1:11
  Scrutiny 26311:12:12
  Work 26311:12
Advertising 3231:2:31
Advice
  Date noting of payments 3737:1:52
  Disposing of book order 2233:4:58
  Seeking regarding book order 2233:4:55
  Work on special deposit 26324:8
Advising
  Allotment 2136:7:81
  Allotment balance 2136:7:78
  Circulation section 2831:5:56
  Direct payment 3737:31:51
  Draft payment 3737:35:561
  Foreign money order 3737:35:53
  Local payment 3737:32:51
  Loss of tickets 26311:14:43
  Maintenance section 26324:8:12
  Reference section 2837:37
Advisory committee, Local 3116
Age exemption obtaining 3232:1:36
Agenda
  Circulating 3133:1:66
  File of committee section 318
  File of staff council 338
  Final work 3133:2
  Preliminary work 3133:1
  Supplementing 3133:2:62
  Writing 3133:1:65
Allocating
  Book fund 3737:6:52
  By budget head 3737:6:51
Allocation work 3737:6
Allotment
  Advising 2136:7:81
  Balance advising 2136:7:78
  File 218
  Preliminary to 2136:6:88
  Sanctioning 2136:6:891
  Watching work 2136:7
  Work 2136:6
Allotted day of the week
  Periodicals 2334:3:46
  Vigilance day 2334:3:51
Alphabetised order cards box
  Order copy completing 2233:3:515
  Unscored cards sorting 2233:3:511

INDEX

Alphabetising
  Bills 2334:7:51
  Current periodicals 2334:3:43
  Order cards 2233:1:52
Alternative time tables 164
Amending attendance register 3432:5:62
Amendments
  Checking 2532:5:56
  Noting 2532:4:56
  Monthly statement 2536:52
Amplifying number 18224
Analysis
  Functional 13
  Job (Second part of each chapter)
  Revision of 126
Annual posting
  Financial diary 2334:2:896
  Scrutinising 3434:81
Annual report 3431
  Completing 3431:86
  Consulting 3431:85
  Data collecting 3431:83
  Drafting 3431:84
  File 348
  Forwarding 3431:87
  Review disposing 3431:88
  Skeleton framing 3431:82
Annual stock verifying 39738:81
Answering query 2631:1:18
Applicants notifying 3231:2:33
Application
  Card
    Filing 26311:12:52
    Specification 267
  Sorting 3231:2:32
Appointing
  Staff 3231:2:35
  Standing binder 39531:85
  Standing vendor for
    Books 2231:85
    Periodical publications 2331
Appointments, Cadre of 3231
Apprenticeship 3923
Aptitude, Individual 1427
Arrangement of records 383
Arranging
  Accepted books 2434:5:52
  Accession cards
    Accessioning work 2434:6:52
    Transmission work 2434:5:55
  Acknowledgments 2434:5:53
  Bills in
    Accession section 2434:5:51
    Accessioning work 2434:6:51
    Accounts section 3737:2:54
    Transmission work 2434:5:51
  Catalogue slips 2537:5:51
  Charged cards 2631:2:383
  Corrected cards 2834:8:57
  Correction collection 2834:1:41
  First impression slips 2534:3:53
  Gift books 2434:5:54
  Instalment books 2434:5:58
    Accession cards 2434:5:57
  Outward correspondence 39332:2
  Periodical publications 2434:5:58
    Accession cards 2434:5:57
  Prepared volumes 2533:8:52
  Replacing shelf 2732
  Shelf register cards
    Maintenance section 2832:3:517
    Technical section 2537:1:52
  Sources 2131:8
  Volumes received in
    Accession section 2434:6:53
    Circulation section 2831:1:42
    Work 2533:8
Arrear
  Indents 2136:6:822
  Listing 39331:6
Art of shelf arrangement 2811
Artificial composite book 2434:4
Ascertaining
  Actuals 2136:6:87
  Binding cost 2831:5:556
  Budget allotment 2136:6:86
  Data for lost books 2831:4:51
  Indents cost 2133:1:55
  New periodicals cost 2136:7:73
  Spent amount 2136:7:77
Assignment
  Adjusting 3432:2:34

Assignment—*contd*
  Consulting 3432:2:31
  Communicating 3432:2:32
  Reporting 3432:2:33
  Schedule file 348
  Work 3432:2
Assistant librarian 3412
  Counter-signature of 384
  File 328
Associations, Professional 3923
Attendance
  Late 166
    Explanation 3432:5:51
  Register 3432:5:12
    Amending 3432:5:62
    Completing 3432:5:42
    Scrutinising 3432:5:41
    Specification 347
    Writing 3432:5:61
Audit of accounts 3717

Back of main card writing 2532:2:54
Back volumes 2337
  File 238
Balance
  Petty cash · 3638:577
  Sheet 3731
    Data furnishing 3731:88
    File 378
    Reviewing 3731:91
Bay guide scrutinising 2833:5:81
Bespeaking 2631:3:34
Bespeaking card
  Box 2631:3:34
  Disposal work 263234:1
  Form 267
  File 268
  Forwarding 263234:1:43
  Picking 263234:1:41
  Receiving 2631:2:14
  Specification 267
  Temporary box 2631:2:14
  Tray 263234:1:41
Bespoken books 263234
  Collection work 263234:8
Bespoken books—*contd*
  Releasing 263234:8:41
  Transmitting 2835:8:626
Bespoken guide changing 263234:8:46
Best'day's work 125
Beware of influential clique 2113
Bibliographical service and shelf study 2738
Big envelope 3937
Billing borrowed book expenditure 26325:2:376
Bills 3737
  Accession numbering 2434:6:54
  Alphabetising 2334:7:51
    and cards transmitting 2233:7:54
    and receipts 393181
  Arranging by accession section
    Accessioning work 2434:6:51
    Transmission work 2434:5:51
  Arranging by accounts section 3737:2:54
  Arrear 3737:1:56
  Binding section 39537
  Calling by stores section 39732:3:81
  Certifying
    Accession section 2432:7:53
    Binding section 39537:64
    Maintenance section 2831:4:54
    Periodical publication section 2334:7:54
    Stores section 39732:3:83
  Classification 3734:2:54
  Distributing 3737:1:45
  in arrears listing 3737:1:56
  Not received group 2432:1:41
  on hand
    and indent checking 2133:1:51
    Checking with 2233:2:54
  Passing by
    Accession section 2432:7
    Accounts section 3737:2
    Binding section 39537:64
    Maintenance section 2831:4:54

Bills—*contd*
Passing by—*contd*
Periodical publication section 2334:7
Stores section 39732:3:83
Register 3737:1:43
Specification 377
Verifying 3737:44:55
Work 3737:1
Registering 3737:1:43
Revising work 3737:44
Revising by
Periodical publication section 2334:7:55
Stores section 39732:3:84
Tallied collection 2432:1:41
Tallying 2432:1:41
Verifying 2432:7:51
Without-supply file 248
Binding
and maintenance section 2835
and size 3959
and technical section 2635
and thickness 3959
Books transmitting 2535:65
Collection 281
Book cards tray 2433:8:56
Card reinserting 2835:8:68
Cost ascertaining 2831:5:556
List
Correcting 39532:64
Scrutinising 2835:8:61
Tallying work 2835:5
Transmitting 39532:68
Materials 3959
Nature of 3959
Order file 3958
Peculiarities
Drafting 2334:4:55
Slip 237
Register
Checking 3737:43:55
Specification 3957
Section 395
Slip 2434:4:53
Preparing 2535:62
Transmitting 39532:63

Binding—*contd*
Specification 3959
Style of 3959
Vital affair 39512
Volumes transmitting 2835:1
Black book 2734
Bond
Custody 9635:658
Form forwarding 26311:14:45
Receiving 26311:14:46
Book
Card 267
Disposing 2533:8:56
Inserting 2835:8:622
Removing 2835:1:53
Ticket 267
Specification 267
Verifying 2832:3:522
Carding
Circulation section 263231:5:34
Technical section 2533:1:56
Enquiry form 227
Fund allocation 3737:6:52
Markets 2211
Order
Final checking work 2233:2
Follow-up pad 2233:32:52
Follow-up work 2233:82
Section 22
Selection
Carding work 2132:2
Consultation
Letter form 217
Work 2132:5
Section 21
Supplement carding 2133:1:523
Supplemental process 2133:1:523
Urgent consulting 2132:5:45
Selection card
Card writing 2132:2:31
Classifying 2132:2:35
Completing 2132:2:37
Filing 2132:2:58
Forwarding 2132:5:51
Revising 2132:2:51

Book—*contd*
Selection card—*contd*
Specification 217
Suggestion noting 2131:2:12
Book selection work 2132:2
and finance 2136
Book supply
Conditions of 221
Receiving work 2233:7
Book to be borrowed, Locating 26325:1:31
Book-binding 3951
Books
From the co-operating libraries 26325
Gift 221
Instalment 221;41, (p 200)
Multivolumed 221
of the counter sequence 263233
on medical leave 281
on shelf, Checking with 2233:2:58
Ordered 2432
Ordinary 221; 233
Out of print 221
Series 221
Standing order 221
Subscription 221
Without
Bills 2432:4:51
File 248
Borrowed book
Collecting 26325:2:31
Expenditure billing 26325:2:376
Forwarding 26325:2:33
Notifying 26325:1:33
Returning work 26325:2
Borrowing
Expenditure noting 26325:1:37
Work 26325:1
Bottom cross reference 18
Bound volumes 39533
Tallying 2835:8:621
Transmitting 39537:68
Box
Alphabetised order cards
Order copy completing 2233:3:515
Box—*contd*
Alphabetised order cards—*contd*
Unsorted cards sorting 2233:3:511
Bespeaking cards 2631:3:34
Cancel listing
Renewal order listing 2334:2:81
Standing order cancelling 2334:2:88
Card checking
Checking with
Bills on hand 2233:2:54
Catalogue 2233:2:55
Exchange list 2233:2:5495
Outstanding orders 2233:2:523
Standing orders 2233:2:524
Order cards alphabetising 2233:1:52
Consolidation slips
Slips consolidating 2532:6:53
Slips picking 2532:6:52
Correction 2534:1:53
Correction slips 2534:3:51
Gift requisition 2233:3:5118
Investigation 2833:1:52
Observation slips 26311:14:44
Reference slips 27385:32
Shelf register cards 2832:3:517
Sorted cards
Accession number tallying 2537:1:53
Catalogue cards sorting 2537:1:51
Stamp 39332:76
Suspense 2432:1:41
Tallied card 2432:1:42
Transmission, Circulation Section
Bespeaking cards
Forwarding 263234:1:43
Picking 263234:1:41
Transmission, Technical section 2537:3:58
Unsorted cards
Catalogue cards sorting 2537:1:51

Box—*contd*
  Unsorted cards—*contd*
    Shelf register cards arranging 2537:1:52
  Unsorted slips 2532:6:56
  Unsupplied cards 2233:8:51
  Week's current
    Current issue
      Perusing 2334:3:456
      Registering 2334:3:44
    Rounding of work 2334:6
Budget 29631
  Amount 2136:6:86
  Ascertaining 2136:6:86
  Correspondence file 368
  Drafting 3631:1:86
  Drafting work 3631:1
  Figure communicating 3631:1:88
  File 368
  Head allocating 3737:6:51
  Preliminary consulting 3631:1:85
  Preliminary drafting 3631:1:83
Bureau of Standards, United States 14
Business, Preparation of 3133

Cabinet
  Admission card 26311:12:52
  Catalogue 2537
  Easing by
    Shelf section 2838:81
    Technical section 2537:4:81
  Reference 27385
  Shelf register 2838
  Specification 257
Cadre
  File 328
  Modifying work 3231:1
  Of appointments 3231
Cadre register 321
  Entering 3232:3:71
  Filling 3232:6:37
  For preparing pay bills 3732:62
  Modifying 3231:1:37
  Posting 3231:2:37
  Specification 327
Call number
  Checking 2531:8:51
  Correction
    Maintenance section 2834
    Technical section 2534
  Examining 2535:51
  Noting 2533:1:52
  Revising 2534:2:51
Call numbering
  Deferred volumes 2531:2:52
  Difficult volumes 2531:2:54
  Normal volumes 2531:2:51
  Work 2531:2
Calling for terms of supply 2231:81
Cancel listing box
  Renewal order listing 2334:2:81
  Standing order cancelling 2334:2:88
Cancelled
  Card marking 2334:2:883
  Order tray 2233:8:54
  Publication
    Check card 2334:3:467
    Definition 2334:3:44
    Registering 2334:3:447
  Stamp 26311:13:12
  Ticket remitting
    Change of ticket work 26311:13:57
    Withdrawal work 26311:3:57
  Tray 2334:2:88
Cancelling
  Order 2233:8:54
  Standing order 2334:2:88
  Ticket
    Change of ticket work 26311:13:12
    Withdrawal work 26311:3:532
Card
  Accession 2132:2:131
  Accession numbering 2434:6:55
  And bills transmitting 2233:7:54
  Book selection 2132:2:31
  Cancelling 2334:2:884
  Check 2315
  Checking box
    Final checking work 2233:2

Card—*contd*
Checking box—*contd*
Order card alphabetising 2233:1:52
Classified index 2316
Consolidation work 2532:3
Correcting by
Maintenance section 2834:2:51
Technical section 2534:4:51
Donation numbering 2434:6:58
Indent 2132:2:31
Inserting 2537:4:51
Inserting work 2537:4
Letter head, Specification 3937
Numbering work 2533:1
Order 2132:2:31
Rearranging
Binding correcting work 2835:2:68
Stack room rearranging work 2833:3:88
Reconciling 2832:1:51
Register 2314
Reinserting
Binding collection 2835:8:68
Topical collection 2836:8:38
Retransferring
Damaged volume 2831:5:58
Lost volume 2831:4:58
Shelf register, Specification 287
Standing order, Specification 227
Surviving
Checking with exchange list 2233:2:5495
Final checking work 2233:2
System of records 138
Tallied group 2432:1:42
Transferring
Correction collection 2834:1:42
Damaged volume 2831:5:48
Lost volume 2831:4:48
Recent additions collection 2832:5:58
Topical collection 2836:1:32
Worn-out volumes 2835:1:52
Carding
Book selection 2132:3

Carding—*contd*
Periodical publication 2334:2:53
Supplemental book selection 2133:1:523
Cash
Balance
Returning 3737:47:56
Verifying 3638:578
Forwarding form 3737:32:51
Specification 377
Receiving 3737:46:56
Work 3737:46
Casual and compensation leave 3234
Casual
Indenting 39736:54
Leave register 3234:44
Catalogue
and indent checking 2133:1:51
Cabinet 2537
Specification 257
Cards
Discussing 2537:2:51
Sorting 2537:1:51
Specification 257
Checking with 2233:2:55
Pad, Specification 257
Printed 394
Cataloguing 2532
Section *see* Technical section
Central executive notifying 3631:1:81
Certificates verifying 3737:44:53
Certified bills transmitting 2432:7:57
Certifying bills
Accession section 2432:7:53
Maintenance section 2831:4:54
Periodical publication section 2334:7:54
Stores section 39732:3:83
Change of ticket
Justification 26311:13:11
Work 26311:13
Changing
Bespoken guide 263234:8:46
Current date 2631:1:46
Due date 2631:2:46
Guide 2631:3:436

Changing—*contd*
  Card 2537:4:82
  Tray guide 2838:84
Chapters, Plan of the 063
Charged
  Cards arranging 2631:2:383
  Tickets filing 2631:3:431
  Tray
    Closing up 2631:3:31
    Work 2631:3
Charging 2631:2:133
  Preliminary to 2631:2:132
  Subsidiary routine 2631:2:133
Check card 2315
  Shifting 2334:3:46
  Specification 237
Checked correction list 39534:63 to 39534:68
Checked list of bound volumes 39533:68
Checking
  Amendments 2532:5:56
  Call number 2531:8:51
  Catalogue slips 2532:6:56
  Consolidated cards 2532:5:53
  Cross reference 2531:8:52
  Cumulative index 2334:5:51
  Donation card 2437:51
  Fresh cards 2532:5:52
  Indent 2133:1:51
  Issue tray 2833:1:51
  Miscellaneous receipt posting 3734:447
  New call number 2534:2:52
  New placings 2531:8:53
  Overdue books 3734:446
  Periodical publications 2334:2:51
  Preliminary book selection 2132:1:38
  Released volumes 2832:5:52
  Shelf 2833:1:52
  Shelf register card 2537:3:53
  With bills on hand 2233:2:54
  With books 2233:2:58
  With catalogue 2233:2:55
  With exchange list 2233:2:5495
Checking—*contd*
  With outstanding order tray 2233:2:523
  With standing order cards 2233:2:524
Checking indent 2133:1:51
  With bills on hand 2133:1:51
  With catalogue 2133:1:51
  With order tray 2133:1:51
  With series entry 2133:1:51
  With title entry 2133:1:51
  With translator, editor etc. 2133:1:51
Checking work
  Book order section 2233:2
  Maintenance section 2833:1
  Technical section
    Cataloguing 2532:5
    Classification 2531:8
Christian holidays 166
Cinderella 11
Circular draft letters
  Planning 393184
  Routine 393343
Circular letter copies forwarding 39343:5
Circulating
  Accession card 2434:6:593
  Agenda 3133:1:66
  Minutes 3135:1:63
  Staff order 3433:32
Circulation section 26
Civility, Lack of 3432:5:14
Claiming special deposit 26324:4:42
Class number for files 18
Classification 2531
  and cataloguing codes 2536
  Consulting 2531:2:53
  Of bills 3737:2:54
Classification section *see* Technical section
Classified
  Card tray 2334:2:51
  Index card 2316
    Specification 237
  Table of files 183
  Volumes sorting 2532:1:51

Classifying
  Book selection card 2132:2:35
  Inward correspondence 39331:2
  Reference guide 27385:35
Closed collection 28131
Closing
  and opening diary 3964
  Early 166
  Routine 39632
  Service register 3232:6:34
Closing up charged tray 2631:3:31
Coat of arms 3937
Code
  Classification and cataloguing 2536
  Correcting 2536:51
  Corrections transmitting 2536:63
  Public finance
    Account section 3711
    Finance section 3617
Collated volume transmitting 2434:5:595
Collating
  Bound volumes 39533:64
  Current issues of periodicals 2334:3:42
  Gift books 2434:4:58
  Ordered books 2434:4:52
  Periodical publications 2434:4:53
  Worn-out volumes 2835:1:44
  Work in accession section 2434:4
Collecting
  Additional data 3133:2:61
  Borrowed book 26325:2:31
  Deposit amount 3635:46
    Special 26324:4:44
  Interest on deposits 3635:661
  Loose issues of periodicals 2334:4:51
  Meeting papers 3133:1:61
  Miscellaneous receipts 3634:46
  Special deposit 26324:4:44
  Topical collection books 2836:1
Collection
  Bill tallied 2432:1:41
  Card tallied 2432:1:42
  Files 1828
Collection—*contd*
  List of 281
  Topical 2836
Colon notation 072
Colour
  Paper for forms 1735
  Top edge of cards 1735
Committee
  Ac hoc 1532
  Local advisory 3116
  Section 31
  Work and librarian 3911
Communicating
  Budget figure 3631:1:88
  Interview result 3231:2:34
  Leave order 3232:3:35
  Re-appropriation sanction 3631:5:68
  Retirement order 3232:6:32
Comparing
  Cut stencil 393343:2
  Extract 393341:2
  Faircopy 393342:2
Compensation leave 3234
Completed registers 381
Completing
  Acquittance roll 3732:78
  Annual report 3431:86
  Attendance register 3432:5:42
  Book selection card 2132:2:37
  Correction work 2534:4
  Faircopy of bill 24322:7:54
  Meeting papers 3133:1:63
  Order copy 2233:3:515
  Work of the periodical publication section 2334:4
    Cumulative index 2334:5:55 to 2334:5:58
    Current issues 2334:4
Complex letters 1898
Composite books, Artificial 2434:4
Composite letters
  Planning 393184
  Routine 393341
Conditions
  Of book supply 221
  Of interlibrary loan 26351

Conference, Professional 3923
Confirmation recommending 3232:1:31
Confirming
  Order 2233:8:52
  Work 3232:1
Conscience box
  Definition 2617
  Dues collection
    Forwarding 26311:4:46
    Receipting 26311:4:12
  Miscellaneous account 3734:47
  Overdue sheet 26311:12:54
  Overduing 2631:3:441
Consolidated
  Cards checking 2532:5:53
  Indent to stores section
    Filing 39736:58
    Issue entering 39736:521
    Stores collecting 39736:522
  Slips box
    Slips
      Consolidation 2532:6:53
      Picking 2532:6:52
Consolidating
  Catalogue
    Cards 2532:3:52
    Slips 2532:6:53
Consolidation
  Cards picking 2532:3:51
  Group 2532:1:51
  Slips picking 2532:6:52
Constants of stores 39713
Constitution file 318
Consultant file 268
Consultation
  Book selection letter 217
  Discharging 2631:2:131
  Work 2132:5
Consulting
  Annual report 3431:85
  Assignment of staff 3432:2:31
  Classification 2531:2:53
  Co-operating libraries 2334:1:83
  Correction list 39534:61
  Current list of periodicals 2334:1:85
Consulting—*contd*
  Distribution of staff 3432:1:31
  Finance diary 2233;3:56
  Indent 39732:1;84
  Intersectional 2233:3:55
  Preliminary budget 3631:1:85
  Refractory cases 2532:4:51
  Urgent book selection 2132:5:45
Consumption rate estimating 39732:1:81
Contingent
  Account totalling
    Annual job 3731:87
    Weekly job 3731:57
  Register
    Specification 377
    Writing 3737:2:57
Co-operating libraries 2635
  Books from 26325
  Consulting 2334:1:83
  Requisitioning from 26325:1:32
Co-operation, Interlibrary 3923
Co-operative library supplies 3942
Copying indent 2132:5:53
Copyright section 2414
Corrected cards
  Arranging 2834:8:57
  Reinserting 2834:8:58
  Sorting 2834:8:56
Corrected volumes
  Shelving 2834:2:53
  Tallying 39534:611
  Transmitting 2534:2:58
Correcting
  Accession card
    Binding work 2835:2:64
    Reinserting work 2834:8:58
  Binding list 39532:64
  Catalogue cards 2534:4:51
  Code 2536:51
  First impression slips 2534:3:52
  Language slips 2534:4:53
  Main card 2534:2:53
  Second impression slips 2534:4:52
  Shelf register card 2834:2:51
  Volumes 2834:2:52

INDEX

Correcting—*contd*
  Work
    Binding 2835:2
    Technical section 2834:2
Correction
  Box 2534:1:53
  Carrying out 2537:2:52
  Collection 28135
    Arranging 2834:1:41
    Card transferring 2834:1:42
    Transmitting 2834:1:43
  Completing work 2534:4
  Diary 2548
  In binding section 39534
  List
    Correcting 39534:64
    Transmitting 39534:68
  of call numbers 2834
  of catalogue entries 2534
  Order file 3958
  Slips
    Disposing 2334:3:48
    Group 2334:3:45
    Transmitting 39534:63
  Verifying 39534:62
  Volumes
    Accepting 2534:1:52
    Transmitting
      Binding section 39534:65
      Maintenance section 2834:1
Correlation *see* Section 5 of each chapter
Correspondence
  Circulation section 39311
  Follow-up work 1896
  Full route 18941
  Inward 393181
  Long range 393182
  No reply 393182
  Outward 393182
  Route 184
  Section 393
  Short range 393182
Cost
  Ascertaining for indents 2133:1:55
  Verifying for
    Periodicals 2334:7:53

Cost—*contd*
  Verifying for—*contd*
    Stores 39732:3:82
Counter
  Collection
    Book 263233
    Issuing from 263233:11
  Custody 2631:1:12
    Discharging 2631:2:17
  Equipment 2612
  Reconditioning work 263231:5
  Unclaimed property
    Forwarding 2631:4:47
    Work 2631:4
  Vigilance 2631:2:11
  Worn-out volumes work 263231:4
Counting
  Duplicate ticket issue 26311:14:18
  Issue 2631:2:38
  Sheet preparing 2631:2:481
  Technical section 2537:1:58
  Tickets renewal 26311:13:18
Coupled
  Bill 3737:2:54
  Book ticket 2631:2:133
  Cards transmitting 2537:3:58
Coupling shelf register card 2537:3:51
Creative
  Forces 1463
  Impulses 1261
  Thinking 124
Cross reference
  Bottom 1897
  Cards
    Specification 257
    Writing 2532:2:52
  Checking 2531:8:52
  For files 1897
  Top 1897
Cross referring
  Inward correspondence 39331:51
  Outward correspondence 39332:51
Cumulative
  Index
    Checking 2334:5:51

Cumulative—*contd*
Index—*contd*
Noting 2334:5:11
Order
Preparing 2334:5:522
Transmitting 2334:5:523
Work 2334:5
Total verifying 3737:7:61
Current
Collection, Definition of 1828
Date changing 2631:1:46
Issue of periodical
Acknowledging 2334:6:55
Alphabetising 2334:3:43
Check card shifting 2334:3:46
Collating 2334:3:42
Cutting and stamping 2334:3:45
Displaying 2334:8:42
Non-supply notifying 2334:6:51
Registering 2334:3:44
Rounding off work 2334:6
Weekly vigilance 2334:3:51
List
Consulting 2334:1:85
Forwarding 2334:1:87
Noting 2334:1:86
Preparing 2334:1:81
Reviewing 2334:1:82
Volumes 2334
Week's display table
Definition 2334:8:4
Guide strip changing 2334:8:25
New issues displaying 2334:8:42
Week's Disposal Pad 2233:82:52
Cut stencil
Comparing 393343:2
Filing 393343:6
Forwarding 393343:3
Cutting and stamping 2334:3:45
Cutting open 2533:2:51
Cycle—Vital (p 92)

Daily
Disbursing 3638:46
Vigilance 2334:3:4698
Damage due to water 39623
Damaged or lost books 26324
Damaged volume
Card retransferring 2831:5:58
Card transferring 2831:5:48
Forwarding 2831:5:551
Work 2831:5
Data
Ascertaining for lost volumes 2831:4:51
Collecting for annual report 3431:83
Furnishing for balance sheet 3731:88
Date Label
Numbering 2533:3:56
Specification 267
Labelling
By circulation section 263231:5:36
By technical section 2533:2:56
Verifying for binding bills 39537:62
Day's work, Best 125
Deciding financial position 2334:2:516
Decisions, Disposal of 3135
Defective
Group 2334:3:44
Publication
Check-card 2334:3:4695
Definition 2334:3:44
Registering 2334:3:494
Supply
Disposing 2432:4:54
Group 2434:4
Notifying 2334:6:54
Defects in binding 39532:62
Deferred
Cards tray 2133:3:58
Disposal files 18921
Disposal pad 1892
Circulation section 26311:3:41
Theory of correspondence
Arrangement 18921
Formation 1852
Order cards tray 2233:3:512
Volumes call numbering 2531:2:52

Delegation of functions 1151
Delivery book 3734:56
  Verifying 39332:431
Deposit
  Account
    Book 377
    Closing 3735:57
    File 378
    Totalling
      Annual job 3731:85
      Weekly job 3731:55
    Writing 3735:46
  Amount
    Collecting 3635:46
    Investing 3635:655
    Remitting 3635:53
  Forwarding 26311:12:46
  Receipt book, Specification 267
  Receipting 26311:12:131
  Refunding 26311:3:535
Description for forms 17
Design
  Form 1713
  Sheet 1712
Despatched faircopy tray 39332:31
  Despatched files
  Acknowledgment verifying
      39332:521
  Forwarding 39332:52
  Tray 39332:31
Despatching 39332:31
Destruction of records 385
Detected ticket reporting 2631:3:514
Detecting ticket 2631:3:414
  Preliminary to 26311:14:44
Detection of duplication of books
  Notifying 2531:4:14
  Work 2531:4
Deviation intimating 3432:6:36
Devices 2531:2:51
Dewey and standardisation 14411
Diary
  Abnormalities in 3434:42
  Correction 2548
  Finance 3746
  Scrutinising 3434:41
  Type of cards 2547
Difference in
  Edition 2233:8:52
  Price 2233:8:52
  Publisher 2233:8:52
Difficult volumes call numbering
    2531:2:54
Direct payment
  Advising 3737:31:51
  File 378
  Forwarding 3737:31:52
  Requisition form 3737:31:51
    Specification 377
  Work 3737:31
Disbursing
  Daily 3638:46
  V P 3638:11
  Weekly 3638:576
Discharging
  Consultation 2631:2:131
  Counter custody 2631:2:17
  Loan 2631:1:131
Discipline work 3432:5
Discrepancy group 2432:1:42
Discussing catalogue cards 2537:2:51
Displaying new issues 2334:8:42
Disposal
  Date 39331:6
  of decisions 3135
  of files, Deferred 18921
  of letters, Modes of 1891
  Pad 18931
    Deferred 1892
    Definition 1828
    Making up 185
  Work
    Bespeaking cards 263234:1
    Unsupplied books 2233:8
Disposing
  Advice of book order 2233:4:58
  Annual report review 3431:88
  Book card 2533:8:56
  Books without bills 2432:4:51
  Correction slip 2334:3:48
  Defective supply 2432:4:54
  Doubtful supply 2432:4:53
  Not due books 2432:4:55
  Rejected items 2133:3:58

Disposing—*contd*
Renewal request 2631:3:432
Slips showing defects in
Periodical publications 2334:6:593
Unsupplied bills 2432:4:52
Distinctive library functions 2
Defined 113
Distributed indents filing 39736:58
Distributing, Week's current box 2334:6:593
Distribution
Indent form for stores 39736
Files 3978
Staff 3432:1
Communicating 3432:1:32
Consulting 3432:1:31
Reporting 3432:1:33
Schedule 348
Docket
Label 1824
Sheet 1824
Docketing, Membership 26311:12:48
Donation
Acknowledging 2437:43
Card
Checking 2437:51
Writing 2437:42
Numbering
Accession card 2434:6:58
Acknowledgment 2434:6:57
Volumes 2434:6:59
Double payment
Accession section 3737:43:55
Periodical publication section 2334:7:58
Standing order for books 22244:7:58
Doubt clearing work 2233:4
Doubtful
Guide 2233:4:55
Supply
Disposing 2432:4:53
File 248
Doubtfuls 2734
Draft
Acknowledgments transmitting 3737:5:55
Advising 3737:35:561
Budget transmitting 3631:1:87
Forwarding form 3737:35:561
Specification 377
Minutes of the staff council 338
Pay bill transmitting 3732:62
Payment file 378
Requisition form 377
Requisitioning 3737:35:55
Drafting
Annual report 3431:84
Binding peculiarities 2334:4:55
Budget 3631:1:86
Letter 186
Drying verandah 39623
Dues
Collection forwarding 26311:4:46
Collection work 26311:4
Demand card specification 267
Fixing 26311:4:11
List preparing 26311:4:71
Receipting 26311:4:12
Reminding 26311:4:75
Duplicate
Copy of bill preparing 3737:2:52
Publication
Definition 2334:3:44
Registering 2334:3:446
Supply
Group 2334:3:446
Notifying 2334:6:56
Ticket issue counting 26311:14:18
Ticketing 26311:14:11
Duplicating 393343:4
Duplicator
Cleaning 393343:7
Trimming 39334:3
Duty
Librarian's
Practical 391
Theory of administration. 135
Staff 136

Earlier weeks' display table
Definition 2334:8
Removal to 2334:8:53
Earliest due week 2233:82:51
Early closing 166
Easing
Cabinet
Maintenance section 2838:81
Technical section 2537:4:81
Shelf 2833:3:81
Educational lecture collection 28137
Devices 2531:2:51
Enemies of libraries 3962
Endorsement
Form specification 3937
Obtaining 3234:41
English Act 3115
Enquirer file 268
Enquiries and quotations 2232
File 228
Enquiring or quotation calling 2232:51
Entering
Card re-register 3232:3:71
Casual leave register 3234:44
Entrance
Gate releasing 2631:1:15
Work 2631:1
Entries verifying in bills 3737:44:54
Enumeration of files 183
Envelopes, Addressing of 39332:32
Equipment
Order book 3737:43:55
Section 396
Equivalent
Finding 3737:35:51
Posting 3737:35:57
Errors in bills file 248
Essence of scientific administration 1252
Establishment *see* Staff section
Estimating
Arrear indents 2136:6:822
Consumption rate 39732:1:81
Indent 2133:1:56
Order cost 2233:3:512
Outstanding orders 2136:6:823
Estimating—*contd*
Payment out of permanent advance 3737:46:51
Periodical publication subscription 2136:6:83
Special deposit 26324:4:41
Standing orders 2136:6:824
Examining
Call number 2535:51
Wrapper by
Accession section 2432:1:11
Periodical publication section 2334:3:411
Exchange
List, Checking with 2233:2:5495
Section 2414 (p 202)
Expenditure
Noting
Borrowing 26325:1:37
Forwarding 26325:2:37
Watching work
Accounts section 3737:7
Finance section 3631:4
Expert opinion obtaining 2136:6:81
Explanation for late attendance
Forwarding 3432:5:52
Obtaining 3432:5:51
Transmitting 3432:5:53
Executive
Central 3631:1:81
Permanent 3114
Exit
Gate releasing 2631:2:15
Work 2631:2
Expiry of tickets reminding 26311:13:85
Extending, Loan period 26325:2:32
External correlation 151
Extract
Comparing 393341:2
Forwarding 393341:3
Extracting
From letters
Routine 393341:1
Theory 1898
From minutes 3135:2:61

INDEX

Factors of planning
  Theory 11
  See section 18 of each chapter
Faircopy
  Bill
    Completing 2432:7:54
    Stamping 3737:2:531
  Comparing 393342:2
  Forwarding 393342:3
  Tray 39332:31
Faircopying
  Planning 393184
  Routine 39334
  Simple draft letters 393342:1
False philosophy 1421
Fascination of
  Administration routine 2714
  Fuss 28145
Favourable omens 1463
Fifth law of library science and
  Correlation 155
  Delegation of functions 1151
  Issue methods 2614
File
  Mark 182
  Number 1822
Files
  Classified table 183
  Collection of
    Record section 383
    Theory 1828
  Enumeration 183
  Library profession 392
  Modes of disposal 1892
  Pad of 1827
  Transfer of 18
  Ultimate 1824
  Vertical 1811
  Work with 184 to 1898
  See section 8 of each chapter
Filing
  Accession cards 2434:6:594
  Acknowledgments 3737:5:42
  Application cards 26311:12:52
  Book selection cards 2132:2:58
  Characteristic 18
  Charged tickets 2631:3:431
Filing—*contd*
  Cut stencil 393243:6
  Gate register 2631:1:411
  Money order receipts 3737:47:538
  New York School 1815
  Order cards 2233:5:522
  Order copy 2233:6:52
  Overdue sheets 26311:12:54
  Permanent advance acknowledgments 3737:5:52
  Reference slips 2738:5:37
  Scored cards 2233:6:58
  Terms 18
  Unrecommended cards 2132:5:58
  Vocation 18
Final
  Agenda work 3133:2
  Checking
    Book order section 2233:2
    Periodical publication section 2334:2:51
  Full supply week 2233:82:51
  Scrutiny of book order 2233:5:521
Finance
  Book selection work 2136
  Diary
    Annual posting 2334:2:896
    Circulation section 264
    Consulting 2233:3:56
    Posting by
      Accounts section 3737:7:51
      Book order section 2233:6:56
      Periodical publication section
        Cumulative index 2334:5:526
        Ordering work 2334:2:56
    Renewing 3631:4:64
    Scrutinising
      Assistant librarian 3437:51
      Finance section 3631:4:61
    Subsidiary 3746
  File 238
  Section 36
Financial position
  Deciding 2334:2:516
  Reviewing 2334:1:84

Fire
  Buckets 39625
  Drill 39627
  Extinguishers 396
  Precaution 39625
First
  Arrival publication
    Check card 2334:3:464
    Definition 2334:3:44
    Registering 2334:3:444
  Law and issue method 2611
  Impression slips
    Arranging 2534:3:53
    Correcting 2534:3:52
    Picking 2534:3:51
    Reinserting 2534:5:52
    Work 2534:3
  Temporary charging tray 2631:2:133
Fixing loose sheets 2334:3:47
Folio
  Letter-head 3937
  Pagination 178
Follow-up work
  Book order 2233:82
  Correspondence 1896
Force 1421
  Opposing 111
Foreign
  Acknowledgments reminding 3737:5:69
    Form 377
  Books 221
  Money order advising 3737:35:53
    Form 377
  Money order writing 3737:35:52
  Payment work 3737:35
Formal library training classes 3923
Forms
  Description 17
  Design consulting 39734:87
  File 3978
  Unprinted 393184
  See section 7 of each chapter
Forms and registers 39734
  and printing section 394
  And stores section 397
Forms and registers—*contd*
  Routine 39734
  Schedule of 397171
  See section 7 of each chapter
Formula, Staff 1145
Forwarding
  Annual report 3431:87
  Bespeaking cards 263234:1:43
  Bond form 26311:14:45
  Book selection cards 2132:5:51
  Borrowed book 266325:2:33
  Circular draft letters 39343:5
  Counter unclaimed property 2631:4:47
  Current list 2334:1:87
  Cut stencil 393343:3
  Damaged volumes 2831:5:551
  Deposit amount 26311:12:46
  Despatched files 39332:52
  Direct payment 3737:31:52
  Draft 3737:35:563
  Dues collection 26311:4:46
  Expenditure noting 26325:2:37
  Explanation for late attendance 3432:5:52
  Extract 393341:3
  Faircopy 393342:3
  Fresh copy 26324:97:18
  Indent 2133:3:511
  Inward correspondence 39331:52
  Marked sources 2132:1:51
  Miscellaneous receipts 3734:56
  Money order 3737:47:531
  Outward correspondence
    Through messenger 39332:43
    To post office 39332:42
  Sanctioned indent 2133:3:52
  Sound volumes 263231:8:38
  Withdrawal files 26311:3:56
  Work of returned volumes 263231:8
  Worn-out volumes 263231:4:48
Four enemies of libraries 3962
Fourth law of library science and
  Card system of records 138
  Files 1812
  Issue method 2614

Fourth law of library science and
—*Contd*
Maintenance section 28137
Rearrangement of books 2833:3:82
Reference service 2713
Freedom 26113
Fresh
Cards
Checking 2532:5:52
Group 2532:1:51
Writing work 2532:2
Copy forwarding 26324:97:18
Men, Apprenticeship 3923
Slips typing 2532:6:51
Full
Job number 123
Route of correspondence 18941
Supply week 2233:82:51
Timed publicity officers 355
Function
Basis of chapter formation 063
Number
Defined 1239
Part of title number 1772
of the notation 071
Functional
Analysis 113
Inequality 116
Planning 112
Functions
Delegation of 1151
Distinctive library 1
Theory 113
General office 3
Theory 113
Library Committees 311
Furniture 39633
Location register 3967
Register 3967

Gap-in-supply
Card specification 237
Check card 2334:3:462
Definition 2334:3:44
Notifying 2334:6:53
Gap-in-supply—*contd*
Registering 2334:3:442
Gate register
Filing 2631:1:411
Putting up 2631:1:412
Renewal 2631:1:31
Scrutinising 2631:1:11
Specification 267
Timing 2631:126
General office functions 3
Theory 113
Gift
Books
Accepting 2437:41
Arranging 2434:5:54
Collating 2434:4:58
Factors in planning 2218
File 228
Routine 2238
Soliciting 2238:51
Unsolicited 2437
Cases picking 2233:3:5118
Publication
Acknowledging 2334:6:55
Check card 2334:3:465
Definition 2334:3:44
Registering 2334:3:445
Requisition box 2233:3:5118
Grace week 2334:3:51
Grade of paper performs 1731
Group
Bill not received 2432:1:41
Consolidation 2532:1:51
Correction slips 2334:3:45
Defective 2334:3:42
Supply 2434:4
Descripensive 2432:1:42
Duplicate supply 2334:3:446
Fresh cards 2532:1:51
Loose sheets 2334:3:45
Linguistic
Fresh cards 2532:1:51
Consolidation 2532:1:51
Normal 2334:3:45
Not due 2432:1:41
Refractory 2532:1:51
Registered 2334:3:44

Group—*contd*
  Sound 2334:3:42
  T C I 2334:3:443
    Waiting 2334:4:52
  Ultimate
    Order copy notes 2233:3:514
    Order writing 2233:5:51
    Unscored cards sorting 2233:3:511
Grouping
  by suppliers 39732:3:85
  by vendors 2334:7:56
  Reference slips 27385:32
Guide
  Cards
    Changing 2537:4:82
    Specification 57
  Changing 2631:3:436
  Doubtful 2233:4:55
  Overdue 2334:3:4698
  Plan scrutinising 2833:5:83
  Reference slips 27385:35
  Strip changing 2334:8:52
  Supplied 2334:3:46
  Tray for unused 2631:3:436
Guiding
  Reference slips 27385:33
  Topical collection 2836:2:34
  Work 2833:5

Hasten slowly 1342
Hindu holidays 166
Holidays 166
Home delivery slips 267
Hourly statistics diary 2648
How to revise 134
Human
  Enemies of libraries 39621
  Memorising 148
  Personality 142
Humanism 28135

I C B 39331:3
I C C 39331:3
I C G 39331:3
I C I 39331:3
I C P 39331:3
Idiosyncrasies of periodicals 24113
Illustrative time scheme *see* Section 6 of each chapter
Increment certificate 3732:61
  Specification 377
Incumbents 3232
Indent 2133
  as inward correspondence 393181
  Card 2132:2:31
  Checking 2133:1:51
  Collecting 39736:512
  Consolidating 39736:515
  Consolidating form 3977
  Copying 2132:5:53
  Distributing 39736:511
  Doubts clearing 2133:1:54
  Drafting 39732:1:86
  Estimating 2133:1:56
  File
    Book order section 218
    Pending 2233:1:51
    Periodical publication section 238
    Stores section 3978
  Forwarding 2133:2:511
    Docket form 237
  Noting 2133:3:51
    Form 217
  Passing work 2133:3
  Reader's ticket for 39736:514
  Register 3937
  Scrutinising work 2133:1
  Slips 3977
  Transmitting 39732:2:81
  Work of store section 39732:1
Index cards writing 2532:2:53
Indian
  Libraries, Ordering book slips 2211
  Publications 2212
India's special opportunity 1454
Individual attitude 1427
Ineligibles 2611
  File 268
Inequality, Functional 116
Influencial clique 2113

INDEX

Initiation of new readers 2733
Inland
  Acknowledgments reminding 3737:5:62
  Money order writing 3737:33:51
  Payment work 3737:33
Insects 39622
Inserting
  Book card
    Circulation section 2631:1;131
    Maintenance section 2835:8:622
    Technical section 2533:8:56
  Catalogue
    Cards 2537:4:51
    Slips 2537:5:52
  Shelf register cards 2838:58
  Work
    Catalogue cards 2537:4
    Catalogue slips 3537:5
Inside numbering 2533:3:52
Inspecting 3438:71
Inspection 3438
  Report file 348
  Reporting 3438:72
Instalment books
  Accession section 24113
  Book order section
    Factors in planning 2218
    Order file 228
    Routine 22343
    Standing order 22343
Instructing new recruits 3433:33
Insuring one's health 3917
Interest
  Collecting 3635:661
  Posting 3635:666
  Transmitting 3635:667
Interlanding
  Resources 3923
  Staff 3923
Interlibrary
  Borrowing file 268
  Co-operation 3923
  Loan
    And five laws 2635
    Conditions 26351
Internal correlation 151
Intersectional consulting 2233:3:55
Interview result communicating 3231:2:34
Inventory reporting 2833:1:54
Investigating
  Reference section 2837:31
  Undischarged card 2835:8:64
  Unfound volumes 2833:1:53
Investigation box 2833:1:52
Investment
  File 368
  Register
    Posting 3635:656
    Specification 367
  Sanction obtaining 3635:651
Inward correspondence
  Acknowledgment verifying 39331:521
  Arrear listing 39331:6
  Classifying 39331:2
  Cross referring 39331:51
  Factors in planning 393181
  Forwarding 39331:52
  General 393181
  Register
    Circulation section 3937
    General 3937
  Registering 39331:3
  Routine 39331
  Sorting 39331:1
Issue
  Box 384
  Counting 2631:2:38
  Diary 2645
  Form for records 384
  Section *see* Circulation section
  Stores 39736:521
  Totalling 2631:2:488
  Tray checking 2833:1:51
Issuing
  From counter collection 263233:11
  On loan 2631:2:16
  Records 38

Jacket numbering 2533:3:51

INDEX

Job
  Analysis
    Theory 12
    See Section 2 of each chapter
  Defined 1211
  Number 1238
    Form number 1773
Junction moment
  Assistant librarian 3435
  Reporting 3435:11
  Theory 163
Junior assistants file 328
Justification of change of ticket 26311:13:11

Kept tickets tray 2631:1:14
Knowledge, Orientation of 2514

L R D 39332:31
Language slips correcting 2534:4:53
Last week's display table 2334:8
Late attendance
  Explanation obtaining 3432:5:51
  Theory 166
  Watching 3432:5:12
Leave
  Account 3232:3:32
  Casual and compensation 3234
  Order communicating 3232:3:35
  Register 327
  Regular 3232:3
  Return from, Noting 3232:3:72
Leisure end of life 1463
Lending libraries file 268
Letter drafting 186
Letters
  Circular 393184
  Composing 393184
  Simple 3931814
Liaison work 391
Librarian 3917
  Duty 135
  File 328
Library
  Binding 3959

Library—*contd*
  Building 396
  Bureau 1441
  Committee *see* Committee section
  Committees of Local Bodies 311
  Equipment 396
  Establishment *see* Staff section
  Four enemies of 3962
  Furniture 39633
  Open access 26113
  Profession 392
  Publicity *see* Publicity section
  Roof of 396
  Rules 269
  Training classes 3923
Life of a form 1731
Lightning speed 2614
Linguistic
  Consolidation group 2532:1:51
  Fresh cards group 2532:1:51
List of collections 2814
Listing renewal order 2334:2:81
Lists 393184
Loan
  Issuing 2631:2:16
  Period extending 26325:2:32
Local
  Advisory Committee 3116
  Body Library Committee 3113
  Payment
    Advising 3737:32:51
    File 378
    Transmitting 3737:47:521
    Watching 3737:47:524
    Work 3737:32
  Variation 04
Locating book to be borrowed 26325:1:31
Long range
  Correspondence 393182
  Despatch register 3937
  Reference 2737
Loose
  Leaves register 382
  Sheets
    Fixing 2334:3:47
    Group 2334:3:45

Loose—*contd*
Issues of periodicals
Collecting 2334:4:51
Shelving work 2334:8
Tallying 2334:4:52
Lost
or damaged volume 26324
File 288
Tickets
Madras University Library 26311:14:44 to 46
Observation slips 26311:14:44
Specification 267
Work 26311:14
Volumes
Card
Retransferring 2831:4:58
Transferring 2831:4:48
Collection 26324:4:44
Work 2831:4
Lower division assistants file 328

Machine trimming 39334:2
Made up volumes transmitting 2334:4:57
Mail
Chief 39311
Stray 1895
Main
Cards
Correcting 2534:2:53
Picking 2534:1:53
Reinserting 2534:5:51
Writing 2532:2:51
On the back 2532:2:54
Collection 2812
Finance diary
Acquittance roll 3731:82
Assistant librarian 3437
Contingent account 3731:57
Expenditure watching 3737:7
Guide writing 2836:2:31
Making up
Disposal pad 1856
Order copy 2233:3:513
Periodical volume 2334:4:53
Maladjustment of work 1427
Margin of tolerance 1452
Marked sources forwarding 2132:1:51
Mecca 1143
Medical certificate requisitioning 3232:1:32
Medium envelope 3937
Meeting
Papers
Collecting 3133:1:61
Completing 3133:1:63
Files 318
Numbering 3133:1:64
Putting up 3133:2:64
Redistributing 3135:2:62
Scrutinising 3133:1:62
Verifying 3135:1:61
Reminding 3133:2:63
Members 26311
Deposit
Account section 3735
Finance section 3635
Files 268
Membership docketing 26311:12:48
Mending 39535
Department 39513
Menials 3432:5:11
Minor mending 263231:4:32
Minutes
Book
Committee section 317
Staff council 337
Circulating 3135:1:63
Extracting 3135:2:61
Work 3135:1
Writing 3135:1:62
Miscellaneous
Account
Acknowledgment file 3734:565
Closing 3734:57
Register 377
Totalling
Annual 3731:84
Weekly 3731:54
Writing 3734:47

Miscellaneous—*contd*
Receipt
Account section 3734
Book 267
Collecting 3634:46
File 378
Finance section 3634
Form 377
Forwarding 3734:56
Transmitting 3634:577
Mis-delivered letters 393181
Mis-spelling of names 2233:8:52
Model library rules 269
Modes of
Disposal of letters 1859
Publicity 35
Modifying cadre register 3231:1:37
Mofussil loan
Forwarding address slips 267
Return address slips 267
Money order
Advice transmitting 3737:47:535
Forwarding 3737:47:531
Payment file 378
Receipt file 378
Receipt filling 3737:47:538
Remittance watching 3737:47:534
Monthly
Amendment statement 2536:52
Supplies
Indent 39736:514
Slip 3977
Indenting 39736:513
Total scrutinising 3434:61
Muchi file 328
Muhammadan holidays 166
Multiplication of collections 2813
Multi-volumed books
Ordering file 228
Planning 2213
Standing order 22342
Mutual adjustment 1426

N R D 39332:31
New
Call number checking 2534:2:52

New—*contd*
Classes noting 2531:2:56
Issues of periodicals
Arranging 2334:8:41
Displaying 2334:8:42
Sorting 2334:3:412
Periodical publications
Cost ascertaining 2136:7:73
Perusing 2334:3:456
Placings checking 2531:8:53
Readers 2733
Recruits 3433:33
Volumes 2832
Shelving 2832:3:53
New York School of Filing 1815
No reply correspondence 393182
Non-supply
Card specification 237
Notifying 51
Issue of periodical 2334:6:51
T C I 2334:6:52
Normal
Group 2334:3:45
Publication
Check card 2334:3:461
Registering 2334:3:441
Volumes call numbering 2531:2:51
Not due
Books 2432:4:55
Group 2432:1:41
Periodicals group 2334:6:58
Publication
Definition 2334:3:44
Registering 2334:3:448
Supply file 248
Notation
For periods 122
Function of 071
Notifying
Applicants 3231:2:33
Borrowed book 26325:1:33
Expenditure 26325:2:376
Central executive 3631:1:81
Defective supply 2334:6:54
Detection 2531:4:14
Duplicate supply 2334:6:56
Gap-in-supply 2334:6:53

Notifying—*contd*
  Maintenance section about
    Correction 2534:1:51
    Lost or damaged book 26324:4:48
  Non-supply
    Issue of periodical 2334:6:51
    T C I 2334:652
  Sections about
    Annual report 3431:81
    Budget 3631:1:82
  Special deposit return 26324:97:32
  Withdrawal
    Cases 26311:3:516
    From bank 3635:54
Noting
  Accession
    Date 2434:6:592
    Number by
      Periodical publication section 2334:4:58
      Technical section 2533:1:51
  Advice date 3737:1:52
  Amendments 2532:4:56
  Borrowing expenditure 26325:1:37
  Call number 2533:1:52
  Current list 2334:1:86
  Cumulative index 2334:5:11
  Forwarding expenditure 26325:2:37
  Indent 2133:3:51
  Leave return 3232:3:72
  New classes 2531:2:56
  Order copy 2233:3:514
  Payment details 3737:1:51
  Regular leave application 3232:3:34
  Renewal 2631:1:133
  Retirement application 3232:6:31
  Sources by
    Book selection section 2131:2:11
    Technical section 2531:2:55
  Suggestion 2131:2:12
  Voucher number 2334:7:58
Number of rules per page 175
Numbering
  Chapters by colon notation 072
Numbering—*contd*
  Date label 2533:3:56
  Forms 177
  Inside 2533:3:52
  Jacket 2533:3:51
  Meeting papers 3133:1:64
  Tag 2533:3:53
  Work for volumes 2533:3

Observation slips for lost tickets
  Box 26311:14:44
  Routine 26311:14:44
  Specification 267
Office functions, General 3
  Theory 113
Old
  Issues shelving 2334:8:54
  Over due charges 2631:1:14
  Open access libraries 26113
Opening
  And closing diary 3964
  Routine 39631
Order
  Cancelling 2233:8:54
  Card
    Alphabetising 2233:1:52
    And selection card 2132:3:31
    Box
      Order copy completing 2233:3:515
      Unscored cards 2233:3:511
    Filing 2233:5:522
    Reconciling 2233:7:53
    Specification 217
    Standing 227
    Tallying 2432:1:42
  Confirming 2233:8:52
  Copy
    Completing 2233:3:515
    Filing 2233:6:52
    Making 2233:3:513
    Noting 2233:3:514
    Transmitting 2233:6:57
  Cost estimating 2233:3:512
  Form
    Local vendors 227

Order—*contd*
Form—*contd*
Outside vendors 227
Standing vendors 227
Obtaining 3234:42
Preparation for
Book order 2233:3
Cumulative index 2334:5:522
Periodical publication 2334:2:52
Transmitting 2233:5:53
Tray 2132:1:38
And indent checking 2133:1:51
Writing 2233:5:51
Ordered books
Collating 2434:4:52
Routine 2432
Ordering book
In Indian libraries 2211
To replace a lost one 2831:4:53
Ordering work
Book ordei section 2233:5
Periodical publication section 2334:2
Orderliness 138
Ordinary books
Doubt clearing file 228
Ordering file 228
Routine 2233
Original indent transmitting 2233:6:51
Out-of-print books 2217
Outstanding order
Cost 2136:6:823
Estimating 2136:6:823
Tray
Checking with 2233:2:523
Order cards filing 2233:5:528
Order confirming 2233:8:52
Supplied cards picking 2233:7:52
Unsupplied cards picking 2233:8:51
Outward correspondence
Arranging 39332:2
Cross referring 39332:51
Forwarding
By messenger 39332:43
Outward correspondence—*contd*
Forwarding—*contd*
To post office 39332:42
Planning 393182
Postal forwarding verifying 39332:421
Routine 39332
Sorting 39332:1
Over due
Checking 3734:446
Guide 2334:3:46
Notice card 267
Noticing 2631:3:445
Register 26311:12:54
Specification 267
Sheet
Filing 26311:12:54
Pad 26311:12:44
Sheeting 26311:12:44
Tickets diary 3747
Checking 3734:446
Over-duing 2631:3:441
Over size collection 28132

Pad
Deferred disposal
Circulation section
Preliminary to refunding 26311:3:52
Withdrawal
Files scrutiny 26311:3:41
Notifying 26311:3:516
Theory 1892
Disposal 1828
Label 1827
Over due sheets 26311:12:44
Transmission 18922
Pagination 178
Paper
Colour 1735
Grade 1731
Size 1736
Parallel movement, Principle of
Cards rearranging 2833:3:88
Theory 2815

Passed bills transmitting
  Accession section 2432:7:57
  Binding section 39537:64
  Maintenance section 2831:4:54
  Periodical publication section 2334:7:57
  Stores section 39732:3:87
Passing work of bills
  Accession section 2432:7
  Binding section 39537:64
  Periodical publication section 2334:7
Passing work of indents 2133:3
Pay
  Amount 3632
    Receiving 3732:66
  Bill
    Account section 3732
    Drafting 3732:61
    Faircopy transmitting 3732:64
    Faircopy 3732:63
    File 378
    Presenting 3732:65
    Revising 3237:67
    Specification 377
Payment details noting 3737:1:51
Pay-order writing 3737:2:532
Peons
  File 328
  Movement regulating 3432:5:11
Period
  Definition 2334:3:51
  Number
    In job number 1238
    Schedule 122
Periodical publications
  Accession cards
    Arranging 2434:5:57
    Sorting 2434:5:56
    Writing 2334:4:56
  Arranging 2434:5:58
  Carding 2334:2:53
  Collating 2434:4:53
  Cost ascertaining 2136:6:83
  Definition 2311
  Idiosyncrasies 24113
  Order transmitting 2334:2:54
Periodical publications—*contd*
  Section 23
  Subscription estimating 2136:6:83
Permanent
  Advance
    Account book 3738:7:56
      Specification 377
    Acknowledging 3738:8:81
    Acknowledgments filing 3737:5:52
    File 378
  Executive 3114
  Files 328
  Papers 3214
  Registers 38
Perpetually current registers 38
Perusing new periodicals 2334:3:456
Petty
  Articles
    Purchasing 39732:2:51
    Requisition 39732:1:51
  Cash
    Account
      Closing 3738:7:57
      Section 3738
      Work 3738:7
      Writing 3738:7:56
    Acknowledgment file 3737:5:52
    Balance receiving 3638:577
    Finance section 3638
Philosophies, False 1421
Picking
  Bespeaking cards 263234:1:41
  Consolidation
    Cards 2532:3:51
    Slips 2532:6:52
  First impression slips 2534:3:51
  Gift cases 2233:3:5118
  Main card 2534:1:53
  Recent additions 2832:5:51
  Topical volumes 2836:1:31
  Unsupplied cards 2233:8:51
  Worn-out volumes 2835:1:41
Pick-up-work
  Circulation section 263231:5
  Elimination of waste 3432:2:34
  Maintenance section 2837

Pick-up-work—*contd*
Shelf study 2837:38
Reference section
Long range reference 2737
Shelf study 2738
Theory 147
Plan of chapters 064
Planning
Factors in
Section 1 of each chapter
Theory 117
Functional 112
Postal forwarding verifying 39332:421
Posting
Acknowledgment
Members deposit 3735:575
Miscellaneous receipt 3734:565
Cadre register 3231:2:37
Equivalent 3737:35:57
Finance diary
Account section 3737:7:51
Book order section 2233:6:56
Periodical publication section
After ordering 2334:2:56
Annual 2334:2:896
Cumulative index 2334:5:526
Interest 3635:666
Investment register 3635:656
Miscellaneous receipt 26311:4:34
Service register 3232:2:81
Voucher number 3737:43:55
Work of voucher number 3737:43
Post-order work 2233:6
Preceding payment scrutinising 2334:7:52
Prejudice to be overcome 1341
Preliminary
Agenda work 3133:1
Checking of books 2132:1:38
Drafting of
Annual report 3431:82
Budget 3631:1:83
Indents for stores 39732:1:83
Selection of books 2132:1:31
Sorting by
Book order section 2233:1:51
Preliminary—*contd*
Sorting by—*contd*
Technical section 2531:1:55
To
Admission 26311:12:11
Allotment 2136:6:88
Charging 2631:2:132
Detecting 26311:14:44
Maintenance section advising 26324:8:12
Refunding 26311:3:52
Special deposit returning 26324:97:31
Work of
Cataloguing 2532:1
Classification 2531:1
Correction 2534:1
Preparation
of
Business 3133
Records 38
Volumes 2533
Work with volumes 2533:2
Prepared volumes arranging work 2533:8
Preparing
Current list 2334:1:81
Dues list 26311:4:71
Order for periodical publications 2334:2:52
Replaced volumes 2831:4:55
Volumes for binding 39532:62
Prepublication ordering file 228
Press material 393181
Printed catalogue 394
Printing
Instructions 3945
Order 3945
Preliminary to order 3944
Register 3947
Verifying 3737:43:55
Section 394
Requesting 39734:88
Stationery indent 3946
Work and store section 3944
Privilege leave *see* Regular leave

Procedure advising on loss of ticket 26311:14:43
Process clip 2531:1:55
Professional matters 3927
Progress
of expenditure
Reviewing 3737:7:74
Verifying 3737:44:56
Watching 3437:57
Report
File 348
Theory 1482
Reporting 3436:61
Public
Accounts code 3711
Finance code 3617
Publications
Indian 2212
Professional 3923
Publicity 35
Punctuality 3432:5:12
Purchase
Foreign publications 2211
Indian publications 2212
Purport number in files 18222
Putting up
Gate register 2631:1:412
Meeting papers 3133:2:64
Puzzles in classification and cataloguing 3914

Quantum of issue 39714
Quarto letter head 3937
Quasi-current collection of files 1828
Query answering 2631:1:18
Quotation
Calling
Book order section 2232:51
Maintenance section 2831:4:52
Tabulating 2232:52

Rate verifying 39537:63
Readers
And Writers Company 1442
New, Initiation of 2733
Readers—*contd*
Ticket 267
Ready reference 2736
Reappropriation
Consulting 3631:5:61
File 368
Sanction communicating 3631:5:68
Seeking 3631:5:65
Work 3631:5
Rearranging
Books in stack room 2833:3:82
Card
Binding correction 2835:2:68
Shelf rearranging 2833:3:88
Work 2833:3
Receipt posting
Checking 3734:447
Circulation section 26311:4:34
Receipting
Deposit 26311:12:131
Miscellaneous dues 26311:4:12
Receiving
Bespeaking card 2631:2:14
Bond 26311:14:46
New volumes 2831:4:54
Mail 184
Over due charge 2631:1:14
Petty cash 3737:46:56
Refund cash 26311:3:531
V P Packet 2334:3:11
Withdrawal notice 26311:3:11
Work
Books 2233:7
Periodical publications 2334:3
Special deposit 26324:4
Stores 39732:3
Reclassification work 2534:2
Reconciling
Cards
Order 2233:7:53
Shelf register 2832:1:51
Time table 3432:6:35
Reconditioning work 263231:5
Records
Collections 1828
Of standards 148

Recruiting work 3231:2
Rectifying shelf 2833:3:43
Redistributing
  Meeting papers 3135:2:62
  Work 3135:2
Reference
  Cabinet 27385
    Reviewing 27385:38
  Catalogue 2831:4:52
  Guide classifying 27385:35
  Investigating 2837:31
  Long range 2737
  Ready 2736
  Section 27
  Advising 2837:37
  Service and librarian 3912
  Slip
    Box 27385:32
    Filing 27385:37
    Grouping 27385:32
    Guide 27385:35
    Guiding 27385:33
    Ready reference 2736
    Specification 277
    Writing 27385:31
  Study 2837
Refractory
  Cases
    Consulting 2532:4:51
    Work 2532:4
  Group 2532:1:51
Refund-cash receiving 26311:3:531
Refunding
  Deposit 26311:3:535
  Preliminary to 26311:3:52
  Special deposit 26324:97
Register Card
  Specification 237
  Theory 2314
  Tray
    Checking order card 2334:2:51
    Current issue registering 2334:3:44
    Renewal order sorting 2334:2:86
  Voucher number noting 3737:43:55
Register card—*contd*
  Tray—*contd*
  Writing 2334:2:53
Register sequence 383
Registered Group 2334:3:44
Registering
  Acknowledgments 3737:5:41
  Bills 3737:1:43
  Current issues of periodicals 2334:3:44
  Inward correspondence 39331:3
Registers and forms
  Schedule 397171
  See section 7 of each chapter
Regular leave
  Application noting 3232:3:34
  Definition 3232:3:3
  Work 3232:3
Reinserting
  Binding collection cards 2835:8:68
  Corrected cards 2834:8:58
  First impression slips 2534:5:52
  Main cards 2534:5:51
  Topical collection cards 2836:8:38
  Work of
    Maintenance section
      Binding correction 2835:8
      Correction work 2834:8
    Technical section 2534:5
Rejected
  Cards tray 2133:3:58
  Items disposing 2133:3:58
Related files 1897
Release dated marking 2836:1:33
Released volumes
  Checking 2832:5:52
  Shelving
    New volumes 2832:5:53
    Topical collections 2836:8:33
  Tallying 2836:8:31
Releasing
  Bespoken books 263234:8:41
  Creative forces 1463
  Entrance gate 2631:1:15
  Exit gate 2631:2:15

Releasing—*contd*
  Work of maintenance section
    New volumes 2832:5
    Topical collection 2836:8
Reminder
  Due check card
    Definition 2334:3:51
    Vigilance 2334:3:512
  For reply 188
  Not-due check card
    Definition 2334:3:51
    Vigilance 2334:3:511
Reminding
  Dues 26311:4:75
  Expiry of tickets 26311:13:85
  Foreign acknowledgments 3737:5:65
  Inland acknowledgments 3737:5:62
  Meeting 3133:2:63
Remittance
  File 368
  Work 3737:47
Remitting
  Cancelled tickets
    Change of tickets 26311:13:57
    Withdrawal 26311:3:57
  Deposit amount 3635:53
Renewal
  Listing tray
    List tallying 2334:2:82
    Listing 2334:2:81
    Order tallying 2334:2:84
    Order writing 2334:2:83
  Noting 2631:1:133
  of
    Gate register 2631:1:31
    Tickets 26311:13:13
  Order
    Address verifying 2334:2:85
    Card 237
    List tallying 2334:2:82
    Listing 2334:2:81
    Sorting 2334:2:86
    Tallying 2334:2:84
    Transmitting 2334:2:87
    Writing 2334:2:83
Request disposing 2631:3:432
Renewing 2631:3:433
  Reordering 2233:8:53
Replaced volumes preparing 2831:4:55
Replacement
  Acknowledgment 3738:8:52
  Cash handing over 3738:8:56
  Receiving 3638:56
  Requisition form 3738:8:51
    Specification 377
  Requisitioning 3738:8:51
  Work 3738:8
Replacing shelf
  Arranging 2732
  Circulation section 263231:8:38
  Reference section 2722
Replacing work 2831:1
Reply
  Due date 1864
  Received date 39331:51
Reporting
  Detected ticket 2631:3:514
  Inventory 2833:1:54
  Weekly progress 3436:61
Requisitioning
  From co-operative library 26325:1:32
  Medical certificate 3232:1:32
  Replacement 3738:8:51
  Sources 2131:2:52
  Reshelving 2835:8:63
Resources
  Circulation section 2632
  Interlending 3923
Retirement
  Application noting 3232:6:31
  Order communicating 3232:6:32
  Work 3232:6
Retransferring
  Card
    Damaged volume 2831:5:58
    Lost volume 2831:4:58
Retransmitting worn-out volumes 2835:2:55
Returned volumes
  Arranging 2831:1:42

Returned volumes—*contd*
Circulation section 263231
Forwarding work 263231:8
Shelving 2831:1:43
Sorting by
Circulation section 263231:4:31
Maintenance section 2831:1:41
Returning
Cash balance 3737:47:56
Special deposit
Balance 26324:97:35
Circulation section 26324:97:197
Finance section 3634:56
Work of borrowed books 26325:2
Wrongly delivered packets 2334:3:12
Revenue 26171
Reviewing
Balance sheet 3731:91
Current list 2334:1:82
Finance diary 3631:4:64
Financial position 2334:1:84
New supply 2233:7:51
Progress of expenditure 3737:7:74
Reference cabinet 27385:38
Work of technical section 2537:2
Revising
Book selection card 2132:2:51
Call number 2534:2:51
Pay bill 3237:67
Periodical publication bill 2334:7:55
Work on bills 3737:44
Revision of
Job analysis 126
Routine 133
Rhythm of work 165
Roman Catholic Holidays 166
Rounding off work 2334:6
Route of correspondence 184
Routine
and librarian 3915
Diary
Account section 3748
Circulation section 2646
Routine—*contd*
Letter 187
See section 3 of each chapter
Rubicon 26112
Rule-of-thumb 3927
Rules of the library 269
Rules per page 175
Ruling of forms 175

S R D 39332:31
Salesmanship in libraries 3155
Sanction
Communicating 3234:43
Obtaining for
Investment 3635:651
Stores 39736:514
Verifying 3737:44:51
Sanctioned indent
File 39736:58
Forwarding 2133:3:52
Sanctioning allotment 2136:6:891
Scale of pay changing 3231:1:32
Schedule of forms and registers 397171
Scientific administration 1252
Scored cards filing 2233:6:58
Scrutinising
Annual posting 3434:81
Attendance register 3432:5:41
Bay guide 2833:5:81
Binding list 2835:8:61
Book order 2233:5:521
Diaries 3434:41
Finance diaries
Assistant librarian 3437:51
Finance section 3631:4:61
Gate register 2631:1:11
Guide plan 2833:5:83
Meeting papers 3133:1:62
Monthly total 3434:61
Preceding payment 2334:7:52
Shelf guides 2833:5:61
Tag 2833:5:43
Tier guide 2833:5:82
Weekly
Progress 3436:51

Scrutinising—*contd*
  Weekly—*contd*
    Totals 3434:51
  Withdrawal files 26311:3:41
  Work of
    Indents 2133:1
    Supply 2432:1
Second
  Impression slips
    Arranging 2537:5:51
    Correcting 2534:4:52
    Inserting 2537:5:52
  Law of Library Science and
    Counter collection issuing 263233:11
    Reference service 271:85
  Temporary charging tray 2631:2:383
Secondary collections 2813
Section number in files 1822
Selected cards tray 2132:1:38
Selection of
  Books 2132
    Preliminary to 2132:1:31
  Current volumes 2334:1
  Periodical publication 2334:1
Sentimental holidays 166
Series
  Books
    Planning 2218
    Routine 22341
  Entry and indent checking 2133:1:51
  Ordering file 228
Service register
  Closing 3232:6:34
  Opening 3232:2:31
  Posting 3232:2:81
  Specification 327
  Work 3232:2
Shelf
  Arrangement 2811
  Checking 2833:1:52
  Easing 2833:3:81
  Guides scrutinising 2833:5:61
  Rectifying 2833:3:43
  Register 2815

Shelf—*contd*
  Register—*contd*
    and accession register 2816
    Cabinet 2838
    Cards
      Arranging by
        Maintenance section 2832:3:517
        Technical section 2537:1:52
      Box 2832:3:517
      Checking 2537:3:53
      Coupling 2537:3:51
      Custody 3913
      Inserting 2838:58
      Sorting 2832:3:516
      Specification 287
      Writing 2532:2:58
  Sources
    Shelving 2131:8:58
    Weeding 2131:8:88
  Study
    Maintenance section 2817
      As pick-up-work 2837:38
    Reference section 2738
  Tidying 2833:3:42
Shelving
  Old issues of periodicals 2334:8:54
  Sources 2131:8:58
  Volumes
    Corrected 2834:2:53
    New 2832:3:53
    Released 2836:8:33
    Returned 2831:1:43
    Topical 2836:2:32
  Work
    Maintenance section
      New volumes 2832:3
      Topical collections 2836:2
    Periodical publication section 2334:8
Shifting check card 2334:3:46
Short range
  Correspondence 393182
  Despatch register 3937
Silver fish 2843

Simple draft letters
  Planning 393184
  Routine 393342
Simplified practice 145
Size
  In binding 3959
  Number in form number 1771
  Paper 1736
Skeleton of annual report 3431:82
Slips
  Arranging 2537:5:51
  Checking 2532:6:56
  Consolidating 2532:6:53
  Correction 2534:3:51
  Disposing 2334:6:593
  Inserting 2537:5:52
    Work 2537:5
Small envelopes 3937
Solicited gift accepting 2238:52
Soliciting gift 2238:51
Sorted cards box
  Accession number tallying 2537:1:53
  Catalogue cards
    Discussing 2537:2:51
    Sorting 2537:1:51
Sorting
  Applications 3231:2:32
  Catalogue cards 2537:1:51
  Classified volumes 2532:1:51
  Corrected cards 2834:8:56
  Instalment book accession cards 2434:5:56
  Inward correspondence 39331:1
  New Issues of periodicals 2334:3:412
  Ordinary book selection cards 2233:1:51
  Outward correspondence 39332:1
  Periodical publications accession cards 2434:5:56
  Preliminary to classification 2531:1:55
  Prepared volumes 2533:8:51
  Renewal order for periodical publications 2334:2:86

Sorting—*contd*
  Returned volumes by
    Circulation section 263231:4:31
    Maintenance section 2831:1:41
  Shelf register cards 2832:3:516
  Sound volumes 263231:8:31
  Unscored cards 2233:3:511
  Work of technical section 2537:1
Sound
  Group 2334:3:42
  Volumes
    Forwarding 263231:8:38
    Sorting 263231:8:31
Source of revenue 26171
Sources
  Acquiring work 2131:2
  Arranging 2131:8
  Book selection section 2131
  File
    Book selection section 218
    Periodical section 238
  Noting by
    Book selection section 2131:2:11
    Technical section
      Call number work 2531:2:55
      Refractory cases 2532:4:55
  Requisitioning 2131:2:52
  Selection slip 2131:2:11
  Shelf
    Shelving 2131:8:58
    Weeding 2131:8:88
  Shelving 2131:8:58
  Slips tray
    Book selection
      Sources noting 21312:2:11
      Sources requisitioning 2131:2:52
    Technical section
      Call numbering work 2531:2:55
      Refractory cases 2532:4:55
  Weeding 2131:8:88
Special
  Action
    Cases 2334:6:592

Special—*contd*
  Action—*contd*
    Due check card
      Definition 2334:3:51
      Vigilance 2334:3:513
  Collections 28131
  Deposit
    Advise work 26324:8
    Claiming 26324:4:42
    Collecting 26324:4:44
    Estimating 26324:4:41
    Expenditure meeting 3634:573
    Receiving work 36324:4
    Refunding work 36324:97
    Return notifying 36324:97:32
    Returning
      Balance 26324:97:35
      Circulation section 26324:97:197
      Finance section 3634:56
      Preliminary to 26324:97:31
  Opportunity of India 1454
Specification
  Binding 3959
  Forms and registers, Section 7 of each chapter
Spent amount ascertaining 2136:7:77
Spirit of Hive 155
Stack room 2833
Staff
  And the assistant librarian 3432
  Assignment work 3432:2
  Council
    and code correction 2536:63
    and library profession 3927
    and printing section 3944
    and work distribution 3432:1:31
    Minutes book 337
    Section 33
    Theory 153
  Discipline work 3432:5
  Distribution work 3432:1
  Duty of 136
  Formula 1145
  Growth in 1144
  Interlanding of 3923
Staff—*contd*
  Order
    Book
      Routine 3433
      Specification 347
    Circulating 3433:32
    Writing 3433:31
  Relation with 142
  Section 32
  Strength changing 3231:1:31
Stamp
  Account register
    Account section 3737:43:55
    Correspondence section 39332:71
    Specification 3937
  Accounting 39332:71
  Affixing 39332:41
  Box 39332:76
  Noting 39332:411
  Ordering 39322:75
  Receiving 39332:76
  Totalling 39332:7
Stamped tray 39332:41
Stamping 2533:2:52
Standardisation
  of practice 3923
  Theory 144
Standing
  Binder 39531
    Appointing 39531:85
  Order 2234
    Books 2218
    Cancelling 2334:2:88
    Card
      Checking with 2233:2:524
      Specification 227
    Cost 2136:6:824
    Estimating 2136:6:824
    Form 237
  Vendors
    Book section 2231
      Appointing 2231:85
      File 228
    Periodical publication section 2331
      File 238

Stationery 397172
Statistical
  Abstracts 385
  Section 398
Stencil cutting 393343:1
Stock
  And issue register
    Account section 3737:43:55
    Specification 3977
    Stores section
      Issue entering 39736:521
      Stores entering 39736:531
  Verification file
    Maintenance section 88
    Stores section 3978
  Verifying of stores
    Annual 39738:81
    Quarterly 39738:731
Stores
  Collecting 39736:522
  Distributing 39736:531
  Reviewing 39738:732
  Section 397
    Printing work 3943
  Tidying up 39738:72
Storing 39738
Stray mail 1895
Strength of staff changing 3231:1:31
Study group file 268
Style of
  Binding 3959
  Writing in library records 1362
Sub-committees
  File 318
  Planning 3115
  Routine 3136
Subramania Ayyar 08
Subscription books
  Planning 2218
  Routine 22344
Subsidiary finance diary 3746
  Posting 3737:7:51
Suggestion
  Noting 2131:2:12
  Transmitting 2537:2:55
  Tray 2131:2:12
Supplement separating 2334:4:54
Supplemental book selection
  Carding 2133:1:523
  Process 2133:1:523
Supplementing the agenda 3133:2:62
Supplied
  Cards picking 2233:7:52
  Guide 2334:3:46
Supplies 39732
Supply
  Calling for terms of 2231:81
  Noting 2233:82:5
  Receiving 2233:7:51
  Scrutinising work 2432:1
  Tabulating the terms of 2231:82
Surprise holidays 166
Surviving card 2233:2
Suspense
  Box 2432:1:41
  Periodical publications work 2334:94

T C I
  Group 2334:3:443
  Not received publication
    Check card 2334:3:4631
    Definition 2334:3:44
    Registering 2334:3:4431
  Notifying of non-supply 2334:6:52
  Received publication
    Check card 2334:3:463
    Definition 2334:3:44
    Registering 2334:3:443
  Reminder card 237
  Waiting group 2334:4:52
Tabulating
  Quotation 2232:52
  Terms of supply 2231:82
Tag
  Numbering 2533:3:53
  Scrutinising 2833:5:43
Tagging
  Circulation section 263231:5:33
  Technical section 2533:2:53
Tallied-card box 2432:1:42
Tallying
  Accession number 2537:1:53

Tallying—*contd*
Bills by
Accession section 2432:1:41
Binding section 39537:61
Binding list 2835:5:61
Bound volumes
Binding section 39533:61
Maintenance section 2835:8:621
Corrected volumes 39534:611
Loose issues 2334:4:52
Order card 2432:1:42
Released topical volumes 2836:8:31
Renewal order 2334:2:84
List 2334:2:82
Volumes
For binding 39532:61
With
Accession card 2531:1:54
Shelf register cards 2832:3:521
Work of book section 2233:1
Work of maintenance section
Binding list 2835:5
New volumes 2832:1
Technical section 25
Counting 2537:1:58
Temporary
Assistants file 328
Bespeaking tray 2631:2:14
Charged tray
First 2631:2:133
Second 2631:2:383
Collections 28145
Papers 321
File 328
Tender for binding
Calling 39531:8
Tabulating 39531:8
Terms of supply of books
Calling 2231:81
Tabulating 2231:82
Tertiary collection 2813
Third law and
Main guide writing 2836:2:31
Maintenance section 2857
Rearrangement 2833:3:82
Third law and—*contd*
Reference service 2713
Topical sequence 2836:2:31
Three cards system 2313
Ticket
Cancelling
Change of ticket case 26311:13:12
Withdrawal case 26311:3:532
Changing work 26311:13
Detecting 2631:3:414
Duplicate 26311:14:11
Justification for change 26311:13:11
Lost
Procedure advising 26311:14:43
Work 26311:14
Madras University Library 26311:12:132
Renewal 26311:13:13
Counting 26311:13:18
Returning 26311:4:13
System of issuing 2615
Tidying
Circulation section 263231:5
Maintenance section 2833:3:42
Tier guide scrutinising 2833:5:82
Time scheme, Section 6 of each chapter
Time-table
Alternative 164
File 348
Reconciling 3432:6:35
Work 3432:6
Timing gate register 2631:1:26
Title entry and indent checking 2133:1:51
Tolerance, Margin of 1451
Tooling verifying 39533:62
Top
Cross reference 1897
Edge, Colour 1735
Topical
Collection
File 288
Guiding 2836:2:34
Planning 28137

Topical—*contd*
Collection—*contd*
Routine 2836
Volumes
Picking 2836:1:31
Shelving 2836:2:32
Total verifying
Accession section 2432:7:52
Accounts section
Bills passing work 3737:2:51
Bills verifying work 3737:44:52
Totalling
Acquittance roll 3731:82
Contingent account
Annual 3731:87
Balance sheet 3731:57
Deposit account
Annual 3731:85
Balance sheet 3731:55
Issue work 2631:2:488
Miscellaneous account
Annual 3731:84
Balance sheet 3731:54
Training class 3923
Transfer of files 18291
Transferring
Cards
Correction sequence 2834:1:42
Damaged volumes 2831:5:48
Lost volumes 2831:4:48
Topical collections 2836:1:32
Worn-out volumes 2835:1:52
Transmission
Box
Circulation section
Cards forwarding 263234:1:43
Cards picking 263234:1:41
Maintenance section 2832:1:51
Pad 18922
Register
Correspondence section 39332:42
Finance section 3634:56
Theory 18942
Work in accession section 2434:5
Transmitting
Accession cards 2832:1:52
Acknowledgments by
Accession section 2437:53
Accounts section 3737:5:51
Bespoken volumes 2835:8:626
Bills and cards 2233:7:54
Binding
Books 2535:65
List 39532:68
Slips 39532:63
Bound volumes 39537:68
Certified bills by
Accession section 2432:7:57
Binding section 39537:64
Maintenance section 2831:4:54
Checked
Correction list 39534:68
List of bound volumes 39533:68
Code corrections 2536:63
Collated volumes 2434:5:595
Corrected volumes 2534:2:58
Correction
Collection 2834:1:43
List 39534:68
Slips 39534:63
Volumes 39534:65
Coupled cards 2537:3:58
Cumulative order 2334:5:523
Draft
Acknowledgments 3737:5:55
Budget 3631:1:87
Paybill 3732:62
Explanation of late attendance 3432:5:53
Interest 3635:667
Local payment 3737:47:521
Made-up volumes 2334:4:57
Miscellaneous receipt 3634:577
Money order advice 3737:47:535
Order 2233:5:53
Copy 2233:6:57
Original indent 2233:6:51
Passed bills of
Periodical publications section 22334:7:57
Stores section 39732:3:87

Transmitting—*contd*
- Passed bills of—*contd*
- Pay bill faircopy 3732:64
- Periodical publication order 2334:2:54
- Renewal order 2334:2:87
- Suggestion 2537:2:55
- Volumes for binding 39532:65
- Week's current box 2334:6:596
- Withdrawal
  - Amount 3635:56
  - Documents 3635:57
- Work of
  - Binding volumes 2835:1
  - Correction volumes 2834:1
- Worn-out volumes 2835:1:55

Tray
- Bespeaking cards 263234:1:41
- Binding collection book cards 2533:8:56
- Cancelled 2334:2:88
  - Order 2233:8:54
- Charged work 2631:3
- Classified cards 2334:2:51
- Deferred
  - Cards 2133:3:58
  - Order cards 2233:3:512
- Despatched file 39332:31
- Faircopy 39332:31
- First temporary charging 2631:2:133
- Guide changing 2838:84
- Kept tickets 2631:1:14
- Order 2132:1:38
- Outstanding order 2233:5:522
- Register card
  - Address writing 2334:2:85
  - Current issue registering 2334:3:44
  - Final checking 2334:2:51
- Rejected cards 2133:3:58
- Renewal listing
  - Order list tallying 2334:2:82
  - Order listing 2334:2:81
  - Order tallying 2334:2:84
  - Order writing 2334:2:83

Tray—*contd*
- Second temporary charging 2631:2:383
- Selected cards 2132:1:38
- Source slips
  - Cataloguing 2532:4:55
  - Classification 2531:2:55
- Stamped 39332:41
- Unused guides 2631:3:436
- Unwanted cards 2233:5:528

Trickery 1422

Type of cards diary 2547

Typewriter machine trimming 39334:2

Typing
- Fresh slips 2532:6:51
- Work of catalogue slips 2532:6

Ultimate
- Economy in binding 39512
- File 1824
- Group of order cards
- Order
  - Order copy noting 2233:3:514
  - Order writing 2233:5:51
  - Unsorted cards sorting 2233:3:511

Unclaimed property work 2631:4

Uncompleted periodical rack 2334:8

Under-size collection 28132

Undisbursed pay
- Receiving 3632:61
- Returning 3632:62

Undischarged cards investigating 2835:8:64

United States of America
- Bureau standards 144
- Money orders to 3737:35:51
- Unprinted forms 393184

Unrecommended cards filing 2132:5:58

Unscored cards sorting 2233:3:511

Unsolicited gift books
- File 248
- Routine
  - Accession section 2437

Unsolicited gift books—*contd*
  Routine—*contd*
    Book order section 2238:52
Unsorted
  Cards box
    Catalogue cards 2537:1:51
    Shelf register cards 2537:1:52
  Slips box 2532:6:56
Unsound supply file 248
Unsupplied
  Bills disposing 2432:4:52
  Book disposing work 2233:8
  Cards
    Box 2233:8:51
    Picking 2233:8:51
Unused guides tray 2631:3:436
Unwanted cards tray 2233:5:522
Upper division assistant's file 328
Urgent book selection consulting 2132:5:45
Used volumes 2831
Users
  File 268
  Routine 2631

V P
  Disbursing 3638:11
  Packet receiving 2334:3:11
Vaishnava holidays 166
Variation of arrangements 2812
Vendors
  Grouping of bills by 2334:7:56
  Order form for
    Foreign 227
    Local 227
    Standing 227
  Standing
    For books 2231
    For periodical publications 2331
Verifying
  Bills
    Accession section 2432:7:51
    Register 3737:44:55
  Book card 2832:3:522
  Cash balance 3638:578
  Certificate 3737:44:53
Verifying—*contd*
  Correction 39534:62
  Cost of periodical publication 2334:7:53
  Cumulative total 3737:7:61
  Data for binding bills 39537:62
  Delivery book 39332:431
  Despatched file acknowledgment 39332:521
  Inward correspondence acknowledgment 39331:521
  Meeting papers 3135:1:61
  Postal forwarding 39332:421
  Progress of expenditure 3737:44:56
  Rate of binding bills 39537:63
  Renewal order address 2334:2:85
  Sanction 3737:44:51
  Total
    Accession section 2432:7:52
    Account section
      Bills passing work 3737:2:51
      Bills revising work 3737:44:52
Vermins 39622
Vertical file 1811
Vigilance
  Book order section 2233:82
  Circulation section 2631:2:11
    Daily 2334:3:4698
  Day 2334:3:51
  Follow up 2233:82:55
  Order
    Copy 2233:82:51
    Dating 2233:82:51
    Destroying 2233:82:88
    Filing 2233:82:52
    Information noting 2233:82:54
    Pad 2233:82:52
    Supply
      Completed pad 2233:82:55
      Noting 2233:82:53
    Work 2233:82
  Reference section 2734
  Weekly 2334:3:51
Volumes
  Accession numbering 2434:6:56
  Arranging 2434:6:53

Volumes—*contd*
Call numbering work 2533:3
Correcting 2834:2:52
Current 2334
Diary 2546
Donation numbering 2434:6:59
For binding 39532
Transmitting 39532:65
Making up 2334:4:53
Preparation of 2533
Voucher
File 378
Number
Noting
Periodical section 2334:7:58
Stores section 39732:3:88
Posting 3737:43:55
Work 3737:43
Numbering 3737:43:51

Waste, Elimination of chapter 34 and Section 4 of each chapter
Watching
Late attendance 3432:5:12
Local payment 3737:47:524
Money order remittance 3737:47:534
Progress of expenditure 3437:57
Work of allotment 2136:7
Water 39623
Weber 1453
Weeding out sources 2131:8:88
Week guide
Definition 2334:3:46
Guide number in 2334:3:46
Shifting 2334:3:518
Weekly
Disbursing 3638:576
Progress scrutinising 3436:51
Totals scrutinising 3434:51
Vigilance 2334:3:51
Week's current box
Definition 2334:3:44
Distributing 2334:6:595
Registering 2334:44

Week's current box—*contd*
Transmitting to
Correspondence section 2334:6:596
Librarian 2334:6:591
Vigilance 2334:3:51
Withdrawal
Amount transmitting 3635:56
Documents
Account section 3735:57
Finance section 3635:57
Files
Forwarding 26311:3:56
Scrutiny 26311:3:41
Notice receiving 26311:3:11
Notifying
Circulation section 26311:3:516
Finance section 3635:54
File 368
Work 26311:3
Withdrawing 3635:55
Work
Accuracy of 137
Item of 1212
Maladjustment of 1427
Number 1236
Rhythm of 165
Worn-out volumes
Card transferring 2835:1:52
Collating 2835:1:44
Forwarding 263231:4:48
Picking 2835:1:41
Retransmitting 2835:2:55
Transmitting 2835:1:55
Work of circulation section 263231:4
Wrapper examining
Accession section 2432:1:11
Periodical publication section 2334:3:411
Writing
Accession card 2334:4:56
Acquittance roll 3732:72
Attendance register 3432:5:61
Back of main card 2532:2:54
Contingent register 3737:2:57
Cross reference cards 2532:2:52

Writing—*contd*
Donation card 2437:42
Index card 2532:2:53
Main
Card 2532:2:51
Guide 2836:2:31
Reference slip 27385:31
Renewal order 2334:2:83
Shelf register card 2532:2:58

Writing—*contd*
Staff order 3433:31
Style 1362
Work of fresh cards 2532:2
Wrong supply
File 246
Work 2432:4
Wrongly delivered packet returning 2334:3:12